Get Updates and More on Nolo.com

Go to this book's companion page at:

 www.nolo.com/back-of-book/PCTM.html

When there's an important change to the law affecting this book, we'll post updates. You'll also find articles and other related materials.

More Resources
from Nolo.com

Legal Forms, Books, & Software
Hundreds of do-it-yourself products—all written in plain English, approved, and updated by our in-house legal editors.

Legal Articles
Get informed with thousands of free articles on everyday legal topics. Our articles are accurate, up to date, and reader friendly.

Find a Lawyer
Want to talk to a lawyer? Use Nolo to find a lawyer who can help you with your case.

⚖ **NOLO**
LAW for ALL

NOLO **The Trusted Name**
(but don't take our word for it)

"In Nolo you can trust."
THE NEW YORK TIMES

"Nolo is always there in a jam as the nation's premier publisher of do-it-yourself legal books."
NEWSWEEK

"Nolo publications…guide people simply through the how, when, where and why of the law."
THE WASHINGTON POST

"[Nolo's]…material is developed by experienced attorneys who have a knack for making complicated material accessible."
LIBRARY JOURNAL

"When it comes to self-help legal stuff, nobody does a better job than Nolo…"
USA TODAY

"The most prominent U.S. publisher of self-help legal aids."
TIME MAGAZINE

"Nolo is a pioneer in both consumer and business self-help books and software."
LOS ANGELES TIMES

17th Edition

Patent, Copyright & Trademark

An Intellectual Property Desk Reference

Attorney Richard Stim

SEVENTEENTH EDITION	APRIL 2022
Cover Design	SUSAN PUTNEY
Book Design	SUSAN PUTNEY
Proofreading	IRENE BARNARD
Index	VICTORIA BAKER

ISSN: 2326-3946 (print)
ISSN: 2332-4368 (online)

ISBN: 978-1-4133-2983-4 (pbk)
ISBN: 978-1-4133-2984-1 (ebook)

This book covers only United States law, unless it specifically states otherwise.

Please note

We believe accurate, plain-English legal information should help you solve many of your own legal problems. But this text is not a substitute for personalized advice from a knowledgeable lawyer. If you want the help of a trained professional—and we'll always point out situations in which we think that's a good idea—consult an attorney licensed to practice in your state.

Dedication

This book is dedicated to Steve Elias, who passed away in 2011. Steve wrote and edited the first three editions at a time when intellectual property was just beginning to surface in mainstream media. His contributions to the legal self-help movement were crucial to its success and the world is a different place for his efforts.

About the Author

Richard Stim is an attorney specializing in intellectual property and the author of several other intellectual property books, including *Getting Permission: Using & Licensing Copyright-Protected Materials Online & Off* (Nolo); *Music Law: How to Run Your Band's Business* (Nolo); and *Profit From Your Idea: How to Make Smart Licensing Deals* (Nolo). He answers intellectual property questions at his blog, Dear Rich (www.dearrichblog.com).

Table of Contents

Introduction 1

    Intellectual Property Law: The Basics 2

    Determining What Rights Apply to Your Work 2

Part 1: **Patent Law** 7

    Patent Law: Overview 9

    Patent Law: Definitions 21

    Patent Law: Forms 161

        Patent Application Basics 161

        Preparing a Design Patent Application 179

Part 2: **Copyright Law** 183

    Copyright Law: Overview 185

    Copyright Law: Definitions 197

    Copyright Law: Forms 365

        Preparing a Copyright Application 365

        Preparing an Electronic (eCO) Copyright Application 369

        Preparing a Traditional Print Copyright Application 370

Part 3: **Trademark Law** 381

    Trademark Law: Overview 383

    Trademark Law: Definitions 395

    Trademark Law: Forms 523

        Preparing a Federal Trademark Application 523

        The Trademark Application: the TEAS System 525

        Example of a TEAS Plus Application 529

Part 4: Trade Secret Law 537

    Trade Secret Law: Overview 539

    Trade Secret Law: Definitions 543

    Trade Secret Law: Forms 599

        Preparing a Nondisclosure Agreement 599

Index 611

Introduction

A photographer questions why an advertising agency can copy her photographs without permission. An inventor is disappointed to learn that he cannot stop a foreign manufacturer from making his patented invention. A woman named Tiffany doesn't understand why she can't name her vintage clothing and jewelry store Tiffany's Trifles.

Welcome to the world of intellectual property.

Writers, inventors, and artists transform ideas into tangible property. When this property qualifies under the law for protection it's known as intellectual property (or IP)—for example, patents, copyrights, trademarks, and trade secrets. Creators of IP are granted specific rights. The author of a book, for instance, can prevent others from copying it; and the owner of a patented invention can prevent others from making, using, or selling the device.

After a time, these exclusive rights can be lost or taken from the owner and given to the public. For example, copyright protection has ended for Mark Twain, and anyone is free to copy his books *Huckleberry Finn* and *The Adventures of Tom Sawyer*. The patent on the original Rollerblade invention has expired, and companies are now free to copy the device.

But not all products of the mind can achieve protection under intellectual property law. Determining what can be protected used to be the exclusive domain of patent, copyright, and trademark lawyers. Unfortunately, few businesses, nonprofits, or educational institutions can afford to call an attorney with every question. And lately, there are a lot of questions. Globalization, digital data, and the Internet have contributed to a greater-than-ever need for information about IP.

But intellectual property is not an inscrutable discipline.

Anybody can understand the basics. This book is proof that IP law is not a mystery. For over 25 years, engineers, scientists, business people, academics, *and* attorneys have used this book as a reference for understanding basic patent, copyright, trademark, and trade secret principles. This helpful desk reference has evolved to include hundreds of definitions, statutes, forms, and bits of how-to information about protecting and preserving intellectual property.

Hopefully, it will make your job easier, your employer more secure, and your business more prosperous.

Intellectual Property Law: The Basics

Intellectual property laws, along with court decisions and regulations, establish rules for the following activities:
- registration and administration of intellectual property
- selling or licensing of intellectual property, and
- resolving disputes between companies making or selling similar intellectual property products and services.

Intellectual property laws don't prevent someone from stepping on an owner's rights. But the laws do give an owner the ammunition with which to take a trespasser to court. This is the most well-known benefit of owning intellectual property: The owner acquires exclusive rights and can file a lawsuit to stop others who use the property without authorization. If the intellectual property owner does not confront the person or company who has acted without permission, the illegal activity will likely continue.

Determining What Rights Apply to Your Work

Intellectual property law consists of several separate and overlapping legal disciplines, each with its own characteristics and terminology. This book is divided into four sections, each for a different type of intellectual property. If you are concerned about your creation, you'll first need to know what form (or forms) of intellectual property protects it.
- **Patent law** establishes three types of patents: **Utility patents** (the most common) are awarded for new processes, machines, manufactures, compositions of matter, or new uses of any of the above. The utility patent owner has the exclusive right to make, use, and sell the invention for a limited term—it expires 20 years after the date the application was filed.

Design patents are awarded to new nonfunctional, ornamental, or aesthetic design elements of an invention or product. A design patent lasts 15 years from issuance, if it was filed on or after May 13, 2015; if filed before that date, it lasts 14 years from issuance.

Plant patents are granted for new asexually reproducible plants (plants reproducible by grafting or cloning). A plant patent expires 20 years from the date the patent was filed.

- **Copyright law** protects expressions of creative ideas such as songs, artwork, writing, films, software, architecture, and video games. Copyright law does not protect ideas and facts, only how those ideas and facts are expressed. Copyright protection lasts a long time, often more than 100 years.

- **Trademark law** protects marketing signifiers such as the name of a product or service or the symbols, logos, shapes, designs, sounds, or smells used to identify it. This protection can last as long as the company continuously uses the trademark in commerce—for example, many trademarks, such as Coca-Cola and General Mills, have been protected for over a century.

- **Trade secret law** commonly protects confidential designs, devices, processes, compositions, techniques, formulas, information, or recipes. A trade secret is any confidential information that gives a business a competitive advantage. Under trade secret law, the owner of this confidential information can prevent others from using it if it was obtained illegally. Trade secret protection lasts for as long as the business maintains the secret.

Is It Primarily Functional or Aesthetic?

Intellectual property rights are often divided between functional elements (protected by utility patents and trade secrets) and nonfunctional elements (protected by trademarks, copyrights, and design patents). Sometimes you can start your analysis of intellectual property protection by asking the question: "Does this creation accomplish a task or goal or is it done primarily to appeal to the senses or provide information or entertainment?"

Legal Basis of Intellectual Property Laws

The sources of intellectual property laws vary according to the subject matter. Copyright and patent laws are derived from powers originating in the U.S. Constitution and are specifically and exclusively implemented by federal statutes. In all of these areas, court decisions provide essential principles governing the application of intellectual property laws. Trademark and trade secret laws originate primarily in federal and state statutes and are also derived from court decisions that apply principles developed by earlier courts as part of the common law.

Forms of Intellectual Property: How They Overlap

Sometimes, trade secret, copyright, patent, and trademark laws intersect for a particular product or service. Some common examples of this are as follows:

- **Trade secret and patent.** It is possible to pursue a patent application while simultaneously maintaining the invention as a trade secret, at least for the first 18 months of the U.S. patent application process. The U.S. Patent and Trademark Office (USPTO) regards applications as confidential until they are published. Unless the applicant files a Nonpublication Request (NPR) at the time of filing and doesn't file for a patent outside the United States, the PTO will publish the application within 18 months of the filing date.

- **Copyright and trademark.** It's not uncommon for an item to be protected under both trademark and copyright law. For example, the expressive artwork in a package design might be protected by copyright, while the overall look and feel of the package might be protected as a form of trademark. Likewise, an advertising commercial might include some material covered by copyright (for example, a jingle) and other material covered by trademark (the product or company name). The difference here is that copyright protects the literal expression, while trademark protects whatever is used to designate the source of a product or service offered in the marketplace.

- **Patent, copyright, and trademark.** Patent law can intersect with copyright and trademark law in the case of certain products. For example, the designer of a toy or jewelry may protect the device's name or appearance (as a trademark), the design of the item (design patent), the appearance of any artwork or graphics (copyright), and the novel, nonobvious functionality of the device (utility patent).

IP Around the World

Most countries in the world have entered into intellectual property treaties that afford members mutual rights. This does not mean that anything protected in the United States will necessarily be protected abroad. However, intellectual property protected in America may achieve protection abroad under the standardized rules established by the various treaties. For example, the Madrid Protocol has standardized the process for obtaining trademark protection among member countries. Similarly, the Berne Convention establishes international copyright principles, and the Paris Convention and the Patent Cooperation Treaty offer harmonization for owners of patents. Trade secrets may receive international protection under GATT (General Agreement on Tariffs and Trade).

Get Updates and More Online

When there are significant changes to the information in this book, we'll post updates online, on a page dedicated to this book: **www.nolo.com/back-of-book/PCTM.html**

Part 1: **Patent Law**

Patent Law: Overview 9

What is a patent? 9

How do inventors benefit from holding a patent? 9

What kinds of patents may be issued? 10

What types of inventions qualify for a utility patent? 10

What is the procedure for applying for a utility patent and a provisional
    patent application? 11

Under what circumstances is a utility patent application approved? 11

How are patent rights enforced? 12

When does a patent expire or otherwise come to an end? 12

What about international protection for U.S. patents? 13

What's new in patent law since the last edition? 14

Patent resources 19

Patent Law: Definitions 21

Patent Law: Forms 161

Patent Application Basics 161

Preparing a Utility Patent Application 161

Who Files the Utility Application? 164

Preparing a Design Patent Application 179

Patent Law: Overview

There are three types of patents: utility patents, design patents, and plant patents. Commonly, when people refer to a patent, they mean a utility patent, which allows the creator of a useful, novel, nonobvious invention to stop others from making, using, or selling that invention for approximately 17 to 18 years.

What is a patent?

A patent is a grant by the U.S. Patent and Trademark Office (USPTO) that allows the patent owner to maintain a monopoly for a limited time on the use and development of an invention.

How do inventors benefit from holding a patent?

Most patent owners make arrangements with an existing company to commercialize an invention. Typically, the arrangement takes the form of a license agreement under which a company (the licensee) is authorized to commercially exploit the invention in exchange for paying the patent owner royalties for each invention sold.

A license may be exclusive (only one company is licensed to exploit the invention) or nonexclusive (several companies are licensed to make and sell it). The license may be for the duration of the patent or for a shorter period of time. Sometimes the patent is sold outright (an assignment) to the company for a lump sum payment.

On occasion, a licensee might sublicense other companies to market or distribute the invention. The right to do this and the extent to which the patent owner will benefit from these sublicenses depends on the agreement between the patent owner and the licensee.

Licenses are often limited by geography (for instance, different licenses for different countries or different parts of one country) and by use. In many cases, one company will trade licenses with other companies—called cross-licensing—so that companies involved in the trade will benefit from each other's technology.

What kinds of patents may be issued?

The U.S. Patent and Trademark Office issues three types of patents:

- **Utility patents.** New, nonobvious, useful inventions that fall into one of five categories—a process, a machine, a manufacture, a composition of matter, or an improvement of an existing idea—may qualify for a utility patent. Often, an invention will fall into more than one of the categories. For instance, computer software can usually be described as a process (the steps that it takes to make the computer do something) and as a machine (a device that takes information from an input device and moves it to an output device). Regardless of the number of categories in which an invention falls, only one utility patent may be issued.
- **Design patents.** New and original designs that ornament a manufactured article can qualify for a design patent. For example, a new shape for a car fender, a novel design for a bottle, or a flashlight design that doesn't improve its functionality would qualify.
- **Plant patents.** The least-frequently issued type of patent is a plant patent—granted for asexually or sexually reproducible plants (such as flowers) that are both novel and nonobvious.

What types of inventions qualify for a utility patent?

Most types of inventions (the term we'll use for innovative ideas) qualify for a utility patent if they offer something new (are novel) and are particularly clever (that is, nonobvious). However, some types of inventions do not qualify for a patent, no matter how nonobvious they are. For instance, mathematical formulas, newly discovered laws of nature, and newly discovered substances that occur naturally in the world traditionally have been considered to be unpatentable.

When deciding whether an invention qualifies for a patent, the USPTO first must determine whether the invention is novel in some way—that is, a new development in at least one or more of its constituent elements—as of the patent application filing date.

If the USPTO determines that the invention is novel, it must make another decision: Is the invention nonobvious? To make this determination, the USPTO asks this question: Would someone skilled in the particular field as of the filing date consider the invention an unexpected or surprising development?

If the invention is found to be both novel and nonobvious, and it fits within one or more of the five statutory categories discussed above, it is likely to receive a patent.

Among the many types of creative works that might qualify for a utility patent are biological inventions; chemical formulas, processes, or procedures; computer hardware and peripherals; computer software; cosmetics; electrical inventions; electronic circuits; food inventions; housewares; machines; magic tricks or techniques; mechanical inventions; medical accessories and devices; medicines; musical instruments; odors; and sporting goods (designs and equipment).

What is the procedure for applying for a utility patent and a provisional patent application?

To seek a U.S. patent, the inventor applies with the USPTO, a branch of the U.S. Department of Commerce.

To obtain an early filing date, the inventor may file what is known as a Provisional Patent Application (PPA). The only requirement for a PPA is that it adequately describe how to make and use the invention. However, to obtain a patent, the inventor must file a formal patent application (within one year of the PPA date if one is filed) that follows technical conventions and contains words and drawings to clearly:

- demonstrate how to make and use the invention
- explain why the invention is different from all previous and similar developments (known as the prior art), and
- describe, with precision, what aspects of the invention deserve the patent (the patent claims).

This patent application will be the subject of some discussion between the applicant and the USPTO patent examiner.

Under what circumstances is a utility patent application approved?

Once a patent application is received by the USPTO, a patent examiner is assigned to the application. The examiner is responsible for deciding whether the application meets all technical requirements, whether the invention qualifies for a patent, and, assuming it does, what the scope of the patent should be.

Usually, communications occur between the applicant and the examiner regarding these issues. Typically, this takes between one and three years and can involve significant amendments by the applicant. The most complex issue to address is whether the invention qualifies for a patent in light of previous developments—that is, whether the invention is novel and nonobvious in light of the prior art.

If the applicant overcomes the examiner's objections, the invention is approved for a patent. Then, the applicant pays a patent issue fee and receives an official copy of the patent.

To keep a patent in effect, three additional fees must be paid over the patent's life. The total patent fee for a small inventor ("small entity"), from application to issue to expiration, is approximately $6,000 to $7,000. For large corporations, it is twice this amount.

How are patent rights enforced?

Once a patent is granted, the owner may enforce it by bringing a patent infringement action (lawsuit) against anyone who makes, uses, or sells the invention without the patent owner's permission. Usually, when a patent infringement action is filed, the alleged infringer counters by attacking the patent's validity. Patents may be held invalid on any of several grounds. The most common are if an alleged infringer can show that the invention wasn't novel or nonobvious, or that the patent examiner made a mistake in issuing the patent.

If the patent is not invalidated, and the defendant is found to have infringed, the court may issue an order (injunction) preventing the infringer from any further use or sale of the infringing device and award damages to the patent owner. Alternatively, the court may work with the parties to hammer out an agreement under which the infringing party will pay the patent owner royalties in exchange for permission to use the infringing device.

When does a patent expire or otherwise come to an end?

The most common reason for a patent to come to an end is that the statutory period during which it is in force expires. For utility and plant patents, the statutory period is 20 years after the application date. Design patents last for 15 years from issuance, or, if filed before May 13, 2015, 14 years from issuance.

Another common reason why patents expire is that the patent owner fails to pay required maintenance fees. Usually, this occurs because attempts to exploit the underlying invention commercially have failed, and the patent owner chooses not to throw good money after bad.

A patent may also be declared invalid (and no longer in force) if it is later shown that the patent application was insufficient, that the applicant committed fraud on the USPTO (usually by lying about or failing to disclose the applicant's knowledge about prior art that would legally preclude the issuance of the patent), or that the inventor engaged in illegal conduct when using the patent—such as conspiring with a patent licensee to exclude other companies from competing with them.

Once a patent has terminated for any reason, the invention described by the patent falls into the public domain: It can be used by anyone without permission. The patent owner has no more rights to the invention than any member of the public. Television and personal computers' primary technologies are good examples of valuable inventions that are no longer covered by in-force patents.

The fact that an invention is in the public domain does not mean that subsequent developments based on the original invention are also in the public domain. Instead, new inventions that improve public domain technology are constantly being conceived and patented. For instance, televisions and personal computers that roll off today's assembly lines employ many recent inventions covered by in-force patents.

What about international protection for U.S. patents?

The right to control or monopolize an invention that a patent owner enjoys in the United States, originates in the U.S. Constitution. It is implemented exclusively by federal laws passed by Congress. These laws define the kinds of patentable inventions and the procedures that must be utilized to apply for, receive, and maintain the patent in full force for its entire period.

All other industrialized countries also offer inventors protection in the form of a patent. While the standards of what is patentable and the period that patents last differ from country to country, several international treaties (including the Patent Cooperation Treaty and the Paris Convention) allow U.S. inventors to obtain patent protection in certain other countries if they take specific required steps, such as filing a patent application in the countries on a timely basis and paying required patent fees.

What's new in patent law since the last edition?

Below are the significant events in patent law since the last edition of this book was published.

Common Patent Acronyms

AIA – America Invents Act

CAFC – Court of Appeals for the Federal Circuit

IPR – Inter Partes Review

PTAB – Patent Trial and Appeal Board

USPTO – United States Patent and Trademark Office.

- **Supreme Court limits assignor estoppel.** Under the doctrine of "assignor estoppel," an inventor who assigns invention rights is precluded from later challenging the validity of the assigned patent when the result "conflicts with an explicit or implicit representation made in assigning patent rights." So, for example, an assignment that prohibits challenging the patent would stop an assignor from later claiming invalidity. But, according to the Supreme Court, "absent that kind of inconsistency, an invalidity defense raises no concern of fair dealing—so assignor estoppel has no place." (*Minerva Surgical, Inc. v. Hologic, Inc.*, 594 U.S. _____ (2021).)

- **No appeal from denial of inter partes review based on 35 U.S. Code Section 315(b).** According to 35 U.S. Code Section 315(b), if someone who is not the patent applicant attempts to challenge it with a request for *inter partes* review (IPR) more than a year after a suit against the requesting party for patent infringement, the IPR will not be instituted. After the Patent Trial and Appeal Board (PTAB) instituted an IPR in this case, the company whose patents were at stake objected that it was barred by 35 U.S. Code Section 315(b). The Supreme Court held that the PTAB's "determination ... whether to institute an inter partes review under this section shall be final and nonappealable." In summary, patent law does not allow an appeal of the PTAB's decision to institute a procedure for challenging the validity of a patent after finding that a one-year time bar does not apply. (*Thryv, Inc. v. Click-To-Call Technologies, LP*, 140 S. Ct. 1367 (2020).)

- **Supreme Court denies attorneys' fees to USPTO.** The U.S. Supreme Court unanimously ruled that the USPTO's attempt to recoup its legal fees violated the American rule, the principle that each party pays for its lawyers. It stated that patent law (specifically 35 U.S. Code § 145) does not permit the USPTO to recover the salaries of its lawyers. (*Peter v. NantKwest, Inc.*, 140 S. Ct. 365, 205 L. Ed. 2d 304, 589 U.S. _____ (Supreme Court, 2019).)

- **Supreme Court rules that PTAB judges are unconstitutionally appointed … but creates a fix.** Decisions made by PTAB's Administrative Patent Judges (APJs) are not reviewable, under the Appointments Clause of the Constitution. (APJs must be "directed and supervised at some level by others who were appointed by Presidential nomination with the advice and consent of the Senate.") Therefore, said the Supreme Court, the APJs are unconstitutional. However, the high court found a fix: giving the USPTO director the discretion to review APJ's decisions. (*Smith & Nephew, Inc. v. Arthrex, Inc.* and *Arthrex, Inc. v. Smith & Nephew, Inc.*, 594 U.S. _____ (2021).)

- **Supreme Court likely to review Section 101 eligibility case.** In *American Axle v. Neapco Holdings*, the CAFC invalidated a drive shaft patent after applying the Supreme Court's two-part "Alice Test." The controversial decision added confusion regarding patents that recite what is known as the "§ 101 natural law exception." The Supreme Court is expected to hear an appeal.

- **CAFC affirms Section 101 patent ineligibility for an abstract idea.** The CAFC analyzed a patent for transmission of advertising data for a set-top box. Applying the two-step Alice test, it determined in step one that the claims were directed to an abstract idea (not an improvement to computer functionality). Because the claims did not "enable computers to operate any more quickly, nor do they solve any technological problem," they were "at most an improvement to the abstract concept of targeted advertising wherein a computer is merely used as a tool." (*Customedia Techs, LLC v. Dish Network Corp.*, 951 F.3d 1359 (Fed. Cir. 2020).)

- **Secondary factors in obviousness analysis cannot be presumed.** When making an obviousness analysis of a bicycle chainring patent, the CAFC held that secondary factors such as commercial success cannot be presumed and that such considerations must have a connection to the patent claims. That is, there must be a sufficient connection between the evidence and the patented invention. (*Fox Factory Inc. v. SRAM LLC*, 944 F.3d 1366 (Fed. Cir. 2019).)

- **PTAB can rule on Section 101 patentability.** Petitioners can request an IPR to disprove the patentability of an issued patent. But they are limited to disproving patent validity under 35 U.S. Code Section 102 (novelty/prior art) or Section 103 (obviousness). Nevertheless, PTAB judges also consider whether the claims contain ineligible subject matter under 35 U.S. Code Section 101 (novelty). In this case, one party appealed after an adverse ruling, claiming that the PTAB was not permitted to rule on Section 101 criteria. The CAFC held that the PTAB does have the power to decide whether a new claim is patentable under Section 101. (*Uniloc 2017 LLC v. Hulu, LLC, Netflix, Inc., et al.* (Fed. Cir. July 22, 2020).)

- **Article III standing required to appeal USPTO decisions.** A party who is dissatisfied with an IPR ruling can appeal it to the CAFC. However, to bring the appeal, parties requesting relief must demonstrate what's called "standing"—almost literally, their right to "stand" before the court. More specifically, appealing to the CAFC requires Article III standing (Article III being the portion of the Constitution establishing the federal court system). Typically, a party demonstrates Article III standing by showing it has suffered an injury. One type of injury, called the doctrine of competitor standing, occurs when the government causes economic injury to one party. In this case, the CAFC rejected the argument that competitor standing doctrine applied to unsuccessful IPR petitioners. In summary, although parties to an IPR are entitled to pursue appeals, they still must show Article III standing. (*AVX Corp. v. Presidio Components Inc.*, 923 F.3d 1357 (Fed. Cir. 2019).)

- **Design patent limited by claims language.** A design patent entitled "Pattern for a Chair" claimed an "ornamental design for a chair." The drawings, however, showed only the pattern, not a chair with the pattern. Defendants used a similar design on a basket. The CAFC prevented the design owner from proceeding against the basket maker because there was no mention of baskets in the application and the design patent was therefore limited to chairs. (*Curver Luxembourg SARL v. Home Expressions Inc.*, CV-2018-2214 (CAFC, September 2, 2019).)

- **An inventor must be a natural person.** A patent application was rejected because the applicant failed to name a natural person (a human being) as the inventor. The application documentation listed the inventor's given name as "DABUS" and the family name as "Invention generated by artificial intelligence." The assignee (and the person who supplied the application) stated that artificial intelligence created the invention autonomously. The USPTO rejected that argument, pointing out that the patent statute identifies the "inventor" as an individual (35 U.S. Code § 115a). (*In re Application No. 16/524,350,* July 29, 2019.)

- **CAFC rules that evidence of competitor copying can be used to show non-obviousness.** Fighting against patent invalidity (due to nonobviousness), a hair-care company offered proof that its hair-bleaching process was copied by a competitor using confidential information. The Patent Trial and Appeals Board concluded that the evidence was irrelevant. On appeal, the CAFC disagreed with the PTAB, holding that copying confidential information without authorization from the patent applicant should be included as a "secondary consideration" when determining nonobviousness. The CAFC remanded the case to the PTAB to consider the evidence of competitor copying. (*Liqwd, Inc. v. L'Oreal USA, Inc.,* No. 18-2152 (Fed. Cir. 2019).)

- **Inequitable conduct can taint a family of patents.** When a patent applicant commits fraud or inequitable conduct in communicating with the USPTO or during the patent application process, a court may later refuse to enforce that patent (the patent is invalidated). Often the tainted patent is part of a group of patents owned by the same party: that is, patents covering similar subject matter. If inequitable conduct occurred only during the prosecution of one patent, associated patents will still be enforceable. However, if the conduct was so bad that the owner's "unclean hands" tainted a family of patents, then, under the doctrine of "infectious unenforceability," all of the patents will be adjudged unenforceable. In *Guardant Health, Inc. v. Foundation Medicine, Inc.,* a Delaware District Court cited this doctrine when it refused to dismiss claims that a family of patents could be invalidated. The court rejected the argument that inequitable conduct must be related only to patent prosecution. (*Guardant Health, Inc. v. Foundation Medicine, Inc.,* 1-17-cv-01616 (D.C. Del. Jan 7, 2020).)

- **A patent owner is bound by admission to USPTO regarding prior art.** The plaintiff, a paint company, had previously admitted to the USPTO that a prior art document disclosed a BPA-free coating. The statement was made during a reexamination proceeding, which was later vacated. The district court determined that a prior admission to the USPTO during a vacated reexamination proceeding is binding on the parties. (*The Sherwin-Williams Company v. PPG Industries, Inc.,* 2-17-cv-01023 (W.D. PA 2021-01-21, Order).)

- **User manual considered publicly accessible print publication.** A company sought to invalidate a patent by introducing a user manual as a prior art printed publication. The patent owner argued that the manual was not publicly accessible. The PTAB disagreed, noting that a manual included with the sale of a product (even with sales of 586 of those products) constituted public accessibility. (*Cisco Systems, Inc. v. Centripetal Networks*, IPR2018-01436, Paper No. 40, January 23, 2020.)

- **USPTO offers a Fast-Track Appeals Pilot Program.** Under the Fast-Track Appeals Pilot Program, appellants can have their ex parte appeals advanced out of turn. To request this, appellants file a petition and pay a $420 petition fee. The PTAB has set a target of issuing a decision within six months from the date the petition is granted, and the ex parte appeal is entered into the pilot program. This pilot program became effective on July 2, 2020 and is scheduled to run until July 2, 2022.

- **Patent refused for invention lacking scientific support.** A group of inventors applied for patents for inventions related to "quantum entanglement." In reviewing the claims, the USPTO determined there was no scientific evidence to support the inventions. The examiner stated that the claims violated the first law of thermodynamics, fundamental chemistry laws, classical physics laws, and the principle of conservation of mass. On appeal, the CAFC supported the USPTO position, stating "concepts that strain scientific principles are properly held to a heightened standard, typically measured by reproducibility of results." The CAFC referred to inventions for perpetual motion machines and cold fusion as having similar patentability problems. (*In re Huping Hu*, 2021 U.S. App. LEXIS 7776.)

- **Patent for online loan application process invalidated as an abstract idea.** Since the Supreme Court's 2014 decision in *Alice v. CLS Bank*, it's been open season on so-called Internet patents—that is, abstract ideas implemented on a generic computer. In this case, the patent owner claimed a process involving receipt of a loan application, a comparison of information, and filling in a second document with the received information. Because the process failed to include a change or improvement in functionality, the district court invalidated the patent under 35 U.S. Code Section 101. (*Mortg. Application Techs., LLC v. Meridianlink, Inc.*, No. 19-CV-704, 2020 WL 1000581 (C.D. Cal. Jan. 6, 2020) *aff'd*. No. 20-1504 (CAFC Jan. 12, 2021).)

- **Ongoing license discussions might preclude a declaratory judgment.** Before an actual lawsuit, a typical scenario is that the patent owner threatens suit via a cease and desist letter, then the accused infringer requests a binding judgment from a court defining the legal relationship between parties. There are advantages to these declaratory actions—they allow the accused infringer to file in a nearby jurisdiction instead of traveling far to defend a lawsuit. A federal court may issue a declaratory judgment only when there is an actual controversy (Article III). In this case, the CAFC refused to hear declaratory judgment actions filed while licensing negotiations were ongoing. The court reasoned that dismissing such cases is consistent with the policy of promoting "extrajudicial dispute resolution." (*Commc'ns Test Design, Inc. v. Contec LLC*, 367 F. Supp. 3d. 350, 360 (E.D. Pa. 2019).)

Patent resources

If you're interested in hands-on, step-by-step instructions on applying for a patent or want more information on patent law, consult one of these Nolo resources:

- *Patent It Yourself,* by David Pressman and David Blau
- *Patent Pending in 24 Hours,* by Richard Stim and David Pressman
- *How to Make Patent Drawings*, by Jack Lo and David Pressman
- *Profit From Your Idea: How to Make Smart Licensing Deals*, by Richard Stim, and
- *Nolo's Patents for Beginners,* by David Pressman and Richard Stim.

You might also find valuable information related to patents at these sites:

- **The USPTO (www.uspto.gov).** This is the place for current policy and statutory changes and transcripts of hearings on various patent law issues. You can also use this site to search patents issued since 1971.
- **Dear Rich: Nolo's Patent, Copyright & Trademark Blog (www.dearrichblog.com).** This intellectual property blog operates as a companion to this book. Answers are provided to common intellectual property questions.
- **Center for Global Innovation/Patent Metrics (www.bustpatents.com).** Directed by Gregory Aharonian, one of the USPTO's most vocal critics, this site provides a free email newsletter, critiques, legal reviews, file wrappers, and information about infringement lawsuits relating to software patents.

Patent Law: Definitions

B elow are definitions of the words and phrases commonly used in patent-related activities.

abandonment of patent application

The USPTO considers a patent application abandoned if the applicant fails to respond on time to actions or requests it initiated.

The USPTO's response to most patent applications is to send the applicant a notice (called an office action) rejecting one or more aspects of the application. The applicant must then amend the application or provide another suitable response within three months to keep the application alive.

In the event an application is treated by the USPTO as abandoned, the applicant may:

- petition the Director of the USPTO to set aside the abandonment decision
- file a substitute application—which means paying additional fees and being given a later filing date (harmful if another applicant applies for a similar invention between the first and second filing dates), or
- forget about the patent and if possible, utilize another available form of intellectual property protection, such as trade secrecy (assuming the invention has not been published or publicly disclosed) or trademark (for example, using a clever name for the invention to capture market share).

Related terms: claims; prosecution of a patent application; substitute patent application.

abstract

This paragraph in the patent application (also known as the "Abstract of the Disclosure") concisely summarizes the invention's general nature, structure, and purpose.

Related terms: *Official Gazette* (OG); patent application.

accused device

An accused device is an invention that is alleged to have been used or sold in a manner that infringes a patented invention.

actual reduction to practice

See reduction to practice.

admissions by inventor

Any statements about an invention, made by the inventor, may be used by the USPTO to reject a patent application or cause a court to rule against the invention's validity. Thus an inventor should avoid writing anything in a patent application or correspondence with the USPTO that derogates the invention. The statement will constitute an admission that can later be introduced by the USPTO or by a competitor to fight the patent.

Related terms: certificate of correction; duty of candor and good faith; file wrapper estoppel.

AEP (Accelerated Examination Program)

Under the Accelerated Examination Program (AEP), the USPTO will advance an application out of turn for examination if the applicant files a Petition to Make Special under the AEP program and the petition is granted. The final disposition of the application typically occurs within 12 months. The AEP program supersedes (although it does not replace) the process whereby applicants file petitions to make special (PTMS). The USPTO has revised the procedures for petitions to make special, except those based on the applicant's health or age. Other petitions to make special (i.e., based on: manufacture, infringement, environmental quality, energy, recombinant DNA, superconductivity materials, HIV/AIDS and cancer, countering terrorism, and biotechnology applications filed by small entities; see MPEP § 708.02) will be processed using the revised AEP procedure. The AEP requires that an applicant file electronically using EFS-Web and Form SB28 at the same time. For more information see the USPTO explanation at www.uspto.gov/patent/initiatives/accelerated-examination.

Related terms: Track One: Prioritized Examination.

AIPLA

The AIPLA (American Intellectual Property Law Association) is the largest organization of intellectual property lawyers in the United States (www.aipla.org).

AIR (Automated Interview Request)

See Automated Interview Request (AIR).

algorithms

An algorithm is a mathematical procedure that can be used to solve a problem or class of problems. Common examples of algorithms are mathematical formulas, geometry axioms, and algebraic equations. Algorithms are not patentable because the patent would create a vast and fundamental monopoly over laws of nature.

> EXAMPLE: The Heisenberg uncertainty principle, a well-known law of nature, states that you cannot design an apparatus to determine a subatomic particle's location and momentum simultaneously. This principle is relevant to many scientific and electrical engineering applications; thus, a patent on it would give the patent owner exclusive control of the development of these applications. Effectively, a patent on the Heisenberg uncertainty principle would either halt progress in any field where the principle applies or force all would-be developers to pay license fees to the patent holder.

The rule against patenting algorithms was applied to computer software because software primarily consists of procedural instructions in a mathematical form that make a computer accomplish a specific and definite result. However, the U.S. Patent and Trademark Office will allow patents on that aspect of software that accomplishes a useful, concrete, and tangible result, and provided that the software process is tied to a particular machine or transforms an article into a different state.

Related terms: laws of nature exception to patents; software patents.
See also Part 2 (Copyright Law): computer software.

Alice Corp. v. CLS

In *Alice Corp. v. CLS Bank International,* the Supreme Court struck a significant blow against software patents when it invalidated a computer-assisted process for exchanging financial obligations, holding that it was an abstract idea, ineligible for patent protection. This decision cast a cloud on many existing software patents and made the future of business method patents unclear. Inventors may no longer simply merge existing ideas within a software context—for example, claim a computer-assisted auction method. (*Alice Corporation Pty. Ltd. v. CLS Bank International et al.*, 573 U.S. 208 (2014).)

Related terms: software patents; Alice Test (Alice/Mayo Test).

Patent Law: Definitions

Alice Test (Alice/Mayo Test)

The Alice Test (also known as the "Alice/Mayo Test") is a two-step method for determining the patentability ("patent eligibility") of inventions that include laws of nature, abstract ideas, or natural phenomena. This test includes the standards set by the Supreme Court in several cases, including *Alice Corporation Pty. Ltd. v. CLS Bank International*, *Mayo v. Prometheus*, and *Association for Molecular Pathology v. Myriad Genetics*.

Step 1: Do the patent claims fall within the statutory subject matter (a process, machine, manufacture, or composition of matter)? If yes, proceed to the second step, which is divided into two parts.

Step 2A: Are the patent claims directed to a law of nature, a natural phenomenon, or an abstract idea (judicial exceptions)? If no, the invention is eligible, and examination should continue for patentability. If yes, proceed to Step 2B.

Step 2B: Do the claims as a whole amount to significantly more than the judicial exception?

EXAMPLE: The CAFC analyzed a patent for transmission of advertising data for a set-top box and determined that the claims were directed to an abstract idea (not an improvement to computer functionality). Because the claims did not "enable computers to operate any more quickly, nor do they solve any technological problem," they were "at most an improvement to the abstract concept of targeted advertising wherein a computer is merely used as a tool." (*Customedia Techs, LLC v. Dish Network Corp.*, 951 F.3d 1359 (Fed. Cir. 2020).)

EXAMPLE: A patent owner claimed a process involving receipt of a loan application, a comparison of information, and filling in a second document with the received information. Because the process failed to include a change or improvement in functionality, the district court invalidated the patent under 35 U.S. Code § 101. (*Mortg. Application Techs., LLC v. Meridianlink, Inc.*, No. 19-CV-704, 2020 WL 1000581 (C.D. Cal. Jan. 6, 2020) *aff'd*. No. 20-1504 (Fed. Cir. Jan. 12, 2021).)

For assistance interpreting the Alice Test criteria, review MPEP Section 2106.

Related terms: *Alice Corp. v. CLS;* laws of nature exception to patents; *Mayo v. Prometheus*; nonstatutory subject matter.

allowance

The decision by the USPTO to award a patent to an applicant is referred to as an allowance (the application is "allowed"). The USPTO sends the applicant a notice of allowance; this usually occurs after the initial claims were amended at least once during the prosecution of the patent application.

Related terms: certificate of correction; prosecution of a patent application.

amendment of patent application

A patent application may be amended (changed) in response to an initial rejection by the U.S. Patent and Trademark Office. Patent examiners often reject the initial application as filed, most commonly because the scope of the patent being applied for is too broad in light of previous developments in that field (the prior art). Other common reasons for rejection are noncompliance with rules governing how the invention must be described in words or portrayed in drawings.

This initial rejection includes an explanation and copies of any patents that seem very similar (called prior art references) and have contributed to the rejection. Upon receiving a rejection, an applicant usually files an amendment, in one part changing the application per the examiner's requirements and in the other part contesting such requirements. Alternatively, an applicant may contest the examiner's decisions completely or file an amendment that completely conforms the application to the examiner's requirements.

Related terms: office action; prosecution of a patent application.

America Invents Act (AIA)

Modifications to the patent law were enacted in September 2011, with the passage of the America Invents Act (also known as the Leahy-Smith America Invents Act). The most significant change is that the U.S. switched to a first-to-file system in March 2013.

Below are the changes resulting from passage of the AIA

The law was enacted over 18 months, and the provisions are listed here in the order each went into effect.

- **Tougher to obtain an *inter partes* reexam.** It is harder to obtain patent reexamination. (The Director can authorize a reexam only if "there is a reasonable likelihood that the petitioner would prevail concerning at least one of the claims challenged in the petition.") And there is no more federal court review of USPTO reexaminations.

- **Easier for prior users to defend.** If you're sued for infringement but you were commercially using the patented technology more than one year before the filing date of the claimed invention, you have a defense against a claim that you infringed (although that defense doesn't invalidate the patent). The Act includes a definition of "commercial use."
- **Goodbye to tax strategy patents.** The USPTO stopped granting patents for strategies for reducing, avoiding, or deferring tax liability.
- **Goodbye, best mode defense.** Before, accused patent infringers often used the "best mode defense." They argued that the patent holder failed to disclose the best mode of carrying out the invention. The best mode defense was eliminated.
- **Hello, virtual website marking.** Virtual marking—the process of using a publicly accessible website to provide a link between a patented invention and its patent number—is now considered as sufficiently providing public notice for that patent.
- **Harder to go after false markers.** It had become standard practice for parties to bring a lawsuit claiming (or making a counterclaim) that an invention was falsely marked, especially if the mark existed on copies of the invention after the patent had expired. The Act provides that privately filed false marking claims (those not brought by the government) require proof of competitive injury. Marking with the number of a patent that covered that product but has expired is no longer considered false marking.
- **New rules when joining defendants.** Joinder of unrelated accused infringers is limited in actions commenced on and after enactment.
- **No patenting humans.** Issuance of patent claims directed to or encompassing a human organism is barred as of enactment.
- **The Luddite penalty.** A new higher fee must be paid by those applicants who do not file utility patent applications electronically.
- **Modifications to the inventor's oath/assignment.** The Act modifies specific requirements regarding the oath or declaration required of an inventor. If an inventor has assigned (or is obligated to assign) an invention, the assignee can apply for the patent.
- **Narrows post-grant reviews.** The Act provides that *inter partes* hearings after a patent has been issued are now limited to challenges for novelty and nonobviousness to issues relating to Sections 102 and 103 of the patent law. Such claims can be based only on prior art consisting of patents and printed

publications and must be filed nine months after the patent is issued. This provision also establishes many additional technical and procedural rules for post-grant reviews, generally making it more challenging to bring post-grant reviews. For example, it prohibits a post-grant review and *inter partes* review if the party filing has filed a related civil action before filing the petition.

- **Changes to Patent Trial and Appeal Board.** The Act sets forth new rules about the Board and provides appeals to the CAFC from certain Board decisions.
- **Submitting "gotcha" documentation.** Before the USPTO grants a patent, the Act allows a third party to submit relevant publications for the patent examiner to consider (commonly referred to as preissuance submissions).
- **Patent owner's right to supplemental exam.** The Act establishes a system of supplemental examinations for a patent owner "to consider, reconsider, and correct information believed to be relevant to the patent."
- **A new look at business patents.** The Act requires the Director to establish a transitional post-grant review proceeding to consider the validity of business-method patents.
- **First to file; not first to invent.** Patents filed 18 months after enactment are subject to new first-to-file and prior art rules, effectively ending centuries of first-to-invent rules. The previous one-year on-sale bar—that permitted sale or disclosure of the claimed invention less than one year before filing—is terminated. However, the Act establishes a limited one-year grace period allowing patent filing even if the inventor (or anyone who obtained the subject matter from the inventor) made certain disclosures of the claimed invention. The novelty and nonobviousness sections of the patent law (Sections 102 and 103) are amended, and existing provisions relating to inventions made abroad and statutory invention registration are terminated.
- **New rules for fighting earlier effective patent filing.** The Act permits a patent owner to bring a "derivation hearing" at the USPTO (replacing interference proceedings) against another patent owner claiming to have the same invention and who has an earlier effective filing date. The derivation hearing must be filed within one year, beginning on the first publication of a claim in the earlier filed application. Alternatively, the patent owner may sue the owner of another patent that claims the same invention and has an earlier effective filing date. These lawsuits can be brought only if the invention claiming priority was derived directly from the person seeking relief.

Patent Law: Definitions

anticipation

An invention is "anticipated" when it is too similar to an earlier invention to be considered novel. Because novelty is a requirement for patentability, anticipated inventions are not patentable.

An invention may be anticipated in any of the following ways:

- Prior publication in such writings as a news article, trade journal article, academic thesis, or prior patent. For example, Fred invents a low-cost kit that permits the car's driver to monitor ten different engine functions while driving. If all of this kit's primary characteristics (elements) had been described by someone else in a publication or patent before Fred filed his application, the invention would be considered anticipated by the published reference. It would be barred from receiving a patent. Note: The America Invents Act established a limited one-year grace period allowing filing if the inventor (or anyone who obtained the subject matter from the inventor) made certain disclosures about the invention.

- By the existence of a prior invention, if all significant elements of the later invention are found in an earlier one predating the application's filing. Suppose Sam "invents" an electric generator driven by the kinetic energy of the car's moving wheels. All essential elements used by Sam in his "invention" can be found in a prior invention (whether patented or not) by Jake. The latter used his invention openly—without suppressing or concealing it—so Sam's generator has been anticipated.

- By placing the invention on sale before an application's being filed. "On sale" means not only an actual sale but any offer of sale. For example, suppose Sam offers to sell his invention to a major car manufacturer before filing a patent application. In that case, the offer will anticipate the invention even if the sale never takes place.

- By public use or display of the invention before filing the patent application. For example, if Fred publicly demonstrated his kit before filing for a patent, the invention would be considered "anticipated" because the earlier public display would render the invention no longer "novel" at the time of applying. However, if the public demonstrations were predominately for experimental purposes, the rule might not apply. Anticipation through public use or display rarely occurs.

Anticipation by a prior invention or printed publication—that is, a prior art reference—can occur only if all of the later invention's basic elements are contained in a single invention or a single publication. For example, if a news article describes some elements of an invention and a prior invention shows the rest, no anticipation has occurred because no single reference contained all the elements.

In a case involving a new use for a composition, the CAFC held that claims were anticipated when (1) the prior references disclosed each element of the claimed invention, and (2) the prior references enabled a person of ordinary skill in the art to practice the invention without undue experimentation (*In re Marin Gleave and Maxim Signaevsky*, 560 F.3d 1331 (Fed. Cir. 2009).) In another case, the CAFC held that prior art—to anticipate an invention—must disclose all elements of a claim and must disclose those elements as they are arranged in the claim. The CAFC analogized to a recipe in which the ingredients must be combined in a particular order. (*Net MoneyIn, Inc. v. Verisign*, 545 F.3d 1359 (Fed. Cir. 2008).)

Note: The previous one-year on-sale bar—that permitted sale or disclosure of the claimed invention less than one year before filing—was terminated after the passage of the AIA in 2011. The Act established a limited one-year grace period allowing filing if the inventor (or anyone who obtained the subject matter from the inventor) makes certain disclosures of the claimed invention.

Related terms: novelty; printed publication as statutory bar; prior art reference; public use.

antishelving clause

This provision in a licensing agreement makes permission to use a patented invention contingent on the willingness of the party receiving the license to use the patent commercially within a designated period (rather than acquiring the patent to put the invention out of commission—that is, "putting it on the shelf ").

antitrust law (federal) and patents

Federal antitrust laws generally prohibit businesses from engaging in monopolistic activities—that is, to engage in practices purposely designed to give the dominant business control over a particular market segment. However, by definition, a patent is a legal monopoly over an invention's production, use, and distribution. In an attempt to reconcile these conflicting legal goals, the United States (and most countries) restricts the ways companies holding patents may use them in the marketplace.

In addition to preventing monopolistic activities, antitrust laws prohibit business practices that restrain the free flow of commerce (called restraint of trade). Among the more common types of patent-related activity that can potentially cause antitrust violations are:

- price-fixing—for example, a patent owner requiring licensees of a patent to charge specific prices for goods manufactured under the patent
- exclusive dealing agreements—for example, a patent owner encouraging patent licensees not to deal with specific customers
- tying agreements—that is, requiring a customer who wishes to purchase the patented invention also to purchase other goods or services as a condition of the purchase; for instance, putting a provision in a license agreement that requires the licensee of a mainframe computer to use the licensor to service the computer would tie the purchase of the computer to the purchase of the service
- requirements contracts, whether mandatory or encouraged by price reductions—for example, prohibiting a purchaser of goods covered by a patent from purchasing comparable items from another source
- patent thickets—a collection of patents owned by various companies that prevent a newcomer from entering a field of technology or invention
- territorial restrictions—for example, restricting licensees to some geographical regions in their marketing of goods covered by the patent, and
- concerted refusal to deal—for example, excluding some potential customers from using the device or process covered by the patent while including others.

Some courts had held that when a drug company with patents pays a generic drug company to stay out of the market (known as a "pay-for-delay" or "reverse payment"), it is permitted to do so under patent law. But the Supreme Court ruled that these deals may be anticompetitive and that patent law doesn't shield them from antitrust laws. (*Federal Trade Commission v. Actavis, Inc.*, 133 S. Ct. 2223 (2013).)

Practically speaking, antitrust laws should not be a concern for most patent owners. Few patents have a large enough impact on the related market or industry to raise the antitrust warning flag. If, however, a patent is so broad in its coverage that the actual ebb and flow of commerce might be affected by it, there is no substitute for good knowledge of antitrust law. This is especially true when important inventions are involved in patent infringement lawsuits because defendants often charge that the plaintiff committed an antitrust violation and therefore cannot enforce the patent.

Related terms: defenses to a patent infringement claim; patent misuse; patent thickets; price-fixing.

appeals

See Patent Trial and Appeal Board (PTAB).

application filing fees

Fees for filing a patent application typically include a filing fee (which is reduced if you file electronically), a search fee, and an examination fee. The fees are reduced by 50% for small entities and reduced by 75% for micro entities. You can determine current fees at the USPTO website: www.uspto.gov/learning-and-resources/fees-and-payment.

Related terms: issue fee; micro entity; small entity.

application issue fees

See issue fee.

Article III standing

See standing.

assignment of a patent

An assignment is a document that transfers a patent owner's rights in exchange for money payable in a lump sum or royalties on future sales of the invention.

Many inventors assign their invention, either to the company they work for under an employment agreement or, in the case of independent inventors, to outside development or manufacturing companies. These assignments typically transfer ownership of any patent that issues on the invention and may (although usually not in the case of employed inventors) provide for compensation for the inventor, although employed inventors, often receive little or no additional compensation because they are getting paid to invent.

As a result of the America Invents Act, a person or organization that has been assigned patent rights can apply as the "applicant." (Before this change, the term "applicant" was always synonymous with the inventor.) Even though an assignee can file, the inventor(s) must still execute an oath or declaration (except in limited circumstances). In addition, an assignment (or an employment agreement) should be recorded no later than when the issue fee is paid.

Patent Law: Definitions

§ 118. Filing by other than inventor

A person to whom the inventor has assigned or is under an obligation to assign the invention may make an application for patent. A person who otherwise shows sufficient proprietary interest in the matter may make an application for patent on behalf of and as agent for the inventor on proof of the pertinent facts and a showing that such action is appropriate to preserve the rights of the parties. If the Director grants a patent on an application filed under this section by a person other than the inventor, the patent shall be granted to the real party in interest and upon such notice to the inventor as the Director considers to be sufficient.

Related terms: licensing of an invention; patent owner.

assignor estoppel

Under the doctrine of "assignor estoppel," an inventor who assigns invention rights is precluded from later challenging the validity of the assigned patent when the result "conflicts with an explicit or implicit representation made in assigning patent rights." So, for example, an assignment that prohibits challenging the patent would stop an assignor from later claiming invalidity. But, according to the Supreme Court, "absent that kind of inconsistency, an invalidity defense raises no concern of fair dealing—so assignor estoppel has no place." (*Minerva Surgical, Inc. v. Hologic, Inc.*, 594 U.S. ___ (2021).)

attorneys' fees

In "exceptional" patent cases, a court may award attorneys' fees to the prevailing party. In 2014, the Supreme Court clarified the term "exceptional," stating that it is "simply [a dispute] that stands out from others with regards to the strength of a company's case or the 'unreasonable manner' in which they made it." This determination (sometimes called an "exceptionality finding") gives judges more leeway to decide when a patent litigant is entitled to attorneys' fees. (*Octane Fitness v. Icon Health and Fitness* and *Highmark v. Allcare Health*, 572 U.S. 559 (2014).) In 2019, the U.S. Supreme Court unanimously ruled that the USPTO's attempt to recoup its legal fees violated the American rule, the principle that each party pays for its lawyers. The Supreme Court held that patent law (specifically 35 U,S, Code § 145) did not permit the USPTO to recover the salaries of its lawyers. (*Peter v. NantKwest, Inc.*, 589 U.S. ___ (2019).)

Attorneys' fee awards are often based on litigation misconduct, although "[A] finding of exceptionality based on litigation misconduct usually does not support a full award of attorneys' fees." (*Rembrandt v. Comcast*, No. 2017-1784 (Fed. Cir. August 15, 2018).)

Attorneys and Agents Registered to Practice Before the U.S. Patent and Trademark Office

See patent attorneys.

Automated Interview Request (AIR)

The Automated Interview Request (AIR) Form is an online form that allows inventors and practitioners to submit an online request for an interview with an examiner. The form is intended to replace the Applicant Initiated Interview Request Form. To use the AIR form, an applicant must agree to communicate via the Internet; and propose a date, time, and type of interview (in person or by telephone). The request for an interview is immediately entered into the record, and the examiner is expected to contact the applicant within two business days.

Bayh-Dole Act

The Bayh-Dole Act, enacted in 1980, permits universities to claim patent rights in inventions created at the university with federal funding. The university may license these discoveries to private industry—a practice some critics have likened to corporate welfare.

As a result of Bayh-Dole, university patent acquisition and licensing has expanded dramatically. Before 1980, U.S. universities acquired fewer than 150 patents per year. However, 20 years later, the University of California alone obtained 324 patents (and earned $261 million in licensing revenue). Regulations for the Bayh-Dole law (35 U.S. Code §§ 200–212) can be found at 37 C.F.R. Part 401.

The key regulations are as follows:

- The university must have written agreements with its faculty and technical staff requiring disclosure and assignment of inventions.
- The university must disclose each new invention to the federal funding agency within two months after the inventor discloses it in writing to the university.
- The decision whether or not to retain title to the invention must be made within two years after disclosing the invention to the agency.
- The university must file a patent application within one year or before the end of any statutory period in which valid patent protection can be obtained in the United States.
- Any company holding an exclusive license to a patent that involves sales of a product in the United States must substantially manufacture the product in the U.S.

Patent Law: Definitions

- In their marketing of an invention, universities must give preference to small business firms (fewer than 500 employees), provided such firms have the resources and capability for bringing the invention to practical application. However, if a large company has also provided research support for the development of the invention, that company may be awarded the license.
- Universities may not assign their ownership of inventions to third parties, except to patent-management organizations.
- Universities must share with the inventor(s) a portion of any revenue received from licensing the invention. Any remaining revenue, after expenses, must be used to support scientific research or education.
- Under certain circumstances, the government can require the university to grant a license to a third party, or the government may take title and grant licenses itself (these are called "march-in rights").

In 2004, in a demonstration of the federal government's power under Bayh-Dole, the Court of Appeals for the Federal Circuit invalidated a patent because the patent owner, a recipient of federal funds, failed to make adequate disclosures regarding its invention as required under the Act. (*Campbell Plastics v. Brownlee*, 389 F.3d 1243 (Fed. Cir. 2004).)

In a 2011 case involving Stanford University and the Roche pharmaceutical company, the Supreme Court was faced with two agreements signed by a university scientist: one in which he promised to assign rights to the university; and another in which he assigned rights to a company that Roche later purchased. The Supreme Court ruled that the agreement in which rights were assigned took precedence over promised rights. Stanford's position was that the inventor's rights automatically vested in the university under the Bayh-Dole Act. Curiously, one of the prerequisites for claiming these rights is that the university has had written agreements with its faculty and technical staff requiring disclosure and assignment of inventions. The ruling won't invalidate past assignments. But problems can occur in cases like this one, where two assignments appear to conflict. In addition, you can expect that universities will stop using language in which inventors promise to assign and instead automatically assign inventions. (*Stanford v. Roche*, 563 U.S. 776 (2011).)

Related terms: march-in rights.

best mode disclosure requirement

See disclosure requirement for patents.

Bilski v. Kappos

Coinventors Bernard Bilski and Rand Warsaw sought to patent a three-step process to limit risks in hedge fund investments. The examiner rejected the applications because the claims merely "manipulated an abstract idea" and solved a "purely mathematical problem." On appeal, the CAFC affirmed the rejection. The CAFC held that for a process claim to be patentable, it must either (1) be tied to a particular machine or apparatus or (2) transform an article into a different state or thing. (*In re Bilski,* 545 F.3d 943 (Fed. Cir. 2008).) The ruling threatened the validity of many business method and software patents. In 2010, the Supreme Court agreed with the CAFC that the Bilski process was unpatentable because it was an abstract idea. However, the Supreme Court rejected the CAFC's view that the so-called "machine or transformation" test should be the sole standard for patentability. ("There are reasons to doubt whether the test should be the sole criterion for determining the patentability of inventions in the Information Age," the Court stated.) The Supreme Court refused to categorically deny patentability to any class or category of otherwise patentable subject matter and in so doing, preserved the status quo and kept alive the concept of software, business method, and other process patents. (*Bilski v. Kappos,* 561 U.S. 593 (2010).)

blocking patent

When patents have claims that overlap each other in a manner that the invention claimed in one patent cannot be used or sold ("practiced" in patent lingo) without infringing the claims of the other patent and vice versa, each patent is referred to as a "blocking patent" since it blocks the use of the other.

Related terms: patent pools.

Board of Patent Appeals and Interferences (BPAI)

A tribunal of administrative judges of the U.S. Patent and Trademark Office that, before 2012, handled appeals of rejected applications and decided who was entitled to a patent whenever an interference occurred (when two or more inventors lay claim to the same invention). This administrative body was dissolved in 2012, and its duties were assumed by the Patent Trial and Appeal Board (PTAB).

Related terms: Court of Appeals for the Federal Circuit (CAFC); final office action; interference; prosecution of a patent application; Patent Trial and Appeal Board (PTAB).

breaking (or busting) a patent

To break a patent means to establish that an existing patent is invalid or unenforceable because of either of the following:

- It was improperly issued by the U.S. Patent and Trademark Office in the first place, or
- The patent owner legally misused it.

Patents are typically broken in the course of defending against a patent infringement charge brought by the patent owner.

Related terms: antitrust law (federal) and patents; defenses to a patent infringement claim; infringement action; patent misuse.

BRI (broadest reasonable interpretation)

Patent claims are reviewed and interpreted for validity during the patent application process (patent prosecution). USPTO examiners must give the words used in the claim the broadest reasonable interpretation (BRI) that is reasonably allowed. This standard—"giving each term in the claim its broadest reasonable construction consistent with the specification"—is incorporated in the federal regulations (37 C.F.R. § 1.56(b)). The Supreme Court held that the USPTO's BRI standard was a "reasonable exercise of Congress's rulemaking authority delegated to the Patent Office." (*Cuozzo Speed Technologies, LLC v. Lee*, 579 U.S. 261 (2016).) The goal of the BRI standard is to establish a clear record of what the applicant intends to claim. (*In re Morris*, 127 F.3d 1048 (Fed. Cir. 1997).) The BRI standard is not applied during court proceedings involving infringement and validity. In such cases, the court is less concerned with what the applicant intended to claim and more interested in how the claims can be interpreted based on a fully developed prosecution record.

Related terms: claims; prosecution of a patent application.

building and testing an invention

Before the passage of the America Invents Act, patent rights were determined by who was first to invent. After conception, the next step is to reduce the invention to practice—that is, to demonstrate that the invention functions for its intended purpose. Building and testing an invention before applying for a patent used to be strongly advised because a working model would more definitively establish the exact nature of the invention and make it much easier to describe the invention in the patent application. It also proved an important date in case a dispute arose as to who was first. Although building and testing may still benefit an inventor, it is of much less importance for determining patent rights for patents filed after March 2013.

Related terms: experimental use of an unpatented invention; interference; reduction to practice.

business methods as statutory subject matter

The business method patent—a term that encompasses novel ways of doing business—has had a tumultuous history and has an uncertain future. For many years it was assumed that methods of doing business were not patentable subject matter. However, in the case of *State Street Bank and Trust v. Signature*, 149 F.3d 1368 (Fed. Cir. 1998), the Court of Appeals for the Federal Circuit ruled that there is no logical basis for the business methods exception and that a business method constitutes statutory subject matter if it produces a useful, concrete, and tangible result. The business method approved of in the State Street case was part of a computer program that facilitates mutual-fund investing.

The patenting of business methods expanded with the Internet as innovators sought monopolies on business processes and software combinations. One of the most well-known is Amazon.com's "One-Click" system, which allows a repeat customer to bypass address and credit card data entry forms when placing an online order. (U.S. Pat. No. 5,960,411.)

Regardless of their categorization, all of these patents seem to have one thing in common: They expand ways of doing business in new technologies. After the State Street case, the number of applications filed in the principal class for business methods (Class 705) exploded.

As business method patents grew in popularity, so did the challenges to their validity. In 2010, one such challenge reached the Supreme Court, which refused to categorically deny patentability to any class or category of otherwise patentable subject matter. In doing so, the Supreme Court preserved the status quo and kept alive the concept of software, business method, and other process patents. (*Bilski v. Kappos*, 561 U.S. 593 (2010).)

In 2014, the future of business method patents became murkier when the Supreme Court declared a software patent invalid. The method employed—a computer-assisted process for exchanging financial obligations—was an abstract idea, ineligible for patent protection. The Supreme Court held that an innovator couldn't simply port an existing process—auction bidding—to the Internet and claim that the resulting combination was the patentable subject matter. (*Alice Corporation Pty. Ltd. v. CLS Bank International et al.*, 573 U.S. 208 (2014).) Sometimes, a business might have been using a particular business method prior to another company acquiring a patent on that method. For example, suppose Business A files for a business method patent. Still, Business B can show that it implemented and commercially used the method publicly more than a year before the filing. In that case, Business B has a good defense against the patent. This defense was created under a 1999 amendment to the patent law. (35 U.S. Code § 273(b).)

The America Invents Act, enacted in September 2011, established a review proceeding to consider the validity of particular "covered business method" (CBM) patents—primarily financial data processing methods.

Related terms: The Alice test (Alice/Mayo test); software patents; statutory subject matter; CBM (covered business method).

CBM (covered business method)

The America Invents Act (AIA) narrowly defines a group of covered business method patents (CBMs) and permits the USPTO to institute a review procedure for them. Section 18 of the America Invents Act (AIA) defines a CBM as "a patent that claims a method or corresponding apparatus for performing data processing or other operations used in the practice, administration, or management of a financial product or service, except that the term does not include patents for technological inventions." Some practitioners believed that the Patent Trial and Appeal Board (PTAB) cast a wider net than the AIA required and reviewed many business methods that did not qualify as CBMs. In *Unwired Planet v. Google*, the Federal Circuit stepped in to reverse a PTAB decision for ignoring the limiting "financial service patents" language. (*Unwired Planet, LLC v. Google Inc.*, 841 F.3d 1376 (Fed Cir. 2016).)

CCPA (Court of Customs and Patent Appeals)

Formerly, this court handled appeals from determinations by the U.S. Patent and Trademark Office. Appeals are now heard by the Court of Appeals for the Federal Circuit (CAFC).

Related terms: Court of Appeals for the Federal Circuit (CAFC).

certificate of correction

The USPTO issues a certificate of correction form when an inventor wishes to make minor technical or clerical corrections in an application after the USPTO has decided to issue the patent. However, these corrections may not consist of new matter that changes the invention covered by the patent.

Related terms: new matter; prosecution of a patent application.

chemicals as patentable subject matter

See composition of matter.

CIP

See continuation-in-part application (CIP).

claim limitations (elements)

Each claim includes a preamble followed by one or more phrases or clauses separated by commas or semicolons. These are referred to as claim elements or claim limitations. These phrases restrict the class of infringing devices to those having the features or qualities described. To stop someone from infringing, the patent owner must demonstrate that the infringing device has all the elements/limitations of at least one claim of the patent.

The Court of Appeals for the Federal Circuit sought to clear up the confusion of the dual terminology when it stated, "In our prior cases, we have used both the term 'element' and the term 'limitation' to refer to words in a claim. It is preferable to use the term 'limitation' when referring to claim language and the term 'element' when referring to the accused device." (*Festo v. Shoketsu*, 234 F.3d 558, 563 n.1 (Fed. Cir. 2000).) Despite this footnote, the Federal Circuit in the *Festo* decision used the two terms interchangeably.

Related terms: claims; printed matter doctrine.

claims

Claims are statements included in a patent application that describe (or "recite") the structure of an invention in precise terms, using a long-established formal style and precise terminology. Claims serve as a way:

- for the USPTO to determine whether an invention is patentable, and
- for a court to determine whether a patent has been infringed (someone has made, used, or sold a patented device without the patent owner's permission).

Patent Law: Definitions

Most patent applications contain more than one claim, each describing the invention from a slightly different viewpoint. Claims may be "independent" (standing on their own) or "dependent" (referring to other claims on which they depend for some or all of their elements). Examples of independent and dependent claims are below.

Each claim must "particularly point out and distinctly claim" the invention for which the patent is being sought. To this end, the USPTO requires that each claim be:

- stated in one unit (a sentence fragment that can and almost always does have numerous clauses and subclauses)
- very specific
- clear
- distinct from other claims, and
- consistent with the narrative description of the patent contained in the patent application.

Claims may be broad or narrow in terms of the scope of the invention they address. The greater the scope of the invention defined in the claims (that is, the broader the claims), the wider the reach of the patent. Similarly, the narrower the scope of a patent claim, the more restricted the reach of the patent—and the easier it is for another inventor to come up with a somewhat similar invention that does not infringe the claim.

EXAMPLE 1: A claim to a new type of writing implement states that the invention is "a hand-held device containing means by which marks may be made on a surface." Because the language of this claim literally reaches every writing implement that ever has been or ever could be manufactured, it would be considered extremely broad. If a patent were issued (extremely unlikely, as discussed below), any subsequent invention held by hand and that made marks on a surface would infringe the claim and therefore the patent.

EXAMPLE 2: Suppose the inventor of a type of writing implement claims the invention as follows: "A 3-inch by ½-inch plastic tube containing liquid and for making an indelible $1/32$-inch line on a flat paper surface." Suppose another company makes a 4-inch-by-¼-inch metal tube containing a charcoal substance capable of making variable width lines on any flat surface. In that case, the claim is not infringed because it recited very specific elements different from the elements of the later invention.

Although broad claims promise to give the inventor more protection, there is a rub: They might preclude issuing a patent. To qualify for a patent, an invention must be both novel (different in some way from previous inventions) and nonobvious (produce an unexpected or surprising result). The broader the claims, the more likely that they overlap with previous developments, and the greater the risk that the invention described in the claims won't be considered novel and nonobvious. (The writing implement discussed in Example 1 above is a good example.) Conversely, narrower claims for an invention provide a greater chance of being considered novel and nonobvious because the claims are less likely to overlap with previous developments.

> EXAMPLE: The first writing implement claim, described earlier, was so broad that it read on (described) prior inventions (such as pencil, chalk, pen, quill, crayon). This fact should preclude issuing a patent and invalidate any patent that did issue on the invention described in that claim. The narrower version of the second writing implement claim, however, tended to exclude many prior inventions. For instance, by limiting the claim to a liquid means, the claim excluded pencils and chalk. The narrower claim would therefore have a better chance of being considered novel and nonobvious.

Because claims must be narrow enough to distinguish the invention from previous developments but broad enough to provide meaningful protection, the primary goal of all patent claim drafters is to draft claims as broadly as possible, given the constraints of the state of prior knowledge or art (inventions and developments).

What is the standard for appealing a district court's interpretation of patent claims? The Supreme Court has held that when a district finding is based on intrinsic evidence (the patent claim and specification, along with the patent prosecution history), the appellate court could review it *de novo*—that is, review it anew and without giving any deference to the trial court's finding. But if the trial court uses extrinsic evidence, the appellate court must give deference and use a higher "clear error" standard of review. (*Teva Pharmaceuticals USA, Inc. v. Sandoz, Inc.*, 574 U.S. 318 (2015).)

The standard for claims review by a court differs from the standard applied by patent examiners. USPTO examiners must review claim terms giving them the broadest reasonable interpretation (BRI) as is reasonably allowed.

Related terms: BRI (broadest reasonable interpretation); dependent claim; independent claim; infringement, patent; limiting reference; means plus function clause; multiple claims; patent application; prior art; specification, defined.

Class Definitions manual

See classification of patents.

classification of patents

The USPTO assigns numbered classes and subclasses to inventions so as to classify patents issued on them and facilitate retrieval of these patents in the course of a patent search. To search prior patents relevant to an invention, one must first determine its proper classification.

There are roughly 300 main classes and an average of more than 200 subclasses under each main class. An invention will fall within at least one of the 66,000 separate classifications and sometimes several.

Fortunately, the USPTO provides resources, available at the USPTO website (www.uspto.gov), to help a patent searcher find the correct classification(s):

- *Index of U.S. Patent Classification.* All 66,000 categories (classes and subclasses) used to classify patented U.S. inventions are listed alphabetically. To conduct a patent search for prior patents relevant to an invention, it is helpful to first determine the class and subclass within which the invention falls.
- *Manual of Classification.* This manual lists by number the 66,000 classes and subclasses used by the USPTO to categorize inventions.
- *Class Definitions.* This manual contains brief definitions of each classification and subclassification used to categorize patents. The manual helps a patent searcher determine the appropriate categories to search in.

In 2015, the USPTO transitioned from its 100-year-old U.S. Patent Classification system (USPC) to an international system known as the Cooperative Patent Classification (CPC). The CPC is derived from the International Patent Classification (IPC). The USPTO patent database continues to present the older USPC as well as current CPC classes. Going forward, however, the USPTO will rely on CPC for classifying new utility patents. (The USPTO will continue to use USPC for classifying design and plant patents.) Both USPC and CPC systems categorize patents by class and then by a subclass.

Related terms: patent search.

coinventors

In situations where an invention is attributable to the creative effort of more than one person, everyone who makes a creative contribution to it (as described in at least one claim in the patent application) is considered a coinventor.

EXAMPLE: Tom and Bonnie jointly conceive of and design a miniature EEG machine (a machine that measures brain waves), which allows its wearers to monitor their brain waves via a wristwatch-like device. Tom and Bonnie get their engineer friend, Clark, to build a test model according to their specifications to make sure the concept is viable. Bonnie and Tom would be listed as "coinventors" of the invention because they were the sole creative contributors to the invention's structure. Clark would not be considered a coinventor, assuming his model was made according to set specifications and did not encompass creative additions to the invention. On the other hand, if Clark had significantly altered the invention's basic specifications and design while building the test model, he might qualify as a coinventor.

In a case involving an invention that provided lumbar supports for car seats, the CAFC ruled that "one who simply provides the inventor with well-known principles or explains state of the art without ever having a firm and definite idea of the claimed combination as a whole does not qualify as a joint inventor." (*Nartron Corp. v. Schukra U.S.A., Inc.*, 558 F.3d 1352 (Fed. Cir. 2009).) In another case, the CAFC held that project members new to a research effort were not inventors because their peers had already formed a definite and permanent idea of the invention even though their knowledge was not scientifically certain. The latecomers to the research effort simply helped the inventors formulate the scientific certainty. As the CAFC indicated, "'knowledge' does not mean proof to a scientific certainty ... the belief that an invention will work is enough to establish a conception." (*Univ. of Pittsburgh of the Commonwealth Sys. of Higher Educ. v. Hedrick*, 573 F.3d 1290 (Fed. Cir. 2009).)

When filing a patent application, it is imperative to identify the inventor or coinventors accurately. Leaving an inventor out or listing someone who doesn't qualify could later cause an issued patent to be declared invalid and unenforceable (if an action is brought in court to enforce the patent). An accurate description of the actual inventors in the patent application is one of the basic requirements for a valid patent.

In 2010, the Third Circuit ruled that a coinventor does not have to make a complete conception of an invention. In that case, a dispute arose as to whether Vanderbilt professors could be added as coinventors on a patent for an inhibitor useful for treating erectile dysfunction. A district court had ruled that the law required that each coinventor have a complete conception of the inhibitor. The Federal Circuit determined this was an error because each coinventor must only engage with the others in some significant way toward that end (The error was considered harmless because Vanderbilt failed to prove its methodology was used in the patent.) (*Vanderbilt University v. ICOS Corp.*, 601 F.3d 1297 (Fed. Cir. 2010).)

Related terms: inventor; patent application.

combination patent

This is a colloquial phrase for patents that are combinations of prior existing inventions or technology. Suppose an inventor combines a public domain bicycle frame with a public domain movable tread design previously utilized on a snowmobile and creates a new type of device that travels efficiently on sand. Because the invention combines two public domain inventions, a patent issued on it will commonly be referred to as a "combination patent."

Earlier court decisions in patent cases suggested that a combination invention had to demonstrate a new or surprising result, called "synergism," before it could qualify for a patent. However, the Court of Appeals for the Federal Circuit has ruled that the phrase "combination patent" has no operational meaning under the patent laws and that virtually all inventions can be said to be combinations of prior existing technology. In short, under the reasoning of this decision, an invention need only meet the basic requirements for a patent (statutory subject matter, novelty, nonobviousness, and utility). The fact that it is a combination of prior developments has no legal effect, and no showing of synergism is required.

Commissioner for Patents

The Commissioner for Patents is the title of the person who manages the patent division of the U.S. Patent and Trademark Office. The previous title for this position was "The Assistant Commissioner for Patents."

Related term: U.S. Patent and Trademark Office (USPTO).

community patent

See European Patent Convention.

composition of matter

A composition of matter is one of the five categories of things (collectively, statutory subject matter) that qualify for a patent. Generally, compositions of matter consist of chemical compositions, conglomerates, aggregates, or other chemically significant substances that are usually supplied in bulk, in liquid, gas, or solid form. They include most new chemicals, new forms of life created by gene-splicing techniques (the genetic mixing constitutes the composition), drugs, road-building compositions, gasoline, fuels, glues, and paper.

Related terms: nonstatutory subject matter; statutory subject matter.

compulsory licensing of a patent

In some countries, a patent owner is legally required to allow others to utilize the invention in exchange for reasonable compensation. Compulsory licensing of a patent doesn't happen in the United States because a U.S. patent owner has the right not to produce, manufacture, create, or implement the invention. This, of course, means that the public might never benefit from the invention—at least, not until the patent has expired.

Under the General Agreement on Tariffs and Trade (GATT), compulsory patent licenses are disfavored.

Related terms: GATT (General Agreement on Tariffs and Trade); licensing of an invention; working a patent.

computer programs and patents

See software patents.

computerized patent search

See patent search, computerized.

conception

Conception is the mental part of inventing, including how an invention is formulated or how a problem is solved. It is a counterpart to "reduction to practice" (meaning that the inventor can demonstrate that it works for its intended purpose). These two events and the dates upon which they occur used to be of great importance when patents were awarded to the first to invent, not the first to file (adopted March 12, 2013). Inventors traditionally document conception (and other elements of the inventing process) by maintaining a notebook.

In 2010, the Third Circuit ruled that a coinventor does not have to make a complete conception of an invention. (*See* coinventors.) (*Vanderbilt University v. ICOS Corp.*, 601 F.3d 1297 (Fed. Cir. 2010).)

Related terms: date of invention; reduction to practice.

concerted refusal to deal

Suppose two or more businesses jointly boycott (discriminate against, refuse to buy from, or refuse to sell to) one or more other businesses. In that case, such activity can be an antitrust violation if commerce has been significantly affected. If a concerted refusal to deal stems from the selective use of one or more patents. These patents may be declared invalid if the antitrust laws have been violated.

> EXAMPLE: The three largest genetic engineering laboratories agree to share their patents through a patent pool arrangement. Competitors are not allowed to use the patents. This exclusion of competitors can constitute a concerted refusal to deal, resulting in the patents being unenforceable.

Related terms: antitrust law (federal) and patents; breaking (or busting) a patent.

confidentiality of patent application

The USPTO treats patent applications as confidential, making it possible to apply for a patent and maintain the underlying information as a trade secret, at least for the first 18 months of the application period. Unless the applicant files a Nonpublication Request (NPR) at the time of filing and doesn't file for a patent outside the United States, the USPTO will publish the application within 18 months of the filing date. Because the USPTO publishes an application, all of the secret information becomes public, and the trade secret status of the application is lost.

If an applicant files an NPR at the time of applying, the information in the patent application will become publicly available only if and when a patent is granted. If the applicant is not filing abroad and the patent is rejected, confidentiality is preserved because the USPTO does not publish rejected applications. If the USPTO approves the patent application, it will be published in the *Official Gazette*. Inventors are willing to accept this trade-off—loss of trade secrecy for patent rights—because the patent can be used to prevent anyone else from exploiting the underlying information.

However, the publication of a patent does not affect trade secret misappropriation claims occurring before publication. In a dispute involving patented technology for an oil drill, a Louisiana district court permitted a trade secret claim to proceed to trial, despite the fact that the USPTO had published the secrets. The defendant argued that trade secret claims were moot because of the disclosure. The court disagreed, holding that the defendant could be liable for trade secret theft that occurred before the USPTO published the secrets. (*Cajun Servs. Unlimited, LLC v. Benton Energy Serv. Co.*, No. 17-0491 S (E.D. La. Apr. 3, 2019).)

If an applicant files an NPR and later files abroad, the applicant must notify the USPTO within 45 days of the foreign filing. The USPTO will then publish the application 18 months after the U.S. filing date (or as soon as possible after the 18-month period), and the applicant must pay a publication fee. If the USPTO is not notified within 45 days, the application will be abandoned unless the applicant demonstrates that the delay was unintentional and pays a stiff fee.

Related terms: patent search; submarine patent.
See also Part 4 (Trade Secret Law): patent application, effect on trade secrets.

constructive reduction to practice

Before March 2013, patents were awarded based on when invention occurred. An essential element in determining when invention occurred was the date "reduction to practice" occurred—typically when the invention was built and tested. However, an invention could also be legally considered to have been reduced to practice even though no actual building and testing had occurred if the inventor filed a patent application or a Provisional Patent Application (PPA) on the invention (constructive reduction to practice). After the passage of the AIA and the introduction of the first-to-file system, the importance of the invention date and reduction to practice has diminished.

Related terms: building and testing an invention; interference; reduction to practice.

continuation application

This type of patent application can keep an original patent application alive after the patent examiner has issued a final office action rejecting one or more of the claims. A "continuation application" must be filed within three months after a patent application is rejected unless an extension is obtained by filing an extension application and paying the appropriate fee.

A continuation application requires a new fee and new claims and will receive a new serial number and filing date. However, in the event an interference (a conflict between two pending applications) occurs, and for purposes of determining the existence of prior art, the inventor will be entitled to the benefit of the original filing date. In other words, if someone else comes up with the same invention between an applicant's original filing date and the continuation application filing date, the original filing date will control and the corresponding invention will be given priority.

The term "continuation application" is often used interchangeably with a "file wrapper continuing application (FWC)."

Patent Law: Definitions

Related terms: continuation-in-part application (CIP); prosecution of a patent application; Request for Continued Examination.

continuation-in-part application (CIP)

A continuation-in-part application (CIP) is filed after an original application and includes new material not covered in the original application. A CIP provides a way for an inventor to supplement an earlier patent application with new matter to cover improvements made since the first filing. The CIP receives the same filing date for matter that it and the original (or parent) application have in common. However, any claim in the CIP that covers the new subject matter is treated as being filed as of the date of the CIP.

Note: Continuation-in-part applications should be distinguished from a continuation application, where applicants reformulate their claims after a rejection by the USPTO.

Related terms: continuation application; final office action; prosecution of a patent application; Request for Continued Examination.

contributory infringement of patent

The unauthorized sale of an item specially designed to work as a material part of a patented invention may be considered a contributory infringement if the item itself lacks independent noninfringing use. Contributory infringement can occur even when the item being sold is itself not patentable. In essence, the contributory infringement doctrine acknowledges that items significantly modified for a patented invention will not generally be sold unless they are being used for an infringing purpose.

EXAMPLE: Bionics, Inc., a manufacturer of artificial human organs, patents and manufactures an artificial kidney containing several unique (but nonpatentable) valves. Suppose Empire Hospital Equipment Ltd. starts selling the modified valve separately. In that case, it can be held to be a contributory infringer of the kidney patent unless it succeeds in showing that the valves have an independent use that does not infringe the kidney invention.

The act of actively inducing another to infringe a patent is also considered an act of infringement.

Related terms: inducing infringement; infringement action; infringement, patent.

Convention application

A patent application may be filed in accordance with the Convention for the Protection of Industrial Property, sometimes known as the Paris Convention. Under this treaty, a patent application must be filed in every country where patent protection is desired within one year of the date that an application is first filed in any other member country. So, if a U.S. patent application has a filing date of February 5, 2020, all additional Convention filings in other countries or jurisdictions, including the Patent Cooperation Treaty and the European Patent Office, must be made by February 5, 2021.

Each Convention filing must be made in the language of the country where it takes place, and separate filing and search fees must be paid. Convention applications in individual countries utilize a different and more costly procedure than Convention applications under the Patent Cooperation Treaty.

Related terms: international patent protection for U.S. inventions; Patent Cooperation Treaty (PCT).

Convention for the Protection of Industrial Property

See Convention application.

Court of Appeals for the Federal Circuit (CAFC)

Often referred to as "Kafka," this special federal court of appeals is responsible for hearing and deciding all appeals from patent infringement actions decided in the U.S. District Courts, as well as all appeals from decisions by the Patent Trial and Appeal Board (PTAB) (a branch of the U.S. Patent and Trademark Office). The CAFC convenes in Washington, DC, and also hears cases in other parts of the United States.

covered business method (CBM)

See CBM (covered business method).

cross-licensing

In a cross-licensing arrangement, two or more owners of separate patents cooperate so that each may use the other's inventions. Because technologies such as automobile manufacturing, genetic engineering, and semiconductor chip fabrication depend heavily on many inventions owned by several different companies, these companies commonly share their patents through cross-licensing agreements. By doing this, they can benefit from the state-of-the-art

Patent Law: Definitions

improvements in the particular field without paying royalties to all the relevant patent owners.

Related terms: improvement inventions; patent pools; patent thickets.

damages, patent infringement

In the event a court determines that a patent has been infringed, the judge or jury may award the patent owner damages for loss of income or for-profits resulting from the infringement from the time the invention was properly marked (when the word "patent" and the patent number were affixed to the invention) or from when the infringer was first put on actual notice of the infringement, whichever occurred first. In the event, the infringement was willful or flagrant (it continued without a reasonable defense after notification by the patent owner, or infringement occurred through direct copying without any ground to believe the plaintiff's patent was invalid), the court may award the plaintiff three times the actual damages established in court plus reasonable attorneys' fees.

When determining lost profits as damages in a patent infringement case, two questions are asked: (1) How many of the infringer's historical sales would not have been made absent the infringing feature or invention? and (2) How many of those sales would have been made by the patent owner if the infringer had not been competing in the marketplace? The Court of Appeals for the Federal Circuit established that as for the first question, when a patent owner seeks damages for more than one patent, the patent owner must distinguish the effects of each patent on marketability. For example, what is the effect if one of several infringing patents were invalid? As for the second question, the court determined that a practical analysis of the marketplace competition requires going beyond broad categories of products and providing evidence of actual competitive patterns for the accused products. (*Ferguson Beauregard/Logic Controls v. Mega Sys.*, 350 F.3d 1327 (Fed. Cir. 2003); *Utah Medical Products v. Graphic Controls Corp.*, 350 F.3d 1376 (Fed. Cir. 2003).)

In no event should the award of damages be "less than a reasonable royalty for the use made of the invention by the infringer..." (15 U.S. Code § 284). In making this calculation, judges either award a royalty based on the entire market value of the infringing device or use various formulas to apportion. The decision depends on whether "the patented feature is the sole driver of customer demand or substantially creates the value of the component parts." (*Power Integrations v. Fairchild Semiconductor International, Inc.*, Nos. 2016-2691, 2017-1875 (Fed. Cir.

September 20, 2018).) In cases where apportionment is necessary, the rate for the complete infringing product is used as a royalty base, and "apportioning through the royalty rate is an acceptable methodology." (*Exmark v. Briggs & Stratton*, 879 F. 3d 1332 (Fed. Cir. 2018).)

U.S. patent owners are not entitled to damages resulting from foreign infringements (unless the patent has been registered in the foreign jurisdiction). However, U.S. patent owners are entitled to foreign profits resulting from exported components intended for assembly in a foreign country. A U.S. patent owner of ocean surveying equipment sued a U.S. company exporting infringing parts of the invention for assembly abroad. The Supreme Court ruled that damages for such infringement entitle the patent owner to lost U.S. profits and lost foreign profits as well. (*WesternGeco v. Ion Geophysical*, 138 S.Ct. 2129, 585 U.S. ___, (2018).)

A court may also increase the damages up to three times (enhanced damages) in cases where one of the parties acted unreasonably. For example, this would be appropriate in the case of a willful infringement in which the party knew what it was doing was illegal but proceeded anyway. The Supreme Court has ruled that judges should exercise their discretion when considering enhanced damages and give greater consideration to the infringer's state of mind (and focus less on the objective reasonableness of the infringer's possible defenses). (*Halo Electronics, Inc. v. Pulse Electronics, Inc.*, 579 U.S. 93 (2016).) Although judges have discretion in this matter, the CAFC has subsequently ruled, "the channel of discretion is narrow and damages are generally reserved for egregious cases of culpable behavior." (*WCM v. IPS*, Nos. 2016-2211, 2016-2268 (Fed. Cir. February 5, 2018).)

§ 284. Damages

Upon finding for the claimant, the court shall award the claimant damages adequate to compensate for the infringement but in no event less than a reasonable royalty for the use made of the invention by the infringer, together with interest and costs as fixed by the court.

When the damages are not found by a jury, the court shall assess them. In either event the court may increase the damages up to three times the amount found or assessed. Increased damages under this paragraph shall not apply to provisional rights under section 154 (d).

The court may receive expert testimony as an aid to the determination of damages or of what royalty would be reasonable under the circumstances.

Related terms: improvement inventions; infringement action.

date of invention

Before March 12, 2013, patents were awarded based on when the invention occurred. For that reason, the date of invention was of great importance. With the passage of the first-to-file rules, the importance has diminished significantly. If a dispute arises for a patent filed before March 2013, the date of invention might still be significant. For those patent owners and applicants, the date of invention is the earliest of the following:

- The date an inventor filed the patent application (provisional or regular).
- The date an inventor can prove that the invention was built and tested (known as "reduction to practice") in the United States or a country that is a member of the North American Free Trade Association (NAFTA) or the World Trade Organization (WTO).
- The date an inventor can prove that the invention was conceived in a NAFTA or WTO country, provided the inventor can also prove diligence in building and testing it or filing a patent application on it.

Related terms: reduction to practice.

declaratory judgment of noninfringement, invalidity, and unenforceability of patent

This type of court ruling is commonly sought when a business wants to commercially utilize an invention but cannot reach a satisfactory licensing agreement with the patent owner. The patent owner threatens a lawsuit via a cease and desist letter. The accused infringer requests a binding judgment from a court defining the legal relationship between the parties. There are advantages to declaratory actions—they allow the accused infringer to file in a nearby jurisdiction versus traveling far to defend a lawsuit. A federal court may issue a declaratory judgment only when there is an actual controversy (Article III). In a 2019 case, however, the CAFC refused to hear declaratory judgment actions filed while licensing negotiations were ongoing. The court reasoned that dismissing such cases is consistent with the policy of promoting "extrajudicial dispute resolution." (*Commc'ns Test Design, Inc. v. Contec LLC*, 367 F. Supp. 3d. 350 (E.D. Pa. 2019).)

Related terms: infringement, patent; licensing of an invention.

defenses to a patent infringement claim

When a patent owner takes legal action to enforce a patent by alleging that it has been infringed (that is, the invention described in the patent has been made, used, or sold without the patent owner's permission), there are several common defenses.

In addition to the most common defense—that the allegedly infringing invention does not infringe on the claims of the patented invention and the two inventions are not substantially similar—the following defenses are also often raised.

Patent Invalidity. A lawsuit for patent infringement almost always becomes two separate battles—one in which the plaintiff claims damage from infringement, and the other in which the defendant attempts to terminate the patent rights by proving the patent is invalid. For example, the Polaroid company sued Kodak for infringement of ten instant photography patents. The court determined that Kodak infringed seven Polaroid patents but that the other three Polaroid patents were invalid.

To prove that a patent is invalid, the defendant must attack the patent based on lack of novelty or nonobviousness—that is, show prior art that anticipates or renders the patent's claims obvious.

Note: The one-year rule, discussed in the case below, terminated in March 2013 when the United States switched to a first-to-file system. Before that date, an inventor had one year from any public disclosure or sale to file a patent. If the inventor failed to meet this one-year deadline, the disclosure or sale could be used against the application as so-called "prior art." The America Invents Act eliminated this broad one-year rule and replaced it with a limited principle: that an inventor had one year from a public disclosure to file a patent, provided that the disclosure was made under the inventor's authority. There is no longer a one-year exception for disclosures or sales not made under the authority of the inventor.

> EXAMPLE: A company was sued for infringement of a patented device for displaying computer text on a television monitor. The company defended itself by proving that more than one year before filing its patent application, the company filing the suit had submitted a proposal to sell the invention. On that basis, the patent was invalidated, and there was no infringement. (*RCA Corporation v. Data General Corporation*, 887 F.2d 1056 (Fed. Cir. 1989).)

In 2011, the Supreme Court refused to alter the standard for invalidating a patent in a battle between tech companies. Microsoft was sued for patent infringement by i4i, a Canadian company, over an XML feature of Microsoft's *Word* software. Microsoft argued that i4i failed to disclose a prior invention that might have invalidated the application (a principle known as the "one-year rule"). The jury was instructed that the patent could only be invalidated if there was "clear and convincing" evidence of invalidity. (*Microsoft Corp. v. i4i Limited Partnership*, 564 U.S. 91 (2011).)

In 2015, the Supreme Court declined to establish a "belief in invalidity" defense to a charge of inducement to infringement. (*Commil v. Cisco*, 575 U.S. 632 (2015).)

Patent Law: Definitions

Inequitable Conduct. Suppose the defendant can prove that a patent owner intentionally misled a patent examiner or should have known that withheld information was material (essential) to the examination process. In that case, the issued patent will be declared invalid.

Exhaustion (First Sale Doctrine). Once a patented item is sold, rights to that item are exhausted, and it is not an infringement to resell it. The defense in this situation is known as the "exhaustion doctrine," (or the "first-sale exemption"). This defense does not apply if the defendant purchased an infringing invention (one that was initially sold without authorization from the patent owner). For example, this defense is unavailable if someone purchases infringing spark plugs and resells them.

Repair Doctrine. It is not an infringement to repair a patented device and replace worn-out unpatented components. It is also not contributory infringement to sell materials used to repair or replace a patented invention. This defense does not apply if the defendant completely rebuilt an invention or repaired an infringing invention.

> EXAMPLE: A company owned a patent for a convertible-top apparatus used in automobiles. The fabric used in the top was not patented. Under the repair doctrine, the sale of fabric to legitimate purchasers of the patented convertible top was not an infringement or contributory infringement. However, a second company was making an infringing version of the convertible-top apparatus. Any repair on the second company's devices was an infringement. The sale of fabric for these infringing devices was a contributory infringement. (*Aro Mfg. Co. v. Convertible Top Replacement Co.*, 365 U.S. 336 (1961).)

File Wrapper Estoppel. The official file containing a patent at the U.S. Patent and Trademark Office is known as a "file wrapper." All statements, admissions, correspondence, or documentation relating to the invention are placed in the file wrapper. If the inventor admits limitations to the invention during the patent application process or disclaims certain rights, those admissions or disclaimers will become part of the file wrapper. The patent owner cannot later sue for infringement over any rights disclaimed in the file wrapper. This defense is known as file wrapper estoppel (or prosecution history estoppel). Estoppel means that a party is prevented from contradicting a former statement or action.

EXAMPLE: A medical company owned a patent for an inflatable thermal blanket. The patent claimed a design that caused the inflated blanket to "self-erect" into a Quonset-hut–like shape, preventing contact of the blanket with the patient. The patent's prosecution history showed that the applicant relinquished rights to any forced-air blanket other than a "self-erecting" convective thermal blanket. On that basis, there could not be an infringement of an allegedly equivalent blanket that rested on a patient and did not inflate itself into a self-supporting structure. (*Augustine Medical Inc. v. Gaymar Industries Inc.*, 181 F.3d 1291 (Fed. Cir. 1999).)

EXAMPLE: The plaintiff, a paint company, had previously admitted that a prior art document disclosed a BPA-free coating to the USPTO. The statement was made during a reexamination proceeding that was later vacated. The district court determined that a prior admission to the USPTO during a vacated reexamination proceeding is binding on the parties. (*The Sherwin-Williams Company v. PPG Industries, Inc.*, 2-17-cv-01023 (W.D. PA 2021-01-21, Order).)

Outside U.S. Borders. Suppose a defendant manufactures and sells an invention in a foreign country. In such a case, a U.S. patent owner cannot stop the manufacture, use, or sale of inventions unless the owner has patented the invention in that country. However, it is an infringement of a U.S. patent:

- to import an infringing device into the United States, or
- to create all of the parts of a patented invention in the United States and ship those parts to a foreign company with instructions for assembly.

Patent Misuse. A patent owner who has misused a patent cannot sue for infringement. Common examples of misuse are violations of antitrust laws or unethical business practices. For example, if a patent owner conspired to fix the price of the patented item, this would violate antitrust laws. If the patent owner later sued for infringement, the defendant could argue that the owner is prohibited from suing because of having misused the patent rights. Tying is a form of patent misuse in which, as a condition of a transaction, the buyer of a patented device must also purchase an additional product.

EXAMPLE: A company had a patent on a machine that deposited salt tablets in canned food. Purchasers of the machine were also required to buy salt tablets from the patent owner. The Supreme Court determined that the seller of the machine misused its patent rights and, on that basis, was prevented from suing for infringement. (*Morton Salt Co. v. G.S. Suppiger Co.*, 314 U.S. 488 (1942).)

Patent Law: Definitions

In 1988, Congress enacted the Patent Misuse Amendments, which require courts to apply a "rule of reason" standard—meaning that the court must view all the relevant factors to determine if the tying arrangement is in any way justified.

In a 2010 case, the Federal Circuit narrowed the scope of patent misuse. Under the Federal Circuit's new standard, there must be evidence of anticompetitive effects associated in addition to restrictions on use. Alleging wrongful conduct is not enough. (*Princo Corp. v. International Trade Commission*, 616 F.3d 1318 (Fed. Cir. 2010).)

Time Limit for Damages. There is no time limit for filing a patent infringement lawsuit, but 35 U.S. Code Section 286 of the patent law states that monetary damages can be recovered only for infringements committed during the six years before the filing of the lawsuit (making it effectively a statute of limitations). Courts used to permit a defense called "laches," in which it is argued that the patent owner waited an unreasonable amount of time to file a lawsuit even if that time were less than six years before filing. In 2017, however, the Supreme Court held that laches could not bar a patent claim brought within the statute of limitations. (*SCA Hygiene Products Aktiebolag v. First Quality Baby Products, LLC*, 580 U.S. ___ (2017).)

Prior User Defense. If you're sued for infringement, but you were commercially using the patented technology more than one year before the filing date of the claimed invention, you have a defense against a claim that you infringed (although that defense doesn't invalidate the patent). The Act includes a definition of "commercial use." (See below.)

Because of the variety of potential defenses to an infringement action, many observers feel that a patent is not worth a great deal if there's significant economic motivation to infringe it. According to this view, the more valuable a patent, the more likely it is that significant economic interests will mount a fierce and expensive court challenge to the patent's validity. Paradoxically, the more difficult it is to enforce a patent, the less it is worth to its rightful owner.

§ 273. Defense to infringement based on prior commercial use

(a) In General. A person shall be entitled to a defense under section 282(b) with respect to subject matter consisting of a process, or consisting of a machine, manufacture, or composition of matter used in a manufacturing or other commercial process, that would otherwise infringe a claimed invention being asserted against the person if—

    (1) such person, acting in good faith, commercially used the subject matter in the United States, either in connection with an internal commercial use or an actual arm's length sale or other arm's length commercial transfer of a useful end result of such commercial use; and

(2) such commercial use occurred at least 1 year before the earlier of either—

    (A) the effective filing date of the claimed invention; or

    (B) the date on which the claimed invention was disclosed to the public in a manner that qualified for the exception from prior art under section 102(b).

(b) Burden of Proof. A person asserting a defense under this section shall have the burden of establishing the defense by clear and convincing evidence.

(c) Additional Commercial Uses.

    (1) PREMARKETING REGULATORY REVIEW. Subject matter for which commercial marketing or use is subject to a premarketing regulatory review period during which the safety or efficacy of the subject matter is established, including any period specified in section 156(g), shall be deemed to be commercially used for purposes of subsection (a)(1) during such regulatory review period.

    (2) NONPROFIT LABORATORY USE. A use of subject matter by a nonprofit research laboratory or other nonprofit entity, such as a university or hospital, for which the public is the intended beneficiary, shall be deemed to be a commercial use for purposes of subsection (a)(1), except that a defense under this section may be asserted pursuant to this paragraph only for continued and noncommercial use by and in the laboratory or other nonprofit entity.

(d) Exhaustion of Rights. Notwithstanding subsection (e)(1), the sale or other disposition of a useful end result by a person entitled to assert a defense under this section in connection with a patent with respect to that useful end result shall exhaust the patent owner's rights under the patent to the extent that such rights would have been exhausted had such sale or other disposition been made by the patent owner.

(e) Limitations and Exceptions.

    (1) PERSONAL DEFENSE.

        (A) IN GENERAL. A defense under this section may be asserted only by the person who performed or directed the performance of the commercial use described in subsection (a), or by an entity that controls, is controlled by, or is under common control with such person.

        (B) TRANSFER OF RIGHT. Except for any transfer to the patent owner, the right to assert a defense under this section shall not be licensed or assigned or transferred to another person except as an ancillary and subordinate part of a good-faith assignment or transfer for other reasons of the entire enterprise or line of business to which the defense relates.

        (C) RESTRICTION ON SITES. A defense under this section, when acquired by a person as part of an assignment or transfer described in subparagraph (B), may only be asserted for uses at sites where the subject matter that would otherwise infringe a claimed invention is in use before the later of the effective filing date of the claimed invention or the date of the assignment or transfer of such enterprise or line of business.

(2) DERIVATION. A person may not assert a defense under this section if the subject matter on which the defense is based was derived from the patentee or persons in privity with the patentee.

(3) NOT A GENERAL LICENSE. The defense asserted by a person under this section is not a general license under all claims of the patent at issue, but extends only to the specific subject matter for which it has been established that a commercial use that qualifies under this section occurred, except that the defense shall also extend to variations in the quantity or volume of use of the claimed subject matter, and to improvements in the claimed subject matter that do not infringe additional specifically claimed subject matter of the patent.

(4) ABANDONMENT OF USE. A person who has abandoned commercial use (that qualifies under this section) of subject matter may not rely on activities performed before the date of such abandonment in establishing a defense under this section with respect to actions taken on or after the date of such abandonment.

(5) UNIVERSITY EXCEPTION.

(A) IN GENERAL. A person commercially using subject matter to which subsection (a) applies may not assert a defense under this section if the claimed invention with respect to which the defense is asserted was, at the time the invention was made, owned or subject to an obligation of assignment to either an institution of higher education (as defined in section 101(a) of the Higher Education Act of 1965 (20 U.S.C. 1001(a)), or a technology transfer organization whose primary purpose is to facilitate the commercialization of technologies developed by one or more such institutions of higher education.

(B) EXCEPTION. Subparagraph (A) shall not apply if any of the activities required to reduce to practice the subject matter of the claimed invention could not have been undertaken using funds provided by the Federal Government.

(f) Unreasonable Assertion of Defense. If the defense under this section is pleaded by a person who is found to infringe the patent and who subsequently fails to demonstrate a reasonable basis for asserting the defense, the court shall find the case exceptional for the purpose of awarding attorney fees under section 285.

(g) Invalidity. A patent shall not be deemed to be invalid under section 102 or 103 solely because a defense is raised or established under this section ....

Related terms: infringement action; infringement, patent; intervening right; statute of limitations, infringement action; unenforceable patent.

defensive publication

Publishing the details of an invention legally transforms the invention into prior art, which in turn precludes others from obtaining a patent on it because it is no longer novel. A defensive publication consists of placing a technical description of an invention in an academic journal, industry publication, or online database issued just for this purpose, such as Technical Disclosure Commons, an online repository for defensive publications (www.tdcommons.org), or the Software Patent Institute, a defensive disclosure program for software-based inventions. Ideally, a defensive publication should include the same detailed technical information as a patent application.

Defensive publications are also used by companies that don't think a particular area of technology (such as software) should be subject to the patent laws and therefore disclose their technology to prevent others from patenting it and extracting royalties.

Related terms: confidentiality of patent application; *Official Gazette* (OG); prior art reference; Software Patent Institute; Statutory Invention Registration (SIR).

dependent claim

The scope of a patent is determined by the way the underlying invention is described in the patent claims (precise, single-sentence statements that articulate the exact nature of the invention). There are two basic types of patent claims: independent and dependent. Independent claims are statements that stand by themselves. Dependent claims are statements that rely on another claim for part of their description. In other words, each dependent claim must be read (interpreted) by incorporating the wording of each claim to which it refers, which may be an independent claim or another dependent claim.

The typical patent application contains several independent claims, each referred to by several additional dependent claims. (Samples of dependent and independent claims are provided in "claims.")

Related terms: claims; independent claim; claim limitations (elements).

derivation hearings

The USPTO permits a patent owner to bring a derivation hearing at the USPTO against another patent owner who claims to have the same invention and who has an earlier effective filing date. The derivation hearing request must be filed within a one-year period beginning on the date of the first publication of a claim in the earlier filed application.

Alternatively, the patent owner may sue the owner of another patent that claims the same invention and has an earlier effective filing date. These lawsuits can be brought only if the invention claiming priority was derived directly from the person seeking relief.

Patent Law: Definitions

§ 135. Derivation proceedings

(a) Institution of Proceeding. An applicant for patent may file a petition to institute a derivation proceeding in the Office. The petition shall set forth with particularity the basis for finding that an inventor named in an earlier application derived the claimed invention from an inventor named in the petitioner's application and, without authorization, the earlier application claiming such invention was filed. Any such petition may be filed only within the 1-year period beginning on the date of the first publication of a claim to an invention that is the same or substantially the same as the earlier application's claim to the invention, shall be made under oath, and shall be supported by substantial evidence. Whenever the Director determines that a petition filed under this subsection demonstrates that the standards for instituting a derivation proceeding are met, the Director may institute a derivation proceeding. The determination by the Director whether to institute a derivation proceeding shall be final and nonappealable.

(b) Determination by Patent Trial and Appeal Board. In a derivation proceeding instituted under subsection (a), the Patent Trial and Appeal Board shall determine whether an inventor named in the earlier application derived the claimed invention from an inventor named in the petitioner's application and, without authorization, the earlier application claiming such invention was filed. In appropriate circumstances, the Patent Trial and Appeal Board may correct the naming of the inventor in any application or patent at issue. The Director shall prescribe regulations setting forth standards for the conduct of derivation proceedings, including requiring parties to provide sufficient evidence to prove and rebut a claim of derivation.

(c) Deferral of Decision. The Patent Trial and Appeal Board may defer action on a petition for a derivation proceeding until the expiration of the 3-month period beginning on the date on which the Director issues a patent that includes the claimed invention that is the subject of the petition. The Patent Trial and Appeal Board also may defer action on a petition for a derivation proceeding, or stay the proceeding after it has been instituted, until the termination of a proceeding under chapter 30, 31, or 32 involving the patent of the earlier applicant.

(d) Effect of Final Decision. The final decision of the Patent Trial and Appeal Board, if adverse to claims in an application for patent, shall constitute the final refusal by the Office on those claims. The final decision of the Patent Trial and Appeal Board, if adverse to claims in a patent, shall, if no appeal or other review of the decision has been or can be taken or had, constitute cancellation of those claims, and notice of such cancellation shall be endorsed on copies of the patent distributed after such cancellation.

(e) Settlement. Parties to a proceeding instituted under subsection (a) may terminate the proceeding by filing a written statement reflecting the agreement of the parties as to the correct inventors of the claimed invention in dispute. Unless the Patent Trial and Appeal Board finds the agreement to be inconsistent with the evidence of record, if any, it shall take action consistent with the agreement. Any written settlement or understanding of the parties shall be filed with the Director. At the request of a party to the proceeding, the agreement or understanding shall be treated as business confidential information, shall be kept separate from the file of the involved patents or applications, and shall be made available only to Government agencies on written request, or to any person on a showing of good cause.

(f) Arbitration. Parties to a proceeding instituted under subsection (a) may, within such time as may be specified by the Director by regulation, determine such contest or any aspect thereof by arbitration. Such arbitration shall be governed by the provisions of title 9, to the extent such title is not inconsistent with this section. The parties shall give notice of any arbitration award to the Director, and such award shall, as between the parties to the arbitration, be dispositive of the issues to which it relates. The arbitration award shall be unenforceable until such notice is given. Nothing in this subsection shall preclude the Director from determining the patentability of the claimed inventions involved in the proceeding.

design around

To design or build a device or process that is similar to but doesn't infringe on a patented invention is referred to as "designing around" the patent. The scope of protection acquired under a patent is determined by the wording of the patent's claims. Thus, any device, process, or substance containing the same elements described in a patent's claims can be said to infringe the patent. Conversely, a device or process that contains fewer or different elements does not infringe the patent (technically, the patent's claims do not "read on," or literally describe, the infringing device). Therefore, by studying the claims associated with a specific patent, it is often possible to build or design a device or process very similar to that described in the patent without legally infringing the patent's claims.

> EXAMPLE: Fred invents and patents a small radiator-type device that uses hot water to dry and warm towels. One of the claims for his invention describes it as consisting of plastic. Bonanza Bathroom Products (BBP) creates a similar device but uses a metal alloy that doubles the ability of the device to retain heat. BBP probably has not infringed Fred's patent because it designed around the invention using a different element that produces a different result.

Patent Law: Definitions

To prevent such "designing around" activity, Fred's patent claim should have been broader to start with. Instead of limiting his invention to plastic, Fred's claim might have described "an inflexible means through which hot water can be channeled at normal domestic water pressures, the heat retained over a period of time, and towels folded over for the purpose of drying."

There is one crucial legal restriction on the ability to design around a patent claim. A court can decide that the differences in the essential elements of the two inventions—in the previous example, the type of substance used and the extra heat retention—are immaterial (unimportant) to the overall invention. In that event, infringement will have occurred under the doctrine of equivalents, which allows infringement to be found when two inventions work in the same way to produce substantially the same result.

Related terms: claims; doctrine of equivalents.

design patents

The USPTO will issue a design patent for any "new, original, and ornamental design for an article of manufacture." (35 U.S. Code § 171.) This includes three types of designs:

- surface ornamentation—that is, a design applied to or embodied in an article of manufacture
- a product shape or configuration, and
- a combination of the first two categories.

U.S. design patents resulting from applications filed on or after May 13, 2015, now have a 15-year term from issuance (instead of 14 years as before). This change resulted from the adoption of the Geneva Act of the Hague Agreement concerning the International Registration of Industrial Designs (Hague Agreement). Also, under the Hague Agreement, it is now possible for U.S. applicants to file a single international design application either with the World Intellectual Property Organization (WIPO) or through the USPTO. Applicants filing international design applications on or after May 13, 2015, can designate the United States for design protection.

Courts have limited design patents to one sense, vision—that is, the appearance presented by the article. A design patent will not be granted for sounds, smells, or tastes that ornament products. In addition, the design must be capable of reproduction and not merely the chance result of a method. A water fountain display—the combined appearance of the water and the underlying sculpture—is suitable subject matter for a design patent because it is definite (even though not permanent) and can be reproduced.

The claims for a design patent are expressed in the drawings and limited by the claims language.

> EXAMPLE: A design patent entitled "Pattern for a Chair" claimed an "ornamental design for a chair." The drawings, however, showed only the pattern, not a chair with the pattern. Defendants used a similar design on a basket. The CAFC prevented the design owner from proceeding against the basket maker because there was no mention of baskets in the application and the design patent was therefore limited to chairs. (*Curver Luxembourg SARL v. Home Expressions Inc.,* CV-2018-2214, (CAFC, September 2, 2019).)

The protected design must be ornamental, not functional.

> EXAMPLE: A personal computer designed to resemble a classical robot might qualify for a design patent as long as the robot characteristics were purely ornamental. But if the robot characteristics were functional in some way—for instance, they provided the computer with mobility—a design patent on these characteristics would be precluded.

Often, two patents will be sought for the same device: a utility patent covering the device's functional characteristics and a design patent protecting the device's ornamental characteristics. In our robot computer example, it might be possible to obtain both types of patents if they cover different aspects of the device.

Although design patents are relatively easy to obtain, the fact that the design, by definition, lacks utility usually makes it easy to create another design that will also be novel and interesting without violating the design patent.

Before 2008, the CAFC used two standards to demonstrate design patent infringement: (1) The Ordinary Observer Test, in which the court compares the allegedly infringing device with design patent drawings to determine whether the allegedly infringing design is substantially similar; and (2) The Point of Novelty Test, in which the court compares the patented design with the prior art to determine "the point of novelty" of the patented design and whether the allegedly infringing design appropriates the novelty.

Patent Law: Definitions

The CAFC terminated the "point of novelty" test in a 2008 case involving a claim of infringement of a nail buffer design, *Egyptian Goddess v. Swisa, Inc.,* 543 F.3d 665, 88 U.S.P.Q.2d 1658 (Fed. Cir. 2008) (*en banc*). Instead, the court held that only an "ordinary observer" test was required. The CAFC also discouraged the "over-verbalization" of design patent claims, preferring more reliance on design patent drawings. In a post-*Goddess* case, a district court applied the new standard to a design patent for a "curvilinear zipper." The district court applied the ordinary observer test, first comparing the differences between the patented design and the infringing design and then considering the differences in relation to the prior art. The conclusion: no infringement. (*Arc'Teryx Equipment, Inc. v. Westcomb Outerwear, Inc.,* 2008 WL 4838141 (D. Utah, November 3, 2008).) The CAFC also extended the ordinary observer test for design patents when determining if a design patent is anticipated by prior art. (*International Seaway Trading Corp. v. Walgreens Corp.,* 589 F.3d 1233, 93 U.S.P.Q.2d 1001 (Fed. Cir. 2009).)

In 2017, the Supreme Court held that when an infringed design patent is a component of an "article of manufacture," the damage award is limited to revenues attributable to the component. Apple had claimed that the Samsung phones infringed the design features of the iPhone and its interface. A jury found for Apple and the court awarded (with interest) $399 million, based on all of Samsung's profits from its phone. The Supreme Court held that damages should not be awarded from the entire profits of Samsung phone sales but only based on the profits attributable to that aspect of the smartphone's appearance that was infringed. (*Samsung Electronics Co. v. Apple Inc.,* 580 U.S. ___ (2016).)

Related terms: design around.

direct infringement of patent

See infringement, patent.

Director of the U.S. Patent and Trademark Office

This is the title of the person who runs the USPTO, a branch of the U.S. Department of Commerce. The full title is Undersecretary of Commerce for Intellectual Property and Director of the U.S. Patent and Trademark Office. Before 2000 the title for this position was the Commissioner of Patents and Trademarks.

Related terms: Commissioner for Patents; U.S. Patent and Trademark Office (USPTO).

Disclosure Document Program (DDP)

This USPTO program, eliminated in February 2007, previously allowed inventors, for a nominal fee, to file a signed document called a "disclosure" that preliminarily described their invention.

disclosure requirement for patents

A patent application must disclose enough about the invention to enable a person with ordinary skill in the art (technology used in the invention) to build or develop it. In addition, a patent application is required to disclose the best means ("best mode") known to the applicant of practicing the invention as of the date of applying. The reason for the disclosure requirement is simple. A disclosure that is detailed enough to enable the invention to be built enhances the public's knowledge of the technology and ideas involved in the invention. In exchange for this public benefit, an inventor earns the right to a statutory monopoly over the right to make, use, and sell the invention.

Before passage of the America Invents Act in September 2011, if the information necessary to build the invention was not sufficiently disclosed in the application (also known as "best mode"), a patent that was issued on the invention might be declared invalid and therefore not enforceable. This was a common defense in infringement actions. The America Invents Act eliminated this defense.

Related terms: patent application.

divisional application

Suppose a patent examiner rejects a patent application because it claims two or more inventions. In that case, the typical inventor response is to restrict the application to one invention of the inventor's choosing. But an inventor who doesn't wish to abandon the other "nonelected" invention can file a separate divisional application to cover it. The divisional application will be entitled to the original application's filing date (which is referred to as the parent application once a divisional application is filed).

What happens if the patent examiner was wrong, and a court later finds that there was, in fact, only one invention, even though the U.S. Patent and Trademark Office (USPTO) issued two (or more) patents on it? Although this violates another patenting rule (the statutory rule against double patenting), both patents will be upheld because the USPTO restricted the original patent application.

§ 121. Divisional applications

If two or more independent and distinct inventions are claimed in one application, the Director may require the application to be restricted to one of the inventions. If the other invention is made the subject of a divisional application that complies with the requirements of section 120 of this title, it shall be entitled to the benefit of the original application's filing date. A patent issuing on an application with respect to which a requirement for restriction under this section has been made, or on an application filed as a result of such a requirement, shall not be used as a reference either in the Patent and Trademark Office or in the courts against a divisional application or against the original application or any patent issued on either of them, if the divisional application is filed before the issuance of the patent on the other application. If a divisional application is directed solely to subject matter described and claimed in the original application as filed, the Director may dispense with signing and execution by the inventor. The validity of a patent shall not be questioned for failure of the Director to require the application to be restricted to one invention.

Related terms: abandonment of patent application; double patenting; nonelected claims; prosecution of a patent application.

doctrine of equivalents

The doctrine of equivalents is a secondary method for deciding whether a patent is being infringed. The common way to assess patent infringement is to compare the literal language of each element of the patent's claims with each element of the allegedly infringing invention. (In patent jargon, the court asks, "Do the patent claims 'read on' the infringing device?") However, even if a patent's claims don't literally "read on" an invention, infringement may be found if the allegedly infringing device is the "equivalent" of the claimed invention—that is, it performs the same function, in the same way, to achieve the same result.

The doctrine of equivalents is intended to prevent designing around a patent on hypertechnical grounds. Unfortunately, there is no logical dividing line between (1) noninfringement based on legitimate designing around an invention, and (2) infringement based on the doctrine of equivalents. It is up to the courts to decide, on a case-by-case basis, whether inventions are substantially equivalent.

In 2000, a federal appeals court barred using the doctrine of equivalents for any amended patent claims. In 2002, the U.S. Supreme Court struck down this absolute bar to the doctrine of equivalents. It replaced it with a less-arbitrary standard, under which all amended claims are presumed to be narrowed to bar the doctrine of equivalents. But this presumption can be rebutted if a patent owner demonstrates that the amendment involved a feature that was "unforeseeable at the time of the application" or "for some other reason" could not be included in the original claim. In that case, the patent owner can use the doctrine of equivalents. (*Festo Corp. v. Shoketsu Kinzoku Kabushiki Co. Ltd.,* 535 U.S. 722 (2002).)

Related terms: design around; *Festo v. Shoketsu;* infringement, patent; negative doctrine of equivalents.

double patenting

If two patents are obtained on (or claim) a single invention, it's called double patenting. Double patenting is not allowed under the patent laws, and both patents can later be invalidated. However, this rule does not apply if double patenting results from a divisional application required by the USPTO because of the USPTO's misperception that two inventions were being described in the original patent (35 U.S. Code § 121).

Related terms: divisional application.

drawings, patent application

Visual representations of an invention must be included in the patent application. These drawings should show all the features described (recited) in the claims.

If an invention is an object (including machines or articles of manufacture), the drawings must show features of the invention that are different from those known in the prior art. A drawing for a process should consist of a flow chart showing its sequence of steps.

Drawings are ordinarily not required for inventions consisting of compositions of matter unless either of the following is true:

- The inventions consist of structures that can be shown in a cross-sectional representation.
- A flow chart showing the process of manufacture is relevant.

Related terms: disclosure requirement for patents; patent application.

duration of patents

Utility patents—the most common kind—expire 20 years after the filing date of the regular formal patent application. This means that the period the patent is actually in force will depend on how long it takes the patent to be examined. For instance, if the regular patent application is filed on December 1, 2019, and the patent issues on December 1, 2022, the patent will be in force for 17 years.

Effective June 2000, every patent is guaranteed an in-force period of at least 17 years. The patent term will be extended for as long as necessary to compensate for any of the following:

- any delay caused by the USPTO failing to examine a new application within 14 months of filing
- any delay caused by the USPTO failing to take any one of the following actions within four months:
  - reply to an amendment or an appeal brief
  - issue an allowance or office action after a decision on appeal, or
  - issue a patent after the issue fee is paid and any required drawings are filed
- any delay caused by the USPTO's failure to issue a patent within three years from filing, unless the delay was due to the applicant filing a continuation application or buying a delay to reply to an office action, or
- any delay due to secrecy orders, appeals, or interferences.

Because the law creating the 20-year patent term became effective June 8, 1995, patents issued before that date—or pending on that date—will expire 20 years from their filing date or 17 years from their issue date, whichever period is longer. (35 U.S. Code § 154(c)(1).)

Design patents last for 15 years from issuance, or, if filed before May 13, 2015, 14 years from issuance. Plant and utility patents last for 20 years from the date of filing.

Related terms: filing date; in force; patent term extension.

duty of candor and good faith

This duty is owed to the USPTO by every patent applicant in connection with the information and disclosures contained in the patent application. Under rules issued by the USPTO, the applicant must disclose:

- all known instances of anticipation (events or references that might cause the USPTO to determine that the invention isn't novel)
- pertinent prior art that might bear on the question of nonobviousness
- the preferred embodiment (best mode) of the invention, and
- any other information known to the applicant that bears on the patentability of the invention and the proper scope of the patent claims.

Failure to comply fully with the duty of candor and good faith can result in rejection of the patent application by the USPTO or a later finding in an infringement action that the applicant committed fraud on the USPTO (if the noncompliance was willful or negligent). In the latter case, the patent may be declared invalid even if the undisclosed information would not have invalidated the patent as such.

> EXAMPLE: In 2010, Patricia invented a device and a process that allowed wind velocities to be differentially measured according to tiny portions of space. The results of the measurements could then be fed into a computer, and the best placement for windmills could be determined. Patricia made the invention for her own home in the country and decided not to patent it due to the plentiful supply of centralized electrical energy. Patricia let some of her neighbors use the invention on an as-needed basis, which may have constituted prior public use of the invention, which in turn could be considered prior art.
>
> Three years later, oil prices soar, and Patricia applies for and receives a patent. In her patent application, she neglects to mention her neighbors' use of the device, a fact she should have disclosed under the applicant's duty to disclose known relevant prior art. In 2015, a leading power company began to market Patricia's device across the country without a license from Patricia. If Patricia sues the company for infringement or her patent, she might find that her patent cannot be enforced. Why? Because she failed to disclose relevant prior art to the USPTO, even though the information in question if disclosed at the time, might not have barred issuance of the patent. If this information comes out at trial, the judge may find that she violated her duty of candor and good faith.

Related terms: anticipation; defenses to a patent infringement claim; disclosure requirement for patents; fraud on the U.S. Patent and Trademark Office.

electronic filing of patent applications

The USPTO has implemented an Electronic Filing System (EFS-Web) that enables the online filing of patent applications, amendments, and other documents. Using it, you can (1) file an application anytime and from anywhere that has Internet access, (2) obtain instant confirmation of receipt of documents by the PTO, (3) send an application to the PTO without having to go to the post office to get an Express Mail receipt or having to wait for a postcard receipt, and (4) file an application without having to prepare an application transmittal, a fee transmittal, receipt postcard, or check or Credit Card Payment Form (CCPF).

To improve application quality and efficiency, the USPTO will transition to DOCX for all filers on January 1, 2022. DOCX is a word-processing file format supported by many popular applications, such as Microsoft *Word*, Google Docs, and LibreOffice. Filing in DOCX provides many benefits in the application process and eliminates the need to convert into a PDF for filing (this eliminates the non-embedded font error, the most common obstacle in uploading a PDF).

elements of invention

See claims.

employed to invent

It is possible that even without a written employment agreement, an employer could own rights to an employee's patent or trade secret under the "employed to invent" doctrine. How might this rule apply? If a person were employed—even without a written employment agreement—for inventing or designing skills or was hired or directed to create an invention, the employer would own all rights to any resulting inventions. This doctrine is derived from a Supreme Court ruling that stated, "One employed to make an invention, who succeeds, during his term of service, in accomplishing that task, is bound to assign to his employer any patent obtained." Most companies prefer to use a written agreement, which is more reliable and easier to enforce than this implied agreement. However, the issue of "employed to invent" still arises.

> EXAMPLE: An engineer had no written employment agreement with his employer. He was assigned as the chief engineer on a project to devise a method of welding a "leading edge" for turbine engines. The engineer spent at least 70% of his time on the project. He developed a hot forming process (HFP) for welding a leading edge and built the invention on his employer's time and using his employer's employees, tools, and materials. The engineer claimed that he was the sole owner of patent rights. A court held that the company owned the patent rights because the engineer was hired for the express purpose of creating the HFP process. That fact, combined with the use of the employer's supplies, payment for the work, and payment by the employer for the patent registration, demonstrated an implied contract to assign the patent rights to the employer. Therefore, even without a written employment agreement, the employer acquired ownership.

enabling disclosure

The description of an invention included ("disclosed") in a patent application must be in sufficient detail as to "enable" a person with ordinary skill in the art to build or develop it ("work it") without having to apply any inventiveness of their own.

Related terms: disclosure requirement for patents.

equivalents, doctrine of

See doctrine of equivalents.

European Patent Convention

This treaty covers patent law relationships, primarily among the members of the European Union (EU), plus a few other countries.

Under the European Patent Convention (EPC), an inventor needs to make only one filing and undergo one examination procedure to obtain patent protection in all member countries. Filings and examinations are conducted by the European Patent Office in Munich, Germany, and The Hague, Netherlands. A patent issued under the EPC lasts for 20 years from the date of application but must be registered in each country.

Related terms: Convention application; Patent Cooperation Treaty (PCT).

European Patent Office

See European Patent Convention.

examiners, patent

See patent examiners.

exclusive patent license

A binding agreement in which a patent owner (the licensor) grants another party (the licensee) the sole (exclusive) right to make, use, or sell an invention covered by the patent is known as an exclusive patent license.

Sometimes the grant of rights is for all purposes, but often it is limited to a specific context. For example, sales may be restricted to the United States, to a particular period, or for a particular purpose. However, the particular right is granted exclusively to the person or business receiving it. For example, a patent owner could grant one company the exclusive right to make and sell the invention in the United States and another company to make and sell it in the European community.

Related terms: geographic patent license; nonexclusive patent license.

Patent Law: Definitions

exhaustion

Patent exhaustion is a legal doctrine that prohibits a patent owner from seeking further patent payments for a product when it has been sold. For example, the patent owner cannot sue the buyer of a patented lawn mower if the buyer later resells the mower (or uses the mower in his gardening business). The principle is also known as the "first sale doctrine," which also applies in copyright law for a similar principle. This principle was reinforced in 2008 by the Supreme Court's ruling in *Quanta v. LG Electronics*, 553 U.S. 617 (2008). In that case, a company (LG) that sold licensed chipsets entered into licenses with direct purchasers. When another company (Quanta) purchased these chipsets from one of LG's customers, LG claimed infringement. The Supreme Court ruled that a patent owner cannot later sue a customer who purchased an authorized copy of a patented product. In other words, the patent owner's rights are exhausted after the sale.

In 2013, the Supreme Court ruled that the patent exhaustion doctrine did not apply in a case involving the resale and self-replication of patented seeds. Monsanto owned patents on seeds resistant to an herbicide (Roundup). Farmers who purchased such seeds from Monsanto agreed not to permit them to self-replicate—that is, the farmer must buy new seeds each year. An Indiana farmer bought mixed seeds (some of which were patented by Monsanto) from a grain elevator. Instead of using the seeds for animal feed as intended, the farmer replanted them and allowed the patented seeds to self-replicate, bypassing the arrangement with Monsanto. The farmer argued that he was permitted to do so under the "exhaustion doctrine," but a unanimous Supreme Court disagreed. The exhaustion doctrine permitted the farmer to resell the seeds as feed but not to replant the seeds. (*Bowman v. Monsanto Co.*, 569 U.S. 278 (2013).)

ex parte reexamination

See reexamination of patent.

experimental use of an unpatented invention

Under pre-AIA rules, an unpatented invention could be used or exhibited in public for experimental purposes—that is, to test or improve the invention. Experimental use was not considered a public use or a disclosure and therefore wouldn't bar a patent under the anticipation rule. However, if the public use was not genuinely experimental, such use would bar a patent unless an application for the patent was filed within one year of the use. For example, a clinical trial application that resulted in a publicly accessible record was not an experimental use. (*In re Natures Remedies*, 315 Fed. App'x. 300 (Fed. Cir. 2009).)

Although patent experts believe that the experimental use exception has continued under the AIA, neither the federal courts nor the USPTO (as of the publication of this edition (2022)) has issued a ruling on the issue. As the USPTO stated in its Examination Guidelines for Implementing the First to File Provisions of the Leahy-Smith America Invents Act (2013), Federal Register/Vol. 78, No. 3.,

"Neither the AIA nor its legislative history expressly addresses whether the experimental use exception applies to public use under AIA 35 USC. 102(a)(1), or to a use that makes the invention available to the public under the residual clause of AIA 35 USC. 102(a)(1). Because this doctrine arises infrequently before the Office and is case-specific when it does arise, the Office will approach this issue when it arises on the facts presented."

Related terms: anticipation; public use.

expert witness

A witness who has special knowledge of a subject so that the court may rely on the expert's opinion. In patent litigation, expert witnesses are commonly used to explain complex scientific or mechanical innovations. In 2005, the Court of Appeals for the Federal Circuit indicated that a patent owner of a complex technology would have difficulty proving infringement unless expert witness testimony were provided. (*Centricut LLC v. Esab Group, Inc.,* 390 F.3d 1361 (Fed. Cir. 2004).)

expiration of patent

See duration of patents.

false marking of invention

See marking of an invention.

Federal Circuit Court of Appeals

See Court of Appeals for the Federal Circuit (CAFC).

Federal Trade Commission proceeding

Under this administrative process, a patent owner can get an order barring devices that infringe the patent from being imported into the United States.

Related terms: international patent protection for U.S. inventions.

Festo v. Shoketsu

In 2000, in a case involving a patent on parts used in robotic arms, a federal appeals court ruled that a patent owner could not assert the doctrine of equivalents if the patent claim at issue had been amended during the application process. The doctrine of equivalents allows a patent owner to stop an infringer who, by using equivalent parts or elements, manages to create an invention that performs the same function in the same manner as a patented invention—for example, if an infringer used aluminum wire when the original patent claimed the use of copper wire.

In 2002, the U.S. Supreme Court struck down this absolute bar to the doctrine of equivalents and replaced it with a less arbitrary standard. Under the Supreme Court's standard, all amended claims are presumed to be narrowed to bar the doctrine of equivalents. But this presumption can be rebutted if a patent owner can demonstrate that the amendment involved a feature that was "unforeseeable at the time of the application" or "for some other reason" could not be included in the original claim. In that case, the patent owner can use the doctrine of equivalents. For example, the patentee could show that, at the time of the amendment, one skilled in the art could not reasonably be expected to have drafted a claim that would have literally encompassed the alleged equivalent. (*Festo Corp. v. Shoketsu Kinzoku Kabushiki Co. Ltd.,* 535 U.S. 722 (2002).)

Related terms: doctrine of equivalents.

field of invention

The "field" of an invention is the classification or subclassification into which an invention falls. For instance, an invention involving gene splicing might be said to be in the "genetic engineering field," while an invention involving computers would fall within the "electronics field."

These terms have no legal significance. The similar phrase "field of search" is related to how patents are categorized for search purposes.

Related terms: classification of patents; patent search.

file wrapper

The file the USPTO maintains for each patent application is known as a file wrapper. This file contains the application itself and copies and notes of all correspondence between the USPTO and the applicant regarding the patent's amendment and issuance. For example, if a letter is sent to the USPTO regarding a pending patent application, it will be added to the applicant's file wrapper.

Related terms: continuation application; file wrapper estoppel; patent application.

file wrapper continuing application (FWC)

See continuation application.

file wrapper estoppel

This is a rule of court under which patent applicants are bound by the statements they make in their patent application and subsequent correspondence and documents filed with the USPTO in the course of prosecuting the application. The term "file wrapper" is jargon for the file the USPTO maintains on an invention, and the term "estoppel" is a legal principle that holds people to their words even if they later want to weasel out of them.

The file wrapper estoppel rule becomes pertinent if the patent owner ever seeks enforcement in court. In that event, the inventor would be prevented from describing the scope of the invention differently from how it was described in earlier documents in the USPTO patent file (again, colloquially referred to as the file wrapper). In short, an inventor is stuck with what's already been told to the USPTO—and cannot later try to broaden a patent's coverage if it has been surrendered by original claim language or in an amendment or a written argument during the earlier prosecution stage.

Because of the file wrapper estoppel rule, it is good practice to follow these two rules:

- Do not say anything negative about an invention in a patent application (your words may come back to haunt you).
- Draft patent claims as broadly as possible in light of the pertinent prior art.

EXAMPLE: Otto invents a medical tool that uses a fiber-optic strand, laser light, specially cloned antibodies, and certain chemicals to detect the presence of various substances in human tissue. In his patent application, Otto drafts his claims very broadly, without a limiting reference to his use of fiber optics. After the USPTO rejects the initial claims, Otto amends his application so that the claims now specify fiber optics as the method of transmitting the laser light. In his cover letter transmitting the amendment to the USPTO, Otto admits that his original claim was wildly overbroad and thanks the examiner for helping him pare his claim down to the appropriate scope. The patent is then granted. Ten years later, Lewis, a famous heart surgeon, makes and uses a similar diagnostic tool, using a magnetic rather than fiber optic means to transmit laser light waves. Suppose Otto brings an infringement action against Lewis, alleging that his patent is sufficiently broad in scope to preclude Lewis's device. In that case, the court will hold Otto to his admission about the overly broad scope of his original claim, as found in the file wrapper, which limits his patent to a fiber optic means.

Related terms: claims; prosecution of a patent application.

filing date

The filing date of a U.S. patent application is indicated on a "filing receipt" that the USPTO sends or emails to the applicant. This date is vital under the first-to-file system effective March 12, 2013, because it establishes priority over later filed inventions regardless of the date of the invention.

The filing date shuts the door on all subsequent developments by other inventors. Any developments occurring after the filing date will not be considered as prior art that could preclude a patent (which must be novel or nonobvious).

The filing date also affects when a patent application must be filed in other countries. For example, if a Convention application is not filed in Germany within one year after the U.S. filing date, German patent protection will not be available. If, however, the applicant files under the Patent Cooperation Treaty within one year of the U.S. filing date, the applicant is allowed a longer period in which to file in Germany.

A Provisional Patent Application (PPA) may be filed up to one year before filing a regular patent application. The PPA filing date will count as the filing date for the invention, provided that the regular patent application is filed within one year. However, the regular patent application filing date—not the PPA filing date—will count as the beginning of the patent term, which expires 20 years from the date of filing, and will also begin the year period in which a patent application must be filed in many foreign jurisdictions.

Related terms: anticipation; interference; international patent protection for U.S. inventions; prosecution of a patent application; Provisional Patent Application (PPA).

filing fees

See application filing fees; issue fee.

final office action

The patent examiner's decision as to whether or not to issue a patent is known as a final office action. Despite the name, final office actions are not necessarily final. A patent examiner can be petitioned to reconsider the application. And, even if the examiner refuses to budge, the applicant can:

- file a continuation application
- agree to amend the application to exclude a claim altogether (if the argument is about a particular claim), or
- appeal the decision to the Patent Trial and Appeal Board (PTAB).

Typically, the final office action occurs after the patent applicant has been afforded at least one opportunity to amend the application (in response to a first office action that raised problems with the application). Most commonly, the applicant will be expected to revise one or more of the amendment's claims, thereby avoiding overlap with prior art that otherwise would preclude a patent from issuing. Also, technical mistakes in how the application describes the invention, how the claims are constructed, and how the drawings depict the invention are typical subjects of an amendment.

Related terms: continuation application; Patent Trial and Appeal Board (PTAB); prosecution of a patent application; first office action.

first office action

This term refers to the patent examiner's first response to a patent application. Often, the first office action involves the rejection of all or most of the claims in an application (in the trade, humorously termed a "shotgun rejection") on the ground that one or more prior art references render the invention obvious. The applicant can file a response within three months (extendable for up to six months) that either amends the claims or satisfactorily explains to the patent examiner why the prior art references found troublesome by the examiner are not pertinent.

Related terms: prosecution of a patent application; final office action.

first sale (patent)

See exhaustion.

FRAND

To establish industry standards that allow devices to communicate and connect universally—for example, HDMI, USB, WIFI, or MP3—companies and their competitors might need to share patents. Companies that own patents that are essential for the industry-standard (known as "standard-essential patents" or SEPs) could have an incentive and disincentive to license (high royalty rates versus competitors' use of SEPs). The willingness of a SEP owner to work with a standard-setting organization (SSO) can affect the success of an entire industry.

To resolve these issues, industries have adopted FRANDs (Fair, Reasonable, and Non-Discriminatory terms) for SSO members (and often, nonmembers).

FRANDs can include rules for use and royalty rates for SEPs. Neither statutes nor government officials create FRANDS. They are contractual—that is, agreements among SSO members or established in SSO governing documents. Although FRANDs involve patents, they are often enforced in state court as a contract claim.

Courts take case-by-case approaches to FRAND disputes. In one case, a court imposed a formula referred to as the smallest-saleable patent practicing unit ("SSPPU") royalty theory. (*FTC v. Qualcomm*, No. 17-CV-00220-LHK (N.D. Cal. May 21, 2019.) In another case, a court rejected a rote formula for fixing a FRAND royalty and based its determination on industry practice and market evidence. (*HTC v. Ericsson*, No. 18-cv-00243 (E.D. Tex. May 23, 2019).)
Related terms: licensing of an invention.

fraud on the U.S. Patent and Trademark Office

Fraud on the UPSTO consists of any behavior by an applicant that attempts to mislead the USPTO in regard to whether the invention deserves a patent. The terminology is often used interchangeably with inequitable conduct, and breach of the duty of candor and good faith. The most common type of fraud is failure to inform the USPTO about one or more relevant prior art references known to the applicant.

An alleged infringer usually raises this issue as a defense. When a patent applicant commits fraud or inequitable conduct when communicating with the USPTO or during the patent application process, a court may later refuse to enforce that patent (meaning the patent is invalidated).

Often the tainted patent is part of a group of patents owned by the same party—that is, patents covering similar subject matter. If inequitable conduct exists only during the prosecution of one patent, associated patents will still be enforceable. However, if the conduct was so bad that the owner's "unclean hands" tainted a family of patents, then, under the doctrine of "infectious unenforceability," all the patents will be judged to be unenforceable. In 2020, a Delaware District Court cited this doctrine in refusing to dismiss claims that a family of patents could be invalidated. The court rejected the argument that inequitable conduct must be related only to patent prosecution. (*Guardant Health, Inc. v. Foundation Medicine, Inc.*, 1-17-cv-01616 (D.C. Del. Jan 7, 2020).)

Related terms: defenses to a patent infringement claim; duty of candor and good faith; infringement action; unenforceable patent.

fully met by a prior art reference

When any single previous development or publication (prior art reference) contains all of the specific elements and limitations set out in a patent claim, the claim is said to be fully met by the prior art. If a claim is fully met, the invention is considered anticipated and is therefore not entitled to a patent.

> EXAMPLE: Unaware of prior developments, Gary invents a mechanical match. When he tries to patent it, however, the U.S. Patent and Trademark Office points out a patent that shows (teaches) all of the elements in the claim describing Gary's device. Because Gary's claims are fully met, his device has been "anticipated" and is not entitled to a patent.

Related terms: claims; novelty; prior art reference.

GATT (General Agreement on Tariffs and Trade)

The General Agreement on Tariffs and Trade (GATT) is an international trade treaty that has had a significant impact on U.S. patent law.

Under GATT, for patents filed after June 7, 1995, the U.S. patent monopoly ends 20 years from the application's filing date, regardless of when the patent issues. However, effective June 2000, every patent is guaranteed an in-force period of at least 17 years. Previously, the patent monopoly lasted for 17 years from the date of issue, regardless of when the application was filed. (Patent applications that were pending—and patents that were in force—as of June 8, 1995, expire 20 years from filing or 17 years from issue, whichever period is longer.)

Another GATT-related rule involves the Provisional Patent Application or PPA. Filing a PPA will legally "reduce an invention to practice," provided that the inventor files an actual patent application within a year of filing the PPA. The reduction to practice date is crucial if an inventor is faced with a competing patent application or a prior art reference with a close date. Formerly, an invention could be reduced to practice only by building and testing it or filing a regular patent application.

GATT also enhanced protection against patent infringement. Before GATT, a patent gave its owner the right to exclude others from making, using, or selling the patented invention. GATT expanded this right to include the situation when anyone else offers for sale or imports a patented invention, or, in the case of a process patent, imports products made abroad by the patented process.

genetic engineering and patents

Ordinarily, patents will not be issued on "inventions" consisting of items or substances found to exist in a natural state. The reason for this is obvious. Something occurring in nature without human intervention cannot have been the product of inventive activity.

There are several categories of patentable inventions that do, however, involve "natural" materials. One category is novel and nonobvious plants created through asexual breeding. Plant patents for new plants involving human inventiveness (breeding skill) are specifically authorized by statute (the patent laws and the Plant Variety Protection Act) in the United States.

Genetic engineering is another field where "natural" materials (that is, bacteria, DNA, or RNA) have been manipulated by humans through gene splicing and cloning techniques (such as Polymerase Chain Reaction or PCR) to produce new organic materials and life forms. These new substances and forms, and the processes used to create them, are also considered to be patentable under the authority of the U.S. Supreme Court's decision in the case of *Diamond v. Chakrabarty*, 447 U.S. 303 (1980), as long as they meet the basic patent requirements of novelty, nonobviousness, and utility.

Because Congress wants basic research in biotechnology to develop as quickly as possible, federal law permits a company to utilize biotechnical inventions patented by another company if the purpose of the use is strictly for research. This is an exception to the general rule that a patent prohibits manufacturing or using an invention covered by an in-force patent. If, however, the company doing the research desires to commercially exploit the substance or process being utilized, it must obtain permission from the patent owner (usually accomplished by paying a license fee).

In 2012, the U.S. Supreme Court determined that certain patent claims for BRCA1 and BRCA2 human genes were invalid. The genes are found in the breast and other tissue cells, where they help repair damaged DNA. The genes are a factor in breast cancer diagnosis. The Supreme Court held that the subject matter was unpatentable because genes are the physical embodiment of [genetic] information. The Supreme Court hypothesized that the creation of a synthetic version of the genes might be patentable. (*Association for Molecular Pathology v. Myriad Genetics, Inc.*, 566 U.S. 12 (2012).) The America Invents Act bars the issuance of patent claims directed to or encompassing a human organism. In a controversial 2015 decision, the Federal Circuit, applying the tests elaborated by the Supreme Court in *Mayo v. Prometheus*, invalidated a patented method for accessing fetal DNA. The Supreme Court refused to hear the case. (*Ariosa Diagnostics, Inc. v. Sequenom, Inc.*, 788 F.3d 1371 (Fed. Cir. 2015).)

Related terms: laws of nature exception to patents; nonstatutory subject matter.

geographic patent license

This type of exclusive license grants its holder (the licensee) the right to make, use, or sell a patented invention only within a specified geographic region. For example, one license might allow its holder to exploit the invention commercially in the United States. In contrast, another license might provide similar rights to another company, to be exercised solely in the European Community countries.

Related terms: exclusive patent license.

Graham v. John Deere

This 1966 Supreme Court case created the guidelines for determining when an invention is nonobvious—a statutory requirement for an invention to be patentable. (*Graham v. John Deere*, 383 U.S. 1 (1966).)

According to the Supreme Court, the following analysis helps to determine whether an invention is nonobvious:

- Determine the scope and content of the prior art.
- Determine the novelty of the invention.
- Determine the skill level of artisans in the pertinent technology (art).
- Against this background, determine the obviousness or nonobviousness of the inventive subject matter.
- Consider relevant secondary factors, such as the commercial success experienced with the invention, whether there was a long-felt but unsolved need for the invention, and whether others tried but failed to produce the invention.

In practice, these guidelines boil down to whether, taking all relevant factors into account, a person reasonably skilled in the art involved in the invention would find the invention to be a surprising or unexpected development at the time it was made.

Related terms: nonobviousness; obviousness; person with ordinary skill in the art (POSITA).

grant of patent

When the USPTO determines that an invention meets legal standards, a patent is "granted" (issued) on an invention.

Patent Law: Definitions

group art unit

The group art unit is an internal division of the U.S. Patent and Trademark Office to which a filed patent application is assigned for examination.

Related terms: prosecution of a patent application; U.S. Patent and Trademark Office (USPTO).

improvement inventions

Technically, almost all inventions are "improvement inventions"—they improve upon other prior inventions.

Patent protection for minor improvements on existing inventions in well-developed fields is relatively easy to obtain. Conversely, in relatively new fields such as genetic engineering, minor improvements might be considered too trivial or obvious to be granted a patent.

This is true primarily because new fields of invention are much more supportive of new developments than established fields, where potential improvement in existing techniques is more obvious.

A patent on an improvement invention covers only the improvement itself and is thus subject to the rights of any holders of in-force patents on the other technology involved. This means that its owner must license the right to use the underlying invention before commercially exploiting the improvement invention. Often this is accomplished by cross-licensing the two patents ("You can use mine if I can use yours"). Cross-licensing is extremely common throughout the industrial world.

> EXAMPLE: A computer manufacturer makes an unexpected and novel improvement on an existing patented data bus (a device included in most microcomputers to move data from one part of the computer to another in an orderly way). The value of this improvement patent will depend heavily upon the degree to which appropriate arrangements can be made with the patent owner on the original data bus. This might not be difficult because the original patent owner will likely want the right to commercially exploit the improvement patent. If so, the parties can enter into a cross-license agreement permitting them to use each other's inventions for agreed-upon compensation. If there were two in-force patents covering the original data bus, the improvement patent owner would have to come to terms with both patent owners to exploit the invention.

Related terms: cross-licensing; patent pools.

independent claim

An independent claim by itself describes an aspect of the invention without reference to any other claim. By contrast, a dependent claim refers to another independent or dependent claim. (Samples of dependent and independent claims are provided in "claims.")

Related terms: claims; dependent claim.

Index of U.S. Patent Classification

See classification of patents.

inducing infringement

35 U.S. Code § 271(b) provides that an act of actively inducing another to infringe a patent shall itself be treated as an act of infringement. To prove inducement to infringe, the patent owner must demonstrate some positive act of inducement on the part of the person being sued. That may include instructing, directing, or advising the third party on how to carry out an infringement.

There must also be an act of infringement.

In a 2011 case, a company, SEB, patented a "cool-touch" deep-fryer whose exterior was cool to the touch. GlobalTech Appliances, operating outside the U.S., copied everything but the cosmetic aspects of the SEB deep-fryer. GlobalTech then branded these deep-fryers for sale by Sunbeam, Montgomery Ward, and others (GlobalTech had vetted its device with a patent attorney but had failed to disclose to the attorney that the device was copied directly from the SEB deep-fryer.) The Supreme Court ruled for the patent owner, SEB. The court said that inducing infringement required knowledge of the existing patent, but that knowledge could be inferred using a legal standard referred to as "willful blindness." The bottom line is that when asking an attorney to render a legal opinion ("Does my deep-fryer infringe?"), don't hide information (like, "I copied this from another deep-fryer"). (*GlobalTech Appliances v. SEB*, 563 U.S. 754 (2011).)

In 2014, the Supreme Court unanimously ruled that there is no liability for induced patent infringement—encouraging someone else to infringe—unless there has been direct (or actual) patent infringement. The plaintiff, Akamai, exclusively licensed a patent for delivering data. Limelight was accused of inducing infringement. However, Limelight never directly infringed the patent because it did not carry out all of the steps claimed in the method. Instead, Limelight's customers carried out one of the steps. Because there was no direct infringement, the Supreme Court concluded there could be no inducement to infringe. (*Limelight Networks, Inc. v. Akamai Technologies, Inc.*, 572 U.S. 915 (2014).)

In a 2015 case, the Supreme Court refused to establish an "of belief in invalidity" defense to a charge of inducement. The high court also ruled that to bring a claim of patent inducement, the patent owner must show proof that "the defendant knew the acts were infringing." (*Commil v. Cisco*, 575 U.S. 632 (2015).)

inequitable conduct

See fraud on the U.S. Patent and Trademark Office; duty of candor and good faith.

infectious unenforceability

See fraud on the U.S. Patent and Trademark Office.

in force

A patent is said to be in force (in effect) if all of the following are true:

- The patent's statutory term has not yet expired.
- Appropriate maintenance fees have been paid when due.
- The patent has not been ruled invalid by the U.S. Patent and Trademark Office or a court.

When a patent is no longer in force, it still is considered prior art when determining whether a later invention qualifies for a patent.

Related terms: patent term extension; reexamination of patent.

Information Disclosure Statement

A statement must be filed with a regular patent application (or within the following three months) that describes all relevant prior art references known to the applicant and provides actual copies of such references when they appear in print. Known as an Information Disclosure Statement, an IDS, or USPTO Form 1449, this gives the USPTO a head start in determining whether the invention deserves a patent. An IDS need not be filed with a Provisional Patent Application.

An applicant's knowing failure to disclose any known and relevant prior art reference is considered fraud on the USPTO. If a patent was granted in this circumstance, it could be held unenforceable in court. However, the deliberately omitted prior art reference might not have resulted in any claim being disallowed.

When examining a patent application, the USPTO conducts its own patent search in addition to what it learns from an applicant's IDS and often picks up omitted prior art references. These references might then be used to reject the application on novelty or nonobviousness grounds, but the USPTO seldom presumes that the omission was intentional. If, however, the USPTO fails to find the omitted prior art reference and proceeds in its ignorance to issue a patent, the reference will usually be brought to light only if an infringement lawsuit is filed. This is because the infringer, as part of its defense, can be counted on to do an exhaustive prior art search (called a validity search) to prove that the patent was improvidently issued and therefore invalid. If the prior art reference is found in the course of this search, the infringer can be expected to argue that the omission was deliberate. If the court agrees, it will invalidate the patent because of fraud on the USPTO, without regard to how the reference affects the invention's novelty and nonobviousness.

Related terms: defenses to a patent infringement claim; patent search; Provisional Patent Application (PPA); validity search.

infringement, patent

Infringement of a utility patent occurs when someone makes, uses, or sells an item covered by the claims of an in-force patent without the patent owner's permission. If a court finds that infringement occurred, every patent infringer can be ordered by a court to stop all infringing activity. Any of the infringers who profited from the infringement may also be found liable for money damages. Only an infringer who had reason to know that a patent was being infringed can be held liable for treble damages as a willful infringer.

> EXAMPLE: Owens Organic Products invents and patents a simple computerized sprinkler system that turns on and off according to the soil's moisture level. Although Phil Prendergast has been independently working on the same invention, he failed to beat Owens to the Patent and Trademark Office and cannot prove that he was the first to invent. However, figuring that Owens will probably never find out, Phil licenses Garden Development Corp. to construct and market his invention in exchange for royalties. Garden Development manufactures and distributes the system wholesale to a chain of retail garden-supply stores, which then sell the sprinklers to consumers who use them in their gardens. Phil, Garden Development, the retail stores, and the consumers are all guilty of patent infringement—even though none except Phil knew about Owens's patent. Phil, Garden Development, and the retail stores may be ordered to stop infringing and pay damages. However, only Phil would be liable for treble damages unless Garden Development and the retail stores knew, or should have known, that their activity infringed Owens's patent.

Patent Law: Definitions

Infringement of a design patent is determined when the allegedly infringing design is substantially the same as the patented design (the Ordinary Observer Test).

Related terms: contributory infringement of patent; infringement action.

infringement action

An infringement action is a lawsuit alleging that one or more parties (defendants) have, without permission, made, used, or sold an invention protected under a patent owned by the party bringing the lawsuit (plaintiff). Patent infringement actions must be filed in the U.S. District Court within a maximum of six years after the date the infringement occurred—or sooner if a delay in filing would cause undue hardship to the defendant.

In 2017, the U.S. Supreme Court held that infringement actions must be filed in districts where the defendant: (1) is incorporated, or (2) has committed acts of infringement and has a regular and established place of business. The decision eliminates "forum shopping" (at the time, 45% of all infringement actions were filed in the Eastern District of Texas). (*TC Heartland LLC v. Kraft Foods LLC,* 581 U.S. ___ (2017).)

Although it is possible to have a jury trial in a patent infringement case, the judge alone is responsible for interpreting the patent claims. (*Markman v. Westview Instruments, Inc.,* 517 U.S. 370 (1996).) The judge or jury then examines the plaintiff's patent and compares the elements recited in its claims with those of the accused infringer's device or process. On this basis, the judge or jury decides whether the plaintiff's claims, as interpreted by the judge, cover the defendant's device or process—that is, fully describe the elements contained in the device or process. If the plaintiff's claims cover ("read on") the device or process, infringement is found. If the claims do not cover the defendant's device or process, then no infringement has occurred.

Even if the claims don't literally read on the infringing device, the judge or jury could find infringement by applying the doctrine of equivalents: The two devices are sufficiently equivalent in what they do and how they do it to warrant a finding of infringement. Also possible, but extremely rare, is the converse: finding no infringement because the two devices are sufficiently dissimilar in what they accomplish or how they work, even though the claims are the same (in patent speak, the negative doctrine of equivalents).

If infringement is found to exist, the judge may:

- issue an injunction (court order) preventing further infringement
- award the patent owner damages for loss of income or for profits resulting from the infringement from the time the invention was properly marked (when the word "patent" and the patent number were affixed to the invention) or from when the infringer was first put on actual notice of the infringement, whichever occurred first, and
- in the event the infringement was willful or flagrant (it continued without a reasonable defense after notification by the patent owner, or infringement occurred through direct copying without any ground to believe the plaintiff's patent was invalid), award the plaintiff three times the actual damages established in court plus reasonable attorneys' fees.

The Supreme Court has determined that a court should not automatically issue an injunction based on a finding of patent infringement. (Alternatively, an injunction should not be denied simply on the basis that the plaintiff does not make, sell, or use the patented invention.) Instead, a federal court must still weigh the four factors traditionally used to determine if an injunction should be granted. (*eBay Inc. v. MercExchange, L.L.C.*, 547 U.S. 388 (2006).)

Patent infringement lawsuits are risky for the patent owner because the defendant will almost always attack the underlying validity of the patent on such grounds as:

- The invention was obvious or lacked novelty when the patent was issued. The defendant proves this by introducing relevant prior art references not picked up by the USPTO in examining the patent application.
- The patent application failed to fully disclose the best mode of the invention, as is required by the patent laws.
- The patent applicant failed to disclose relevant prior art known to the applicant (fraud on the USPTO).

Related terms: breaking (or busting) a patent; contributory infringement of patent; defenses to a patent infringement claim; infringement, patent.

infringement defenses

See defenses to a patent infringement claim.

infringement search

An infringement search is conducted for the purpose of discovering whether an invention infringes an in-force patent. This type of search is typically conducted by an invention developer as a preliminary step to deciding whether to develop a particular invention. It is much narrower in scope than a patentability search, which is concerned with all prior art—including expired patents and relevant unpatented technology. It also differs from a validity search, which typically is conducted by a defendant in a patent infringement lawsuit to discover information that would invalidate the patent.

Related terms: patent search.

injunctions and injunctive relief

See infringement action.

inter partes review (IPR)

Suppose someone—for example, another patent owner, a potential infringer, or the U.S. Patent and Trademark Office (USPTO)—seeks to reexamine an existing patent to determine its validity. In such a case, an IPR can be brought at the USPTO. This type of administrative hearing is less expensive, less formal, and faster than challenging a patent owner in court. In addition, decisions are rendered by technical specialists, not juries.

The Director can authorize an IPR only if "there is a reasonable likelihood that the petitioner would prevail with respect to at least one of the claims challenged in the petition." (35 U.S. Code § 314(A).) Such proceedings are limited to challenges for novelty and nonobviousness—that is, to issues relating to Sections 102 and 103 of the patent law. These claims can be based only on prior art consisting of patents and printed publications and must be filed nine months after the patent is issued. Patent law also establishes many additional technical and procedural rules, making it more challenging to bring IPRs.

In 2017, the Supreme Court held that the USPTO has the final say as to whether to institute an IPR)—that is, the decision as to whether or not to institute an IPR is not appealable. The Supreme Court also held that the USPTO's "broadest reasonable interpretation" (BRI) standard was a "reasonable exercise of the rulemaking authority that Congress delegated to the Patent Office." (*Cuozzo Speed Technologies, LLC v. Lee*, 579 U.S. 261 (2016).) More recently, there has been a flurry of IPR decisions including the following:

- **IPR patent challenges are constitutional.** The Supreme Court ruled, in a 7–2 decision, that post-grant challenges to patent validity do not violate the Fifth Amendment's "taking" prohibition. The holding, which supported the PTAB's decision-making power, effectively concluded that patents are a government franchise, not necessarily a property right. (*Oil States Energy v. Greene's Energy Group*, 138 S.Ct. 1365, 584 U.S. ___((2018).)

- **CAFC okays IPRs for pre-AIA patents.** In the *Oil States* decision, the Supreme Court ruled that it was constitutional to subject a post-AIA patent (a patent issued after the adoption of the America Invents Act) to IPR. In *Celgene Corp. v. Peter*, the CAFC held "that the retroactive application of IPR proceedings to pre-AIA patents is not an unconstitutional taking under the Fifth Amendment." In other words, it is constitutional to maintain an IPR proceeding for pre-AIA patents. (*Celgene Corp. v. Peter*, Nos. 2018-1167-1171 (CAFC, July 30, 2019).)

- **PTAB must determine the patentability of all of the petitioner's disputed claims.** In a 5–4 decision, the Supreme Court held that when the PTAB initiates an IPR, it must resolve the patentability of all of the claims the petitioner has questioned. In other words, "the PTAB must address every claim the petitioner has challenged," and cannot "partially institute" an IPR review. *(SAS Institute Inc. v. Iancu*, 138 S.Ct. 1348, 584 U.S. ___ (2018).)

- **CAFC determines the real party in interest for IPRs.** The CAFC ruled that the PTAB applied an improper standard when determining the real party in interest for the purposes of instituting IPR proceedings. The CAFC held that "[T]he focus of the real-party-in-interest inquiry is on the patentability of the claims challenged in the IPR petition, bearing in mind who will benefit from having those claims canceled or invalidated." (*Applications in Internet Time v. RPX Corporation*, 897 F.3d 1336 (2018).)

- **CAFC rules against tribal sovereign immunity in IPRs.** Allergen, a drug company, transferred patents to a Native American tribe and then claimed sovereign immunity to avoid an attack on its patents. The CAFC ruled that tribal sovereign immunity cannot be asserted to end IPR proceedings. (*St. Regis Mohawk Tribe v. Mylan Pharmaceuticals*, 896 F.3d 1322 (2018).)

- **No sovereign immunity for state governments in IPR proceedings.** A state university argued that its patents could not be challenged in an IPR proceeding because of sovereign immunity. The CAFC disagreed, holding that sovereign immunity did not apply in USPTO enforcement actions. (*Regents of the Univ. of Minnesota v. LSI Corp.*, 926 F.3d 1327 (Fed. Cir. 2019).)

Patent Law: Definitions

- **The federal government is not a "person" for purposes of IPRs.** The three types of administrative patent reviews provided by the AIA—*inter partes* reviews, post-grant reviews, and covered business method reviews—are available to any "person" who wants to challenge a patent's validity. At issue was whether a government agency qualified as a person. In a 6–3 decision, the Supreme Court followed precedent and held that the government was not a person for purposes of the AIA. (*Return Mail, Inc. v. United States Postal Service*, 139 S. Ct. 1853 (2019).

- **No appeal from denial of IPR based on 35 U.S. Code § 315(b).** If a request for an IPR comes more than a year after a suit against the requesting party for patent infringement, the IPR will not be instituted. The Supreme Court held that patent law does not allow an appeal of the PTAB's decision to institute a procedure for challenging the validity of a patent after finding that a one-year time bar does not apply. (*Thryv, Inc. v. Click-To-Call Technologies, LP*, 140 S. Ct. 1367 (2020).)

- **PTAB can rule on Section 101 patentability.** Petitioners (anyone who can request an IPR) are limited to disproving patent validity under 35 U.S. Code Section 102 (novelty/prior art) or Section 103 (obviousness). Even though petitioners are limited to Section 102 and Section 103, PTAB judges also consider whether the claims contain ineligible subject matter under 35 U.S. Code Section 101 (inventions patentable). (*Uniloc 2017 LLC v. Hulu, LLC, Netflix, Inc., et al.* (Fed. Cir. July 22, 2020).)

- **Article III standing required to appeal USPTO decisions.** If one party is dissatisfied with an IPR ruling, it can appeal it to the CAFC. However, the party requesting relief must demonstrate it has standing (almost literally, the right to "stand" before the court). More specifically, appealing to the CAFC requires Article III standing (Article III being the portion of the Constitution that established the federal court system). Typically, a party demonstrates Article III standing by showing it has suffered an injury. One type of injury—the doctrine of competitor standing—occurs when the government causes economic injury to one party. In this case, the CAFC rejected the argument that the competitor standing doctrine applied to unsuccessful IPR petitioners. In summary, although parties to an IPR are entitled to pursue appeals, they still must show Article III standing. (*AVX Corp. v. Presidio Components Inc.*, 923 F.3d 1357 (Fed. Cir. 2019).)

§ 311. Inter partes review

(a) In General. Subject to the provisions of this chapter, a person who is not the owner of a patent may file with the Office a petition to institute an inter partes review of the patent. The Director shall establish, by regulation, fees to be paid by the person requesting the review in such amounts as the Director determines to be reasonable, considering the aggregate costs of the review.

(b) Scope. A petitioner in an inter partes review may request to cancel as unpatentable 1 or more claims of a patent only on a ground that could be raised under section 102 or 103 and only on the basis of prior art consisting of patents or printed publications.

(c) Filing Deadline. A petition for inter partes review shall be filed after the later of either—

(1) the date that is 9 months after the grant of a patent or issuance of a reissue of a patent; or

(2) if a post-grant review is instituted under chapter 32, the date of the termination of such post-grant review.

§ 312. Petitions

(a) Requirements of Petition. A petition filed under section 311 may be considered only if—

(1) the petition is accompanied by payment of the fee established by the Director under section 311;

(2) the petition identifies all real parties in interest;

(3) the petition identifies, in writing and with particularity, each claim challenged, the grounds on which the challenge to each claim is based, and the evidence that supports the grounds for the challenge to each claim, including—

(A) copies of patents and printed publications that the petitioner relies upon in support of the petition; and

(B) affidavits or declarations of supporting evidence and opinions, if the petitioner relies on expert opinions;

(4) the petition provides such other information as the Director may require by regulation; and

(5) the petitioner provides copies of any of the documents required under paragraphs (2), (3), and (4) to the patent owner or, if applicable, the designated representative of the patent owner.

(b) Public Availability. As soon as practicable after the receipt of a petition under section 311, the Director shall make the petition available to the public.

§ 313. Preliminary response to petition

If an inter partes review petition is filed under section 311, the patent owner shall have the right to file a preliminary response to the petition, within a time period set by the Director, that sets forth reasons why no inter partes review should be instituted based upon the failure of the petition to meet any requirement of this chapter.

Patent Law: Definitions

§ 314. Institution of inter partes review

(a) Threshold. The Director may not authorize an inter partes review to be instituted unless the Director determines that the information presented in the petition filed under section 311 and any response filed under section 313 shows that there is a reasonable likelihood that the petitioner would prevail with respect to at least 1 of the claims challenged in the petition.

(b) Timing. The Director shall determine whether to institute an inter partes review under this chapter pursuant to a petition filed under section 311 within 3 months after—

   (1) receiving a preliminary response to the petition under section 313; or

   (2) if no such preliminary response is filed, the last date on which such response may be filed.

(c) Notice. The Director shall notify the petitioner and patent owner, in writing, of the Director's determination under subsection (a) and shall make such notice available to the public as soon as is practicable. Such notice shall include the date on which the review shall commence.

(d) No Appeal. The determination by the Director whether to institute an inter partes review under this section shall be final and nonappealable.

Related terms: reexamination of patent.

interference

An "interference" is an administrative proceeding that was formerly conducted to determine who got a patent when there were two pending applications both claiming the same invention. The America Invents Act terminated interferences as of March 2013 and provided two options: a "derivation hearing" at the USPTO, or lawsuits by the patent applicants in federal court.

Related terms: derivation hearings.

International Bureau of the World Intellectual Property Organization

This administrative arm of the World Intellectual Property Organization (WIPO) in Geneva, Switzerland, is designated by the Patent Cooperation Treaty of 1970 as the clearinghouse for international patent applications.

Related terms: Patent Cooperation Treaty (PCT).
See also Part 4 (Trade Secret Law): World Intellectual Property Organization (WIPO).

international patent protection for U.S. inventions

U.S. inventors can gain patent protection in countries outside the United States in two ways:

- by filing separately in each country where protection is desired under rules established by the Paris Convention, or
- by filing an "international application" with the International Bureau of the World Intellectual Property Organization, an office established under the Patent Cooperation Treaty (PCT). This single filing establishes a filing date good in all member countries, although the patent owner must file separate "national" applications in each member country where the owner wants coverage. The European Patent Office is considered a single entity for PCT purposes.

Although other treaties exist between the United States and certain countries concerning reciprocal patent protection, the two mentioned above provide the primary international protection for U.S. inventors.

Related terms: Convention application; European Patent Convention; Federal Trade Commission proceeding; Patent Cooperation Treaty (PCT).

Internet, patent searching

See patent search, computerized.

Internet patent

The term "Internet patent" has, for the most part, been supplanted by the term "business method patent," though technically, an Internet patent is a subset of business method patents. The term is typically used to describe a group of utility patents issued for software programs and for methods of doing business, most of which relate to Internet uses. The most notorious example of an Internet patent is Amazon.com's "One-Click" system, which allows a repeat customer to bypass address and credit card data entry forms when placing an online order. (U.S. Pat. No. 5,960,411.)

For most of the 20th century, the courts and USPTO believed that business methods could not be patented. But in 1998, a federal court ruled that patent laws were intended to protect any method, whether or not it required the aid of a computer, so long as it produced a "useful, concrete, and tangible result." (*State Street Bank & Trust Co. v. Signature Financial Group, Inc.*, 149 F.3d 1368 (Fed. Cir. 1998).) Thus in one stroke, the court legitimized both software patents and methods of doing business, opening the way for these so-called Internet patents. Regardless of their categorization, business method, software, and Internet patents have one thing in common: They were all affected by the Supreme Court's 2010 ruling in *Bilski v. Kappos*. The Supreme Court rejected the view held by the CAFC that the so-called "machine or transformation" test should be the sole standard for patentability. The Supreme Court refused to categorically deny patentability to any class or category of otherwise patentable subject matter, preserved the status quo, and kept the concept of Internet, software, business method, and other process patents alive. (*Bilski v. Kappos*, 561 U.S. 593 (2010).)

In 2014, the Supreme Court made it more challenging to obtain software-based Internet patents when it declared a particular software patent invalid. The method employed—a computer-assisted process for exchanging financial obligations— was an abstract idea, ineligible for patent protection. (*Alice Corporation Pty. Ltd. v. CLS Bank International et al.*, 573 U.S. 208 (2014).) Subsequent case law established the criteria for the two-step test for determining patentability (known as the "Alice Test" or "Alice/Mayo Test").

Related terms: business methods as statutory subject matter; software patents; Alice Test (Alice/Mayo Test).

intervening right

When an in-force patent is reissued based on broadened claims, there exists the possibility that someone relying on the wording of the claims in the original patent developed or used a device that would not have infringed the original patent, but that does infringe the reissue patent. When this occurs, the infringing business is said to have "intervening" rights, which preclude an infringement suit under the new broadened claims. However, these intervening rights are considered personal to the business in question and cannot be transferred to another business or owner.

Related terms: defenses to a patent infringement claim; reissue patent.

invalid patent

See defenses to a patent infringement claim; unenforceable patent.

invention

An invention is generally considered to be any thing, process, or idea that:

- is not generally and currently known
- without too much skill or ingenuity can exist or be reduced to tangible form or used in a tangible thing
- has some value or use to society, and
- was thought up or discovered by someone.

Related terms: inventor; patent.

inventor

An inventor is a person (human being) who contributes significant creative input into an invention. Until September 2012, an application for a patent on an invention had to be made in the inventor's name (or the names of all inventors if there were more than one), even if a commercial or nonprofit organization actually owned the invention. Failing to accurately name the real inventors in a patent application could result in an issued patent later being declared invalid. However, as of September 2011, assignees of invention rights may apply for the patent rather than the inventor.

An inventor must be a natural person. For example, one patent application listed the inventor's given name as "DABUS" and the family name as "Invention generated by artificial intelligence." The USPTO rejected the application because the applicant failed to name a natural person (a human being) as the inventor. The assignee (and the person who supplied the application) stated that artificial intelligence created the invention autonomously. But the USPTO pointed out that the patent statute identifies the "inventor" as an individual. (35 U.S. Code § 115a; (*In re Application No. 16/524,350*, July 29, 2019.)

§ 118. Filing by other than inventor

A person to whom the inventor has assigned or is under an obligation to assign the invention may make an application for patent. A person who otherwise shows sufficient proprietary interest in the matter may make an application for patent on behalf of and as agent for the inventor on proof of the pertinent facts and a showing that such action is appropriate to preserve the rights of the parties. If the Director grants a patent on an application filed under this section by a person other than the inventor, the patent shall be granted to the real party in interest and upon such notice to the inventor as the Director considers to be sufficient.

Related terms: coinventors; patent applicant; patent owner; prosecution of a patent application; shop rights.

issue fee

In addition to the fees required for filing a patent application, additional fees must be paid for the patent to issue after allowance by the U.S. Patent and Trademark Office. The fees depend on the applicant's classification: large entity, small entity, or micro entity. However, if a small entity has made an assignment to a large entity, hefty entity fees must be paid. For current fees, check the USPTO website (www.uspto.gov).

Related terms: application filing fees; prosecution of a patent application.

joint inventors

See coinventors.

junior party in interference proceedings

When an interference is scheduled by the USPTO, the inventor who was last to file a patent application is the junior party.

Related terms: interference.

jury, role of in patent infringement cases

See infringement action.

KSR v. Teleflex

Teleflex owned a patent that combined two well-known components—a gas pedal that can be adjusted relative to the driver's seating position and an electronic (as opposed to a mechanical) sensor that senses and transmits to the vehicle's throttle computer the position of the pedal. Teleflex sued its competitor, KSR International, of Canada, for supplying General Motors with adjustable gas pedals with its sensors for use with electronic throttle controls.

The Supreme Court decided that when elements, techniques, items, or devices are combined, united, or arranged, and when, in combination, each item performs the function it was designed to perform, the resulting combination—something the court called "ordinary innovation"—is obvious and therefore, not patentable. In summary, ordinary tasks that engineers perform in the course of their usual day-to-day activities might not be patentable. (*KSR v. Teleflex*, 550 U.S. 398 (2007).)

laboratory notebook

See notebook, inventor's.

large entity

A for-profit company with over 500 employees is considered a large entity by the U.S. Patent and Trademark Office (USPTO). When a large entity owns the patent rights to an invention or is entitled to have ownership of these rights transferred to it, the fees payable to the USPTO for various aspects of the patent application and prosecution process are double those for small entities.

Related terms: issue fee; maintenance fees; micro entity; small entity.

laws of nature exception to patents

This rule states that general scientific and mathematical principles are not patentable, even if they meet the other statutory requirements for patentability (such as utility, novelty, and nonobviousness). Laws of nature are considered to be part of the public domain rather than products of human inventiveness.

Related terms: algorithms; genetic engineering and patents; naturally occurring substances as nonpatentable; nonstatutory subject matter; statutory subject matter.

lay judge

Patent law practitioners use this term to refer to any judge sitting in a patent case who is not a patent attorney or especially experienced in patent law.

lay patent searchers

See patent searcher.

letters patent

See patent deed.

licensing of an invention

The process by which an owner permits another party to make, use, or sell a patented invention is most often a written document called a license. A license of patent rights can be either an exclusive license (only the licensee is entitled to exercise the rights set out in the license) or a nonexclusive license (the licensee may exercise the rights set out in the license but cannot prevent others from exercising the same right under a different license).

Related terms: assignment of a patent; exclusive patent license; nonexclusive patent license.

limiting reference

A limiting reference consists of any element in a patent claim that operates to both define the invention and, by defining it, limit its scope.

Related terms: claims.

machines as patentable subject matter

Generally defined as any devices with moving parts, machines are one of the five categories of inventions (statutory subject matter) that can be patented. Electronic circuits are also considered machines, even though their parts, strictly speaking, don't move.

Patent Law: Definitions

Related terms: statutory subject matter.

maintenance fees

To keep an issued patent in effect, fees must be paid to the USPTO (or the patent office of another country where a utility patent has been obtained). Maintenance fees are due 3.5, 7.5, and 11.5 years after the grant of the utility patent. They are not required for plant patents or design patents, or for a reissue patent if the patent being reissued did not require maintenance fees. For current maintenance fees, check the USPTO website (www.uspto.gov).

Related terms: large entity; micro entity; small entity.

Manual of Classification

See classification of patents.

Manual of Patent Examining Procedure (MPEP)

The MPEP is a manual of internal procedures followed by USPTO examiners in processing patent applications (often termed "The Examiner's Bible"). The MPEP is available online at the USPTO website (www.uspto.gov).

Related terms: classification of patents; patent application.

manufactures as patentable subject matter

Relatively simple objects that don't have working or moving parts, "manufactures," sometimes also called "articles of manufacture," are one of the five categories of inventions (statutory subject matter) that can be patented. There can be some overlap between the "machines" and "manufactures" categories—especially in the case of inventions involving electronic circuits, which lack moving parts but are frequently classified as machines because of how they operate.

Examples of more typical manufactures include erasers, desks, houses, wires, tires, books, cloth, chairs, containers, and transistors.

Related terms: statutory subject matter.

march-in rights

The U.S government retains the right (though rarely uses it) to use an invention that has been developed as a result of a government contract if the actual inventor fails to develop and exploit the invention sufficiently.

Related terms: Bayh-Dole Act; patent owner; shop rights.

marking of an invention

Affixing the marks "Patent Pending" or "Pat. Pend." to an invention after a patent application or provisional patent application has been filed, or affixing the patent number after a patent has been issued, is known as marking the invention.

The marks "Patent Pending" or "Pat. Pend." have no immediate legal significance. Still, they place potential infringers on notice that should a patent ultimately issue, they will not be allowed to make, use, or sell the invention without the patent owner's permission. During the patent pending period, an inventor cannot stop an infringer or collect damages. However, under the recent 18-month publication statute (see "confidentiality of patent application"), an inventor whose application is published before issuance may obtain royalties from an infringer from the date the application is published. There are two requirements: (1) the application later issues as a patent; and (2) the infringer had actual notice of the published application. (35 U.S. Code §§ 122, 154.) An infringer will have actual notice of a publication if upon seeing the published application. This can be accomplished by sending a copy to the infringer by registered mail. Otherwise, the inventor has no rights whatsoever against infringers during the pendency period—only the hope of a future monopoly, which doesn't commence until a patent issues.

Marking an invention with a patent number (for example, "patent #5,040,387" or "pat. #5,040,387") after a patent is issued puts infringers on notice that any use of the invention could result in an injunction and damages. If an infringement action is later filed, the patent owner will be able to collect damages from the date the owner began properly marking the invention. By contrast, if the invention is not marked, damages may be collected only when the infringer received actual notice (usually in the form of a demand letter from the patent owner) or the date the patent infringement suit was first filed, whichever occurred earlier.

Many inventors prefer not to place the patent number on their invention.

Why? Because marking the invention makes it easier for a competitor to obtain a copy of the patent and design around it. A competitor might have a much more difficult time locating the patent on an unmarked invention. Some patent holders just use the mark "patent" without an accompanying number to avoid this problem. However, this doesn't have any legal clout since this type of notice is not legally sufficient to start the period running for which damages may be recovered. As with an unmarked invention, damages on an inadequately marked invention are recoverable only for the period after the infringer received actual notice or after the suit was filed.

Patent Law: Definitions

The America Invents Act initiated two changes regarding patent marking:

- **Virtual marking.** Virtual marking is the process of using a publicly accessible website to provide a link between a patented invention and its patent number. After September 2011, this is considered as sufficiently providing public notice for that patent.
- **Harder to claim false marking defense.** The America Invents Act provides that privately filed false marking claims (those claims not brought by the government) will require proof of competitive injury. Marking with the number of a patent that covered that product but has expired will no longer be considered false marking.

Related terms: confidentiality of patent application; infringement action; patent pending.

Markman v. Westview Instruments

This U.S. Supreme Court case (517 U.S. 370 (1976)) ruled that the judge rather than the jury is responsible for interpreting patent claims in a patent infringement case. Since the scope of the claims can often determine the outcome of an infringement case, the jury's power in such cases has been sharply diminished.

mathematical formulas

See algorithms.

Mayo v. Prometheus

This 2012 U.S. Supreme Court decision invalidated various patents (two DNA gene patents and a patent for a method for determining drug efficacy) because they covered only natural phenomena. The Supreme Court stated that a process including a law of nature is patentable only if it includes "additional features that provide practical assurance that the process is more than a drafting effort to monopolize the law of nature itself." The *Mayo* case is commonly linked with *Association for Molecular Pathology v. Myriad Genetics, Inc.*, in which the Supreme Court held that isolating a naturally occurring DNA segment does not make it patentable. The cases helped establish the criteria for the two-step test for determining patentability for natural phenomena (known as the "Alice Test" or "Alice/Mayo Test"). (*Mayo v. Prometheus*, 566 U.S. 66 (2012); *Association for Molecular Pathology v. Myriad Genetics*, 569 U.S. 576 (2013).)

Related terms: *Alice Corp. v. CLS.*

Means plus function clause

This refers to a way of defining an invention in a patent claim that describes an element of the invention in terms of its function (how a function is performed) rather than in terms of its structure.

The use of a means plus function clause broadens the claim and makes the claim harder to design around since a patent on the "means" will then support all possible structures that can perform the specified function. A means plus function clause must include the term "means" followed by the specific function of the element.

> EXAMPLE: One of the claims in a patent application filed on fundamental multimedia search technology begins by stating: "A computer search system for retrieving information, comprising: ... *means for storing* interrelated textual information and graphical information."

In this claim element, the words "means for storing ... information" theoretically are broad enough to include a CD-ROM, a computer hard disk, or any other information storage method that exists now or might exist in the future. However, the scope of this or any other claim using a means plus clause is not as unlimited as the words seem to suggest. When determining the scope of a claim containing a means plus function clause, the USPTO and courts look to other references to the invention contained in the patent or patent application and limit the reach of the claim to those references. Also, because historically, there has been some dispute as to how broadly means plus function claims can read (that is, how many devices/processes they can cover), it is often wise to draft one set of claims using means function clauses and a duplicate set of claims citing specific devices and processes so that the patent will be both as broad and as specific as the USPTO will allow.

A 2007 court decision emphasized that every means and non-means component in the patent claims portion of a patent application must also be clearly described and identified in the specification. (*Biomedino, LLC v. Waters Technologies Corp.*, 490 F.3d 946, 950 (Fed. Cir. 2007).)

Related terms: claims; prosecution of a patent application.

MedImmune v. Genentech

In 2007, the Supreme Court ruled that a licensee in good standing can challenge the validity of the patents it has licensed without breaking the license agreement before doing so. In other words, without a contractual clause limiting such behavior, the licensee has an unfettered right to prove that the underlying patent

Patent Law: Definitions

is void. The Supreme Court did not limit this holding to patents—indicating that perhaps trademark and copyright licensees can also challenge the validity of the title. (*MedImmune v. Genentech*, 549 U.S. 118 (2007).)

methods as patentable subject matter

See processes (or methods) as patentable subject matter.

micro entity

A patent applicant who qualifies as a micro entity pays the lowest USPTO fees (approximately one-quarter of regular fees and one-half of small entity fees). To qualify as a micro entity, the filer must be a small entity and must meet the following criteria:

(1) The applicant has not been named as the inventor on a total of more than four utility patents (regular utility patents, not provisional patent applications), design patents, or plant patents. This also does not include certain international PCT applications and applications owned by a previous employer. In addition, the applicant had to have had a gross income in the previous year of less than three times the median household income reported by the Bureau of the Census. (The median household income has been hovering around $78,000 in recent years.) If the patent application has been assigned, the assignee needs to have had a gross (not net) income of less than three times the U.S. median household income; or

(2) The majority of the patent filer's employment income is from an Institution of Higher Learning, or the applicant has assigned or is obliged to assign the patent to an Institution of Higher Learning. An Institution of Higher Learning is a public or nonprofit, accredited institution that admits postsecondary students for programs of not less than two years.

How do you determine micro entity status for multiple inventors? The rules apply individually to each joint inventor. So, no joint inventor can have been named an inventor on more than four applications. No joint inventor can have a gross income (as defined by the IRS) exceeding three times the median household income for the preceding calendar year. (As of 2020, the median income was $78,500, so an inventor's gross income could not exceed approximately $235,500.

Related terms: small entity.

misuse

See patent misuse.

multiple claims

A single patent application may contain two or more claims describing a single invention. A patent application typically contains more than one claim because there is often more than one way a single invention can be novel or useful.

> EXAMPLE: A robotics invention that keeps a running account of a kitchen's ingredients can be viewed as a device for maintaining general inventory, a specific process of managing a kitchen's stock of food, and a new physical manifestation of certain robotics principles. At least three different independent claims might be used to describe the invention in these different ways.

Related terms: claims; dependent claim; independent claim.

narrowing a claim

A claim in a patent application that a patent examiner initially rejected as too broad (over the prior art) may be redrafted (narrowed) so that the claim no longer overlaps with the prior art and, therefore, describes a novel and non-obvious invention. Narrowing can be done by adding more elements to the claim or reciting the existing elements more specifically.

Related terms: claims; first office action.

naturally occurring substances as nonpatentable

Items or substances that exist in a natural state are not eligible for patent protection (they are nonstatutory subject matter). In other words, the discovery of natural substances and processes does not by itself qualify as an invention. However, if natural substances are manipulated and repackaged to meet specific human needs—as is true with many drugs—they may qualify as patentable inventions.

The rule prohibiting the patenting of naturally occurring substances previously was used to bar patents on most living matter. However, the late 20th century saw the development of technologies that allow the genetic alteration of living plants and animals into something different from a "naturally occurring substance." Accordingly, patents have been issued on such items as genetically manipulated DNA molecules, enzymes, proteins, bacteria, viruses, plants, and even a mouse and the processes of manipulation themselves.

Patent Law: Definitions

However, there are limits on what is granted. In 2012, the U.S. Supreme Court invalidated various patents (two DNA gene patents and a patent for a method for determining drug efficacy) because they covered only natural phenomena. (*Association for Molecular Pathology v. Myriad Genetics, Inc.,* 569 U.S. 12 (2012); *Mayo v. Prometheus,* 566 U.S. 10 (2012).)

In 2015, the Federal Circuit applied the Alice/Mayo test and invalidated a patented method for accessing fetal DNA. *(Ariosa Diagnostics, Inc. v. Sequenom, Inc.,* 788 F.3d 1371 (Fed. Cir. 2015).)

Related terms: genetic engineering and patents; nonstatutory subject matter; plant patents; Alice Test (Alice/Mayo Test).

negative doctrine of equivalents

Under this doctrine, a later device or process may be held to not infringe the patent on an earlier invention, even though the patent's claims fully cover ("read on") the later device or process, if the structure, function, or result of the two inventions is substantially different.

This is the rarely used converse of the doctrine of equivalents, which requires a finding of infringement when an invention and a later item are the same, even though the patent's claims do not, strictly speaking, cover the later item.

Related terms: doctrine of equivalents; infringement action.

new combinations of old inventions

See combination patent.

new matter

Technical information about an invention not included in the original patent application is referred to as new matter. Once an application has been filed, the USPTO does not allow an applicant to add new matter that would change the scope and nature of the invention. This is because the filing date often determines the date of the invention. If new matter could continually be added to an application, the filing date would no longer serve this purpose.

However, an applicant for a patent who wants to bring new matter before the USPTO may do so by filing a special supplementary application called a continuation-in-part application.

Related terms: continuation-in-part application (CIP); filing date; patent application.

new-use invention

A new-use invention consists of a new way to use an old device or process, such that the new use is nonobvious—generally remote or surprising to one skilled in the art.

> EXAMPLE: Utilizing a known physical property of color dyes that causes them to expand at a different rate when applied to cloth, Tony invents a new process for transferring color patterns into textiles. Assuming that the process is considered nonobvious, it will be entitled to a patent as an old principle's "new use."

Related terms: nonobviousness; statutory subject matter.

nondisclosure of patent applications by U.S. Patent and Trademark Office

See confidentiality of patent application.

nonelected claims

A patent may claim only one invention. An applicant may voluntarily choose (elect) not to prosecute a claim or claims in a pending patent application in response to a patent examiner's decision that the application impermissibly claims two inventions. However, an applicant can file a "divisional application" on the nonelected claims so that they are not abandoned.

Related terms: abandonment of patent application; divisional application; double patenting.

nonexclusive patent license

A nonexclusive patent license is an agreement by which a patent owner (the "licensor") authorizes (licenses) another (the "licensee") to make, use, or sell the patented invention but retains the right to license it to others as well. For example, the inventor of a new, more efficient fuel injection system would most likely grant nonexclusive licenses to all the major car companies able to utilize the system, rather than just license it to one company on an exclusive basis.

Related terms: antishelving clause; exclusive patent license; infringement action.

nonobviousness

The quality of nonobviousness refers to the ability of the invention to produce unexpected or surprising new results—results that were not anticipated by the prior art. (The statute that sets forth the nonobviousness requirements is found in 35 U.S. Code § 103.)

To be patentable, an invention must be nonobvious to a person with ordinary skill in the art. Thus, an invention involving video technology would need to be considered nonobvious to a video engineer thoroughly familiar with prior art in the video field.

Analyzing an invention for nonobviousness is difficult primarily because it is a subjective exercise. In addition, whether or not an invention is nonobvious is supposed to be determined as of the date a provisional or regular patent application is filed.

The patent examiner makes the initial determination of whether an invention is (was) nonobvious in deciding whether a patent should issue. The patent examiner typically approaches this task by examining all pertinent prior art references that existed as of the date of invention. Because the patent examiner is usually knowledgeable in the area of the patent being examined, such expertise may also be brought to bear as a person with ordinary skill in the art.

However, once a patent issues, the patent may be attacked (usually in court) on the ground that the patent examiner made a mistake on the question of nonobviousness. In this situation, both sides will typically produce experts who provide opposing opinions ("Yes, it was nonobvious"; "No, it wasn't"). The inventor will also attempt to establish that the invention enjoyed commercial success or solved an unperceived need and should therefore be considered nonobvious based on actual developments in the marketplace, regardless of what the experts say. In some cases, the court may consider evidence of competitor copying.

> **EXAMPLE:** A hair-care company offered proof that its hair-bleaching process was copied by a competitor using confidential information. The PTAB concluded that the evidence was irrelevant. On appeal, the CAFC disagreed, holding that copying confidential information without authorization from the patent applicant should be included as a "secondary consideration" when determining nonobviousness. (*Liqwd, Inc. v. L'Oreal USA, Inc.*, No. 18-2152 (Fed. Cir. 2019).)

In addition to this evidence, the court will evaluate from scratch the prior art existing at the time of the filing of the application. One danger of relying on this type of retrospective analysis is that the experts and judge will be unconsciously affected by the intervening technical improvements. The invention might later be considered obvious even though it wasn't at the time of filing.

In 2007, the U.S. Supreme Court attempted to clarify the issue of nonobviousness regarding combination inventions. The Supreme Court recognized that most, if not all, patentable inventions rely on known building blocks and combinations that, in some sense, are already known. The Court held that when elements, techniques, items, or devices are combined, and when, in combination, each item performs the function it was designed to perform—something the court called "ordinary innovation"—the result may not be patentable. (*KSR v. Teleflex*, 550 U.S. 398 (2007).)

The CAFC applied the *KSR* standard in a case involving a glass sexual aid, concluding that a person of ordinary skill would have known that the results of particular glass experimentation were predictable. (*Ritchie v. Vast Resources, Inc.*, 563 F.3d 1334 (Fed. Cir. 2009).) The CAFC also applied the *KSR* standard in *Aerosol and Specialty Container, Inc. v. Limited Brands, Inc.*, 555 F.3d 984 (Fed. Cir. 2009). In that case, the court reviewed a candle tin whose cover could also serve as the candle's base. The court held that prior art references, when combined, made the candle claims obvious.

In 2009, the Federal Circuit provided hopeful news: nonobviousness determinations can be based on common sense. The court invalidated a patent for email distribution. The patent claimed a method for managing bulk email distribution to consumers, including selecting recipients, sending emails to that group, and tabulating the number of emails successfully transmitted. If the number did not exceed a certain minimum, the last step repeated the previous steps. The district court summarized the last step as obvious since it was based on the commonsense principle, "If at first you don't succeed, try again." (*Perfect Web Technologies, Inc. v. InfoUSA, Inc.*, 587 F.3d 1324 (Fed. Cir. 2009).)

§ 103. Conditions for patentability; nonobvious subject matter

A patent for a claimed invention may not be obtained, notwithstanding that the claimed invention is not identically disclosed as set forth in section 102, if the differences between the claimed invention and the prior art are such that the claimed invention as a whole would have been obvious before the effective filing date of the claimed invention to a person having ordinary skill in the art to which the claimed invention pertains. Patentability shall not be negated by the manner in which the invention was made.

Related terms: *Graham v. John Deere*; obviousness; person with ordinary skill in the art (POSITA); statutory subject matter.

Nonpublication Request (NPR)

The USPTO treats patent applications as confidential, so it is possible to apply for a patent and maintain the underlying information as a trade secret, at least for the first 18 months of the application period. The USPTO will publish a patent application 18 months after the earliest claimed filing date but will not publish it if, at the time of filing, the inventor files a Nonpublication Request (NPR) stating that it will not be foreign-filed. (The 18-month publication statute was enacted to make U.S. patent laws more like those of foreign countries.) If an inventor does not file the NPR, the application will be published after 18 months, and the trade secret status of the application will be lost. If the inventor files an NPR and decides to foreign-file the application later, the NPR must be rescinded within 45 days.

If the inventor files an NPR, the information in the patent application becomes publicly available only if and when a patent issues. Suppose the patent is refused so that the application is not published. In that case, the competition will not know about the invention, and any competitive advantage inherent in that fact can be maintained.

nonstatutory subject matter

To qualify for a patent, an invention must fit into one or more categories established by the federal patent laws (statutes). The categories are compositions of matter, processes, machines, manufactures, and new uses of inventions falling within any of the first four categories. Inventions that don't fall within any of these classes are said to be "nonstatutory subject matter" and are not patentable. Examples of nonstatutory subject matter are:

- processes done entirely by human motor coordination, such as choreographed dance routines
- printed matter that has no unique physical shape or structure associated with it
- naturally occurring matter, even though its external characteristics may be modified, and
- abstract scientific principles, mathematical formulas, and natural laws (algorithms) or ideas that don't produce a useful, concrete, or tangible result.

The term "nonstatutory subject matter" has a second, less obvious meaning: Any invention that doesn't qualify for a patent for any reason is also termed nonstatutory subject matter. So even if an invention fits within one of the five statutory categories above, it would still be considered nonstatutory subject matter if it failed to meet the additional basic patent qualifications of novelty, non-obviousness, and utility.

Related terms: algorithms; genetic engineering and patents; laws of nature exception to patents; naturally occurring substances as nonpatentable; statutory subject matter.

not invented here (NIH) syndrome

A handicap to inventors trying to market their inventions is the refusal by many companies to buy, develop, or distribute inventions owned by outside inventors—inventions that are "not invented here."

This all-too-common policy is often attributable to corporate ego: If it wasn't invented here, it can't be any good. But, in addition, it can be the understandable result of the sincere desire to avoid potential and expensive disputes over who owns the patents held or applied for by the company. By never looking at outsiders' inventions, a business can partially protect itself from such claims.

Related terms: infringement action; patent owner.

notebook, inventor's

Many inventors maintain a journal in which they record when and how they conceived of an invention and specify all procedures, dates, actions, failures, successes, contacts, and other events that occur in testing the invention.

Related terms: interference; Provisional Patent Application (PPA).

notice of allowance

A notice of allowance is sent to an applicant when a patent examiner decides that a patent should issue on an invention (technically, "the claims are allowed").

Related terms: office action; prosecution of a patent application.

notice of references cited

This form is sent by the USPTO to a patent applicant, citing the various prior art references used by the USPTO as a basis for rejecting the application's claims. Copies of the references are also enclosed, so the applicant can respond to the rejection by either explaining why they don't apply or amending the rejected claims.

Related terms: office action; prior art reference; prosecution of a patent application.

Patent Law: Definitions

novelty

An invention must have novelty to qualify for a patent. In this context, "novelty" means that the invention is different from the prior art (that is, all previous products, devices, methods, and documents describing these things). An invention is considered different from the prior art—and therefore novel—when no single prior art item describes all of the invention's elements. The statute setting out the novelty requirement is 35 U.S. Code Section 102.

Even if an invention is novel in that it is different from the prior art, it can still flunk the novelty test if it has been described in a published document or put to public use before a patent application is filed.

Although an invention might meet the novelty test, it still can be denied a patent if the patent examiner finds that the invention is obvious. That is, it isn't innovative enough to deserve a patent.

§ 102. Conditions for patentability; novelty

(a) Novelty; Prior Art. A person shall be entitled to a patent unless—

    (1) the claimed invention was patented, described in a printed publication, or in public use, on sale, or otherwise available to the public before the effective filing date of the claimed invention; or

    (2) the claimed invention was described in a patent issued under section 151, or in an application for patent published or deemed published under section 122(b), in which the patent or application, as the case may be, names another inventor and was effectively filed before the effective filing date of the claimed invention.

(b) Exceptions—

    (1) DISCLOSURES MADE 1 YEAR OR LESS BEFORE THE EFFECTIVE FILING DATE OF THE CLAIMED INVENTION. A disclosure made 1 year or less before the effective filing date of a claimed invention shall not be prior art to the claimed invention under subsection (a)(1) if—

      (A) the disclosure was made by the inventor or joint inventor or by another who obtained the subject matter disclosed directly or indirectly from the inventor or a joint inventor; or

      (B) the subject matter disclosed had, before such disclosure, been publicly disclosed by the inventor or a joint inventor or another who obtained the subject matter disclosed directly or indirectly from the inventor or a joint inventor.

    (2) DISCLOSURES APPEARING IN APPLICATIONS AND PATENTS. A disclosure shall not be prior art to a claimed invention under subsection (a)(2) if—

      (A) the subject matter disclosed was obtained directly or indirectly from the inventor or a joint inventor;

(B) the subject matter disclosed had, before such subject matter was effectively filed under subsection (a)(2), been publicly disclosed by the inventor or a joint inventor or another who obtained the subject matter disclosed directly or indirectly from the inventor or a joint inventor; or

(C) the subject matter disclosed and the claimed invention, not later than the effective filing date of the claimed invention, were owned by the same person or subject to an obligation of assignment to the same person.

(c) Common Ownership Under Joint Research Agreements. Subject matter disclosed and a claimed invention shall be deemed to have been owned by the same person or subject to an obligation of assignment to the same person in applying the provisions of subsection (b)(2)(C) if—

(1) the subject matter disclosed was developed and the claimed invention was made by, or on behalf of, 1 or more parties to a joint research agreement that was in effect on or before the effective filing date of the claimed invention;

(2) the claimed invention was made as a result of activities undertaken within the scope of the joint research agreement; and

(3) the application for patent for the claimed invention discloses or is amended to disclose the names of the parties to the joint research agreement.

(d) Patents and Published Applications Effective as Prior Art. For purposes of determining whether a patent or application for patent is prior art to a claimed invention under subsection (a)(2), such patent or application shall be considered to have been effectively filed, with respect to any subject matter described in the patent or application—

(1) if paragraph (2) does not apply, as of the actual filing date of the patent or the application for patent; or

(2) if the patent or application for patent is entitled to claim a right of priority under section 119, 365(a), or 365(b), or to claim the benefit of an earlier filing date under section 120, 121, or 365(c), based upon 1 or more prior filed applications for patent, as of the filing date of the earliest such application that describes the subject matter.

Related terms: anticipation; nonobviousness; prior art.

obviousness

The quality of an obvious invention is such that a person with ordinary skill in the art could reasonably believe that the invention was to be expected at the time of its conception. An obvious invention (that is, one that lacks the quality of nonobviousness) doesn't qualify for a patent.

EXAMPLE: A new metal that is significantly lighter and stronger than current alloys hits the market. It is "obvious" that someone will build a bicycle containing the material since lightness is a desirable aspect of high-quality bicycles. Thus, while the inventor of the metal might qualify for a patent, the developer of the new bicycle made from that metal will not.

The Supreme Court has clarified nonobviousness standards in two cases, *Graham et al. v. John Deere Co. of Kansas City et al.*, 383 U.S. 1 (1966) and *KSR v. Teleflex*, 550 U.S. 398 (2006).

Related terms: nonobviousness; person with ordinary skill in the art (POSITA); prior art; *Graham v. John Deere*; *KSR v. Teleflex*.

office action

A letter sent by a patent examiner to an applicant regarding the pending application is called an office action. Usually, one or two office actions are sent per patent application. The first office action typically describes what's wrong with the application and why it can't be allowed. Most often, the first office action rejects the application because of:

- lack of novelty (35 U.S. Code § 102)
- obviousness (35 U.S. Code § 103), or
- claim indefiniteness (35 U.S. Code § 112).

The applicant can amend the application to overcome the rejection as long as no new subject matter is added. If the application is accepted as amended, a notice of allowance will be sent (that is, a patent is granted). If the application is still not acceptable, the patent examiner will send a final office action that partially or entirely rejects the application.

Related terms: final office action; first office action; prosecution of a patent application.

Official Gazette (OG)

The *Official Gazette* consists of two weekly online publications produced by the U.S. Patent and Trademark Office (USPTO). There is one for trademarks and another for patents. Each is colloquially known as the OG.

The patent edition contains official announcements concerning USPTO policy and patent rules and information on patents issued that week. For each patent, the *Official Gazette* contains:

- its patent number
- all inventors' names and addresses

- the assignee (usually a company to which the inventor has transferred ownership of the patent), if any
- the filing date
- the application's serial number
- the international classification number
- the U.S. classification number
- the prominent figure or drawing
- the number of claims, and
- a sample claim or abstract.

The *Official Gazette* contains the essence of the invention, not the entire patent. The full text of the patent contains far more technical information.

Anyone wishing to keep up with the patents being issued in a specific field should regularly read the *Official Gazette*, an online new-patent service available through the USPTO's website (www.uspto.gov).

Related terms: abstract; Patent and Trademark Resource Centers (PTRCs); patent search.

one-year rule (on-sale bar)

Section 102(b)(1) of the America Invents Act states that certain disclosures made one year or less before the filing date of a patent application shall not be considered prior art if "the disclosure was made by the inventor or a joint inventor or by another who obtained the subject matter disclosed directly or indirectly from the inventor or a joint inventor; or the subject matter disclosed had, before such disclosure, been publicly disclosed by the inventor or a joint inventor or another who obtained the subject matter disclosed directly or indirectly from the inventor or a joint inventor." In other words, a patent application will not be rejected because of certain disclosures made less than one year before filing and under the authority of the inventor. The adoption of the AIA eliminated the previous "one-year" rule, under which patent applicants were granted a one-year period before filing during which any of the following activities were permitted:

- any public use of the invention by the inventor
- an actual sale of the invention
- an offer to sell the invention, or
- any description of the invention by the inventor in a published document.

Related terms: anticipation; filing date; novelty; patent application; Provisional Patent Application (PPA); public use; statutory bar.

Patent Law: Definitions

online patent searching

See patent search, computerized.

operability

An invention must (theoretically at least) work in order to qualify for a utility patent. Although this does not mean the device must be built and working, it does mean that the patent application must disclose sufficient information to demonstrate the theoretical operability of the invention.

A patent examiner who believes an invention will not work (is non-operable) can require proof of its operability (such as a demonstration) before the patent application will be allowed. However, the fact that a patent has been issued on an invention does not guarantee that the invention will work—only that it appears on paper to work.

Related terms: disclosure requirement for patents; utility patents.

opposing a patent (international rules)

In most countries, a party may register its opposition to a pending patent application after it has been officially published. If the opposing party can establish that relevant prior art exists, an opposition proceeding is held to determine whether a patent should be issued. This process opens up the initial patent determination to all interested parties.

Related terms: defenses to a patent infringement claim; infringement action; reexamination of patent.

ordinary skill in the art

See person with ordinary skill in the art (POSITA).

ownership of patent

See patent owner.

PAD

See Patent Application Declaration (PAD).

parent application

During the prosecution of a patent, an applicant might need to file additional applications such as a divisional application, a substitute application, a continuation application, a continuation-in-part application, or an application for a reissue patent. If one of these subsequent applications is filed, the original application will be referred to as the parent application.

> EXAMPLE: Rory applies for a patent for a tennis racket with an electronic device embedded in the handle that keeps track of the score. The patent examiner rejects the application because it claims two inventions—the racket/device combination and the device itself. Rory then restricts his application by withdrawing or canceling the claims to the device itself and files a divisional application. In this scenario, the application that now claims only the combination will be considered the parent application.

Related terms: continuation application; divisional application; double patenting; prosecution of a patent application; reissue patent; substitute patent application.

Paris Convention

See Convention application; European Patent Convention.

patent

A patent is a right provided by a government that allows an inventor to prevent others from manufacturing, selling, or using the patent owner's invention. This right covers the invention as described explicitly in the patent application's claims allowed by the USPTO or other patent-examining agencies in other countries.

Physically, a U.S. patent consists of the following:

- a cover sheet bearing the patent number; the name of the invention as provided by the inventor; the name of all inventors; the name of the assignee (the person or company to whom the patent has been assigned), if any; the application filing date; a list of the prior art references found by the patent examiner to be pertinent to the invention; and the patent abstract (a concise summary of the invention)
- one or more pages containing drawings of the invention submitted by the patent applicant
- the patent specification as submitted in the patent application (a detailed narrative description of the invention's structure and function), and
- the patent claims as finally approved by the patent examiner.

The original physical patent issued by the USPTO is termed a "patent deed" or "letters patent" and has a blue ribbon and gold seal for adornment. The physical patent retained by the USPTO and others interested in the patent is often termed a "patent copy" or a "soft copy" and lacks the adornment found on the patent deed. As with a college diploma or deed, the patent has no intrinsic value in any of its forms. The patent derives its value from the offensive rights it provides in the event of an infringement.

Related terms: claims; infringement action; prosecution of a patent application.

patent agents

Patent agents are nonattorneys with technical training who are legally permitted—under a license issued by the U.S. Patent and Trademark Office (USPTO)—to draft, file and prosecute patent applications on behalf of inventors. If necessary, a patent agent also can represent applicants before the Patent Trial and Appeal Board (PTAB). However, if a patent becomes the subject of litigation in court, only a patent attorney may appear on behalf of the inventor.

Related terms: patent attorneys; patent searcher.

Patent and Trademark Office

See U.S. Patent and Trademark Office (USPTO).

Patent and Trademark Resource Centers (PTRCs)

The USPTO has designated about 25 Patent and Trademark Resource Centers (PTRCs) (formerly called Patent and Trademark Depository Libraries (PTDLs)) throughout the country to house copies of U.S. patent and trademark materials and to make them available to the public. The PTRCs provide access to the EAST (Examiner Assisted Search Tool) and WEST (Web-based Examiner Search Tool). These USPTO searching tools enable full-text searching of all U.S. patents. However, some PTRCs charge for using the terminals, and the charges can add up to a considerable amount. (Note, you can use the EAST terminals at the USPTO headquarters in Virginia for free.) Find out more about each PTRC's features by checking the USPTO website or calling the respective library.

Related terms: patent search; patent search, computerized.

patent applicant

The inventor or assignee who files the patent application (and, often, who will own the patent if the application is granted) is termed the patent applicant. Patent applicants typically are independent inventors who choose to build and distribute their inventions, companies to which independent inventors have sold (assigned) their invention, or large R&D companies that employ the actual inventor. As a result of the America Invents Act, a person or organization that has been assigned patent rights can apply as the "applicant." (Before this change, the term "applicant" was always synonymous with the inventor.) Even though an assignee can file, the inventor(s) must still execute an oath or declaration (except in limited circumstances). In addition, an assignment (or an employment agreement) should be recorded no later than when the issue fee is paid.

Related terms: coinventors; inventor; patent application; patent owner.

patent application

An inventor must transmit a collection of documents to the USPTO, either electronically or by mail, to obtain a patent. Usually included in a patent application (and depending on whether it is filed electronically or via mail) are:

- drawings
- a specification (a sample is provided in the Forms section at the end of this part of the book)
- one or more patent claims
- an abstract
- a Patent Application Declaration (PAD)
- an Information Disclosure Statement (IDS)
- a transmittal letter
- a check for the filing fee
- a fee transmittal form, and
- a self-addressed receipt postcard.

A regular patent application can also include a Petition to Make Special (to speed the processing), an assignment and assignment cover sheet (if its owner sold the invention), and a transmittal letter claiming the Provisional Patent Application filing date, if a PPA was filed.

Patent Law: Definitions

An applicant can file electronically or by mailing a paper application. Besides lower fees—a "non-electronic filing fee" for filing with paper—there are other advantages to filing a patent application with the USPTO's Electronic Filing System (EFS-Web). Using it, you can (1) file an application anytime and from anywhere that has Internet access, (2) obtain instant confirmation of receipt of documents by the PTO, (3) send an application to the PTO without having to go to the post office to get an Express Mail receipt or having to wait for a postcard receipt, and (4) file an application without having to prepare an application transmittal, a fee transmittal, receipt postcard, or check or Credit Card Payment Form (CCPF).

The filing date applies to this application and will provide the starting date for determining the patent term (20 years from the date of filing). However, if a Provisional Patent Application was filed, its filing date will provide the basis for determining the invention's novelty.

If an application is filed by mail, then one to two weeks after the application is mailed, the applicant will receive the receipt postcard back from the USPTO with the filing date and number stamped on it. This means that the USPTO has established a separate file (called a file wrapper), in which the application and all future correspondence between the applicant and the USPTO will be kept.

Once a regular patent application is on file, the applicant is in the patent prosecution stage, which averages 18 months but can take much longer in specific cases.

Related terms: electronic filing of patent applications; prosecution of a patent application; Provisional Patent Application (PPA).

Patent Application Declaration (PAD)

A Patent Application Declaration (PAD) is a written statement made under penalty of perjury that must accompany a patent application. In the statement, the patent applicant states (avers) that:

- The applicant is the first and true inventor.
- The applicant has reviewed and understands the specification and claims.
- The applicant has disclosed all information material to the examination of the application.

Related terms: duty of candor and good faith; fraud on the U.S. Patent and Trademark Office; patent application; prosecution of a patent application.

patent attorneys

Patent attorneys must be licensed to practice law and be licensed by the USPTO to practice before it. Patent attorneys prepare and prosecute patent applications, represent clients in interference proceedings, and bring and defend patent-related lawsuits in federal court.

Patent attorneys are required to have a technical higher education degree and a legal background and must pass a USPTO examination to obtain their license. A complete listing of all licensed patent attorneys can be obtained in the USPTO publication *Attorneys and Agents Registered to Practice Before the U.S. Patent and Trademark Office.*

Related terms: infringement action; interference; patent agents.

patent claim

See claims.

Patent Cooperation Treaty (PCT)

This international agreement establishes streamlined procedures for obtaining uniform patent protection in its member countries. The PCT is administered by the World Intellectual Property Organization (WIPO) in Geneva, Switzerland. U.S. inventors applying for PCT patent protection can file with the U.S. Patent and Trademark Office, which has been designated a receiving office of the International Bureau.

In addition to filing the one PCT application, an inventor must file a national patent application in every country where patent protection is desired. However, the primary advantages of using the PCT's procedures are as follows:

- By filing one PCT application, the applicant obtains a filing date that is good in every member country in which they ultimately seek patent protection.
- An initial international patent search is conducted on the PCT application, and the member countries will rely heavily on this search. Thus, the applicant is saved the great expense and delay that can result from having to conduct separate searches in each country and convince each country's patent examining agency that an invention is novel and nonobvious over the prior art.
- The PCT applicant need not decide whether to prosecute the international application in the individual countries until 18 months after the initial patent application filing in the original country.

Patent Law: Definitions

For more specific information on filing under the Patent Cooperation Treaty, a booklet called the "PCT Applicant's Guide" can be obtained from the World Intellectual Property Organization (www.wipo.org).

Related terms: International Bureau of the World Intellectual Property Organization; international patent protection for U.S. inventions.
See also Part 4 (Trade Secret Law): World Intellectual Property Organization (WIPO).

patent deed

This official document, sometimes termed "letters patent," is sent to applicants by the U.S. Patent and Trademark Office when their patent issues.

Related terms: final office action; notice of allowance; patent.

patent examination process

See prosecution of a patent application.

patent examiners

U.S. Patent and Trademark Office examiners are employees who examine patent and trademark applications. On the patent side, the examiners correspond with applicants and decide whether inventions deserve patents. All patent examiners must have a technical degree in some field, such as electrical engineering, chemistry, or physics. Many are also attorneys.

Related terms: U.S. Patent and Trademark Office (USPTO).

patent infringement action

See infringement action.

patent issue fees

See issue fee.

patent license agreements

See exclusive patent license; nonexclusive patent license.

patent misuse

The use of a patent in a manner that violates federal patent or antitrust laws can result in the patent being declared invalid or unenforceable by a court. Most often, the issue of patent misuse is raised as a defense to a patent infringement action. If the court in such an action finds that the patent was misused, it will not enforce the patent unless the owner can show that the misuse was involuntary and completely cured ("purged"). If the misuse was an antitrust violation, however, no such cure is possible and the patent will simply be invalid.

In 2010, the Federal Circuit narrowed the scope of patent misuse in a case involving compact disc patents. Under the Federal Circuit's new standard, there must be evidence of anticompetitive effects in addition to restrictions on use. Alleging wrongful conduct is not enough. (*Princo Corp. v. International Trade Commission*, 616 F.3d 1318 (Fed. Cir. 2010).)

Related terms: antitrust law (federal) and patents; breaking (or busting) a patent; defenses to a patent infringement claim; duty of candor and good faith; fraud on the U.S. Patent and Trademark Office; infringement, patent.

patent number

Each patent allowed by the USPTO is given a number.

Related terms: marking of an invention.

patent number marking

See marking of an invention.

patent owner

The inventor is usually the patent owner unless the invention and patent rights were assigned (ownership rights were transferred to another person or entity—for instance, because the invention arose during an employment relationship).

Many inventors assign ownership of their invention to development or manufacturing companies in exchange for compensation in a lump sum or royalties on sales realized from the invention. These assignments typically also include ownership of the patent, whether already issued or to be issued in the future.

Large companies, and often universities and laboratories, usually require employees to assign their future inventions to the institution as a condition of employment. Under these assignments, the institution will be considered the patent owner. In some states, such requirements are prohibited for inventions that:

- were made on the employee's own time
- did not involve the use of the employer's equipment, supplies, facilities, or trade secret information, and
- do not relate to the employer's business and do not result from any work prepared by the employee or relate to the employer's actual or demonstrably anticipated research or development.

Even if an inventor retains the right to the invention and is considered the patent owner, employers retain the right (called "shop rights") to make and use an invention created during the employment relationship and with the employer's tools and facilities.

Related terms: assignment of a patent; coinventors; shop rights.

patent pending

Once a patent application (regular or provisional) has been filed in the U.S. Patent and Trademark Office, the invention has patent pending status. The inventor can then mark the device "patent pending" to deter potential competitors from copying it by informing them that it might soon receive a patent. However, unless and until a patent is issued, an inventor has no right to prevent others from making, using, and selling the invention. In other words, simply applying for a patent does not earn the applicant the right to behave like a patent owner.

However, under the 18-month publication statute (see "confidentiality of patent applications"), an inventor whose application is published before issuance may obtain royalties from an infringer from the date the application is published. There are two requirements: (1) the application later issues as a patent, and (2) the infringer had actual notice of the published application. (35 U.S. Code §§ 122, 154.) An infringer will have actual notice of a publication upon seeing the published application. This can be accomplished by sending a copy to the infringer by registered mail. Otherwise, the inventor has no rights whatsoever against infringers during the pendency period.

The patent pending label allows an inventor to show the invention to a potential developer without fear that the developer will rip it off and later claim to be the actual inventor. This is especially useful when a developer refuses to sign a nondisclosure agreement for fear of a later lawsuit by the inventor.

Before June 8, 1995, obtaining patent pending status involved the considerable expense of preparing and filing a full patent application. Under the Provisional Patent Application program, however, patent pending status can be acquired for much less.

Related terms: marking of an invention; not invented here (NIH) syndrome; office action; opposing a patent (international rules); Provisional Patent Application (PPA).

patent pools

Under a patent pool arrangement, two or more companies license their patents to each other or to third parties. This allows the participating companies to share their intellectual property by giving them access to each other's patents on a reciprocal basis.

Patent pools run a risk of violating the antitrust laws if they are not open to all competitors in a particular industry. For this reason, some patent pools seek approval from the U.S. Department of Justice. The DOJ, in response, provided the following criteria for analyzing patent pools under antitrust laws:

- Patents must be clearly identified and should be available for licensing individually as well as in a package as chosen by a potential licensee.
- The patents in the pool must be valid and must not have been expired.
- The patent pool should be limited to technically essential patents, which by definition are not competing; and an independent expert should assess whether a patent is essential.
- The patent pool should have limited duration.
- The royalties proposed by the arrangements should be reasonable.
- Worldwide non-exclusive licenses should be available.
- Licensees should be free to develop and use alternative patents.
- Licensees should grant back non-exclusive, non-discriminatory licenses to use patents that are essential to comply with the technology, and
- Pool participants must not collude on prices outside the scope of the pool, e.g., on downstream products.

Related terms: antitrust law (federal) and patents; concerted refusal to deal; cross-licensing; FRAND; patent thickets.

patent prosecution

See prosecution of a patent application.

patent search

The term "patent search" refers to a hunt for documents that will help to decide whether a particular invention meets patent standards. While a patent search usually starts with the patent database (all previously issued patents), it also covers other types of documents that might describe the invention being searched, such as journal articles and scientific papers.

There usually are three discrete types of patent searches:

- **Patentability searches.** This kind of search is ordinarily conducted by, or on behalf of, an inventor to familiarize the inventor with previous developments in the field of invention and help the inventor determine whether it is worthwhile to develop the invention and apply for a patent in the first place. Also, once a patent application is filed, the USPTO will conduct its own patentability search in the course of examining the application.
- **Infringement searches.** An infringement search is usually much narrower in scope than a patentability search. It is conducted to decide whether a particular invention will infringe an in-force patent.
- **Validity searches.** The defendant usually conducts this search in a patent infringement case to discover documents that will adversely bear on the validity of the patent as issued.

All patents issued by the USPTO since 1972 are now available online through several different public and private services. The USPTO website (www.uspto.gov) is a free online full-text searchable database of patents and drawings covering January 1976 to the most recent weekly issue date.

In addition, you can search the USPTO database with a speedier search engine using **Google Patent Search** (www.google.com/patents). Google has entered the free patent searching business by converting the entire image database of U.S. patents (from 1790 to the present) in a format that's easy to search. Google plans to include patent applications, international patents, and U.S. patents issued over the last few months.

Below are several fee-based patent search engines:

- **Derwent** (https://clarivate.com/derwent)
- **LexisNexis** (www.lexisnexis.com)
- **IP.com** (www.ip.com), and
- **PatBase** (www.patbase.com).

All prior art is relevant to a patent application—even patents issued decades ago and that have long since expired. For this reason, it might be necessary to search for pre-1972 patents and the patents in the computer database—all of which were issued after that date. This would especially be true for gadget-type inventions that might resemble something invented hundreds of years ago. For instance, the finger grooves in certain old swords were considered prior art for the finger indentations found in many modern automobile steering wheels.

Pre-1972 patents are not ordinarily relevant to patent searches involving inventions based on modern technologies such as computers and software, integrated circuits, superconductivity, nanotechnology, artificial intelligence, robotics, and bioengineering. For these types of inventions, an online computer search should do the entire job.

Patent searches are usually carried out by entering specific keywords into a computer search. For example, if your search involves a bicycle chain, you might ask for a listing of all patents that contain the words "bicycle" and "chain," where "bicycle" comes before "chain." When the list appears, you can then view the full text of any entry on the list or any selected portion (such as the abstract of patent, drawing, claims, or specification).

If you find that no patent contains the words "bicycle" and "chain" in that order, then you will need to reformulate your request (try "bipedal vehicle" and "wheel pulling device"). Often it takes several attempts to cover all possible words used in all relevant patents. Unless you come up with all the correct words, you might miss patents and thus perform an incomplete search.

A copy of a patent can be acquired by:

- contacting the USPTO by phone or fax, ordering from the USPTO website, or writing a letter listing the number of the patent to Commissioner for Patents, Washington, DC 20231, along with a payment for the price per patent (see the Fee Schedule at the USPTO website) times the total number of patents being ordered, or
- downloading a text copy or image copy of the patent, if available, from the Google or USPTO search sites.

Related terms: infringement search; nonobviousness; novelty; Patent and Trademark Resource Centers (PTRCs); patent searcher; patentability search; prior art; validity search.

patent searcher

Several individuals and firms specialize in conducting patent searches. In the United States, patent searchers tend to be concentrated in Washington, DC, and Virginia because the USPTO library is nearby. It is, therefore, the best place to conduct a patent search.

Patent Law: Definitions

There are three options for getting a patent search done by someone else:

- patent attorneys
- patent agents, and
- lay searchers.

Patent attorneys usually have their favorite searchers and can help you assess the results of the search. However, this is the most expensive option.

A less costly option is a patent agent. Patent agents are licensed by the USPTO and have demonstrated their competence by passing a USPTO-administered test.

Related terms: patent agents; patent attorneys; patent search.

patent term extension

Under 35 U.S. Code Sections 155 and 156, the statutory period during which a patent is in force can be extended if the inventor's ability to realize a gain from the invention will be adversely affected by a regulatory process. For instance, a new drug or food might be withheld from the market for several years because of a requirement that the Food and Drug Administration must approve such items as safe and effective.

Related terms: duration of patents.

patent thickets

A patent thicket is a collection of patents—often owned by different companies— that must be licensed in order to commercialize a new technology. The name refers to the fact that new companies in the tech industry must "hack" their way through in order to get into the marketplace. For example, companies performing gene research often encounter a network of overlapping patent rights. A patent thicket has the effect of limiting the players in an industry and, because of that, it raises antitrust concerns.

Related terms: antitrust law (federal) and patents.

Patent Trial and Appeal Board (PTAB)

The PTAB is an administrative arm of the USPTO, established in 2012 (replacing the Board of Patent Appeals and Interferences). It consists of an appeals division that reviews final rejections by patent examiners and a trial division that hears a range of USPTO-related disputes such as derivation hearings and *inter partes* reviews. PTAB cases are decided upon by Administrative Patent Judges (APJs).

In 2021, the Supreme Court determined that the PTAB APJs were unconstitutional because the Appointments Clause of the Constitution requires that APJs be "directed and supervised at some level by others who were appointed by Presidential nomination with the advice and consent of the Senate." The Supreme Court provided a fix, by authorizing the USPTO Director to give discretionary review to decisions rendered by APJs. (*Arthrex, Inc. v. Smith & Nephew, Inc.*, 594 U.S. ___ (2021).)

patent troll

"Patent troll" is a disparaging term for someone who sues for patent infringement but does not make or sell any products using the patented technology. In other words, the patent troll is in the business of suing companies but not in the business of making or selling anything. Other terminology used to describe those who practice trolling includes PME (Patent Monetization Entity) and PAC (Patent Assertion Company). Patent trolls are sometimes disliked because they seek licensing fees considered disproportionate to the patent's value. They are often well funded and can dig in during litigation (while the defendants might settle to save money).

In a case that affected the dynamics of patent troll litigation, eBay was sued by a company that owned several auction patents. The patent owner sought a permanent injunction, which was granted by the Court of Appeals for the Federal Circuit (CAFC). Patent trolls typically rely on the fear of permanent injunctions to elicit licensing fees. eBay appealed the case, and the Supreme Court determined that courts should not automatically issue an injunction based on a finding of patent infringement. (Alternatively, an injunction should not be denied simply on the basis that the plaintiff does not make, sell, or use the patented invention.) Instead, a federal court must still weigh the four factors traditionally used to determine if an injunction should be granted. The case is seen as a blow to patent trolls. (*eBay v. MercExchange, L.L.C.*, 547 U.S. 388 (2006).)

In 2011, an alleged patent troll saw two of its Internet browser patents invalidated when it went after various big-tech companies (Adobe, Amazon, Google, Yahoo) seeking licensing fees. The defendants succeeded in invalidating the patents by locating sufficient prior art to prove that the two browser patents were obvious at the time the patent was filed. Among the expert witnesses for the defense was Tim Berners-Lee, the "inventor" of the World Wide Web. (*Eolas Technologies Inc. v. Adobe Systems Inc.*, 810 F. Supp.2d 795 (E.D. Texas 2011).)

Patent Law: Definitions

In 2014, the U.S. Supreme Court took two swings at patent troll litigation. First, it lowered standards regarding the award of attorneys' fees, by giving judges more leeway to decide when a patent case is "exceptional," thereby entitling a litigant to attorneys' fees. (*Octane Fitness v. Icon Health and Fitness* and *Highmark v. Allcare Health*, 572 U.S. 559 (2014).) Second, the Supreme Court held that a patent would be invalid for indefiniteness if its claims failed to define the scope of the invention with "reasonable certainty," thus making it easier to invalidate the patent. (*Nautilus, Inc. v. Biosig Instruments, Inc.*, 572 U.S. 898 (2014).) In 2017, the Supreme Court dealt a jurisdictional blow against patent trolls. In *TC Heartland v. Kraft Foods*, the Court unanimously ruled that patent owners can sue corporate defendants only in districts where the defendant: (1) is incorporated or (2) has committed acts of infringement and has a regular and established place of business.

Before that, a ruling by the Federal Circuit permitted national companies to be sued in any district in the country, which led to the trollish preference for the friendly juries located in the Eastern District of Texas (by 2015, 45% of all patent cases were filed there). The Supreme Court's decision eliminates "forum shopping" in patent cases. (*TC Heartland LLC v. Kraft Foods LLC*, 581 U.S. ___ (2017).)

patentability

Patentability refers to an innovation's capability to receive patent rights.

To qualify for a utility patent, an invention must:

- fit within one of the five (statutory) subject matter classes
- be novel
- be nonobvious, and
- have some usefulness.

To qualify for a design patent, the innovation's design must:

- be new and original,
- be nonobvious, and
- serve as an ornamental design for a useful article of manufacture (that is, have no practical function other than ornamentality).

To qualify for a plant patent, the plant must be:

- new and original,
- nonobvious, and
- asexually reproduced (not from seeds).

Related terms: nonstatutory subject matter; statutory subject matter.

patentability search

Once an invention is conceived, the inventor will usually conduct (or have conducted) a search of previous and existing patents and other documents that might describe the invention to discover whether the invention is novel and nonobvious enough over the prior art to qualify for a patent. A search conducted for this purpose is commonly termed a patentability search. The primary reason for a patentability search is to avoid wasting time and money developing an invention that is not patentable.

Related terms: classification of patents; novelty; patent search; patent search, computerized; patent searcher; prior art reference.

patentable subject matter

See statutory subject matter.

patents as prior art

Whether patents are expired or in force, and whether they were issued in the United States or other countries, all patents are considered prior art when determining whether an invention qualifies for a patent.

Related terms: anticipation; prior art; prior art reference.

PCT

See Patent Cooperation Treaty (PCT).

person with ordinary skill in the art (POSITA)

A POSITA (also known as PHOSITA—a person having ordinary skill in the art) is a hypothetical person whose educational or occupational credentials would make them competent in the field of the invention. For example, an electrical engineer would be a person with ordinary skill concerning integrated circuits. In contrast, a prosthetics engineer would be a person with ordinary skill in the art of designing knee braces.

This hypothetical person would view a particular invention as a standard to make some critical determinations. Among the questions that must be answered in deciding whether a patent should issue, or whether an in-force patent is valid are:

- whether a person with ordinary skill in the art would find the invention an obvious development in light of the relevant prior art (the technology and knowledge existing at the time the invention was first conceived), and
- whether the patent application sufficiently discloses the nature of the invention to permit a person with ordinary skill in the art to build it in a routine manner.

Related terms: disclosure requirement for patents; *Graham v. John Deere*; nonobviousness.

Petition to Make Special

An applicant can, under certain circumstances, have an application examined sooner than the ordinary course of the USPTO examination (one to three years). Before 2008, this was accomplished by filing a "petition to make special" (PTMS), together with a supporting declaration. In 2007, the USPTO introduced a process for filing petitions to make special (PTMS) known as the Accelerated Examination Program (AEP). Under the new procedures, the USPTO will advance an application out of turn for examination if the applicant files a grantable petition to make special under the accelerated examination program (AEP). The USPTO is similarly revising the procedures for other petitions to make special, except those based on the applicant's health or age. Other petitions to make special (i.e., based on manufacture, infringement, environmental quality, energy, recombinant DNA, superconductivity materials, HIV/AIDS and cancer, countering terrorism, and biotechnology applications filed by small entities will be processed using the revised AEP procedure; see MPEP § 708.02). AEP requires that an applicant file electronically using EFS-Web and Form SB28 at the same time. For more information, see www.uspto.gov/patent/initiatives/accelerated-examination.

Related terms: AEP (Accelerated Examination Program); patent applicant; patent application; Track One: Prioritized Examination.

PHOSITA

See person with ordinary skill in the art (POSITA).

plant patents

Since 1930, the United States has been granting plant patents under the Plant Patent Act to any person who first appreciates the distinctive qualities of a plant and reproduces it asexually. Asexual reproduction means reproducing the plant by a means other than seeds, usually by grafting or cloning the plant tissue. If a plant cannot be duplicated by asexual reproduction, it cannot be the subject of a plant patent. In addition, the patented plant must also be novel and distinctive. Generally, this means that the plant must have at least one significant distinguishing characteristic to establish it as a distinct variety. For example, a rose may be novel and distinctive if it is nearly thornless and has a unique two-tone color scheme. Tuber-propagated plants (such as potatoes) and plants found in an uncultivated state cannot receive a plant patent. (35 U.S. Code §§ 161–164.)

There is a limit on the extent of plant patent rights. Generally, a plant patent can be infringed only when a plant has been asexually reproduced from the actual plant protected by the plant patent. In other words, the infringing plant must have more than similar characteristics—it must have the same genetics as the patented plant.

A human-made plant can also be the subject of a utility patent. These plants can be reproduced either sexually (by seeds) or asexually. For example, utility patents have been issued for elements of plants such as proteins, genes, DNA, buds, pollen, fruit, plant-based chemicals, and the processes used in the manufacture of these plant products. To obtain a utility patent, the plant must be made by humans and fit within the statutory requirements (utility, novelty, and nonobviousness).

The patent must describe and claim the specific characteristics of the plant for which protection is sought. Sometimes the best way to meet this requirement is to deposit seeds or plant tissue at a specified public depository. For example, many countries have international depositories for such purposes.

Although a utility patent is more complicated and time-consuming to acquire than a plant patent, it is considered to be a more potent form of protection. For example, a plant protected by a utility patent can be infringed if it is reproduced either sexually or asexually. Since the utility patent owner can prevent others from making and using the invention, does this mean the purchaser of a patented seed cannot sell the resulting plants to the public? No, the purchaser can sell the plants but cannot manufacture the seed line.

Related terms: genetic engineering and patents; nonstatutory subject matter.

Plant Variety Protection Act

This statute authorizes the U.S. Department of Agriculture to grant patent protection for certain types of plants.

Related terms: plant patents.

POSITA

See person with ordinary skill in the art (POSITA).

post-grant review (PGR)

The PTO provides three procedures by which a patent can be challenged: *inter partes* review (IPR), post grant review (PGR), and ex parte reexamination. In a PGR, the proceedings are handled by the Patent Trial and Appeal Board (PTAB) and anyone (except the patent owner) may challenge the patent. The filing fees are steep, approximately $50,000, and the process takes about a year. The parties may appeal the decision to the CAFC.

practicing an invention

See reduction to practice; working a patent.

preinvention assignments

Some employment agreements have a provision requiring an employee to assign any inventions to an employer. Because these employment agreements are signed before the employee creates the invention, they are sometimes referred to as preinvention assignments.

Eight states, including California, impose restrictions on the permissible scope of assignments of employee-created inventions, so as to protect employees. These restrictions apply only to "inventions" an employee creates—that is, items for which a patent is sought. These limitations on employee invention assignments are usually not very generous to employees. The only inventions an employee can't be required to assign to the employer are actual independent inventions—those that are developed entirely without company resources and that don't relate to the employee's work or the employer's current business or anticipated future business. The following states impose restrictions:

- California (Cal. Lab. Code § 2870)
- Delaware (Del. Code Ann. tit. 19 § 805)
- Illinois (Ill. Rev. Stat. Chapter 140, §§ 301–303)
- Kansas (Kansas Stat. Ann. §§ 44–130)
- Minnesota (Minnesota Stat. Ann. § 181.78)
- North Carolina (N.C. Gen. Stat. §§ 66-57.1, 66-57.2)
- Utah (Utah Code Ann. §§ 34-39-2, 34-39-3), and
- Washington (Wash. Rev. Code Ann. §§ 49.44.140, 49.44.150).

In a 2010 case, the Federal Circuit ruled that an employment agreement is not conclusive as to a preinvention assignment. A scientist signed an employee invention agreement that required that inventions created during employment would belong to his employer unless:

(1) the invention was developed entirely on his own time

(2) equipment, supplies, facility, or trade secret of the company was not used in its development, and

(3) it did not relate to the business or the company's actual or demonstrably anticipated research or development, or it did not result from any work performed by [him] for the company.

The scientist invented a method of sequencing DNA on his own time using his home computer and without taking advantage of any company trade secrets. The Federal Circuit determined that under California law, the scientist need only meet either of the two requirements established in the third criterion. The court determined the invention did not result from work performed for the company, and on that basis, there was no assignment. (*Applera Corp. Applied Biosystems Group v. Illumina, Inc.*, 2009–1260, 2010 WL 1169936 (Fed. Cir. Mar. 25, 2010).)

preliminary look at prior art

This preliminary investigation by inventors consists of checking online search engines, stores, catalogs, reference books, product directories, and similar sources to discover whether a proposed invention already exists. Such preliminary looks should be done before investing time and money developing an invention.

If a preliminary look finds no relevant previous development, then work on the invention may be initiated, with a more comprehensive patentability search to follow before significant resources are expended.

Related terms: patent search; patentability search.

presumption of validity

In an infringement suit brought by a patent owner against an alleged infringer, it is legally presumed that the patent owner's patent is valid. Practically, this means the legal responsibility (burden) is on alleged infringers to prove that the patent is invalid if they want to raise this defense.

Related terms: defenses to a patent infringement claim; infringement action.

price fixing

If two or more separate businesses agree (formal or informal) to maintain their prices at a certain level, it is known as price fixing. Price fixing is considered a restraint of trade, which is a violation of the antitrust laws. A patent owner who uses the patent monopoly to fix prices may also be deemed guilty of misusing the patent and accordingly lose patent rights.

Related terms: antitrust law (federal) and patents; concerted refusal to deal; patent misuse.

printed matter doctrine

A claim limitation that recites the content of printed matter is considered to have little or no weight when determining an invention's patentability unless the printed matter "is functionally related to the substrate on which the printed matter is applied." The printed matter—for example, a printed instruction sheet for a medical device—must functionally relate to what's in the claims. The USPTO and the courts sometimes apply this judicially created doctrine using a two-step test: Is the claim limitation directed to printed matter? If yes, should the printed matter be given patentable weight? (*In re Thomas L. DiStefano, III*, 808 F.3d 845 (Fed Cir. 2015).) Under recent case law, the scope of printed matter has been expanded to include claim limitations involving mental steps (providing information and recommendations). (*Praxair Distribution, Inc. v. Mallinckrodt Hospital Products IP LTD.*, 890 F.3d 1024 (Fed. Cir. 2018).) In another case, the Federal Circuit held that markings on dice constituted printed matter, similar to the markings on a deck of cards. (*In re Marco Guldenaar Holding B.V.*, 911 F.3d 1157 (Fed Cir. 2018).)

Related terms: claims; claim limitations (elements).

printed publication as a statutory bar

Under patent law, published writings are considered prior art references, so a previous publication that discusses or describes the essential ideas, functional means, or structures that underlie an invention can render that invention ineligible for a patent (the patent is barred by statute from issuing). In order to qualify as prior art, a printed publication must be "publicly accessible." The PTAB has defined two types of public accessibility: searchability (for example, in a database, or catalog); and dissemination (distribution via sales, conferences, or trade shows).

> EXAMPLE: A company sought to invalidate a patent by introducing a user manual as a prior art printed publication. The patent owner argued that the manual was not publicly accessible. The PTAB disagreed, noting that a manual included with the sale of a product (even with sales of 586 of those products) constituted public accessibility. (*Cisco Systems, Inc. v. Centripetal Networks*, IPR2018-01436, Paper No. 40, January 23, 2020.)

There is an exception to this rule (35 U.S. Code § 102(b)) that provides that a disclosure made by the inventor one year or less before the application filing date is not prior art. In addition, a third-party disclosure one year or less before the filing date is not prior art if the content of the disclosure was directly or indirectly obtained from the inventor. However, practitioners consider reliance on this rule to be risky, mainly because it doesn't appear to apply to variations on the disclosure. If, for example, a third-party modifies and improves a disclosure made by an inventor, that third-party disclosure may be considered prior art against the original invention.

Related terms: anticipation; one-year rule (on-sale bar); statutory bar.

prior art

"Prior art" refers to all previous developments that are used by the U.S. Patent and Trademark Office and the courts (in the event of an infringement action) to decide whether a particular invention is sufficiently novel and nonobvious to qualify for a U.S. patent.

Prior art relevant to a particular invention ordinarily includes:
- any published writing (including any patent) that was publicly available before the patent application filing date,
- any U.S. patent with a filing date earlier than the date of invention, or
- any public or commercial use, sale, or knowledge of the invention before the application filing date.

Any specific instance of prior art is generally referred to as a prior art reference.

There is an exception to this rule (35 U.S. Code § 102(b)) that provides that a disclosure made by the inventor one year or less before the application filing date is not prior art. In addition, a third-party disclosure one year or less before the filing date is not prior art if the content of the disclosure was directly or indirectly obtained from the inventor. (See the statute below for the specific language.)

§ 102. Conditions for patentability; novelty

(a) Novelty; Prior Art. A person shall be entitled to a patent unless—

    (1) the claimed invention was patented, described in a printed publication, or in public use, on sale, or otherwise available to the public before the effective filing date of the claimed invention; or

    (2) the claimed invention was described in a patent issued under section 151, or in an application for patent published or deemed published under section 122(b), in which the patent or application, as the case may be, names another inventor and was effectively filed before the effective filing date of the claimed invention.

(b) Exceptions—

(1) DISCLOSURES MADE 1 YEAR OR LESS BEFORE THE EFFECTIVE FILING DATE OF THE CLAIMED INVENTION. A disclosure made 1 year or less before the effective filing date of a claimed invention shall not be prior art to the claimed invention under subsection (a)(1) if—

(A) the disclosure was made by the inventor or joint inventor or by another who obtained the subject matter disclosed directly or indirectly from the inventor or a joint inventor; or

(B) the subject matter disclosed had, before such disclosure, been publicly disclosed by the inventor or a joint inventor or another who obtained the subject matter disclosed directly or indirectly from the inventor or a joint inventor.

(2) DISCLOSURES APPEARING IN APPLICATIONS AND PATENTS. A disclosure shall not be prior art to a claimed invention under subsection (a)(2) if—

(A) the subject matter disclosed was obtained directly or indirectly from the inventor or a joint inventor;

(B) the subject matter disclosed had before such subject matter was effectively filed under subsection (a)(2), been publicly disclosed by the inventor or a joint inventor or another who obtained the subject matter disclosed directly or indirectly from the inventor or a joint inventor; or

(C) the subject matter disclosed and the claimed invention, not later than the effective filing date of the claimed invention, were owned by the same person or subject to an obligation of assignment to the same person.

(c) Common Ownership Under Joint Research Agreements. Subject matter disclosed and a claimed invention shall be deemed to have been owned by the same person or subject to an obligation of assignment to the same person in applying the provisions of subsection (b)(2)(C) if—

(1) the subject matter disclosed was developed and the claimed invention was made by, or on behalf of, 1 or more parties to a joint research agreement that was in effect on or before the effective filing date of the claimed invention;

(2) the claimed invention was made as a result of activities undertaken within the scope of the joint research agreement; and

(3) the application for patent for the claimed invention discloses or is amended to disclose the names of the parties to the joint research agreement.

(d) Patents and Published Applications Effective as Prior Art. For purposes of determining whether a patent or application for patent is prior art to a claimed invention under subsection (a)(2), such patent or application shall be considered to have been effectively filed, with respect to any subject matter described in the patent or application—

(1) if paragraph (2) does not apply, as of the actual filing date of the patent or the application for patent; or

(2) if the patent or application for patent is entitled to claim a right of priority under section 119, 365(a), or 365(b), or to claim the benefit of an earlier filing date under section 120, 121, or 365(c), based upon 1 or more prior filed applications for patent, as of the filing date of the earliest such application that describes the subject matter.

Related terms: anticipation; nonobviousness; novelty; patentability; prior art reference.

prior art reference

Any printed publication, prior patent, or other document that contains a discussion or description relevant to an invention for which a patent is currently being sought or enforced is a prior art reference.

When applying for a patent, an applicant who knows of any prior art references must submit an Information Disclosure Statement (IDS). All such references must be listed, and to which copies of these references must be appended.

In the event a patent examiner rejects one or more claims on the ground they are anticipated by (or are obvious over) the prior art, the U.S. Patent and Trademark Office sends out a Notice of Prior Art References, with copies of the actual references attached, which identifies the prior art references upon which the rejection is based.

Related terms: anticipation; Information Disclosure Statement; prior art.

Prioritized Examination

See Track One: Prioritized Examination.

processes (or methods) as patentable subject matter

Ways of doing or making things (termed processes or methods) are one of the five categories of statutory subject matter—that is, types of inventions that can be patented. Processes always have at least two steps, each of which expresses some activity or occurrence. Examples include heat-treatment processes, chemical reactions, surgical techniques, gene-splicing procedures, applied robotics, and computer software.

To be patentable, a process must produce a useful, concrete, and tangible result.

Related terms: nonstatutory subject matter; software patents; statutory subject matter.

Patent Law: Definitions

product-by-process claim

A patent claim for a product is defined in terms of the method (or the manipulative steps) used to manufacture the product. Even though product-by-process claims are limited by and defined by the process, their patentability is based on the product itself (because the patentability of a product does not depend on its method of production). If the product in the product-by-process claim is the same as or obvious from a prior art product, the claim is unpatentable even though a different process made the prior product. (*In re Thorpe,* 777 F.2d 695 (Fed. Cir. 1985).) Previously, the use of a product-by-process claim was limited to situations where the product could not be defined or distinguished from the prior art except by reference to the process of creating the product. The Court of Appeals for the Federal Circuit ruled that in an infringement analysis, a product-by-process claim would be limited by the process in the claim. (*Abbott Labs v. Sandoz,* 566 F.3d 1282 (Fed Cir. 2009).) *See also* MPEP Section 2113 (Product-by-Process Claims).

prosecution of a patent application

Once a regular patent application has been filed, the whole gamut of procedures that must be followed to obtain the patent is referred to as the prosecution of a patent application. (The patent prosecution process does not apply to Provisional Patent Applications (PPAs).)

The first step in the patent prosecution process is when the USPTO patent examiner assigned to the application sends the applicant a written form (called the first office action). This sometimes takes place up to a year after the application is received. This form will typically deny all or most of the application's claims on a variety of grounds.

If the rejection was due to lack of novelty (35 U.S. Code § 102), the office action will identify the reasons. If the rejection was due to obviousness over the relevant prior art (35 U.S. Code § 103), the office action will list the prior art references in a Notice of Prior Art References. In both Section 102 and 103 rejections, the USPTO will attach copies of the relevant prior art references and designate the claims to which the references pertain.

Note: If a valid PPA was previously filed on the invention, and the PPA filing date is claimed in the regular patent application, the examiner will use that earlier date to assess the prior art and base a rejection only on prior art references that came before it.

Claims also may be rejected under 35 U.S. Code Section 112 because they are too broad or are formulated incorrectly. The inventor will be provided the opportunity to make amendments suggested by the examiner. On occasion, the patent examiner will determine that the application impermissibly claims two or more inventions. In this case, the applicant will be informed in the first office action that it's necessary to "elect" (choose to include) the claims covering one of the inventions in the original (parent) application and optionally file one or more divisional applications for the nonelected claims (the ones that weren't kept in the parent application) that recite the additional inventions.

Sometimes, an inventor will improve the invention while the application is pending or seek to broaden or better define the claims. If so, the inventor can file a continuation-in-part (CIP) application incorporating the changes.

Whatever the recommendations made by the patent examiner and the reasons given for the claims being rejected, the applicant must either file a response to the first office action within three months or pay a fee and obtain up to a three-month extension. If the applicant fails to do either, the application will be deemed abandoned.

Once the applicant has responded, the patent examiner will respond again, usually with a final office action. This will either reject all of the claims with suggested modifications that would make them allowable or reject some of the claims and accept others. If amended claims are rejected on anticipation or obviousness grounds, any pertinent prior art references that were not cited the first time around will be listed (and copies sent). Suggestions might also be made for how to narrow claims that are too broad.

After the final office action, the applicant has five basic choices:
- amend the claims as suggested by the patent examiner
- request that the patent examiner reconsider one or more of the decisions contained in the final office action
- appeal to the Patent Trial and Appeal Board (PTAB)
- file a continuation application (essentially a new application with new claims, with the benefit of the original filing date for the purpose of determining the effect of relevant prior art references), or
- file a Request for Continued Examination (RCE), which effectively removes the final action so that the applicant can submit further amendments, for example, new claims, new arguments, a new declaration, or new references.

Patent Law: Definitions

Whatever the choice, it must be done within three months of the final office action, or an extension (up to three months) must be obtained. Otherwise, the application will be deemed legally abandoned. If the USPTO has not published the application, it won't serve as a prior art reference after being abandoned—unless the applicant makes a defensive publication.

The applicant will receive a Notice of Allowability, assuming that the final action results in an allowance of one or more claims, either as drafted or as amended in response to the final office action. This will be followed or accompanied by a formal Notice of Allowance and a form specifying the issue fee that is due. At this time, it is still possible to file minor amendments. Also, if any amendments to claims that have occurred in the course of prosecution are not covered by the formal Patent Application Declaration signed by the applicant, a Supplemental Declaration should also be filed.

Suppose the issue fee is sent to the USPTO within three months of the formal Notice of Allowance. In such a situation, the applicant will receive a patent deed (a decorative document describing the patent with a USPTO seal on the front) and a regular photocopy of the patent. Although the formal patent prosecution process is now over, the inventor might later wish to amend the in-force patent in some material way, perhaps because a new ramification is spotted or the inventor now sees that one or more of the claims could have been made broader. If the amendment broadens one or more claims, and the application is filed within two years of the patent issue date, a reissue patent may be obtained. This will carry the same issue date as the original patent but will incorporate the claims as amended.

Related terms: claims; continuation application; continuation-in-part application (CIP); filing date; issue fee; office action; patent application; Provisional Patent Application (PPA); reconsideration request; reissue patent; Request for Continued Examination; supplemental declaration.

Provisional Patent Application (PPA)

An inventor may file an interim patent application (a provisional patent application or PPA) to reduce the invention to practice constructively. Suppose the PPA sufficiently discloses the invention, and a regular patent application is filed within one year of the PPA's filing date. The inventor would then benefit from the PPA filing date for the purpose of deciding whether prior art is relevant and, in the event an interference exists, who is entitled to the patent. In addition, the inventor gets the full 20-year term from the date the regular application is filed.

The PPA needs to contain only a portion of the information presently required in a patent application specification—a complete description of the invention (structure and operation) and any drawings that are necessary to understand the description. The PPA need not include claims, formal drawings, a Patent Application Declaration, or an Information Disclosure Statement. To claim the benefit of the PPA's filing date, the applicant must file an amendment in the regular patent application referring to the earlier-filed PPA. As of this book's most recent update (October 2021), filing a PPA at USPTO costs $75 for micro-entities, $150 for small entities, and $300 for large entities.

Thus an inventor can potentially afford to get an invention registered with the USPTO and have a year to show the invention to potential developers before filing a regular patent application. An inventor who files a PPA may claim patent pending status.

In a 2010 case, the Federal Circuit determined that the filing date of a provisional patent application establishes prior art references. An inventor, Giacomini, filed a patent application claiming a method of selectively storing sets of electronic data. Another inventor, Tran, filed a patent application after Giacomini for a similar invention. However, Tran's application was based on a provisional patent application that accurately described the invention and was filed before Giacomini's application. In that case, the Federal Circuit held that Tran, as "first inventor," could claim patent rights and use his patent application as prior art against Giacomini. (*In re Giacomini,* 612 F.3d 1380 (Fed. Cir. 2010).)

Related terms: filing date; patent application; patent pending; prosecution of a patent application.

PTO

See U.S. Patent and Trademark Office (USPTO).

PTRC

See Patent and Trademark Resource Centers (PTRCs).

public domain

When an idea, design, or expression does not belong to anyone under the patent (or copyright) laws, it is said to exist in the public domain. Anyone may use it for any purpose without obtaining permission from its originator or author.

Any invention that is published, put in public use, sold, or placed on sale more than one year before filing a patent application is considered to be in the public domain. Also in the public domain are inventions whose patents are no longer in force (the patent period has expired).

Related terms: anticipation; defensive publication; one-year rule (on-sale bar); printed publication as a statutory bar; prior art; Statutory Invention Registration (SIR).

public use

When an invention is worked (used by the inventor in the presence of one or more members of the public in a nonconfidential context), it is considered to have been publicly used. Public use of an invention before filing a patent application (or a provisional patent application) constitutes a statutory bar to a patent under the anticipation doctrine.

There are exceptions to the public use rule for:

- experimental tests (to develop and improve an invention). Although patent experts believe that the experimental use exception has continued under the AIA, neither the federal courts nor the USPTO (as of the publication of this edition (2020)) has issued a ruling on the issue, and

- uses that are not, in fact, public (for instance, when witnesses to the use sign nondisclosure agreements or are otherwise required to maintain secrecy). However, an inventor's "secret sale" of an invention to a third party qualifies as prior art. (*Helsinn Healthcare S.A. v. Teva Pharmaceuticals USA, Inc.,* 139 S. Ct. 628 (2019).)

Although there is a limited one-year grace period for disclosures made by the inventor, there is no such grace period for public use or public sales not made by the inventor. Also, the public use (or sale) functions as prior art even if it is outside the United States.

Related terms: anticipation; experimental use of an unpatented invention; one-year rule; statutory bar.

publicly accessible

See printed publication as a statutory bar.

read on

In the patent context, "read on" means to literally describe. A patent is infringed if the patent's claims read on (literally describe) all elements of the infringing device.

Related terms: anticipation; claims; infringement, patent.

recite

When the claims of a prior patent literally describe or "read on" the elements of a later invention, the claims are said to "recite" such elements.

Related terms: read on.

reconsideration request

A patent applicant can request that the patent examiner reconsider an application whose claims were rejected in the final office action. If this reconsideration request is rejected, the applicant may:

- amend the claims in the manner suggested by the patent examiner, if this option was presented to the applicant in the office action
- appeal to the Patent Trial and Appeal Board (PTAB), or
- file a continuation application.

Related terms: continuation application; final office action; prosecution of a patent application.

reduction to practice

After conception, the inventor's next step is to reduce the invention to practice—that is, to demonstrate that it can function for its intended purpose. The question of when an inventor reduced an invention to practice is of little importance now that the U.S. has adopted the first-to-file system, but reduction to practice was, before March 17, 2013, an important marker for determining the date of invention and occurred if the inventor:

- built and tested the invention (called actual reduction to practice)
- filed a Provisional Patent Application (PPA) on the invention (called constructive reduction to practice), or
- filed a regular patent application (also a constructive reduction to practice).

Related terms: constructive reduction to practice; Provisional Patent Application (PPA).

reexamination of patent (ex parte reexamination)

The USPTO may hold a formal proceeding in which it reexamines an in-force patent to determine whether newly cited prior art references adversely affect the patent's validity. A patent may be reexamined at any time while it is in force. Anyone may petition for reexamination. Upon request, the requester's identity will be kept confidential. (The statute establishing the reexamination process is 35 U.S. Code § 302.)

The Director will authorize a re-exam only if "there is a reasonable likelihood that the petitioner would prevail with respect to at least one of the claims challenged in the petition."

Related terms: nonobviousness; prior art reference; *inter partes* review (IPR).

references

See prior art reference.

regular patent application

See patent application.

reissue patent

To revise the specification or claims of an in-force patent, the patent owner may apply for a reissue patent. If it seeks to broaden the claims, the reissue patent must be applied for within two years of the issue date of the original patent. If issued, the reissue patent takes the place of the original patent and expires when that patent would have.

Reissue patents can be used to correct any significant error in the claims of the original patent or to narrow or broaden its claims. Reissue patents are relatively rare, because the push and pull of the patent prosecution process tends to make the claims both accurate and as broad as the U.S. Patent and Trademark Office will allow.

Related terms: intervening right; patent application.

rejection of patent application

See office action.

repair doctrine

Anyone authorized to make, use, or sell a patented device is also permitted to repair and replace unpatented components. This right is asserted as an affirmative defense in a patent infringement lawsuit. The defense does not apply to wholly rebuilt inventions, unauthorized inventions, or items made or sold without authorization of the patent owner.

Request for Continued Examination

A Request for Continued Examination (RCE) is filed when a patent applicant wishes to continue prosecuting an application that has received a final office action. Filing the RCE with another filing fee effectively removes the final action so that the applicant can submit further amendments, for example, new claims, new arguments, a new declaration, or new references.

An RCE must cover the same invention as the parent or basic application, and the parent or basic application must be abandoned when a continuation is filed. When an RCE continuation is filed, the USPTO uses the same file jacket and papers as the parent or basic filing. After an RCE is filed, prosecution of the same application simply continues as if there were no final action. The RCE is entitled to the benefit of the filing date of the parent or prior application for purposes of overcoming prior art.

It is also possible to file a continuation of an RCE. It's theoretically possible to file a complete sequence of RCEs or continuation applications. However, an RCE is not an end-run around a previous objection by the USPTO.

The RCE or continuation will be quickly rejected unless the inventor comes up with a genuinely different slant on or definition of the invention that the USPTO did not previously consider. When a patent issues on an RCE, the heading of the patent will not indicate that it's based on the RCE.

An RCE must be mailed before the period for response to the final rejection expires or before any extensions expire. The RCE can be mailed on the last day of the period for response.

reverse engineering

The process of figuring out how a device is built by taking it apart and studying its components.

See also Part 4 (Trade Secret Law): reverse engineering and trade secrets.

search of patentability

See patentability search.

secrecy of patent application

See confidentiality of patent application.

SEP (standard-essential patent)

See FRAND.

Patent Law: Definitions

sequence listing

For biotech inventions, the USPTO requires an attachment to a patent application that includes a sequence listing of a nucleotide or amino acid sequence. The applicant attaches this information on separate sheets of paper and refers to the sequence listing in the application. (PTO Rule 77.)

shelving of invention

See antishelving clause.

shop rights

Most employers acquire ownership of invention rights created by employees either through written employment agreements (preinvention assignments) or under the "employed to invent" rule. In another situation, the employer may not acquire ownership of a patent but may acquire a limited right to use these innovations, known as a shop right. Under a shop right, the employee retains ownership of the patent, but the employer can use the invention without paying for it. A shop right can occur only if the employee uses the employer's resources (materials, supplies, time) to create an invention. Other circumstances might be relevant, but the use of employer resources is the most critical criterion. Shop right principles are derived from state laws and precedents in court cases. Ordinarily, the shop right claim arises when an inventor sues a former employer for patent infringement. The employer defends itself by claiming a shop right.

Related terms: employed to invent; march-in rights; nonexclusive patent license; patent owner; preinvention assignments.

shotgun rejection of claims

This slang term refers to the U.S. Patent and Trademark Office's (USPTO's) habit of rejecting all claims in its first office action (its first formal response to the application) on the premise that it will deal more seriously with the application if and when the applicant submits amended claims or a more detailed explanation of why the existing claims should be allowed. Although discouraging, a shotgun rejection does not necessarily mean that an applicant should abandon patenting the invention. As mentioned, a shotgun rejection has much more to do with standard USPTO practices than with the merits of a particular patent application.

Related terms: first office action; prosecution of a patent application.

single application rule

See divisional application.

small entity

A for-profit company with 500 or fewer employees, a nonprofit organization, or an independent inventor is referred to by the USPTO as a small entity. The USPTO charges small entities half the fees charged large entities for filing a patent application and for issuing and maintaining the patent. A small entity qualifies for these lower fees provided that the company or inventor has not assigned or licensed, or agreed to assign or license, its patent rights to a large entity (a for-profit company with over 500 employees). The America Invents Act created a special class of small entities—the micro-entity—entitled to further reduced fees.

Related terms: issue fee; large entity; maintenance fees; micro entity.

smart money

The colloquial phrase "smart money" is used by patent attorneys to describe the extra damages that can be imposed on defendants found guilty of willful or flagrant infringement. These extra damages—up to three times the actual damages established in court—are awarded to teach the infringers a lesson and make them "smart."

Related terms: infringement action; willful infringement.

software-based inventions

See software patents.

software patents

Patents don't issue on software itself, they issue on "software-based" inventions that use innovative software to produce a useful, concrete, and tangible result.

When first faced with applications for patents on software-based inventions in the 1950s, the USPTO routinely rejected them on the grounds that software consists of mathematical algorithms (abstract methods for solving problems not tied to a particular use or concrete structure), which were considered to be unpatentable for the same reason abstract laws of nature are unpatentable.

In the late 1980s, however, the USPTO began granting patents on inventions that rely heavily on innovative software. Now the USPTO issues software patents on software if the patent application describes the software in relation to computer hardware and related devices and limits the software to specific uses.

Software-based inventions that have qualified for patents often involve software that connects to and runs hardware components. For example, consider a device that monitors a patient's heart functions, feeds the raw information

Patent Law: Definitions

into a computer where a program analyzes the information according to a set of algorithms and causes the results of this analysis to be displayed on a monitor in a format that shows whether the person is at risk for a heart attack. While none of the components of this invention would qualify for a patent (the physical items have already been invented, and the algorithm itself is unpatentable), the overall invention did qualify for a U.S. patent, even though the software was the critical aspect of the invention.

It is also possible to obtain a patent on the process or method used by software and the machine aspect of the invention—that is, the combined software and hardware. For instance, the heart monitor invention described above received a patent on a machine claim (a claim that described the structure which produced the result) as well as a method claim (a claim that described the process by which the structure worked). Other examples of software-based inventions that have received patents are a device that converts sound waves into smooth waveforms for display on an oscilloscope (a rasterizer) and software that moves the cursor on a computer screen.

In 2010, the Supreme Court kept alive software patents when it rejected the view held by the CAFC that the so-called "machine or transformation" test should be the sole standard for patentability. The Supreme Court preserved the status quo and kept alive the concept of software patents (as well as a business method and other process patents). (*Bilski v. Kappos*, 561 U.S. 593 (2010).)

In 2014, the Supreme Court's decision in *Alice Corp. v. CLS Bank International* cast a cloud over many existing software patents. The Supreme Court invalidated a software patent because the method employed—a computer-assisted process for exchanging financial obligations—was an abstract idea, ineligible for patent protection. The decision sets the stage for invalidation of numerous software patents that simply applied an obvious existing idea to a software or computer setting. (*Alice Corporation Pty. Ltd. v. CLS Bank International et al.*, 573 U.S. 208 (2014).)

Although the *Alice* decision narrowed patentability for software, it was not the death knell for developers that earlier decisions were, notably the Federal Circuit's 2016 decision in *Enfish v. Microsoft*. In that case, the Federal Circuit reversed a lower court decision finding Enfish's patents invalid. The Federal Circuit held that the claims did not cover abstract ideas and that physical elements are not a prerequisite for a software claim to be patentable. (*Enfish, LLC v. Microsoft Corp.*, 2016 U.S. App. LEXIS 8699, 2016 WL 2756255 (Fed. Cir. May 12, 2016); *DDR Holdings, LLC v. Hotels.com, L.P.*, 773 F.3d 1245 (Fed. Cir. 2014).)

In any case, most software-based inventions do not qualify for patents because they are considered obvious over the prior art and must therefore be protected in another manner—usually under trade secret or copyright laws.

Virtually all patents that have been obtained on software-based inventions are utility patents, although design patents have been issued on computer screen icons.

Related terms: algorithms; business methods as statutory subject matter; nonstatutory subject matter; *State Street Bank and Trust v. Signature Financial Group.*

sovereign immunity

Sovereign immunity is a principle that a government is immune from civil suit or criminal prosecution. For purposes of patent law, it refers to the fact that state governments cannot be liable for patent infringement (Congress had previously amended the patent laws to circumvent state sovereign immunity but the amendments were invalidated in 1999 by the Supreme Court. In one case, the State of Florida was sued by a patent holder for utilizing a patented financing methodology. (*Fla. Prepaid Postsecondary Educ. Expense Bd. v. College Sav. Bank,* 527 U.S. 627 (1999).)

Neither the federal government nor local municipal or county governments enjoy similar sovereign immunity. Moreover, civil patent remedies can be pursued against any government employee (federal, state, or local) who commits infringement in their individual capacity. Finally, a state institution should not assume it has carte blanche to commit patent infringement. State laws vary, and some states waive or limit sovereign immunity in certain situations.

State sovereign immunity does not apply to USPTO administrative hearings such as *inter partes* review. For example, a state university argued that its patents could not be challenged in an IPR proceeding because of sovereign immunity. The CAFC disagreed, holding that sovereign immunity did not apply in USPTO enforcement actions. (*Regents of the Univ. of Minnesota v. LSI Corp.,* 926 F.3d 1327 (Fed. Cir. 2019).)

Native Americans have limited sovereignty under the Indian Civil Rights Act, which prevents actions against an Indian tribe in federal court for deprivation of substantive rights (except for habeas corpus proceedings). However, like state governments, tribes cannot assert sovereignty in *inter partes* review proceedings. Allergen, a drug company, transferred patents to a Native American tribe and then claimed sovereign immunity to avoid an attack on its patents. The CAFC ruled that tribal sovereign immunity cannot be asserted to end IPR proceedings. (*St. Regis Mohawk Tribe v. Mylan Pharmaceuticals,* 896 F.3d 1322 (2018).)

Patent Law: Definitions

specification, defined

The narrative portion of a patent application is called a specification, and includes descriptions of:

- the type of invention
- the pertinent prior art (previous developments in the technology utilized in the invention) known to the applicant
- the purpose of the invention
- the invention itself (for example, how it's constructed and what it's made of)
- the operation of the invention (how it works), and
- any accompanying drawings.

The specification also includes the patent claims and an abstract: a one-paragraph summary of the specification as defined by the patent laws. (A sample specification is provided in the Forms section at the end of this part of the book.)

Essentially, the specification must provide enough information about the invention so that a person having ordinary skill in the art (proficient in the particular area of expertise involved in the invention) could build it without having to be "inventive." Because the specification is where the entire disclosure of the invention is made, it (rather than the claims) is commonly used to determine whether the patent has anticipated a later invention.

§ 112. Specification

This statute sets out the detailed requirements for how an invention must be described in a patent application, known as the specification and claims.

The specification shall contain a written description of the invention, and of the manner and process of making and using it, in such full, clear, concise, and exact terms as to enable any person skilled in the art to which it pertains, or with which it is most nearly connected, to make and use the same and shall set forth the best mode contemplated by the inventor of carrying out his invention.

The specification shall conclude with one or more claims particularly pointing out and distinctly claiming the subject matter which the applicant regards as his invention.

A claim may be written in independent or, if the nature of the case admits, in dependent or multiple dependent form.

Subject to the following paragraph, a claim in dependent form shall contain a reference to a claim previously set forth and then specify a further limitation of the subject matter claimed. A claim in dependent form shall be construed to incorporate by reference all the limitations of the claim to which it refers.

A claim in multiple dependent form shall contain a reference, in the alternative only, to more than one claim previously set forth and then specify a further limitation of the subject matter claimed. A multiple dependent claim shall not serve as a basis for any other multiple dependent claim. A multiple dependent claim shall be construed to incorporate by reference all the limitations of the particular claim in relation to which it is being considered.

An element in a claim for a combination may be expressed as a means or step for performing a specified function without the recital of structure, material, or acts in support thereof, and such claim shall be construed to cover the corresponding structure, material, or acts described in the specification and equivalents thereof.

Related terms: claims; disclosure requirements for patents.

SSO (standard-setting organization)

See FRAND.

standing

The party bringing a lawsuit must have the legal capacity to "stand" before the court. That is, the plaintiff must allege a sufficient interest in the dispute. If a party lacks standing, the case will be dismissed without the court having considered the issues. Parties in federal court must meet the Constitutional standing requirement of Article III (the portion of the Constitution establishing the federal court system). Typically, a party demonstrates Article III standing by showing it has suffered an injury.

State Street Bank and Trust v. Signature Financial Group

In this 1998 case (149 F.3d 1368 (Fed. Cir. 1998)), the Court of Appeals for the Federal Circuit made it much easier to obtain a patent on computer software and on methods of doing business. The software invention at issue in this case was designed solely to make financial calculations dealing with advantageous mutual fund investing techniques. In the past, such a program would have been considered to be nothing more than a mathematical algorithm, which does not constitute statutory subject matter. However, in *State Street,* the court ruled that the mathematical algorithms are nonpatentable only when they are nothing more than abstract ideas consisting of disembodied concepts that are not useful. In the court's words: "Today we hold that the transformation of data, representing discrete dollar amounts, by a machine through a series of mathematical calculations into a final share price, constitutes a practical application of a mathematical algorithm, formula, or calculation, because it produces a useful, concrete, and tangible result—a final share price momentarily fixed for recording and reporting purposes and even accepted and relied upon by regulatory authorities and in subsequent trades."

The court also shed new light on the long-held belief that methods of doing business do not constitute statutory subject matter. The court pointed out that the patent statutes do not expressly exclude business methods from being patentable and that no authoritative case law supported the concept.

Related terms: *Bilski v. Kappos*; business methods as statutory subject matter.

statement of prior art references

See Information Disclosure Statement.

statute of limitations, the infringement action

There is no time limit (statute of limitations) for filing a patent infringement lawsuit. Still, monetary damages can be recovered only for infringements committed during the six years before filing the lawsuit. For example, if a patent owner sues after ten years of infringement, the owner cannot recover monetary damages for the first four years of infringement.

§ 286. Time limitation on damages

Except as otherwise provided by law, no recovery shall be had for any infringement committed more than six years prior to the filing of the complaint or counterclaim for infringement in the action.

In the case of claims against the United States Government for use of a patented invention, the period before bringing suit, up to six years, between the date of receipt of a written claim for compensation by the department or agency of the Government having authority to settle such claim, and the date of mailing by the Government of a notice to the claimant that his claim has been denied, shall not be counted as part of the period referred to in the preceding paragraph.

Related terms: defenses to a patent infringement claim.

statutory bar

A statutory bar is any federal statutory provision that requires the U.S. Patent and Trademark Office or a court to disqualify an invention for a patent. Among the most common types of statutory bars are:

- the rule that prior patents, or other printed publications that describe the invention, may preclude the invention from being considered novel
- the rule that a later invention is precluded from receiving a patent by an earlier invention that contains all of the same elements

- the rule that a patent may not be obtained on an invention if the application has been abandoned by the inventor, and
- the rule that a description in a printed publication, public use, or on-sale status of the invention before the application filing date precludes a patent from issuing.

Related terms: anticipation; one-year rule (on-sale bar); printed publication as statutory bar; prior art reference; public use.

Statutory Invention Registration (SIR)

Prior to 2013, a patent applicant could abandon an application and prevent anyone else from getting a patent on the underlying invention by, in effect, putting the invention in the public domain. This was done by converting a patent application to a Statutory Invention Registration. As a result of the passage of the America Invents Act, the SIR procedure was no longer available after March 2013.

It is also possible to turn an invention into a prior art reference (thereby placing it in the public domain) by publishing an article on it or listing it with an invention register. The effective date of the reference will be the date of publication.

Related terms: defensive publication; interference.

statutory subject matter

The U.S. Patent and Trademark Office issues utility patents, design patents, and plant patents. To qualify for a utility patent, an invention must fit into at least one of five categories defined in 35 U.S. Code Section 101. Qualifications for a design or plant patent are not, however, governed by these statutory categories.

The statutory categories for utility patents are:
- compositions of matter
- manufactures (or articles of manufacture)
- machines (or apparatuses)
- processes (or methods), and
- new and useful improvements of any of the above categories.

Any invention that does not fall within at least one of these categories does not qualify for a utility patent, no matter how novel or nonobvious it may otherwise prove to be. On the other hand, it is unnecessary to define precisely which category applies to a particular invention as long as the patent examiner concludes that at least one of them does.

> **EXAMPLE:** A patent application on an automated database invention that answers legal questions can be viewed as claiming a machine (apparatus) or a process (method). Because the invention can fit within one or the other of these categories, it is deemed statutory subject matter.

To qualify for a utility patent, an invention must be novel, useful, and nonobvious, in addition to fitting within at least one of the five statutory categories. The phrase "statutory subject matter" is often used to refer not only to inventions that fall within one of the five statutory classes but to those that satisfy these other patent requirements as well.

Statutory subject matter does not include inventions that lack scientific support.

> **EXAMPLE:** A group of inventors applied for patents for inventions related to "quantum entanglement." In reviewing the claims, the USPTO determined there was no scientific evidence to support the invention claims. The examiner stated that the claims violated the first law of thermodynamics, fundamental chemistry laws, classical physics laws, and the principle of conservation of mass. On appeal, the CAFC supported the USPTO position, stating "concepts that strain scientific principles are properly held to a heightened standard, typically measured by reproducibility of results." The CAFC referred to inventions for perpetual motion machines and cold fusion as having similar patentability problems. (*In re Huping Hu*, 2021 U.S. App. LEXIS 7776.)

Related terms: nonstatutory subject matter; prosecution of a patent application.

submarine patent

A patent may be deliberately held up in the USPTO by the applicant. In contrast, the technology covered by the patent is developed by companies that don't know of the pending application. Then, once the patent issues, it is like a submarine, suddenly emerging from the patent office and forcing users of the invention to pay hefty license fees. Two changes in patent law have substantially eliminated the possibility of submarine patents. In 1995, the patent laws were amended to limit the duration of patents to 20 years from the date of filing. In 1999, the patent laws were amended to require publication of patent applications within 18 months of filing unless the patent applicant will not be filing the patent application in a foreign country.

Related terms: confidentiality of patent application.

substitute patent application

Inventors sometimes file a new patent application after abandoning an earlier application on the same invention. For example, suppose an applicant who failed to respond to the USPTO's first office action within three months refiles a duplicate application. The later application would be considered a substitute for the abandoned parent application. The substitute application does not get the benefit of the original filing date, so any prior art that has surfaced in the meantime can operate to anticipate the invention and thus bar the patent from issuing.

Related terms: abandonment of patent application; parent application.

supplemental declaration

When claims are broadened or changed in any substantial way in the course of successful patent prosecution, the applicant must file a supplemental declaration with the U.S. Patent and Trademark Office after receiving a notice of allowance. Under oath, the inventor must:

- specify which claims have been altered in the course of the prosecution, and
- declare that the applicant was the inventor of the subject matter contained in the altered claims and knows of no prior art that would anticipate the claims as altered.

Related terms: prosecution of a patent application.

teach the invention

When a prior publication, invention, or patent discusses the elements of, or technology associated with, an invention for which a patent is being sought, it is said to "teach" the invention.

temporary presence exception

This rule permits foreign ship and aircraft owners with otherwise infringing technology to dock or land here without being sued provided: (1) the ship or aircraft enters the U.S. on a temporary or accidental basis, and (2) the patented technology or device is used exclusively for the needs of the ship or aircraft.

Title 35 of the United States Code

This part of the United States Code (sometimes abbreviated as U.S.C. or U.S. Code) contains the patent statutes. The entire code can be found in 35 United States Code Annotated (U.S.C.A.) or 35 United States Code Service, Lawyers Edition (U.S.C.S.).

Patent Law: Definitions

Track One: Prioritized Examination

The USPTO offers Track One, a process for fast-tracking a utility or plant patent application for an additional fee: $4000/$2000/$1000 (Large Entity/Small Entity/Micro Entity). Unlike the USPTO's other fast-tracking process, known as the Accelerated Examination Program (AEP), Track One has fewer requirements and doesn't involve performing a preexamination search. Track One is available for a fee at the time of filing an original utility or plant application. A single request for prioritized examination may be granted for a Request for Continued Examination (RCE) in a plant or utility application. The USPTO reports that the program is especially popular with independent inventors who benefit from micro-entity status. Applicants who satisfy the requirements for Track One and pay the required fees typically receive a final disposition within 12 months after being granted Track One status. The USPTO accepts up to 12,000 Track One cases per year.

Related terms: AEP (Accelerated Examination Program).

transfer of a patent or patent application

See assignment of a patent.

transmittal letter for patent application

See patent application.

treaties on international patent protection

See Convention application; international patent protection for U.S. inventions; Patent Cooperation Treaty (PCT).

treble (triple) damages for patent infringement

See infringement action.

troll

See patent troll.

tying

In some circumstances, patent owners may violate the antitrust laws by using their patents to unfairly require that companies purchasing the patented technology also purchase unpatented products. For example, let's say a clothing manufacturing company patents a new machine for sewing buttons. The clothing company licenses the machine and insists that manufacturers buy buttons from it as a condition of the license. In general, deciding whether a particular activity violates antitrust laws involves such variables as the actors' intent, the degree of harm done to other companies, and the level of commerce that is affected (local, state, national, or international). In a 2005 case, the Court of Appeals for the Federal Circuit established a rebuttable presumption that the company requiring the tying of products has sufficient market power to make the action an antitrust violation. (*Independent Ink v. Illinois Tool Works,* 396 F.3d 1342 (Fed. Cir. 2005).)

Related terms: antitrust law (federal) and patents.

unenforceable patent

A patent may be declared unenforceable if the alleged infringer can show that the patent owner has misused the patent. Among the specific types of misuse that can render a patent unenforceable are:

- falsely marking an invention, such as putting a patent number on it that doesn't apply
- illegal or unfair licensing practices, or
- fraud on the U.S. Patent and Trademark Office (USPTO), such as failing to include a pertinent prior art reference in the patent application.

Patents may be declared invalid if a court finds any of the following:

- The USPTO didn't discover or properly analyze relevant prior art references that affect the novelty or nonobviousness of the invention (in short, the invention didn't qualify for a patent).
- The invention doesn't or won't work.
- The disclosure of the invention in the patent application contains insufficient information to teach an ordinary person skilled in the art to build the invention.
- The patent claims are vague and indefinite.
- The patent was issued to the wrong inventor.
- Antitrust violations occurred.
- Any other facts exist that operate to retroactively invalidate the patent.

In 2014, the Supreme Court held that a patent would be invalid for indefiniteness if its claims failed to define the scope of the invention with "reasonable certainty," a decision benefiting those seeking to invalidate a patent. (*Nautilus, Inc. v. Biosig Instruments, Inc.,* 572 U.S. 898 (2014).)

Related terms: defenses to a patent infringement claim.

Patent Law: Definitions

unobviousness

See nonobviousness.

U.S. Patent and Trademark Office (USPTO)

An administrative branch of the U.S. Department of Commerce, the U.S. Patent and Trademark Office (www.uspto.gov), is responsible for overseeing and implementing the federal laws on patents and trademarks. Also known as the USPTO or Patent Office, this agency is responsible for examining, issuing, classifying, and maintaining records of all patents issued by the United States. It also serves as a filing agency for Patent Cooperation Treaty (PCT) applications.

The USPTO publishes online the *Official Gazette* (both the patent and trademark versions), a weekly periodical that describes newly issued patents, new regulations, and other information of interest to patent practitioners. The USPTO also maintains a library in which a complete patent search may be conducted by classification.

Related terms: Patent Cooperation Treaty (PCT).

usefulness, required for patents

See utility patents.

utility

See utility patents.

utility model

This provision in Japanese and German law states that inventions that do not qualify for a regular patent may nonetheless receive some protection for a shorter period of time.

utility patents

Patents may issue on inventions that have some usefulness (utility) even if the use is humorous, such as a musical condom or a device to hold your big toes together to prevent sunburned inner thighs. However, the invention must work, at least in theory. Thus, a new drug that hasn't been tested or a new chemical for which no use is now known will not receive a patent. Design patents and plant patents, the other two types of patents obtained in the United States, do not require utility.

Related terms: design patents; plant patents; statutory subject matter.

validity search

A patent search may be conducted after a patent has been issued for the purpose of discovering any fact that might be used to invalidate and thus break the patent. Usually conducted by the defendant in a patent infringement action, a validity search is often more thorough than the initial patentability search conducted by the inventor before filing a patent application, which was used to determine whether the invention was anticipated.

Related terms: defenses to a patent infringement claim; patent search.

willful infringement

Willful patent infringement occurs when someone deliberately and in "wanton disregard" of the patent owner's rights copies a patented invention. Willfulness is usually demonstrated when an infringer copies an invention without any grounds for believing that the patent is invalid or when an infringer continues unauthorized copying after being notified of the infringement. In cases of willful infringement, the court may award the plaintiff three times the actual damages established in court plus reasonable attorneys' fees. In 2016, the Supreme Court held that when determining willfulness, courts should emphasize the state of mind of the infringer and less on the objective reasonableness of the infringer's possible defenses. (*Halo Electronics, Inc. v. Pulse Electronics, Inc.*, 579 U.S. ___ (2016).)

Previously, a court would infer willful infringement occurred if an alleged patent infringer did not produce or obtain an opinion of counsel regarding the use of an infringing invention. The Court of Appeals for the Federal Circuit reversed this 20-year precedent when it ruled that the absence of an opinion of counsel is only one of several factors to be considered when determining whether patent infringement is willful. (*Knorr-Bremse Systeme fuer Nutzfahrzeuge GmbH v. Dana Corp. et al.*, 383 F.3d 1337 (Fed.Cir. 2004).)

Related terms: damages, patent infringement; infringement, patent.

working a patent

Developing and commercially exploiting the underlying invention covered by a patent is known as working a patent. In many countries outside the United States, a patent owner's failure to work the patent within a specific period of time can result in the owner's being forced to grant a license (called a compulsory license), at government-set fees, to any party that wants to be licensed.

Related terms: compulsory licensing of a patent.

Patent Law: Definitions

World Intellectual Property Organization (WIPO)

See International Bureau of the World Intellectual Property Organization; Patent Cooperation Treaty (PCT).

World Trade Organization (WTO)

This organization was created by the General Agreement on Tariffs and Trade (GATT) for the purpose of enforcing the intellectual property and other trade agreements contained in that treaty.

Related terms: GATT (General Agreement on Tariffs and Trade).

Patent Law: Forms

Patent Application Basics

This section explains the basic principles involved in filing a utility patent application and a design patent application. We also provide a completed example of both types of patents. Applicants can also obtain help from the instructions provided at the USPTO website (www.uspto.gov).

Note: To improve application quality and efficiency, the USPTO will be transitioning to a different filing format, DOCX, on January 1, 2022. You will no longer need to convert documents to PDF. DOCX is a word-processing file format supported by popular applications such as Microsoft *Word*, Google Docs, and LibreOffice. According to the USPTO, filing in DOCX provides many benefits in the application process and eliminates the need to convert into a PDF for filing. (This also eliminates the non-embedded font error, the most common obstacle in uploading a PDF.)

Preparing a Utility Patent Application

Preparing a utility patent application follows the same basic procedure whether one files electronically (via EFS-WEB system) or by mail. There are several advantages to filing electronically, including paying lower fees. (Applicants who file by mail must pay a non-electronic filing fee of $400 for large entities and $200 for small and micro entities.) Either way, two documents are at the heart of every utility application:

- **The Specification.** This document describes the invention so that someone knowledgeable in the field of the invention can make and use it without any further experimenting. It also discloses the "best mode" of creating and using the invention. In other words, the specification is a statement that explains the best way to make and use an invention. If the inventor knew of a better way (or "best mode") and failed to disclose it, that failure could result in the loss of patent rights. The specification consists of several sections including:
    - title

- background of the invention—this usually includes cross-references to any related applications, references to a microfiche appendix, a statement regarding federally sponsored research or development, the field of the invention, and a discussion of prior art
- summary of the invention—this usually includes the objects (what the invention accomplishes) and advantages (why the invention is superior to the prior art) of the invention
- description of the drawings
- a detailed description of the invention and how it works
- abstract—a concise, one-paragraph summary of the structure, nature, and purpose of the invention, and
- claims. Of all the elements, claims are often the hardest to draft (and most challenging to decipher). One reason is that claims follow strict grammatical requirements: They are sentence fragments, always start with an initial capital letter, and contain one period and no quotation marks or parentheses (except in mathematical or chemical formulas). Claims are usually made up of independent and dependent claims. One claim is stated as broadly as possible (the "independent claim") and then followed by successively narrower claims designed to specifically recite possible variations on the invention ("dependent claims"). The independent claim stands by itself, while a dependent claim always refers back and incorporates the language of another independent or dependent claim.

- **Drawings.** Patent drawings (also known as "drawing sheets") are visual representations of the invention that must be included with the application if necessary to explain the invention. The drawings must show every feature recited in the claims. There are strict standards for patent drawings regarding materials, size, form, symbols, and shading. For help in preparing drawings, consult *How to Make Patent Drawings*, by Jack Lo and David Pressman (Nolo). If you'd prefer to have a patent draftsperson prepare the drawings, expect to pay between $75 to $150 per drawing sheet.

In addition to the Specification and Drawings, the application must include specific data and fees. Below are the paper forms that are required. Much of this is incorporated directly into the EFS-WEB program, so if filing electronically, you will provide this information in an online form. These paper forms include:

Patent Law: Forms

- **Transmittal Form.** The Transmittal Form serves as a cover letter for the application. It describes what is being filed, the names of the inventors, the number of pages, the fee, and other information used by the USPTO to categorize the filing. All of the inventors must sign the transmittal form. (All of the USPTO forms required for an application are downloadable from the USPTO website, at www.uspto.gov.)
- **Fee Transmittal Form.** This form provides information about your fee, including whether you are claiming Small Entity Status. (Most inventors claim this reduced-fee status unless they have transferred their invention rights to a for-profit business with more than 500 employees.)
- **Credit Card Transmittal Form.** You must complete this additional form if you are paying by credit card.
- **Fee.** You can pay by personal check, money order, or credit card. Check the USPTO website for current fees. The fee depends on several variables, including the number of independent and dependent claims, whether the applicant qualifies for Micro Entity Status or Small Entity Status, and whether an assignment is being filed (transferring rights from the inventor to another entity). You can review current filing fees at the USPTO website.
- **Patent Application Declaration (PAD).** The PAD certifies the accuracy of the statements in the application—in other words that you are telling the truth.

In addition to these documents, the following documents might also be included in the utility patent application:

- **Information Disclosure Statement.** This should be included if you know of any relevant prior art. You don't have to include it with the application; you can file it within three months after you apply.
- **Petition to Make Special.** Include this if you want to accelerate the examination process by a few months. You can request it only if you meet one of the requirements in the patent law—for example, your invention relates to HIV/AIDS or cancer research, counters terrorism, or results in significant energy savings, or if the applicant's health is poor.
- **Assignment and Cover Sheet.** Include this if you are transferring ownership of the patent. You don't have to provide it with the application; you can file it any time.
- **Return Receipt Postcard.** This is optional, but it provides proof that the USPTO received the application.

Patent Law: Forms

Who Files the Utility Application?

A patent application may be filed in the name of the actual inventor or inventors or the assignee. If there is more than one inventor, each becomes an applicant for the patent, and each automatically owns equal shares of the invention and any resulting patents.

Inventorship can be different from legal ownership. Often, all or part of the ownership rights to the invention and the patent application must be transferred to someone else, either an individual or a legal entity. For example, some inventors are hired to invent for companies; they might be required to transfer ownership of any inventions they create as a condition of employment. To make the transfer, the inventor must legally transfer the interest by filing an assignment, either with the patent application or afterward. Some inventors prefer to wait until they have received a serial number for the application before filing the assignment.

Even if the patent doesn't indicate the assignment, the assignment will still be effective if the USPTO has recorded it.

Should You Do Your Own Utility Patent Application or Hire a Professional?

Many inventors have obtained patents on their own, often using the method David Pressman devised in his book, *Patent It Yourself* (Nolo). Preparing your patent requires considerable diligence. If you have sufficient funds but don't have the time or writing skills to do it yourself, you might be better off hiring a professional.

Of course, you can do some of the work yourself and hire a professional to do the rest. You can, for example, draft your application then have an attorney review it, or hire an attorney only if your application runs into problems with a USPTO examiner. Or you can familiarize yourself with the patent drafting rules so that you can save time explaining your invention and preparing your patent.

An example of a completed patent specification is provided below.

Interested in Filing a Provisional Patent Application?

If you are interested in preparing a provisional patent application (PPA), you can prepare and file the PPA yourself using the book *Patent Pending in 24 Hours*, by Richard Stim and David Pressman.

Patent Law: Forms

Specification of Sample Patent Application

A2-Koppe

Lam.SB

Patent Application of

Lou W. Koppe

for

TITLE: PAPER-LAMINATED PLIABLE CLOSURE FOR FLEXIBLE BAGS

CROSS-REFERENCE TO RELATED APPLICATIONS   Not Applicable

FEDERALLY SPONSORED RESEARCH   Not Applicable

SEQUENCE LISTING OR PROGRAM   Not Applicable

BACKGROUND OF THE INVENTION—FIELD OF INVENTION

This invention relates to plastic tab closures, specifically to such closures which are used for closing the necks of plastic produce bags.

BACKGROUND OF THE INVENTION

Grocery stores and supermarkets commonly supply consumers with polyethylene bags for holding produce. Such bags are also used by suppliers to provide a resealable container for other items, both edible and inedible.

Originally these bags were sealed by the supplier with staples or by heat. However, consumers objected since these were of a rather permanent nature: The bags could be opened only by tearing, thereby damaging them and rendering them impossible to reseal.

Thereafter, inventors created several types of closures to seal plastic bags in such a way as to leave them undamaged after they were opened. U.S. patent 4,292,714 to Walker (1981) discloses a complex clamp which can close the necks of bags without causing damage upon opening; however, these clamps are prohibitively expensive to manufacture. U.S. patent 2,981,990 to Balderree (1961) shows a closure which is of

Patent Application of Lou W. Koppe for "Paper-Laminated
Pliable Closure for Flexible Bags" continued

expensive construction, being made of PTFE, and which is not effective unless the bag has a relatively long "neck."

Thus, if the bag has been filled almost completely and consequently has a short neck, this closure is useless. Also, being relatively narrow and clumsy, Balderree's closure cannot be easily bent by hand along its longitudinal axis. Finally, his closure does not hold well onto the bag, but has a tendency to snap off.

Although twist closures with a wire core are easy to use and inexpensive to manufacture, do not damage the bag upon being removed, and can be used repeatedly, nevertheless they simply do not possess the neat and uniform appearance of a tab closure, they become tattered and unsightly after repeated use, and they do not offer suitable surfaces for the reception of print or labeling. These ties also require much more manipulation to apply and remove.

Several types of thin, flat closures have been proposed—for example, in U.K. patent 883,771 to Britt et al. (1961) and U.S. patents 3,164,250 (1965), 3,417,912 (1968), 3,822,441 (1974), 4,361,935 (1982), and 4,509,231 (1985), all to Paxton. Although inexpensive to manufacture, capable of use with bags having a short neck, and producible in break-off strips, such closures can be used only once if they are made of frangible plastic since they must be bent or twisted when being removed and consequently will fracture upon removal. Thus, to reseal a bag originally sealed with a frangible closure, one must either close its neck with another closure or else close it in makeshift fashion by folding or tying it. My own patent 4,694,542 (1987) describes a closure which is made of flexible plastic and is therefore capable of repeated use without damage to the bag, but nevertheless all the plastic closures heretofore known suffer from a number of disadvantages:

(a) Their manufacture in color requires the use of a compounding facility for the production of the pigmented plastic. Such a facility, which is needed to compound the primary pigments and which generally constitutes a separate production site, requires the presence of very large storage bins for the pigmented raw granules. Also, it presents great difficulties with regard to the elimination of the airborne powder which results from the mixing of the primary granules.

(b) If one uses an extruder in the production of a pigmented plastic—especially if one uses only a single extruder—a change from one color to a second requires purging the extruder of the granules having the first color by introducing those of the second color. This process inevitably produces, in sizable volume, an intermediate product of an undesired color which must be discarded as scrap, thereby resulting in waste of material and time.

(c) The colors of the closures in present use are rather unsaturated. If greater concentrations of pigment were used in order to make the colors more intense, the plastic would become more brittle and the cost of the final product would increase.

Patent Application of Lou W. Koppe for "Paper-Laminated
Pliable Closure for Flexible Bags" continued

(d) The use of pigmented plastic closures does not lend itself to the production of multicolored designs, and it would be very expensive to produce plastic closures in which the plastic is multicolored—for example, in which the plastic has stripes of several colors, or in which the plastic exhibits multicolored designs.

(e) Closures made solely of plastic generally offer poor surfaces for labeling or printing, and the label or print is often easily smudged.

(f) The printing on a plastic surface is often easily erased, thereby allowing the alteration of prices by dishonest consumers.

(g) The plastic closures in present use are slippery when handled with wet or greasy fingers.

(h) A closure of the type in present use can be very carefully pried off a bag by a dishonest consumer and then attached to another item without giving any evidence of such removal.

BACKGROUND OF INVENTION—Objects and Advantages

Accordingly, besides the objects and advantages of the flexible closures described in my above patent, several objects and advantages of the present invention are:

(a) to provide a closure which can be produced in a variety of colors without requiring the manufacturer to use a compounding facility for the production of pigments;

(b) to provide a closure whose production allows for a convenient and extremely rapid and economical change of color in the closures that are being produced;

(c) to provide a closure which both is flexible and can be brightly colored;

(d) to provide a closure which can be colored in several colors simultaneously;

(e) to provide a closure which will present a superior surface for the reception of labeling or print;

(f) to provide a closure whose labeling cannot be altered;

(g) to provide a closure which will not be slippery when handled with wet or greasy fingers; and

(h) to provide a closure which will show evidence of having been switched from one item to another by a dishonest consumer—in other words, to provide a closure which makes items tamper-proof.

Further objects and advantages are to provide a closure which can be used easily and conveniently to open and reseal a plastic bag without damage to the bag, which is simple to use and inexpensive to manufacture, which can be supplied in separate tabs en masse or in break-off links, which can be used with bags having short necks, which can be used repeatedly, and which obviates the need to tie a knot in the neck of the bag or fold

Patent Application of Lou W. Koppe for "Paper-Laminated
Pliable Closure for Flexible Bags" continued

the neck under the bag or use a twist closure. Still further objects and advantages will become apparent from a consideration of the ensuing description and drawings.

SUMMARY

In accordance with the present invention, a bag closure comprises a flat body having a notch, a gripping aperture adjacent the notch, and a layer of paper laminated on its side.

DRAWINGS—FIGURES

In the drawings, closely related figures have the same number but different alphabetic suffixes.

Figs 1A to 1D show various aspects of a closure supplied with a longitudinal groove and laminated on one side with paper.

Fig 2 shows a closure with no longitudinal groove and with a paper lamination on one side only.

Fig 3 shows a similar closure with one longitudinal groove.

Fig 4 shows a similar closure with a paper lamination on both sides.

Fig 5 shows a similar closure with a paper lamination on one side only, the groove having been formed into the paper as well as into the body of the closure.

Figs 6A to 6K show end views of closures having various combinations of paper laminations, longitudinal grooves, and through-holes.

Figs 7A to 7C show a laminated closure with groove after being bent and after being straightened again.

Figs 8A to 8C show a laminated closure without a groove after being bent and after being straightened again.

DRAWINGS—Reference Numerals

10	base of closure	12	lead-in notch
14	hole	16	gripping points
18	groove	20	paper lamination
22	tear of paper lamination	24	corner
26	longitudinal through-hole	28	neck-down
30	side of base opposite to bend	32	crease

DETAILED DESCRIPTION—FIGS. 1A AND 1B—PREFERRED EMBODIMENT

A preferred embodiment of the closure of the present invention is illustrated in Fig 1A (top view) and Fig 1B (end view). The closure has a thin base 10 of uniform cross

Patent Application of Lou W. Koppe for "Paper-Laminated
Pliable Closure for Flexible Bags" continued

section consisting of a flexible sheet of material which can be repeatedly bent and
straightened out without fracturing. A layer of paper 20 (Fig 1B) is laminated on one
side of base 10. In the preferred embodiment, the base is a flexible plastic, such as
poly-ethylene-tere-phthalate (PET—hyphens here supplied to facilitate pronunciation)
available from Eastman Chemical Co. of Kingsport, TN. However, the base can consist of
any other material that can be repeatedly bent without fracturing, such as polyethylene,
polypropylene, vinyl, nylon, rubber, leather, various impregnated or laminated fibrous
materials, various plasticized materials, cardboard, paper, etc.

At one end of the closure is a lead-in notch 12 which terminates in gripping points 16
and leads to a hole 14. Paper layer 20 adheres to base 10 by virtue either of the extrusion
of liquid plastic (which will form the body of the closure) directly onto the paper or
the application of heat or adhesive upon the entirety of one side of base 10. The paper-
laminated closure is then punched out. Thus the lamination will have the same shape as
the side of the base 10 to which it adheres.

The base of the closure is typically .8 mm to 1.2 mm in thickness, and has overall
dimensions roughly from 20 mm x 20 mm (square shape) to 40 mm x 70 mm (oblong
shape). The outer four corners 24 of the closure are typically beveled or rounded to avoid
snagging and personal injury. Also, when closure tabs are connected side-to-side in a long
roll, these bevels or roundings give the roll a series of notches which act as detents or
indices for the positioning and conveying of the tabs in a dispensing machine.

A longitudinal groove 18 is formed on one side of base 10 in Fig 1. In other
embodiments, there may be two longitudinal grooves—one each side of the base—or
there may be no longitudinal groove at all. Groove 18 may be formed by machining,
scoring, rolling, or extruding. In the absence of a groove, there may be a longitudinal
through-hole 26 (Fig 6L). This through-hole may be formed by placing, in the extrusion
path of the closure, a hollow pin for the outlet of air.

Figs 2-5—Additional Embodiments

Additional embodiments are shown in Figs 2, 3, 4, and 5; in each case the paper
lamination is shown partially peeled back. In Fig 2 the closure has only one lamination
and no groove; in Fig 3 it has only one lamination and only one groove; in Fig 4 it has
two laminations and only one groove; in Fig 5 it has two laminations and one groove, the
latter having been rolled into one lamination as well as into the body of the closure.

Figs 6A-6B—Alternative Embodiments

There are various possibilities with regard to the relative disposition of the sides which
are grooved and the sides which are laminated, as illustrated in Fig 6, which presents end
views along the longitudinal axis. Fig 6A shows a closure with lamination on one side only
and with no groove; Fig 6B shows a closure with laminations on both sides and with no

Patent Application of Lou W. Koppe for "Paper-Laminated
Pliable Closure for Flexible Bags" continued

groove; Fig 6C shows a closure with only one lamination and only one groove, both being on the same side; Fig 6D shows a closure with only one lamination and only one groove, both being on the same side and the groove having been rolled into the lamination as well as into the body of the closure; Fig 6E shows a closure with only one lamination and only one groove, the two being on opposite sides; Fig 6F shows a closure with two laminations and only one groove; Fig 6G shows a closure with two laminations and only one groove, the groove having been rolled into one lamination as well as into the body of the closure; Fig 6H shows a closure with only one lamination and with two grooves; Fig 6I shows a closure with only one lamination and with two grooves, one of the grooves having been rolled into the lamination as well as into the body of the closure; Fig 6J shows a closure with two laminations and with two grooves; Fig 6K shows a closure with two laminations and with two grooves, the grooves having been rolled into the laminations as well as into the body of the closure; and Fig 6L shows a closure with two laminations and a longitudinal through-hole.

Operation—Figs 1, 6, 7, 8

The manner of using the paper-laminated closure to seal a plastic bag is identical to that for closures in present use. Namely, one first twists the neck of a bag (not shown here but shown in Fig 12 of my above patent) into a narrow, cylindrical configuration. Next, holding the closure so that the plane of its base is generally perpendicular to the axis of the neck and so that lead-in notch 12 is adjacent to the neck, one inserts the twisted neck into the lead-in notch until it is forced past gripping points 16 at the base of the notch and into hole 14.

To remove the closure, one first bends it along its horizontal axis (Fig 1C—an end view—and Figs 7 and 8) so that the closure is still in contact with the neck of the bag and so that gripping points 16 roughly point in parallel directions. Then one pulls the closure up or down and away from the neck in a direction generally opposite to that in which the gripping points now point, thus freeing the closure from the bag without damaging the latter. The presence of one or two grooves 18 or a longitudinal through-hole 26 (Fig 6L), either of which acts as a hinge, facilitates this process of bending.

The closure can be used to reseal the original bag or to seal another bag many times; one simply bends it flat again prior to reuse.

As shown in Figs 1C, 7B, and 8B (all end views), when the closure is bent along its longitudinal axis, region 30 of the base will stretch somewhat along the direction perpendicular to the longitudinal axis. (Region 30 is the region which is parallel to this axis and is on the side of the base opposite to the bend.) Therefore, when the closure is flattened again, the base will have elongated in the direction perpendicular to the longitudinal axis. This will cause a necking down 28 (Figs 1D, 7C, and 8C) of the base, as well as either a telltale tear 22, or at least a crease 32 (Figs 7A and 8A) along the axis of

Patent Application of Lou W. Koppe for "Paper-Laminated
Pliable Closure for Flexible Bags" continued

bending. Therefore, if the closure is attached to a sales item and has print upon its paper lamination, the fact that the closure has been transferred by a dishonest consumer from the first item to another will be made evident by the tear or crease.

Figs 7A and 8A show bent closures with and without grooves, respectively. Figs 7C and 8C show the same closures, respectively, after being flattened out, along their longitudinal axes, paper tear 22 being visible.

Advantages

From the description above, a number of advantages of my paper-laminated closures become evident:

(a) A few rolls of colored paper will contain thousands of square yards of a variety of colors, will obviate the need for liquid pigments or a pigment-compounding plant, and will permit the manufacturer to produce colored closures with transparent, off-color, or leftover plastic, all of which are cheaper than first-quality pigmented plastic.

(b) With the use of rolls of colored paper to laminate the closures, one can change colors by simply changing rolls, thus avoiding the need to purge the extruder used to produce the closures.

(c) The use of paper laminate upon an unpigmented, flexible plastic base can provide a bright color without requiring the introduction of pigment into the base and the consequent sacrifice of pliability.

(d) The presence of a paper lamination will permit the display of multicolored designs.

(e) The paper lamination will provide a superior surface for labeling or printing, either by hand or by machine.

(f) Any erasure or alteration of prices by dishonest consumers on the paper-laminated closure will leave a highly visible and permanent mark.

(g) Although closures made solely of plastic are slippery when handled with wet or greasy fingers, the paper laminate on my closures will provide a nonslip surface.

Figs 7A and 8A show bent closures with and without grooves, respectively. Figs 7C and 8C show the same closures, respectively, after being flattened out, along their longitudinal axes, paper tear 22 being visible.

Conclusion, Ramifications, and Scope

Accordingly, the reader will see that the paper-laminated closure of this invention can be used to seal a plastic bag easily and conveniently, can be removed just as easily and without damage to the bag, and can be used to reseal the bag without requiring a new closure. In addition, when a closure has been used to seal a bag and is later bent and removed from the bag so as not to damage the latter, the paper lamination will tear or

Patent Application of Lou W. Koppe for "Paper-Laminated
Pliable Closure for Flexible Bags" continued

crease and thus give visible evidence of tampering, without impairing the ability of the closure to reseal the original bag or any other bag. Furthermore, the paper lamination has the additional advantages in that:

• it permits the production of closures in a variety of colors without requiring the manufacturer to use a separate facility for the compounding of the powdered or liquid pigments needed in the production of colored closures;

• it permits an immediate change in the color of the closure being produced without the need for purging the extruder of old resin;

• it allows the closure to be brightly colored without the need to pigment the base itself and consequently sacrifice the flexibility of the closure;

• it allows the closure to be multicolored since the paper lamination offers a perfect surface upon which can be printed multicolored designs;

• it provides a closure with a superior surface upon which one can label or print;

• it provides a closure whose labeling cannot be altered or erased without resulting in telltale damage to the paper lamination; and

• it provides a closure which will not be slippery when handled with wet or greasy fingers, the paper itself providing a nonslip surface.

Although the description above contains many specificities, these should not be construed as limiting the scope of the invention but as merely providing illustrations of some of the presently preferred embodiments of this invention. For example, the closure can have other shapes, such as circular, oval, trapezoidal, triangular, etc.; the lead-in notch can have other shapes; the groove can be replaced by a hinge which connects two otherwise unconnected halves; etc.

Thus the scope of the invention should be determined by the appended claims and their legal equivalents, rather than by the examples given.

CLAIMS: I claim:

1. In a bag closure of the type comprising a flat body of material having a lead-in notch on one edge thereof and a gripping aperture adjacent to and communicating with said notch, the improvement wherein said closure has a layer of paper laminated on one of its sides.

   2. The closure of claim 1 wherein said body of material is composed of polyethyleneterephthalate.

   3. The closure of claim 1 wherein said body is elongated and has a longitudinal groove which is on said one side of said body and extends the full length of said one side, from said gripping aperture to the opposite edge.

4.   The closure of claim 3 wherein said groove is formed into and along the full length of said lamination.

5.   The closure of claim 1 wherein said body is elongated and has a longitudinal groove which is on the side of said body opposite to said one side thereof and extends the full length of said one side, from said gripping aperture to the opposite edge.

6.   The closure of claim 1 wherein said body is elongated and has two longitudinal grooves which are on opposite sides of said body and extend the full lengths of said sides, from said gripping aperture to the opposite edge.

7.   The closure of claim 6 wherein the groove on said one side of said body is formed into and along the full length of said lamination.

8.   The closure of claim 1 wherein said body has a paper lamination on both of said sides.

9.   The closure of claim 8 wherein a groove is on one side of said body and extends the full length of said one side, from said gripping aperture to the opposite edge.

10.   The closure of claim 8 wherein two grooves, on opposite sides of said body, extend the full lengths of said sides, from said gripping aperture to the opposite edge.

11.   The closure of claim 10 wherein said grooves are rolled into and along the full lengths of said laminations, respectively.

12.   The closure of claim 1 wherein said paper lamination is colored.

13.   The closure of claim 1 wherein said body is elongated and has a longitudinal through-hole.

14.   A bag closure of the type comprising a flat body of material having a lead-in notch on one edge thereof, a gripping aperture adjacent to and communicating with said notch, characterized in that one of its sides has a layer of paper laminated thereon.

15.   The closure of claim 14 wherein said body of material is composed of polyethyleneterephthalate.

16.   The closure of claim 14 wherein said body is elongated and has a longitudinal groove on said one side of said body and which extends the full length of said one side, from said gripping aperture to the opposite edge.

17.   The closure of claim 14 wherein said body is elongated and has a longitudinal groove which is on the side of said body opposite to said one side thereof and extends the full length of said one side, from said gripping aperture to the opposite edge.

Patent Application of Lou W. Koppe for "Paper-Laminated
Pliable Closure for Flexible Bags" continued

18. The closure of claim 14 wherein said body is elongated and has two longitudinal grooves which are on opposite sides of said body and extend the full lengths of said sides, from said gripping aperture to the opposite edge.

19. The closure of claim 14 wherein said body has a paper lamination on both of said sides.

20. The closure of claim 19 wherein a groove is on one side of said body and extends the full length of said one side, from said gripping aperture to the opposite edge.

21. The closure of claim 19 wherein two grooves, on opposite sides of said body, extend the full lengths of said sides, from said gripping aperture to the opposite edge.

22. The closure of claim 14 wherein said paper lamination is colored.

23. The closure of claim 14 wherein said body is elongated and has a longitudinal through-hole.

24. A method of closing a plastic bag, comprising:

(a) providing a bag closure of the type comprising a flat body of material having a lead-in notch on one edge thereof, a gripping aperture adjacent to and communicating with said notch, and a layer of paper laminated on one of its sides,

(b) providing a plastic bag and inserting contents into said plastic bag,

(c) twisting said plastic bag so that it forms a neck portion to hold said contents from falling out of said plastic bag,

(d) inserting said bag closure onto said neck portion of said plastic bag so that said neck portion of said plastic bag passes said lead-in notch and into said gripping aperture,

whereby said bag closure can be easily marked to identify and/or price said contents in said plastic bag.

25. The method of claim 24 wherein said flat body of material is composed of polyethyleneterephthalate.

26. The method of claim 24 wherein said layer of paper is colored.

Abstract: A thin, flat closure for plastic bags and of the type having at one edge a V-shaped notch (12) which communicates at its base with a gripping aperture (14). The base (10) of the closure is made of a flexible material so that it can be repeatedly bent, without fracturing, along an axis aligned with said notch and aperture. In addition, a layer of paper (20) is laminated on one or both sides of the closure. The axis of the base may contain one or two grooves (18) or a through-hole (26), either of which acts as a hinge to facilitate bending.

1/4

FIG.IA FIG.IB FIG.IC FIG.ID

FIG.2 FIG. 3 FIG. 4

FIG.5

FIG.6D   FIG.6G   FIG.6I   FIG.6K

3/4

FIG.6A   FIG.6B   FIG.6C   FIG.6E

FIG.6F   FIG.6H   FIG.6J   FIG.6L

4/4

FIG.7A

FIG.7B

FIG.7C

FIG. 8A

FIG.8B

FIG.8C

Preparing a Design Patent Application

Preparing and filing a design patent is relatively simple—especially when compared to preparing and filing a utility patent. If you're a self-starter with a do-it-yourself mindset, you can, with a bit of work, prepare your design patent application and save anywhere from $500 to $1,000. Below, we present basic instructions for preparing a design patent application. If you want more information, read *Patent It Yourself* (Nolo), or read and download the design patent information provided at the USPTO website, at www.uspto.gov. Even if you prepare the rest of the application yourself, however, you might need to hire a patent draftsperson to create professional drawings.

If you're not the do-it-yourself type, you can always hire an attorney or patent agent to review and analyze your design and advise whether pursuing a design patent is worthwhile. The attorney or agent can prepare the application.

If there is a problem at the USPTO—for example, an examiner challenges your application—the attorney or agent can respond and keep the application on track.

If you don't want to do it all yourself, you'll have to pay between $750 and $1,500 for:

- an attorney to draft the application
- a patent draftsperson to create the drawings, and
- the filing fees.

Unless you pay for expedited processing of your application, you will have to wait approximately one to two years for your design patent. What's more, you cannot use it to stop others from copying your design until the patent has been granted. (The USPTO has indicated that it will place design patents on a faster track than utility patents, which can take two to three years.) Design patents automatically expire 15 years after they're issued (except for those filed before May 13, 2015, which last 14 years from issuance), and you cannot renew them.

As the inventor, only you have the right to apply for the patent. (The USPTO often refers to the designer as the inventor and to the design as the invention.) Even if you signed away your rights to someone else or were employed to create the design, you must still be listed as the inventor and sign the application. However, the issued patent application will indicate that your rights have been assigned. If someone else contributes to a new, nonobvious element of your design, that person is a coinventor, and the two of you should reach an agreement as to ownership of the patent.

Patent Law: Forms

If you're employed to create designs, your employer might own rights in any resulting design patents. Who owns the design depends on the contents of your employment agreement, your employer's policies, whether you used your employer's time and resources to create the design, and state laws regarding employee ownership rights.

The design patent application consists of:

- The Specification—a short written document describing your design. The specification is quite simple to prepare. We've provided a sample one for a table design created by a furniture designer. The elements of the specification are reasonably straightforward. Here's a quick breakdown:
  - Preamble—one or two boilerplate sentences announcing that you're seeking a design patent.
  - Specification—the place to introduce your design by name. A basic title such as "glass bowl," "puppet," or "steel table" will work best.
  - Cross References to Related Applications—here, you indicate whether you have filed a previous design patent application to which this one is related.
  - Statement Regarding Federally Sponsored R & D—indicate whether the design was prepared under a government grant or as part of government research.
  - Description of the Figure(s) of the Drawings—describe the view presented in each drawing sheet.
  - Feature Description—provide a short description of your design; for example, "My candle is characterized by a pinwheel effect that gradually slopes outward."
- The Drawing(s) showing the appearance of your design. Design patent drawings are technical and stylized. Each element—for example, stippling (use of dots), linear shading (use of lines), and distinctive patterns (for indicating colors)—has a special meaning. You are allowed to provide informal drawings, such as rough sketches or photographs, with your design patent application. Still, no one will examine your application until you provide formal drawings similar to those shown in this chapter. To avoid delay, we recommend that you provide formal drawings in the first place.

Patent Law: Forms

(The only time you should furnish informal drawings is when you are in a hurry to obtain an early filing date but haven't had a chance to draft the drawings.) With some drawing skills or computer graphics knowledge, you can prepare formal drawings for your design patent application. In their book *How to Make Patent Drawings* (Nolo), Jack Lo and David Pressman explain how to prepare these drawings using computer software or pen and ink. One chapter is devoted solely to design patent drawing rules. If you prefer to have a professional draft your drawings, you can accomplish this relatively inexpensively (about $80 per drawing sheet; each sheet may contain one or two figures). Designs are commonly depicted in different views—for example, top views, side views, or disassembled views. You should present as many views as are necessary to demonstrate your design. Each view provides another way of "seeing" the design. Each view is given a discrete figure number (abbreviated as "Fig" in patent law). Keep in mind that the design patent protects only what is disclosed in the drawings. If you later change the design substantially, you can't protect it unless you apply for a new design patent.

- the Design Patent Application Transmittal—a cover sheet that accompanies your application. You must submit a cover sheet with your design patent application. The USPTO has prepared one that we recommend you use. To obtain it, go to the USPTO home page at www.uspto.gov and click "Patents" on the left side of the screen. Under "Apply for a Patent," click "Forms," then follow the instructions to download Form SB0018.

- the Declaration—an oath provided by the designer. The declaration, Form SB/01, is a two-page form that you can download from the USPTO website. Check the box "Declaration Submitted With Initial Filing" and provide the title of your design. On page 2, list the designers and their addresses. Sign the declaration where it is marked "Inventor's Signature."

- the Fee Application Transmittal Form. The Fee Transmittal, Form SB/17, is a one-page form that you can download from the USPTO website. Indicate your method of payment.

- a fee (check current fees).

Design Patent Application—Preamble, Specification, and Claim

Mail Stop Designs—United States Patent and Trademark Office
Commissioner for Patents
P.O. Box 1450
Alexandria, VA 22313-1450

PREAMBLE:

The petitioner whose signature appears on the declaration attached respectfully requests that Letters Patent be granted to such petitioner for the new and original design set forth in the specification.

SPECIFICATION:

Petitioner has invented a new, original, and ornamental design for a table entitled "I Cannot Tell a Lie Table," of which the following is a specification. Reference is made to the accompanying drawings which form a part hereof, the figures of which are described below.

CROSS-REFERENCE TO RELATED APPLICATIONS: None

STATEMENT REGARDING FEDERALLY SPONSORED RESEARCH: None

DRAWING FIGURES:

Fig 1 is a perspective view of my new table design

Fig 2 is a right side view of my new table design

Fig 3 is a top view of my new table design

Fig 4 is a left end view of my new table design

FEATURE DESCRIPTION: My table design is characterized by wooden hatchets, hanging wooden cherries, and the written expression "I cannot tell a lie."

CLAIM: I (We) Claim:

The ornamental design for a table as shown and described.

Express Mail Label # EU121293846US

Date of Deposit: 2020 _____

Part 2: Copyright Law

Copyright Law: Overview 185

    What is a copyright? 185

    How is a copyright created? 186

    Who owns a copyright? 186

    Can copyrights be divided or transferred? 187

    How long does copyright protection last? 188

    What happens if a copyright is infringed? 188

    When can a copyrighted work be used without an owner's permission?.......... 189

    What laws cover copyright protection in the United States and
        other countries? 190

    What's new in copyright law since the last edition? 190

    Copyright resources... 196

Copyright Law: Definitions.. 197

Copyright Law: Forms... 365

    Preparing a Copyright Application..365

    Preparing an Electronic (eCO) Copyright Application 369

        Submitting Deposit Copies 370

    Preparing a Traditional Print Copyright Application 370

Copyright Law: Overview

Copyright law protects a variety of original expressions, including art, sculpture, literature, music, songs, choreography, crafts, poetry, software, photography, movies, video games, videos, websites, architecture, and graphics. Protection occurs automatically—that is, you acquire copyright once you fix the work in a medium—but this automatic protection can be enhanced by registering the work with the U.S. Copyright Office.

Copyright lasts for the life of the work's creator (its author) plus 70 years. In cases where the creator is a business, the copyright lasts between 95 and 120 years. Most nations of the world offer copyright protection to works by U.S. citizens and nationals, and the United States offers its copyright protection to the citizens and nationals of these same nations.

What is a copyright?

A copyright gives the owner of a creative work the right to keep others from unauthorized use of the work. Under copyright law, a creative work (often referred to as a "work of authorship") must meet all of these three criteria to be protected:

- It must be original—that is, the author must have created rather than copied it.
- It must be fixed in a tangible (concrete) medium of expression—for example, it should be recorded or expressed on paper, audio or videotape, computer disk, clay, or canvas.
- It must have at least some creativity—that is, it must be produced by an exercise of human intellect. There is no hard and fast rule as to how much creativity is enough. To give an example, it must go beyond the creativity found in the telephone white pages, which involve a nondiscretionary alphabetic listing of telephone numbers rather than a creative selection of listings.

Copyright does not protect ideas or facts; it protects only the unique way in which ideas or facts are expressed. For instance, copyright might protect an author's science fiction novel about a romance between an earthling and a space alien, but the author cannot stop others from using the underlying idea of an intergalactic love affair.

How is a copyright created?

A creative work is protected by copyright the moment it assumes a tangible form—which in copyright circles is referred to as being "fixed in a tangible medium of expression." Contrary to popular belief, providing a copyright notice or registering the work with the U.S. Copyright Office is *not* necessary to obtain essential copyright protection. But, there are some steps that can be taken to enhance the creator's ability to sue or stop others from copying:

- Place a copyright notice on a published work. The copyright notice, or "copyright bug" as it is sometimes called, commonly appears in this form: "© (year of publication) (author or other basic copyright owner)." Placing this notice on a published work (distributed to the public without restriction) prevents others from claiming that they did not know that the work was covered by copyright. This can be important if the author is forced to file a lawsuit to enforce the copyright, since it is much easier to recover significant money damages from a deliberate (as opposed to innocent) copyright infringer.

- Register works with the U.S. Copyright Office. Timely registration—within three months of the work's publication date, or before the infringement actually begins—creates a legal presumption that the copyright is valid and, if accomplished prior to someone copying the work, allows the copyright owner to recover up to $150,000 (and possibly attorneys' fees) without proving any actual monetary harm. Registration may be accomplished online or by filing a paper form and depositing one or two samples of the work (depending on what it is) with the U.S. Copyright Office.

- Currently, the fee to register is $45 if you file electronically and provided you're registering one work created by one person who also owns the copyright. All other electronic application filings are $65. Paper application filings are $125.

Who owns a copyright?

With three important exceptions, a copyright is owned by the person who created the work. In copyright lingo, these people are all called "authors."

The exceptions are:

- If a work is created by an employee in the course of employment, it is called a "work made for hire," and the copyright is owned by the employer (which employer is considered the "author" for copyright purposes).
- If the work is commissioned (created by an author working as an independent contractor), and the parties sign a written work-made-for-hire agreement, the copyright will be owned by the commissioning party as long as the work falls within one of the statutory categories of commissioned works that can qualify as works made for hire.
- If the author sells ("assigns") the copyright to someone else, the purchasing person or business owns the copyright.

Can copyrights be divided or transferred?

A copyright actually encompasses a bundle of separate exclusive rights, including the exclusive right to:

- reproduce the work
- display or perform the work
- distribute the work, and
- prepare adaptations of the work (derivative works).

A copyright owner who wishes to exploit a work commercially typically transfers one or more of these rights to the publisher or other entity who will be responsible for getting the work to market. It is also common for the copyright owner to place some limitations on the exclusive rights being transferred. For example, the owner might limit the transfer to a specific period of time, allow the right to be exercised only in a specific part of the country or world, or require that the right be exercised only on certain computer platforms.

When all copyright rights are transferred unconditionally, it is ordinarily termed an "assignment." When only some of the rights associated with the copyright are transferred, it is known as a "license." An exclusive license exists when the right being licensed can be exercised only by the licensee and no one else. If the license allows others to exercise the same rights being transferred in the license, the license is said to be nonexclusive.

Buyers of exclusive and nonexclusive copyright rights are allowed to record the transfers in the U.S. Copyright Office. This helps to protect the buyers in case the original copyright owner later decides to transfer the same rights to another party.

How long does copyright protection last?

As a result of the Copyright Term Extension Act of 1998, most copyrights for works published after January 1, 1978, last for the life of the author plus 70 years. However, in the following circumstances, the copyright lasts between 95 and 120 years, depending on the date the work is published:

- The work belongs to the author's employer under work-made-for-hire principles.
- The work was commissioned under a work-made-for-hire agreement (and fits within one of the categories of works that qualify for work-made-for-hire treatment).
- The author publishes and registers the work anonymously or under a pseudonym.

After copyright expires, the work goes into the public domain, meaning it becomes available for anyone's use.

For works created before 1978, the duration times are different:

- If the work was published before 1926, it is in the public domain (available for use without permission). (Note: On January 1, 2019, for the first time since 1998, expiring copyrighted works entered the public domain. So, in 2019, works first published in the U.S. before 1924 entered the public domain. In 2022, works first published before 1927 will enter the public domain, and so forth.)
- If the work was published between 1926 and 1963 and not renewed, it is in the public domain.
- If the work was published between 1926 and 1963 and it was renewed, the copyright lasts 95 years from the date of first publication.
- If the work was published between 1964 and 1977, the copyright lasts for 95 years from the date of publication.
- If the work was created before 1978 and published before December 31, 2002, the copyright lasts the longer of either (a) life of the author plus 70 years, or (b) until December 31, 2047; if created before 1978 and not published before December 31, 2002, the copyright lasts for the life of the author plus 70 years.

What happens if a copyright is infringed?

In the event someone infringes (violates) the exclusive rights of a copyright owner, the owner is entitled to sue in federal court and ask the court to:

- issue orders (restraining orders and injunctions) to prevent further violations
- award money damages if appropriate, and
- in some circumstances, award attorneys' fees.

Whether the lawsuit will be effective and whether damages will be awarded depends on whether the alleged infringer succeeds in raising one or more legal defenses to the charge. Common legal defenses to copyright infringement are:

- Too much time has elapsed between the infringing act and the lawsuit (the statute of limitations defense).
- There is no infringement; it is fair use.
- The infringement was innocent (the infringer had no reason to know the work was protected by copyright).
- The infringing work was independently created (that is, it wasn't copied from the original).
- The copyright owner authorized the use in a license.

When can a copyrighted work be used without an owner's permission?

Some unauthorized uses of a copyrighted work are considered fair use. The unauthorized use is excused because the work is being used for a transformative purpose such as research, scholarship, criticism, or journalism. When determining whether an unauthorized use should be excused on the basis of fair use, a court will use several factors, including the purpose and character of the use, amount and substantiality of the portion borrowed, and effect of the use on the market for the copyrighted material.

It's important to understand that fair use is a defense rather than an affirmative right. This means that a particular use only gets established as a fair use if the copyright owner decides to file a lawsuit and the court upholds the fair use defense. There is, therefore, no way to find out in advance whether something will or won't be considered a fair use. Of course, if the copyright owner is willing to grant permission for the use, then the uncertainty surrounding the use goes away. For this reason, most people who propose to use a copyrighted work do what they can to obtain permission and rely on the fair use defense only if permission is not granted or the copyright owner can't be located.

What laws cover copyright protection in the United States and other countries?

In the United States, copyright protection derives from the U.S. Constitution, which requires that original works of authorship be protected by copyright. The current (and exclusive) source of this protection is the federal Copyright Act of 1976, as amended. There are no state copyright laws.

Copyright protection rules are fairly similar worldwide due to several international copyright treaties, the most important of which is the Berne Convention. Under this treaty, all member countries (over 100 countries, including virtually all industrialized countries) must afford copyright protection to authors who are nationals of any member country. This protection must last for at least the life of the author plus 50 years and must be automatic, without the need for the author to take any legal steps to preserve the copyright.

In addition to the Berne Convention, the GATT (General Agreement on Tariffs and Trade) treaty contains a number of provisions that affect copyright protection in signatory countries. Together, the Berne Copyright Convention and the GATT treaty allow U.S. authors to enforce their copyrights in most industrialized nations and allow the nationals of those nations to enforce their copyrights in the United States.

What's new in copyright law since the last edition?

Below are some changes in copyright law that have occurred since the last edition.

- **Congress cannot terminate states' sovereign immunity.** The Constitution provides the states with protection from copyright lawsuits, that is, with "sovereign immunity." Congress sought to end that with the Copyright Remedy Clarification Act ("CRCA"). However, in an appeal from a copyright infringement lawsuit against North Carolina, which had, without permission, publicized privately commissioned videos and photos of a shipwreck recovery, the Supreme Court held that Article 1 of the Constitution prohibits Congress from limiting the sovereign immunity of state governments. (*Allen v. Cooper*, 140 S. Ct. 994 (2020).)

- **Annotations in state laws are not protectible by copyright.** The Supreme Court held that the "government edicts doctrine"—a principle that prevents judges and legislators from claiming authorship in judicial opinions or laws—also applies to annotations prepared and adopted by a state legislature. (*Georgia v. Public.Resource.Org, Inc.*, 140 S. Ct. 1498 (2020).)

- **Naming an individual author in a compilation registration is not required for the work's author to bring an infringement lawsuit.** A book publisher exceeded the license requirements of a photo permission agreement, and a photographer sued for copyright infringement. The Second Circuit acknowledged that exceeding the license amounted to infringement and limited damages to no more than three years before the lawsuit. Because a group registration for a compilation registers each of the individual works, the photographer did not need to be named as an author in the publisher's compilation registration to bring an infringement lawsuit. (Note: In any case, the author of a compilation is typically the editor or curator of the group of works.) (*Sohm v. Scholastic Inc.*, 2020 WL 2375056 (2d Cir. May 2020).)

- **Ninth Circuit rejects "inverse ratio" rule.** In an appeal regarding the Led Zeppelin song, "Stairway to Heaven," the Ninth Circuit rejected the "inverse ratio" doctrine—a judge-made rule saying that the more substantial the evidence of access, the less is required to show substantial similarity—and ruled in favor of Led Zeppelin. (*Skidmore v. Led Zeppelin*, 952 F.3d 1051 (9th Cir. 2020).)

- **Nonfiction author cannot claim rights to "fictionalized" facts.** The copyright owner of a biography of the Four Seasons singing group argued that the producers of a musical about the singing group borrowed more than facts from the biography because some of the facts were "fiction." The Ninth Circuit disagreed, holding "Copyright protects the creative labor of authors; it does not protect authors' post-completion representations about the lack of veracity of their own avowedly truthful work." (*Corbello v. Valli*, 974 F. 3d 965 (9th Cir. 2020).)

- **Issue of lyric originality is a question of fact.** The Ninth Circuit reversed and remanded a district court case that alleged the lyrics from a Taylor Swift song, "Shake It Off" (2014), were copied. The Ninth Circuit stated that originality is a question of fact and not suitable for a motion to dismiss. (*Hall v. Swift*, _____ F.3d _____ (9th Cir. 2019).)

- **A coauthorship dispute is a matter of federal jurisdiction.** According to the Fifth Circuit, ruling in a case regarding a cosmetics book, the federal courts have exclusive jurisdiction over initial ownership and coauthorship of copyright disputes. (*Di Angelo Publications, Inc. v. Kelley*, No. 20-20523 (5th Cir. 2021).)

- **Floor plans are not "pictures" for copyright purposes.** The Eighth Circuit reversed and remanded a case where real estate agencies claimed the right to reproduce floor plans based on Section 120(A) of the copyright law. ("The copyright in an architectural work that has been constructed does not include the right to prevent the making, distributing, or public display of pictures, paintings, photographs, or other pictorial representations of the work if the building in which the work is embodied is located in or ordinarily visible from a public place.") The Eighth Circuit held open the possibility that fair use might succeed as a defense against a claim of floor plan infringement. (*Designworks Homes, Inc. v. Columbia House of Brokers Realty, Inc.*, No. 19-3608 (8th Cir. 2021).)

- **Copyright sublicenses can be implied.** A commercial photographer issued an unrestricted license that included the freedom to sublicense. The photographer later sued, claiming that the sublicenses must be in writing. Considering this issue for the first time, the First Circuit held that the parties' conduct could imply sublicenses. (*Photographic Illustrators Corp. v. Orgill Inc.* 953 F. 3d 56 (1st Cir. 2020).)

- **Personal planner layout not protected by copyright.** The Tenth Circuit held that the layout of a personal planner—for example, introductory statements, color-coded monthly calendars, and lined pages for making notes—was an idea, not the expression of an idea, and therefore, not protected by copyright. (*Craft Smith, LLC v. EC Design, LLC*, 969 F.3d 1092 (10th Cir. 2020).)

- **Statute of limitations claim accrues once ownership is disputed.** A producer claimed to be a coauthor of the Jerry Seinfeld TV series, *Comedians in Cars Getting Coffee*. In 2012, Seinfeld disputed that claim and told the producer his contribution amounted to a work made for hire. The producer did not file an infringement lawsuit until 2018, and the case was dismissed because of copyright law's three-year statute of limitations. (*Charles v. Seinfeld*, No. 18-1196 (S.D.N.Y. Feb. 26, 2021).)

- **Use of RSS feed does not imply a license to reproduce.** A news aggregator copied a medical blog and defended itself, arguing that a license was implied because the blog was distributed by an RSS feed (a standardized method of syndicating blogs and podcasts). The Eleventh Circuit disagreed and upheld a verdict of infringement. (*Midlevelu, Inc. v. ACI Information Group*, No. 20-10856 (11th Cir. 2021).)

- **Control panel design is not copyrightable.** Although a company obtained a copyright registration for its control panel design for a clothes drier, a district court ruled that the work was a useful article and copyright was invalid. The court held that a showing of utility could overcome the registration's presumption of validity. (*Town & Country Linen Corp., et al. v. Ingenious Designs LLC*, No. 18-5075 (S.D.N.Y. 2020).)
- **Failure to acquire assent dooms browserwrap agreement.** An online gambling app tried to enforce an arbitration provision buried within its terms-of-use agreement. Because the online gambling site failed to acquire user-assent and failed to prove constructive or actual notice of the terms ("the user would need Sherlock Holmes's instincts to discover the Terms"), the Ninth Circuit refused to enforce the provision. (*Wilson v. Huuuge, Inc.*, No. 18-36017, 2019 U.S. App. LEXIS 37952 (9th Cir. 2019).)

Social Media

- **Embedding considered an infringement of "display right."** A New York federal court held that when Sinclair Broadcasting and others embedded a polar bear video found on social media on their own websites, they violated the photographer's display right. The ruling opposes the Ninth Circuit's "server test," which held that embedding does not infringe unless copies are made and stored on a server. (*Nicklen v. Sinclair Broad. Grp.*, No. 20-10300 (JSR) (S.D.N.Y. 07/30/2021).)
- **Embedding celebrity photos is transformative and, therefore, fair use.** A photographer's photo of Cardi B, posted without authorization by the celebrity on Instagram and later embedded in an article discussing Cardi B's cosmetic business, was held to be fair use. The court held that the use was transformative (the original use was to show the celebrity at a fashion show) and did not affect the market for the photograph. (*Walsh v. Townsquare Media, Inc.*, No. 19-4958, 2020 WL 2837009 (S.D.N.Y. 2020).)
- **New York courts issue conflicting decisions on Instagram Terms of Use.** In a surprising decision, a New York federal court ruled that once a photographer posted her picture as "public" to Instagram, she gave up exclusive licensing rights. The court reasoned that because Instagram's Terms of Use provide for nonexclusive sublicensing rights, the photographer could not halt embedding of the photo by a news website. (*Sinclair v. Ziff Davis*, 454 F. Supp. 3d 342

(S.D.N.Y. 2020).) A New York district court reached the opposite conclusion when an Instagram photographer sued *Newsweek* for infringement. The court held that the Instagram Terms of Use did not grant a sublicense between *Newsweek* and Instagram. (*McGucken v. NEWSWEEK LLC*, 464 F. Supp. 3d 594 (S.D.N.Y. 2020).) In light of the *McGucken* decision, the judge in *Sinclair v. Ziff Davis* granted the photographer's motion for reconsideration.

- **Embedding photo of tennis star is fair use.** Tennis professional Caroline Wozniacki posted a photo of herself on Instagram announcing her retirement. The Instagram photo was later embedded at a tennis website. The district court granted a motion to dismiss the photographer's copyright infringement claim, holding that the website's embedding constituted fair use. (*Boesen v. United Sports Publications, Ltd.*, No. 20-1552 (E.D.N.Y. 2020).)

Substantial Similarity

- **No substantial similarity.** The Second Circuit determined no substantial similarity between a video game developer's proposed game and the television program *Star Trek: Discovery*. (*Abdin v. CBS Broadcasting Inc.*, 971 F. 3d 57 (2d Cir. 2020).) An author and performance coach sued the makers of the TV show, *Billions*. The Second Circuit dismissed the case using the "more discerning observer" test to find no substantial similarity. (*Shull v. TBTF Productions, Inc.* No. 20-3529 (2d Cir. 2021).) A district court dismissed an infringement lawsuit brought by a comic book author who claimed that Nickelodeon copied elements of the comic in a children's TV show, *Rusty Rivets*. Although some of the characters shared similar names, the court found no substantial similarities. (*Knowles v. Spin Master, Inc.*, No. 18-5827 (C.D. Cal. 2019).) A New York district court found no substantial similarity between two short stories set in Paris and a remake of *Rosemary's Baby*. (*Montgomery v. Holland*, 408 F. Supp. 3d 353 (S.D.N.Y. 2019).)

Fair Use

- **Google's use of JAVA API is fair use.** Like most software applications, Oracle's JAVA SE program contains coding tools (Application Programming Interface or API) that allow the program to connect to, or be accessed by, various platforms. The Supreme Court held that Google's copying of the Java SE API included only those lines of code that were needed to allow programmers to work in a new and transformative program. In other words, Google's limited API borrowing was fair use. (*GOOGLE LLC v. Oracle America, Inc.*, 141 S. Ct. 1183 (2021).)

- **Using eight seconds of a three-minute children's song is fair use.** A documentary about burlesque didn't infringe when it used eight seconds of a 190-second children's song. The use was transformative and the amount used (though the heart of the composition) was not more than required. According to the Second Circuit, fair use does not obligate a defendant to use the shortest possible snippet to convey its message. (*Brown, et al. v. Netflix, Inc., et al.,* No. 20-2007 (2d Cir 2020).)
- **Use of Prince photograph for Warhol silkscreen not fair use.** The Second Circuit held that Andy Warhol's use of a Prince photograph was derivative, not transformative, reversing a fair use decision by the district court. (*Andy Warhol Foundation for the Visual Arts, Inc. v. Goldsmith,* ___ F.3d ___ (2d Cir. Aug. 24, 2021).)
- **Modification of "crotch shot" photo is fair use.** A New York district court held that the *Huffington Post's* satirical modifications to a John Hamm "crotch shot" photograph was transformative and constituted fair use. (*Schwartzwald v. Oath Inc.,* No. 19-CV-9938 (S.D.N.Y. Sep. 10, 2020).)
- **Reproducing clips from a movie in an acting reel is fair use.** After completing a film, an actress incorporated clips from the movie in her acting reel (an actor's video resume). The film's director sued the actress for infringement. A district court ruled that the actress was excused under fair use principles—most notably, because the acting reels wouldn't interfere with the film's market or profitability. (*Bain v. Film Indep.,* Inc. No. 18-4126 (C.D. Cal. 2020).)
- **Mash-Up of *Star Trek* and Dr. Seuss not fair use.** The Ninth Circuit determined that "Oh, the Places You'll Boldly Go!"—a proposed mash-up of TV's *Star Trek* and a Dr. Seuss book, *Oh, the Places You'll Go!*—was not fair use. The proposed work was not a parody because it did not critique or comment on the Dr. Seuss work. Instead, the authors simply intended to make a humorous book by combining characters from *Star Trek* with layouts and illustrations lifted directly from the Dr. Seuss book. (*Dr. Seuss Enterprises v. ComicMix, LLC,* No. 19-55348 (9th Cir. 2020).)
- **Incorporation of a screenshot in an opinion article is fair use.** A photographer's picture for a controversial article about dating was not infringed when a writer published an opinion piece that included a screenshot of the article and picture. The district court held that the use was transformative and unlikely to harm the market for the picture. (*Yang v. Mic Network, Inc.,* No. 18-7628, 2019 WL 4640263 (S.D.N.Y. 2019).)

VARA

- **The Second Circuit includes temporary works within the VARA standard of "recognized stature."** The Visual Artists Rights Act (VARA) permits an artist to prevent the destruction of art that has achieved "recognized stature." Upholding a $6.75 million judgment for New York graffiti artists, the Second Circuit held that VARA makes no distinction between temporary and permanent works when determining whether a work has achieved recognized stature. (*Castillo v. G&M Realty LP,* 950 F. 3d 155 (2d Cir. 2020).)

Copyright resources

You can find valuable information about copyright by using any of the following Web resources:

- **Nolo (www.nolo.com).** Nolo offers self-help information about a wide variety of legal topics, including copyright law.
- **Copyright Office (www.copyright.gov).** The U.S. Copyright Office's website offers forms, circulars, and a wide range of helpful copyright information.
- **Copyright & Fair Use (https://fairuse.stanford.edu).** Operated by the Stanford University Libraries, this site provides a through overview of copyright and fair use.
- **Dear Rich: Nolo's Patent, Copyright & Trademark Blog (www.dearrichblog.com).** Have a question about copyright law? This intellectual property blog operates as a companion to this book.

Copyright Law: Definitions

n this section, we provide concise definitions of the words and phrases commonly used when dealing with copyrights.

abridgment

See derivative work.

abstractions test

See plot, protection of.

access

In order to prove infringement, the copyright owner must first demonstrate that the infringer had access to the work. That is, the infringer had a reasonable opportunity to view or hear the copyrighted work. If the infringement involves identical copies, such as photographs copied from a magazine, access may be presumed and need not be proven. That's because in cases of verbatim copying, it is virtually impossible that two works could have been independently created.

> EXAMPLE: The makers of Beanie Babies successfully sued a company marketing a pig bean bag known as "Preston the Pig" that was identical to the Beanie Baby known as "Squealer." The similarity between the two was so close as to create a reasonable presumption of access. (*Ty Inc. v. GMA Accessories Inc.,* 132 F.3d 1167 (7th Cir. 1997).)

When the copies are not identical, access can be proven in various ways.

> EXAMPLE 1: The owners of copyright in popular children's characters proved access because the representatives of a fast-food chain had visited their head-quarters and discussed use of the characters in commercials. (*Sid & Marty Krofft Television Prods., Inc. v. McDonald's Corp.,* 562 F.2d 1157 (9th Cir. 1977).)

EXAMPLE 2: The owners of the song "He's So Fine" sued George Harrison, alleging that Harrison's song "My Sweet Lord" infringed their copyright. It was determined that Harrison had access to "He's So Fine" because the song was on the British pop charts in 1963 during the same period when a song by the Beatles was also on the British charts. (*Abkco Music, Inc. v. Harrisongs Music, Ltd.*, 722 F.2d 988 (2d Cir. 1983).)

As a general rule, the more popular a work, the easier it is to prove access. Conversely, if a work was not published, the copyright owner has a harder time proving access.

Proving access ordinarily requires direct evidence. For example, a T-shirt company alleged access by its claim that a representative of the company that made Bratz dolls attended the Los Angeles County Fair where the T-shirt company had a display. The Ninth Circuit Court of Appeals dismissed this as a mere "bare possibility" because there was no direct evidence of the representative seeing the design or of the design being widely disseminated. (*Art Attacks Ink LLC v. MGA Entertainment Inc.*, 581 F.3d 1138 (9th Cir. 2009).) What the courts are seeking is "significant, affirmative and probative evidence" of a 'particular chain of events,' sufficient to permit a reasonable jury to infer access." (*Horizon Comics Productions, Inc. v. Marvel Entertainment, LLC.*, No. 16-CV-2499 (J.P.O.) (S.D.N.Y. July 15, 2019).)

Of course, in order to prove access, the party alleging infringement should be able to demonstrate a chronology that makes sense.

EXAMPLE: Two men alleged that they had sent their version of a song to a talent scout representing Britney Spears and claimed it was later infringed by the Spears song "What U See Is What U Get." However, the undisputed evidence at trial showed that Spears had recorded her version several months before the two men had even submitted their composition. (*Cottrill v. Spears*, 2003 U.S. Dist. LEXIS 8823 (E.D. Pa. 2003).)

Until 2020, the Ninth Circuit followed the "inverse ratio" rule, which says that the stronger the evidence of access, the less evidence is required to prove substantial similarity. (The rule had been rejected in other circuits.) In an appeal regarding the Led Zeppelin song, "Stairway to Heaven," the Ninth Circuit overruled the inverse ratio precedent, stating it "defies logic and creates uncertainty for the courts and the parties." The court also noted that the access concept has been diluted by the era of digital connectivity. (*Skidmore v. Led Zeppelin*, 952 F.3d 1051 (9th Cir. 2020).)

Related terms: infringement (copyright); infringement action.

actual damages

See damages for copyright infringement.

adaptations or alterations

See derivative work.

advertising injury

This is the title of a provision in insurance contracts (usually found in comprehensive general liability policies used by most businesses) that often triggers coverage for the defense of copyright or trademark claims. Typically, the provision is worded to provide coverage when "infringing upon another's copyright, trade dress or slogan in your advertisement" (quoting from the ISO Comprehensive General Liability Form). Although initially written (and interpreted) broadly, such provisions now commonly include strict exclusions relating to intellectual property infringement. The key for triggering insurance coverage is for the policyholder to demonstrate a causal connection between the business's advertising and the infringement—for example, an artist might allege that the policyholder's unauthorized distribution and marketing of a promotional T-shirt infringes one of the artist's works.

affirmative rights

Many people use the term "protections" to refer to the benefits that go along with ownership of copyrights and other intellectual property such as trade secrets, patents, and trademarks. For example, one might say, "My poem is protected by copyright." However, some commentators prefer to describe these legal protections as "affirmative rights," because works are not protected unless the owners affirmatively exercise their rights if their copyright is infringed.

Affirmative rights include the owner's right to file a lawsuit, the right to recover damages, and the right to obtain an injunction (a court order preventing the infringer from taking certain actions, such as using or selling the infringing material). Although observing this linguistic difference could lead to a better understanding of how intellectual property laws work, this book mostly uses the more accepted and commonly used term "protection."

all rights reserved

This phrase was required as part of a copyright notice by the Buenos Aires Convention international treaty. Until recently, the term appeared in many copyright notices in an attempt to secure complete protection under that treaty. However, all signatory countries to the Buenos Aires Convention are now also members of other international agreements that don't require the "all rights reserved" phrase, so it is no longer required.

Related terms: international copyright protection.

Altai case

See infringement (copyright).

anonymous

An author's contribution to a work is anonymous if the author (a natural person) is not identified on the copies or phonorecords (audio recordings) of the work. Copyright protection for anonymous and pseudonymous works lasts 95 years from the date of publication or 120 years from creation, whichever is shorter. However, if the name of the author is disclosed in the records of the Copyright Office, the work will be protected for the author's life plus 70 years.

> EXAMPLE: The 1995 best-seller *Primary Colors* was published anonymously. The media eventually determined that the book's author was Joe Klein, a writer for *Newsweek* magazine. If Mr. Klein died in 2030 without disclosing his name to the Copyright Office, the term of copyright for *Primary Colors* would end in 2090 (95 years from publication). If Mr. Klein disclosed his name, protection would extend until 2100 (70 years from his death.)

Copyright Act: § 101. Definitions

An "anonymous work" is a work on the copies or phonorecords of which no natural person is identified as author.

Related terms: author; duration of copyrights; pseudonym.

anthologies, copyrightability of

See compilations.

APIs (application programming interface code)

See software.

Apple Computer, Inc. v. Franklin

In this influential 1983 court decision, a federal Court of Appeals for the first time extended copyright protection to computer operating systems consisting of object code embedded in read-only memory chips, or ROMs. (*Apple Computer, Inc. v. Franklin Computer Corporation,* 714 F.2d 1240 (3d Cir. 1983), *aff'd,* 35 F.3d 1435 (1994).)

Related terms: software.

Apple Computer, Inc. v. Microsoft Corp.

This seminal case established that the metaphor—your computer screen is a desktop in which you can click on icons to accomplish tasks—employed by the Macintosh user interface was an unprotectable idea. Further, most of the individual elements that made up this desktop metaphor were not protected by copyright, either because they were functional rather than original expression or because they were unprotectable ideas. (*Apple Computer, Inc. v. Microsoft Corp.,* 717 F. Supp. 1428 (N.D. Cal. 1989), 779 F. Supp. 133 (N.D. Cal. 1992), *aff'd,* 35 F.3d 1435 (9th Cir. 1994).)

Related terms: software.

architectural work

The appearance, architectural plans, drawings, or photographs of an architectural work (a building) created after 1990 cannot be reproduced without the consent of the owner of copyright in the architectural work—usually the architect or developer. There are some exceptions. For example, if the building is located in a place that is ordinarily visible to the public, photos or pictures of the building can be taken, distributed, or publicly displayed. Standard features such as common bathroom or kitchen design elements are not protected.

In 2021, the Eighth Circuit reversed and remanded a case in which real estate agencies claimed the right to reproduce floor plans, arguing they were "pictures" permitted under Section 101 of U.S. copyright law. Although the Eighth Circuit ruled against the real estate agencies, the court held open the possibility that fair use might succeed as a defense against a claim of floor plan infringement. (*Designworks Homes, Inc. v. Columbia House of Brokers Realty, Inc.,* No. 19-3608 (8th Cir. 2021).)

Copyright Law: Definitions

Even if a building contains sculptural elements like vampire figures, you can still photograph those elements and in one case, it was permissible to use such architectural elements as part of the backdrop in a Batman movie. (*Leicester v. Warner Bros.*, 232 F.3d 1212 (9th Cir. 2000).) As with all copyright infringement, the copyright owner must demonstrate that the alleged infringer had access to the plans or design. For example, in one case, the Tenth Circuit Court of Appeals found no evidence that the defendant architect had access to the plaintiff's plans and concluded that any similarities in the designs of two homes were because both architects took direction and ideas from the same person. (*La Resolana Architects P.A. v. Reno, Inc.*, 555 F.3d 1171 (10th Cir. 2009).)

Copyright Act: § 101. Definitions
An "architectural work" is the design of a building as embodied in any tangible medium of expression, including a building, architectural plans, or drawings. The work includes the overall form as well as the arrangement and composition of spaces and elements in the design, but does not include individual standard features.

Copyright Act: § 120. Scope of exclusive rights in architectural works
This statute governs when architectural works may be reproduced, altered, or destroyed.
(a) **Pictorial Representations Permitted.**—The copyright in an architectural work that has been constructed does not include the right to prevent the making, distributing, or public display of pictures, paintings, photographs, or other pictorial representations of the work, if the building in which the work is embodied is located in or ordinarily visible from a public place.
(b) **Alterations to and Destruction of Buildings.**—Notwithstanding the provisions of section 106 (2), the owners of a building embodying an architectural work may, without the consent of the author or copyright owner of the architectural work, make or authorize the making of alterations to such building, and destroy or authorize the destruction of such building.

archival copies

The Computer Software Protection Act of 1980 defines archival copies as copies of software made by a software owner strictly for backup purposes—that is, to use if something happens to the original copy. The Act permits a computer program owner to make archival copies of the program as long as the owner retains the original copy of the program. But if the purchaser sells or gives away the original software to a new owner, all archival copies must either be included in the transfer or destroyed. The intention is to prevent two or more people from legally possessing copies of a program that has been purchased from the copyright owner only once.

arrangements, musical

See musical works and sound recordings distinguished.

asserted truth doctrine

See estoppel, copyright.

assignment of copyright

The transfer of all or a portion of a copyright to a new owner is referred to as an assignment. Usually, an assignment involves the permanent transfer of the entire copyright, as when a freelance writer assigns all copyright interests in a particular article to a magazine. But an assignment can also transfer less than the whole copyright. For example, an author might assign the right to promote, display, and distribute a novel to a publisher while reserving the right to create derivative works (such as a screenplay) from that novel.

As a broad rule, assignments are unconditional transfers of the rights in question, without limitations on how long the transfer lasts or the conditions under which the rights may be used. By contrast, licenses give permission for a party to use a copyright under certain specified conditions for a defined period of time. For works published after January 1, 1978, any assignment by the author may be terminated by the author, the author's surviving spouse, or the author's children or grandchildren 35 years after publication or 40 years after the transfer, whichever comes first.

Related terms: licensing of copyrights; termination of transfers; transfers of copyright ownership.

attorneys' fees

In an infringement action, copyright owners who timely register their copyright (either before an infringing activity has begun, or within three months of first publication of the work) may qualify to have their attorneys' fees and court costs paid by an unsuccessful defendant. However, if the defendant prevails, the defendant may seek attorneys' fees regardless of whether the plaintiff timely registered. The Supreme Court has placed some conditions on the recovery of attorneys' fees in copyright infringement lawsuits. First, a court may not award attorneys' fees as a matter of course. Second, a court may not treat prevailing

Copyright Law: Definitions

plaintiffs and prevailing defendants differently. Third, multiple factors are to be considered, including: frivolousness, motivation, objective unreasonableness, and the need in particular circumstances to advance considerations of compensation and deterrence. The objective reasonableness of bringing the lawsuit or making a defense is "an important factor" but not a controlling one. (*Kirtsaeng v. John Wiley & Sons*, 579 U.S. ___ (2016).) Attorneys' fees may also be recovered under the Digital Millennium Copyright Act (17 U.S. Code § 1202), and (without registration), under the Visual Artists Rights Act (17 U.S. Code § 106A(a)).

Related terms: infringement action, registration.

attribution

Many people mistakenly believe that they can use copyrighted material as long as they credit the author. Providing the author's name for a quotation will not, by itself, excuse someone from a charge of infringement (or qualify the use as a fair use). That said, judges and juries may take attribution into consideration. For example, an author who provides attribution may be considered more favorably when a judge or jury makes a fair use determination or awards damages.

There is no requirement for attribution when reproducing public domain works. In a 2003 case, a film company had created film footage that had fallen into the public domain. When the footage was reproduced in another documentary, the film company argued that it should be credited. Why? Because the failure to do so would violate trademark laws, because it would confuse consumers as to the source of the footage. The U.S. Supreme Court disagreed and ruled that people who use public domain materials don't violate trademark laws by failing to provide credit to the creator of the materials. In other words, if you use public domain works, you don't need to provide attribution. (*Dastar Corp. v. Twentieth Century Fox Film Corp.*, 539 U.S. 23 (2003).)

Related terms: credit line.

Audio Home Recording Act

The Audio Home Recording Act of 1992 (AHRA) requires the manufacturers of certain digital devices to register with the Copyright Office and pay a statutory royalty on each device and piece of media sold. The Act is, for the most part, outdated because it covers only devices that are designed or marketed for the primary purpose of making digital musical recordings, such as DAT players and minidisc players—technologies that no longer account for much of the marketplace.

Had personal computers or CD burners been included in the AHRA, much of the battle about musical downloading might have been circumvented by a system that accounted for copying of musical compositions. Under the AHRA manufacturers also are obligated to use a copyright management system that permits a copy to be made from an original only (or first-generation copy). By following these rules, manufacturers immunize themselves against lawsuits claiming copyright infringement. Consumers are also immune from claims of infringement when using devices covered by the AHRA so long as the copying is done for noncommercial use.

Related terms: MP3.

audiovisual works

The Copyright Act defines audiovisual works as ones consisting of "a series of related images intended to be shown on machines such as projectors, viewers, or electronic equipment, with accompanying sounds, if any, whether the works are recorded on film, tape, or other material." (17 U.S. Code § 101.) The Copyright Act specifically protects movies, videotapes, videodiscs, CD-ROM multimedia packages, training films, and computer games as audiovisual works.

Related terms: Copyright Act of 1976; Form PA.

author

Under copyright law, the "author" of a work is either:

- the person who creates the work
- the person or business that pays another to create the work in the employment context, or
- the person or business that commissions the work under a valid work-made-for-hire contract.

For example, a songwriter might author a song, a movie producer might author a movie, a computer programmer might author a program, and a toy designer might author a toy (a toy's appearance might be protectable). In all these situations, however, if the creator does not work independently, but creates the work in an employment relationship or under a valid work-made-for-hire contract, the employer or person paying for the work is the author for copyright purposes. The author is the initial owner of the work and remains the owner unless the ownership rights are transferred, most likely by an assignment.

Related terms: assignment of copyright; transfers of copyright ownership; work made for hire.

Copyright Law: Definitions

authorized use as defense

One defense to infringement is that the owner granted permission for the use—in other words, that it was authorized. Usually, authorization is proven with a written agreement. But even in the absence of a written agreement, a defendant can argue that the use was authorized orally or was implied by the actions of the copyright owner. Were such a case to go to court, the judge would seek to determine the conditions under which the license or transfer was granted, what was transferred, and to whom.

Related terms: infringement (copyright); infringement action; transfers of copyright ownership.

automated databases

See computer databases.

based on an earlier work

See derivative work.

Berne Convention

Originally drafted in 1886, the Berne Convention is an international treaty that standardizes basic copyright protection among all of the countries signing it (currently over 100 member countries). For copyright purposes, a member country will afford the same treatment to an author from another country as it does to authors in its own country. In addition, each member country has agreed to protect what are called the author's "moral rights" in the work (generally, the right to proclaim or disclaim authorship and the right to protect the reputation of the work) and to extend copyright protection for at least the life of the author plus 50 years. No notice of copyright or other formality is required for basic copyright protection under the Berne Convention.

Under the General Agreement on Tariffs and Trade (GATT) treaty, enacted into U.S. law in December 1994, all signatories to GATT must also adhere to the Berne Convention if they don't already do so.

Related terms: GATT (General Agreement on Tariffs and Trade); Universal Copyright Convention (U.C.C.).

best edition of a work

To register a work with the U.S. Copyright Office, the author must deposit the best edition of the work with the application. The "best edition of a work" is usually the best-quality version of the work available at the time of registration or deposit. The U.S. Copyright Office has published a circular explaining the best version of a work for different types of deposits. Download Circular 7b from the U.S. Copyright Office's website (www.copyright.gov).

Copyright Act: § 101. Definitions
The "best edition" of a work is the edition, published in the United States at any time before the date of deposit, that the Library of Congress determines to be most suitable for its purposes.

Related terms: deposit with U.S. Copyright Office; U.S. Copyright Office.

BitTorrent

BitTorrent is an Internet software protocol that is especially efficient when transferring large files such as music, movies, or videogames. Although the BitTorrent software is legal and free to use, unauthorized BitTorrent transfers are sometimes difficult for copyright owners to stop. That's because the complete file is rarely stored in one piece; instead, the file is broken into identically sized pieces that are stored on different computers. The file is reassembled as the user makes a download. In 2010, a district court determined that BitTorrent protocols—when used to facilitate infringement—violated copyright law in the same manner as other peer-to-peer infringements despite the lack of a central server containing infringing copies of the material. (*Columbia Pictures Industries, Inc. v. Fung,* 447 F. Supp.2d 306 (C.D. Cal. 2009).) BitTorrent sites are usually not anonymous, and IP addresses (the unique numerical address for each computer) can be tracked by copyright owners with access to tracking logs.

blank forms

Since the U.S. Supreme Court's decision in *Baker v. Selden* (101 U.S. 99 (1879)), courts have considered blank forms to be unprotectable. The principle has been adopted in 37 C.F.R. 202.1(b), which states that registration will not be entertained for "blank forms, such as timecards, graph paper, account books, diaries, bank checks, scorecards, address books, report forms, order forms and the like, which are designed for recording information and do not in themselves convey information." This rule is based on the idea that these documents are either functional works, ideas, or works that can only be expressed in a limited number of ways. For example, the Eleventh Circuit determined that blank forms used for emergency room purposes were not copyrightable because the forms did not convey information. (*Utopia Provider Systems, Inc. v. Pro-Med Clinical Systems, LLC*, 596 F.3d 1313 (11th Cir. 2010).) And in 2020, the Tenth Circuit held that the layout of a personal planner—color-coded monthly calendars, and lined pages for making notes—was an idea, not the expression of an idea, and therefore, not protected by copyright. (*Craft Smith, LLC v. EC Design, LLC*, 969 F.3d 1092 (10th Cir. 2020).)

blog

A blog is a website (or portion of a website) where users typically post chronological journal entries. Blogs range from personalized vanity sites (for example, a teenager's diary, and so on) to corporate communication tools (for example, a business bulletin board). Each blog post usually contains one or more hyperlinks to other sites or references. In terms of copyright law, the same legal principles that apply to websites apply to blogs—that is, reproduction of unauthorized materials requires permission unless excused by fair use principles, and the use of links that encourage infringement can give rise to copyright infringement claims.

bootlegging of live performance

In 1994, as part of the implementation of the GATT Agreement, the United States passed legislation that allows a performer or record company to prevent the unauthorized recording of a live performance, even if the performer or record company does not own a copyright in any of the songs being performed. (17 U.S. Code § 1101.) Under this law, performers or record companies did not have to register with the Copyright Office in order to receive protection, and there was no limit on how long the protection lasts. In 2007, the Second Circuit upheld the law despite the fact that some critics contended the law provided "seemingly perpetual protection for unfixed musical performances." (*United States v. Martignon*, 492 F.3d 140 (2d Cir. 2007).)

browserwrap agreement

See end-user license.

Buenos Aires Convention

The Buenos Aires Convention establishes copyright reciprocity between the United States and most Latin American nations. However, because all of these member nations are now also members of larger international treaties that supersede the Buenos Aires Convention, this treaty has little, if any, remaining significance.

When the Buenos Aires Convention had more importance, it guaranteed copyright protection in its member countries if the statement "all rights reserved" was placed on all expressions for which copyright protection was being claimed. This is why the "all rights reserved" phrase appears as a part of so many copyright notices on published works, even if there is no longer any legal reason for it.

Related terms: international copyright protection.

caching

A "cache" refers to a storage area (usually temporary) where digital data is stored, enabling rapid access. It's commonly used to store an archival copy of an image of part or all of a website. With cached technology it is possible to search webpages that the website owner has permanently removed from display. In one case an attorney/author sued Google when the company's cached search results provided end users with copies of copyrighted works. The court held that Google did not infringe. Google was considered passive in the activity—users chose whether to view the cached link. Also, Google had an implied license to cache webpages because owners of websites have the ability to turn on or turn off the caching of their sites using tags and code. In this case, the attorney/author knew of this ability and failed to turn off caching, making his claim against Google more tenuous. (*Field v. Google Inc.*, 412 F. Supp.2d 1106 (D. Nev. 2006).)

Related terms: website.

CASE Act

The Copyright Alternative in Small-Claims Enforcement Act of 2020 (the CASE Act) creates a forum for small copyright claims. The law, enacted in 2021, requires the Copyright Office to create the Copyright Claims Board to decide copyright disputes. The board is authorized to hear copyright infringement claims, actions for a declaration of noninfringement, claims that a party knowingly sent false takedown notices, and related counterclaims. Damages awarded by the board are capped at $30,000. Participation in board proceedings is voluntary, and parties may choose instead to have a claim or defense heard in court. If the parties agree to have their dispute heard by the board, they give up the right to be heard before a court and the right to a jury trial.

The Act provides for various procedures, requests for information from the other party, and requests for the board to reconsider a decision. The board may issue monetary awards based on actual or statutory damages. The parties shall bear their own attorneys' fees and costs except where there is bad faith

Copyright Law: Definitions

misconduct, and such awards shall be limited to $5,000. A board's final determination precludes relitigating the claims in court or at the board, but parties may apply to a federal district court for review of the decision.

CDA

See Communications Decency Act § 230 (47 U.S. Code § 230).

cease and desist letter

The opening salvo in any copyright dispute is usually a cease and desist letter from the copyright owner's attorney. This letter typically informs the alleged infringer of the validity and ownership of the copyrighted work, the nature of the infringement, and the remedies that are available to the copyright holder unless the infringement is halted.

Related terms: damages for copyright infringement; infringement (copyright); infringement action.

certificate of registration

When the U.S. Copyright Office approves a copyright application for registration, it mails the author (or other owner) a certificate of registration. This certificate consists of the information in the copyright application, a copyright registration number, a registration date, the U.S. Copyright Office seal, and the signature of the Register of Copyrights.

If the copyright owner sues another party for infringement, the certificate can be used to prove that the copyright is valid. There is also a legal presumption that the certificate contains true statements—for example, the year the work was created, the fact of authorship, and whether other works are incorporated in the work being copyrighted. Copyright owners must register their work prior to suing for infringement under the provisions of 17 U.S. Code Section 411(a). (*Fourth Estate Public Benefit Corp. v. Wall-Street.com, LLC.*, 586 U.S. ___ (2019).)

Related terms: infringement (copyright); infringement action; supplemental registration.

characters, fictional

Fictional characters can be protected separately from their underlying works as derivative copyrights, provided that they are sufficiently unique and distinctive— for example, James Bond, Fred Flintstone, Hannibal Lecter, and Snoopy. Judge

Learned Hand established the standard for character protection in *Nichols v. Universal Pictures Corp.*, 45 F.2d 119 (2d Cir. 1930), when he stated that, "… the less developed the characters, the less they can be copyrighted; that is the penalty an author must bear for marking them too indistinctly."

For example, alien characters stranded on earth is a popular and recurring theme as portrayed in *My Favorite Martian, Starman, Paul, Alien Nation, Transformers, District 9, Predators,* and *The Man Who Fell to Earth.* The idea of a stranded alien character, without embellishment, is not protectable.

> EXAMPLE: A relatively unknown play (*Lokey From Maldemar*) featured an alien with powers of levitation and telepathy, stranded on earth and pursued by authoritarian characters. The playwright sued the owners of the movie *E.T.—The Extra-Terrestrial,* claiming that her character was infringed by the E.T. character. A federal court disagreed, ruling that that the character from Lokey was too indistinct to merit protection. (*Litchfield v. Spielberg,* 736 F.2d 1352 (9th Cir. 1984).)

However, once the stranded alien acquires more distinctive characteristics—for example, a big-headed, long-necked alien with a glowing finger who murmurs "Phone home"—it is distinct enough to merit protection and its owners can prevent others from using his image and expression. (*Universal Studios, Inc. v. J.A.R. Sales, Inc.,* 216 U.S.P.Q. 679 (C.D. Cal. 1982); *Universal Studios, Inc. v. Kamar Indus. Inc.,* 217 U.S.P.Q. 1165 (S.D. Tex. 1982).)

Exploitation of fictional characters is a crucial source of revenue for entertainment and merchandising companies. Characters such as Superman and Mickey Mouse are the foundations of massive entertainment franchises and are commonly protected under both copyright and trademark law.

Objects that emulate character qualities may also be protected as copyrightable characters. In 2015, the Ninth Circuit protected the Batmobile under copyright law, noting that it has "physical as well as conceptual qualities" and is "sufficiently delineated" to be recognizable. (*DC Comics v. Mark Towle,* 802 F.3d 1012 (9th Cir. 2015).)

The protection afforded to fictional characters sometimes clashes with the fair use right to comment upon or criticize those characters. This is particularly common in parody cases. For example, one court refused to permit an X-rated parody, *Scarlett Fever,* that used characters from *Gone with the Wind.* (*Metro-Goldwyn-Mayer, Inc. v. Showcase Atlanta Cooperative Productions, Inc.,* 479 F. Supp. 351 (N.D. Ga. 1979).

Another court permitted publication of a novel using characters from *Gone with the Wind* but written from a slave's perspective. (*Suntrust Bank v. Houghton Mifflin Co.,* 268 F.2d 1257 (11th Cir. 2001).) The disparity in the two opinions—both based on *Gone with the Wind*—might be due to the fact that in one work the characters were lampooned in a broad sexual farce, while in the other the characters were used to provoke discussion about racial stereotypes.

Related terms: derivative work; parody and fair use.
See also Part 4 (Trademark Law): characters as trademarks.

charts, copyrightability of

See flow charts, registration of.

choreography and pantomime

Choreography is the composition and arrangement of dance movement and patterns, often accompanied by music. A registrable choreographic work should be capable of being performed and usually includes direction for movement. Popular dance steps such as the cha-cha and other simple routines are not copyrightable.

Pantomime or "mime" is considered a mute performance with expressive communication. Because it is a form of acting that consists mostly of gestures, there is an overlap in the categorization of pantomime and dramatic works. Traditionally, pantomime and choreographic works are fixed in a system of written notation, but the copyright act provides that they also may be fixed in any tangible medium including film, video, or photographs.

Like all copyrightable works, choreographic and pantomimic productions can qualify for copyright protection when fixed in a tangible medium of expression such as film, video, written score, or recording. To register these types of works with the U.S. Copyright Office, the owner must use Form PA.

Although choreography and pantomime disputes are rare under copyright law, they arise occasionally.

EXAMPLE: The works of dancer Martha Graham came under scrutiny in 2002 when a federal court ruled that the bulk of her dance compositions (45 out of 61) belonged to the Martha Graham Center for Contemporary Dance because she had composed them while she worked as an employee for the Center. In addition, ten of her dance compositions were found to be in the public domain. (*Martha Graham School and Dance Foundation, Inc. v. Martha Graham Center for Contemporary Dance, Inc.,* 224 F. Supp.2d 567 (2002).)

When registering a choreographic work or pantomime, the applicant typically submits either video, a text, and photographic/drawing description, or classic dance notation. Registration of dance routines is subject to scrutiny. The actor Alfonso Ribeiro, of *The Fresh Prince of Bel Air*, filed a suit against the creators of Fortnite—Epic Games—alleging imitation of his special dance moves, namely, "The Carlton." When he sought to register this work, however, the Copyright Office rejected the application on the grounds that the Carlton consisted of a simple combination of three dance steps.

Related terms: Form PA; parody and fair use; registration.

clearinghouses, copyright

Copyright clearinghouses organize and license works by their members. A person who wants to use one of these works contacts the clearinghouse and— depending on how the organization is structured—pays a fee and acquires a limited right to use the work for a specific purpose. Clearinghouses speed up the permissions process by providing a central source for a class or type of work. For example, Copyright Clearance Center (www.copyright.com) provides permission for written materials. BMI (www.bmi.com) and ASCAP (www.ascap.com) provide permission for musical performances. Harry Fox Agency (www.harryfox.com) provides permission to reproduce songs. Getty (www.gettyimages.com) is one of several clearinghouses that grant permission to use photographs. Art Resource (www.artres.com) grants permission for famous artwork. The Cartoonbank (www.cartoonbank.com) is one of several clearinghouses that license cartoons.

Related terms: permission.

clickwrap agreement

See end-user license.

coauthors

Two or more people who have contributed significant creative input to a work of expression are legally considered coauthors. Coauthorship can take several forms and the most common is a joint work, where the authors intend that their separate contributions be merged into a unified whole. Coauthors of a joint work share in the copyright of the whole work equally, unless they have signed a joint ownership agreement that provides differently. Absent an agreement to the contrary, any coauthor may use the expression covered by the copyright without permission of other coauthors but must account to the other coauthors and equally share with them any profits realized from the use.

Other forms of coauthorship appear in collective works and derivative works with more than one author, where each author owns only the copyright of the material he or she created:

- **Collective works.** Coauthors intend to keep their contributions separate—for instance, where one coauthor is separately credited for chapters 1 through 10 and the other coauthor is credited for chapters 11 through 20.
- **Coauthored derivative works.** Two or more authors create separate works and only later decide to combine them in one work.

Related terms: collaboration agreement (coauthor agreement); collective work; derivative work; joint work.

collaboration agreement (coauthor agreement)

When coauthors want to specify their rights, obligations, and percentage of copyright ownership and revenues, they enter into a collaboration (or coauthor) agreement. Without a collaboration agreement or other evidence to the contrary, a court will presume that the coauthors share equally.

Related terms: coauthors; collective work; joint work.

collective work

A work such as a periodical, anthology, wiki, or encyclopedia, in which a number of separate and independent works are assembled into one work, is referred to as a collective work. (17 U.S. Code § 101.) A collective work is a type of compilation, but, unlike other compilations such as a directory or book of quotes, the underlying elements assembled into a collective work can be separately protected; for example, a collection of short stories by John Updike or a collection of "greatest disco hits" recordings from the 1970s. Other examples of collective works would include a newspaper, a group of film clips, or a poetry anthology. To create a collective work, either public domain materials must be used or the owners of the copyrights in the constituent parts must give their permissions. Assuming that these rules are followed, the creativity involved in organizing and selecting the constituent materials is itself subject to independent copyright protection.

> EXAMPLE: Phil prepares an anthology of what he considers to be the best American poems published in the years 1900 and 2000, calling this collective work *American Poetry—A Century of Difference*. Each poem from 2000 is a separate and independent work protected by its own copyright. To use these poems, Phil must get the permission of each copyright owner. But because copyright protection has

run out on the 1900 poems, they are now in the public domain and Phil can use them without obtaining anyone's permission. Once all needed permissions are assembled, Phil has created a new protectable collective work and owns a copyright in the choice and organization of the poems, but not in any specific poem.

Many collective works have been preserved in digital format. However, when a collective work (or compilation) is provided in conjunction with a software program—for example, a program that organizes or creates clip art versions of images on a disk—two separate copyrights are at work. One copyright is in the collective work, for example, the collection of images, and the other copyright is in the underlying program. In order to assert rights in both, each must be separately registered. (*Xoom, Inc. v. Imageline, Inc.,* 323 F.3d 279 (4th Cir. 2003).)

Copyright Act: § 101. Definitions
A "collective work" is a work, such as a periodical issue, anthology, or encyclopedia, in which a number of contributions, constituting separate and independent works in themselves, are assembled into a collective whole.

Related terms: compilations; original work of authorship.

commissioned work

See work made for hire.

common law copyright

Prior to 1978, copyright law protected only published works. Unpublished works were protected under rules known as common law copyright (also sometimes referred to as "state copyright"). The 1976 Copyright Act (effective 1978) extended protection to unpublished works and replaced common law copyright rules. Issues of common law copyright rarely arise.

Related terms: Copyright Act of 1909; Copyright Act of 1976.

Communications Decency Act § 230 (47 U.S. Code § 230)

The Communications Decency Act (CDA), signed into law in 1996, was intended to restrict a minor's access to sexually explicit materials online. However, the Supreme Court gutted the bill when it struck down the anti-obscenity provisions. (*Reno v. American Civil Liberties Union,* 521 U.S. 844 (1997).) Among the provisions that survived was Section 230, which stated in part, "No provider or user of an interactive computer service shall be treated as the publisher or speaker of any information provided by another information content provider." This

Copyright Law: Definitions

provision allows online services that publish third-party content to escape liability (even if notified of the wrongdoing). One exception to this blanket liability is that Section 230 shall not "be construed to limit or expand any law pertaining to intellectual property." So, for example, a provider who is notified of copyright infringing material posted at its site must take steps to remove the content or face the potential of vicarious liability.

Related terms: vicarious liability (copyright).

compilations

A compilation is a work formed by selecting, collecting, and assembling preexisting materials or data in a novel way that forms an original work of authorship. Examples of compilations are databases (collections of information arranged in a way to facilitate updating and retrieval), anthologies, and collective works. (17 U.S. Code § 101.)

The creative aspects of a compilation—such as the way it is organized and the selection of the materials to be included—are entitled to copyright protection whether or not the individual parts are in the public domain or are subject to another owner's copyright.

> EXAMPLE: Harry assembles sheet music of national anthems (public domain) for a music book. If Harry simply published the anthems in alphabetical order without enhancing or organizing them in a special way or combining them with other materials, the collection would not be protected, because it is not considered to be creative. If, on the other hand, Harry compiled a selection of his anthems for countries that have been at war with each other ("Battling Anthems"), the compilation (but not the music) is more likely to qualify for copyright protection, because the act of selecting the anthems involved some creative work on Harry's part. If it did qualify, Harry could stop others who copied his work from creating a similar compilation.

Copyright Act: § 101. Definitions

A "compilation" is a work formed by the collection and assembling of preexisting materials or of data that are selected, coordinated, or arranged in such a way that the resulting work as a whole constitutes an original work of authorship. The term "compilation" includes collective works.

Copyright Act: § 103. Subject matter of copyright: Compilations and derivative works

(a) The subject matter of copyright as specified by section 102 includes compilations and derivative works, but protection for a work employing preexisting material in which copyright subsists does not extend to any part of the work in which such material has been used unlawfully.

(b) The copyright in a compilation or derivative work extends only to the material contributed by the author of such work, as distinguished from the preexisting material employed in the work, and does not imply any exclusive right in the preexisting material. The copyright in such work is independent of, and does not affect or enlarge the scope, duration, ownership, or subsistence of, any copyright protection in the preexisting material.

Related terms: collective works, damages for copyright infringement; *Feist Publications Inc. v. Rural Telephone Service Co.*; original work of authorship.

compulsory license

In order to reproduce, perform, or distribute a copyrighted work, permission must be obtained from the copyright owner. However, in a few circumstances—known as compulsory licenses—a copyright owner's permission is not required provided that the user follows certain rules and pays fees set by law. Such compulsory licenses are commonly used by satellite TV providers, cable providers, webcasters, and music companies.

One of the most common uses of a compulsory license is in the music industry. Once a song has been recorded and distributed to the public on recordings, any person or group is entitled to record and distribute the song without obtaining the copyright owner's consent, provided they pay a fee and meet copyright law requirements.

In order to take advantage of this compulsory license, a notice must be sent to the copyright owner along with a fee set by the Copyright Office known as the statutory fee or statutory rate. The fee for physical recordings and permanent downloads is currently 9.1 cents per song (or 1.75 cents per minute of playing time). To verify the current rate, check the Copyright Office's online rate list at http://copyright.gov/licensing/m200a.pdf. If a song is three minutes long and an artist makes 1,000 MP3s of the song, the fee paid to the song's owner would be $91. A recording artist does not have to use the compulsory license, and many recording artists seek permission directly from the song owner and negotiate for a lower rate.

> EXAMPLE: Lou writes and releases the song "Up the Stairs." Later, Barry decides he wants to record "Up the Stairs." If Barry is willing to pay the statutory fee, he does not need to ask Lou for permission—but if he wants to pay less per copy, he must obtain permission from Lou.

Keep in mind that the compulsory license for recording music (the mechanical license) only authorizes the use of the song for nondramatic musical compositions and you could not, under the compulsory license, use the song for dramatic purposes such as in an opera or an overture to a musical. The compulsory license only applies to physical copies (phonorecords) and digital downloads (permanent downloads) distributed to the public. Therefore, it cannot be used to record a song for use on a television show's soundtrack. In that case, permission must be obtained from the copyright owner. It is possible to obtain compulsory licenses online through companies such as SongFile (www.songfile.com), a division of the Harry Fox agency.

Under the terms of a compulsory license, the licensee is permitted to make a new arrangement of the composition as long as the basic melody or fundamental character of the work is not altered.

> EXAMPLE: Sammy composes and records a country ballad. Later, Pauline, a punk rap star, acquires a compulsory license and records Sammy's song but changes the words and eliminates the melody. Sammy can have Pauline's compulsory license revoked and prevent the recording from being distributed further or played.

Under the 2018 Music Modernization Act, a new music licensing collective (MLC) will take effect in 2021. Once in place, the MLC will act as a toll booth for Spotify, Pandora, SoundCloud, and other streaming music providers. These providers will pay the MLC for each use of a song, and the MLC will compensate the owners accordingly.

In a different context, and without regard to the type of work involved, the concept of a compulsory license can arise in a copyright infringement action. A court has the power to order a copyright owner to grant a license to an innocent infringer instead of ordering the infringement stopped.

Finally, in countries that subscribe to the Universal Copyright Convention (U.C.C.), including the United States, an author may be required to grant a compulsory license to a subscribing government to translate his or her work into that country's primary language if no translation has been published within seven years of the work's original date of publication. This rule precludes copyright owners in most countries from preventing the translation of works covered by their copyrights into different languages.

Related terms: derivative work; innocent infringement of copyright; mechanical rights; musical works and sound recordings distinguished.

Computer Associates Int'l v. Altai

See infringement (copyright).

computer databases

A computer database, sometimes known as an automated database, is a collection of information or resources placed in a computer and organized to allow for rapid updating and retrieval. Examples of computer databases are:

- a mailing list organized so that mailings can be made according to certain criteria such as the residential area, average personal income, or interests of the recipient
- a compilation of articles published on a particular subject (for example, female Parkinson's disease sufferers over 80) organized so that people can quickly retrieve and read the article dealing with their particular point of interest, and
- a listing of all items in a store's inventory arranged to permit an analysis by such variables as supplier, kind of product, price, and length of time in stock.

Computer databases commonly consist both of materials protected by copyright and materials that are said to be in the public domain, either because their copyright has run out or because they consist of ideas and facts that themselves do not receive copyright protection.

Despite the fact that the database owner might not own any copyright interest in any of the material in the database, the structure and organization of the database itself can qualify as an original work of authorship and thus be subject to copyright protection as a compilation.

Although the original expression implicit in the structure and organization of a computer database is entitled to copyright protection, the labor and cost associated with building a database is not protected by copyright. For instance, the labor and cost associated with compiling an alphabetical telephone directory does not protect the information in the directory from being copied by others, because there was no creativity exercised in building the database.

Similarly, copyright owners of a software program that gathers public domain information cannot seek to extend database protection over the information that the users gather with the software.

Copyright Law: Definitions

EXAMPLE: A company owned by the Multiple Listing Service (MLS) sought public data about real estate from county and municipal assessors. Several municipalities refused to furnish it, claiming that to do so would violate the copyright of a rival company that had already solicited and categorized the information in a database using customized software. The Seventh Circuit Court of Appeals ruled that the process of furnishing (or extracting) the raw data did not violate copyright law and did not create a derivative work. (*Assessment Technologies of WI LLC v. WIREData Inc.*, 350 F.3d 640 (7th Cir. 2003).)

Computer databases can be registered with the U.S. Copyright Office. For more information on preparing the registration, see Copyright Office Circulars 65 and 66.

Related terms: compilations; *Feist Publications Inc. v. Rural Telephone Service Co.*; Form TX.

computer software

See software.

Computer Software Protection Act of 1980

See archival copies; software.

Computer Software Rental Amendments Act of 1990

See first sale doctrine.

contributory infringement

Contributory infringement occurs when someone knows of (or should have known of) infringing activity and induces or substantially contributes to it. Technology developments brought the issue of contributory infringement further to the forefront. In the 1980s the issue arose as to whether the sale of videocassette recorders amounted to contributory infringement because the manufacturer knew that some buyers of the device used it for infringing purposes. The Supreme Court held that manufacturers of devices that are capable of substantial noninfringing uses should not be held liable as contributory infringers. (*Sony Corp. of America v. Universal City Studios, Inc.*, 464 U.S. 417 (1984).) Thirty years later, the Supreme Court held that a company that distributes software that enables file sharing on peer-to-peer networks, could be considered a contributory infringer. (*Metro-Goldwyn-Mayer Studios, Inc. v. Grokster, Ltd.*, 545 U.S. 913, 936-37 (2005).)

Similarly, by combining instant messaging with a peer-to-peer music sharing network, AOL committed contributory infringement. (*In re Aimster*, 334 F.3d 643 (7th Cir. 2003).) Another line of contributory infringement cases deals with the liability of entities that rent space to infringers. For example, a department store owner that rented space with the knowledge that some of is tenants were selling bootleg merchandise was a contributory infringer. (*Shapiro, Bernstein and Co. v. H.L. Green Co.*, 316 F.2d 304 (2d Cir. 1963).) Similarly, a flea market operator that leased stalls with knowledge that some vendors were selling infringing merchandise was liable as a contributory infringer. (*Fonovisa, Inc. v. Cherry Auction, Inc.*, 76 F.3d 259 (9th Cir. 1996).)

Related terms: vicarious liability (copyright).

copies

For purposes of the copyright law, a copy is the physical form in which an expression is retained over time, no matter how brief. This includes such things as photocopies, tape recordings, photographs, manuscripts, printings, molds (for example, for plastic toy designs), computer hard drives, thumb drives, videotapes, videodiscs, CDs, and DVDs. The placing of a program in dynamic computer memory (RAM) for a brief period of time has also been treated as copying, which can constitute an infringement under the copyright act. (*Mai v. Peak*, 991 F.2d 511 (9th Cir. 1993).)

The Copyright Act defines copies as "material objects, other than phonorecords, in which a work is fixed by any method now known or later developed, and from which the work can be perceived, reproduced, or otherwise communicated, either directly or with the aid of a machine or device." (17 U.S. Code § 101.)

The right to prepare copies of an original work of authorship—that is, put the work into some fixed form—is one of the primary rights protected by the overall copyright.

Copyright Act: § 101. Definitions

"Copies" are material objects, other than phonorecords, in which a work is fixed by any method now known or later developed, and from which the work can be perceived, reproduced, or otherwise communicated, either directly or with the aid of a machine or device. The term "copies" includes the material object, other than a phonorecord, in which the work is first fixed.

Related terms: copyright; infringement (copyright); photocopies.

Copyright Law: Definitions

copyfraud

This term, coined by a law professor, is applied to those parties that deliberately assert copyright ownership when they do not own such rights. Typically, this occurs when someone attempts to control the use of public domain materials— for example, by prohibiting copying of artwork clearly in the public domain. Although copyright law criminalizes fraudulent uses of copyright notices (Section 506(c)) and punishes false statements in copyright registrations (Section 506(e)), there is no specific prohibition for this form of copyright misuse.

Copyleft

Copyleft refers to a grassroots movement formed in protest to perceived abuses of copyright—for example, cases brought under the Digital Millennium Copyright Act or the extension of copyright per the Copyright Term Extension Act. Comprising librarians, legal scholars, historians, artists, musicians, archivists, website creators, and many others, the Copyleft seeks through public awareness and litigation to rebalance the rights of authors and the public under copyright law. Leaders of the Copyleft such as professors Larry Lessig and Jonathan Zittrain believe that copyright has become a permission-based enterprise and that it should be returned to its Jeffersonian roots—that is, to encourage rather than stifle creativity. The Copyleft movement was a strong supporter of Eric Eldred and his unsuccessful effort to terminate the 1998 copyright extension. (*Eldred v. Ashcroft,* 537 U.S. 186 (2003).)

Related terms: Creative Commons; *Eldred v. Ashcroft.*

copyright

A copyright consists of a bundle of rights held by the author or developer of an original work of authorship. The term "copyright" applies both to the entire bundle of rights and to any individual right or part of an individual right:

- the exclusive right to make copies
- the exclusive right to authorize others to make copies
- the exclusive right to make derivative works (that is, similar works based on the original, such as translations or updated versions)
- the exclusive right to sell (market) the work
- the exclusive right to display the work
- the exclusive right to perform the work (such as plays and musical compositions), and
- the exclusive right to obtain court relief in the event others infringe (violate) these rights.

Each of these exclusive rights can be sold separately through transfers of copyright ownership. For example, a transfer might give a party the exclusive right to make derivative works from an original work. In addition, each right may be divided, giving different parties exclusive rights during different periods of time or in different geographical areas.

Under the laws of most countries, any original work of authorship is considered the property of its owner; others are prevented from using this property without the owner's consent. The owner is usually the originator of the work—the actual author or somebody who paid for the work under an employment agreement or work-made-for-hire contract. Sometimes, however, full ownership is transferred to somebody else before the work is finished. For instance, it is common for freelance software programmers to assign all of their copyright rights in a program to the publisher before programming begins, in exchange for advance royalties or payments to be received in phases as the project progresses. Usually termed a "grant of rights," this type of transfer shifts ownership of the copyright from the author to the publisher.

Among the categories of expressive works that are protected by copyright throughout the world are:

- literary works
- audiovisual works
- computer software
- graphic works
- musical arrangements, and
- sound recordings.

In short, practically any type of expression that can be fixed in a tangible medium of expression is eligible for copyright protection, assuming it is original and has at least some creativity. It is important to understand, however, that copyright law protects only the expression itself—not the underlying facts, ideas, or concepts. This means it is often possible to legitimately produce an expression very similar to one that is already protected by copyright, as long as the original expression itself is not copied or used as a basis for the later work. The more factual in nature the original work, the more similar the second work can be without infringement occurring. Conversely, works of fiction are more susceptible to infringement claims, because they tend to involve far more original expression than do nonfiction works.

Copyright Law: Definitions

Although a copyright owner's permission must be obtained to make copies for commercial purposes, it is sometimes possible to copy without permission in situations collectively labeled as "fair use." These tend to be for educational and nonprofit purposes—situations where there is little or no commercial motive for using the material and the use of the material won't interfere with the natural market for the work being used.

Under the Copyright Act of 1976, an original work of authorship gains copyright protection the instant it becomes fixed in a tangible form. This means that such protection is available for both published and unpublished works. The protection lasts for:

- the life of the author plus 70 years, or
- 95 years from the date of publication or 120 years from the date of creation, whichever is shorter, if the author is an employer or commissioner of a work made for hire, or if the author uses a pseudonym or remains anonymous.

In addition to the automatic protection extended a copyright owner by the law, it is possible to gain crucially important protective benefits in the United States by placing a proper copyright notice on the work and registering it with the U.S. Copyright Office. If the registration occurs in a timely manner (either within three months of publication or before the infringing activity begins), it is easier for the copyright owner to obtain effective relief against infringers.

Related terms: copyright owner; duration of copyrights; fair use; infringement (copyright); timely registration; transfers of copyright ownership.

Copyright Act of 1909

This federal statute governed copyrights in the United States between 1910 and 1978. Works first published prior to January 1, 1978, are still covered by the 1909 Act, unless the copyright has expired. The main practical differences between the 1909 Copyright Act and the 1976 Copyright Act (which replaced the 1909 Act) are:

- The 1909 Act granted protection only to published works. The 1976 Act extends its protection to both published and unpublished works.
- Protection under the 1909 Act could be permanently lost if even a single copy was distributed without the proper notice of copyright. The 1976 Act provided that the absence of a proper notice could be cured under certain circumstances. Moreover, as of March 1989, there is no longer any requirement for a notice.

Note: The GATT (General Agreement on Tariffs and Trade) restored copyright protection for works of foreign authors that fell into the public domain in the United States prior to March 1989 because of faulty notice. These restored copyrights have the same duration as they would have had if they not been considered to be in the public domain.

Related terms: common law copyright; copyright; Copyright Act of 1976; notice of copyright; restored copyright under GATT.

Copyright Act of 1976

This comprehensive federal statute governs copyright protection for original works of authorship created after January 1, 1978. Found in Title 17, U.S. Code, Sections 100 and following, the 1976 Copyright Act (as amended from time to time) is the exclusive source of copyright law in the United States for works published after January 1, 1978. It preempts (replaces) all state laws that affect rights covered by this Act.

Related terms: audiovisual works; copyright; Copyright Act of 1909; infringement action; original work of authorship.

copyright and patent compared

Copyright law protects all forms of expression fixed in a tangible medium, but not the underlying ideas. Patents protect ideas that take the form of useful, novel, and nonobvious inventions—for instance, production methods, devices, substances, and mechanical processes.

Copyright and patent do intersect, however, in two important areas:

- **Product design.** Both copyright and design patent law may be used to protect a product's design, as long as the design does not affect how the product functions. A design patent is more time-consuming and expensive to obtain than a copyright, but it offers a broader scope of protection. That's because under design patent law, you can stop anyone who uses the same design; but under copyright law, you can stop only those who copy your design, not those who independently create the same design. On the other hand, copyright protection lasts for the life of the author, whereas design patent protection lasts for only 15 years from the date the patent issues. As mentioned, these two approaches to protecting original designs are not exclusive of each other. For instance, a truly innovative but functionless design for a computer might qualify for both copyright protection (as a pictorial, graphic, or sculptural work) and for a design patent (as a purely ornamental design of an article of manufacture).

- **Software.** Both copyright and patent may be used to protect software. A copyright may protect the program's literal expression and perhaps its structure, sequence, and organization. A patent may issue on the program's innovative approach to solving a particular problem or producing a particular result in a computer or other type of machine, such as a robot or remote vehicle. As with designs, patent protection is broader than that afforded by copyright because the patent creates a monopoly over the ideas covered by the patent, whereas the copyright protects only the expression itself. In addition, a copyright owner can stop only someone who has copied the software. A patent owner can stop anyone who is making, selling, or using the software, regardless of whether it has been copied or developed independently.

Related terms: software; pictorial, graphic, and sculptural works.
See also Part 1 (Patent Law): design patents; software patents.

copyright claimant

A copyright claimant is the party considered to be the basic owner of the copyright in a work being registered with the U.S. Copyright Office. The copyright claimant may be any of the following:
- the actual author of the work
- an employer (also considered the actual author) whose employee created the work in the scope of employment
- a party who commissioned a work made for hire, as defined in the Copyright Act (also considered the actual author)
- a party to whom all rights in a work have been assigned, or
- a party who has come to own all of the exclusive rights that make up the copyright.

The name of the copyright claimant must be included in the copyright registration form filed with the U.S. Copyright Office as part of the registration process.

Related terms: registration.

copyright infringement

See infringement (copyright).

copyright management information (CMI)

Copyright management information (CMI) is information conveyed with a copyrighted work that identifies the owner and nature of that copyright. The Digital Millennium Copyright Act of 1998 prohibits the removal or falsification of CMI as well as the distribution of such altered works. The Act specifically defines copyright management information as:

- The title and other information identifying the work, including the information set forth on a notice of copyright.
- The name of, and other identifying information about, the author of a work.
- The name of, and other identifying information about, the copyright owner of the work, including the information set forth in a notice of copyright.
- With the exception of public performances of works by radio and television broadcast stations, the name of, and other identifying information about, a performer whose performance is fixed in a work other than an audiovisual work.
- With the exception of public performances of works by radio and television broadcast stations, in the case of an audiovisual work, the name of, and other identifying information about, a writer, performer, or director who is credited in the audiovisual work.

In 2011, the Third Circuit determined that the CMI rules also applied to non-digital works.

> EXAMPLE: A photographer's copyrighted picture of two nude radio "shock jocks" was published in the *New Jersey Monthly*. The radio station that employed the men scanned and posted the photo online (after removing the photo credit that ran alongside the photo known in the trade as a "gutter credit"). The station then encouraged listeners to download the photo, modify it, and resubmit the photos to the station for posting. The Third Circuit ruled that the "gutter credit" qualified as CMI and cutting it off the photo violated the DMCA. (*Murphy v. Millennium Radio Group*, 650 F.3d 295 (3d Cir. 2011).)

In 2018, the Ninth Circuit held that removing CMI wasn't enough, by itself, to justify a claim. The party asserting the violation must offer specific evidence that the removal of the CMI impaired the copyright owner's ability to police possible infringement. (*Stevens v. Corelogic, Inc.*, 899 F.3d 666 (9th Cir. 2018).)

Related terms: Digital Millennium Copyright Act (1998); digital rights management (DRM).

Copyright Law: Definitions

copyright notice

See notice of copyright.

copyright office

See U.S. Copyright Office.

copyright owner

"Copyright owner" refers to the person or entity listed as the owner in the U.S. Copyright Office and on any notice attached to the copyrighted work. This is either the original author or a person or entity to whom all rights under the copyright have been transferred.

"Copyright owner" also refers to a person or entity who owns one or more of the five exclusive rights that make up the whole copyright, and who therefore has a right to sue infringers of that right. These constituent rights, which may be separately owned and assigned (sold), consist of:

- the right to reproduce (copy) the work
- the right to prepare derivative works
- the right to distribute copies of the work
- the right to perform the work, and
- the right to display the work.

EXAMPLE: June writes a novel and owns the copyright on the expression contained in it. June grants an exclusive worldwide license (permission) to Henry to publish and distribute her novel. She also gives Ernest the exclusive right to prepare a screenplay (a derivative work) based on the novel. Because these rights are exclusive, both Henry and Ernest are legally considered copyright owners.

In addition to separately licensing basic copyright rights, a copyright owner can separately license subparts of each right.

EXAMPLE: Vixen Publications purchases the entire copyright in Andrew's book before it is written, in exchange for a royalties advance. Vixen is now the copyright owner and has the right to transfer parts of its copyright ownership to others. Vixen licenses exclusive German language book rights to a German publisher, exclusive French language book rights to a French publisher, and exclusive Russian language book rights to a Russian publisher. Each of the entities receiving exclusive rights under these licenses would also be considered a copyright owner.

Although different people or entities can own different rights based on a copyright and be considered copyright owners, there is only one actual "copyright." Unless the original owner (the author, employer, commissioner of a work made for hire, or assignee of all rights) transfers all of the exclusive rights set out above to one or more parties, that original owner is still considered by the U.S. Copyright Office to be the copyright owner.

Copyright Act: § 201. Ownership of copyright

(a) Initial Ownership.—Copyright in a work protected under this title vests initially in the author or authors of the work. The authors of a joint work are co-owners of copyright in the work.

(b) Works Made for Hire.—In the case of a work made for hire, the employer or other person for whom the work was prepared is considered the author for purposes of this title, and, unless the parties have expressly agreed otherwise in a written instrument signed by them, owns all of the rights comprised in the copyright.

(c) Contributions to Collective Works.—Copyright in each separate contribution to a collective work is distinct from copyright in the collective work as a whole, and vests initially in the author of the contribution. In the absence of an express transfer of the copyright or of any rights under it, the owner of copyright in the collective work is presumed to have acquired only the privilege of reproducing and distributing the contribution as part of that particular collective work, any revision of that collective work, and any later collective work in the same series.

Related terms: author; copyright claimant; standing (to sue); transfers of copyright ownership.

copyright protection

See affirmative rights.

copyright registration

See registration.

copyright registration forms

The Copyright Office provides applicants for registration with two methods of copyright registration. Applicants may (1) file using the online eCO system (currently $45 to $65 per application); or (2) file using traditional paper forms (currently $125 per application) such as Form TX for nondramatic literary works, including computer programs, Form PA for audiovisual works, Form VA for graphic art and sculptural works, Form SR for sound recordings, and Form SE for serials and periodicals. Copyright forms can be downloaded from the copyright office website (www.copyright.gov).

Copyright Law: Definitions

Related terms: registration.

Copyright Remedy Clarification Act ("CRCA")

See sovereign immunity.

creation of work

Once a work is created, it's entitled to copyright protection. But when is a work created?

Rule 1: Creation of a work occurs when it first becomes "fixed" in some form.

Rule 2: Drafts and other intermediate forms in the development of a work receive copyright protection just like the underlying work does.

Rule 3: Each new version of an original work is a separate creation.

EXAMPLE: Todd creates complex charts showing the relationships among scientific concepts in different fields. Todd often carries an idea for a particular chart around in his head for weeks before he jots it down in physical (tangible) form. Once his idea becomes fixed in a tangible form, whether on paper, programmed on a computer, or constructed out of plastic or other materials, Todd has created a work of authorship. Todd typically changes and improves the physical representation of his original idea. Each new version of Todd's chart becomes an original work as of the moment it becomes fixed in a tangible form. As long as Todd is working on a given chart, he has created only one work, despite a number of incremental changes. If, however, Todd produces his chart both in a print version and in a specially tailored computerized slide show, he would have two different versions of the same work and could obtain separate copyright protection for each. Separate copyrights might also be available for two different charts based on the same idea, regardless of the medium used.

Copyright Act: § 101. Definitions

A work is "created" when it is fixed in a copy or phonorecord for the first time; where a work is prepared over a period of time, the portion of it that has been fixed at any particular time constitutes the work as of that time, and where the work has been prepared in different versions, each version constitutes a separate work.

Related terms: derivative work; fixed in a tangible medium of expression.

Creative Commons

The Creative Commons is a nonprofit enterprise that encourages copyright owners to share their works with the public in various innovative ways including dedications to the public domain or through a series of licenses. For example, under one system, copyright owners can elect to use what the Commons calls "Founders' Copyright"—the original copyright term adopted by the first copyright law in 1790. This consists of an initial term of 14 years after publication, and an additional 14 years if the copyright owner wants it. The copyright owner fills out an online application and sells the copyright to the Creative Commons for $1, and then the organization gives the owner an exclusive license to the work for 14 or 28 years. If desired, users of the dedicated works can be required to provide attribution to the original author. In these cases, a failure to provide attribution can lead to a copyright infringement lawsuit. (*Philpott v. Alternet Media*, No. 18-04479 (N.D. Cal. 2018).) Works so dedicated to the public domain are listed in the Creative Commons website so people can find them easily For detailed information, see the Creative Commons website (https://creativecommmons.org).

Related terms: Copyleft.

credit line

A written acknowledgment of authorship is referred to as a credit line. When authors give permission for somebody else to use a portion or an entire work, they commonly condition the permission on including a line crediting the original author in the new work. Credit lines may become part of a work's copyright management information (CMI) and removal of this information may violate the Digital Millennium Copyright Act.

Related terms: attribution; copyright management information (CMI).

criminal copyright infringement

Infringement of a copyright can be treated as a federal crime under the Copyright Act (17 U.S. Code § 506) if it is done intentionally and with full knowledge that an infringement is occurring. As a practical matter, the U.S. Department of Justice only brings criminal charges against copyright infringers when a substantial amount of money is at stake and the purpose of the infringement is commercial gain.

An infringer who commits one or more infringements during a 180-day period for "purposes of commercial advantage or private financial gain" can be fined and imprisoned for one to five years depending upon the value of the infringements. Repeat violations can result in fines and imprisonment for up to ten years.

Regardless of whether there is financial gain, an infringer can be liable for fines and up to three years in jail if the infringement is ten or more copies of one or more copyrighted works that have a total retail value of $2,500. Repeat offenders can be liable for jail time of up to six years.

The government will also prosecute anyone who knowingly and willfully aids in a criminal infringement. The government will not prosecute innocent infringers, that is, persons who had a good-faith reason to believe that copying was permitted, although those persons can still be subject to a civil lawsuit.

Willful violators of the Digital Millennium Copyright Act (and those who do it for purposes of financial gain) can be subject to fines of not more than $500,000 or imprisonment for not more than five years, or both, for the first offense, and fines of not more than $1,000,000 or imprisonment for not more than ten years, or both, for any subsequent offense.

Finally, the Family Entertainment and Copyright Act of 2005 made it a crime to videotape or transmit video signals from inside a movie theater, and to knowingly place a copyrighted computer program, musical work, motion picture, or other audiovisual work or sound recording on a computer network accessible to the public for purposes of copying. And in 2020, the Protecting Lawful Streaming Act made it a felony to operate as a "digital transmission service"— a commercial entity that primarily functions to stream unauthorized copyrighted material. The Act sets a maximum penalty of up to ten years, imprisonment, plus fines if convicted. The Act will primarily benefit national sports franchises and motion picture makers.

Copyright Act: § 506. Criminal offenses
This statute authorizes criminal penalties for certain types of copyright infringement and establishes fines for certain dishonest copyright-related activities.
(a) **Criminal Infringement.** Any person who infringes a copyright willfully either—
   (1) for purposes of commercial advantage or private financial gain, or
   (2) by the reproduction or distribution, including by electronic means, during any 180-day period, of 1 or more copies or phonorecords of 1 or more copyrighted works, which have a total retail value of more than $1,000, shall be punished as provided under section 2319 of title 18, United States Code. For purposes of this subsection, evidence of reproduction or distribution of a copyrighted work, by itself, shall not be sufficient to establish willful infringement.
(b) **Forfeiture and Destruction.** When any person is convicted of any violation of subsection (a), the court in its judgment of conviction shall, in addition to the penalty therein prescribed, order the forfeiture and destruction or other disposition of all infringing copies or phonorecords and all implements, devices, or equipment used in the manufacture of such infringing copies or phonorecords.
(c) **Fraudulent Copyright Notice.** Any person who, with fraudulent intent, places on any article a notice of copyright or words of the same purport that such person knows to be false, or who, with fraudulent intent, publicly distributes or imports for public

distribution any article bearing such notice or words that such person knows to be false, shall be fined not more than $2,500.

(d) **Fraudulent Removal of Copyright Notice.** Any person who, with fraudulent intent, removes or alters any notice of copyright appearing on a copy of a copyrighted work shall be fined not more than $2,500.

(e) **False Representation.** Any person who knowingly makes a false representation of a material fact in the application for copyright registration provided for by section 409, or in any written statement filed in connection with the application, shall be fined not more than $2,500.

(f) **Rights of Attribution and Integrity.** Nothing in this section applies to infringement of the rights conferred by section 106A(a).

customs, preventing importing of infringing works

See importing of infringing works.

damages for copyright infringement

Money damages in copyright infringement actions are commonly awarded under three legal theories, actual damages, profits, and statutory damages:

- **Actual damages.** Also called compensatory damages, this consists of the dollar amount of any demonstrable loss the copyright owner suffered as a result of the infringing activity. This loss may be from lost sales, lost licensing revenue, or any other provable financial loss directly attributable to the infringement.

- **Profits.** This consists of any money made by the infringer as a result of the infringement. These damages are awarded only if they exceed the amount of profits lost by the copyright owner (actual damages) as a result of the infringement. In establishing the infringer's profits, the copyright owner must present proof only of the infringer's gross revenue, and the infringer is required to prove his or her deductible expenses and the elements of profit attributable to factors other than the copyrighted work.

    EXAMPLE: A book on self-defense, authored by Susan, contains a practical chapter on how to purchase and care for a handgun. Rachel also writes a book on self-defense and substantially borrows from Susan's chapter on handguns without first obtaining her permission. Rachel has infringed Susan's copyright. A court could award Susan actual damages if Susan proves that she lost sales of her book because people bought Rachel's book instead, at least in part because of the handgun chapter. Alternatively, if Susan has licensed chapters of her books to other authors, the amount she normally receives for such licensing could be her actual damages. In addition, the court could award Susan any profits that Rachel realized from the infringement to the extent such profits exceeded the amount of Susan's lost profits.

- **Statutory damages.** In many copyright cases, both actual damages and profits are difficult to prove. For that reason, the Copyright Act provides for statutory damages—that is, damages in an amount set by law. However, only a person who has registered a work with the U.S. Copyright Office before the infringement (or within three months of publication) may opt for statutory damages. Suppose a company registers a work after the work is infringed. The company can't recover statutory damages. But what if the same infringer commits a different act of infringement after registration? The Fifth Circuit has held that statutory damages are not available for either violation. (*Southern Credentialing Support Services, LLC v. Hammond Surgical Hospital, LLC*, No. 18-31160 (5th Cir. 2020).)

For infringements that can't clearly be proven as either innocent or willful, statutory damages may be from $750 to $30,000 per infringement depending on the circumstances. The amount will depend on the seriousness of the infringing act and the financial worth of the infringer. On the other hand, an innocent infringer might have to pay as little as $200, while an intentional infringer might have to pay as much as $150,000 for a single infringement of one work.

In the case of collective works registrations, determining statutory damages requires that the court determine whether the registration encompasses "one work" or several works (each qualifying for a statutory award). What usually matters most is whether the collective work functions primarily as a composite whole or whether each of the works can stand alone. The Second and Seventh Circuits have a slightly different standard: "whether the copyright holder marketed and distributed the multiple protected works as individual works or as a compendium of works." (*Sullivan v. Flora, Inc.*, No. 17-2241 (7th Cir. Aug. 21, 2019).)

On occasion, the award of statutory damages may seem out of proportion to the actual injury. For example, a record company sued an individual for illegally downloading 24 songs. Such songs were available for purchase for one dollar a song. Nevertheless, the Eighth Circuit determined that the jury award of $222,000 in statutory damages for the infringement of the songs ($9,250 per song) did not violate copyright law. (*Capitol Records Inc. v. Thomas-Rasset*, 692 F.3d 899 (2012).)

Copyright Act: § 504. Remedies for infringement: Damages and profits

(a) In General.—Except as otherwise provided by this title, an infringer of copyright is liable for either—

   (1) the copyright owner's actual damages and any additional profits of the infringer, as provided by subsection (b); or

   (2) statutory damages, as provided by subsection (c).

(b) Actual Damages and Profits.—The copyright owner is entitled to recover the actual damages suffered by him or her as a result of the infringement, and any profits of the infringer that are attributable to the infringement and are not taken into account in computing the actual damages. In establishing the infringer's profits, the copyright owner is required to present proof only of the infringer's gross revenue, and the infringer is required to prove his or her deductible expenses and the elements of profit attributable to factors other than the copyrighted work.

(c) Statutory Damages.—

   (1) Except as provided by clause (2) of this subsection, the copyright owner may elect, at any time before final judgment is rendered, to recover, instead of actual damages and profits, an award of statutory damages for all infringements involved in the action, with respect to any one work, for which any one infringer is liable individually, or for which any two or more infringers are liable jointly and severally, in a sum of not less than $750 or more than $30,000 as the court considers just. For the purposes of this subsection, all the parts of a compilation or derivative work constitute one work.

   (2) In a case where the copyright owner sustains the burden of proving, and the court finds, that infringement was committed willfully, the court in its discretion may increase the award of statutory damages to a sum of not more than $150,000. In a case where the infringer sustains the burden of proving, and the court finds, that such infringer was not aware and had no reason to believe that his or her acts constituted an infringement of copyright, the court in its discretion may reduce the award of statutory damages to a sum of not less than $200. The court shall remit statutory damages in any case where an infringer believed and had reasonable grounds for believing that his or her use of the copyrighted work was a fair use under section 107, if the infringer was:

     (i) an employee or agent of a nonprofit educational institution, library, or archives acting within the scope of his or her employment who, or such institution, library, or archives itself, which infringed by reproducing the work in copies or phonorecords; or

     (ii) a public broadcasting entity which or a person who, as a regular part of the nonprofit activities of a public broadcasting entity (as defined in subsection (g) of section 118) infringed by performing a published nondramatic literary work or by reproducing a transmission program embodying a performance of such a work.

(d) Additional Damages in Certain Cases.—In any case in which the court finds that a defendant proprietor of an establishment who claims as a defense that its activities were exempt under section 110 (5) did not have reasonable grounds to believe that its use of a copyrighted work was exempt under such section, the plaintiff shall be entitled to, in addition to any award of damages under this section, an additional award of two times the amount of the license fee that the proprietor of the establishment concerned should have paid the plaintiff for such use during the preceding period of up to 3 years.

Related terms: criminal copyright infringement; infringement action; injunctions; innocent infringement of copyright; profits as damages.

dance

See choreography and pantomime.

databases, copyright of

See computer databases.

de minimis

This term, derived from the Latin expression, "*de minimis non curat lex*," ("the law does not concern itself with trifles") is applied in two ways under copyright law. As used by the U.S. Copyright Office, the term characterizes changes in an existing work that are too small to warrant a separate registration. U.S. Copyright Office regulations allow only one registration per version of a work. If an author makes several minor changes to a work and tries to register the new version, the U.S. Copyright Office will consider the changes "*de minimis*" and reject the attempted new registration.

The term is also used in copyright litigation. If a court determines that the infringement is insubstantial, the copying will be excused as *de minimis*. This is not a fair use defense; it is a defense based solely upon the inconsequential amount of infringing material. For example, several photographs appeared briefly in the film *Seven*. A court determined that a lay observer would have been unable to identify them. Therefore, the momentary use of the photos was so insubstantial that the copyright was not infringed. (*Sandoval v. New Line Cinema Corp.*, 147 F.3d 215 (2d Cir. 1998).) In 2018, a New York District Court similarly ruled that a fleeting shot of barely visible graffiti painted on a dumpster, appearing in the HBO series *Vinyl*, was a *de minimis* use and did not amount to infringement. (*Gayle v. Home Box Office, Inc.*, No. 1:2017cv05867 (S.D.N.Y. May 1, 2018).)

A *de minimis* insubstantiality defense is not always successful.

EXAMPLE: A storage business was unaware of the existence of an infringing photo (of an Indianapolis landscape) on one of its servers. The server was obtained as part of a business acquisition and the storage business had never used the image. A photographer/lawyer (considered by some to be a copyright troll) discovered the photo and filed a lawsuit. The district court ruled for the storage business that the infringement was trivial and therefore, *de minimis*. But the Ninth Circuit reversed the decision. The Court of Appeals held that because the entire photo had been copied, the *de minimis* defense could not apply. (*Bell v. Wilmott Storage Servs., LLC,* No. 19-55882 (9th Cir. 2021).)

Related terms: derivative work; single registration rule.

deep linking

See linking.

defective copyright notice

Until March 1, 1989, works published in the United States needed a copyright notice for the copyright to remain in force. A defective notice could and did permanently nullify copyright protection for many works. However, after the March 1, 1989, date, no notice is required, but only recommended (to give people notice that the work is protected by copyright).

A correct notice is either the little "©" or the words "Copyright" or "Copr." followed by the date and the author's name. In the case of a sound recording, the proper symbol is a "P" in a circle.

A defective copyright notice might be one with an error in or omission of the author's name, the copyright symbol, or the date (an error of more than one year).

Related terms: innocent infringement of copyright; international copyright protection; notice of copyright; omission of copyright notice.

defenses to copyright infringement

The common defenses to an allegation of copyright infringement are:

- The use was a "fair use," that is, was for a transformative purpose such as a parody, or in a critical commentary.
- The allegedly infringing work was independently created, that is, it wasn't copied.
- The statute of limitations has run (the plaintiff waited too long to file suit—filing must be within three years of discovering the infringement).

- The work (or the portion) copied was in the public domain.
- The use was authorized, that is the copyright owner gave permission.
- The plaintiff doesn't own the copyright.

Related terms: authorized use as defense; fair use; independent creation; innocent infringement of copyright; public domain; statute of limitations.

deposit with U.S. Copyright Office

Part of the copyright registration process requires the deposit of actual copies, photographs, or other representations of an original work of authorship with the U.S. Copyright Office. For most categories of published works, it is necessary to deposit two copies of the work's best edition. For some types of works, however, including computer programs, motion pictures, and most unpublished works, only one copy need be deposited. The form a deposit must take differs according to the media in question but must generally be sufficient to identify the work being registered. Users of the Copyright Office's electronic filing system (eCO) should upload one digital copy of a published work (if the applicant meets the deposit requirements) or mail in two hard copies of a published work. The eCO program provides a preprinted mailing label.

The failure to submit the deposit materials won't terminate copyright protection. If the required deposit is not made within three months after receiving a demand from the Copyright Office, the owner may be subjected to:

- a fine of not more than $250 for each work
- the total retail price of the work demanded or, in the absence of a retail price, the reasonable cost of acquiring the work, and
- for willful or repeated failure to comply with the demand, a fine of $2,500.

Related terms: identifying material; registration.

derivative work

A derivative work is one based upon preexisting material to which enough original creative work has been added so that the new work represents an original work of authorship. The term (as defined in 17 U.S. Code § 101) encompasses any form into which a work may be recast, transformed, or adapted.

The author of a derivative work must obtain permission from the owner of the copyright in the earlier work to copy, sell, or distribute the derivative work. For example, a foreign language translation of a book is based on the book as it was originally written and is subject to the copyright in the original version; a movie that borrows the main characters, the story line, and some dialogue from a novel is based on that novel and is subject to that novel's copyright; and a song that has substantially the same melody as an earlier song is based on that song, even if the words are different, and is subject to the earlier song's copyright.

As a broad rule, the more expression a subsequent work uses from an earlier work, the more likely it is to be considered a derivative work and therefore subject to the earlier work's copyright. However, assuming permission is obtained from the owner of the copyright in the earlier work, the derivative work is itself subject to copyright protection as an independent work.

Examples of derivative works are:

- an English translation of a book written in French
- a computer program rewritten in a different programming language
- a movie based on a play or book
- condensed or abridged versions of articles, such as those found in *Reader's Digest*
- annotations to literary works (for example, *CliffsNotes*), and
- a jazz version of a popular tune.

Derivative works may also be fictionalizations, recordings, or even editorial revisions. Compilations and collective works are not normally considered derivative works because they are collections of different underlying works, rather than a new work based upon an original work.

The exclusive right to make derivative works is an important part of the bundle of rights that make up every copyright. Absent an explicit transfer of this right by a written license, or by permission from the owner (voluntary or forced in the case of a compulsory license), no one else can exercise it except for personal use.

> EXAMPLE: Joe wants to adapt a popular novel into an interactive iPad app. Because the app will be based on the novel, it will constitute a derivative work and therefore cannot legally be marketed without permission from the novel's copyright owner.

Copyright Act: § 101. Definitions

A "derivative work" is a work based upon one or more preexisting works, such as a translation, musical arrangement, dramatization, fictionalization, motion picture version, sound recording, art reproduction, abridgment, condensation, or any other form in which a work may be recast, transformed, or adapted. A work consisting of editorial revisions, annotations, elaborations, or other modifications which, as a whole, represent an original work of authorship, is a "derivative work."

Copyright Act: § 103. Subject matter of copyright: Compilations and derivative works

(a) The subject matter of copyright as specified by section 102 includes compilations and derivative works, but protection for a work employing preexisting material in which copyright subsists does not extend to any part of the work in which such material has been used unlawfully.

(b) The copyright in a compilation or derivative work extends only to the material contributed by the author of such work, as distinguished from the preexisting material employed in the work, and does not imply any exclusive right in the preexisting material. The copyright in such work is independent of, and does not affect or enlarge the scope, duration, ownership, or subsistence of, any copyright protection in the preexisting material.

Related terms: collective work; copyright; independent creation; infringement (copyright).

Digital Millennium Copyright Act ("DMCA")

This federal statute addresses a number of copyright issues created by the use of the Internet. Among other things, it outlaws attempts to get around processes, methods, or devices that limit copying of copyrighted works. For example, if a copyright owner installs a digital rights management (DRM) system that limits copying of a motion picture, and a user circumvents the system (even without copying the underlying movie), a violation of the DMCA has occurred. In short, the DMCA has made it possible for a person to violate copyright law without infringing a copyright. The act has numerous exceptions allowing for override of DRMs. (*See entry below*: digital rights management (DRM).)

In addition to DRM rules, the DMCA has many other requirements including:

- The DMCA prohibits the production, marketing, or sales of a product or service designed to circumvent these technological protections. For example, the movie industry was able to use the DMCA to prohibit circumvention of DVD technology when it stopped a programmer from distributing a software code designed to decode DVDs and permit their copying. (*Universal City Studios Inc. v. Corley*, 273 F.3d 429 (2d Cir. 2001).)

- The DMCA puts restrictions on the import, distribution, and sales of analog video cassette recorders and camcorders that don't have a certain type of copy-proof technology.

- The DMCA prohibits the falsification of copyright management information and the distribution of works that contain such falsified information.

- The DMCA contains a number of provisions relating to transmission of copyrighted materials over Internet service providers (ISPs). The DMCA takes ISPs off the hook for infringement for transient transmissions automatically passing through their computers. Under its "safe harbor" provisions, the DMCA also allows ISPs to escape liability for infringement regarding more permanent materials if they promptly remove infringing materials upon request. The DMCA sets up a procedure in case the owner of the removed materials protests. In exchange for escaping liability for infringement, service providers must designate an agent to accept service of legal papers. The DMCA also relieves ISPs from liability for unknowingly linking to a site that does contain infringing material. In 2016, the Copyright Office revised the registration process, requiring websites to renew their registration every three years. Finally, the DMCA authorizes U.S. district court clerks to issue subpoenas to service providers requiring them to identify an alleged online infringer.

The DMCA is often used by angry copyright claimants seeking to have an ISP remove infringing works under its "notice and takedown" procedures, described above. To protect against the unjustified use of this provision, Congress provided section 512(f), which permits Internet publishers to bring affirmative claims against copyright owners who knowingly and materially misrepresent that infringement has occurred. In a 2004 case, two ISPs successfully used this provision to fight back against a DMCA notice and takedown procedure instigated by Diebold over the republication of an email archive. The emails from Diebold engineers allegedly sounded an alarm over flaws in Diebold's electronic voting machines. A court ruled that the republication of the emails was a fair use because there was no commercial harm and no diminishment of the value of the works. (*Online Privacy Group v. Diebold*, 72 U.S.P.Q.2d 1200 (N.D. Cal. 2004).)

In 2008, a district court ruled that prior to requesting a takedown notice, a copyright owner must consider the likelihood of a claim of fair use. In that case, Universal Music issued a takedown notice for a video of a child dancing to the song, "Let's Go Crazy," by Prince. The owner of the video claimed that because Universal didn't consider the issue of fair use, Universal could have not had a "good faith belief" they were entitled to a takedown. Faced with this novel issue, a district court agreed that the failure to consider fair use when sending a DMCA notice could give rise to a claim of failing to act in good faith. The Ninth Circuit affirmed this decision and held that the owner must have made a "subjective good faith" analysis regarding fair use. The Ninth Circuit also held that a copyright owner who neglects to make this fair use analysis is liable for damages for copyright misrepresentation." (*Lenz v. Universal Music Corp.*, 801 F.3d 1126 (2015).)

In 2012, a court of appeals clarified one aspect of the DMCA for ISPs—that "awareness" of infringement was not the same as a "duty to police." Viacom sued YouTube claiming that YouTube failed to police its content even though the company had followed the DMCA procedures of implementing a procedure to respond to takedown notices from copyright owners and removing infringing content of which it was aware. The Second Circuit held that a general awareness of infringement did not trigger a duty to police postings under the DMCA. The Second Circuit held that YouTube was responsible only if it knew of specific infringements or deliberately insulated itself from knowledge of such infringement by its users. (*Viacom International Inc. v. YouTube Inc.,* 676 F.3d 19 (2d Cir. 2012).)

In 2016, the Second Circuit held that the DMCA safe harbor rules applied to state copyright (pre-1972 sound recordings) as well as to federal copyright. The court also held that the burdens of proof for an ISP claiming a safe harbor involves factual issues that trigger varying burdens of proof.) (*Capitol Records LLC et al v. Vimeo LLC*, No. 14-1048. (2d Cir. 2016).)

In 2017, the Ninth Circuit reversed and remanded a district court grant of "safe harbor" to a celebrity website over its use of copyrighted photos. At issue was whether the website (or its agents) had a say in the photo choices and whether the site knew the photos were protected ("red flagged"). (*Mavrix Photographs, LLC. v. LiveJournal*, No. 14-56596 (9th Cir. 2017).)

The DMCA allows a copy of a computer program to be made for the purpose of repairing or maintaining a computer. In addition, the DMCA contains new laws regarding the licensing of motion pictures and phonorecordings and the innovative designs of vessel hulls.

Violations of the DMCA can result in civil remedies consisting of injunctive relief, actual damages, and statutory damages. Repeat violators may be tagged with treble damages. A willful violation of the DMCA for personal or financial gain can result in stiff criminal penalties (up to ten years in prison).

The first criminal prosecution under the DMCA occurred when the U.S. government indicted Dmitri Sklyarov for creating and distributing software that could permit electronic book owners to convert the Adobe *eBook* format. A jury later acquitted Sklyarov of all criminal charges.

One of the more novel attempts at applying the DMCA occurred in 2003 when a printer manufacturer, Lexmark, sued a rival company, Static Control Components, which sold replacement toner cartridges. Lexmark's printers contained a software program that read information embedded on a chip in the toner cartridge. If the toner wasn't "authorized" (made by Lexmark or a licensee), the toner cartridge would not work in the printer. Static Control created Smartek chips that sent a message to the Lexmark printer authorizing the use of its toner cartridges. Lexmark argued that the Smartek chips circumvented Lexmark technology in violation of the DMCA. In March 2003, a district court in Kentucky agreed with Lexmark and enjoined Static Control from selling its Smartek chip or incorporating it in cartridges. That decision was later vacated by a federal Court of Appeals. (*Lexmark International Inc. v. Static Control Components Inc.,* 387 F.3d (6th Cir. 2004).) In a different case, the federal Circuit Court of Appeals upheld the dismissal of a case involving garage door openers in which a company unsuccessfully argued that a competitor's ability to offer universal remote control devices was prohibited under the DMCA. (*Chamberlain Group, Inc. v. Skylink Techs., Inc.,* 381 F.3d 1178 (Fed. Cir. 2004).)

Related terms: Copyleft; digital rights management (DRM).

digital rights management (DRM)

A term that encompasses various processes or methods of restricting usage of (or access to) a copyrighted work. Initially DRM technologies were created solely to prevent copying of software, but since the late 1990s they have been used in conjunction with creative works such as music, books, databases, and movies. DRMs are implemented at the discretion of the copyright owner. Cracking, reproducing, or tampering with DRM technologies has resulted in several lawsuits, usually brought under the Digital Millennium Copyright Act (which prohibits such activities). For example, the DRM system used on DVDs known as Content Scrambling System (CSS) was the subject of considerable litigation, as was the DRM system used to limit copying of Adobe *eBooks*. Despite claims made by their creators, no DRM has yet proven uncrackable.

Circumventing DRM is not excused just because DRM-cracking tools are widely available. In a 2010 case, Apple sued a company that had circumvented its DRM system. The defendant company argued in defense that tools for cracking the DRM were widely available and that therefore, the DRM itself was so ineffective as to be meaningless. The court disagreed and held that if the DRM could not be circumvented without outside information or tools, it would be considered as effective DRM. (*Apple Inc. v. Psystar Corp.,* 673 F. Supp.2d 931 (N.D. Cal. 2009).)

The DMCA contains numerous exceptions allowing for override of DRMs, including:

- works exempted by the Copyright Office, under rules to be issued in the future
- nonprofit libraries, archives, and educational institutions that need to decide whether to add the protected work to their collections
- reverse engineering for the purpose of determining interoperability (the ability of computer programs to exchange information, and of such programs mutually to use the information that has been exchanged)
- legitimate encryption research
- legitimate security testing
- law enforcement and intelligence activities, and
- legitimate consumer privacy needs (the need to disable the protective device in order to prevent the unwanted acquisition of personal information or the tracking of activities on the Internet).

Additional exemptions have subsequently been added including the right to:

- copy video from DVDs, Blu-ray discs, and other sources for various educational purposes as well as criticism and commentary
- make e-books accessible to the visually impaired through third-party read-aloud software
- unlock new and used phones, tablets, mobile hotspots, and wearable devices to use on different wireless networks
- jailbreak mobile devices to add or remove particular apps
- jailbreak smart TVs to install third-party software
- tinker with the embedded software in cars and trucks for diagnosis, repair, and personalization (and extends to their telematics and entertainment systems)
- conduct security research on software in cars, voting machines, and medical devices
- resume playing video games that required an authorization from a server that's no longer online
- use the plastic feedstock of your choice in a 3-D printer
- inspect the data collected about you by networked medical devices
- jailbreak voice assistant devices to allow them to run legal programs

- access the software in home appliances and smart-home gadgets to diagnose, maintain, and repair it, and
- disable digital locks to conduct security research on software subject to restrictions.

Related terms: CMI; Digital Millennium Copyright Act ("DMCA").

display a work

The exclusive right to display an original work of authorship is one of the bundle of rights that together form the overall copyright. (17 U.S. Code § 101.) The Copyright Act of 1976 defines "display" as: "to show a copy of it, either directly or by means of a film, slide, television image, or any other device or process or, in the case of a motion picture or other audiovisual work, to show individual images nonsequentially" (as in movie previews).

> EXAMPLE: Marylou photographs Juan's copyrighted print for the purpose of using it in her photography show. Because Juan has the exclusive right to display his work, Marylou must obtain Juan's permission before she displays the photo.

This particular right has become increasingly important as more creative works have been placed into digital form for display through the Internet and through the large online services that charge users for the time they spend viewing displayed materials.

Related terms: copyright.

dramatic works

In the copyright sense, a dramatic work is one that carries a story line and is intended to be performed before an audience, either directly or through use of a tangible medium such as paper, film, videotape, or videodisc. Dramatic works include movies, plays, satires, comedies, and pantomimes. Like other original works of authorship, they are fully protectable by copyright.

Related terms: original work of authorship.

droit moral

See moral rights.

Copyright Law: Definitions

duration of copyrights

How long a copyright lasts in the United States depends on when the work covered by the copyright was first created or published:

- **Works created on or after January 1, 1978.** Under the Copyright Act of 1976, copyrights on works created on or after January 1, 1978, last for a defined period of time. If the "author" is an individual, and the work appears under that person's name, the copyright lasts for the life of the author plus 70 years. If the "author" is an employer or the commissioner of a work made for hire, or uses a pseudonym or remains anonymous, the copyright lasts for 95 years from the date of publication or 120 years from the date the work was first created, whichever comes first.

- **Works created or published before January 1, 1978.** If the work was published before 1978, the copyright lasts for 95 years from the date of publication, assuming the copyright was (or is) timely renewed (by filing a renewal application with the U.S. Copyright Office). The copyright in works created before 1978 lasts at least to December 31, 2047, if published before December 31, 2002. All unpublished works created by authors who died 70 or more years ago are now in the public domain in the United States. This is so whether the author was American or a non-American. Unpublished works made for hire created more than 120 years ago are also in the U.S. public domain.

Countries that are members of the Berne Convention and countries that have signed the GATT treaty (which requires its members to honor the Berne Convention's copyright protection standards) extend copyright protection for the life of the author plus a minimum of 50 years. The countries in the European Union also extend copyright protection for the life of the author plus 70 years.

The value of works such as books, films, art, and songs (that is, their ability to generate copyright fees) might last well beyond the term of the copyright, in which case the author's inheritors are out of luck. On the other hand, computer-related works seem likely to be more short-lived, so copyright protection will probably last for more than enough time to protect them for their entire commercial life expectancy.

Below is a chart that shows the duration of copyrights for different publishing dates.

Copyright Duration Chart

Date and Nature of Work	Copyright Term
Published before 1926*	The work is in the public domain
Published 1926* through 1963 and never renewed	The work is in the public domain
Published 1926* through 1963 and timely renewed	95 years from the date of first publication
Published 1964 through 1977	95 years from the date of publication (renewal term automatic)
Created before 1978 but never published	Life of the author plus 70 years or 120 years from creation for unpublished works made for hire, and unpublished or pseudonymous works
Created before 1978 and published 1978 through 2002	The greater period of either (a) life of the author plus 70 years, or (b) until January 1, 2048
Created after 1977 (or created before 1978 but first published after 2002)	Life of author + 70 years

* In 2019, works first published in the U.S. in 1923 (that is, published before 1924) entered the public domain. In 2020, works first published in 1924 (that is, published before 1925) entered the public domain, and so forth.

Copyright Act: § 302. Duration of copyright: Works created on or after January 1, 1978

(a) **In General.**—Copyright in a work created on or after January 1, 1978, subsists from its creation and, except as provided by the following subsections, endures for a term consisting of the life of the author and 70 years after the author's death.

(b) **Joint Works.**—In the case of a joint work prepared by two or more authors who did not work for hire, the copyright endures for a term consisting of the life of the last surviving author and 70 years after such last surviving author's death.

(c) **Anonymous Works, Pseudonymous Works, and Works Made for Hire.**—In the case of an anonymous work, a pseudonymous work, or a work made for hire, the copyright endures for a term of 95 years from the year of its first publication, or a term of 120 years from the year of its creation, whichever expires first. If, before the end of such term, the identity of one or more of the authors of an anonymous or pseudonymous

Copyright Law: Definitions

work is revealed in the records of a registration made for that work under subsections (a) or (d) of section 408, or in the records provided by this subsection, the copyright in the work endures for the term specified by subsection (a) or (b), based on the life of the author or authors whose identity has been revealed. Any person having an interest in the copyright in an anonymous or pseudonymous work may at any time record, in records to be maintained by the Copyright Office for that purpose, a statement identifying one or more authors of the work; the statement shall also identify the person filing it, the nature of that person's interest, the source of the information recorded, and the particular work affected, and shall comply in form and content with requirements that the Register of Copyrights shall prescribe by regulation.

(d) **Records Relating to Death of Authors.**—Any person having an interest in a copyright may at any time record in the Copyright Office a statement of the date of death of the author of the copyrighted work, or a statement that the author is still living on a particular date. The statement shall identify the person filing it, the nature of that person's interest, and the source of the information recorded, and shall comply in form and content with requirements that the Register of Copyrights shall prescribe by regulation. The Register shall maintain current records of information relating to the death of authors of copyrighted works, based on such recorded statements and, to the extent the Register considers practicable, on data contained in any of the records of the Copyright Office or in other reference sources.

(e) **Presumption as to Author's Death.**—After a period of 95 years from the year of first publication of a work, or a period of 120 years from the year of its creation, whichever expires first, any person who obtains from the Copyright Office a certified report that the records provided by subsection (d) disclose nothing to indicate that the author of the work is living, or died less than 70 years before, is entitled to the benefits of a presumption that the author has been dead for at least 70 years. Reliance in good faith upon this presumption shall be a complete defense to any action for infringement under this title.

Related terms: *Eldred v. Ashcroft;* GATT (General Agreement on Tariffs and Trade); international copyright protection; Sonny Bono Copyright Term Extension Act; work made for hire.

electronic filing of copyright applications

Using the eCO electronic filing system, users can file a copyright application online (currently for $45 to $65). The process is fairly straightforward (and discussed in the Forms portion of this text, following this section). You may upload a digital copy of your work (if you qualify), or you may mail in hard copies of your deposit materials.

Eldred v. Ashcroft

During the past four decades, Congress has extended copyright terms 11 times. After the Sonny Bono Copyright Term Extension Act added a 20-year term extension, Eric Eldred and other users of public domain commercial materials sued, claiming that Congress's continual extensions of the copyright term violated the Constitution. In 2003, the U.S. Supreme Court disagreed and ruled the 20-year copyright extension did not violate the U.S. Constitution. (*Eldred v. Ashcroft*, 537 U.S. 186 (2003).)

Related terms: Copyleft; duration of copyrights; Sonny Bono Copyright Term Extension Act.

embedding

Embedding is the process of incorporating a file from one source onto another location without making a copy. For example photos are commonly embedded (a process previously referred to as "inlining" or "mirroring") when the HTML code for a posted photo (Site 1) is included with the code for a second site (Site 2). The photo is displayed at both sites, but it is stored only on Site 1's server. Embedding is used by search engines when they produce small low-resolution versions of images ("thumbnails") and provide links to full-size versions of the same images.

In a 2003 case, the Ninth Circuit Court of Appeals held that a form of embedding—Google's practice of creating small reproductions ("thumbnails") of images and placing them on its own website—was permitted as a fair use. The thumbnails were much smaller and of much poorer quality than the original photos and served to index the images and thereby help the public access them. (*Kelly v. Arriba Soft Corp.*, 336 F.3d 811 (9th Cir. 2003).)

A similar result was reached by the Ninth Circuit Court of Appeals in a case involving Google. The court determined that Google's use of thumbnails was permitted as a fair use in a case involving reproductions of images from an adult men's magazine website. The Ninth Circuit went even further when it introduced the "server test," which posits there is no copyright liability for content that is stored on another website's server. (*Perfect 10, Inc. v. Amazon.com, Inc.*, 508 F.3d 1146 (9th Cir. 2007).)

On social media, links, photos, video, and music are commonly embedded by users. Although the embedding of Instagram posts and Twitter tweets is ordinarily considered to be a fair use, a New York district court disagreed. In a case involving embedding of a tweeted photo of quarterback Tom Brady, the court rejected the server test. "When defendants caused the embedded tweets to appear on their websites, their actions violated plaintiff's exclusive display right," the judge wrote. "The fact that the image was hosted on a server owned and operated by an unrelated third party (Twitter) does not shield them from this result." (*Goldman v. Breitbart News Network, LLC*, 302 F. Supp. 3d 585 (S.D.N.Y. 2018).) Below are summaries of some recent embedding cases.

- A New York federal court held that embedding a polar bear video on social media violated the photographer's display right. The ruling opposes the Ninth's Circuit "server test," according to which embedding does not infringe unless copies are made and stored on a server. (*Nicklen v. Sinclair Broad. Grp.*, No. 20-10300 (JSR) (S.D.N.Y. 2021).)

- A photographer's photo of Cardi B, posted without authorization by the celebrity on Instagram and later embedded in an article discussing Cardi B's cosmetic business, was held to be fair use. The court held that the use was transformative (the original use was to show the celebrity at a fashion show) and did not affect the market for the photograph. (*Walsh v. Townsquare Media, Inc.*, No. 19-4958, 2020 WL 2837009 (S.D.N.Y. 2020).)

- Tennis professional Caroline Wozniacki posted a photo of herself on Instagram announcing her retirement. The Instagram post (featuring the plaintiff's photograph) was later embedded at a tennis website. The district court granted a motion to dismiss the photographer's copyright infringement claim, holding that the website's embedding constituted fair use. (*Boesen v. United Sports Publications, Ltd.*, No. 20-1552 (E.D.N.Y. 2020).)

end-user license

Copyright owners, particularly software and website publishers, might want to limit how purchasers use their products and services. For example, a software maker might insist that customers use its app only for personal, not commercial, purposes. To impose these restrictions, most publishers use a contract known as an end-user license agreement (EULA).

These EULAs were originally known as "shrinkwrap licenses" because—at least in the early days of software production—the user would consent to the EULA (visible on the back of the package) by breaking the box's shrinkwrap. A user who proceeded to use the program was deemed to accept the terms. A user who didn't want to accept the terms could return the program to the manufacturer for a refund.

Nowadays, most EULAs are known as a "clickwrap agreements" or "browserwrap agreements," because the user enters into the agreement online and must click to accept the conditions before accessing a website or using software.

What is the end-user agreeing to do (or not do)? The provisions of the EULA differ in name (terms and conditions, terms of use, terms of service) and differ in purpose (for example, disclaiming liability, restricting use of content, setting rules of behavior). Often, they establish dispute resolution procedures. But if the copyright owner fails to obtain assent or provide effective notice of these provisions, a court is unlikely to enforce them.

> **EXAMPLE:** An online gambling app tried to enforce an arbitration provision buried within its terms-of-use agreement. Because the online gambling site failed to acquire user-assent and failed to prove constructive or actual notice of the terms ("the user would need Sherlock Holmes's instincts to discover the Terms"), the Ninth Circuit refused to enforce the provision. (*Wilson v. Huuuge, Inc.*, No. 18-36017, 2019 U.S. App. LEXIS 37952 (9th Cir. 2019).)

Initially, there was doubt as to whether EULAs could be enforced in court, especially if the provisions were inconsistent with the Copyright Act. The reason for doubt is because the typical EULA isn't negotiated between seller and purchaser at the time of sale, and so the purchaser shouldn't be held to its terms, especially if the user must waive rights under the Copyright Act. For example, some licenses may prohibit the user from copying the software, even though the Copyright Act permits the purchaser to make an archival copy.

In 1996, a federal Court of Appeal ruled that shrinkwrap licenses are valid as long as a user who disagrees with the terms can return the product for a refund. The court also ruled that a license restricting rights that a purchaser would have otherwise had under the Copyright Act is legal. (*ProCD v. Zeidenberg*, 86 F.3d 1447 (7th Cir. 1996).)

The same standards apply to clickwrap agreements: "[C]lickwrap license agreements are an appropriate way to form contracts." (*i.Lan Systems Inc. v. Netscout Service Level Corp.*, 183 F. Supp.2d 328 (D. Mass., 2002).) In a case involving America Online, a court upheld a clickwrap agreement between AOL and a Massachusetts man requiring that legal disputes with AOL be settled in Virginia. (*Hughes v. AOL*, 2002 U.S. Dist. LEXIS 9569 (D. Mass. 2002).)

A EULA was ineffective in a case involving the Adobe Software company. In 2001, a federal court ruled that, despite the language of an Adobe license agreement, the purchaser of a bundle of Adobe software programs could resell the individual components (separate programs on CDs). (*Softman Products Co. LLC v. Adobe Systems Inc.,* 171 F. Supp.2d 1075 (C.D. Cal. 2001).) The district court in that case determined that Adobe had sold, rather than licensed, its products to distributors, permitting the resale of the components under the first sale doctrine.

In 2000, federal legislation—the Electronic Signatures in Global and International Commerce Act—was enacted, which helped remove some of the uncertainty that previously plagued e-contracts and prevented a contract from being challenged simply because it was created electronically. Some proponents of software licenses urged passage of the Uniform Computer Information Transaction Act (UCITA), a proposed law that would legitimize all software licenses. However, the UCITA was adopted in only two states, Virginia and Maryland.

Another company, as a condition of its EULA, prohibited reverse engineering of its software. To the dismay of software programmers, a federal court upheld this provision. (*Bowers v. Baystate Technologies, Inc.,* 320 F.3d 1317 (Fed. Cir. 2003).)

Even more disconcerting for many scholars and consumers was the introduction of nonsoftware EULAs. For example, a book publisher used a shrinkwrap agreement to prohibit the resale of books. A museum required viewers to waive the right to claim fair use when copying material from its website. (Both of these rights—resale and fair use—are otherwise permitted under the Copyright Act.)

Related terms: software; licensing of copyrights; UCITA.

ephemeral recording

Under some circumstances, the Copyright Act permits making copies of works for purposes of later transmission. For example, a disc jockey is permitted to copy a song from compact disc to tape in order to prepare a radio broadcast. These ephemeral recordings are commonly used in radio, cable, and Internet broadcasting.

EULA

See end-user license.

exclusive copyright rights

A copyright owner is exclusively entitled to a bundle of rights consisting of:
- the right to reproduce (copy) the work
- the right to prepare derivative works
- the right to distribute copies of the work

- the right to perform the work, and
- the right to display the work.

Copyright Act: § 106. Exclusive rights in copyrighted works
Subject to sections 107 through 122, the owner of copyright under this title has the exclusive rights to do and to authorize any of the following:
(1) to reproduce the copyrighted work in copies or phonorecords;
(2) to prepare derivative works based upon the copyrighted work;
(3) to distribute copies or phonorecords of the copyrighted work to the public by sale or other transfer of ownership, or by rental, lease, or lending;
(4) in the case of literary, musical, dramatic, and choreographic works, pantomimes, and motion pictures and other audiovisual works, to perform the copyrighted work publicly;
(5) in the case of literary, musical, dramatic, and choreographic works, pantomimes, and pictorial, graphic, or sculptural works, including the individual images of a motion picture or other audiovisual work, to display the copyrighted work publicly; and
(6) in the case of sound recordings, to perform the copyrighted work publicly by means of a digital audio transmission.

Related terms: copyright; infringement action; licensing of copyright.

exclusive license

See licensing of copyright.

expedited registration

The U.S. Copyright Office has a special procedure to register a work if a copyright owner needs the registration quickly. Only three reasons are permitted for receiving special handling: pending or prospective litigation, customs matters, or contract or publishing deadlines that necessitate the expedited issuance of a certificate. Expedited registration—called "special handling" by the U.S. Copyright Office—costs an additional $800 for registration and $550 for recordation. For more on special handling, review Circular 10 at the Copyright Office.

Copyright owners must register their work prior to suing for infringement under the provisions of 17 U.S. Code Section 411(a). (*Fourth Estate Public Benefit Corp. v. Wall-Street.com, LLC.*, 586 U.S. ____ (2019).)

Related terms: infringement (copyright).

estoppel, copyright

Copyright estoppel is an affirmative defense to copyright infringement. It's based on the principle that if the copyright owner misled the defendant into believing something that wasn't true (and the defendant relied on that to their detriment), the copyright owner is later prevented (or "estopped") from taking advantage of that misrepresentation. For example, if a photographer assures a blogger that it's okay to freely reproduce a photo and then sues the blogger, the photographer could be estopped from recovering. In the Ninth Circuit, a version of copyright estoppel is referred to as the "Asserted Truth Doctrine": when the writer of a factual work later claims that some of the facts were fictionalized. This is done because it's not a violation to borrow facts from nonfiction, but it can be a violation to borrow fictional elements.

> EXAMPLE: The copyright owner of a biography of the Four Seasons singing group argued that the producers of a musical about the singing group borrowed more than facts from the biography because some of the facts were "fiction." The Ninth Circuit disagreed, holding, "Copyright protects the creative labor of authors; it does not protect authors' post-completion representations about the lack of veracity of their own avowedly truthful work." (*Corbello v. Valli*, 974 F. 3d 965 (9th Cir. 2020).)

Related Terms: factual works.

expression, protection of, under copyright law

See copyright; original work of authorship.

factual works

Factual works are those that legitimately may be classified as nonfiction. Histories, instruction manuals, trade catalogs, travel guides, and biographies are all examples of factual works. Under copyright law, factual works receive less (or "narrower") protection than works of fiction because the underlying facts are legally considered to be in the public domain. Therefore, factual works do not contain as much protectable material as fictional works.

> EXAMPLE: Tim writes a travel book on the Comoros Islands, a small island country off the east coast of Africa. In this book, he catalogs all the usual items, including lodging, tourist sites, and food. A year later, Alice publishes a competing book that contains much of the same information plus some additional facts about the Comorean political system. Tim writes Alice, accusing her of copyright infringement. Alice responds that she used Tim's book to visit the Comoros and that because his facts were remarkably accurate, she had no choice but to include them in her book. Because facts such as those found in Alice's and Tim's books are in the public domain, Alice has not infringed Tim's copyright.

In a 2009 case involving a play and a book—both examining the death of Pope John Paul I—a New York district court ruled that historical facts, theories interpreting those facts, and plots based on the chronology of historical events are unprotectable. (*Crane v. Poetic Products, Ltd.*, 593 F. Supp.2d 585 (S.D.N.Y. 2009).)

Related terms: *Feist Publications Inc. v. Rural Telephone Service Co.*; merger doctrine.

fair use

The fair use doctrine permits the unauthorized use of copyrighted material if it is used for certain purposes such as criticism, commentary, or parody. The Copyright Act permits any person to make "fair use" of a published or unpublished copyrighted work—including the making of unauthorized copies—in these contexts:

- in connection with criticism of or comment on the work
- in the course of news reporting
- for teaching purposes, or
- as part of scholarship or research activity.

As a practical matter, fair use is primarily an affirmative defense to a claim of copyright infringement—that is, the defense is that even if the defendant copied the work, there is no liability, because the infringing activity was excusable as a fair use of the original work. However, it is also unique among copyright defenses. As the Ninth Circuit stated, "fair use is uniquely situated in copyright law so as to be treated differently than traditional affirmative defenses." (*Lenz v. Universal Music Corp.*, 801 F.3d 1126 (2015).) In *Lenz*, the court held that before a copyright owner issues a DMCA notice, the owner must have made a "subjective good faith" analysis regarding fair use. The Ninth Circuit also held that a copyright owner who neglects to make this fair use analysis is liable for damages for copyright misrepresentation.

Whether or not a particular instance of copying without permission qualifies as a fair use is decided on a case-by-case basis and depends on four basic factors. These are:

- the purpose and character of the use, including whether such use is of a commercial nature or for nonprofit, educational purposes
- the nature of the copyrighted work
- the amount and substantiality of the portion used in relation to the copyrighted work as a whole, and
- the effect of the use upon the potential market for, or value of, the copyrighted work.

Copyright Law: Definitions

Below we examine each of these factors separately. Note that when we use the term "defendant" we are referring to the person accused of infringement.

The **first factor** is considered the most important and requires an analysis as to whether the use is transformative. That is, did the defendant change the original by adding new expression or meaning? Did the defendant add value to the original by creating new information, new aesthetics, new insights and understandings? If the use was transformative, this weighs in favor of a fair use finding. In a parody, for example, the parodist transforms the original by holding it up to ridicule. The brief use of photographs in a film was considered to be transformative because the images were used in furtherance of the creation of a distinct aesthetic and overall mood. The defendant's work doesn't have to transform the original work's expression as long as the purpose is transformative, for example, scholarship, research, education, or commentary.

In a 2012 case, the painter Richard Prince created a collage using—in one collage—35 images from a photographer's book. The artist also used 28 of the photos in 29 additional paintings. In some instances, the full photograph was used while in others, only the main subject of the photo was used. The Second Circuit Court of Appeals held that to qualify as a transformative use, Prince's work did not have to comment on the original photographer's work (or on popular culture), concluding that 25 of Prince's artworks qualified as fair use. (*Cariou v. Prince*, 714 F.3d 694 (2d Cir. 2013).)

In a 2014 case, the Second Circuit held that scanning books to create a searchable database was a "quintessentially transformative" fair use. Many colleges, universities, and nonprofits had offered their book collections to HathiTrust, a nonprofit that created a ten-million-book database. The Second Circuit ruled that HathiTrust was permitted under fair use principles to electronically scan its copyrighted books to create a full-text searchable database. (*Authors Guild, Inc. v. HathiTrust*, 755 F.3d 87 (2d Cir. 2014).)

Determining what is transformative—and the degree of transformation—can be challenging. For example, the creation of a Harry Potter encyclopedia was determined to be "slightly transformative" (because it made the Harry Potter terms and lexicons available in one volume), but this transformative quality was not enough to justify a fair use defense in light of the extensive verbatim use of text from the Harry Potter books. (*Warner Bros. Entertainment, Inc. v. RDR Books*, 575 F. Supp.2d 513 (S.D.N.Y. 2008).)

The use of a comedy routine within a drama would seem to be transformative, but that's not always the case. The heirs of the comedy team Abbott and Costello sued the producers of the Broadway drama *Hand to God* over the play's use of the "Who's on First" comedy routine. The Second Circuit held that a use is not transformative simply because the new work "serves a purpose or conveys an overall expression, meaning, or message different from the copyrighted material it appropriates." Instead, "the critical inquiry is whether the new work uses the copyrighted material itself for a purpose, or imbues it with a character, different from that for which it was created." (*TCA Television Corp. v. McCollum*, No. 16-134-cv, (2d Cir. 2016).)

Borrowing software code may be a transformative use, as well. For example, Oracle's JAVA SE program contains coding tools (Application Programming Interface or API) that allow the program to connect to, or be accessed by, various platforms. The Supreme Court held that Google's copying of the Java SE API included only those lines of code that were needed to allow programmers to work in a new and transformative program. In other words, Google's limited API borrowing was fair use. (*Google LLC v. Oracle America, Inc.*, 141 S. Ct. 1183 (2021).)

See also: transformative use.

When considering the **second factor**—nature of the copyrighted work—a court will typically consider whether the work being copied is informational or entertaining in nature. As the Supreme Court indicated, "copying a news broadcast may have a stronger claim to fair use than copying a motion picture." Why? Because copying from informational works such as scholarly, scientific, or news journals encourages the free spread of ideas and encourages the creation of new scientific or educational works, all of which benefits the public. In addition, a defendant has a stronger case of fair use if material is copied from a published work rather than an unpublished work. The scope of fair use is narrower with respect to unpublished works because of the author's right to control the first public appearance of this artistic expression.

As for the **third factor**—amount and substantiality of portion used—the more that is taken from a work, the more difficult it becomes to justify it as a fair use. For example, in one case the court found that copying more than half of an unpublished manuscript was not considered a fair use. When considering the amount and substantiality of the portion taken, the court considers not just the quantity of the material taken, but its quality. Determinations regarding "quality" or "substantiality" are subjective and can be difficult to reconcile. For example, the copying of one minute and 15 seconds of a 72-minute Charlie Chaplin film, which was used in a news report about the comedian's death, was considered substantial and not a fair use. However, in another case, the court determined that copying 41 seconds from a boxing match film was not substantial and permitted it as a fair use in a movie biography of Muhammad Ali. In 2021, the Second Circuit ruled that a documentary about burlesque didn't infringe when it used eight seconds of a 190-second children's song. The amount used (though the heart of the composition) was not more than required. According to the Second Circuit, fair use does not obligate a defendant to use the shortest possible snippet to convey its message. (*Brown, et al. v. Netflix, Inc., et al.,* No. 20-2007 (2d Cir. 2020).)

In certain rare cases, copying of a complete work may be considered a fair use. (*Universal City Studios v. Sony Corp.,* 464 U.S. 417 (1984).) For example, the Supreme Court in the Sony case permitted off-the-air copying of complete television programs by consumers who owned video recorders (VCRs).

As for the **fourth factor**—effect of the use on the potential market—a judge must consider the effect on the actual and potential market for the copyrighted work. This consideration goes beyond the past intentions of the author or the means by which the author is currently exploiting the work. For example, in one case a photograph was adapted into a wood sculpture without authorization from the photographer. The fact that the photographer never considered converting the photograph into a sculpture was irrelevant. What mattered was that the potential market existed, as demonstrated by the fact that the defendant earned hundreds of thousands of dollars selling such sculptures.

Some uses are not considered to undermine the potential market.

EXAMPLE 1: After completing a film, an actress incorporated clips from the movie in her acting reel (an actor's video resume). The film's director sued the actress for infringement. A district court ruled that the actress was excused under fair use principles: most notably, the acting reels wouldn't interfere with the film's market or profitability. (*Bain v. Film Indep., Inc.* No. 18-4126 (C.D. Cal. 2020).)

EXAMPLE 2: A photographer's picture for a controversial article about dating was not infringed when a writer published an opinion piece that included a screenshot of the article and picture. The district court held that the use was unlikely to harm the market for the motion picture. (*Yang v. Mic Network, Inc.,* No. 18-7628, 2019 WL 4640263 (S.D.N.Y. 2019).)

Copying a magazine cover for purposes of a comparative advertisement is a fair use, because the comparative advertisement does not undermine the sales or need for the magazine. Another court found that the appearance of a poster in the background of a television series for less than 30 seconds did not harm the potential market for the poster.

Similarly, a court held that a search engine's practice of creating small reproductions ("thumbnails") of images and placing them on its own website (known as "embedding") did not undermine the potential market for the sale or licensing of those images. One of the reasons for this fair use ruling was that the thumbnails were much smaller and of much poorer quality than the original photos and served to index the images and help the public access them. (*Kelly v. Arriba Soft Corp.,* 336 F.3d 811 (9th Cir. 2003).)

A similar result was reached by the Ninth Circuit Court of Appeals in a case involving Google. The court determined that Google's use of thumbnails was permitted as a fair use in a case involving reproductions of images from an adult men's magazine website. (*Perfect 10, Inc. v. Amazon.com, Inc.,* 508 F.3d 1146 (9th Cir. 2007).)

In a case involving the reproduction of concert posters within a book, the Second Circuit Court of Appeals determined that the reduced reproduction of concert posters within the context of a timeline was a fair use. (*Bill Graham Archives v. Dorling Kindersley Ltd.,* 448 F.3d 605 (2d Cir. 2006).) In a related case, a district court held that the reproduction of movie monster magazine covers, in a book about the cover artist, was a fair use. (*Warren Publishing Co. v. Spurlock d/b/a Vanguard Productions,* 645 F. Supp.2d 402 (E.D. Pa. 2009).)

The failure to exploit a market can influence a fair use determination. A group of publishers claimed that Georgia State University (GSU) infringed their rights by using digital excerpts in their course packs. On appeal, the Eleventh Circuit held that GSU's use could not have negatively affected the potential market for digital excerpts because the publishers had not fully exploited digital licensing. The Appeals Court also held that the district court erred when it ruled that copying less than a chapter or 10% of a book is a safe harbor from copyright infringement. (*Cambridge University v. Patton,* 769 F.3d 1232 (11th Cir. 2014).)

In addition to these four fair use factors, a court may consider other factors, if relevant. The drafters of the Copyright Act of 1976 were careful to advise that the four fair use factors were intended only as a guideline and the courts are free to adapt the doctrine to particular situations on a case-by-case basis.

Copyright Law: Definitions

In some cases, however, the facts preclude raising the defense at all. For example, a defendant in a music file sharing case could not claim a fair use defense because he had failed to provide evidence that his copying of music files involved any transformative use (an essential element in proving fair use). The court held that "In the end, fair use is not a referendum on fairness in the abstract. ..." (*Capitol Records Inc. v. Alaujan*, 593 F. Supp.2d 319 (D. Mass. July 27, 2009).)

A thorough source of fair use information is the Copyright and Fair Use site (https://fairuse.stanford.edu) operated by the Stanford University Libraries. In 2015, the Copyright Office created a comprehensive searchable database of fair use cases (www.copyright.gov/fair-use/fair-index.html).

Related terms: transformative use.

Copyright Act: § 107. Limitations on exclusive rights: Fair use

Notwithstanding the provisions of sections 106 and 106A, the fair use of a copyrighted work, including such use by reproduction in copies or phonorecords or by any other means specified by that section, for purposes such as criticism, comment, news reporting, teaching (including multiple copies for classroom use), scholarship, or research, is not an infringement of copyright. In determining whether the use made of a work in any particular case is a fair use the factors to be considered shall include—

(1) the purpose and character of the use, including whether such use is of a commercial nature or is for nonprofit educational purposes;

(2) the nature of the copyrighted work;

(3) the amount and substantiality of the portion used in relation to the copyrighted work as a whole; and

(4) the effect of the use upon the potential market for or value of the copyrighted work.

The fact that a work is unpublished shall not itself bar a finding of fair use if such finding is made upon consideration of all the above factors.

Related terms: infringement (copyright); infringement action; embedding; published work; transformative use.

false representation in copyright registration application

A deliberate lie on a copyright registration form, such as a false statement that no preexisting works are included in the work being registered, may invalidate the legal effect and benefits of the registration. On the other hand, an innocent mistake should not invalidate the registration if the copyright owner makes timely moves to correct it.

Related terms: fraud on the Copyright Office; supplemental registration.

Family Entertainment and Copyright Act of 2005

This Act—a collection of provisions reflecting the interests of various lobbying groups—(1) makes it a criminal violation of copyright law to videotape or transmit video signals from inside a movie theater, (2) exempts from copyright and trademark claims those who filter movies to eliminate objectionable content, (3) makes it a crime to knowingly place a copyrighted computer program, musical work, motion picture or other audiovisual work, or sound recording on a computer network accessible to the public for purposes of copying, (4) directs the Copyright Office to establish a preregistration procedure for works that have not yet been published, (5) establishes rules for the National Film Preservation Act, and (6) permits, during the last 20 years of any term of copyright of a published work, certain rights of reproduction and distribution of copyrighted works for libraries or archives engaged in the preservation, scholarship, or research of those works.

Related terms: duration of copyrights; filtering.

fanfiction (fan fiction, fanfic)

Fanfiction is fiction written by a fan of a movie, book, TV show, or other work. The fanfiction writer borrows characters, environments, and plot elements— known as the "canon" or "bible"—and creates original derivative works incorporating these elements, often focusing on unexpected aspects of the plot, sexual activities or orientation, or minor characters. Although fanfiction has been around since the 1960s (beginning with *Star Trek*), it has exploded on the Web with the posting of millions of fanfiction stories and videos ranging from popular sources (*Harry Potter, Star Wars*) to unexpected inspiration (Bill Nye, the science guy).

Characters and plot lines may be protected by copyright law, and if their appearance in fanfiction is not excused as a fair use, then it is infringement. This places copyright owners in an awkward position: If they sue to stop unauthorized use, they will be pursuing the fans who helped popularize the original work. That's why most copyright owners tolerate fanfiction and rarely pursue claims of infringement. For example, Paramount Studios (owner of *Star Trek*) was tolerant of *Star Trek* fanfiction (and even provided guidelines to help fans avoid lawsuits). But in 2015, Paramount sued Axanar Productions, a company formed by a group of fans attempting to make professional-quality *Star Trek* fanfiction movies. Axanar had produced a 20-minute trailer based on *Star Trek* stories and featuring actors from previous *Star Trek* films. Axanar collected over $1 million in crowdfunding revenue for production of a full-length film. In 2017, a district court held that

Axanar's use of *Star Trek* settings, characters, and themes was not a fair use. *Paramount Pictures Corp v. Axanar Productions, Inc.*, No. 2:15-CV-09938-RGK-E, (C.D. Cal. 2017). The parties settled, and Axanar agreed to abide by Paramount's revised fan-film guidelines: Paramount will not hassle fanfiction *Star Trek* movies provided that they are less than 15 minutes long, they don't use the name Star Trek in their title, and that they use commercially available costumes and props. Fundraising for such films is capped at $50,000.

Some fanfiction may be excused as a fair use, although based on case law the deck is stacked against fanfiction writers. For example, in a case involving the author J.D. Salinger, an author wrote a book in which a character known as Mr. C was allegedly modeled after the character of Holden Caulfield, from Salinger's *Catcher in the Rye*. It was not a fair use because, according to the court, aging the character and placing him in present day did not add something new, particularly because the character's personality remains intact as derived from the original work. (*Salinger v. Colting*, 641 F. Supp.2d 250 (S.D.N.Y. 2009), vacated and remanded on different grounds; *Salinger v. Colting*, 607 F.3d 68 (2d Cir. 2010).)

A similar result occurred when an author borrowed Dr. Seuss characters to retell the story of the O.J. Simpson trial. (*Dr. Seuss Enterprises v. Penguin Books USA, Inc.*, 109 F.3d 1394 (9th Cir. 1997).) An opposite result was reached in a case involving the legendary Civil War novel *Gone with the Wind*. An author wrote a book called *The Wind Done Gone*, which chronicled the diary of a woman named Cynara, the illegitimate daughter of a plantation owner, and Mammy, a slave who cares for the owner's children. The author of *The Wind Done Gone* copied *Gone with the Wind*'s characters, famous scenes, and other elements from the plot and dialogue and descriptions. The court held that *The Wind Done Gone* was protected by the fair use privilege because "its aim is to comment upon or criticize a prior work by appropriating elements of the original in creating a new artistic, as opposed to scholarly or journalistic, work." (*Suntrust Bank v. Houghton Mifflin Co.*, 268 F.2d 1257 (11th Cir. 2001).) Regardless of these results, one generalization seems appropriate: Once a fanfiction creator engages in a for-profit work that might compete with or divert revenue from the original property, the copyright owner is more likely to file a lawsuit.

Related terms: characters, fictional; derivative work; fair use.

Feist Publications Inc. v. Rural Telephone Service Co.

In this court case, a publisher of a residential telephone directory sued a competitor who had copied the directory verbatim. The Supreme Court ruled that the original phone directory was not protected under copyright because:

- it consisted of facts in the public domain (the residence and phone number of each person listed in the directory), and
- the information was not arranged in a creative manner (the listings were in alphabetical order).

Although the phone book publisher argued that it wasn't fair to allow a competitor to capitalize on the labor and expense that had gone into the original directory, the Supreme Court ruled that copyright protects only original expression, not labor and expense. (*Feist Publications Inc. v. Rural Telephone Service Co.,* 499 U.S. 340 (1991).)

Related terms: compilations; computer databases.

filtering

Filtering is the process by which an individual can skip or mute over objectionable content in audio or video content of motion pictures. The technology was created to allow parents the ability to bypass content such as graphic violence, sex, nudity, and profanity during DVD playback. In September 2002, several Hollywood movie studios and directors sued the manufacturer of the process, claiming that the process violated trademark and copyright law. However, in 2005, the lawsuit became moot when President George W. Bush signed into effect the Family Entertainment and Copyright Act of 2005, which includes a provision, The Family Movie Act of 2005, creating an exemption from copyright or trademark infringement for anyone who uses this technology for home viewing.

Related terms: Family Entertainment and Copyright Act of 2005.

filtration test

See infringement (copyright).

first sale doctrine

The first sale doctrine permits the purchaser of a legal copy of a copyrighted work to treat that copy in any way desired, as long as the copyright owner's exclusive copyright rights are not infringed. This means the copy can be destroyed, sold,

Copyright Law: Definitions

given away, or rented. A common example is the rental of movie videos, where the store purchasing the videotapes is entitled to rent them out without paying any royalties to the owner of the copyright rights in the movie. If, however, the store made additional copies of the movie and also rented them out, the underlying copyright would be infringed. The term "first sale doctrine" comes from the fact that the copyright owner maintains control over a specific copy only until it is first sold.

As with many areas of copyright law, there is some confusion as to the boundaries of the first sale doctrine. Two cases involving the framing of artwork seem to have arrived at different results.

EXAMPLE 1: A company purchased a book of prints by the painter Patrick Nagel, then cut out the individual images in the book and mounted them in frames for resale. The Ninth Circuit Court of Appeals in California held that this practice was an infringement and was not permitted under the first sale doctrine. (*Mirage Editions, Inc. v. Albuquerque A.R.T. Co.*, 856 F.2d 1341 (1988).) A similar result was reached in *Greenwich Workshop Inc. v. Timber Creations, Inc.*, 932 F. Supp. 1210 (C.D. Cal. 1996).

EXAMPLE 2: A company purchased notecards and mounted them on tiles. A federal court in Illinois determined that this practice was not an infringement and was permitted under the first sale doctrine. (*Lee v. Deck the Walls, Inc.*, 925 F. Supp. 576 (N.D. Ill. 1996).) The Seventh Circuit affirmed this decision and singled out the Ninth Circuit for criticism. (*Lee v. ART Co.*, 125 F.3d 580 (7th Cir. 1997).) A similar result occurred in *C.M. Paula Co. v. Logan*, 355 F. Supp. 189 (D.C. Texas 1973).

Under these rulings, a person in California cannot mount individual images from an art book, while a person in Illinois can mount individual notecards. Should it matter whether the object that is mounted is from an art book or from a note card? In the California case, the justices felt that mounting the Nagel images separately created a derivative work. In the Illinois case, the judge did not believe that mounting an image on a tile created a derivative work, because the image was not altered or modified.

Another first sale decision added some confusion regarding the rights of software companies. A federal court ruled that the purchaser of a bundle of software programs could resell the individual components (separate programs on CDs). (*Softman Products Co. LLC v. Adobe Systems Inc.*, 171 F. Supp.2d 1075 (C.D. Cal. 2001).)

There are exceptions to the first sale doctrine. As a result of lobbying by the computer and music industries, the rental of computer programs and sound recordings is prohibited. The sound recording exception is limited to musical works; it does not extend to audiobooks. (*Brilliance Audio, Inc. v. Haights Cross Communications, Inc.*, 2007 474 F.3d 365 (6th Cir. 2007).) It is also not permissible under the first sale doctrine to destroy a fine art or photographic work that meets the requirements of the Visual Artists Rights Act (for example, signed and numbered photographs created in limited editions of 200 or fewer copies).

The first sale doctrine does not apply if the copyrighted work is made and sold outside the United States. In a 2008 case, Costco bought Omega watches (with copyrighted designs) outside the U.S. and resold them in U.S. stores. When sued for infringement, the company used a first-sale defense. The Ninth Circuit Court of Appeals rejected that defense, holding that the first sale doctrine—the freedom to resell copyrighted goods—did not apply when the goods are made and first sold outside the U.S. (*Omega v. Costco*, 541 F.3d 982 (9th Cir. 2008).)

In 2013, the U.S. Supreme Court ruled that there are no geographic limitations on the first sale doctrine. In that case, a Thai student came to the U.S. to study and engaged in a business arrangement with his family in Thailand. They would send him the books purchased in Thailand and he would resell them in the U.S. market. The student expanded the business and eventually earned $100,000 profit. U.S. publishers sued the student, arguing that the first sale doctrine did not apply to "gray market goods"—lawfully made goods that were imported into (but not made in) the United States. The Supreme Court disagreed and ruled for the student, stating that as long as the copies were lawfully made—under the direction of the copyright holder—there was no requirement that the books be manufactured in the United States. (*Kirtsaeng v. John Wiley & Sons, Inc.*, 568 U.S. 519 (2013).)

The Ninth Circuit reached a similar result in 2015 when a watch company sued for infringement after its watches were imported into the U.S. without permission. The Ninth Circuit barred the company's claim because the right to control importation expired after a "first sale" of the watches occurred prior to importation. (*Omega S.A. v. Costco Wholesale Corporation*, 541 F.3d 982 (9th Cir. 2015).)

A district court struck down a provision of the California Resale Royalty Act (CRRA) that required a seller of fine art to pay the artist a 5% royalty from the proceeds of a sale. The court held that the Copyright Act's first sale doctrine preempts this state law. (*Sam Francis Foundation et al. v. Christie's Inc.*, No. 2:11-cv-08605 (C.D. Cal. 2016).)

Copyright Act: § 109. Limitations on exclusive rights: Effect of transfer of particular copy or phonorecord

(a) Notwithstanding the provisions of section 106 (3), the owner of a particular copy or phonorecord lawfully made under this title, or any person authorized by such owner, is entitled, without the authority of the copyright owner, to sell or otherwise dispose of the possession of that copy or phonorecord …

   (A) Notwithstanding the provisions of subsection (a), unless authorized by the owners of copyright in the sound recording or the owner of copyright in a computer program (including any tape, disk, or other medium embodying such program), and in the case of a sound recording in the musical works embodied therein, neither the owner of a particular phonorecord nor any person in possession of a particular copy of a computer program (including any tape, disk, or other medium embodying such program), may, for the purposes of direct or indirect commercial advantage, dispose of, or authorize the disposal of, the possession of that phonorecord or computer program (including any tape, disk, or other medium embodying such program) by rental, lease, or lending, or by any other act or practice in the nature of rental, lease, or lending. Nothing in the preceding sentence shall apply to the rental, lease, or lending of a phonorecord for nonprofit purposes by a nonprofit library or nonprofit educational institution. The transfer of possession of a lawfully made copy of a computer program by a nonprofit educational institution to another nonprofit educational institution or to faculty, staff, and students does not constitute rental, lease, or lending for direct or indirect commercial purposes under this subsection.

   (B) This subsection does not apply to—

      (i) a computer program which is embodied in a machine or product and which cannot be copied during the ordinary operation or use of the machine or product; or

      (ii) a computer program embodied in or used in conjunction with a limited purpose computer that is designed for playing video games and may be designed for other purposes.

Related terms: end-user license; work of visual art.

fixed in a tangible medium of expression

In the United States and most other countries, an original work of authorship first qualifies for copyright protection when it is reduced to some physical form or representation—that is, when it is fixed in a tangible medium of expression. Under the Copyright Act of 1976, a work is considered fixed in a tangible medium of expression when "its embodiment in a copy or phonorecord, by or under the authority of the author, is sufficiently permanent or stable to permit it to be perceived, reproduced, or otherwise communicated for a period of more than transitory duration."

When a computer program is first reduced to paper or electronic patterns on a disk, it becomes fixed in a tangible medium of expression and is protected under the copyright laws. Similarly, when a song is recorded, a holograph photographed, a movie filmed, a video game recorded on tape, or an ornamental design molded, each is fixed in a tangible medium of expression and protected by copyright.

A work consisting of sounds, images, or both that is being transmitted live is considered "fixed" if some record of the work is being made simultaneously with its transmission. A live transmission of a baseball game is therefore subject to copyright protection at the instant of transmission, because the images being broadcast are also captured on videotape or sound recording.

Although copyright protection arises the instant a work becomes fixed, many countries, including the United States, allow the copyright owner to take additional steps to strengthen this protection, such as including a correct notice of copyright and registering the copyright with a government agency.

Copyright Act: § 101. Definitions

A work is "fixed" in a tangible medium of expression when its embodiment in a copy or phonorecord, by or under the authority of the author, is sufficiently permanent or stable to permit it to be perceived, reproduced, or otherwise communicated for a period of more than transitory duration. A work consisting of sounds, images, or both, that are being transmitted, is "fixed" for purposes of this title if a fixation of the work is being made simultaneously with its transmission.

Related terms: copyright; international copyright protection; registration.

flow charts, registration of

Flow charts that constitute original works of authorship qualify for copyright protection and may be registered with the U.S. Copyright Office. When registering flow charts, it is necessary to categorize them as a literary work (used for flow charts that communicate information primarily through text) or a visual arts work (used for charts that communicate information primarily through a graphic arrangement of symbols and boxes).

Related terms: registration.

Form CA

The U.S. Copyright Office requires Form CA for supplemental registrations, including the correction of errors.

Related terms: registration; supplemental registration; U.S. Copyright Office.

Form CO

Form CO, a multipurpose application, debuted in 2008 and was discontinued in 2012.

Form GRAM (Group Registration for Works on an Album of Music)

If you want to register a group of musical works (with or without lyrics), you must submit the online application for "Musical Works from an Album." This application can be used only to register musical works (including any lyrics). It cannot be used to register sound recordings.

Form GRTX (Group Registration of Short Online Literary Works)

In 2020, the Copyright Office debuted a new group registration option for short online literary works such as blog entries, social media posts, and short online articles. Applicants are required to use a new registration application form specifically designed for this option.

Form GRUW (Group Registration of Unpublished Works)

In 2019, the Copyright Office implemented a group-registration option for unpublished works. Group Registration for Unpublished Works (GRUW) may be used to register up to ten unpublished works for a single fee. Applicants are required to use a new application form specifically designed for this group option and submit the application and required digital deposit copies through the electronic Copyright Office (eCO) registration portal.

Form PA

Form PA is a paper form used to register all works involving the performing arts, including dramatic works, audiovisual works (such as movies, audiotapes, and training films), and multimedia products that feature a graphical user interface.

Related terms: musical works and sound recordings distinguished; registration; U.S. Copyright Office.

Form RE

The U.S. Copyright Office requires Form RE to renew copyrights on works first published prior to January 1, 1978.

Related terms: duration of copyrights; registration; U.S. Copyright Office.

Form SE (short, regular, and group)

The U.S. Copyright Office provides several versions of the SE form for the registration of works consisting of newspapers, serials, or periodicals such as magazines. Which form to use depends on a number of factors, including the number of items to be registered, the period of time for which the items are to be registered, and whether the constituent parts of the items are works made for hire.

Related terms: registration; U.S. Copyright Office.

Form SR

Form SR is a paper form used to register published and unpublished sound recordings.

Related terms: musical works and sound recordings distinguished; registration; U.S. Copyright Office.

Form TX

Form TX is a paper form used to register all works classified as literary and nondramatic. These include books, poems, computer programs and documentation, essays, and articles.

Related terms: registration; U.S. Copyright Office.

Form VA

Form VA is a paper form used to register all sculptural or graphic works, such as paintings, photographs, and designs.

Related terms: pictorial, graphic, and sculptural works; registration; U.S. Copyright Office.

framing

Framing occurs when one website displays a webpage of another company usually within a bordered area on its own site (similar to the "picture-in-picture" feature offered on some televisions). For example, when a user enters a search engine request, the search engine might display the contents of an online store within the search engine's website, framed by the search engine's text and logos. When a website is framed within another website, the URL or domain name of the website within the frame is not displayed, and users are not able to bookmark the site.

Framing can trigger a dispute under copyright and trademark law theories because a framed site arguably alters the appearance of the content and creates the impression that its owner endorses or voluntarily chooses to associate with the framer. A court fight involving two dental websites failed to fully resolve the issues. Applied Anagramic Inc., a dental services website, framed the content of a competing site. The frames included information about Applied Anagramic as well as its trademark and links to all of its webpages. A federal district court ruled that a website containing a link that reproduced webpages within a frame may constitute an infringing derivative work. The court reasoned that the addition of the frame modified the appearance of the linked site, and such modifications could, without authorization, amount to infringement. (*Futuredontics Inc. v. Applied Anagramic Inc.,* 46 U.S.P.Q.2d 2005 (C.D. Cal. 1997).)

The Ninth Circuit Court of Appeals might have provided the final word on framing. According to the court, the relevant test as to whether framing amounts to infringement is the "server test"—that is, whether the alleged infringing site hosted and physically transmitted the framed content. The court rejected the "incorporation test"—that is, whether the framed content is incorporated in the alleged infringer's site. Google's framing was found not to infringe because it provided only a method for the user's computer to retrieve the framed content. (*Perfect 10, Inc. v. Amazon.com, Inc.,* 508 F.3d 1146 (9th Cir. 2007).)

Related terms: Digital Millennium Copyright Act; embedding; inlining and thumbnails; linking.

fraud on the Copyright Office

Fraud on the Copyright Office exists if the applicant for copyright deliberately misstates or omits a fact that, if known, might have caused the Copyright Office to reject the application. This allegation is typically put forth by a defendant charged with infringement, or alternatively by a party seeking to acquire registration in the face of a previously issued (and fraudulently obtained) registration. If a court finds fraud on the Copyright Office, the registration will be invalidated.

Related terms: false representation in copyright registration application.

freedom of speech and copyright protection

The First Amendment to the U.S. Constitution prohibits the government from placing restrictions on a person's freedom of speech, except in certain situations. Copyright laws, however, prohibit speech that would infringe on somebody's copyright. For example, a court can issue an injunction to prevent the publication of material that would damage a copyright owner by infringing on a copyright. These two legal rules sometimes conflict and one of the means of resolving the issue is the fair use defense in copyright. For example, educators, news reporters, and scholars can invoke the statutory defense of fair use when they use small amounts of copyrighted material as part of teaching, criticizing, or commenting on the copyrighted material.

Related terms: fair use.

freelancer rights

See *New York Times v. Tasini.*

GATT (General Agreement on Tariffs and Trade)

Commonly known as GATT, the General Agreement on Tariffs and Trade is a comprehensive free-trade treaty signed by 117 nations, including almost every developed country. GATT created an international regulatory body known as the World Trade Organization (WTO) to enforce compliance with the agreement.

The portion of GATT that affects copyright law (and other forms of intellectual property) is contained in a special agreement known as Trade Related Aspects of Intellectual Property Rights (TRIPS for short). Probably the most important provision of the TRIPS agreement is that all members of GATT must now adhere to the Berne Convention (except for the Berne requirement that moral rights be respected), even if they haven't signed it. This means that 12 countries that were not members of the Berne Convention—including Haiti, Indonesia, Kuwait, Malaysia, and some of the countries of the former Soviet Union—now agree to offer basic copyright protection under that treaty because of their GATT membership.

Other important GATT provisions applicable to all members include:

- Live musical performances must be protected from unauthorized distribution (bootlegging) through the means of fixing the performance in a tangible medium (tape, video, and so on) or communicating the performance to the public by wireless means.
- Computer programs are to be treated as literary works under the Berne Convention.
- Works by foreign authors that entered the public domain in the United States because of their failure to comply with certain U.S copyright formalities are to have restored copyright protection.

Copyright Law: Definitions

- Substantive penalties for copyright infringement are to be provided, including injunctive relief that prevents further infringement and adequate monetary damages for past infringement.
- Members must implement procedures that stop infringing materials from crossing the borders of other member countries.
- Software copyright owners may prevent the commercial rental of their protected works.

In 2012, the Supreme Court upheld one provision of GATT when it ruled that it was permissible for Congress to allow certain foreign works to have limited copyright protection restored. (*Golan v. Holder*, 565 U.S. 302 (2012).)

Related terms: Berne Convention; international copyright protection; restored copyright under GATT; Universal Copyright Convention (U.C.C.).

Google v. Oracle

Oracle sued Google for $9 billion, claiming that Google's Android operating system improperly used JAVA application programming interface code ("APIs"). APIs are bits of software that interface with programs to trigger software functions. The District Court found that Google's use of JAVA components was "fair use," primarily because APIs exist to interface with other codes and are traditionally borrowed as industry protocols. On appeal, the Federal Circuit ruled that the use of APIs was not a fair use because it wasn't minimal or transformative. (*Oracle Am., Inc. v. Google LLC*, 886 F.3d 1179 (Fed. Cir. 2018).) The Supreme Court had the final word, holding that Google's copying of the Java SE API was a fair use because it included only those lines of code that were needed to allow programmers to work in a new and transformative program. (*Google v. Oracle America, Inc.*, 141 S. Ct. 1183 (2021).)

grant of rights

This phrase, commonly used in license agreements and other contracts pertaining to intellectual property, refers to the rights being transferred under the agreement. For example, an author makes a grant of rights when she licenses all print rights to her publisher in advance of publication.

Related terms: assignment of copyright; transfers of copyright ownership.

graphic and pictorial works

See pictorial, graphic, and sculptural works.

Grokster (Metro-Goldwyn-Mayer, Inc. v. Grokster Ltd.)

See peer-to-peer.

hot news doctrine

This refers to a legal theory that goes beyond copyright and prohibits the theft of "hot news." It's based on the 1918 case of *International News Service v. Associated Press* in which a rival news agency "stole" and "rewrote" AP news articles. Some states still uphold this approach; others consider it invalid. To qualify as the theft of hot news, the theft must be of "time-sensitive" news and must not involve material protected under copyright law. If the material is protected under copyright, the hot news doctrine is inapplicable and considered "pre-empted" under copyright law. That's what happened in a 2011 case, when Barclays Bank complained that its research reports qualified as hot news. The Second Circuit disagreed and ruled that the claim was preempted by copyright law. *(Barclays Capital, Inc. v. TheFlyOnTheWall.com, Inc.,* 650 F.3d 876 (2d Cir. 2011).)

HTML

HTML (Hypertext Markup Language) is a collection of computer symbols and codes that are used to create documents that can be displayed on the Internet. HTML works in conjunction with a Web browser—a software program such as Google *Chrome,* Mozilla *Firefox,* or Microsft *Edge* that allows users to surf the Internet. Although typical HTML commands such as "bold" or "indent" are not protectable under copyright law, the visual or literary expression resulting from complex HTML code—for example, as manifested in the appearance of websites—is protected under copyright law.

ideas, not protected under copyright

Ideas as such are not protected through the copyright process. Only the actual expression of an idea is subject to copyright protection.

> EXAMPLE: Janice authors a new computer program that permits a homemaker to keep a running inventory of household goods. If Kim likes the idea and independently writes a competing program, no copyright infringement has occurred, because Kim copied Janice's idea, but not the expressive aspect of the program.

Copyright Law: Definitions

Other legal doctrines, such as patent law and trade secret law, are available to protect some ideas in certain contexts. For example, an idea that adds to a business's competitive position and is not generally known or used in the trade may be treated as a trade secret, and others may be prevented from disclosing or using it without permission. Similarly, an idea may qualify for protection as a utility patent if it is novel, nonobvious, and useful and has either been reduced to practice (that is, demonstrated to work) or been adequately described in a patent application. An idea for a design may also qualify for a patent if it is for a nonfunctional ornamental design of a manufactured product.

Copyright Act: § 102(b). Subject matter of copyright: In general

(b) In no case does copyright protection for an original work of authorship extend to any idea, procedure, process, system, method of operation, concept, principle, or discovery, regardless of the form in which it is described, explained, illustrated, or embodied in such work.

Related terms: copyright and patent compared.

See also Part 4 (Trade Secret Law): idea submission; ideas as trade secrets.

identifying material

To register a copyright, it is ordinarily necessary to deposit at least one, and often two, complete copies of the work with the U.S. Copyright Office. However, some kinds of works (for instance, holographs and virtual reality scenarios) are not easy to deposit. In other cases, the author might wish to maintain certain ideas as trade secrets and fears their disclosure if a true or complete copy of the work is to be deposited.

To accommodate the needs of registrants in such situations, the U.S. Copyright Office will accept a deposit of only a portion of the work or a representation of the entire work. The portion deposited is labeled as "identifying material" in order to satisfy the deposit requirement in the copyright law. Examples of identifying material include photographic prints, transparencies, photostats, drawings, or similar two-dimensional reproductions visible without the aid of a machine.

To deposit software, the U.S. Copyright Office will accept the first and last 25 pages of a program as identifying material, if the program runs beyond 50 pages. For databases, identifying material consists of a portion of each file in the database.

In addition to these rules, the U.S. Copyright Office is willing to provide special relief for individual deposits on a case-by-case basis. For instance, if a software developer wants to deposit source code but doesn't want to disclose certain trade secrets, the U.S. Copyright Office will allow the developer to black out certain portions of the code so that it cannot easily be understood and copied by potential infringers. Deposits accomplished under the special relief doctrine are also considered to be "identifying material."

Related terms: deposit with U.S. Copyright Office; object code; source code; special relief.

implied license (copyright)

See licensing of copyrights.

importing of infringing works

U.S. copyright and customs laws authorize the U.S. Customs and Border Protection agency (CBP) to prevent material that infringes a U.S. copyright from entering the United States. Under GATT, all member countries are supposed to enact a similar procedure.

In the United States, the procedure is supposed to work like this: The copyright owner records his or her work with CBP. Any imported copies that are the same as or highly similar to the recorded works are temporarily seized. The copyright owner is informed of the seizure and provided time in which to obtain a court order barring the materials from being imported to the United States.

As a practical matter, this remedy is seldom used, due to the inability of CBP to check imports carefully against recorded copyrights. However, CBP will act if alerted by the copyright owner.

U.S. customs law also authorizes copyright owners to file a complaint with the International Trade Commission to have infringing works excluded from the United States on the ground their importation would constitute an unfair method of competition.

Related terms: international copyright protection.

indecent or immoral works, not protected

Copyright protection is not available for works that a court or the U.S. Copyright Office deems to be indecent or immoral. The current position of U.S. Copyright Office is to accept registration for even fairly explicit material and to let the courts decide the issue if anyone objects.

Copyright Law: Definitions

independent creation

When an author independently creates a work, it is considered original, even though it might be highly similar to another work created by someone else. Accordingly, if a defendant in an infringement lawsuit can prove independent creation, the infringement action will fail, even if the plaintiffs have proved the necessary elements for infringement (substantial similarity and access).

Although some situations are relatively clear-cut, there is also a large gray area where it is difficult to tell whether subsequent works are independent creations or derivatives of earlier ones. In the latter case, permission to use the earlier work would be required.

> EXAMPLE: Tim writes a book in English that is similar to one Antoine has written in French, but it is not, strictly speaking, a translation. Is this an independent creation? No, if the court finds that Tim's book was based on the French one, and yes, if the court finds that Tim's book was created without relying on or borrowing from Antoine's book. Which of these results will occur depends on the degree of similarity between the works, whether Tim had access to Antoine's work, and the probability of Tim's independently creating a similar work.

Determining whether a work is an independent creation or a derivative work is especially difficult in the cases of:

- **Computer graphics.** Expression can easily be reduced to digital form, allowing incremental modifications (called "morphing" in the case of moving images) to be made easily, with the result that one expression can be transformed into another without a clear line of demarcation.
- **Musical sampling.** Sounds can be digitally captured and then modified and mixed to a point that the result has very little resemblance to any of the original material.

Related terms: based on an earlier work; copyright; derivative work; infringement (copyright).

infringement (copyright)

Copyright infringement occurs when a copyrighted work is reproduced, distributed, performed, publicly displayed, or made into a derivative work without the permission of the copyright owner. Some examples of infringement are copying a software program, sampling a song, modifying a photo, posting an eBook, or downloading a video without the authorization of the copyright owner.

Whether or not a work will be found to have infringed largely depends on these factors:

- Was the work that was copied the subject of a proper copyright? This factor is typically satisfied if the work was independently created, has enough creativity, and is fixed in a tangible medium.
- Did the infringer copy the work? In the absence of an admission that copying occurred, did the author of the second work have access to the copyrighted work?
- Are the two works substantially similar? Has enough been taken in quality and quantity from the copyrighted work to amount to a theft of intellectual property?

Substantial Similarity. Judging substantial similarity is the task of the jury in a court proceeding. They must determine whether the infringement tipping point has occurred. One of the first cases to define this standard involved a litigious songwriter who was convinced that Cole Porter had sent "stooges" to steal his songs. Justice Jerome Frank, writing for the Second Circuit, stated, "The question, therefore, is whether defendant took from plaintiff's works so much of what is pleasing to the ears of lay listeners, who comprise the audience for whom such popular music is composed, that defendant wrongfully appropriated something which belongs to the plaintiff." (*Arnstein v. Porter*, 154 F.2d 464 (2d Cir. 1946).)

Sometimes an infringement analysis requires separating the similarities into two categories:

- **literal similarities,** when elements of the content (words, images, music) are copied directly; for example, bootlegged movies, duplicated images, verbatim text copying; and
- **non-literal similarities,** for example, copying a plotline, creating a sequel, or borrowing the look, feel, and functionality of a software program.

EXAMPLE: The owners of *Star Wars* sued the owners of the television show *Battlestar Galactica* for copyright infringement. There was no duplication of *Star Wars* dialogue in the television show, but there were many non-literal similarities. In their brief to the court, the owners of *Star Wars* listed 34 such non-literal similarities. For example, the central conflict of each story is a war between the galaxy's democratic and totalitarian forces; a friendly robot who aids the democratic forces is severely injured (*Star Wars*) or destroyed (*Battlestar*) by the totalitarian forces; there is a romance between the hero's friend (the cynical fighter

Copyright Law: Definitions

pilot) and the daughter of one of the leaders of the democratic forces; and there is a scene in a cantina (*Star Wars*) or casino (*Battlestar*) in which musical entertainment is offered by bizarre, nonhuman creatures. On the basis of the 34 non-literal similarities, the owners of *Star Wars* were able to prove infringement. (*Twentieth Century-Fox Film Corp. v. MCA Inc.*, 715 F.2d 1327 (9th Cir. 1983).)

The stronger the similarity, the greater the chance that a court will find that infringement occurred. A greater similarity is usually required for factual, or nonfiction, works to be considered infringing than is required for works of fiction. In order to analyze the many ways that copyright can be infringed (such as borrowing characters, dialogue, musical sections, snipping code, embedding pictures, lifting text, and so on), courts have developed methods for measuring similarity. Due to varying standards in different federal circuits, many of these methods use different terms and language to accomplish the same result: separating and comparing protectible and nonprotectible elements.

- **Objective/subjective** (also known as the extrinsic-intrinsic test). A standard approach to similarity is to first identify the aspects of the two works that are subject to copyright protection and objectively (extrinsically) compare them. During this phase, expert testimony may be introduced. For example, in a case involving alleged infringement of the Marvin Gaye song "Got to Give It Up," by Robin Thicke's "Blurred Lines," the court permitted expert testimony as to melodies, rhythms, harmonies, structures, and lyrics of the two. Next, the jury subjectively (intrinsically) analyzed and compared the two works from a lay perspective (that of the ordinary, reasonable person) to determine that Thicke's song amounted to infringement. (*Williams v. Gaye*, 885 F.3d 1150 (9th Cir. 2018).)
- **Lay observer** (also known as the ordinary observer test). Substantial similarity exists where an average lay observer would recognize the alleged copy as having been appropriated from the copyrighted work. (*Original Appalachian Artworks, Inc. v. Toy Loft, Inc.*, 684 F.2d 821, 824 (11th Cir.1982).) In such cases, expert testimony is usually not necessary. For example, in *Original Appalachian Artworks*, a lay observer test was used to determine that a doll manufacturer had created ripoffs of the Cabbage Patch dolls.
- **More discerning observer.** Like the objective/subjective test, the court removes the unprotectable elements before considering the similarity of the defendant's work to the copyrighted work. The court is measuring

"substantial similarity between those elements, and only those elements, that provide copyrightability to the allegedly infringed [work]." (*Shull v. TBTF Productions, Inc.,* No. 20-3529 (2d Cir. 2021).) In *Shull*, an author and performance coach sued the makers of the TV show, *Billions*, claiming the TV show had infringed her coaching guide. The Second Circuit dismissed the case, determining that the similarities between the two works—stock characters with generalized qualities and a financial setting—were unprotectible, and what remained as copyrightable was not infringed.

- **Filtration** (also known as the Abstraction-Filtration-Comparison test or *Altai* test). In the case of *Computer Associates Int' l v. Altai*, 982 F.2d 693 (2d Cir. 1992), a federal appellate court first applied a now commonly used technique called "filtration" to distinguish those aspects of software or software interfaces that are protected by copyright from those that are not. (The *Altai* case itself dealt with whether a computer program interface was entitled to copyright protection.) Often used in cases of software piracy, this test has three steps: eliminate from a software-related work such unprotectable elements as ideas, elements dictated by efficiency (that is, where there is no other sensible way to write the code or handle the task), material from the public domain, and elements determined by external factors (such as the nature of the mechanical specifications of the computer on which the program is intended to run, compatibility requirements, manufacturers' design standards, and intended user base). What's left of the work is then examined to see whether it qualifies for copyright protection. After the *Altai* court applied the filtration process to the interface in question, nothing was left to protect; thus, copyright protection was denied.

Substantial similarity can traverse different media, often in the creation of infringing derivative works.

> EXAMPLE: The photographer Art Rogers created a photograph entitled "Puppies," which features a man and a woman sitting on a bench and holding eight puppies. The artist Jeff Koons purchased two postcards of the image and, without obtaining Mr. Rogers's authorization, created a wood sculpture based on the image. Even though Koons had demonstrated sufficient originality in his statues, a lay observer would conclude that the statues were derived from, and substantially similar to the photograph. (*Rogers v. Koons*, 960 F.2d 301 (2d Cir. 1992).)

Related terms: derivative work; fair use; infringement action; registration; standing (to sue); scènes à faire doctrine.

infringement action

Once a copyright owner suspects infringement, the owner may file a lawsuit against the infringer for damages in a federal court. Copyright owners must register their work prior to suing for infringement under the provisions of 17 U.S. Code Section 411(a). (*Fourth Estate Public Benefit Corp. v. Wall-Street.com, LLC*, 586 U.S. ___ (2019).)

Infringement actions offer the successful plaintiff the possibility of a wide variety of judicial relief, depending on the circumstances and whether the work is registered with the U.S. Copyright Office. In addition to awarding financial damages, the court is authorized to grant immediate but temporary relief in the form of a temporary restraining order and, pending a full-scale trial, more extended relief in the form of an injunction. Either or both of these devices can halt publication or distribution of the offending work.

The preliminary injunction can be vital to a copyright owner's interests, because a regular injunction (or permanent injunction) can be obtained only as a part of a final judgment, which can take years. A preliminary injunction used to be relatively easy to obtain, once substantial evidence had been presented to the court showing a probability that an infringement was occurring. However, that standard appears to have changed. In a 2010 case, the Second Circuit held that the old test no longer applied in light of the Supreme Court's ruling in *eBay v. MercExchange, L.L.C.*, a patent case in which the Supreme Court ruled that showing a likelihood of infringement was not enough; the party seeking the preliminary injunction must apply a more traditional four-factor test. (*Salinger v. Colting*, 607 F.3d 68 (2d Cir. 2010).) The four factors to be considered are: whether the moving party will suffer irreparable injury; whether there is an adequate remedy available at law; the balance of hardships; and public interest considerations. (*TD Bank v. Hill*, No. 16-2897 (3d Cir. Jul. 1, 2019).)

In addition to court orders prohibiting further infringing activity, plaintiffs may be awarded a money award known as damages. This can consist of actual losses suffered as a result of the infringement and the profits realized by the defendant because of the infringement. As an alternative to seeking damages and profits, copyright owners who have timely registered their copyright may pursue statutory damages, which can be awarded without any proof of harm or defendant's profits.

Copyright owners who timely register their copyright and/or record their ownership interest may qualify to have their attorneys' fees and court costs paid by an unsuccessful defendant. However, if the defendant is successful and prevails, the defendant may seek attorneys' fees regardless of whether the plaintiff timely registered.

According to the Supreme Court, the award of court costs (or "full costs" as used in the Copyright Act) was not meant to go beyond the six categories in the federal statute authorizing district courts to award costs. (28 U.S. Code §§ 1821 and 1920.) The categories include: (1) fees of the clerk and marshal; (2) fees for printed or electronically recorded transcripts; (3) fees and disbursements for printing and witnesses; (4) fees for exemplification and the costs of making copies; (5) docket fees; and (6) compensation of court-appointed experts, and compensation of interpreters. (*Rimini Street v. Oracle U.S.A.*, 139 S. Ct. 873 (2019).)

Copyright Act: § 503. Remedies for infringement: Impounding and disposition of infringing articles

(a) At any time while an action under this title is pending, the court may order the impounding, on such terms as it may deem reasonable, of all copies or phonorecords claimed to have been made or used in violation of the copyright owner's exclusive rights, and of all plates, molds, matrices, masters, tapes, film negatives, or other articles by means of which such copies or phonorecords may be reproduced.

(b) As part of a final judgment or decree, the court may order the destruction or other reasonable disposition of all copies or phonorecords found to have been made or used in violation of the copyright owner's exclusive rights, and of all plates, molds, matrices, masters, tapes, film negatives, or other articles by means of which such copies or phonorecords may be reproduced.

Copyright Act: § 505. Remedies for infringement: Costs and attorney's fees

In any civil action under this title, the court in its discretion may allow the recovery of full costs by or against any party other than the United States or an officer thereof. Except as otherwise provided by this title, the court may also award a reasonable attorney's fee to the prevailing party as part of the costs.

Related terms: access; attorneys' fees; damages for copyright infringement; defenses to copyright infringement; infringement (copyright); injunctions; registration; standing (to sue).

injunctions

Once copyright infringement is established, courts often are willing to issue an order (termed an injunction) to prevent the infringer from making or distributing further unauthorized copies of the original work of authorship. To the extent that the infringing work heavily relies on the infringed work, an injunction can have a severely adverse economic impact on the infringer.

EXAMPLE: When Apple Computer Inc. obtained an injunction preventing Franklin Computer from further copying the Apple Computer operating system, Franklin was effectively unable to market its computers, because they would not work without using the infringing material. (*Apple Computer, Inc. v. Franklin Computer Corporation*, 714 F.2d 1240 (3d Cir. 1983).)

Injunctions come in three forms:

- **Temporary injunctions or temporary restraining orders (TROs).** These are technically restricted to a situation when the plaintiff is on the brink of suffering irreparable injury and needs to stop some immediate action pending further consideration of the case. TROs typically last only for a week or two until the court can consider whether to grant a preliminary injunction.
- **Preliminary injunctions.** Courts will issue a preliminary injunction if the plaintiff makes a strong showing that the plaintiff is likely to prevail at the trial of the case and the plaintiff will suffer greater economic harm than the defendant if such interim relief is not granted. Preliminary injunctions can last as long as it takes to get to trial—sometimes years.
- **Permanent injunctions.** These are permanent prohibitions against using or distributing the unauthorized work.

Prior to a Supreme Court ruling regarding patents (*eBay Inc. v. MercExchange, L.L.C.*, 547 U.S. 388 (2006)), courts tend to presume that a likelihood of copyright infringement caused irreparable injury and often issued TROs and preliminary injunctions if infringement appeared likely. A more modern approach is to require that the plaintiff prove both a likelihood of infringement, *and* irreparable harm. The Third Circuit confirmed that irreparable harm cannot be presumed in copyright cases and that the classic four-factor injunction standard should be used. (*TD Bank v. Hill*, No. 16-2897 (3d Cir. Jul. 1, 2019).)

If an injunction is issued, the court will usually require the plaintiff to post a bond to compensate the defendant for any harm caused by the injunction if later on the defendant ends up winning the case. Whether or not preliminary relief is granted, the court will determine after a trial whether injunctive relief is appropriate on a more permanent basis.

As a practical matter, losing a preliminary injunction often spells defeat for the defendant, regardless of the legal strength of the case. This is because few defendants can afford to keep the allegedly infringing work off the market pending trial and also meet the costs of a full-blown defense to the infringement charges. Because by definition a judge has already determined that infringement will mostly likely be found to exist when the case goes to trial, defendants normally find it economically prudent to settle early on the plaintiff's terms and get on with their business.

Copyright Act: § 502. Remedies for infringement: Injunctions

(a) Any court having jurisdiction of a civil action arising under this title may, subject to the provisions of section 1498 of title 28, grant temporary and final injunctions on such terms as it may deem reasonable to prevent or restrain infringement of a copyright.

(b) Any such injunction may be served anywhere in the United States on the person enjoined; it shall be operative throughout the United States and shall be enforceable, by proceedings in contempt or otherwise, by any United States court having jurisdiction of that person. The clerk of the court granting the injunction shall, when requested by any other court in which enforcement of the injunction is sought, transmit promptly to the other court a certified copy of all the papers in the case on file in such clerk's office.

Related terms: *Apple Computer, Inc. v. Franklin*; damages for copyright infringement; infringement action.

innocent infringement of copyright

Innocent infringement—when an author honestly believes, based on the circumstances, that a work is not protected under copyright—does not excuse infringement. It is, however, a mitigating factor when determining the remedies for infringement. For example, a court may halt the activity but may not be inclined to award damages. Innocent infringement should be distinguished from the fair use doctrine. Under fair use, there is no infringement because of the nature of the material and the context in which it was used, not because of the author's belief as to whether the work was copyrighted.

Related terms: fair use; omission of copyright notice.

instructional text

A literary, pictorial, or graphic work that is prepared for use in day-to-day instructional activities is an instructional text. For example, a textbook would be an instructional text, but a novel used in a literature class would not be an instructional text. Instructional text is one of the enumerated categories listed for determining whether a work can qualify as a commissioned work made for hire. This distinction is important because if a work was commissioned and it did not fall within one of the enumerated categories, it would not be a work made for hire even if there was a signed agreement stating that the work was made for hire. If a work qualifies as a work made for hire, the copyright is owned by the hiring party, not the author.

Related terms: work made for hire.

insurance, copyright

See advertising injury.

international copyright protection

Over 120 nations have signed treaties in which they agree to extend reciprocal copyright protection to works authored by nationals of the other signing countries as well as works first published in one of the other signing countries. This reciprocal approach is commonly called "national treatment."

The two main copyright treaties are the Berne Convention and the Universal Copyright Convention (U.C.C.), both of which the United States has signed. To the extent the provisions of these two treaties overlap, the author is entitled to the more liberal protection available—usually found in the Berne Convention.

Most countries of the world have ratified GATT (General Agreement on Tariffs and Trade), which binds them to comply with the provisions of the Berne Convention (except for its moral rights provision) whether or not they are already members. The GATT treaty makes the Berne Convention by far the more important international treaty; the U.C.C. plays an increasingly minor role in international copyright protection.

Besides establishing reciprocal protection rights, the Berne Convention also establishes the minimum protections that must be afforded and specifies that no formalities—such as copyright notice—are required for gaining such protection. The Berne Convention does not impose on any country a definition of what can and cannot be copyrighted, but virtually all of the signatory countries (and GATT members) will fully protect such traditional items as books, art works, movies, and plays. In addition, GATT requires that all members treat computer programs as literary works under the Berne Convention.

Authors seeking to invoke international protection under the Berne Convention (authors in the U.S. and in most large, industrialized nations, including all nations that ratify the GATT treaty) need not apply any copyright notice to their works.

Authors seeking to invoke international copyright protection under the Universal Copyright Convention (the relatively few countries that have not signed the Berne Convention or the GATT treaty) must use the following notice: "© (year of publication) (author or other basic copyright owner)."

For example, the correct U.C.C. notice for this book would be: "© 2022 Richard Stim." Or, if Nolo owned the copyright, the correct notice would be: "© 2022 Nolo."

Related terms: Berne Convention; GATT (General Agreement on Tariffs and Trade); Universal Copyright Convention (U.C.C.).

Internet Service Provider (ISP)

An Internet Service Provider (ISP)—also sometimes referred to as an Online Service Provider (OSP)—is any business that provides access to the Internet. That includes big access providers like AOL, Yahoo!, and Google, or it can refer to companies that provide website hosting, commercial Wi-Fi services, or FTP services. ISPs can sometimes be held accountable for copyright violations for material posted by subscribers and users but are usually protected by the "safe harbor" provisions of the Digital Millennium Copyright Act.

Related terms: Digital Millennium Copyright Act ("DMCA").

inverse ratio rule

Until 2020, the Ninth Circuit followed this judge-made rule that the more substantial the evidence of access, the less that was required to show substantial similarity. The Ninth Circuit rejected the rule in an appeal regarding the Led Zeppelin song, "Stairway to Heaven." (*Skidmore v. Led Zeppelin*, 952 F.3d 1051 (9th Cir. 2020).)

joint copyright ownership

See joint work.

joint work

Under the Copyright Act of 1976, a joint work is defined as "a work prepared by two or more authors who intend to merge their contributions into inseparable or interdependent parts of the whole." (17 U.S. Code § 101.) The U.S. Copyright Office will accept for registration works that meet this statutory definition and will treat the authors as having equal rights to register and enforce the copyright, regardless of what the joint authors arrange among themselves.

> EXAMPLE: Tom and Mary have a partnership agreement, under which Tom owns three-fourths of the copyright and Mary one-fourth. If the copyright is registered with the U.S. Copyright Office with Tom and Mary listed as coauthors, they will be simply listed as coauthors without reference to their independent, unequal ownership arrangement. However, the partnership agreement will govern issues that might arise between Tom and Mary, such as who gets what share of the any royalties earned on the work, who is entitled to license the work to others, and who can sue to enforce the copyright.

Related terms: coauthors.

laches

See statute of limitations.

laws, judicial opinions, and model codes, copyrightable subject matter

There has long been a judicial consensus that neither the opinions of judges, nor the statutes enacted by Congress or state legislatures, can be protected by copyright. This principle is derived from a Supreme Court opinion, *Wheaton v. Peters*, 33 U.S. 591 (1834). Although anyone is free to quote or reproduce these statutes and legal opinions, various publishers and reporting systems have claimed proprietary rights to the way these statutes and opinions are annotated or organized. For example, West Publishing unsuccessfully argued that its page numbering system could not be copied onto CD-ROMs by a rival publisher. (*Matthew Bender & Co. v. West Publishing Co.*, 158 F.3d 674 (2d Cir. 1998).) In 2020, the Supreme Court held that the "government edicts doctrine"—a principle that prevents judges and legislators from claiming authorship in judicial opinions or laws—also applies to the annotations prepared and adopted by a state legislature. (*Georgia v. Public.Resource.Org, Inc.*, 140 S. Ct. 1498 (2020).) These decisions and their underlying rationale—that the laws and opinions created by public officials belong in the public domain—do not necessarily apply to model codes. Model codes are regulations created by a private business that may later be adopted by a public entity.

> EXAMPLE: The Southern Building Code Congress International (SBCCI) is a nonprofit organization that develops modern building, fire, and mechanical codes. These codes are adopted by municipalities, and the SBCCI earns revenues by publishing and selling the codes or licensing the codes for publication. In 1997, Peter Veeck, the operator of a website, posted the building codes for two small towns in North Texas. The SBCCI sued for copyright infringement. In 2002, the Fifth Circuit Court of Appeals ruled that a company that creates a model code may not claim copyright in it once the code has been adopted into law. (*Veeck v. Southern Building Code Congress International, Inc.*, 293 F.3d 791 (5th Cir. 2002).)

Related terms: factual works; merger doctrine; public domain.

Library of Congress

With few exceptions, under the Copyright Act of 1976 an author is required to deposit at least one copy of his or her published work with the Library of Congress. This requirement is automatically met if the work is registered with the U.S. Copyright Office, which requires a deposit of either one or two copies of the best edition of the work, depending on the type of work. However, even if an author decides not to register a work with the U.S. Copyright Office, the author ordinarily has an obligation to make the Library of Congress deposit, except for computer programs and certain other types of works. Failure to make the deposit carries no penalty unless the Library of Congress makes a demand. In that case, failure to deposit within three months may result in a relatively nominal fine.

Copies of works deposited for copyright registration or in fulfillment of the mandatory deposit requirement are available to the Library of Congress for its collections. The Library reserves the right to select or reject any published work for its permanent collections based on the research needs of Congress, the nation's scholars, and of the nation's libraries. For more information on the Library's selection policies, contact: Library of Congress, Collections Policy Office, 101 Independence Avenue, SE, Washington, DC 20540.

Related terms: best edition of a work; deposit with U.S. Copyright Office.

license fee, payable by innocent infringer

See innocent infringement of copyright.

license recordation

See recordation of copyright transfers.

licensing of copyrights

A copyright license is a method by which the owner of a copyright (the "licensor") gives permission for another (the "licensee") to use or copy an original work of authorship. A license is a "permission agreement" not a transfer of ownership.

A license may be either exclusive or nonexclusive and can be restricted by territory, time, media, purpose, or by virtually any other factor desired by the parties.

Copyright Law: Definitions

Exclusive licenses. An exclusive license, which must be in writing, is a contract in which a copyright owner authorizes another person or entity (called the licensee) to exclusively exercise one or more of the rights (or portion of such rights) that belong to the copyright owner under the copyright. The licensee is said to "own" the rights granted in the license and is often referred to as a "copyright owner."

EXAMPLE: Jeanette, a U.S. author, publishes a successful cookbook specializing in East African recipes. Aaron believes the book will sell well in other countries and approaches Jeanette for permission to sell it on the international market. Jeanette may choose to grant Aaron an exclusive license to copy, distribute, and translate (prepare derivative works from) the book for marketing in all countries outside of the United States. She might, instead, license Aaron to market the book only in one or a few countries—for example, France, the Canadian province of Quebec, and all Caribbean and African countries where French is a primary language. In addition to foreign rights, Jeanette is interested in finding someone to help her market the book to cooking stores within the United States. To reach this market, she grants an exclusive license to a cookware wholesaler. Finally, she exclusively licenses a cookbook publisher to publish and distribute the book to the book trade (exclusive of cooking stores) in the United States.

Under an exclusive license, the licensee as a "copyright owner" has the right to file an infringement action in court to stop all infringing activities, assuming that the copyright was properly registered, and the license was recorded with the U.S. Copyright Office. Exclusive licenses must almost always be in writing to be valid. In all cases, licenses should be recorded with the U.S. Copyright Office.

Nonexclusive licenses. A copyright owner grants a nonexclusive license when the owner (licensor) authorizes another person or institution (the licensee) to exercise one or more of the rights belonging to the owner under the copyright on a shared (nonexclusive) basis. Legally, no transfer of copyright ownership takes place under a nonexclusive license, because the licensee shares the right with the original owner and, perhaps, with additional nonexclusive licensees. Although a nonexclusive license need not be in writing to be valid, most are.

EXAMPLE: Steve builds an electronic legal dictionary featuring intellectual property terminology for the purpose of selling it to law firms. Rather than selling the dictionary outright, Steve distributes it under nonexclusive licenses that permit licensee law firms to make copies for use in personal computers belonging to the law office staff (a site license). The nonexclusive license prohibits a licensee from transferring the dictionary to another firm and requires payment of a set amount each year for renewal of the license. Under this arrangement, thousands of law firms might be nonexclusive licensees, but none of them would be considered a copyright owner, because none has the exclusive right to use and therefore enforce the copyright.

Implied licenses. Licenses can be implied from the parties' conduct and reasonable expectations. For example, if a written license expired, but the parties continued as if it hadn't, the license for the extended use would be implied. An implied license is always nonexclusive. Sublicenses (when a licensee grants a license) can also be implied.

EXAMPLE: A commercial photographer issued an unrestricted license that included the freedom to sublicense. The photographer later sued, claiming that the sublicenses must be in writing. Considering this issue for the first time, the First Circuit held that the parties' conduct could imply sublicenses. (*Photographic Illustrators Corp. v. Orgill Inc.*, 953 F. 3d 56 (1st Cir. 2020).)

Related terms: standing (to sue); transfers of copyright ownership.

limited publication

A work is *not* considered "published" under the Copyright Act if it is a limited publication. The Ninth Circuit described limited publication as when one "communicates the contents of a [work] to a definitely selected group and for a limited purpose, and without the right of diffusion, reproduction, distribution, or sale." (*White v. Kimmel*, 193 F.2d 744, 746 (9th Cir. 1952).) The limited publication concept was more relevant prior to 1989 when publication without copyright notice resulted in a loss of copyright.

linking

Any component of a webpage that connects the user to another webpage or another portion of the same webpage is a link (also known as "hyperlink"). Clicking on underlined text or a graphic image activates most links. It is a violation of the law to create a link that contributes to unauthorized copying of a copyrighted work if the linking party knew or had reason to know of the unauthorized copying and encouraged it.

> EXAMPLE: A website posted infringing copies of a church's copyrighted handbook at its site. The website was ordered to remove the handbook but subsequently provided links to other sites that contained infringing copies of the handbook. These links were different from traditional links, because the website knew and encouraged the use of the links to obtain unauthorized copies. The linking activity constituted contributory copyright infringement. (*Intellectual Reserve, Inc. v. Utah Lighthouse Ministry, Inc.*, 75 F. Supp.2d 1290 (D. Utah 1999).)

A link that bypasses a website's home page and instead goes to another page within the site is often called a "deep link." The consensus among copyright experts is that deep linking is not copyright infringement—after all, the author of a novel can't prevent readers from reading the end first if they so desire, so why should a website owner have the right to determine in what order a user can access a website? Some well-known websites such as Amazon.com welcome deep links. However, some websites—even the listener-friendly National Public Radio—have asserted rights against deep linkers under both copyright and trademark law principles. In 2002, a Danish court prevented a website from deep linking to a newspaper site. In 2003, Germany weighed in on the issue when its federal court ruled that deep linking was not a violation of German copyright law. (*Handelsblatt v. Paperboy*, Federal Superior Court of Germany (Bundesgerichtshof) 17 July 2003.)

Related Terms: embedding.

literary works

"Literary works" is one of the broad categories of material protected under the copyright laws. The phrase has little legal significance and is used primarily to classify materials that must be registered with the U.S. Copyright Office in a copyright application.

According to the U.S. Copyright Act of 1976, literary works are "works, other than audiovisual works, expressed in words, numbers, or other verbal or numerical symbols or indicia, regardless of the nature of the material objects, such as books, periodicals, manuscripts, phonorecords, film, tapes, disks, or cards in which they are embodied." (17 U.S. Code § 101.)

Examples of literary works include computer programs, books, poems, plays, newspapers, magazines, software documentation, training films consisting primarily of dialogue, and flow charts consisting primarily of text.

Related terms: registration.

mandatory deposit

See deposit with U.S. Copyright Office.

manufacturing clause

The manufacturing clause is a now-defunct U.S. statute that barred the importation of more than 2,000 copies of any nondramatic literary material written in English by an American author, unless it had been manufactured in the United States or Canada. The manufacturing clause has not been in effect since the 1980s.

mask work

See Semiconductor Chip Protection Act of 1984.

mechanical rights

The right to reproduce a song on physical or digital media such as MP3s, compact disc, vinyl recordings, or DVD (collectively known as phonorecords) is referred to as a mechanical right. In contrast, broadcasting a song over the radio, TV, or Internet or incorporating a song in a movie, video, or video game is not a mechanical right; it is known as a performance right.

Every time a song is "pressed" (or fixed) on a phonorecord, the songwriter is entitled to a payment for this mechanical right, known as a mechanical royalty. Mechanical royalty rates are set by law (known as the statutory rate), but artists and songwriters are free to negotiate a lower rate. The advantage of paying the statutory rate is that an artist does not have to seek permission to record the song provided that certain requirements are met (see "compulsory license").

Sometimes a songwriter accepts less than the statutory rate. Why? Often the songwriter has no choice because it is a condition of a recording agreement or because it is the only way to attract a specific artist to record the song.

The current fee for recordings is 9.1 cents per song (or 1.75 cents per minute of playing time). To verify the current rate, check the Copyright Office's online rate list at www.copyright.gov/licensing/m200a.pdf. A recording artist does not have to use the compulsory license, and many recording artists seek permission directly from the song owner and negotiate for a lower rate.

Related terms: compulsory license; music publisher.

merger doctrine

This court-made rule severely limits copyright protection—or denies it altogether—to a work that involves very little creativity if its ways of expressing the ideas in the work are very limited. For example, there are limited ways to express the instructions for activating a fire alarm, or how to perform a yoga pose. When it is very difficult to separate the expression in a work from the underlying ideas, the two are said to merge. Under the merger doctrine, a work will be protected only against verbatim copying, assuming there is any protectable expression at all in the work.

The merger doctrine has been the basis for a series of court decisions that deny protection to computer user interfaces, for example *Computer Associates Int'l v. Altai,* 982 F.2d 693 (2d Cir. 1992). The merger doctrine also applies to factual works such as histories, biographies, and scientific treatises.

Related terms: *Feist Publications Inc. v. Rural Telephone Service Co.;* infringement (copyright).

microcode and copyright

Microcode is software embedded in a computer chip for the purpose of performing the computer's basic purpose: to process information. One court has ruled that microcode is subject to copyright protection. (*NEC Corp. v. Intel Corp.,* 10 U.S.P.Q.2d 1177 (N.D. Cal. 1989).) However, this protection is likely to be limited to "virtually identical copying," as it was in the *Intel* case, because microcode is very much determined by external constraints such as heat and space, and the underlying unprotectable idea would therefore be merged with any protectable expression in the code.

Related terms: software; merger doctrine.

mistakes in registration, correction of

See supplemental registration.

money damages in infringement action

See damages for copyright infringement.

moral rights

Every copyright owner who lives or publishes in a country that has signed the Berne Convention is supposed to have moral rights that are personal to the author and that cannot, therefore, be taken away or abridged. Sometimes referred to by the French term "*droit moral*," these rights include the author's right to:

- proclaim authorship of a work
- disclaim authorship of a work, and
- object to any distortion, mutilation, or other modification of the work that would be injurious to the author's reputation as an author.

Even though the United States is a signatory nation to the Berne Convention, it doesn't specifically recognize moral rights, taking the position that a number of different U.S. statutes provide equivalent and adequate protection. For instance, Section 106 of the Copyright Act, as amended, provides that the artist of a work of visual art (as defined by the statute) can control whether his or her name is on the art and object if the integrity of the work is threatened. And under a federal statutory scheme that primarily governs trademarks (known as the Lanham Act), an author may sue anyone who misrepresents authorship.

Most art law experts believe this piecemeal approach to moral rights leaves the moral rights provision in the Berne Convention largely unimplemented in the United States. Although the moral rights provision of the Berne Convention applies to all works of expression, it is seldom an issue in any area other than the visual arts.

California sought to offer moral rights to artists with the California Resale Royalty Act (CRRA). In 2016, a district court struck down a provision of the CRRA that required a seller of fine art to pay the artist a 5% royalty from the proceeds of a sale, holding that the provision was preempted by federal copyright law. The decision was upheld by the Ninth Circuit. (*Close v. Sotheby's, Inc.*, 909 F.3d 1204 (9th Cir. 2018).)

Related terms: Berne Convention; international copyright protection; work of visual art.

See also Part 3 (Trademark Law): Lanham Act.

Copyright Law: Definitions

motion pictures, copyrights

According to Section 101 of the Copyright Act of 1976, as amended, "Motion pictures are audiovisual works consisting of a series of related images which, when shown in succession, impart an impression of motion, together with accompanying sounds, if any." Motion pictures are entitled to copyright protection under the audiovisual work category and may be registered with the U.S. Copyright Office.

Related terms: best edition of a work; registration of copyright.

MP3

The most common system for music downloads from the Internet is known as MPEG 1 Layer 3, or "MP3" for short. MP3 technology compresses sound files so that approximately 60 minutes of music can be stored on 32 megabytes of computer memory.

Internet sites that facilitate the copying, transfer, or sale of unauthorized MP3s have been the subject of lawsuits from the recording industry. In 2000, both MP3.com and Napster.com—a file sharing system—were the subjects of record company litigation. In both cases, judges rejected fair use arguments and found that the websites facilitated the distribution of unauthorized recordings. In other words, even though a company does not store or offer unauthorized recordings at its website, the company is still violating copyright law if it has established a system that allows others to infringe copyrights.

By 2003, several legitimate—that is, authorized—distributors of MP3s (and similar formats) began offering pay-to-use or subscription-based services. Most notable was the Apple iTunes website that became the leading site for acquiring legitimate copies of songs. Despite Apple's success—and despite lawsuits brought by the Recording Institute of America (RIAA) against individual users of file sharing networks—file sharing sites offering unauthorized copies have continued to maintain their popularity with a large segment of Internet music fans and it is estimated that 95% of the music that is downloaded is unauthorized. In 2005, the Supreme Court determined that individuals or companies who own or permit the use of networks that promote copyright infringement are liable for the resulting acts of infringement by third parties using the network. (*Metro-Goldwyn-Mayer, Inc. v. Grokster Ltd.,* 545 U.S. 913 (2005).)

In 2005, Congress made it a criminal violation of copyright law to knowingly place an MP3 or other computer program, musical work, motion picture or other audiovisual work, or sound recording on a computer network accessible to the public for purposes of copying.

Related terms: Audio Home Recording Act; peer-to-peer.

Music Modernization Act (MMA) of 2018

The MMA incorporated three pieces of legislation that alter copyright law as follows:

New music licensing collective. The MMA simplifies the licensing rules for digital music providers and creates a new music licensing collective (MLC), which should take effect in 2021. Once in place, the MLC will act as a toll booth for Spotify, Pandora, SoundCloud and other digital music providers. These providers will pay the MLC for each use of a song and the MLC will compensate the owners accordingly. The MLC will also identify copyrighted material embodied in sound recordings, locate the copyright owners of such material, administer copyright owners' ownership claims, and assist with the setting of royalty rates and terms.

Pre-1972 recordings covered by copyright. Prior to the MMA, pre-1972 sound recordings were protected under state law, making them ineligible to collect the digital performance right granted to sound recordings in 1995. The MMA extends the public performance right to pre-1972 recordings, thereby requiring digital music providers to compensate those recording artists and song owners.

Music producers collect royalties directly. Individuals who create sound recordings (producers, engineers, mixers) can now seek royalties directly from SoundExchange, rather than pursuing the sound recording artists and performers for payment.

music publisher

Music publishers own song copyrights and collect revenue, handle business formalities, sue infringers, and look for new ways to exploit songs. Music publishers acquire ownership of song copyrights when the songwriter transfers copyright ownership in exchange for payments or an ongoing royalty. Most music publishers offer an up-front sum or "advance" to the songwriter and share the revenue with the songwriter as the song earns money. That is, the songwriter continues to earn a percentage of the revenue through the life of the copyright.

musical works and sound recordings distinguished

There are two types of copyrights for music: musical works copyrights, which protect songs and compositions, and sound recording copyrights, which protect the manner in which music is arranged and recorded—that is, the sounds fixed on the recording. These forms of copyright protection create two overlapping sources of income. Songwriters earn income from the exploitation of songs. Recording artists and record companies earn money from the sale of recordings. The same person or business can own both types of copyrights, but the musical works copyright is usually owned by the songwriter or a music publisher, and the sound recording copyright is usually owned by a record company.

national treatment

This approach to international copyright protection, taken by the Berne Convention and other major copyright treaties, requires a signatory country to extend to nationals of other signatory countries the same copyright protection as is extended to its own citizens.

Related terms: Berne Convention; international copyright protection.

new version

See derivative work; single registration rule.

New York Times v. Tasini

This 2001 Supreme Court case (*New York Times v. Tasini*, 533 U.S. 483), stands for the principle that permission is required from freelance writers if their material is published as part of an unrevised collective work in new media, not specifically covered in the original freelance agreement.

A group of freelance authors who wrote articles for the *New York Times*, *Time*, and several other publications sued these publications when their articles were reproduced without their consent on the LexisNexis database and when microfilm reproductions of the publications were also reproduced on two CD-ROM products.

The freelance authors argued that their contracts did not grant permission for these uses of the material. The publishers argued that the freelancers' permission was not required, because the act of placing the articles on electronic databases constituted modified versions of the collective works. In 2001, the Supreme

Court rejected the publishers' argument, reasoning that electronic databases such as LexisNexis are not revisions of collective works (such as the *New York Times),* because the databases store and retrieve articles individually—articles that are part of a vast database of diverse texts. They do not store intact copies of newspapers or other collective works as originally published. In contrast, the court suggested that microfilm copies of newspapers and other collective works are revisions of the collective works, because copies of entire intact editions are stored together on the microfilm rolls.

Under *Tasini,* permission from the writers would not be required if the republication in the new media qualified as reproduction or modification of the collective work (magazine, newspaper, or other publication). For example, permission would not be needed if a newspaper was published both in print form and online, because the online edition would surely qualify as a revision of the original print edition.

But what about republishing articles and other materials on CD-ROMs? In *Tasini*, the Supreme Court had affirmed the right of freelance writers to prevent publishers from reprinting their works in computer databases. But in that case, the Supreme Court also stated that image-based reproductions of periodicals, such as microfilm and microfiche, are permissible under the Copyright Act because the articles appear in the exact position in which they appeared in print.

Applying that logic in a case against *National Geographic* magazine, the Eleventh Circuit Court of Appeals ruled that *National Geographic* could reproduce archived works on CD-ROMs and DVDs (although not in computer databases, absent permissions) without seeking additional permissions from freelance photographers. (*Greenberg v. National Geographic Society,* 244 F.3d 1267 (11th Cir. 2007).) Therefore, the rule appears to be that where a magazine or newspaper is simply scanned onto media with no conversion or reconstruction, no additional permissions are required by the publishers from freelancers. But if the material is reconstructed— for example, as when preparing text articles for a database, or pulling photos out of articles for a slideshow—then the publisher must seek additional permission.

news reporting, fair use

See fair use.

nonexclusive license

See licensing of copyright.

notice of copyright

Often referred to as a "legend" or "bug," a notice of copyright is the little "©" plus the date of publication and author's name.

For works published in the United States after March 1, 1989, no such copyright notice is required for copyright protection within the United States. Nor is a notice required in any of the other countries that have signed either the Berne Convention or GATT. However, the notice is still useful to:

- remind others that the work is protected by copyright
- preclude the use of the "innocent infringer" defense in a copyright infringement case, and
- point a would-be user of the work in the right direction for permission to use it.

For works published in the United States prior to March 1, 1989, a copyright notice is required to preserve the copyright in the work.

To provide adequate notice where such notice is desired, the copyright notice must be placed where it will easily be seen by a person viewing the work—that is, it must provide "reasonable notice of the claim of copyright." Under guidelines published by the U.S. Copyright Office:

- For literary works, notice may appear on either the front or the back of the title page.
- For software, notice may appear on the disk or other media or in the program itself, or it may be placed to appear when the program appears on the computer screen.
- For audiovisual works, notice may appear on the screen with the credits.
- For phonorecords, audiotapes, and CDs, notice may appear on the record cover or CD and tape enclosures.

There is no limit to the number of different places a copyright notice can appear.

Copyright Act: § 401. Notice of copyright: Visually perceptible copies

This statute explains the proper form for a copyright notice, as well as when, where, and why a copyright notice should be placed on a work of expression.

(a) General Provisions.—Whenever a work protected under this title is published in the United States or elsewhere by authority of the copyright owner, a notice of copyright as provided by this section may be placed on publicly distributed copies from which the work can be visually perceived, either directly or with the aid of a machine or device.

(b) Form of Notice.—If a notice appears on the copies, it shall consist of the following three elements:

(1) the symbol © (the letter C in a circle), or the word "Copyright," or the abbreviation "Copr."; and

(2) the year of first publication of the work; in the case of compilations, or derivative works incorporating previously published material, the year date of first publication of the compilation or derivative work is sufficient. The year date may be omitted where a pictorial, graphic, or sculptural work, with accompanying text matter, if any, is reproduced in or on greeting cards, postcards, stationery, jewelry, dolls, toys, or any useful articles; and

(3) the name of the owner of copyright in the work, or an abbreviation by which the name can be recognized, or a generally known alternative designation of the owner.

(c) Position of Notice.—The notice shall be affixed to the copies in such manner and location as to give reasonable notice of the claim of copyright. The Register of Copyrights shall prescribe by regulation, as examples, specific methods of affixation and positions of the notice on various types of works that will satisfy this requirement, but these specifications shall not be considered exhaustive.

(d) Evidentiary Weight of Notice.—If a notice of copyright in the form and position specified by this section appears on the published copy or copies to which a defendant in a copyright infringement suit had access, then no weight shall be given to such a defendant's interposition of a defense based on innocent infringement in mitigation of actual or statutory damages, except as provided in the last sentence of section 504 (c)(2).

Copyright Act: § 402. Notice of copyright: Phonorecords of sound recordings
This statute governs how, when, where, and why to place a copyright notice on a phonorecord (the media on which sounds are fixed for the purpose of distribution essentially, and reproduction).

(a) General Provisions.—Whenever a sound recording protected under this title is published in the United States or elsewhere by authority of the copyright owner, a notice of copyright as provided by this section may be placed on publicly distributed phonorecords of the sound recording.

(b) Form of Notice.—If a notice appears on the phonorecords, it shall consist of the following three elements:

(1) the symbol P (the letter P in a circle); and

(2) the year of first publication of the sound recording; and

(3) the name of the owner of copyright in the sound recording, or an abbreviation by which the name can be recognized, or a generally known alternative designation of the owner; if the producer of the sound recording is named on the phonorecord labels or containers, and if no other name appears in conjunction with the notice, the producer's name shall be considered a part of the notice.

(c) Position of Notice.—The notice shall be placed on the surface of the phonorecord, or on the phonorecord label or container, in such manner and location as to give reasonable notice of the claim of copyright.

(d) Evidentiary Weight of Notice.—If a notice of copyright in the form and position specified by this section appears on the published phonorecord or phonorecords to which a defendant in a copyright infringement suit had access, then no weight shall be given to such a defendant's interposition of a defense based on innocent infringement in mitigation of actual or statutory damages, except as provided in the last sentence of section 504 (c)(2).

Related terms: defective copyright notice; innocent infringement of copyright; omission of copyright notice.

object code

Most computers work through the use of compilers, which translate programs written in a programming language (called source code) into a language that the computer can recognize (called object code). The source code typically consists of words and a formal grammatical syntax. The object code consists of ones and zeros which, in all respects, are equivalent to the source code's meaning and syntax but feed the program to the computer in a binary form (one = on and zero = off), which the computer can then process and act on. This is much like translating a written message into short and long Morse Code signals for telegraphic transmission.

Although object code is unintelligible to most human readers, the courts have held that it qualifies for copyright protection as a form of expression and, as such, can be registered with the U.S. Copyright Office. The reason to register object code rather than source code is that because source code can be readily understood by skilled readers, registering it might give away trade secrets that have been maintained in the software.

When someone registers object code rather than source code, the U.S. Copyright Office places the registration under what's termed "the rule of doubt." This means that because the U.S. Copyright Office can't read or understand what was deposited, it expresses no opinion on whether the object code qualifies for copyright protection. In short, the U.S. Copyright Office does not consider the object code deposit the best edition of the underlying work and expressly favors the source code as a computer program deposit instead.

The U.S. Copyright Office offers a number of alternatives to the deposit of pure object code, which are designed to preserve trade secrets in a program while providing the U.S. Copyright Office with something intelligible to its employees. For example, acceptable deposits include parts of the source code with strategic sections blacked out, or a mix of source code and object code.

Related terms: software; deposit with U.S. Copyright Office; source code.
See also Part 4 (Trade Secret Law): trade secret, defined.

omission of copyright notice

Although the use of a copyright notice on copies is no longer required in the United States as of March 1, 1989, for many years previous to that, omission of the notice voided copyright protections. A work of authorship published prior to January 1, 1978, without the proper notice of copyright qualified for no copyright protection. A work published between January 1, 1978 and March 1, 1989 without the proper notice of copyright lost its copyright protection unless the work was republished after March 1, 1989. But even then, the old copies remained unprotected unless the work was registered with the U.S. Copyright Office within five years of its original publication, and an earnest attempt was made to have correct notices placed on all copies that were already distributed.

While works publicly distributed in the United States after March 1, 1989, do not need a notice to protect the copyright, it is still a good idea to include one. If a copyright infringement lawsuit becomes necessary and the work has the correct notice on it, the infringer will not be able to claim an innocent infringement—a legal status that makes it far harder for the copyright owner to recover damages.

Under GATT, works that entered into the public domain in the United States because they lacked a proper copyright notice may have their copyright restored if they were otherwise protected by the Berne Convention when created.

Copyright Act: § 405. Notice of copyright: Omission of notice on certain copies and phonorecords

(a) **Effect of Omission on Copyright.**—With respect to copies and phonorecords publicly distributed by authority of the copyright owner before the effective date of the Berne Convention Implementation Act of 1988, the omission of the copyright notice described in sections 401 through 403 from copies or phonorecords publicly distributed by authority of the copyright owner does not invalidate the copyright in a work if—

(1) the notice has been omitted from no more than a relatively small number of copies or phonorecords distributed to the public; or

(2) registration for the work has been made before or is made within five years after the publication without notice, and a reasonable effort is made to add notice to all copies or phonorecords that are distributed to the public in the United States after the omission has been discovered; or

(3) the notice has been omitted in violation of an express requirement in writing that, as a condition of the copyright owner's authorization of the public distribution of copies or phonorecords, they bear the prescribed notice.

(b) Effect of Omission on Innocent Infringers.—Any person who innocently infringes a copyright, in reliance upon an authorized copy or phonorecord from which the copyright notice has been omitted and which was publicly distributed by authority of the copyright owner before the effective date of the Berne Convention Implementation Act of 1988, incurs no liability for actual or statutory damages under section 504 for any infringing acts committed before receiving actual notice that registration for the work has been made under section 408, if such person proves that he or she was misled by the omission of notice. In a suit for infringement in such a case the court may allow or disallow recovery of any of the infringer's profits attributable to the infringement, and may enjoin the continuation of the infringing undertaking or may require, as a condition for permitting the continuation of the infringing undertaking, that the infringer pay the copyright owner a reasonable license fee in an amount and on terms fixed by the court.

(c) **Removal of Notice.**—Protection under this title is not affected by the removal, destruction, or obliteration of the notice, without the authorization of the copyright owner, from any publicly distributed copies or phonorecords.

Related terms: defective copyright notice; innocent infringement of copyright; notice of copyright.

open source

Open source loosely describes software that is created free of proprietary rights and royalty restrictions. Proponents of open source seek to collaborate and build upon code freely and to provide the software to the public without restrictions. There is an organized movement, the Open Source Initiative (OSI) (www.opensource.org), that established open source standards. Despite the restriction-free premise of open source software, its proponents often take the position that the software is subject to one of two general open source licenses: a general public license (GPL) and a lesser-used general public license (LGPL).

One of the most popular open source software codes is Linux, an operating system initially developed by Linus Torvalds that runs on various hardware platforms including PCs and Macs. Because it is distributed for free, Linux has become a popular choice for some operating systems. Several companies have also been successful selling versions of Linux licensed under GPLs. However, the freedom associated with Linux (and the open source movement) has been threatened by a rash of lawsuits by companies that own or claim to own copyrights on portions or versions of Linux.

original work of authorship

Under the Copyright Act, an "original work of authorship" encompasses, with a few exceptions, any type of expression independently conceived of by its creator. The Copyright Act requires two elements: (1) that the work is independently created; and (2) that the work is sufficiently creative (17 U.S. Code § 102). As long as a particular expression has been independently arrived at, it need not be original in the sense of "new." For example, if Thomas never heard of or read *One Flew Over the Cuckoo's Nest,* by Ken Kesey, but somehow managed to write a play very similar to it, Thomas's play would qualify as "original" and would thus be subject to copyright protection. Of course, when one work is very much like another, the odds favor the likelihood that copying occurred.

Among the many creations that qualify as works of authorship are sheet music, movies, recordings, video productions, video games, cartoons, artistic designs, magazines, and books. Software also counts as a work of authorship, in both source code and object code form.

A few categories of expression do not qualify as "original works of authorship" either because they are too short to deserve copyright protection, or they involve little or no creativity or originality. Among these are titles of books, movies, and songs; short phrases and slogans; printed forms; common shapes; compilations of facts; and works consisting entirely of information that is public domain property—for instance, lists and tables taken from public documents or other common sources. Typically, the decision as to whether there is sufficient creativity is made by the Copyright Office, as occurred in 2018 when the Copyright Office Review Board rejected an application for pattern swatches for luxury cars.

Related terms: compilations; *Feist Publications Inc. v. Rural Telephone Service Co.*

Copyright Law: Definitions

orphan work

An orphan work is one that is owned by a hard-to-find copyright owner. For example, in 1975, a child sends a drawing to Elvis Presley. In 2008, a biographer wants to include the drawing in a Presley biography. The problem for publishers (as well as libraries and academics) is that the artist can't be found, and the publisher doesn't want to reproduce the image without permission. A work categorized as an orphan work does not lose its copyright protection. Two bills proposed in Congress in 2007 to provide limited uses of orphan works met with opposition from artist rights organizations and did not pass.

Related terms: software.

overlapping transfers of copyright

Overlapping transfers of copyright rights occur when a copyright owner:

- transfers all or part of the same exclusive right to two or more separate parties
- transfers an exclusive right when that right has already been the subject of a nonexclusive license, or
- grants a nonexclusive license involving a right that has already been transferred by an exclusive license.

The following rules determine ownership in these situations:

- In a case of conflicting exclusive rights, the first right granted is entitled to the protection if the right is recorded in the U.S. Copyright Office within one month of the underlying work's publication (within two months if the right was granted outside of the United States).
- If the exclusive right is not recorded on time, the first transfer recorded is entitled to protection (even if it was the second one granted), as long as the grantee received it in good faith (without knowledge of the earlier one).
- Whether recorded or not, a nonexclusive written license will coexist with a later transfer of an exclusive right.
- Whether recorded or not, a nonexclusive written license will coexist with an exclusive right that was transferred earlier if both the grant of the non-exclusive license occurred before the earlier transfer was recorded and the recipient of the nonexclusive license did not know of the earlier exclusive-rights transfer.

Related terms: licensing of copyright; recordation of copyright transfers.

ownership of copyright

See copyright owner.

pantomimes and choreographic works, copyrights

See choreography and pantomime.

parody and fair use

Parody occurs when one work ridicules another work (usually a well-known one) by imitating it in an amusing or comedic way. Normally, under U.S. law and the First Amendment to the Constitution, Americans perceive public ridicule such as this as a form of free speech. However, to the extent that the parody copies material protected by copyright, a parody may also be considered as copyright infringement. Courts reconcile these two legal interests by excusing unauthorized parodies under the principle of fair use.

Not all parodies qualify. The courts first decide whether a particular work qualifies as parody. If so, the court then determines whether the work qualifies as a fair use. If it does, then the parodist is not liable for the infringement.

To determine whether a work is a parody, the courts decide whether the work actually comments on the original work or just invokes the original work as a means of calling attention to itself in the marketplace. The key question to be addressed in deciding whether a work is a parody is whether the new work "adds something new, with a further purpose or different character altering the first with new expression, meaning, or message; it asks in other words whether and to what extent the new work is transformative." (*Campbell v. Acuff-Rose*, 510 U.S. 569 (1994).)

EXAMPLE: The Paramount motion picture company released an advertisement for the movie *Naked Gun 33⅓* that showed Leslie Nielsen's face superimposed on the famous nude photo of a pregnant Demi Moore (which originally appeared on the cover of *Vanity Fair* magazine). Annie Leibovitz, the photographer, sued Paramount for copyright infringement. In holding the work to be a parody, the Court held that the "ad may reasonably be perceived as commenting on the seriousness and even pretentiousness of the original." The Court went on to note that the parody differed from the original "in a way that may, reasonably, be perceived as commenting, through ridicule, on what a viewer might reasonably think is the undue self-importance conveyed by the subject of the Leibovitz photograph." (*Leibovitz v. Paramount Pictures Corp.*, 137 F.3d 109 (2d Cir. 1998).)

Copyright Law: Definitions

At the same time, a work does not become a parody simply because the author models characters after those found in a famous work. For example, in a case involving the author J.D. Salinger, an author wrote a book in which a character known as Mr. C was allegedly modeled after the character of Holden Caulfield, from Salinger's *Catcher in the Rye*. After Salinger sued, the sequel's author claimed that his work was a parody, an argument rejected by the district court primarily because the work was not transformative. Aging the character and placing him in present day does not add something new, particularly because the character's personality remains intact as derived from the original work. (*Salinger v. Colting*, 641 F. Supp.2d 250 (S.D.N.Y. 2009).) (Note, the district court's decision in *Salinger v. Colting* was vacated and remanded by the Second Circuit (*Salinger v. Colting*, 607 F.3d 68 (2d Cir. 2010).) The Second Circuit agreed with the district court regarding its fair use analysis but vacated the judgment because the district court failed to incorporate new standards regarding preliminary injunctions.)

Once a work is found to be a parody, the court then must go on to decide whether the other tests used to determine fair use apply to the case. Briefly, these tests are:

- the purpose and character of the use, including whether such use is of a commercial nature or is for nonprofit educational purposes
- the nature of the copyrighted work
- the amount and substantiality of the portion used in relation to the copyrighted work as a whole, and
- the effect of the use upon the potential market for or value of the copyrighted work.

It is often difficult to discern whether a work is a parody. Cases involving Dr. Seuss and the book *Gone with the Wind* (below) show how difficult it can be to know for sure whether a parody qualifies as a fair use.

EXAMPLE 1: Two authors wrote a book called *The Cat NOT in the Hat! A Parody by Dr. Juice*. The book told the story of the O.J. Simpson trial through poems and sketches similar to those in the famous *The Cat in the Hat* children's stories by Dr. Seuss. The work was narrated by Dr. Juice, a character based on Dr. Seuss, and contained a character called "The Cat NOT in the Hat." The owners of the copyrights in Dr. Seuss sued for copyright infringement. The authors claimed that their work was a fair use of the Dr. Seuss stories because it was a parody.

They argued that by applying Dr. Seuss's style to adult subject matter, their work commented on the "naiveté of the original" Dr. Seuss stories as well as on society's fixation on the O.J. Simpson trial. The court disagreed. It said that a parody was a literary or artistic work that imitates the characteristic style of an author for comic effect or ridicule. *The Cat NOT In the Hat!* didn't qualify, because the authors' poems and illustrations merely retold the Simpson tale. Although they broadly mimicked Dr. Seuss's characteristic style, they did not hold it up to ridicule or otherwise make it an object of the parody. The court opined that the authors used the Seuss characters and style merely to get attention or avoid the drudgery of working up something fresh. It upheld an injunction that barred Penguin Books from distributing 12,000 books it had printed at an expense of $35,000. (*Dr. Seuss Enterprises v. Penguin Books USA, Inc.*, 109 F.3d 1394 (9th Cir. 1997).)

EXAMPLE 2: In a case involving the legendary Civil War novel *Gone with the Wind*, an author wrote a book, called *The Wind Done Gone*, that chronicles the diary of a woman named Cynara, the illegitimate daughter of a plantation owner, and Mammy, a slave who cares for his children. Without obtaining permission from the copyright owner of *Gone with the Wind*, the author of *The Wind Done Gone* copied the prior book's characters, famous scenes, and other elements from the plot and dialogue and descriptions. The Margaret Mitchell estate sued both the publisher and author for copyright infringement.

The court held that *The Wind Done Gone* was protected by the fair use privilege, and thus the Mitchell estate could not obtain a court order halting its publication. The court concluded that *The Wind Done Gone* was a parody because "its aim is to comment upon or criticize a prior work by appropriating elements of the original in creating a new artistic, as opposed to scholarly or journalistic, work." *The Wind Done Gone* satisfied this test because it was a specific criticism of and rejoinder to the depiction of slavery and the relationships between blacks and whites in *Gone with the Wind*. (*Suntrust Bank v. Houghton Mifflin Co.*, 268 F.2d 1257 (11th Cir. 2001).)

In one of the stranger decisions regarding parody and fair use, a California district court ruled that a parody did not need to be funny to qualify as fair use. In that case, a pro-life video organization created two antiabortion videos by borrowing video clips from a pro-choice video and juxtaposing them with actual abortion footage. The court characterized the videos as parodies despite the fact they did not meet the classic definition of a parody—something that humorously mimics or ridicules another's work. In a unique holding, the court held that a parody need not be humorous, but may merely comment on, or criticize the original. (*Northland Family Planning Clinic v. Center for Bio-Ethical Reform*, 868 F. Supp.2d 962 (C.D. Cal. June 15, 2012).) Can a parody that's based on fair use be separately copyrightable? In a case involving a parody of the surfer-thriller *Point Break*, the Second Circuit held that if the author of the unauthorized work provides sufficient original material and is otherwise qualified under fair use rules, the resulting work will be protected under copyright. (*Keeling v. Hars*, 809 F.3d 43 (2d Cir. 2015).)

Related terms: fair use; infringement (copyright).

patent and copyright

See copyright and patent compared.

peer-to-peer

Peer-to-peer file sharing networks, the most popular of which are currently based on the BitTorrent protocol, permit access to (and free distribution of) electronic files, usually consisting of copyrighted music, films, and software. These networks commonly permit users to either communicate directly with each other (not using central servers) or to allow users to reassemble files, the elements of which are stored on many computers, using BitTorrent protocols.

In other words, these networks and the data they manage often lack a central location from which material is transmitted and received; all participants are both clients and servers. In 2005, the Supreme Court determined that individuals or companies who own or permit the use of such networks, with the goal of promoting their use to infringe copyright, are liable for the resulting acts of infringement by third parties using the network. (*Metro-Goldwyn-Mayer, Inc. v. Grokster Ltd.*, 545 U.S. 913 (2005).)

Also striking a blow against peer-to-peer file sharing, Congress passed the Family Entertainment and Copyright Act of 2005 which, among its provisions, made it a criminal violation to knowingly place a copyrighted computer program, musical work, motion picture or other audiovisual work, or sound recording on a computer network accessible to the public for purposes of copying.

In 2005, a woman was sued for copyright infringement for downloading 30 songs using peer-to-peer file sharing software. She argued that her activity was a fair use because she was downloading the songs to determine if she wanted to later buy them. Because numerous sites, such as iTunes, permit listeners to sample and examine portions of songs without downloading, the court rejected this "sampling" defense. (*BMG Music v. Gonzalez*, 430 F.3d 888 (7th Cir. 2005).)

Defendants in a peer-to-peer file sharing case might also have difficulty asserting a fair use defense. One defendant was denied that right because he had failed to provide evidence that his copying of music files involved any transformative use (an essential element in proving fair use). (*Capitol Records Inc. v. Alaujan*, 593 F. Supp.2d 319 (D. Mass. 2009).)

In 2013, the Ninth Circuit determined that BitTorrent protocols violated copyright law in the same manner as other peer-to-peer infringements (for example, as used in the *Grokster* case*)* despite the lack of a central server containing infringing copies of the material. (*Columbia Pictures Industries, Inc. v. Fung*, 710 F.3d 1020 (9th Cir. 2013) (C.D. Cal. 2009).)

Related terms: BitTorrent; Family Entertainment and Copyright Act of 2005.

performing a work

The exclusive right to perform a work is one of the bundle of rights that make up a copyright. To perform a work publicly has a much broader meaning under copyright law than the common concept of a performance. The drafters of the Copyright Act stated that "to perform a work means to recite, render, play, dance, or act it, either directly or by means of any device or process or, in the case of a motion picture or other audiovisual work, to show its images in any sequence or to make the sounds accompanying it audible." Section 101 of the Copyright Act states that to perform a work "publicly" means that there is performance of the work where the public is gathered, or the work is transmitted or otherwise communicated to the public. (17 U.S. Code § 101.)

Examples of public performance include:

- A disc jockey plays a phonorecord in a nightclub.
- A novelist reads aloud from her work at a bookstore.
- A dancer presents a performance during halftime at a football game.
- A motion picture company authorizes a showing of its latest film.
- A songwriter performs an original composition at a nightclub.
- A radio station plays a record containing a copyrighted song.
- A television station broadcasts a television show.
- A cable TV company receives a television station broadcast and rebroadcasts it via cable transmission.

The performance right does not extend to pictorial, graphic, or sculptural works, because these works cannot be performed; they can only be displayed, so these rights are covered by the display right. In 1994, the Copyright Act was amended to include digital performance rights for sound recordings and to prevent the bootlegging of live musical performances.

Related terms: exclusive copyright rights; infringement (copyright); public performance of a work.

performing music at a business

Performing rights societies collect fees from establishments where music is performed, such as clothing stores, bars, or restaurants. The "performance" of a song has a broad meaning encompassing live concerts; playing of a recording at a business or club; and transmission of a song via radio, television, cable, or digital signals.

Some businesses are exempt from these pay-for-play rules. Businesses that play the radio or television do not have to pay performance fees if they meet one or more of the criteria below:

- The business is a restaurant or bar under 3,750 square feet.
- The business is a retail establishment under 2,000 square feet.
- The business, regardless of size, has no more than six external speakers, but not more than four per room, or four televisions measuring 55 inches or less, but not more than one per room.

The exemptions above apply only to establishments that play radio and television. Establishments playing prerecorded music, such as compact discs, must still pay performance fees. Permission is not required to play a song in a record store or if the song is played via licensed jukebox.

Related terms: mechanical rights; musical works and sound recordings distinguished; performing a work; performing rights societies.

performing rights societies

Performing rights societies monitor the performance of music (whether it is live concerts, playing of a recording at a business or club, or transmission of a song via radio, television, cable, or digital signals). These societies then collect royalties from those who perform the music and distribute them to copyright owners (known as "performance royalties"). For the most part (see below) the collection of payments is on behalf of song owners, not sound recording owners. That's because, except for digital audio transmissions, there is no public performance right associated with sound recordings; it is only associated with musical compositions (songs).

It would be impractical for the proprietors of radio and TV stations or nightclubs to contact each song owner for permission each time a song was to be publicly performed. Performing rights societies were established in order to negotiate and collect these fees. In the United States, a song owner affiliates with one of three performing rights societies: ASCAP, BMI, or SESAC. These societies act as agents for song owners, surveying radio stations on a regular basis and using the surveys as a basis for payments to songwriters. TV stations furnish logs of music played, and agreements are also made with club owners where phonorecords are played or with concert halls where live music is performed.

Since 1996, owners of sound recordings have had a performance right for digital audio transmissions—specifically interactive digital services as popularized on the Internet (for example, Pandora and Spotify). These royalty payments are collected from webcasters by SoundExchange and distributed to sound recording owners.

Related terms: mechanical rights; musical works and sound recordings distinguished; performing a work; performing music at a business.

permanent download

Companies such as Apple and Amazon sell digital music files of a song or an album that a user can download. The Copyright Act refers to these as permanent digital downloads (17 U.S. Code § 115) (also called digital permanent downloads or DPDs). Typically, these files are in the form of MP3s that may be retained and played on a permanent basis.(37 C.F.R. § 385.2.)

permission

Many kinds of media publications—small and large—use words, music, and imagery that are protected by copyright laws. Is permission required for all uses of someone else's work? For example, is permission needed to reproduce a photo taken by a club member, a friend, or a relative? The short answer is, "yes." Copyright protection extends to any original work regardless of who created it and permission is required for reproduction, display, or distribution of the work.

The reason for acquiring permission is to avoid a lawsuit. The copyright owner controls the use of the work, and a person who uses it without permission could be sued for financial damages. If a friend or family member has consented to the use, the concern over a lawsuit diminishes, as does the need for a written permission agreement. An oral consent is valid, although an email or written consent is preferred as it is easier to prove in the event of a dispute. Sometimes the process of acquiring consent can be simplified by using the services of a copyright clearinghouse.

It is wise to operate under the assumption that all art, music, and writings are protected by copyright law. A work is not in the public domain simply because it has been posted on the Internet (a popular fallacy) or because it lacks a copyright notice (another fallacy). As a general rule, permission is needed to reproduce copyrighted materials including photos, writing, music, and artwork.

Do not assume that clip art, shareware, freeware, or materials labeled "royalty-free" or "copyright-free" can be distributed or copied without authorization. Read the terms and conditions in the "click to accept" agreement or "readme" files ordinarily accompanying such materials to be certain that an intended use is permitted. One company failed to honor the terms of a clickwrap agreement and was found liable for illegally distributing three volumes of software clip art. Also, don't assume that because a site permits the download of a story that this story can be posted on another website. Each type of activity—emailing, copying, printing, and posting—requires authorization.

Permission is sometimes needed to reproduce a trademark including any word, symbol, or device that identifies and distinguishes a product or service. For example, the word "McDonald's," the distinctive yellow arches, and the Ronald McDonald character are all trademarks of the McDonald's company. Permission would be needed to use these trademarks at a commercial website if consumers are likely to be confused by the use or if the commercial use damages the reputation of McDonald's.

Related terms: clearinghouses, copyright; end-user license.

phonorecords

The U.S. Copyright Act of 1976 defines phonorecords not only as the traditional "record" but also as audiotape recordings, compact discs, permanent downloads, and any future technology for reproducing sound. The statute covers "material objects in which sounds, other than those accompanying … [an] audiovisual work, are fixed by any method now known or later developed, and from which the sounds can be perceived, reproduced, or otherwise communicated, either directly or with the aid of a machine or device. [It] … includes the material object in which the sounds are first fixed." (17 U.S. Code § 101.)

An original work of authorship contained on a phonorecord may be registered as a sound recording with the U.S. Copyright Office on Form SR. To register a group of sound recordings, you must submit the online application for "Sound Recordings from an Album." This application may be used to register two to 20 sound recordings. It may also be used to register photographs, artwork, or liner notes that were first published with the same album. Instructions on how to access this application are at www.copyright.gov.

Copyright Act: § 101. Definitions

"Phonorecords" are material objects in which sounds, other than those accompanying a motion picture or other audiovisual work, are fixed by any method now known or later developed, and from which the sounds can be perceived, reproduced, or otherwise communicated, either directly or with the aid of a machine or device. The term "phonorecords" includes the material object in which the sounds are first fixed.

"Sound recordings" are works that result from the fixation of a series of musical, spoken, or other sounds, but not including the sounds accompanying a motion picture or other audiovisual work, regardless of the nature of the material objects, such as disks, tapes, or other phonorecords, in which they are embodied.

Related terms: compulsory license; Form SR; musical works and sound recordings distinguished; registration.

photocopies

The photocopy machine is a familiar part of life in America, and copyrights are frequently infringed by its use. Because much photocopying occurs in private and doesn't involve commercial distribution, this type of infringement is seldom discovered. Also, unless the copyright owner has been damaged in some manner or profits were gained from the infringement, an infringement lawsuit is usually out of the question. The increased popularity of scanners, and electronic books, and the diminishing popularity of print books and copy machines, make photocopy infringement less of a priority for copyright owners.

Nevertheless, in situations where photocopying is discovered by a copyright owner and it appears that sales of the item being copied may be adversely affected, a copyright lawsuit may be the result. For instance, in the case of *Basic Books, Inc.*

v. Kinko's Graphics Corp., 758 F. Supp. 1522 (S.D.N.Y. 1991), a group of seven major publishers obtained a $510,000 judgment against a duplicating business for copying excerpts from books without permission, compiling them into "course packets," and selling them to college students. Almost 20 years later, the same issues and the same result occurred in *Blackwell Publishing, Inc. v. Excel Research Group,* 661 F. Supp.2d 786 (E.D. Mich. 2009).

Related terms: copies; fair use; infringement action.

photography

Photographic images are protectable under copyright law whether in print or digital format. The photographer is considered the author and original owner of copyright. Absent an agreement transferring rights, a person who is photographed does not acquire copyright ownership in the photo. However, a person who is the subject of the photograph may be able to prevent its reproduction under legal theories such as the right of publicity, defamation, or invasion of privacy.

Along with the right to control reproduction, the photographer acquires the right to create derivatives of the work. These derivatives may even be three-dimensional. For example, the photographer Art Rogers created the photograph entitled "Puppies," which features a man and woman sitting on a bench and holding eight puppies. The artist Jeff Koons purchased two postcards of the image and, without obtaining Mr. Rogers's authorization, created a wood sculpture based on the image. Even though Koons had demonstrated sufficient originality in his statues, he could not sell his works because he failed to obtain permission from the photographer of the underlying copyrighted work. (*Rogers v. Koons,* 960 F.2d 301 (2d Cir. 1992).) On the other hand, Andy Warhol's series of silkscreens of the musician Prince, using photos by Lynn Goldsmith as his source material, was considered fair use. According to the court, "The Prince Series works can reasonably be perceived to have transformed Prince from a vulnerable, uncomfortable person to an iconic, larger-than-life figure." (*Andy Warhol Found. for Visual Arts, Inc. v. Goldsmith,* 17-cv-2532 (J.G.K.) (S.D.N.Y. Jul. 1, 2019).)

What's protectable about a photograph? It's not the subject matter per se. Everyone, for example, can photograph the Golden Gate Bridge or a presidential candidate. But other elements in the making of a photograph may be protectable. In one decision, a district court judge ruled that photographic elements such as rendition (the technical choices made when photographing a subject) and timing—taking a picture at the right time and right place—may be original and protectable elements in some photographs. For example, a photographer could potentially infringe the famous photo of servicemen installing the flag at Iwo Jima by recreating the photographic elements using models. (*Mannion v. Coors Brewing Company*, 377 F. Supp.2d 444 (S.D.N.Y. 2005).)

At the same time, a photograph that is merely a "slavish reproduction" of an existing work is unlikely to be protected under copyright. For example, a federal judge ruled against a company trying to claim copyright in a perfect reproduction of a public domain painting. (*Bridgeman Art Library Ltd. v. Corel Corp.*, 25 F. Supp.2d 412 (S.D.N.Y. 1997).) In a similar vein, the Tenth Circuit Court of Appeals held that a detailed three-dimensional computer photo-perfect replication of an automobile—in this case, a Toyota—did not demonstrate sufficient originality such that the software company that created the imagery could claim copyright. (*Meshwerks Inc. v. Toyota Motor Sales U.S.A. Inc.*, 528 F.3d 1258 (10th Cir. 2008).) Apparently, photos of human teeth meet the standards of copyright. A Boca Raton dentist was able to stop a competitor from copying "before-and-after" photos of a patient. (*Pohl v. MH SUB I LLC*, No. 18-13233 (11th Cir. May. 1, 2019).)

Two cases highlight the confusion regarding registration of collections of photographs. In one case, a photographer licensed 150 works to Corbis. Corbis included the photos in a group registration of approximately 12,000–16,000 photographs. A district court ruled that the photographer could not rely on the group registration because it identified Corbis as the author of the works, not the photographer. Because each author must be identified, the compilation registration did not register copyrights in the individual works. (*Bean v. Houghton Mifflin Publishing, Co.*, 95 U.S.P.Q.2d 1489 (D. Ariz. 2010).) A related result occurred in *Muench Photography, Inc. v. Houghton Mifflin Harcourt Publishing*, 712 F. Supp.2d 84 (S.D.N.Y. 2010). In that case, a New York district court ruled that copyright registration in an automated database of photographs must contain the names of each of the photographers in order for an individual photographer to sue for infringement.

In 2018, the Copyright Office simplified the rules regarding registration of photo collections, permitting photo registrations as a group or a database. (37 C.F.R. § 202.3(b)(5)). In its new regulations the Copyright Office established that group registrants can seek statutory damages for individual images, while database registrants can seek only a single statutory award, no matter how many images are infringed. In short, group registration of photos is a better choice for photographers.

Related terms: embedding.

pictorial, graphic, and sculptural works

Works of expression using graphic and physical representations of objects and ideas, rather than text, are entitled to copyright protection. The Copyright Act covers "two-dimensional and three-dimensional works of fine, graphic, and applied art, photographs, prints and art reproductions, maps, globes, charts, technical drawings, diagrams, and models." (17 U.S. Code § 101.)

The original design of a toy, package, implement, or other product can qualify for copyright protection if it is created for expressive rather than functional purposes. For instance, a pitcher designed as a unicorn may be subject to copyright protection as long as the unicorn shape is not directly related to the pitcher's function—that is, the unicorn shape does not affect how the pitcher stores and pours liquids. Whether or not a design is functional or expressive can only be decided on a case-by-case basis. (Functional works are also known as "useful articles.")

Copyright Act: § 101. Definitions
"Pictorial, graphic, and sculptural works" include two-dimensional and three-dimensional works of fine, graphic, and applied art, photographs, prints and art reproductions, maps, globes, charts, diagrams, models, and technical drawings, including architectural plans. Such works shall include works of artistic craftsmanship insofar as their form but not their mechanical or utilitarian aspects are concerned; the design of a useful article, as defined in this section, shall be considered a pictorial, graphic, or sculptural work only if, and only to the extent that, such design incorporates pictorial, graphic, or sculptural features that can be identified separately from, and are capable of existing independently of, the utilitarian aspects of the article.

A "useful article" is an article having an intrinsic utilitarian function that is not merely to portray the appearance of the article or to convey information. An article that is normally a part of a useful article is considered a "useful article."

Related terms: copyright and patent compared; Form VA; registration of copyright; useful article.
See also Part 1 (Patent Law): design patents; Part 3 (Trademark Law): trade dress.

piracy

A colloquial term without legal significance, piracy is used to describe the illegal activity of willful copyright infringers.

Related terms: criminal copyright infringement; infringement (copyright).

placement of copyright notice

See notice of copyright.

plagiarism

Deliberately passing off somebody else's original expression or creative ideas as one's own is colloquially known as plagiarism. Plagiarism can be a violation under the copyright laws if original expression is copied.

Often, however, plagiarism does not violate any law but marks the plagiarist as an unethical person in the political, academic, or scientific community where the plagiarism occurs.

Related terms: infringement (copyright); original work of authorship.

plot, protection of

Copyright will protect the plot of a novel or other fiction work, provided that the author's expression is somehow separable from the underlying premise or concept of the plot. For example, the idea of boy-meets-girl, boy-loses-girl, boy-gets-girl plot is not protectable. But the embellished plot variations of that premise or theme—such as *When Harry Met Sally*, or *An Affair to Remember*—can achieve protection. The standard was best described by Judge Learned Hand in *Nichols v. Universal Pictures,* 45 F.2d 119 (2d Cir. 1930). In that case the author of the popular play, *Abie's Irish Rose,* sued the producers of a movie, *The Cohens and the Kellys.* Both plots involved children of Irish and Jewish families who marry secretly because their parents are prejudiced. At the end of each work there is a reconciliation of the families, based upon the presence of a grandchild. Beyond that, the works had little in common except for ethnic clichés.

Judge Hand established a standard to separate the idea from the expression. He used the term "abstraction," which is a process of removing or separating something. He stated: "Upon any work, and especially upon a play, a great number of patterns of increasing generality will fit equally well, as more and more of the incident is left out." In other words, every narrative work is built around an underlying idea, in this case the basic plot summary. The idea might be similar to other plots—many people believe there are only between seven and 30 basic plots—but the author's embellishments, the series of details and incidents that separate the idea from similar plots, trigger copyright protection.

EXAMPLE: A writer sued the makers of the movie *E.T.—The Extra Terrestrial*. The writer claimed that the film infringed her musical play, *Lokey from Maldemar,* a social satire designed to "illustrate the disunity of man, divided by egotism." The district court applied the abstractions test and determined that the only similarity between the works was the basic idea of the plot line—aliens with powers of levitation are stranded on earth, pursued by authoritarian characters, and finally bid their earthly friends farewell. (*Litchfield v. Spielberg,* 736 F.2d 1352 (9th Cir. 1984).)

podcasting

Podcasting—a term derived from the popular audio player, the iPod—is the process of scheduling an audio file for automatic download. The process permits listeners, for example, to arrange for automatic delivery of radio shows, audio-books, music, or other audio programs. Because podcasting involves digital distribution, performance, duplication, and transfer, the process can trigger the same gamut of copyright issues raised by MP3 downloads and digital copying.

preemption

Under Section 301 of the Copyright Act, states are prohibited from creating or enforcing laws that are equivalent to any of the exclusive rights granted under copyright law. This principle—known as preemption (or "pre-emption")—is sometimes used by a defendant in a lawsuit who claims that a state lawsuit should be dismissed because it actually involves a right similar to copyright— for example, a dispute involving the right of publicity or a shrinkwrap license.

preliminary injunctions

See injunctions.

preregistration of copyright

The U.S. Copyright Office has instituted a preregistration procedure for certain classes of works that have a history of pre-release infringement. According to the Copyright Office, preregistration serves as a placeholder for limited purposes, mainly where a copyright owner needs to sue for infringement while a work is still being prepared for commercial release. Preregistration is not a substitute for registration, and its use is appropriate only in certain circumstances.

A work submitted for preregistration must meet three conditions:

- The work must be unpublished.

- The work must be in the process of being prepared for commercial distribution in either physical or digital format—that is, film copies, CDs, computer programs to be sold online—and the applicant must have a reasonable expectation of this commercial distribution.
- The work must fall within the following classes of works determined by the Register of Copyrights to have had a history of infringement prior to authorized commercial distribution. The works determined to be eligible under this requirement are: motion pictures, sound recordings, musical compositions, literary works being prepared for publication in book form, computer programs (which can include video games), and advertising or marketing photographs.

Preregistration is not a form of registration but is simply an indication of an intent to register a work once the work has been completed and/or published. When the work has been completed, it may be registered as an unpublished work, and when it has been published, it may be registered as a published work.

A person who has preregistered a work must register the work within one month after the copyright owner becomes aware of infringement and no later than three months after first publication. If full registration is not made within the prescribed time period, a court must dismiss an action for copyright infringement that occurred before or within the first two months after first publication.

To preregister, a copyright owner must apply online; no paper application form is available. The effective date is the day on which the completed application and fee for an eligible work have been received in the Copyright Office.

Related term: Family Entertainment and Copyright Act of 2005.

printed forms, not copyrightable

Printed forms do not usually qualify for copyright protection because they are designed for recording information and do not in themselves convey information or original expression. In other cases, the forms contain information that can be expressed only in a limited number of ways (for example, a job application form) and such works will not be protected under the merger doctrine—that is the idea and expression are merged.

Related terms: copyright; merger doctrine; original work of authorship.

Copyright Law: Definitions

Prioritizing Resources and Organization for Intellectual Property Act of 2008 (PRO-IP Act)

This Act was primarily intended to offer new tools with which IP owners of trademarks and copyrights can fight counterfeiting. The copyright tools include: the authority for impoundment and forfeiture of documents and goods relating to infringement and trafficking activities; enhanced criminal penalties for trafficking in counterfeit goods or services; application of U.S. copyright laws to the export of infringing materials; and mandatory awards of treble damages and attorneys' fees for providing goods or services necessary for infringement with the intent that the recipient of such goods or services actually commit infringement.

The Act also established that a copyright registration certificate can satisfy the registration requirement even if it contains inaccurate information, unless: (1) "the inaccurate information was included on the application for copyright registration with knowledge that it was inaccurate"; and (2) "the inaccuracy of the information if known would have caused the register of copyrights to refuse registration." (17 U.S. Code § 411(b)(1).) A copyright owner who fails to meet these registration standards could face invalidation of the copyright, the inability to pursue copyright infringement claims, or an award of attorneys' fees. (*Gold Value Int'l Textile, Inc. v. Sanctuary Clothing, LLC*, 925 F.3d 1140 (9th Cir. 2019).)

Related terms: registration.

profits as damages

Profits reaped by an infringer as a result of a copyright infringement (called defendant's profits) are one possible element of monetary damages a court may require the infringer to pay the copyright owner. Defendant's profits will be awarded only where these profits exceed the amount of profits lost by the copyright owner as a result of the infringement.

To establish the amount of an infringer's profits, the plaintiff copyright owner first must prove the defendant's gross profits from the sales of the infringing goods or services. The defendant then is entitled to deduct his or her demonstrable costs from the gross revenues from selling the infringing material. The resulting amount is then compared with the plaintiff's lost profits, if any. Damages that will be awarded will be the greater of defendant's profits attributable to the infringement or the plaintiff's lost profits.

EXAMPLE: Janet infringed Jeffrey's copyright by stealing his dissertation and publishing it first. Jeffrey proves that he lost $20,000 in publishers' advances and royalties based on the reasonably anticipated sale of the dissertation as a scholarly book. Because Janet's publisher did a super job selling foreign rights, she ended up with $35,000. Janet would have to pay Jeffrey $35,000, because her profits were greater. However, if instead Janet's net profits were only $15,000, she would have to pay him $20,000, his lost profits, because his lost profits were greater than her actual ones.

Related terms: damages for copyright infringement.

programs, computer, copyright of

See software.

pseudonym

A "pseudonymous work" is one on which the author is identified under a fictitious name. Copyright laws protect an author who publishes a work under a pseudonym almost as well as (and in some cases better than) they do an author who uses his or her real name. The main difference is that the copyright will last 95 years for a pseudonymous work, instead of the author's life plus 70 years for an author-identified work.

Related terms: anonymous; author; duration of copyrights.

public domain

Any work of authorship that is not protected under copyright law is said to fall within the public domain. This means that anyone can use the work without obtaining permission from the author or the author's heirs. There are several common reasons why works may be considered to be in the public domain:

- The work was published before 1926*.
- The work was published between 1926* and 1963 and never renewed.
- The work consists solely of facts or ideas. (Facts and ideas are not protected by copyright, although the means used to express them may be protected to some extent.)
- The work was published before 1978 and lacked a proper copyright notice. (But the copyright in many of these works has been restored.)
- The work was published between 1978 and 1989, the notice on the work was defective, and inadequate efforts were made to correct the defects. (Copyrights by non-U.S. authors covered by the Berne Convention that expired for this reason can be restored under GATT.)

- The copyright owner deliberately placed the work in the public domain by making a statement to that effect.
- The work was prepared by an officer or employee of the United States Government as part of that person's official duties.
- The work was created before 1978 but not published before December 31, 2003, and the author has been dead more than 70 years.

Although it was once a rule that works in the public domain could never be protected under copyright law, in 1994 Congress passed the General Agreement on Tariffs and Trade (GATT), which restored U.S. copyright protection to certain foreign works that entered the public domain in the United States because of their failure to comply with U.S copyright formalities. In 2012, the Supreme Court upheld the law and ruled that it was permissible for Congress to allow these foreign works to have limited copyright protection. (*Golan v. Holder,* 565 U.S. 1 (2012).)

* In 2019, works first published in the U.S. in 1923 (in other words, published before 1924) entered the public domain. In 2020, works first published in 1924 (in other words, published before 1925) entered the public domain, and so forth.

Related terms: factual works; *Feist Publications Inc. v. Rural Telephone Service Co.*; original work of authorship; restored copyright under GATT; work of the U.S. Government.

public performance of a work

Among the bundle of rights making up a copyright is the exclusive right to publicly perform or display an original work of authorship. The Copyright Act considers a public performance to be: (1) when a work is performed or displayed at a place open to the public or at any place where a substantial number of persons outside of a normal circle of a family and its social acquaintances is gathered; or (2) when a performance or display of the work is transmitted or otherwise communicated to the public, by means of any device or process. (17 U.S. Code § 101.)

In 2009, a court held that it is not a public performance of a song when the song is used as a ringtone. ASCAP, a society that collects money for songwriters, claimed that Verizon's sale of ringtones amounted to violation of the public performance right and required payment of licensing fees. A New York court decided that the ringtones—which were stored on user's phones—were exempt from public performance licensing under 17 U.S. Code Section 110(4). (*In re Application of Cellco Partnership,* 663 F. Supp.2d 363 (S.D.N.Y. 2009).)

Copyright Act: § 101. Definitions

To perform or display a work "publicly" means—

(1) to perform or display it at a place open to the public or at any place where a substantial number of persons outside of a normal circle of a family and its social acquaintances is gathered; or

(2) to transmit or otherwise communicate a performance or display of the work to a place specified by clause (1) or to the public, by means of any device or process, whether the members of the public capable of receiving the performance or display receive it in the same place or in separate places and at the same time or at different times.

Related terms: copyright; infringement (copyright); licensing of copyright.

publication

See published work.

published work

An original work of authorship is considered published under the Copyright Act only when it is first made available to the public on an unrestricted basis. It is thus possible to display a work or distribute it with restrictions on disclosure of its contents, without actually "publishing" it (or what is sometimes referred to as a "limited publication").

> EXAMPLE: Andres writes an essay called "Blood Bath" about the war in Iraq and distributes it to five human rights organizations under a nonexclusive license that places restrictions on their right to disclose the essay's contents. "Blood Bath" has not been "published" in the copyright sense.

Does posting material on the Internet for unrestricted access amount to publication? Although the Copyright Office does not take an official position on the issue, it is generally considered that unrestricted Internet displays amount to publication. In 2002, a federal court ruled that the posting of a website on the Internet amounted to publication. This ruling enabled the website owner to collect statutory damages from an infringer who copied the website. (*Getaped.com v. Cangemi,* 188 F. Supp.2d 398 (S.D.N.Y. 2002).)

Published and unpublished works are both entitled to copyright protection, but there are some legal distinctions, such as:

- For works created after 1977, if the "author" is an employer or the commissioner of a work made for hire, or uses a pseudonym or remains anonymous, the copyright lasts for 95 years for published works and 120 years for unpublished works.

- The publication date sets the time running for a timely registration of the copyright with the U.S. Copyright Office.
- It is more difficult for an infringer to claim fair use when the infringed work is unpublished because the infringing publication deprives its copyright owner of the right to determine its publication date.
- A valid copyright notice on a published work can prevent the claim of innocent infringement from being raised in a copyright infringement lawsuit.

Copyright Act: § 101. Definitions

"Publication" is the distribution of copies or phonorecords of a work to the public by sale or other transfer of ownership, or by rental, lease, or lending. The offering to distribute copies or phonorecords to a group of persons for purposes of further distribution, public performance, or public display, constitutes publication. A public performance or display of a work does not of itself constitute publication.

Related terms: fair use; international copyright protection; limited publication; notice of copyright; registration.

recordation of copyright transfers

Recordation refers to the filing of documents that evidence the ownership or transfer of copyright or of specific rights associated with copyright. When one or more exclusive copyright rights are transferred, it is important for the recipient of the rights to record the transfer immediately with the U.S. Copyright Office. This is because the first party to record has greater rights in the event of conflicting or overlapping transfers.

Recordation also provides all persons with "constructive notice" of the transfer of rights. This means that the law will presume infringers should have found out about it, even if they didn't actually know. Without recordation, although the owner of transferred rights can sue an infringer, it can be hard to prove that the infringement was not innocent.

To record a transfer, the new owner must file with the U.S. Copyright Office a written document describing the work involved and the transfer granted and bearing the signature of the person granting the transfer.

Related terms: overlapping transfers of copyright; transfers of copyright ownership.

recordings, sound

The U.S. Copyright Office calls all sound recordings "phonorecords," no matter what medium is actually used.

Related terms: phonorecords.

Register of Copyrights

This is the official title of the person who heads the U.S. Copyright Office.

Related terms: registration; U.S. Copyright Office.

registration

Registration occurs when the Copyright Office receives all of the required application materials associated with an author's claim and approves the application.

Registration is not required to obtain copyright protection; that occurs automatically when a work of authorship is fixed in a tangible medium of expression. Nevertheless, registration is recommended because it provides several advantages in case of infringement:

- If a copyright is registered either before an infringing activity has begun, or within three months of first publication of the work, the copyright owner may collect statutory damages for the infringement, plus attorneys' fees, if the issue ends up in court. These benefits often make the difference between an owner being able to afford litigation and having to forgo copyright rights.
- In an infringement action, the registered copyright owner is presumed to be the actual owner, and the statements in the registration application are presumed to be true. Such presumptions make it easier to present a viable court case, because they put the burden on the other side to disprove the plaintiff's right to relief.
- Copyright owners must register their work prior to suing for infringement. (See below.)

The registration process is relatively simple. It requires three elements: a completed application form, deposit materials, and payment of a fee. An applicant can register online, or prepare a written application form and mail it in.

Using the Copyright Office's eCO system, you can file an application for $45 to $65. The process is fairly straightforward (and discussed in the Forms portion of this text, following this section). The applicant may upload a digital copy of the work (if the applicant qualifies), or in the case of most published works, the applicant mails in two physical copies to the Copyright Office.

The U.S. Copyright Office provides a number of preprinted forms, for different types of works. The filing fee for these forms is $125 (apparently to discourage their use).

The U.S. Copyright Office provides a number of preprinted forms, for different types of works. The filing fee for these forms is $85 (apparently to discourage their use).

- Form TX is used for all nondramatic literary works, including software code.
- Form PA is used for published and unpublished works of the performing arts, such as musical and dramatic works, pantomimes, motion pictures, and graphically based multimedia works on CD-ROM.
- Form VA is used for the visual arts.
- Form SR is used for sound recordings.
- Form SE (there are several variations) is used for serials like newspapers, periodicals, and journals.

All forms can be downloaded from the Copyright Office's website at www. copyright.gov. Users of print forms must send the forms to the Copyright Office with a proper deposit of the work itself, or with material that satisfactorily identifies the work (called identifying material). The Copyright Office has specific regulations governing the form of the deposit. Special rules apply in the case of computer software, phonorecordings, and mask works.

In certain cases, the Copyright Office grants "special relief" by waiving formal deposit or other registration requirements. This means, for example, that the Copyright Office will accept deposits in a different medium or form from what is normally required. There are no specific rules for when specific relief will or will not be granted.

Assuming that the registration materials are properly completed, the Copyright Office will normally register the work and send a certificate of registration. On the other hand, if information is either left out of the form or clearly erroneous on its face, the Copyright Office will send the form back and indicate how to correct it.

After registration, information provided in the initial registration can be corrected or updated by filing a supplemental registration form (Form CA).

Registration is a prerequisite to filing an infringement action (17 U.S. Code § 411(a).) In 2019, the Supreme Court held that a Certificate of Registration is required as a condition of filing an infringement action. The copyright owner had filed a suit after it had applied for but not received a registration. The Supreme Court also held that once copyright is registered, the owner can recover retroactively for infringement. (*Fourth Estate Public Benefit Corp. v. Wall-Street.com, LLC.*, 586 U.S. ___ (2019).) Registration is not required to file an infringement lawsuit for non-U.S. works that meet the definition of Berne

Convention works (that is, when the author is a national of a Berne Convention country and the work was first published in a Berne Convention country). (See 17 U.S. Code § 101.) Registration is also not required to file an infringement lawsuit for works of visual art (fine art limited editions of 200 or fewer copies as defined in 17 U.S. Code, Sections 101 and 106A).

Copyright Act: § 411. Registration and infringement actions

This statute requires, with some exceptions, that a copyright be registered with the U.S. Copyright Office before a lawsuit for copyright infringement may be filed.

(a) Except for an action brought for a violation of the rights of the author under section 106A (a), and subject to the provisions of subsection (b), no action for infringement of the copyright in any United States work shall be instituted until registration of the copyright claim has been made in accordance with this title. In any case, however, where the deposit, application, and fee required for registration have been delivered to the Copyright Office in proper form and registration has been refused, the applicant is entitled to institute an action for infringement if notice thereof, with a copy of the complaint, is served on the Register of Copyrights. The Register may, at his or her option, become a party to the action with respect to the issue of registrability of the copyright claim by entering an appearance within sixty days after such service, but the Register's failure to become a party shall not deprive the court of jurisdiction to determine that issue.

(b) In the case of a work consisting of sounds, images, or both, the first fixation of which is made simultaneously with its transmission, the copyright owner may, either before or after such fixation takes place, institute an action for infringement under section 501, fully subject to the remedies provided by sections 502 through 506 and sections 509 and 510, if, in accordance with requirements that the Register of Copyrights shall prescribe by regulation, the copyright owner—

   (1) serves notice upon the infringer, not less than 48 hours before such fixation, identifying the work and the specific time and source of its first transmission, and declaring an intention to secure copyright in the work; and

   (2) makes registration for the work, if required by subsection (a), within three months after its first transmission.

Copyright Act: § 412. Registration as prerequisite to certain remedies for infringement

This statute establishes the penalty for failure to timely register a copyright with the U.S. Copyright Office and states when a registration will be considered timely.

In any action under this title, other than an action brought for a violation of the rights of the author under section 106A (a) or an action instituted under section 411 (b), no award

Copyright Law: Definitions

of statutory damages or of attorney's fees, as provided by sections 504 and 505, shall be made for—

(1) any infringement of copyright in an unpublished work commenced before the effective date of its registration; or

(2) any infringement of copyright commenced after first publication of the work and before the effective date of its registration, unless such registration is made within three months after the first publication of the work.

Related terms: copyright owner; deposit with U.S. Copyright Office; identifying material; infringement (copyright); infringement action; preregistration of copyright; special relief; timely registration.

registration of copyright license

See recordation of copyright transfers.

registration of copyrights in unpublished works

See unpublished work.

reliance party, when copyright restored

See restored copyright under GATT.

renewal of copyright

See duration of copyrights.

restored copyright under GATT

Until the United States became a member of the Berne Convention in March 1989, works originating in Berne Convention countries often lost their copyright in the United States because they failed to observe certain formalities required by U.S. copyright laws, such as copyright notices. Under the General Agreement on Tariffs and Trade (GATT), copyright protection has been restored in all such works. In 2012, the Supreme Court upheld the law and ruled that it was permissible for Congress to allow these previously public domain foreign works to be restored to copyright protection. (*Golan v. Holder*, 565 U.S. 1 (2012).) However, parties who used these restored works without permission in reliance on the fact that they weren't protected by copyright (called reliance parties) cannot be sued for copyright infringement and may continue using the works under certain circumstances if they pay a reasonable license fee to the restored copyright owner under a type of compulsory license.

Related terms: GATT (General Agreement on Tariffs and Trade).

revocation of license

Most copyright licenses contain conditions under which the license must be exercised. If these conditions are broken, the copyright owner ordinarily has a right to revoke the license. The license revocation should always be done in writing. Any exercise of the licensed right after revocation will constitute an infringement of the copyright.

Revocation of a license should not be confused with the right to terminate transfers under the Copyright Act. In that situation (and in addition to any provisions in the license itself), the original copyright owner (or his or her heirs) has a legal right to terminate any transfer after 35 to 40 years have passed.

Related terms: licensing of copyrights; termination of transfers.

rule of doubt

The U.S. Copyright Office allows object code (for software registrations) to be deposited in connection with a computer program registration. There is, however, an express understanding that doubt exists as to whether the code qualifies for copyright protection should litigation later ensue. In essence, the U.S. Copyright Office is saying, "We will let you deposit object code, but because we can't read or understand it, we won't commit ourselves as to its copyrightability."

If the registration is accomplished under the rule of doubt, the copyright owner might be unable to claim the presumption of ownership—an important benefit of registration—should the issue end up in court because of an alleged copyright infringement.

Related terms: software; special relief.

safe harbor

See Digital Millennium Copyright Act ("DMCA").

sampling

The digital recording process has made it possible to "sample" a portion of a sound recording. These digital samples can be manipulated to replay once or twice or repeat as a "loop" throughout a new recording. The unauthorized use of a sample almost always infringes the sound recording copyright and might infringe the musical works copyright held on the underlying sampled music.

Whether the use qualifies as an infringement depends upon the portion sampled and its qualitative or quantitative importance to the copyrighted work. Initially, U.S. courts took a rigid approach prohibiting any use of digital samples. Then, in a 1997 case, a court determined that the rap group Run DMC's use of a drum sample from a 1973 recording was not infringing. (*Ruff 'N' Rumble Mgmt. v. Profile Records, Inc.,* 42 U.S.P.Q.2d 1398 (S.D.N.Y. 1997).)

However, the pendulum swung against sampling in a 2004 case when the Sixth Circuit Court of Appeals ruled that the use of a two-second sample was an infringement of the sound recording copyright. The court went even further, stating that when it came to sound recording there was no permissible minimum sanctioned under copyright law. (*Bridgeport Music v. Dimension Films,* 383 F.3d 390 (6th Cir. 2004).) No other courts have yet endorsed this extreme view of sound recording protection, which ignores the defense of fair use.

In a 2017 case involving spoken word sampling, the musician Drake sampled a 1982 jazz recording on which Jimmy Smith stated, "Jazz is the only real music that's gonna last/All that other bullshit is here today and gone tomorrow. But jazz was, is and always will be." Drake edited the sample so that on his recording, it states, "Only real music's gonna last. All that other bullshit is here today and gone tomorrow." In Smith's recording, his words spoke of the supremacy of jazz; Drake converted their meaning for a broader class of "real music." The court held that the use was transformative and permitted as a fair use. (*Estate of James Oscar Smith v. Cash Money Records, Inc.* No. 1:2014cv02703 (S.D.N.Y. 2017).) The decision was affirmed by the Second Circuit in 2020.

Although industry custom requires that two licenses be obtained to sample recorded music (from the sound recording and musical work owners), a federal court ruled in 2002 that the use of a six-second flute sample, repeated throughout a Beastie Boys song, "Pass the Mic," required permission only from the sound recording owner, not from the composer. (*Newton v. Diamond,* 2002 U.S. Dist. LEXIS 10247 (C.D. Cal., 2002).)

Sound recordings were not protected by copyright law until 1972. The use of a musical sample from a work created prior to 1972 would not be an infringement of a sound recording copyright, although it might be a violation of applicable state laws (or what is sometimes referred to as "common law copyright"). In order to avoid claims of infringement, popular artists seek sample clearance from copyright owners.

scènes à faire

The scènes à faire doctrine says that when an element of a work is a customary or stock component of a discipline or genre, it is not protectible. For example, a fish-out-of-water plot, a trench-coated detective character, a cemetery setting, a blues guitar riff, or a vignette photo filter are all unprotectable unless distinguished by expressive additions.

Related terms: infringement (copyright).

secondary infringement

See contributory infringement; vicarious liability.

Semiconductor Chip Protection Act of 1984

This statute protects semiconductor chip manufacturers against the unauthorized copying or use of semiconductor chips and the templates that are used to manufacture them.

Semiconductor chips are a complex combination of tiny circuits that are designed to manipulate electronic data. They are mass-produced from multi-layered three-dimensional templates that are called "chip masks" in the trade and "mask works" under the Semiconductor Chip Protection Act.

Mask works (and the resulting semiconductor chips) are difficult and expensive to design, but very easy to copy. Accordingly, semiconductor chip manufacturers have long sought protection of these devices as a form of intellectual property. Because technological advances in these chips have been incremental in nature, most improvements have been considered obvious and, therefore, not patentable. Before 1984, the chips did not qualify for copyright protection, due to the fact that their design was considered functional rather than expressive. To plug this gap, Congress passed the Semiconductor Chip Protection Act.

Under this statute, the owner of the exclusive rights in the mask work (typically the manufacturer) is given an exclusive ten-year right to:
- reproduce the mask work
- import or distribute a semiconductor chip product in which the mask work is embodied, and
- license others to exercise these rights.

These rights are forfeited, however, if the owner fails to register the mask work with the U.S. Copyright Office within two years of its commercial exploitation anywhere in the world.

Copyright Law: Definitions

A party who innocently purchases a semiconductor chip product that has been manufactured in violation of these exclusive rights is not liable for copyright infringement but must pay a reasonable royalty for each unit the innocent party imports or distributes after notice of the infringement.

Related terms: software; innocent infringement of copyright.

server test

See embedding.

shrinkwrap agreement

See end-user license.

simultaneous publication

Previous to March 1, 1989, the United States belonged to the Universal Copyright Convention (U.C.C.) but not to the Berne Convention. If an author wished to obtain protection under both the Berne Convention and the U.C.C., he or she could do so by causing the initial publication of the work to simultaneously occur in the United States and a Berne Convention country, such as Canada. In March 1989, however, the United States joined the Berne Convention, so U.S. authors have no further reason for simultaneous publication.

Related terms: Berne Convention; international copyright protection; Universal Copyright Convention (U.C.C.).

single (eCO) application

In 2014, the Copyright Office modified the eCO application process by introducing a two-tiered approach to online registration: "Single" and "Standard" applications. Single applications are for one work by one author (not made for hire) who is also the sole owner of all rights in the work. Standard applications are for all other electronic registrations. Single application fees are currently $35; Standard application fees are $55. eCO filers are now prompted to answer "yes" or "no" to three statements to determine the appropriate application (Single or Standard) for registering their work. Filers have the opportunity to change to the Standard Application if it becomes apparent that the Single application is not appropriate. Using the Single application when a work does not meet the requirements will result in processing delays, an additional fee, and a later effective date of registration. If the Copyright Office determines that a work does not meet the Single application requirements, the filer will be contacted at the email address listed on the application with instructions on how to pay the additional fee and resubmit on the Standard application.

single registration rule

The U.S. Copyright Office normally allows only one registration for each original work of authorship. There are exceptions, however. A new registration is permitted when an unpublished work is later published. A new registration is also allowed to substitute an author's name.

Changes, updates, or translations of a given work will merit a second registration only if they are substantial enough in quantity or quality to qualify the work as a new version. Practically, unless the modified work is significantly changed or contains a great deal of new material, the original registration should provide adequate protection. However, certain minor or technical changes in an existing registration sometimes warrant filing a supplemental registration.

If a new version is registered, that registration applies only to the new material contained in the work. The material taken from the original work is still covered under the original registration.

Related terms: best edition of a work; supplemental registration.

site license

Some software publishers grant a single license to a company that allows a set number of copies of the software to be installed on individual computers. For instance, if a company with 100 employees wants its employees to use a particular graphics program, it can either buy 100 copies of the program or try to get a site license that would permit use of 100 copies of the software at a reduced rate per copy.

Related terms: software; end-user license; licensing of copyrights.

software

Under a 1980 amendment to the copyright law, software is protected in the same manner as other original works of authorship. Any computer program, defined as "a set of statements or instructions to be used directly or indirectly in a computer to bring about a certain result," can be protected by copyright if it constitutes an original work of authorship. The 1980 amendment also specifies situations in which computer programs may be copied and altered without permission of the copyright owner.

The early years of software protection consisted of battles of protection for code in object code form, for example as mechanically reproduced in a silicon chip as part of an integrated circuit (ROM chips), and in templates (mask works) used in making ROM chips. Most disputes were resolved in favor of copyright protection for software regardless of its form (that is, whether it is source code or object code), and regardless of whether it is embedded in a chip or exists as an independent work on a computer disk. The leading case in this area is *Apple Computer, Inc. v. Franklin Computer Corporation*, 714 F.2d 1240 (3d Cir. 1983). (Under a different line of cases, software can also be protected by patent law.)

Since the early 1980s, many questions have arisen about what aspects of software could receive copyright protection. Some of the issues have been:

- Should copyright protection be limited to the literal code as written, or is the structure, sequence, and organization of software code also entitled to copyright protection? In *Whelan v. Jastrow*, 797 F.2d 1222 (3d Cir. 1986), a federal circuit court of appeals held that protection for software code goes beyond the code's literal expression and extends to its structure, sequence, and organization. Other courts have found this approach unworkable and have adopted the filtration approach taken in *Computer Associates Int' l. v. Altai*, 982 F.2d 693 (2d Cir. 1992). That approach separates the code's ideas and other public domain elements from its expression and then extends protection only to the expression.

- What aspects of computer screen displays, and graphical user interfaces (GUIs) are entitled to copyright protection? The filtration approach taken in the *Altai* case has been used by a number of courts to decide which aspects of a program interface are protected by copyright. The most prominent of these cases involved a suit by Apple against Microsoft, which claimed that the Microsoft Windows operating system violated a copyright owned by Apple in the Macintosh interface. (*Apple Computer, Inc. v. Microsoft Corp.*, 717 F. Supp. 1428 (N.D. Cal. 1989), 779 F. Supp. 133 (N.D. Cal. 1992).) Using the filtration approach, the court eliminated from copyright protection most individual elements of the Macintosh interface and refused to provide protection for the interface as a whole. In short, Microsoft won, and Apple lost. The overall result of applying the filtration approach to computer user interfaces has been to afford computer user interfaces very little copyright protection.

- How much originality must a factual database have in order to qualify for copyright protection? In *Feist Publications Inc. v. Rural Telephone Service Co.*, 111 S. Ct. 1282 (1991), the U.S. Supreme Court ruled that an alphabetically arranged telephone directory involved insufficient creativity to qualify for copyright. As a result, the Copyright Act could not be used to compensate Feist Publications Inc. for the labor and expense involved in originally compiling the directory. The question remains, however, as to how much creativity is required to qualify a factual database for copyright. By its very nature, this issue can be decided only on a case-by-case basis.

- Is it fair use to copy those portions of programs that make it possible to interface with other programs? Oracle sued Google for $9 billion claiming that Google's *Android* operating system improperly used JAVA application programming interface code ("APIs"). APIs are bits of software that interface with programs to trigger software functions. The District Court found that Google's use of JAVA components was "fair use," primarily because APIs exist to interface with other codes and are traditionally borrowed as industry protocols. On appeal, the Federal Circuit ruled that the use of APIs was not a fair use because it wasn't minimal or transformative. (*Oracle Am., Inc. v. Google LLC*, 886 F.3d 1179 (Fed. Cir. 2018).) The Supreme Court had the final word, and held that Google's copying of the Java SE API was a fair use because it included only those lines of code that were needed to allow programmers to work in a new and transformative program. (*Google LLC v. Oracle America, Inc.*, 141 S. Ct. 1183 (2021).)

Related terms: *Apple Computer, Inc. v. Franklin*; *Apple Computer, Inc. v. Microsoft Corp.*; copyright; infringement (copyright); infringement action.

Sonny Bono Copyright Term Extension Act

This Act, signed by the president on October 26, 1998, extended the copyright term in the United States by 20 years for all works published after January 1, 1998. The act also extended the duration of the copyright term on works created or published prior to 1978.

In 2003, the U.S. Supreme Court ruled that the 20-year copyright extension did not violate the U.S. Constitution. (*Eldred v. Ashcroft*, 537 U.S. 186 (2003).)

Related terms: Copyleft; duration of copyrights; *Eldred v. Ashcroft*.

Copyright Law: Definitions

sound recordings

See phonorecords.

source code

Source code refers to the program code in which a programmer writes a software program. Source code can be written in various computer languages (for instance, Cobol, C++, Visual Basic) and contains not only the commands for the computer, but also the programmer's comments regarding the purpose and meaning of the different lines of code. It is relatively easy for a skilled computer programmer to examine the source code for a particular program and figure out how to produce the same result with a different program. Thus, access to source code will reveal a program's trade secrets and allow a competitor to use its ideas in a competing program.

For this reason, programmers like to keep their source code as confidential as possible. Accordingly, when registering a program with the U.S. Copyright Office, many software authors prefer to deposit only object code, which is extremely difficult to decipher because it appears in the form of ones and zeros, hexadecimal, or some other inscrutable form.

Nevertheless, the U.S. Copyright Office considers a program's source code to be the best edition of the work and, accordingly, prefers it as a deposit. In fact, the U.S. Copyright Office will accept a deposit of portions of the source code with critical parts blacked out, or a mixture of source code and object code. But the U.S. Copyright Office will also accept a deposit of the object code under what is called the rule of doubt—that is, it has no opinion as to whether the registered code qualifies for copyright protection, because it can't read it.

Related terms: software; object code; open source; registration; rule of doubt.

sovereign immunity

Sovereign immunity is a principle that a government is immune from civil suit or criminal prosecution. For purposes of copyright, it refers to the fact that state governments cannot be liable for copyright infringement. For example, in 2000 a suit was dismissed in which a man sued the University of Houston (a state-run institution) for copyright infringement. (*Chavez v. Arte Publico Press,* 204 F.3d 601 (5th Cir. 2000).)

Congress sought to correct this situation by passing the "Copyright Clarification Act" (1990) (17 U.S. Code § 511), which provides that no state is immune from suit in federal court for copyright violations. However, in 2020, the Supreme Court held that under Article 1 of the Constitution, Congress could not limit the sovereign immunity of state governments. (*Allen v. Cooper*, 140 S. Ct. 994 (2020).) Neither the federal government nor local municipal or county governments enjoy similar sovereign immunity. Moreover, civil copyright remedies can be pursued against any government (federal, state, or local) employee who commits infringement in his or her individual capacity. Finally, a state institution should not assume it has freedom to commit copyright infringement. State laws vary, and some states will waive or limit sovereign immunity in certain situations.

special relief

The U.S. Copyright Office sometimes gives a special variance to depart from its usual requirements for copyright registration or deposit. This variance is known as "special relief." Applicants for copyright registration might have one or many reasons to seek exemptions from the formal requirements for registration and deposits—for example, an unusual shape, size, or composition of the work to be deposited or the need to maintain a trade secret expressed by the work. Often the U.S. Copyright Office will grant such special relief to applicants who request it and explain in a cover letter to their registration application why they need it.

Related terms: best edition of a work; deposit with U.S. Copyright Office; registration.

standard (eCO) application

In 2014, the Copyright Office modified the eCO application process by introducing a two-tiered approach to online registration: so-called "Single" and "Standard" applications. Single Applications are for one work by one author (not made for hire) who is also the sole owner of all rights in the work. Standard applications are for all other online electronic registrations. Single application fees are currently $35; Standard application fees are $55. eCO filers are now prompted to answer "yes" or "no" to three statements to determine the appropriate application (Single or Standard) for registering their work.

Related term: common law copyright.

Copyright Law: Definitions

Copyright Law: Definitions

standing (to sue)

The party bringing a lawsuit must have the legal capacity to "stand" before the court. In most cases, this means demonstrating that the party has suffered harm as a result of the violation of a statute. If a party lacks standing, the case will be dismissed without the court having considered the issues. Standing under the Copyright Act is set forth in Section 501(b), which states that the "legal or beneficial owner of an exclusive right under a copyright is entitled . . . to institute an action for any infringement of that particular right committed while he or she is the owner of it." In other words, standing is bestowed upon the owner of the copyright or an exclusive licensee. For example, a stock photo company that was the exclusive licensing agent for copyrighted photos had standing to bring claims of direct infringement under the Copyright Act. (*Minden Pictures, Inc. v. John Wiley & Sons, Inc.*, 795 F.3d 997 (9th Cir. 2015).) Though it probably doesn't need to be said, standing is bestowed only upon humans, not animals. (*Naruto v. Slater*, 888 F.3d 418 (9th Cir. 2018).) The *Naruto* case involved an Indonesian crested macaque who took several photos of itself when a photographer left his camera unattended.

states, copyright infringement suits against

See sovereign immunity.

statute of limitations

A statute of limitations sets the legal time limit by which a person bringing an infringement lawsuit must file the suit. In civil copyright cases, this limit provides that you can't file suit more than three years after the discovery of the infringement, or after it reasonably should have been discovered. (In criminal copyright cases, the government must bring an action within five years after the infringement occurred.) The theory behind the statute of limitations is that plaintiffs can't be allowed to "sit on their rights" and accumulate damages but must act reasonably promptly to prevent further damage once it is discovered.

Because it is not always easy to discover the existence of a copyright infringement, it's fairly common to file a lawsuit after the three-year deadline, claiming recent discovery. Unfortunately, the courts do not always agree on what types of acts start the calendar running for purposes of the three-year statute of limitations period.

In one case, for example, the Supreme Court permitted an author/screenwriter's heirs to wait 18 years before filing a copyright infringement lawsuit against the owners of the film, *Raging Bull*. As noted, the copyright law provides that when there are ongoing infringements—as in this case, where copies of *Raging Bull* continue to be sold—the copyright owner may bring the lawsuit within three years of *any* infringement (and can collect damages for only the preceding three years). Lower court decisions had prevented the heirs' lawsuit under a principle known as laches (an equitable principle saying that it's unfair to proceed with a lawsuit after one party has waited an unreasonable amount of time to bring the claim). In light of the federal statute of limitations, however, the Supreme Court ruled that it was inappropriate to apply laches. The Court held, "This Court has never applied laches to bar in their entirety claims for discrete wrongs occurring within a federally prescribed limitations period." (*Petrella v. Metro-Goldwyn-Mayer*, Inc., 572 U.S. 633 (2014).)

Copyright Act: § 507. Limitations on actions

(a) **Criminal Proceedings.**—Except as expressly provided otherwise in this title, no criminal proceeding shall be maintained under the provisions of this title unless it is commenced within 5 years after the cause of action arose.

(b) **Civil Actions.**—No civil action shall be maintained under the provisions of this title unless it is commenced within three years after the claim accrued.

statutory damages under copyright act

See damages for copyright infringement.

streaming

Services such as Spotify, Netflix, Pandora, and Hulu transmit their content in a steady stream of compressed data packets, allowing the user to begin playback without having to wait for the whole production to be transmitted. In other words, the user does not retain a copy. Although there was some confusion as to whether streaming constituted infringement—or whether, for example, streaming was subject to cable TV rules—the Second Circuit held that unauthorized streaming of video is a violation of the performance right. (*WPIX, Inc. v. IVI, Inc.*, 691 F.3d 275 (2d Cir. 2012).) Similar rulings have held that unauthorized streaming of music is infringement, as well. (*Bluewater Music Servs. Corp. v. Spotify U.S. Inc.*, Case No. 3:17-cv-01051-JPM (W.D. Tenn. Sep. 28, 2018).) In 2020, the Protecting Lawful Streaming Act (18 U.S. Code § 2319C) made it a felony to operate a for-profit streaming "digital transmission service" whose primary purpose is to stream unauthorized content. The transmission service must be primarily designed for streaming copyrighted works without authorization, or have no commercial purpose other than to stream copyrighted works without authorization. The Act sets a maximum penalty of up to ten years' imprisonment, and additional fines if convicted.

Related terms: webcasting.

substantial similarity

See infringement (copyright).

supplemental registration

Certain errors in a copyright registration may be corrected, changed, or amplified by filing a supplemental registration. Form CA, a downloadable form that you can fill out on your computer and print out, is available for this purpose.

Supplemental registration is appropriate for both trivial mistakes and more serious errors, such as:

- The author's name was misspelled.
- The author's birth date was incorrect.
- The title of the work has changed since the original registration.
- The owner's address has changed.
- An unpublished work was registered as published.
- The author or copyright claimant was misidentified, omitted, or has a changed name (not because of a transfer).
- Some aspect of the application information needs clarification.

The first three of these situations are trivial and need not be changed for the copyright to remain valid. An address change need not be noted for legal purposes, but an accurate address will obviously enable potential licensees and transferees to locate the copyright owner. The other errors, and the need to correct them, are more important, because they affect both the validity of the copyright and the owner's ability to vindicate his or her rights in court.

Related terms: single registration rule.

Tasini

See New York Times v. Tasini.

Tattoos

In 2005, a tattoo artist sued to prevent basketball player Rasheed Wallace from displaying a tattoo the artist had designed and inked in Nike commercials. The case settled prior to a ruling on the copyrightability of ink on flesh. In 2011, Warner Bros. was sued by a tattoo artist after a movie (*Hangover II*) included a character with a tattoo identical to the one created for boxer Mike Tyson. Warner Bros. was set to digitally remove the tattoo, but the case settled before that was necessary. Prior to settlement, the district court refused to halt the release of the film and at the hearing the judge acknowledged that Warner Bros. was unlikely to succeed on a fair use defense. The case aroused interest as to the issue of whether the human body constituted a "tangible medium of expression" as required by copyright law, and whether the tattoo artist impliedly licenses or relinquishes the display right. In 2020, a tattoo company sued a videogame maker because five players (out of 400) in a basketball simulation game included tattoos for which the tattoo company held exclusive licenses. Because the tattoos could barely be seen in the game (accounting for less than .0003% of the game data), the court held that the videogame maker's reproduction was a fair use. (*Solid Oak Sketches, LLC v. Visual Concepts, LLC et al.*, No. 16-00724, (S.D.N.Y. 2020).)

temporary restraining order (TRO)

See infringement action; injunctions.

termination of transfers

For works published after January 1, 1978, any exclusive copyright right that has been transferred by the author—for example, the author had assigned or licensed the rights to a publisher—may be terminated by the author, the author's surviving spouse, or the author's children or grandchildren, provided that the termination occurs after 35 years from publication of the work or 40 years after the transfer is made, whichever comes first. However, the termination must occur within five years of the date the author or heirs become eligible to do so, or the right to terminate is lost forever. This termination right does not apply to works made for hire.

> EXAMPLE: Bill composes a song and grants the rights to record and market the song to Ecotopia Enterprises. The transfer takes effect January 1, 1995. When first published in January 1996, the song becomes a classic, continuously recorded by a succession of artists. In 2031, Bill will have the right to terminate the "grant of rights" and recapture full ownership of the copyright. However, if Bill fails to exercise this option to terminate by 2036, he will lose it.

Copyright Law: Definitions

Although all copyright transfers after 1977 may be terminated through this process, any derivative works that have been legally prepared in the meantime will continue to belong to their authors, rather than reverting to the original copyright owner. For instance, if under a broad grant of rights from Bill (which included the right to use the song for all legal purposes) Ecotopia had prepared and marketed a television series based on the song, all rights to the television series will remain with Ecotopia or anyone to whom it transferred the series.

Related terms: licensing of copyrights.

terms and conditions/terms of use

See end-user license.

thin copyright

When a work features a limited number of original features, the copyright is said to be "thin," and the owner can stop others from copying only those original features, not other unprotectable elements. For example, in one case, a California glass artist created glass-in-glass jellyfish sculptures. The works were successful—some sold for hundreds of thousands of dollars—and another glass artist who saw them began making similar works. The California glass artist sued, but a court ruled against him, stating that he could not prevent others from depicting the natural shape of jellyfish, their naturally bright colors, or their vertical-swimming appearance. Nor could the artist prevent others from portraying jellyfish in glass. On that basis, the artist had a thin copyright and could prevent only near-exact duplications of his work. (*Satava v. Lowry,* 323 F.3d 805 (9th Cir. 2003).) A similar determination was made in a case in which a photographer of a vodka bottle claimed infringement when the vodka company used similar lighting and setting to create a similar photograph. (*Ets-Hokin v. Skyy Spirits,* 323 F.3d 763 (9th Cir. 2003).)

timely registration

To obtain all the benefits of registration, a work must be registered with the U.S. Copyright Office within certain time limits. Timely registration entitles a copyright owner to statutory damages and attorneys' fees in an infringement suit, which may make affordable a suit that is otherwise prohibitively expensive and risky.

For a published work, timely registration must occur within three months of first publication or before the infringement begins. For unpublished works, registration is timely as long as it occurs before the infringement begins.

Copyright owners must register their work prior to suing for infringement under the provisions of 17 U.S. Code Section 411(a).

Related terms: copyright; registration.

Trade Related Aspects of Intellectual Property Rights (TRIPS)

See GATT (General Agreement on Tariffs and Trade).

transfers of copyright ownership

According to the Copyright Act, a transfer of copyright ownership is any grant of an exclusive right, or an assignment, mortgage, exclusive license, or any other conveyance of a copyright or of any of the exclusive rights constituting a copyright. A transfer does not include a nonexclusive license.

Because a copyright consists of a bundle of rights that can be divided, a transfer can involve the entire copyright or only a portion of it. For example, a grant of rights can be limited by time, geography, or media. The right to make copies of an original work, the right to sell the work, the right to display the work, and the right to make derivative works of the work are also separate transferable rights.

> EXAMPLE: Ruth writes a book called *Nurse Ruth*. She registers the copyright with the U.S. Copyright Office and lists herself as the owner. Although Ruth could publish and market the book herself, more likely she will let others do the job for her. For example, she might execute a written license giving Able Publishers the exclusive right to sell, display, and make copies of the book. She might also transfer some or all of the remaining rights (for instance, film, radio and TV, and magazine) to Able, or she can choose to transfer some of them to others, retaining for herself only a few or perhaps only the exclusive right to make derivative works.

In fact, an almost infinite number of transfers can occur for a copyrighted work. The only prerequisites for a transfer of ownership are that:

- The transfer must be in writing.
- The transfer must be signed by the owner.
- The right that is transferred must be an exclusive grant.

> EXAMPLE 1: Ruth retains at least one of the exclusive copyright rights in the book *Nurse Ruth*, so she remains the owner of the "copyright" as far as the U.S. Copyright Office is concerned and continues to have her name on the notice of copyright. Although Able Publishers may own a number (but not all) of the rights and is considered a legal copyright owner, it owns only the exclusive rights transferred in the license and is not named as owner in the U.S. Copyright Office or on the notice of copyright.

Copyright Law: Definitions

EXAMPLE 2: Ruth decides to transfer all of her copyright rights in *Nurse Ruth* to Able Publishers (including the right to make derivative works). Able is the new "owner" in the U.S. Copyright Office and on the copyright notice. On the other hand, if Ruth transfers all rights to Able except the derivative works, which she transfers to someone else (her sister Edna, perhaps), Ruth will still be the "owner," even though she has transferred all her rights to other people. This is because the U.S. Copyright Office considers the original owner to remain the owner unless all of the copyright rights are transferred together to a single person or entity.

Although transfers can be valid without being recorded with the U.S. Copyright Office, it is better practice to record them. This record will serve as evidence in case of an argument about the scope of the rights granted. Also, the date of recordation helps determine which transfer prevails in case of overlapping transfers.

Copyright Act: § 201. Ownership of copyright

(d) Transfer of Ownership.—

(1) The ownership of a copyright may be transferred in whole or in part by any means of conveyance or by operation of law, and may be bequeathed by will or pass as personal property by the applicable laws of intestate succession.

(2) Any of the exclusive rights comprised in a copyright, including any subdivision of any of the rights specified by section 106, may be transferred as provided by clause (1) and owned separately. The owner of any particular exclusive right is entitled, to the extent of that right, to all of the protection and remedies accorded to the copyright owner by this title.

(e) Involuntary Transfer.—When an individual author's ownership of a copyright, or of any of the exclusive rights under a copyright, has not previously been transferred voluntarily by that individual author, no action by any governmental body or other official or organization purporting to seize, expropriate, transfer, or exercise rights of ownership with respect to the copyright, or any of the exclusive rights under a copyright, shall be given effect under this title, except as provided under title 11.

Copyright Act: § 204. Execution of transfers of copyright ownership

This statute sets out the requirements for transfers of copyright ownership (assignments).

(a) A transfer of copyright ownership, other than by operation of law, is not valid unless an instrument of conveyance, or a note or memorandum of the transfer, is in writing and signed by the owner of the rights conveyed or such owner's duly authorized agent.

(b) A certificate of acknowledgement is not required for the validity of a transfer, but is prima facie evidence of the execution of the transfer if—

(1) in the case of a transfer executed in the United States, the certificate is issued by a person authorized to administer oaths within the United States; or

(2) in the case of a transfer executed in a foreign country, the certificate is issued by a diplomatic or consular officer of the United States, or by a person authorized to administer oaths whose authority is proved by a certificate of such an officer.

Related terms: overlapping transfers of copyright; recordation of copyright; termination of transfers.

transformative use

In 1994, the Supreme Court heard a case involving a rap group, 2 Live Crew. The group had borrowed the opening musical tag and the words (but not the melody) from the first line of the song "Pretty Woman" ("Oh, pretty woman, walking down the street"). The rest of the lyrics and the music were different. In a decision that surprised many in the copyright world, the Supreme Court ruled that the borrowing was fair use. Part of the decision was colored by the fact that so little was borrowed. But the Supreme Court also added a new dimension to the fair use analysis. It focused on one of the four fair use factors—the purpose and character of the use—and emphasized that the most important aspect of the fair use analysis was whether the purpose and character of the use was "transformative."

In the 2 Live Crew case, the use of the lyrics was transformative because they poked fun at the norms of what was "pretty." Justice Souter wrote: "... the enquiry focuses on whether the new work merely supersedes the objects of the original creation, or whether and to what extent it is 'transformative,' altering the original with new expression, meaning, or message. The more transformative the new work, the less will be the significance of other factors, like commercialism, that may weigh against a finding of fair use." (*Campbell v. Acuff-Rose Music*, 510 U.S. 569 (1994).)

In the two decades that have passed, the standards of transformative continue to evolve. Still, the status of a transformative work seems to be defined by two questions:

Has the material taken from the original work been transformed by adding new expression or meaning?

Was value added to the original by creating new information, new aesthetics, new insights, and understandings?

Below are some summaries of cases involving "transformative claims."

- **The Harry Potter encyclopedia** (Not transformative). Although the creation of a Harry Potter encyclopedia was determined to be "slightly transformative" (because it made the Harry Potter terms and lexicons available in one volume), this transformative quality was not enough to justify a fair use defense. An important factor in the court's decision was the extensive verbatim use of text from the Harry Potter books. (*Warner Bros. Entertainment, Inc. v. RDR Books*, 575 F. Supp.2d 513 (S.D.N.Y. 2008).)
- **Monster Movie art** (Transformative). A publisher of monster magazines from the 1950s, '60s, and '70s sued the creator and publisher of a book, *Famous Monster Movie Art of Basil Gogos*. (Gogos created covers for the magazines.) The book publisher had obtained licenses from the artist directly, but not from the magazine publisher, who claimed copyright under work-made-for-hire principles. The district court determined that the use was transformative. The use was for a biography/retrospective of the artist, not simply a series of covers of magazines devoted to movie monsters. In addition, the magazines were no longer in print, and the covers amounted to only one page of the magazine, not the "heart" of the magazine. (*Warren Publishing Co. v. Spurlock d/b/a Vanguard Productions*, 645 F. Supp.2d 402, (E.D. Pa. 2009).)
- **Ed Sullivan clip** (Transformative). A seven-second clip from the Ed Sullivan TV show was used in a staged musical history (*The Jersey Boys*) based on the career of the musical group the Four Seasons. The use was transformative. ("Being selected by Ed Sullivan to perform on his show was evidence of the band's enduring prominence in American music," the judge wrote in the ruling. "By using it as a biographical anchor, [the defendant] put the clip to its own transformative ends.") Further, the use caused no financial harm to the copyright owners of the show. (*SOFA Entertainment, Inc. v. Dodger Productions, Inc.*, 709 F.3d 1273 (9th Cir. Mar. 11, 2013).)
- **Prince collages** (Transformative). The painter Richard Prince created a collage using—in one collage—35 images from a photographer's book. The artist also used 28 of the photos in 29 additional paintings. In some instances the full photograph was used while in others only the main subject of the photo was used. The Second Circuit Court of Appeals held that to qualify as a transformative use, Prince's work did not have to comment on the original photographer's work (or on popular culture). The Court of Appeals concluded that 25 of Prince's artworks qualified as fair use and remanded the case to determine the status of the remaining five artworks. (*Cariou v. Prince*, 714 F.3d 694 (2d Cir. 2012).)

- **Nonprofit immigration use** (Transformative). A nonprofit organization posted a newspaper article about police discrimination on its website. The newspaper assigned its right in the article to a third party, Righthaven, which filed the lawsuit. The court's reasoning that the nonprofit's use was transformative was influenced by the fact that Righthaven had acquired the copyright and was not in the newspaper business (it appeared to be in the "litigation business"). For that reason, the court reasoned that the nonprofit's use was transformative because its purpose was to educate the public about immigration issues, whereas Righthaven had no such purpose for the article (because it was not in the news business). And also, because Righthaven was not in the news business, it could show no harm from the defendant's dissemination of the article. (*Righthaven LLC v. Jama*, No 2:2010-cv-01322, 2011 WL 1541613 (D. Nev. April. 22, 2011).)

- **Naked Demi** (Transformative). A movie company used a photo of a naked pregnant woman onto which it superimposed the head of actor Leslie Nielsen. The photo was a parody using similar lighting and body positioning to a famous photograph taken by Annie Leibovitz of the actress Demi Moore for the cover of *Vanity Fair* magazine. The movie company's use was transformative because it imitated the photographer's style for comic effect or ridicule. (*Leibovitz v. Paramount Pictures Corp.*, 137 F.3d 109 (2d Cir. N.Y. 1998).)

- **Dr. Seuss** (Not transformative). An author mimicked the style of a Dr. Seuss book while retelling the facts of the O.J. Simpson murder trial in *The Cat NOT in the Hat! A Parody by Dr. Juice*. The Ninth Circuit Court of Appeals determined that the book was a satire, not a parody, because the book did not poke fun at or ridicule Dr. Seuss. Instead, it merely used the Dr. Seuss characters and style to tell the story of the murder. In short, the author's work was nontransformative and commercial. (*Dr. Seuss Enterprises, L.P. v. Penguin Books USA, Inc.*, 109 F.3d 1394 (9th Cir. 1997).)

- **Dr. Seuss II** (Not transformative). The Ninth Circuit determined that "Oh, the Places You'll Boldly Go!"—a proposed mash-up of TV's *Star Trek* and a Dr. Seuss book, *Oh, the Places You'll Go!*—was not transformative. The proposed work was not a parody because it did not critique or comment on the Dr. Seuss work. Instead, the authors simply intended to make a humorous book by combining characters from *Star Trek* with layouts and illustrations lifted directly from the Dr. Seuss book. (*Dr. Seuss Enterprises v. ComicMix, LLC*, No. 19-55348 (9th Cir. 2020).)

- **Posting on social media** (Not transformative). In an anniversary tribute on Facebook, a Fox news producer posted an iconic unmodified photo of firefighters hoisting a flag after the 9/11 bombings ("Raising the Flag at Ground Zero"). The photo was juxtaposed with an image of soldiers raising the flag at Iwo Jima and the caption #neverforget. After the photographer sued, Fox claimed fair use for the posting, arguing that posting on social media is by its nature transformative because such postings promote comment and criticism. The district court rejected the argument and held that the posting was not a fair use. (*North Jersey Media Group Inc. v. Jeanine Pirro and Fox News Network, LLC,* 74 F. Supp.3d 605 (S.D.N.Y. 2015).)

- **Court-filed briefs reproduced in legal database** (Transformative). In *White v. West Publishing,* a district court ruled that legal databases such as Westlaw and Lexis could incorporate legal briefs into their databases. The searchable use of court-filed documents was transformative (and therefore excusable as a fair use) because the lawyers created the briefs to assist their clients, while the legal services were using the briefs as research tools. (*White v. West Publishing,* 29 F. Supp.3d 396 (S.D.N.Y. 2014).)

- **Recreating three scenes from *Deep Throat*** (Transformative). The recreation of three scenes from the film, *Deep Throat,* was a fair use when made for a biographical film about actress Linda Lovelace. The court was persuaded by the fact that the recreated scenes were used in a nonpornographic film biography about an actress who ultimately railed against pornography. This use illustrated a strong transformative purpose and demonstrated that the copyright owner of *Deep Throat* would be unlikely to lose revenue from this nonpornographic use. (*Arrow Productions, LTD v. The Weinstein Company LLC,* 44 F. Supp.3d 359 (S.D.N.Y. 8/25/14).)

- **Book scanning to create a database** (Transformative). In a 2014 case, the Second Circuit held that scanning books to create a searchable database was a "quintessentially transformative" fair use. Many colleges, universities, and nonprofits had offered their book collections to HathiTrust, a nonprofit that created a ten-million-book database. The Second Circuit ruled that HathiTrust was permitted under fair use principles to electronically scan its copyrighted books to create a full-text searchable database. (*Authors Guild, Inc. v. HathiTrust,* 755 F.3d 87 (2d Cir. 2014).)

- **Landlord sues former tenant for infringement** (Transformative). A disgruntled former commercial tenant (Chevaldina) used an unflattering photo of her former landlord (Katz) in 25 critical blog posts. Katz purchased the copyright in the photo and sued Chevaldina for infringement. The use was considered noncommercial, and transformative because, in the context of the blog post's surrounding commentary, Chevaldina used Katz's "compromising appearance to ridicule and satirize his character." (*Katz v. Chevaldina*, No. 14-14525 (11th Cir. 2015).)

- **Book digitization** (Transformative). Google made digital copies of books submitted to it by libraries, scanned them, and made them available to search through its Google Books service, so that users could—for free—identify relevant words, terms, or snippets from the scanned text. Google also allowed participating libraries to retain the copies they submitted. Google's digitization was deemed a transformative use because it provided limited information about the books without allowing users more complete access to the works. (*Authors Guild v. Google, Inc.*, No. 13-4829 (2d Cir. 2015).

- **Drake wins sampling lawsuit** (Transformative). The musician Drake sampled several spoken word phrases from a 1982 jazz recording by Jimmy Smith. The court held that the use was transformative because in Smith's recording, his words spoke of the supremacy of jazz; Drake converted their meaning for a broader class of "real music." (*Estate of James Oscar Smith v. Cash Money Records*, Inc. No. 1:2014cv02703 (S.D.N.Y. 2017).)

- **Taking of "Who's on First" in play** (Not transformative). The heirs of the comedy team Abbott and Costello sued the producers of the Broadway play *Hand to God* over the play's use of the "Who's on First" comedy routine. Although a lower court had permitted it as a fair use, the Second Circuit disagreed, holding that a use is not transformative simply because the new work "serves a purpose or conveys an overall expression, meaning, or message different from the copyrighted material it appropriates." Instead, "the critical inquiry is whether the new work uses the copyrighted material itself for a purpose, or imbues it with a character, different from that for which it was created." (*TCA Television Corp. v. McCollum*, No. 16-134-cv, (2d Cir. 2016).)

- **Copying portions of interface programs permitted** (Transformative). Oracle sued Google for $9 billion, claiming that Google's *Android* operating system improperly used JAVA application programming interface code ("APIs"). APIs are bits of software that interface with programs to trigger software functions. The District Court found that Google's use of JAVA components was "fair use," primarily because APIs exist to interface with other codes and are traditionally borrowed as industry protocols. However, on appeal, the Federal Circuit ruled that the use of APIs was not a fair use because it wasn't transformative. (*Oracle Am., Inc. v. Google LLC*, 886 F.3d 1179 (Fed. Cir. 2018).) The Supreme Court reversed and held that Google's copying of the Java SE API included only those lines of code that were needed to allow programmers to work in a new and transformative program. In other words, Google's limited API borrowing was fair use. (*Google LLC v. Oracle America, Inc.*, 141 S. Ct. 1183 (2021).)

- **B.I.G. exalts "Party and Bullsh*t"** (Transformative). Notorious B.I.G., a rap artist, borrowed the phrase "party and bullshit" from an album by The Last Poets. B.I.G.'s use was considered transformative because it "exalts 'party and bullshit' rather than condemning it," (as did The Last Poets). (*Oyewole v. Ora*, 291 F. Supp. 3d 422 (S.D.N.Y. 2018).)

- **Warhol use of Prince photos** (Not transformative). In 1984, Andy Warhol created a series of silkscreens of the musician Prince, using photos by Lynn Goldsmith as his source material. According to the district court, "The Prince Series works can reasonably be perceived to have transformed Prince from a vulnerable, uncomfortable person to an iconic, larger-than-life figure." (*Andy Warhol Found. for Visual Arts, Inc. v. Goldsmith*, 17-cv-2532 (J.G.K.) (S.D.N.Y. July 1, 2019).) On appeal, the Second Circuit held that Andy Warhol's use of the Prince photograph was derivative, not transformative, reversing the fair use decision by the district court. (*Andy Warhol Foundation for the Visual Arts, Inc. v. Goldsmith*, ___ F.3d ___ (2d Cir. Aug. 24, 2021).)

- **News reproduction of Trump-photobombed wedding picture** (Not transformative). A wedding guest photographed President Trump as he "crashed" a wedding at Trump's golf course in New Jersey. The photo appeared on Instagram and was subsequently reproduced by CNN, TMZ, and several other media companies. The court rejected the theory that the use was transformative simply because the photographer took the photo for personal use, not news use. (*Otto v. Hearst Comm.*, 1:17-cv-04712-GHW-JLC (S.D.N.Y. 2018).)

- **Competitor's reproduction of bond trader photo** (Not transformative). A photographer created a portrait of a bond trader for *Forbes* magazine. Subsequently *Barron's*, a competitor of *Forbes*, reproduced the photo without permission. The court did not consider the use by a competitor to be transformative: "[U]sing a photo for the precise reason it was created does not support a finding that the nature and purpose of the use was fair." (*Michael Grecco Productions, Inc. v. Valuewalk, LLC.* 345 F. Supp. 3d 482 (S.D.N.Y. 2018).)

- **Tagging photos and making them searchable is not enough** (Not transformative). VHT, who licensed real estate photos to Zillow, claimed Zillow exceeded its license by displaying the photos after the sale, and at a second website for home renovations. The Court of Appeals ruled that making the images searchable did not fundamentally transform their original purpose of displaying the property. (*VHT, Inc. v. Zillow Group, Inc.*, 918 F. 3d 723 (9th Cir. March 15, 2019).)

translation rights

See compulsory license; derivative work.

UCITA

The Uniform Computer Information Transaction Act (UCITA) is an unpopular model code intended to create uniformity in the way in which courts treat software licenses. UCITA has been adopted in different forms in only two states, Virginia and Maryland. The Act was met with considerable opposition—the American Bar Association wouldn't endorse it and four states even adopted "anti-UCITA" laws.

Related terms: end-user license.

Universal Copyright Convention (U.C.C.)

This is an international copyright treaty that offers national treatment to any work first published in a U.C.C. member country or by a national of any U.C.C. country. In addition, it limits the formalities that a U.C.C. country may require to confer copyright protection. A member country may require only that the work carry this notice of copyright: "© (year of first publication) (name of the author)."

The U.C.C. also requires that each member country offer a minimum copyright duration of at least the life of the author plus 25 years. With one exception, each author is also given the exclusive right to translate his or her own work. If, however, the work is imported to another U.C.C. treaty country and not translated within seven years of the work's original publication, the government of that country may authorize a translation into that country's language under a compulsory licensing system (along with payment of a fair fee).

Copyright Law: Definitions

Although the U.C.C. continues to have some importance in areas not covered by the Berne Convention, the Berne Convention is normally the governing international treaty, especially because the GATT treaty provides that all of its signatories agree to be bound by the Berne Convention.

Related terms: Berne Convention; GATT (General Agreement on Tariffs and Trade); international copyright protection.

unpublished work

An original work of authorship that is fixed in a tangible medium of expression but has not yet been made available to the general public without restriction is considered to be an unpublished work and automatically qualifies for copyright protection. Displaying a work—for example, exhibiting a painting in a gallery—or distributing a work with restrictions on disclosure—for example, distributing galleys of a book under the terms of a nondisclosure agreement—are also not considered publications.

Unpublished works may be registered with the U.S. Copyright Office, but the more common practice is to wait until a work is published before registering. If the registration occurs before an infringement of the unpublished works begins, the copyright owner may recover statutory damages and possibly attorneys' fees.

All unpublished works created by authors who died 70 or more years ago are now in the public domain in the United States. This is so whether the author was American or a non-American. Unpublished works made for hire created more than 120 years ago are also in the U.S. public domain. Unpublished works that were created after 1977 that are works made for hire are protected for 120 years.

Note: It is more difficult for an infringer to claim fair use when the infringed work is unpublished because the infringing publication deprives its copyright owner of the right to determine its publication date.

useful article

Copyright law doesn't protect useful articles, meaning objects like a belt or a lamp that have "an intrinsic utilitarian function that is not merely to portray the appearance of the article or to convey information." (17 U.S. Code § 101.) The appearance or design of a useful article will be protected by copyright (as a pictorial, graphic, or sculptural work), provided that the design is separable and capable of existing independently of useful features of the article (referred to as "separability"). For example, the design of a belt buckle is conceptually separable from a belt, and therefore protectable. (*Kieselten-Cord v. Accessories by Pearl, Inc.*, 632 F.2d 989 (2d Cir. 1980).) In a case called *Universal Furniture International, Inc. v. Collezione Europa USA, Inc.* (618 F.3d 417 (4th Cir. 2010)), the Fourth Circuit ruled that highly ornate furniture design can be separable and copyrightable despite its utilitarian function. In *Lanard Toys Ltd. v. Novelty, Inc.* (375 Fed. App'x. 705 (9th Cir. 2010)), the Ninth Circuit held that there was sufficient evidence to demonstrate that a launcher and flying toy were copyrightable despite their function.

In *Star Athletica, L.L.C. v. Varsity Brands, Inc.* (137 S. Ct. 1002 (2017)), the Supreme Court held that the surface decoration of a cheerleader uniform was protectable, and also fashioned a separability test. Basically, a feature incorporated into the design of a useful article is eligible for copyright protection if the feature (1) can be perceived as a two- or three-dimensional work of art separate from the useful article and (2) would qualify as a protectable pictorial, graphic, or sculptural work—either on its own or fixed in some other tangible medium of expression—if it were imagined separately from the useful article into which is incorporated.

In one of the first applications of the Supreme Court's separability test, the Third Circuit held that a full-body banana costume was protected by copyright law. (*Silvertop Assocs. Inc. v. Kangaroo Mfg. Inc.*, No. 18-2266 (3d Cir. Aug. 1, 2019).) (Designs of useful articles may also qualify for design patent protection.)

Related terms: pictorial, graphic, and sculptural works.

U.S. Copyright Office

Established by Congress, the U.S. Copyright Office—a branch of the Library of Congress—oversees the implementation of the federal copyright laws. It issues regulations, processes applications for registration of copyrights, and accepts and (for some types of works) stores deposits made in connection with registration. The U.S. Copyright Office also issues opinions on whether certain types of items are subject to copyright protection.

The U.S. Copyright Office has a website (www.copyright.gov) where you can download forms and find a great deal of useful copyright information.

The mailing address for the U.S. Copyright Office is:

Register of Copyrights
U.S. Copyright Office
101 Independence Avenue, SE
Washington, DC 20559-6000

Copyright Law: Definitions

version

See derivative work; single registration rule.

visual artists' rights

See work of visual art.

vicarious liability (copyright)

Vicarious liability occurs when someone supervises and profits from copyright infringement without committing it directly. One of the earliest cases occurred when a dance hall hired an orchestra to provide music to its patrons. The dance hall was held liable for the unauthorized public performance of songs played by that orchestra. (*Dreamland Ballroom, Inc. v. Shapiro, Bernstein & Co.*, 36 F.2d 354 (7th Cir. 1929).) Vicarious liability requires two elements: (1) the right and ability to supervise or control the infringing activity; and (2) a direct financial benefit from that activity. For example, Napster, a peer-to-peer music sharing service, was held vicariously liable for infringements by its users because it could control, and it profited from, the offenses. (*A&M Records, Inc. v. Napster, Inc.*, 239 F.3d 1004 (9th Cir. 2001).) Vicarious liability (along with contributory infringement) is considered "secondary infringement."

Related terms: contributory infringement.

webcasting

Webcasting is the digital audio transmission of music over the Internet. There are various types of webcasting systems: interactive sites (in which the listener requests music), passive sites (in which the station chooses the play lists), subscription sites (in which listeners pay a fee), and nonsubscription sites. Webcasters can also include terrestrial stations—commercial and noncommercial AM and FM radio stations— that simulcast musical programming over the Internet.

The Copyright Royalty Board (CORB) (formerly the Copyright Arbitration Royalty Panel (CARP)) recommends rates and terms for the statutory license for eligible nonsubscription services. Under CORB guidelines, in order for these services to play recordings (including simultaneous Internet retransmissions of over-the-air AM or FM radio broadcasts), a webcaster must pay a royalty per song played. Simulcasts of noncommercial radio stations (AM or FM) incur a per-song royalty.

In 2002, the Copyright Office announced an agreement between rival web- casting groups that set rates for small commercial webcasters. Small commercial webcasters—those that meet the eligibility requirements established in 17 U.S. Code, Sections 112 and 114—may operate under rates and terms set forth in the negotiated agreement, or they may operate under the rules previously established by the Copyright Office.

Unhappy with rates established by Congress in 2007, webcasters sought to modify the arrangement for payment of royalties with the digital music industry's licensing agent, SoundExchange. Two agreements were made—the Webcaster Settlement Act of 2008 and the Webcaster Settlement Act of 2009—that gave an alternative set of rates to pureplay webcasters—Internet broadcasters whose primary business is streaming audio, for example Pandora.com and Spotify.com.

For the period from 2016 to 2020, the CORB established new rates that webcasters will pay to SoundExchange for the use of sound recordings in their digital transmissions over the Internet and to mobile devices. For commercial webcasters, the CORB set $.0017 as the per-performance rate (that is, the rate per song, or per listener) for nonsubscription streaming, and $.0022 per performance for subscription streaming. For most webcasters, including broadcasters, this represents a drop of approximately one-third the rates previously paid.

The Music Modernization Act (MMA), signed into law in 2018, simplifies the licensing rules for digital music providers and creates a new music licensing collective (MLC), which should take effect in 2021. Once in place, the MLC will act as a toll booth for Spotify, Pandora, SoundCloud, and other digital music providers. These providers will pay the MLC for each use of a song, and the MLC will compensate the owners accordingly. The MLC will also identify copyrighted material embodied in sound recordings, locate the copyright owners of such material, administer copyright ownership claims, and assist with the setting of royalty rates and terms.

website

A website is a collection of pages or documents, stored on a server, and accessible and viewable over the Internet. A website is usually written in a computer language known as HTML and is accessed by typing in a domain name such as www.nolo.com. Although the website is written in computer code, it incorporates, displays, and performs many media, including text, photography, music, animation, sound, artwork, and movies. All of these media may contain copyrightable expressions. To that extent, the website's creator must obtain permission to use these media. The unauthorized use of these materials is an infringement unless permitted as a fair use.

Copyright Law: Definitions

In turn, a website or webpage is protected under copyright law and may be registered with the Copyright Office. The procedure for registration is established in Copyright Circular 66, which is available at the Copyright Office website (www.copyright.gov). Copyright protection for a website does not extend to the layout or "look and feel" or design of the site. In other words, the website's style cannot be protected under copyright law. But it is possible that the style or style features can be protected as trade dress under trademark laws.

Related terms: caching; Digital Millennium Copyright Act ("DMCA").

work made for hire

For purposes of the Copyright Act, a work made for hire is:

- a work created by an employee within the scope of employment, or
- certain works specified in the Copyright Act (see below) created by an independent author under a written contract specifying that the project is a work made for hire.

Copyright of a work made for hire belongs either to the party who commissioned it or the party who employed the creator, not the party who created it.

Works made for hire most typically result when an employee authors an article, computer program, or other original work of authorship within the scope of employment (an employee work for hire). "Within the scope of employment" means that it is the kind of work the employee is paid to perform, it is prepared substantially within work hours at the workplace, and it is prepared, at least in part, to serve the employer.

Unless an employer and employee agree otherwise, anything an employee creates outside the scope of employment is not a work made for hire. This is so even if the work arises out of the employee's activities on the employer's behalf.

> EXAMPLE: Ned uses company time to write a training manual for his employer. The employer owns the copyright in the manual as a work made for hire. By contrast, if Ned used his own time to write the manual, Ned would own the copyright, even though the manual's main purpose was to help Ned's employer.

Who is an employee for purposes of the work-made-for-hire rule? If a court determines that an employment relationship exists, even if the author is not technically employed, the work-made-for-hire rule treats the author as an employee for the purpose of determining copyright ownership. The courts examine 11 factors to decide whether an employment relationship exists. All of the factors address who has the right to control the manner and means by which the work is created. These factors are:

1. the skill required to do the work
2. the source of tools and materials used to create the work
3. the duration of the relationship
4. whether the commissioning person has the right to assign additional projects to the creative party
5. who determines when and how long the creative party works
6. the method of payment
7. who decides which assistants will be hired and who pays them
8. whether the work is in the ordinary line of business of the person who commissions it
9. whether the creative party has his/her own business
10. whether the creative party receives employee benefits from the commissioning person, and
11. the tax treatment of the creative party.

If there is no employment relationship, there is a second method of acquiring work for hire status, which occurs if both parties sign a written work-for-hire agreement, and the work fits within one of the following nine categories of works (a commissioned work for hire) (17 U.S. Code § 101):

1. a work specially ordered or commissioned for use as a contribution to a collective work
2. a part of a motion picture or other audiovisual work, such as a screenplay
3. a translation
4. a supplementary work
5. a compilation
6. an instructional text
7. a test
8. answer material for a test, or
9. an atlas.

EXAMPLE: Nolo plans to publish a series of educational texts on copyright, trademark, and patent law. They hire Charles, an author who is not employed by Nolo, to write the books. For Nolo to own copyright as a work made for hire, Charles will have to sign a work-made-for-hire agreement and the resulting texts must fall within one of the enumerated work-made-for-hire categories. It's possible that the texts may qualify as "instructional texts," but only if they are intended to be used in day-to-day teaching activities. If the texts do not fall within one of the enumerated categories, the works will not be works made for hire even though a work-made-for-hire agreement has been signed. In that event, the only other method by which Nolo could acquire copyright ownership is to require Charles to assign his rights under his publishing agreement.

To qualify as a commissioned work made for hire, the parties should sign the written agreement prior to completion of the work. On occasion, written agreements signed after completion of the work are acceptable if "there was unanimous intent among all concerned that the work for hire doctrine would apply, notwithstanding that some of the paperwork remained not fully executed." For example, a court of appeals held that check endorsements confirming work made for hire status that were signed at the time of payment were suitable to categorize completed artwork by Patrick Nagel as works made for hire. (*Playboy Enterprises, Inc. v. Dumas*, 53 F.3d 549 (2d Cir. 1995).) However, the Second Circuit refused to accept a written agreement executed five years after a series of film reviews were created and published in *The New Republic*. (*Estate of Kauffmann v. Rochester Inst. of Tech.*, Docket No. 18-2404-cv (2d Cir. Aug. 1, 2019).)

The duration of copyrights on works for hire is different from that on copyrights for author-owners. A copyright on a work made for hire lasts for the shorter of 75 years from the date of publication or 120 years from the date of creation in the case of unpublished works.

Copyright Act: § 101. Definitions

A "work made for hire" is—

(1) a work prepared by an employee within the scope of his or her employment; or

(2) a work specially ordered or commissioned for use as a contribution to a collective work, as a part of a motion picture or other audiovisual work, as a translation, as a supplementary work, as a compilation, as an instructional text, as a test, as answer material for a test, or as an atlas, if the parties expressly agree in a written instrument signed by them that the work shall be considered a work made for hire. For the purpose of the foregoing sentence, a "supplementary work" is a work prepared for publication as a secondary adjunct to a work by another author for the purpose of introducing, concluding, illustrating, explaining, revising, commenting upon, or assisting in the use of the other work, such as forewords, afterwords, pictorial illustrations, maps, charts, tables, editorial notes, musical arrangements, answer

material for tests, bibliographies, appendixes, and indexes, and an "instructional text" is a literary, pictorial, or graphic work prepared for publication and with the purpose of use in systematic instructional activities.

In determining whether any work is eligible to be considered a work made for hire under paragraph (2), neither the amendment contained in section 1011(d) of the Intellectual Property and Communications Omnibus Reform Act of 1999, as enacted by section 1000(a)(9) of Public Law 106–113, nor the deletion of the words added by that amendment—

(A) shall be considered or otherwise given any legal significance, or

(B) shall be interpreted to indicate congressional approval or disapproval of, or acquiescence in, any judicial determination, by the courts or the Copyright Office. Paragraph (2) shall be interpreted as if both section 2(a)(1) of the Work Made For Hire and Copyright Corrections Act of 2000 and section 1011(d) of the Intellectual Property and Communications Omnibus Reform Act of 1999, as enacted by section 1000(a)(9) of Public Law 106–113, were never enacted, and without regard to any inaction or awareness by the Congress at any time of any judicial determinations.

The terms "WTO Agreement" and "WTO member country" have the meanings given those terms in paragraphs (9) and (10), respectively, of section 2 of the Uruguay Round Agreements Act.

Related terms: copyright; duration of copyrights.

work of the U.S. government

All works prepared by an officer or employee of the U.S. government as part of that person's official duties are considered part of the public domain and are not entitled to copyright protection. This rule does not apply to state or local governmental employees.

Copyright Act: § 101. Definitions

A "work of the United States Government" is a work prepared by an officer or employee of the United States Government as part of that person's official duties.

Related terms: public domain.

work of visual art

All art works (photos, paintings, and so on) are protected under copyright. But certain visual art that is produced in a single copy or limited edition of 200 copies or fewer signed and numbered copies receives special protection under an amendment to the Copyright Act known as the Visual Artists Rights Act (VARA). (17 U.S. Code § 106A.)

VARA amends the Copyright Act by defining a "work of visual art" as: (1) a painting, drawing, print, or sculpture, existing in a single copy, in a limited edition of 200 copies or fewer that are signed and consecutively numbered by the author, or, in the case of a sculpture, in multiple cast, carved, or fabricated sculptures of 200 or fewer that are consecutively numbered by the author and bear the signature or other identifying mark of the author; or (2) a still photographic image produced for exhibition purposes only, existing in a single copy that is signed by the author, or in a limited edition of 200 copies or fewer that are signed and consecutively numbered by the author.

VARA incorporates certain rules developed in Europe to protect the moral rights of artists. European law grants certain rights to artists based upon moral principles. For example, the creator of a work of fine art (or the artist's heirs) can share in subsequent sales of the work and can prevent the destruction or mutilation of a work. Under these principles, known as *droit de moral*, the artist's rights continue after the sale of the art. An unknown artist who sold a work inexpensively could share in revenues if the work later appreciated in value.

The United States refused to recognize moral rights for most of the 20th century. However, in order to join in an international treaty known as the Berne Convention, Congress amended the Copyright Act in 1990 to include VARA. VARA incorporates two of the features of European *droit de moral*: attribution and integrity. Attribution is the right to claim or disclaim authorship of a work. That is, the artist has a right to demand that credit be given or that credit be removed from an artwork. The right of integrity is the right to prevent distortion, mutilation, or other modification of the work. These rights are independent of the other rights granted under copyright law.

What's Protected and What's Not Protected by VARA	
Protected by VARA	**Not Protected by VARA**
A limited edition of 20 copies of a silkscreen, numbered and signed by the artist.	A silkscreen image reprinted on 1,000 posters.
A sculpture of Noah's ark.	Miniature replicas of Noah's ark sold by a mail order company.

What happens if an oil painting is reproduced in a museum booklet or in a magazine review? Does that mass production remove the work from VARA status? No; the artist could still exert VARA rights over the oil painting. However, the artist could not prevent destruction or mutilation of the reprints in the booklet, because these would not be covered by VARA, although they would still be covered under normal copyright principles.

Under Section 106A, the creator of a work of visual arts can prevent the "intentional distortion, mutilation, or other modification of that work which would be prejudicial to his or her honor or reputation." This is the most powerful right granted under the VARA provisions. For example, if a collector buys a limited edition photograph (that is, fewer than 200 prints were made), the collector cannot destroy it without permission from the artist. If the work is destroyed, the artist can sue under VARA and recover damages.

The rule regarding destruction does not apply if: (1) the work was created prior to enactment of the VARA provisions on December 1, 1990; (2) the artist specifically waives the rights in a written statement signed by the artist and owner of the artwork; or (3) the destruction or modification results from the passage of time or because of the materials used to construct the work. For example, certain works such as ice sculptures and sand sculptures self-destruct, and the owner would have no obligation to affirmatively prevent such destruction.

Under certain circumstances, the person who employs an artist or commissions artwork acquires copyright ownership. This principle is known as work made for hire. If artwork is created as work made for hire, there are no VARA rights. That is, although normal copyright law applies to the work, neither the artist nor the person commissioning the work can claim rights of integrity or attribution under VARA.

VARA permits an artist to prevent the destruction of art that has achieved "recognized stature." Upholding a $6.75 million judgment for New York graffiti artists, the Second Circuit held that VARA makes no distinction between temporary and permanent works when determining whether a work has achieved recognized stature. (*Castillo v. G&M Realty L.P.,* 950 F.3d 155 (2d Cir. 2020).)

The rights granted under VARA—attribution and integrity—are not transferable. Only the artist can exert these rights. Although copyright protection normally lasts for the life of the author plus 70 years, the rights granted under VARA last only for the life of the artist. That is, once the artist has died, the work can be destroyed under VARA without the destroyer seeking consent from the artist's estate.

Keep in mind as well that, as one court put it, "Not every artist has rights under VARA, and not everything called 'art' is protected by such rights." When an artist attempted to claim rights under VARA for a political banner commissioned by an advocacy group, a court noted that Congress has specifically excluded advertising and promotional materials, and that the banner, even though it involved political advertising, was within this exemption. (*Pollara v. Seymour,* 344 F.3d 265 (2d Cir. 2003).)

At least one court has ruled that in order for VARA to apply, the work at issue must have more than "artistic merit" or "some level of local notoriety"; it must be of "recognized stature" as an artistic work. In that case, the court permitted unauthorized dismantling of a 6,000-pound swan sculpture, (*Scott v. Dixon,* 309 F. Supp.2d 395 (E.D.N.Y. 2004).)

On the other hand, graffiti murals have been protected under VARA. A New York district court determined that graffiti works painted on buildings had the "recognized stature" to qualify as a protected artwork under the Visual Artists Rights Act (VARA). The works, known as the 5Pointz project, were whitewashed by the developer of the building. The court awarded the artists $6.7 million, the maximum statutory damages, for 45 of the murals. (*Cohen v. G&M Realty L.P.,* 13-CV-5612 (FB) (E.D.N.Y. Jun. 22, 2018)).

Unfinished artwork is also protected by VARA. A Swiss artist, unhappy with the manner in which his art was being installed in a museum, sued under the Visual Artists Rights Act (VARA). The First Circuit determined that VARA was intended to protect the integrity of works of art, even those that are not completed. (*Massachusetts Museum of Contemporary Art Foundation, Inc. v. Buchel,* 593 F.3d 38 (1st Cir. 2010).)

Some states, such as California, have passed more comprehensive statutes regarding art preservation and resale. Under the California statute (California Civil Code Sections 986–989), for example, an artist is entitled to 5% of the resale of a work of fine art. These rights survive for 20 years after the death of the artist. New York and eight other states also have laws that grant certain rights to artists.

The legality of these resale statutes was disputed in 2016, when a federal district court struck down a provision of the California Resale Royalty Act (CRRA) that required a seller of fine art to pay the artist a 5% royalty from the proceeds of a sale. The decision was based on the fact that because the first sale doctrine is federal law, it preempts state laws that interfere with that right. (*Sam Francis Foundation et al v. Christie's Inc.,* No. 2:11-cv-08605 (C.D. Cal. 2016).)

Copyright Act: § 101. Definitions

A "work of visual art" is—

(1) a painting, drawing, print, or sculpture, existing in a single copy, in a limited edition of 200 copies or fewer that are signed and consecutively numbered by the author, or, in the case of a sculpture, in multiple cast, carved, or fabricated sculptures of 200 or fewer that are consecutively numbered by the author and bear the signature or other identifying mark of the author; or

(2) a still photographic image produced for exhibition purposes only, existing in a single copy that is signed by the author, or in a limited edition of 200 copies or fewer that are signed and consecutively numbered by the author.

A work of visual art does not include—

  (A) (i) any poster, map, globe, chart, technical drawing, diagram, model, applied art, motion picture or other audiovisual work, book, magazine, newspaper, periodical, data base, electronic information service, electronic publication, or similar publication;

    (ii) any merchandising item or advertising, promotional, descriptive, covering, or packaging material or container;

    (iii) any portion or part of any item described in clause (i) or (ii);

  (B) any work made for hire; or

  (C) any work not subject to copyright protection under this title.

Copyright Act: § 106A. Rights of certain authors to attribution and integrity

(a) **Rights of Attribution and Integrity.**—Subject to section 107 and independent of the exclusive rights provided in section 106, the author of a work of visual art—

  (1) shall have the right—

    (A) to claim authorship of that work, and

    (B) to prevent the use of his or her name as the author of any work of visual art which he or she did not create;

  (2) shall have the right to prevent the use of his or her name as the author of the work of visual art in the event of a distortion, mutilation, or other modification of the work which would be prejudicial to his or her honor or reputation; and

  (3) subject to the limitations set forth in section 113 (d), shall have the right—

    (A) to prevent any intentional distortion, mutilation, or other modification of that work which would be prejudicial to his or her honor or reputation, and any intentional distortion, mutilation, or modification of that work is a violation of that right, and

    (B) to prevent any destruction of a work of recognized stature, and any intentional or grossly negligent destruction of that work is a violation of that right.

Copyright Law: Definitions

(b) Scope and Exercise of Rights.—Only the author of a work of visual art has the rights conferred by subsection (a) in that work, whether or not the author is the copyright owner. The authors of a joint work of visual art are co-owners of the rights conferred by subsection (a) in that work.

(c) Exceptions.—(1) The modification of a work of visual art which is a result of the passage of time or the inherent nature of the materials is not a distortion, mutilation, or other modification described in subsection (a)(3)(A).

(2) The modification of a work of visual art which is the result of conservation, or of the public presentation, including lighting and placement, of the work is not a destruction, distortion, mutilation, or other modification described in subsection (a)(3) unless the modification is caused by gross negligence.

(3) The rights described in paragraphs (1) and (2) of subsection (a) shall not apply to any reproduction, depiction, portrayal, or other use of a work in, upon, or in any connection with any item described in subparagraph (A) or (B) of the definition of "work of visual art" in section 101, and any such reproduction, depiction, portrayal, or other use of a work is not a destruction, distortion, mutilation, or other modification described in paragraph (3) of subsection (a).

Related terms: Copyright Act of 1976; work made for hire.

World Trade Organization (WTO)

See GATT (General Agreement on Tariffs and Trade).

Copyright Law: Forms

Preparing a Copyright Application

There are two ways to file a copyright application:
- file online (using the Copyright Office's electronic eCO system), or
- file a traditional printed copyright form (Forms PA, TX, VA, SR, etc.), each of which is specific to the type of work (for example, Form TX is only for text works).

Which is right for you?

- If you're comfortable with electronic filing—that is, preparing and filling out forms online—the eCO system is less expensive than using paper forms, and will likely result in faster turnaround. Currently, the fee to register is $45 if you file electronically and provided you're registering one work created by one person who also owns the copyright. All other electronic application filings are $65.
- If you are used to the traditional application or feel more comfortable using a form that is specific to your type of work, use the familiar forms (Forms VA, TX, PA, SE, or SR) and pay a higher fee ($125 per application).
- If you're registering a group of works, review the new group filing options that the Copyright Office began debuting in 2019. These include: Form GRAM (Group Registration for Works on an Album of Music) used to register musical works, including any lyrics (but it cannot be used to register sound recordings); Form GRTX (Group Registration of Short Online Literary Works) for short online literary works such as blog entries, social media posts, and short online articles; and Form GRUW (Group Registration of Unpublished Works) for up to ten unpublished works.

On the following pages, examples of the various copyright application forms are provided, along with a few screenshots from the electronic filing procedure. Regardless of which type of application is used, the information required for an application is the same. The primary differences in the two types of applications are how and in what order the information is collected.

The Copyright Office provides extensive help for the application process. There are downloadable circulars that explain registration procedures for every type of work—for example, the Copyright Office provides advice on registering comic books, software, songs, websites, and much more. The eCO electronic system is also heavily documented with online guidance. For example, the Copyright Office website offers a *PowerPoint* presentation, FAQs, and more. All of this can be found at www.copyright.gov. An explanation for each of the primary methods of filing is provided below. Note, the fees for each application may have changed. Check with the Copyright Office for current fees.

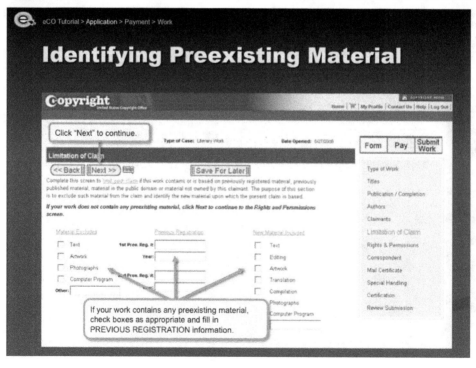

Preparing an Electronic (eCO) Copyright Application

The eCO application process has a two-tiered approach to online registration: "Single" and "Standard" applications. Single Applications are for one work by one author (not made for hire) who is also the sole owner of all rights in the work. Standard Applications are for all other registrations. eCO filers will now be prompted to answer "yes" or "no" to three statements to determine the appropriate application (Single or Standard) for registering their work. Filers will have the opportunity to change to the Standard Application if it becomes apparent that the Single Application is not appropriate for the work being registered. Using the Single Application when a work does not meet the requirements will result in processing delays, an additional fee, and a later effective date of registration. If the Copyright Office determines that a work does not meet the Single Application requirements, the filer will be contacted at the email address listed on the application with instructions on how to pay the additional fee and resubmit on the Standard Application.

Once that election has been completed, the electronic copyright (eCO) application process has three parts. The applicant:

- completes the online interview
- pays the fee (payment can be made by credit/debit card, Automated Clearinghouse (ACH), or by setting up a deposit account), and
- uploads or mails copies of the work. One can upload unpublished works, works published only electronically, published works for which the deposit requirement is ID material, or published works for which there are special agreements required. All other works must be sent by U.S. Postal Service (USPS). You will be instructed to print out a shipping slip to be attached to the work for delivery by the USPS.

In order to use eCO, the user must disable pop-up blockers and third-party toolbars.

Need help? The Copyright Office has done a nice job of explaining the process and making it user-friendly. There is an excellent tutorial and set of FAQs to walk you through the electronic filing process. In addition, the eCO process is peppered with helpful drop-down menus, as well as hypertext links that provide pop-up explanations for each aspect of the application process.

Copyright Law: Forms

You will also need to create a user account and password. The eCO system includes a special "Save for Later" feature that will preserve your work in the event you sign off and then sign on at a later time. Keep in mind that payment is required before the system will prompt you to upload your work as an electronic file or print out a shipping slip if you plan to submit a hard copy of your work.

Submitting Deposit Copies

A payment confirmation page will appear as soon as payment is completed. Click the Continue button at the top right of the screen and do one of the following:

- If you intend to mail or hand deliver hard copies of your work(s), click the Create Shipping Slip link. Then click on the blue Shipping Slip link to view and print out a shipping slip to be attached to your work(s). Be sure to attach a shipping slip directly to each work or set of works that you submit.
- If you intend to upload a copy of your work(s) electronically, click the Upload Deposit link. Then browse and select the file(s) you wish to upload.

The "browse and select" window will not appear if your pop-up blocker is enabled. For a list of acceptable electronic file types go to www.copyright.gov/eco/help-file-types.html. Above are some screenshots with explanations to give you an idea of how eCO functions.

Preparing a Traditional Print Copyright Application

The traditional copyright application forms—Form TX, Form VA, Form PA, Form SE, and Form SR—can be downloaded from the Copyright Office website. The Forms are in PDF format and each downloadable application form is considered "fillable," meaning that you can type information directly into the form visible on your screen. Although you can print the completed form, you can't save the data. So, once you turn off the computer or close the program, you'll lose any information you typed into the form. The fees for filing these print forms are currently $125 per application.

After you've completed the application, print the two pages of the form onto one sheet of paper printed head to head (top of page 2 is directly behind the top of page 1) using both sides of a single sheet. You must use either an ink-jet or laser printer (lasers are preferable). Forms printed by a dot matrix printer will not be accepted by the Copyright Office. Below are the basic requirements for completing these forms.

Title of the Work

Space 1 requires that you provide the title and alternate or previous title of your work. The Copyright Office requires the title in order to index the work in its records. Nondescriptive titles such as "Work Without a Title" can be used. If you're registering a group of works, use a title that indicates it's a collection—for example, "12 Summer Stories." The alternate or previous title refers to any additional title under which someone searching for the registration might look.

Nature of Work

Space 1 of Form VA also requires information about the "nature of the work." Provide a brief description—for example, needlework, mosaic, jewelry design, fabric design, or three-dimensional sculpture.

Publication as a Contribution

If your work is textual and was first published as part of a serial publication or as part of a collective work—for example, your work first appeared in *Rosie* magazine—present the required information about the magazine.

The Author

Copyright law refers to you—the person who created the work—as "author." Provide your name in Space 2 unless you wish to be anonymous or pseudonymous. Also provide your date of birth and nationality. Repeat this procedure in subsequent spaces for anyone who coauthored your work. A coauthor is someone who, at the time the work was created, made a copyrightable contribution.

Works Made for Hire

If you created this work by yourself, and you were neither commissioned to make it nor working for a business at the time, check "no" under the question, "Was this contribution to the work a work made for hire?" Otherwise, review the information about works made for hire in "Copyright Law: Overview" and "Copyright Law: Definitions."

Nature of Authorship

Generally, this means the extent of your authorship. For example, if you wrote a book, you would type "Entire Text" in Form TX. On Form VA, check the box that most closely describes your work, for example, 3-Dimensional Sculpture or Jewelry Design.

Copyright Law: Forms

Creation and Publication

In Space 3, provide information about the dates of creation and first publication of the work. Your work was created on the day you completed it—the date you stood back and said, "I'm done." Give the full date (that is, month, day, and year) when the work was published. If you're unsure, it's okay to write "approximately" (for example, "approximately June 4, 2008").

The Copyright Claimant

In Space 4, provide information about the person claiming copyright—probably you or your business. Use your or your business's full legal name and address.

Transfer

If the person named as copyright claimant is not the same as the person in Space 2 (the "Author"), explain how the transfer from author to claimant occurred. For example, if you created the work but then transferred the rights in it to your corporation, you would write, "by written contract" or "by written assignment." (Don't attach the transfer documents. These should be recorded separately or at a later date with the Copyright Office.) The procedure for recording such documents is described in Circular 12, issued by the Copyright Office.

Previous Registration

Here in Space 5, you must indicate any previous copyright registrations for this work or for earlier versions of the work. The Copyright Office is only concerned with whether this work or a previous version has been *registered*, not whether it's gained any other copyright protection. If it hasn't been registered, check the "No" box.

Basis for Seeking New Registration

If you checked the "Yes" box earlier in Space 5, then check the box that best describes why you're seeking a new registration—for example, if this is a changed version of the work, or if this the first application submitted by you as copyright claimant.

Previous Registration Number and Year of Registration

If this work was previously registered, indicate the registration—the number listed on the upper right-hand corner of the registration beginning with the letters VA, for example, VA-13-800.

Derivative Work or Compilation

In Space 6, you must determine whether the work you're registering is a derivative work or a compilation.

A derivative work is a modification of a previous work (regardless of whether the previous work was registered). For example, if you wrote a short story and then later used the same material and converted it to a novel, or you carved a wood block design, then created a second design adding additional flora, the second design would be a derivative.

A compilation is a collection of material—for example, a book titled *The 100 Greatest Essays on Dentistry*—in which someone assembled, selected, or organized the preexisting materials without transforming them. The author of a compilation seeks to protect the collection, not the individual works.

If you're registering a derivative work, complete 6a and 6b. If you are registering a compilation, complete 6b.

Deposit Accounts and Correspondence

If you have a deposit account—an account for applicants registering works on a regular basis—complete this section (Space 7). (It's usually not worth obtaining a deposit account unless you are registering hundreds of works.) Otherwise, skip this portion and provide your correspondence information so the examiner can contact you if any questions arise.

Certification

Check the Author box in Space 8 if you're filling out the form and if you are the person (or one of the persons) named in Space 2 of the application. In some circumstances, you may also prepare the application if you're someone other than the author. For example, the author may be deceased and you've been granted legal power to prepare the registration on behalf of the author's family.

Check Other Copyright Claimant if you're filling out the application and you're the copyright claimant in Space 4 (that is, you obtained your copyright ownership by purchasing or licensing it from the creator).

Check Owner of Exclusive Rights if you're filling out the application and you own a limited right—for example, the exclusive right to reproduce the work for a period of years—but you're not the author or the copyright claimant.

Check Authorized Agent if you're filling out the form as the authorized representative of the author, claimant, or owner of exclusive rights.

Copyright Law: Forms

Signature

After you check the appropriate box in Space 8, type or print your name and date in Space 9 and sign it where marked. Bear in mind that by signing the application, you will be certifying to the Copyright Office that the information contained in the application is correct to the best of your knowledge. A "false representation of a material fact" in a copyright application may result in a fine of up to $2,500.

Mailing Information

After the application has been processed, it will be mailed back in a window envelope, and the space entitled "Mailing Information" will be your own address, showing through.

The Fee

A filing fee is required along with the application and deposit material. The fee is currently $45 to $65 per online application, and $125 per paper application. But check the Copyright Office for current fee information before sending your application. You can pay by personal check, cashier's check, or money order, but don't send cash. If your checking account has insufficient funds, the Copyright Office will not proceed with registration or will revoke the registration if it has already been issued.

Including Copies of Your Work With the Registration Application

You must include copies or images of your work with your application. As a general rule, one copy is deposited for unpublished works; two for published. If your work is three-dimensional, send two-dimensional "identifying material" such as photographs of your works. The photographs should clearly and accurately represent the work. If you've ever sent in jury photos of a work, you've already got a good idea of how to achieve this.

Sending Your Registration Application

If you are concerned about delays or that mail will be lost, you might want to send your parcel by U.S. Express Mail or some other overnight courier. This does not guarantee faster processing, but it does guarantee proof of receipt.

If you must have your application dealt with quickly after it reaches the Copyright Office, review the procedures for expediting copyright applications at the Copyright Office website.

Sample Form PA (front)

Privacy Act Notice: Sections 408-410 of title 17 of the *United States Code* authorize the Copyright Office to collect the personally identifying information requested on this form in order to process the application for copyright registration. By providing this information you are agreeing to routine uses of the information that include publication to give legal notice of your copyright claim as required by 17 U.S.C. §705. It will appear in the Office's online catalog. If you do not provide the information requested, registration may be refused or delayed, and you may not be entitled to certain relief, remedies, and benefits under the copyright law.

Form PA
For a Work of Performing Arts
UNITED STATES COPYRIGHT OFFICE

REGISTRATION NUMBER

PA   PAU

EFFECTIVE DATE OF REGISTRATION

Month   Day   Year

DO NOT WRITE ABOVE THIS LINE. IF YOU NEED MORE SPACE, USE A SEPARATE CONTINUATION SHEET.

1

TITLE OF THIS WORK ▼

And Then You Die

PREVIOUS OR ALTERNATIVE TITLES ▼

NATURE OF THIS WORK ▼ See instructions

Screenplay

2

a

NAME OF AUTHOR ▼

David Griffith

DATES OF BIRTH AND DEATH
Year Born ▼ 1945   Year Died ▼

Was this contribution to the work a "work made for hire"?
☐ Yes
☒ No

AUTHOR'S NATIONALITY OR DOMICILE
Name of Country
OR { Citizen of U.S.A
     Domiciled in

WAS THIS AUTHOR'S CONTRIBUTION TO THE WORK
Anonymous? ☐ Yes ☒ No
Pseudonymous? ☐ Yes ☒ No
If the answer to either of these questions is "Yes," see detailed instructions.

NOTE
Under the law, the "author" of a "work made for hire" is generally the employer, not the employee (see instructions). For any part of this work that was "made for hire" check "Yes" in the space provided, give the employer (or other person for whom the work was prepared) as "Author" of that part, and leave the space for dates of birth and death blank.

NATURE OF AUTHORSHIP Briefly describe nature of material created by this author in which copyright is claimed. ▼
Entire text

b

NAME OF AUTHOR ▼

DATES OF BIRTH AND DEATH
Year Born ▼   Year Died ▼

Was this contribution to the work a "work made for hire"?
☐ Yes
☐ No

AUTHOR'S NATIONALITY OR DOMICILE
Name of Country
OR { Citizen of
     Domiciled in

WAS THIS AUTHOR'S CONTRIBUTION TO THE WORK
Anonymous? ☐ Yes ☐ No
Pseudonymous? ☐ Yes ☐ No
If the answer to either of these questions is "Yes," see detailed instructions.

NATURE OF AUTHORSHIP Briefly describe nature of material created by this author in which copyright is claimed. ▼

c

NAME OF AUTHOR ▼

DATES OF BIRTH AND DEATH
Year Born ▼   Year Died ▼

Was this contribution to the work a "work made for hire"?
☐ Yes
☐ No

AUTHOR'S NATIONALITY OR DOMICILE
Name of Country
OR { Citizen of
     Domiciled in

WAS THIS AUTHOR'S CONTRIBUTION TO THE WORK
Anonymous? ☐ Yes ☐ No
Pseudonymous? ☐ Yes ☐ No
If the answer to either of these questions is "Yes," see detailed instructions.

NATURE OF AUTHORSHIP Briefly describe nature of material created by this author in which copyright is claimed. ▼

3

a YEAR IN WHICH CREATION OF THIS WORK WAS COMPLETED 2014 Year This information must be given in all cases.

b DATE AND NATION OF FIRST PUBLICATION OF THIS PARTICULAR WORK Complete this information ONLY if this work has been published. Month ____ Day ____ Year ____ Nation

4

COPYRIGHT CLAIMANT(S) Name and address must be given even if the claimant is the same as the author given in space 2. ▼

David Griffith
666 Hollywood Blvd.
Hollywood, CA 90000

TRANSFER If the claimant(s) named here in space 4 is (are) different from the author(s) named in space 2, give a brief statement of how the claimant(s) obtained ownership of the copyright. ▼

DO NOT WRITE HERE
OFFICE USE ONLY

APPLICATION RECEIVED

ONE DEPOSIT RECEIVED

TWO DEPOSITS RECEIVED

FUNDS RECEIVED

MORE ON BACK ▶ • Complete all applicable spaces (numbers 5-9) on the reverse side of this page.
• See detailed instructions.   • Sign the form at line 8.

DO NOT WRITE HERE
Page 1 of ____ pages

Sample Form PA (back)

EXAMINED BY _____	FORM PA
CHECKED BY _____	
☐ CORRESPONDENCE Yes	FOR COPYRIGHT OFFICE USE ONLY

DO NOT WRITE ABOVE THIS LINE. IF YOU NEED MORE SPACE, USE A SEPARATE CONTINUATION SHEET.

PREVIOUS REGISTRATION Has registration for this work, or for an earlier version of this work, already been made in the Copyright Office?

☒ **Yes** ☐ **No** If your answer is "Yes," why is another registration being sought? (Check appropriate box.) ▼ If your answer is No, do **not** check box A, B, or C.

a. ☐ This is the first published edition of a work previously registered in unpublished form.

b. ☐ This is the first application submitted by this author as copyright claimant.

c. ☐ This is a changed version of the work, as shown by space 6 on this application.

If your answer is "Yes," give: **Previous Registration Number** ▼   **Year of Registration** ▼

5

DERIVATIVE WORK OR COMPILATION Complete both space 6a and 6b for a derivative work; complete only 6b for a compilation.

Preexisting Material Identify any preexisting work or works that this work is based on or incorporates. ▼

Material Added to This Work Give a brief, general statement of the material that has been added to this work and in which copyright is claimed. ▼

a 6

See instructions before completing this space.

b

DEPOSIT ACCOUNT If the registration fee is to be charged to a Deposit Account established in the Copyright Office, give name and number of Account.

Name ▼   **Account Number** ▼

a 7

CORRESPONDENCE Give name and address to which correspondence about this application should be sent. Name/Address/Apt/City/State/Zip▼

David Griffith
666 Hollywood Blvd.
Hollywood, CA 90000

Area code and daytime telephone number 213) 666-6666   Fax number (   )

Email

b

CERTIFICATION* I, the undersigned, hereby certify that I am the

Check only one ▶

☒ author
☐ other copyright claimant
☐ owner of exclusive right(s)
☐ authorized agent of _____
Name of author or other copyright claimant, or owner of exclusive right(s) ▲

of the work identified in this application and that the statements made by me in this application are correct to the best of my knowledge.

8

Typed or printed name and date ▼ If this application gives a date of publication in space 3, do not sign and submit it before that date.

David Griffith   Date May 1, 2017

Handwritten signature (X) ▼

x _____

Certificate will be mailed in window envelope to this address:	Name ▼ David Griffith	YOU MUST: • Complete all necessary spaces • Sign your application in space 8
	Number/Street/Apt ▼ 666 Hollywood Blvd.	**SEND ALL 3 ELEMENTS IN THE SAME PACKAGE:** 1. Application form 2. Nonrefundable filing fee in check or money order payable to Register of Copyrights 3. Deposit material
	City/State/Zip ▼ Hollywood, CA 90000	**MAIL TO:** Library of Congress Copyright Office-PAD 101 Independence Avenue SE Washington, DC 20559-6230

9

*17 U.S.C. §506(e): Any person who knowingly makes a false representation of a material fact in the application for copyright registration provided for by section 409, or in any written statement filed in connection with the application, shall be fined not more than $2,500.

Form PA–Full Rev 02/2009 Print 05/2010 — 50,000 Printed on recycled paper   U.S. Government Printing Office: 2010-357-993/80,085

Sample Form TX (front)

Copyright Office fees are subject to change. For current fees, check the Copyright Office website at www.copyright.gov, write the Copyright Office, or call (202) 707-3000.

Form TX
For a Nondramatic Literary Work
UNITED STATES COPYRIGHT OFFICE

REGISTRATION NUMBER

TX	TXU

EFFECTIVE DATE OF REGISTRATION

Month	Day	Year

DO NOT WRITE ABOVE THIS LINE. IF YOU NEED MORE SPACE, USE A SEPARATE CONTINUATION SHEET.

1

TITLE OF THIS WORK ▼

A Fish Story

PREVIOUS OR ALTERNATIVE TITLES ▼

PUBLICATION AS A CONTRIBUTION If this work was published as a contribution to a periodical, serial, or collection, give information about the collective work in which the contribution appeared.   **Title of Collective Work ▼**

If published in a periodical or serial give: **Volume ▼**   **Number ▼**   **Issue Date ▼**   **On Pages ▼**

2

a

NAME OF AUTHOR ▼
Felix Founder

DATES OF BIRTH AND DEATH
Year Born ▼ 1965   Year Died ▼

Was this contribution to the work a "work made for hire"?
☐ Yes
☒ No

AUTHOR'S NATIONALITY OR DOMICILE
Name of Country
OR { Citizen of ▶ U.S.A.
Domiciled in ▶

WAS THIS AUTHOR'S CONTRIBUTION TO THE WORK
Anonymous? ☐ Yes ☐ No
Pseudonymous? ☐ Yes ☐ No
If the answer to either of these questions is "Yes," see detailed instructions.

NATURE OF AUTHORSHIP Briefly describe nature of material created by this author in which copyright is claimed. ▼
Entire text of unpublished novel

NOTE
Under the law, the "author" of a "work made for hire" is generally the employer, not the employee (see instructions). For any part of this work that was "made for hire" check "Yes" in the space provided, give the employer (or other person for whom the work was prepared) as "Author" of that part, and leave the space for dates of birth and death blank.

b

NAME OF AUTHOR ▼

DATES OF BIRTH AND DEATH
Year Born ▼   Year Died ▼

Was this contribution to the work a "work made for hire"?
☐ Yes
☐ No

AUTHOR'S NATIONALITY OR DOMICILE
Name of Country
OR { Citizen of ▶
Domiciled in ▶

WAS THIS AUTHOR'S CONTRIBUTION TO THE WORK
Anonymous? ☐ Yes ☐ No
Pseudonymous? ☐ Yes ☐ No
If the answer to either of these questions is "Yes," see detailed instructions.

NATURE OF AUTHORSHIP Briefly describe nature of material created by this author in which copyright is claimed. ▼

c

NAME OF AUTHOR ▼

DATES OF BIRTH AND DEATH
Year Born ▼   Year Died ▼

Was this contribution to the work a "work made for hire"?
☐ Yes
☐ No

AUTHOR'S NATIONALITY OR DOMICILE
Name of Country
OR { Citizen of ▶
Domiciled in ▶

WAS THIS AUTHOR'S CONTRIBUTION TO THE WORK
Anonymous? ☐ Yes ☐ No
Pseudonymous? ☐ Yes ☐ No
If the answer to either of these questions is "Yes," see detailed instructions.

NATURE OF AUTHORSHIP Briefly describe nature of material created by this author in which copyright is claimed. ▼

3

a YEAR IN WHICH CREATION OF THIS WORK WAS COMPLETED This information must be given
2014 ◀ Year in all cases.

b DATE AND NATION OF FIRST PUBLICATION OF THIS PARTICULAR WORK
Complete this information ONLY if this work has been published.
Month ▶   Day ▶   Year ▶   ◀ Nation

4

See instructions before completing this space.

COPYRIGHT CLAIMANT(S) Name and address must be given even if the claimant is the same as the author given in space 2. ▼
Felix Founder
1000 Bonito Way
Tampa, FL 10000

TRANSFER If the claimant(s) named here in space 4 is (are) different from the author(s) named in space 2, give a brief statement of how the claimant(s) obtained ownership of the copyright. ▼

APPLICATION RECEIVED

ONE DEPOSIT RECEIVED

TWO DEPOSITS RECEIVED

FUNDS RECEIVED

DO NOT WRITE HERE OFFICE USE ONLY

MORE ON BACK ▶ • Complete all applicable spaces (numbers 5-9) on the reverse side of this page.
• See detailed instructions.   • Sign the form at line 8.

DO NOT WRITE HERE
Page 1 of _____ pages

Sample Form TX (back)

EXAMINED BY		FORM TX
CHECKED BY		
☐ CORRESPONDENCE Yes		FOR COPYRIGHT OFFICE USE ONLY

DO NOT WRITE ABOVE THIS LINE. IF YOU NEED MORE SPACE, USE A SEPARATE CONTINUATION SHEET.

PREVIOUS REGISTRATION Has registration for this work, or for an earlier version of this work, already been made in the Copyright Office?
☐ Yes ☒ No If your answer is "Yes," why is another registration being sought? (Check appropriate box.) ▼

a. ☐ This is the first published edition of a work previously registered in unpublished form.

b. ☐ This is the first application submitted by this author as copyright claimant.

c. ☐ This is a changed version of the work, as shown by space 6 on this application.

If your answer is "Yes," give: **Previous Registration Number** ▶   **Year of Registration** ▶

5

DERIVATIVE WORK OR COMPILATION
Preexisting Material Identify any preexisting work or works that this work is based on or incorporates. ▼

a **6**

See instructions before completing this space.

Material Added to This Work Give a brief, general statement of the material that has been added to this work and in which copyright is claimed. ▼

b

DEPOSIT ACCOUNT If the registration fee is to be charged to a Deposit Account established in the Copyright Office, give name and number of Account.
Name ▼   **Account Number** ▼

a **7**

CORRESPONDENCE Give name and address to which correspondence about this application should be sent. Name / Address / Apt / City / State / Zip ▼

b

Felix Founder
1000 Bonito Way
Tampa, FL 10000
Area code and daytime telephone number ▶ **813-123-4567**   Fax number ▶
Email ▶

CERTIFICATION* I, the undersigned, hereby certify that I am the
Check only one ▶
    ☒ author
    ☐ other copyright claimant
    ☐ owner of exclusive right(s)
    ☐ authorized agent of _____

of the work identified in this application and that the statements made by me in this application are correct to the best of my knowledge.

Name of author or other copyright claimant, or owner of exclusive right(s) ▲

8

Typed or printed name and date ▼ If this application gives a date of publication in space 3, do not sign and submit it before that date.

Felix Founder   Date ▶   May 1, 2017

Handwritten signature ▼

Certificate will be mailed in window envelope to this address:	Name ▼ **Felix Founder**	YOU MUST: • Complete all necessary spaces • Sign your application in space 8
	Number/Street/Apt ▼ **1000 Bonito Way**	SEND ALL 3 ELEMENTS IN THE SAME PACKAGE: 1. Application form 2. Nonrefundable filing fee in check or money order payable to *Register of Copyrights* 3. Deposit material
	City/State/Zip ▼ **Tampa, FL 10000**	MAIL TO: Library of Congress Copyright Office 101 Independence Avenue SE Washington, DC 20559-6222

9

*17 USC §506(e): Any person who knowingly makes a false representation of a material fact in the application for copyright registration provided for by section 409, or in any written statement filed in connection with the application, shall be fined not more than $2,500.

Form TX – Full   Rev: 11/2006   Print: 11/2006 – 30,000   Printed on recycled paper   U.S. Government Printing Office: 2006-xx-xxx/60,xxx

Sample Form VA (front)

Copyright Office fees are subject to change.
For current fees, check the Copyright Office
website at www.copyright.gov, write the Copyright Office, or call (202) 707-3000.

Form VA
For a Work of the Visual Arts
UNITED STATES COPYRIGHT OFFICE

REGISTRATION NUMBER

_____

VA   VAU

EFFECTIVE DATE OF REGISTRATION

_____

Month   Day   Year

DO NOT WRITE ABOVE THIS LINE. IF YOU NEED MORE SPACE, USE A SEPARATE CONTINUATION SHEET.

1

Title of This Work ▼   NATURE OF THIS WORK ▼ See instructions

All About Everything   Photographs

Previous or Alternative Titles ▼

Publication as a Contribution If this work was published as a contribution to a periodical, serial, or collection, give information about the collective work in which the contribution appeared. **Title of Collective Work ▼**

If published in a periodical or serial give: Volume ▼   Number ▼   Issue Date ▼   On Pages ▼

2

NAME OF AUTHOR ▼   DATES OF BIRTH AND DEATH
                                   Year Born ▼   Year Died ▼

a Mike Minolta   1970

NOTE

Was this contribution to the work a "work made for hire"?
☐ Yes
☒ No

Author's Nationality or Domicile
Name of Country
OR { Citizen of U.S.A.
     Domiciled in

Was This Author's Contribution to the Work
Anonymous?   ☐ Yes ☒ No
Pseudonymous? ☐ Yes ☒ No
If the answer to either of these questions is "Yes," see detailed instructions.

Under the law, the "author" of a "work made for hire" is generally the employer, not the employee (see instructions). For any part of this work that was "made for hire" check "Yes" in the space provided, give the employer (or other person for whom the work was prepared) as "Author" of that part, and leave the space for dates of birth and death blank.

Nature of Authorship Check appropriate box(es). **See instructions**
☐ 3-Dimensional sculpture   ☐ Map   ☐ Technical drawing
☐ 2-Dimensional artwork   ☐ Photograph   ☐ Text
☐ Reproduction of work of art ☒ Jewelry design ☐ Architectural work

b Name of Author ▼   Dates of Birth and Death
                                   Year Born ▼   Year Died ▼

Was this contribution to the work a "work made for hire"?
☐ Yes
☐ No

Author's Nationality or Domicile
Name of Country
OR { Citizen of
     Domiciled in

Was This Author's Contribution to the Work
Anonymous?   ☐ Yes ☐ No
Pseudonymous? ☐ Yes ☐ No
If the answer to either of these questions is "Yes," see detailed instructions.

Nature of Authorship Check appropriate box(es). **See instructions**
☐ 3-Dimensional sculpture   ☐ Map   ☐ Technical drawing
☐ 2-Dimensional artwork   ☐ Photograph   ☐ Text
☐ Reproduction of work of art ☐ Jewelry design ☐ Architectural work

3

a Year in Which Creation of This Work Was Completed
2014 Year
This information must be given ONLY if this work in all cases.

b Date and Nation of First Publication of This Particular Work
Complete this information ONLY if this work has been published.
Month May   Day 11   Year 2014
U.S.A.   Nation

4

COPYRIGHT CLAIMANT(S) Name and address must be given even if the claimant is the same as the author given in space 2. ▼

Mike Minolta
100 Grant St.
Chicago, IL 50000

See instructions before completing this space.

Transfer If the claimant(s) named here in space 4 is (are) different from the author(s) named in space 2, give a brief statement of how the claimant(s) obtained ownership of the copyright. ▼

APPLICATION RECEIVED

ONE DEPOSIT RECEIVED

TWO DEPOSITS RECEIVED

FUNDS RECEIVED

DO NOT WRITE HERE OFFICE USE ONLY

MORE ON BACK ▶ • Complete all applicable spaces (numbers 5-9) on the reverse side of this page.
• See detailed instructions.   • Sign the form at line 8.

DO NOT WRITE HERE
Page 1 of _____ pages

Copyright Law: Forms

Sample Form VA (back)

EXAMINED BY	FORM VA
CHECKED BY	

| CORRESPONDENCE ☐ Yes | FOR COPYRIGHT OFFICE USE ONLY |

DO NOT WRITE ABOVE THIS LINE. IF YOU NEED MORE SPACE, USE A SEPARATE CONTINUATION SHEET.

PREVIOUS REGISTRATION Has registration for this work, or for an earlier version of this work, already been made in the Copyright Office?

☐ Yes ☒ No If your answer is "Yes," why is another registration being sought? (Check appropriate box.) ▼

a. ☐ This is the first published edition of a work previously registered in unpublished form.

b. ☐ This is the first application submitted by this author as copyright claimant.

c. ☐ This is a changed version of the work, as shown by space 6 on this application.

If your answer is "Yes," give: **Previous Registration Number** ▼   **Year of Registration** ▼

5

DERIVATIVE WORK OR COMPILATION Complete both space 6a and 6b for a derivative work; complete only 6b for a compilation.

a. Preexisting Material Identify any preexisting work or works that this work is based on or incorporates. ▼

b. Material Added to This Work Give a brief, general statement of the material that has been added to this work and in which copyright is claimed. ▼

6
a
b

See instructions before completing this space.

DEPOSIT ACCOUNT If the registration fee is to be charged to a Deposit Account established in the Copyright Office, give name and number of Account.

Name ▼   **Account Number** ▼

7
a

CORRESPONDENCE Give name and address to which correspondence about this application should be sent. Name/Address/Apt/City/State/Zip ▼

Mike Minolta
100 Grant St.
Chicago, IL 50000

Area code and daytime telephone number **312 555-5555**   Fax number (   )

Email

b

CERTIFICATION* I, the undersigned, hereby certify that I am the

check only one ▶ {
☒ author
☐ other copyright claimant
☐ owner of exclusive right(s)
☐ authorized agent of _____
Name of author or other copyright claimant, or owner of exclusive right(s) ▲
}

of the work identified in this application and that the statements made by me in this application are correct to the best of my knowledge.

8

Typed or printed name and date ▼ If this application gives a date of publication in space 3, do not sign and submit it before that date.

Mike Minolta   Date **July 1, 2017**

Handwritten signature (X) ▼

X _____

| Certificate will be mailed in window envelope to this address: | Name ▼ Mike Minolta Number/Street/Apt ▼ 100 Grant St. City/State/ZIP ▼ Chicago, IL 50000 | **YOU MUST:** • Complete all necessary spaces • Sign your application in space 8 **SEND ALL 3 ELEMENTS IN THE SAME PACKAGE:** 1. Application form 2. Nonrefundable filing fee in check or money order payable to *Register of Copyrights* 3. Deposit material **MAIL TO:** Library of Congress Copyright Office 101 Independence Avenue SE Washington, DC 20559-6000 |

9

*17 USC §506(e): Any person who knowingly makes a false representation of a material fact in the application for copyright registration provided for by section 409, or in any written statement filed in connection with the application, shall be fined not more than $2,500.

Form VA Rev: 07/2006 Print: 07/2006—30,000 Printed on recycled paper   U.S. Government Printing Office: 2004-320-958./60,126

Part 3: **Trademark Law**

Trademark Law: Overview...383

What are trademarks and service marks?...383

What is trade dress?...383

What is trademark law?..384

What kinds of trademarks and service marks receive protection under
trademark law?...384

What cannot be protected under trademark law?...385

How is trademark ownership determined? 387

What about federal registration of a mark? 387

How can you tell if a mark proposed for use is already being used
by another business? 389

Do mark owners need to provide notice to the public?...................................389

How is ownership of a mark enforced? 390

Can a trademark owner stop use of a similar mark on unrelated goods? 390

What's new in trademark law since the last edition? 391

Trademark resources..393

Trademark Law: Definitions..395

Trademark Law: Forms..523

Preparing a Federal Trademark Application 523

The Trademark Application: the TEAS System..525

Disclaimers...527

Example of a TEAS Plus Application 529

Trademark Law: Overview

Trademark law consists of the legal rules by which businesses protect the names, logos, and other commercial signifiers used to identify their products and services. One of the principal goals of trademark law is to prevent consumers from being confused in the marketplace. Another goal is to prevent a business from trading off another business's goodwill. (Goodwill is that intangible quality or standard that creates consumer loyalty.)

What are trademarks and service marks?

A trademark is a distinctive word, phrase, logo, graphic symbol, or other device used to identify the source of a product or service and to distinguish it from any competitors. Some examples of trademarks are Tesla for cars, Frito-Lay for food products, and iTunes for music services.

A trademark can be more than just a brand name or logo. It can include other nonfunctional but distinctive aspects of a product or service that tend to promote and distinguish it in the marketplace, such as shapes, letters, numbers, sounds, smells, or colors. Titles, character names, or other distinctive features of movies, television, and radio programs can also serve as trademarks when used to promote a product or service.

For all practical purposes, a service mark is the same as a trademark—except that trademarks promote products while service marks promote services. Some familiar service marks include Chipotle (food service), FedEx (delivery service), Netflix's logo (television network service), and the Olympic Games's multicolored interlocking circles (international sporting event).

What is trade dress?

Trademark law protects more than names and logos. The law also offers some protection to distinctive shapes (the Coca-Cola bottle) or packaging (the choice of blue on the Tiffany box). Likewise, a service may be identified by its distinctive decor (Hard Rock Café, Old Navy clothing store). Collectively, these types of identifying features are commonly termed "trade dress." Functional aspects of trade dress cannot be protected under trademark law.

What is trademark law?

Trademark law addresses the overlapping and conflicting uses of trademarks, service marks, and trade dress by different businesses. The rules for resolving these disputes usually favor whichever business was first to use the name, logo, or trade dress on a category of goods within a geographic area. These rules come from decisions by federal and state courts (the common law) and from U.S. government statutes known collectively as the Lanham Act.

The Lanham Act also establishes the trademark registration system and provides for judicial remedies in cases of trademark infringement. In addition to the Lanham Act, most states provide for some means of registering trademarks with a state agency and allow for remedies in case of infringement.

Finally, federal and state courts have applied their own set of rules to activity deemed "unfair competition," which usually occurs when one business competes unfairly with another. Trademark laws are a subset of unfair competition laws. Trademark law also addresses treaties signed by a number of countries that make it easier to obtain international trademark protection.

What kinds of trademarks and service marks receive protection under trademark law?

Trademark law confers the most protection to distinctive names, logos, and other marketing devices. Trademarks become distinctive (or strong) in two ways: They are born distinctive (inherently distinctive) or they achieve distinction through sales and advertising. Inherently distinctive trademarks don't describe the goods or services for which they are used—for example, Arrow for shirts or Uber for transportation services.

Trademarks that are classified as inherently distinctive consist of:

- creatively unique logos or symbols
- words that are created specifically to be a trademark ("fanciful" marks), such as Exxon, Pepsi, or Google
- common words that are used in a surprising or unexpected manner ("arbitrary marks"), such as Amazon for retail services or Diesel for clothing, and
- words that cleverly connote qualities about the product or service without literally describing these qualities ("suggestive" marks), such as Combat for insect traps or Safari for Internet browsers.

If a mark describes some aspect of the goods or the services (a weak mark), it can become distinctive (or strong) from sales and advertising, often over several years. Typical examples are:

- terms that attempt to literally describe the product or its characteristics (Vision Center for an optics store, Yogaworks for fitness services, Park 'N Fly for airport parking services)
- surnames (Sears, Gallo, Newman's Own), and
- geographic terms (Bank of America, Mutual of Omaha).

Descriptive marks become distinctive if they achieve significant public recognition through exposure in the marketplace. A mark that has become distinctive in this way is said to have acquired a "secondary meaning."

What cannot be protected under trademark law?

There are five common instances in which a company cannot acquire trademark protection for a term or logo:

- **Nonuse.** Trademark rights are derived from the continued use of a mark in commerce. If there is a significant break in the chain of trademark usage, the owner may lose rights under a principle known as abandonment. Abandonment can occur in many ways, but the most common way is nonuse, that is, the mark is no longer used in commerce and there is sufficient evidence that the owner intends to discontinue use of the mark. For example, the owner of a mark for hotel services closed its hotels and failed to use the mark on similar services for a period of 30 years. This was sufficient proof that the owner abandoned the mark. Under the Lanham Act, a trademark is presumed to be abandoned after three years of nonuse. This presumption does not mean that the mark is automatically classified as abandoned after three years of nonuse. It means that the burden of proof shifts to the owner of the mark to prove it is not abandoned. The owner must prove an intention to resume commercial use.
- **Generics and genericide.** A generic term describes an entire group or class of goods or services. For example, the terms "computer," "eyeglasses," and "eBook" are all generic. The public associates these terms with a type of goods, not a specific brand (e.g., there are many brands of tablets—Apple, Google, and Samsung—but there is no brand known simply as Tablet). If protection were granted to generics, one company would have a monopoly

and could stop all others from using the name of the goods. For example, if only one company could use the term "Jam," any other company would be prevented from using that term with their brand of jam. Consumers are used to seeing a generic term used in conjunction with a trademark (for example, Avery labels or Canon printers). From a grammatical point of view, generics are generally nouns, trademarks are generally adjectives, and the generic term almost always follows the trademark. On some occasions a company invents a new word for a product (for example, Kleenex for a tissue). That term may function so successfully as a trademark that the public eventually comes to believe that it is the name of the goods, not the trademark. This is what happened with the term "cellophane." This word, originally a registered trademark of the DuPont corporation became so popular that consumers began to think of cellophane as the generic term for clear plastic sheets. Other famous terms that moved from trademark to generic are "aspirin," "yo-yo," "escalator," "thermos," and "kerosene." The process of moving from trademark to generic is referred to as genericide.

- **Confusingly similar marks.** A mark will not be registered or otherwise protected under trademark law if it so resembles another mark currently registered or in use in the United States as to cause confusion among consumers. This standard, known as "likelihood of confusion," is a foundation of trademark law. Many factors are weighed when considering likelihood of confusion. These factors are derived from the case of *Polaroid Corp. v. Polarad Elect. Corp.*, 287 F.2d 492 (2d Cir. 1961). However, the most important "confusion factors" are generally the similarity of the marks, similarity of the goods, degree of care exercised by the consumer when purchasing, intent of the person using the similar mark, and any actual confusion that has occurred.

- **Weak marks.** A weak (or descriptive) trademark will not be protected unless the owner can prove that consumers are aware of the mark and associate it with their product or service ("secondary meaning"). There are three types of weak marks: descriptive marks, geographic marks that describe a location, and marks that are primarily surnames (last names). When an applicant attempts to register a weak mark, the U.S. Patent and Trademark Office (USPTO) will permit the applicant to submit proof of distinctiveness or to move the application from the Supplemental Register to the Principal Register. If the applicant fails to prove distinctiveness (known as secondary meaning), the USPTO will reject the application. An applicant who disagrees with the USPTO decision can appeal it to the federal district court.

- **Functional features.** Trademark law, like copyright law, will not protect functional features. Trademark disputes about this issue (sometimes referred to as functionality) arise in cases involving product shapes or product packaging (sometimes referred to as trade dress). Unfortunately, there is no simple definition for "functional," because this area of law is always evolving. Broadly speaking, a functional feature is essential to the usability of a product. That is, the feature is necessary for the item to work. When the feature is not necessary for the item to work, it will be protected under trademark law. For example, the cases for smartphones come in many variations (the designs) and all are intended to shield the phone from damage (the function). If the design is not dictated by the ability of the case to protect the phone, the design may become a trademark. (The design might also be protectable as a design patent.)

How is trademark ownership determined?

As a general rule, a mark is owned by the business that is first to use it in a commercial context—that is, the first to associate the mark with a product or service. After the first use, the owner might be able to prevent others from using it, or a similar trademark, for their goods and services as long as the owner continues to use the mark in connection with its goods and services. The rights of the trademark owner, particularly for a trademark that is not registered with the federal government, may be limited by the geographic extent of the use.

First use can also be established by filing an intent-to-use (ITU) trademark registration application with the U.S. Patent and Trademark Office. The filing date of this application will be considered the date of first use if the applicant puts the mark into actual use within required time limits (between six months and three years, depending on the reasons for the delay and whether the applicant seeks and pays for extensions) and follows up to obtain an actual registration.

What about federal registration of a mark?

Registering a trademark or service mark with the USPTO makes it easier for the owner to protect it against would-be copiers and puts the rest of the country on notice that the mark is already taken. The registration process involves filling out an online application and paying an application fee. The fee ranges from $250 to $350 per class. As of October 5, 2019, all applications must be filed electronically using the USPTO's TEAS system. Be prepared to work with an official of the USPTO to correct any errors in the application.

To qualify a mark for registration with the USPTO, the mark's owner first must put it into use "in commerce that Congress may regulate." This means the mark must be used on a product or service that crosses state, national, or territorial lines or that affects commerce crossing such lines—as would be the case with a catalog business or a restaurant or motel that caters to interstate or international consumers. If an intent-to-use application is being filed (the applicant intends to use the mark in the near future but hasn't begun using it yet), another document must be filed for a fee once the actual use begins, showing that the mark is being used in commerce (as defined above).

Once the USPTO receives a trademark registration application, it determines the answers to these questions:

- Does the application have to be amended (because of errors) before it can be examined?
- Is the mark the same as or similar to an existing mark used on similar or related goods or services?
- Is the mark on a list of prohibited or reserved names?
- Is the mark generic—that is, does the mark describe the product or service itself rather than its source?
- Is the mark descriptive—that is, does it consist of words or images that are ordinary or that literally describe one or more aspects of the underlying goods or services?

When the USPTO can answer all of these questions in the negative, it will publish the mark in the *Official Gazette* (an online publication of the USPTO) as being a candidate for registration. Existing trademark and service mark owners may object to the registration by filing an opposition. If this occurs, the USPTO will schedule a hearing to resolve the dispute. Even if existing owners don't challenge the registration of the mark at this stage, they may later attack the registration in court if they believe the registered mark infringes one they already own.

If there is no opposition, and use in commerce has been established, the USPTO will place the mark on the list of trademarks known as the Principal Register if it is considered distinctive (either inherently or because the applicant has shown that the mark has acquired secondary meaning). Probably the most important benefit of placing a mark on the Principal Register is that anybody who later initiates use of the same or a confusingly similar mark will be presumed by the courts to be a "willful infringer" and therefore liable for money damages. However, it is still possible to obtain basic protection for a mark from the federal courts under the Lanham Act without prior registration.

If a mark consists of ordinary or descriptive terms (that is, it isn't considered distinctive), it may be placed on a different list of trademarks and service marks known as the Supplemental Register. Placement of a mark on the Supplemental Register produces significantly fewer benefits than those offered by the Principal Register but still provides notice of ownership. Also, if the mark remains on the Supplemental Register for five years—that is, the registration isn't canceled for some reason—and also remains in use during that time, it may then be placed on the Principal Register under the secondary meaning rule (secondary meaning will be presumed).

How can you tell if a mark proposed for use is already being used by another business?

A "trademark search" is an investigation to discover potential conflicts between a proposed mark and an existing one. Typically done before or at the beginning of a new mark's use, a trademark search reduces the possibility of inadvertently infringing a mark belonging to someone else.

Often, a professional search agency is used to conduct the trademark search—by first checking both federal and state trademark registers for identical or similar marks and then checking journals, telephone books, and magazines to see whether the mark is in actual use. It is also possible to conduct a preliminary online trademark search to determine if a trademark is distinguishable from other federally registered trademarks. This can be accomplished using the USPTO's free searchable TESS (Trademark Electronic Search System) database. Using TESS, a trademark owner has free access to records of federally registered marks or marks that are pending (applications undergoing examination at the USPTO). At the USPTO website (www.uspto.gov), click "Searching Trademarks" under Trademarks.

Privately owned fee-based online trademark databases often provide more current USPTO trademark information.

Do mark owners need to provide notice to the public?

Many owners like to put a "TM" (or "SM" for service mark) next to their mark to let the world know that they are claiming ownership of it. There is no legal necessity for providing this type of notice—nor are any specific legal benefits acquired by its use. The use of the mark, not the use of the symbol, is the act that confers rights.

The "R" in a circle (®) is a different matter entirely. The Lanham Act prohibits use of this notice (or any other signifier indicating federal registration such as "Reg. U.S. Pat. & TM Office") with a trademark unless the trademark has been registered with the USPTO. Once a trademark is federally registered, the owner should apply the "R" in a circle to signify its registration. Failure to use the notice with a federally registered mark may limit the damages that can be recovered in an infringement lawsuit.

How is ownership of a mark enforced?

The owner of a trademark has the burden of enforcing trademark rights. Whether or not a trademark is federally registered, the owner may sue to prevent someone else from using it or a confusingly similar mark. Courts will examine such factors as:

- whether the trademark is being used on competing goods or services (goods or services compete if the sale of one is likely to preclude the sale of the other)
- whether consumers would likely be confused by the concurrent use of the two companies' trademarks, and
- whether the products or services are offered in the same part of the country or are distributed through the same channels.

If the mark is infringing and the mark's owner can prove a financial loss or show that the competitor gained economically as a result of the improper use, the competitor might have to pay the owner damages based on the profit or loss. If the court finds the competitor intentionally copied the owner's trademark, the infringer might have to pay other damages, such as punitive damages, fines, or attorneys' fees. On the other hand, if the trademark's owner has not been damaged, a court has discretion to allow the competitor to also use the mark under very limited circumstances, which are designed to avoid the possibility of consumer confusion.

Can a trademark owner stop use of a similar mark on unrelated goods?

Under a principle known as "dilution," owners of a famous trademark may prevent it from being used by others on unrelated goods if both of the following are true:

- The mark is well known.
- The later use would dilute the mark's strength—that is, impair or tarnish its reputation for quality or render it common through overuse in different contexts (even if it is unlikely that any consumers would be confused by the second use).

What's new in trademark law since the last edition?

Below are the major changes in trademark law since this book's previous edition was published.

- **Trademark Modernization Act of 2020.** The Trademark Modernization Act (TM Act) provides several changes to U.S. trademark law:
  - **It establishes the evidentiary burden for obtaining an injunction.** The TM Act resolves a circuit court split by creating a presumption of irreparable harm when a party demonstrates likelihood of confusion, making it easier for some parties to obtain an injunction.
  - **It changes some procedures for trademark owners at the USPTO.** Third parties who object to an application can now submit evidence if it is connected to a ground for refusal. The TM Act also provides examining attorneys with flexibility in setting response times, including deadlines shorter than six months.
  - **It establishes procedures for cancelling fraudulent and "deadwood" registrations.** To address a flood of fraudulent foreign trademark applications, Section 1 of the Lanham Act was amended to include a process for submitting a letter of protest against registration of a mark. The TM Act also establishes an "expungement " procedure, which allows third parties to seek cancellation of a registration on the grounds that the mark was never used with the claimed goods or services. At the same time, the TM Act permits cancellation if the mark has never been used in commerce. Finally, the TM Act creates a system for ex parte reexamination of a registration based on nonuse.
- **A court can award damages based on profits without finding willful infringement.** Fossil, a manufacturer of fashion accessories, was found to have used infringing fasteners in its products. Because the jury did not find that Fossil acted willfully, the district court refused to award Fossil's profits as damages to the fastener company. The U.S. Supreme Court reversed and ruled that willfulness is not required as a condition for obtaining an infringer's profits. "Reading words into a statute should be avoided, especially when they are included elsewhere in the very same statute." (*Romag Fasteners, Inc. v. Fossil, Inc.* 140 S. Ct. 1492 (2020).)

- **A generic term combined with ".com" is not always generic.** The USPTO had a *per se* rule against trademark registration for a generic term combined with ".com," concluding that the combination was generic. Following this rule, a trademark examiner rejected registration for BOOKING.COM for a travel booking company. The Supreme Court struck down the rule that 'generic.com' terms are incapable of identifying a source. The Supreme Court concluded that, "Because 'Booking.com' is not a generic name to consumers, it is not generic." The takeaway: "Whether a compound term is generic turns on whether that term, taken as a whole, signifies to consumers a class of goods or services." (*USPTO v. Booking.com B.V.*, 140 S. Ct. 2298 (2020).)

- *Res judicata* **does not bar a party from asserting a defense that it could have raised in a prior suit.** In a trademark dispute over the use of the term "LUCKY," the Second Circuit concluded that one of the parties was prohibited from raising an unlitigated defense that it should have raised earlier. The court relied on *res judicata*—the legal principle that once a matter that has been adjudicated it can't be pursued further by the same parties. In a unanimous ruling, the Supreme Court held that a party is not precluded from raising defenses when a subsequent lawsuit raises different claims from earlier litigation. (*Lucky Brand Dungarees, Inc. v. Marcel Fashions Grp., Inc.*, 140 S. Ct. 1589 (2020).)

- **Punitive damages can be awarded only when there are actual damages.** Monster Energy Company prevailed in a trademark lawsuit with a competitor. However, the jury awarded $0 in actual damages and $5,000,000 in punitive damages. On appeal, the Ninth Circuit held that a jury may award punitive damages only if there are also actual damages. (*Monster Energy Co. v. Integrated Supply Network, LLC*, No. 19-55760 (9th Cir. Jul. 22, 2020).)

- **Mall landlords liable for tenant's counterfeit sales.** Oakley, maker of Ray-Ban and Oakley sunglasses, sued a mall owner for contributory trademark infringement. The defendants owned and managed an indoor mall where counterfeit Oakley merchandise was sold. Despite three raids by law enforcement and numerous letters from Oakley, the mall owners refused to take any action, such as policing the mall lessees, and as a result, the Eleventh Circuit found the mall landlords liable as contributory infringers. (*Luxottica Group v. Airport Mini Mall, LLC.*, 932 F.3d 1303 (11th Cir. August 2019).)

- **Use of "SPORTS FUEL" by Gatorade is a fair use.** SportFuel, a supplement company, sued Gatorade over its use of "GATORADE: THE SPORTS FUEL COMPANY." When Gatorade registered the mark, it disclaimed

"Sports Fuel Company." The Seventh Circuit held that Gatorade's use of the "sports fuel" terminology was descriptive and trademark fair use. (*SportFuel, Inc. v. PepsiCo, Inc.*, No. 18-3010 (7th Cir. 2019).)

- **Multicolor trademarks on product packaging do not require proof of secondary meaning.** The Federal Circuit determined that a multicolor mark on product packaging did not have to meet the same standards as a single-color mark on product designs (the *Qualitex* standard). The Federal Circuit held that multicolor packaging marks could be inherently distinctive, and unlike the *Qualitex* standard, registrable without proof of secondary meaning. (*In re: Forney Industries, Inc.*, 955 F.3d 940 (2020).)

Trademark resources

If you're interested in protecting your trademark or service mark, you might want to consult *Trademark: Legal Care for Your Business & Product Name,* by Stephen Fishman (Nolo). This book shows how to choose a distinctive name, conduct a trademark search, register a mark with the USPTO, and protect the mark once it's in use.

Many trademark materials are available online, including:

- Nolo (www.nolo.com), which offers self-help information about a wide variety of legal topics, including trademark law.
- U.S. Patent and Trademark Office (www.uspto.gov), the place to go for recent policy and statutory changes and transcripts of hearings on various trademark law issues. This site also offers three useful online programs: TESS, TEAS, and TSDR. TESS is a searchable database of federally registered trademarks; TSDR provides information on the status of pending registrations, as well as serving as an advanced electronic portal to PDF viewing, downloading, and printing of documents for hundreds of thousands of trademark applications; and TEAS is a system for electronic filing of trademark registrations.
- International Trademark Association (INTA) (www.inta.org), which provides trademark services, publications, and online resources.
- Martin Schwimmer's Trademark Blog (www.schwimmerlegal.com), the most interesting (and popular) source of daily trademark news.
- The TTABlog (http://thettablog.blogspot.com), the most thorough analysis of Trademark Trial and Appeal Board (TTAB) rulings.
- Dear Rich: An Intellectual Property Blog (www.dearrichblog.com). This blog operates as a companion to this book. Answers are provided to common IP questions.

Trademark Law: Definitions

I n this section we provide definitions of the words and phrases commonly used in trademark law. Note that we use the word "mark" to refer broadly to trademarks, service marks, certification marks, and collective marks—that is, for any distinguishing identifier.

abandonment of mark

Abandonment—the loss of trademark rights due to nonuse—commonly occurs when the trademark owner stops using the mark in commerce and fails to show an intent to use it again.

Under the Lanham Act, a mark registered with the U.S. Patent and Trademark Office is presumed abandoned if it is not used for a continuous period of three years or more. This means that the mark's owner cannot prevent someone else from using the mark unless the owner can convince a court that the mark really wasn't abandoned, despite the lack of use. Some reasons that may be acceptable for this purpose are:

- temporary financial difficulty
- bankruptcy proceedings, or
- the need for a product revision.

For example, Google was able to demonstrate that a software company had abandoned its ANDROID DATA mark (despite its continued registration of the mark) by showing that the software company had three years of nonuse and failed to demonstrate plans for use. (*Specht v. Google, Inc.,* 758 F. Supp.2d 570 (N.D. Ill. 2010).)

A company can also prove that a mark is not abandoned by furnishing documents that indicate the company intended to resume use or by the continued existence of customer goodwill.

> EXAMPLE: The owners of the Rambler trademark (for cars) were able to demonstrate that the trademark had not been abandoned even though the company had not manufactured any new automobiles in many years. They proved nonabandonment by demonstrating that there were many Rambler autos (and related supplies) bearing the mark still in use, signs featuring the trademark were still posted, and many consumers still wanted Rambler products as evidenced by Rambler fan clubs. (*American Motors Corp. v. Action Age, Inc.,* 178 U.S.P.Q. 377 (T.T.A.B. 1973).)

Proving abandonment can be difficult and expensive. It is also affected by a procedure known as a Section 8 affidavit, a document that must be filed by the owner in order to demonstrate continued use. The abandonment presumption is located in the definitions section of the Lanham Act. (15 U.S. Code § 1127.)

In 2020, in response to a flood of bad faith registrations, primarily from foreign registrants, Congress passed the Trademark Modernization Act (TMA). The TMA makes it easier to challenge applications and registrations based on nonuse, including by procedure for submitting a letter of protest against registration of a mark and for canceling (through an ex parte reexamination) and expunging (ex parte) a registration on grounds that the mark was not used with the claimed goods or services.

Abandonment of a trademark is different from abandonment of a trademark application (see below). In the latter, the owner fails to complete the trademark application process, and rights to the trademark are not necessarily lost.

The Lanham Act: § 1127. (§ 45) Construction and definitions

A mark shall be deemed to be "abandoned" if either of the following occurs:

(1) When its use has been discontinued with intent not to resume such use. Intent not to resume may be inferred from circumstances. Nonuse for 3 consecutive years shall be prima facie evidence of abandonment. "Use" of a mark means the bona fide use of such mark made in the ordinary course of trade, and not made merely to reserve a right in a mark.

(2) When any course of conduct of the owner, including acts of omission as well as commission, causes the mark to become the generic name for the goods or services on or in connection with which it is used or otherwise to lose its significance as a mark. Purchaser motivation shall not be a test for determining abandonment under this paragraph.

Related terms: abandonment of trademark application; continuous use of mark; loss of mark; naked license; opposing and canceling a trademark registration; Trademark Modernization Act of 2020; ex parte expungement; ex parte reexamination.

abandonment of trademark application

The U.S. Patent and Trademark Office (USPTO) considers a trademark application abandoned if the applicant fails to respond in a timely manner to actions or requests initiated by the USPTO. An application may also be abandoned for procedural failures—for example, an intent-to-use applicant fails to file a statement of use. It's possible to monitor trademark application progress and status online at the USPTO's website (www.uspto.gov). To do so, click "Trademarks" on the home page. Then, from the drop-down menu, click

"Checking Registration Status & Viewing Documents," which will access the TSDR (Trademark Status and Document Retrieval System). In the event an application has been abandoned, an owner who would still like to seek federal registration can either petition the USPTO to have it revived or begin the application process anew (in hopes that previous obstacles can be overcome).

Under rules resulting from enactment of the Madrid Protocol, the USPTO has the ability to grant a "partial abandonment." This occurs if the applicant fails to respond to a refusal limited only to certain goods/services in an application or registration. Previously, this failure to respond would have caused the entire application to be abandoned.

Also, under Madrid Protocol rules, if more than two months have passed since the Notice of Abandonment was mailed, it can be revived only if the applicant claims it was not received and the applicant has been checking the status of the application or registration at least every six months after filing the application. Even if a petition to revive is successful, related international rights under the Madrid Protocol are likely to be terminated. In other words, if a U.S. application or registration becomes abandoned, related international registrations will likely be abandoned as well.

The Trademark Modernization Act of 2020 (TMA) establishes an "expungement procedure," which will allow third parties to seek cancellation of a registration on the grounds that the mark was never used with the claimed goods or services. At the same time, the TMA permits cancellation if the mark has never been used in commerce. Finally, the TMA creates a system for ex parte reexamination of a registration based on nonuse.

Related terms: abandonment of mark.

Acceptable Identification of Goods and Services Manual

When filing an application for federal trademark registration or deciding whether one mark infringes another, it is useful to classify the mark in question according to the kinds of goods or services it is used with. There are 45 classes of goods and services (34 for goods, 11 for services) that are used by the U.S. Patent and Trademark Office (USPTO) for this purpose. Because of the limited number of classes, it is often difficult to tell which class a particular good or service fits within. To help this process along, the International Trademark Association has published the *Acceptable Identification of Goods and Services Manual*, an alphabetical listing of hundreds of discrete goods and services with appropriate descriptions and suggested classification numbers. The *Manual* is available on the USPTO's website (www.uspto.gov).

aesthetic functionality

Aesthetic functionality refers to visually appealing but unprotectable features of a trademark. For example, the wide mouth spout of a milk product might be distinctive and aesthetically pleasing, but it is primarily a functional feature and not protected under trademark law. Similarly, the bright yellow color of a tennis ball is visually appealing but it is primarily functional, allowing players to see the ball in diminished light.

affidavit of use

See Section 8 Declaration; Section 15 Declaration.

Allegation of Use for Intent-to-Use Application, With Declaration

When a trademark application is filed on an intent-to-use basis, the actual registration won't occur until you file a document with the USPTO stating that the mark is now in actual use and pay an additional fee. The form to use for this purpose is called Allegation of Use for Intent-to-Use Application. The Allegation of Use form may be filed at any time prior to the date the USPTO authorizes the publication of the proposed mark, and any time after the USPTO issues a Notice of Allowance. It may not be filed between those two dates.

Amendment to Allege Use

See Allegation of Use for Intent-to-Use Application, With Declaration.

Anticybersquatting Consumer Protection Act

The Anticybersquatting Consumer Protection Act (ACPA) was enacted in order to protect businesses against the practice of cybersquatting. (15 U.S. Code § 1125(d).) A cybersquatter registers a well-known trademark as a domain name, hoping to later profit by reselling the domain name back to the trademark owner. This law authorizes a trademark owner to sue an alleged cybersquatter in federal court and obtain a court order transferring the domain name back to the mark's owner. In some cases, the cybersquatter must pay money damages. In order to stop a cybersquatter, the mark's true owner must prove all of the following:

- The domain name registrant had a bad-faith intent to profit from the mark.
- The mark was distinctive at the time the domain name was first registered.
- The domain name is identical or confusingly similar to the mark.
- The mark qualifies for protection under federal trademark laws—that is, the mark is distinctive and its owner was the first to use the mark in commerce.

If the person or company who registered the domain name had reasonable grounds to believe that the use of the domain name was fair and lawful, they would avoid a court decision that they acted in bad faith. In other words, if the accused cybersquatter can demonstrate a reason to register the domain name other than to sell it back to the trademark owner for a profit, then a court will probably determine the domain was not acquired in bad faith. Besides proving a defendant's bad-faith intent to profit, the ACPA requires that the trademark owner demonstrate that the trademarks were distinctive or famous at the time the alleged cybersquatter registered the domain names. (*ZP No. 314, LLC v. ILM Capital, LLC*, No. 16-00521-B (S.D. Ala. 2019).)

In addition to the rules provided under the ACPA, domain name owners can alternatively use the dispute resolution procedures that are overseen by ICANN, the international agency that oversees domain names. ICANN offers a Uniform Dispute Resolution Procedure (UDRP), an arbitration procedure that is usually resolved within two months.

Related terms: cybersquatting; domain names.

antidilution statutes

See dilution.

arbitrary mark

A word or phrase is classified as an arbitrary trademark if the choice is unrelated to any quality or characteristics of the goods or services. For example, Penguin (books), Arrow (shirts), and Beefeater (gin) are arbitrary terms in relation to the products they advertise and therefore stand out because they are original and surprising. Arbitrary marks are considered to be inherently distinctive, entitling them to the highest degree of trademark protection available.

Related terms: distinctive mark.

assignment of mark

An assignment is a permanent transfer of ownership rights and goodwill associated with a mark. Assignments commonly occur when a company is sold. An assignment may also occur as part of a bankruptcy or may be used as a security interest when a business seeks to obtain a loan.

Once the assignment is made, the business buying the trademark rights (the "assignee") becomes the owner, and the seller (the "assignor") has no further ownership interest. On some occasions, an assignment may be transferred back to the original owner if certain conditions are met. The Lanham Act requires the assignment of a registered mark to be in writing. Assignments should be recorded with the U.S. Patent and Trademark Office (USPTO), and the new owners can obtain new certificates of registration in their names. Using the USPTO's ETA system (Electronic Trademark Assignment), a trademark owner must file a trademark assignment electronically. To search the assignment database, use AOTW (Assignments on the Web), which enables the user to query by many different variables.

Keep in mind that recording a trademark assignment doesn't prove its validity. The USPTO does not examine trademark assignments; it simply records them. Therefore, the simple act of recording the assignment is not determinative of the assignment's validity and doesn't guarantee its enforceability. (*Richards v. Burgett, Inc.*, 2011 WL 6156838 (N.D. Ill. December 12, 2011).)

The Lanham Act: § 1057. (§ 7) Certificates of registration

(b) Certificate as prima facie evidence

… A certificate of registration of a mark may be issued to the assignee of the applicant, but the assignment must first be recorded in the Patent and Trademark Office. In case of change of ownership the Director shall, at the request of the owner and upon a proper showing and the payment of the prescribed fee, issue to such assignee a new certificate of registration of the said mark in the name of such assignee, and for the unexpired part of the original period.

The Lanham Act: § 1060. (§ 10) Assignment

This statute sets out the conditions under which a mark that has been, or is to be, registered may be sold (assigned) to another party.

(a) (1) A registered mark or a mark for which an application to register has been filed shall be assignable with the good will of the business in which the mark is used, or with that part of the good will of the business connected with the use of and symbolized by the mark. Notwithstanding the preceding sentence, no application to register a mark under section 1051 (b) of this title shall be assignable prior to the filing of an amendment under section 1051 (c) of this title to bring the application into conformity with section 1051 (a) of this title or the filing of the verified statement of use under section 1051 (d) of this title, except for an assignment to a successor to the business of the applicant, or portion thereof, to which the mark pertains, if that business is ongoing and existing.

(2) In any assignment authorized by this section, it shall not be necessary to include the good will of the business connected with the use of and symbolized by any other mark used in the business or by the name or style under which the business is conducted.

(3) Assignments shall be by instruments in writing duly executed. Acknowledgment shall be prima facie evidence of the execution of an assignment, and when the prescribed information reporting the assignment is recorded in the United States Patent and Trademark Office, the record shall be prima facie evidence of execution.

(4) An assignment shall be void against any subsequent purchaser for valuable consideration without notice, unless the prescribed information reporting the assignment is recorded in the United States Patent and Trademark Office within 3 months after the date of the assignment or prior to the subsequent purchase.

(5) The United States Patent and Trademark Office shall maintain a record of information on assignments, in such form as may be prescribed by the Director.

(b) An assignee not domiciled in the United States may designate by a document filed in the United States Patent and Trademark Office the name and address of a person resident in the United States on whom may be served notices or process in proceedings affecting the mark. Such notices or process may be served upon the person so designated by leaving with that person or mailing to that person a copy thereof at the address specified in the last designation so filed. If the person so designated cannot be found at the address given in the last designation, or if the assignee does not designate by a document filed in the United States Patent and Trademark Office the name and address of a person resident in the United States on whom may be served notices or process in proceedings affecting the mark, such notices or process may be served upon the Director.

Related terms: certificate of registration; goodwill; Lanham Act; ownership of mark in the United States.

attorneys' fees in trademark infringement actions

Previously, courts would award attorneys' fees only in "exceptional" trademark infringement lawsuits. To qualify as such a case, the defendant must have acted willfully, intentionally, or maliciously. In 2014, the Supreme Court ruled on a similar attorneys' fees provision in patent law and redefined "exceptional" as "simply [a dispute] that stands out from others with regards to the strength of a company's case or the 'unreasonable manner' in which they made it." This ruling gave judges more leeway to decide when a litigant is entitled to attorneys' fees. (*Octane Fitness, LLC v. ICON Health & Fitness, Inc.*, 572 U.S. 545 (2014).) The federal circuits applied the rule to trademark law as well as patent law. (*SunEarth Inc. v. Sun Earth Solar Power Co.*, 839 F.3d 1179 (9th Cir. 2016).)

Attorneys' fees may also be awarded if infringement occurred as a result of a breach of contract or license that itself provides for attorneys' fees. In these cases, there is no need to show willfulness.

Related terms: infringement (trademark); innocent infringer; Lanham Act.

average reasonably prudent consumer

In deciding trademark conflicts, courts often try to imagine whether an average reasonably prudent consumer would likely be confused by the two marks. This viewpoint is particularly helpful in deciding:

- if an infringed mark is distinctive enough to warrant protection by the court, and
- whether the infringing mark would be likely to mislead or confuse the public.

If a court determines that a hypothetical consumer would be likely to know the infringed mark because of its distinctiveness and also would be confused by the use of the infringing mark, then infringement may be found.

In a trademark infringement action where consumer confusion is alleged, the parties typically conduct consumer polls to discover the actual views of the "average consumer" and introduce the results of such polls in support of their case.

Related terms: likelihood of confusion.

award, use of trademark in ratings or

A company that receives a rating or award might desire to include information about that award (or an image of the award) in its advertising—for example, an app developer might want to feature an "Apple Design Award" in its ads or on its packaging. Because such uses are commercial and might confuse consumers, permission should be acquired before using another company's trademark. Most companies that provide ratings or awards have guidelines for the use of their marks in advertising. Some require a written agreement from the user; some have a policy not to permit the use of their trademarks for other companies' products regardless of the rating, review, or award. For example, Consumers Union, the publisher of *Consumer Reports*, disfavors use of its trademark in product advertisements.

brandverbing (trademark verbing)

Brandverbing is a marketing strategy by which a business encourages the use of its trademark as a verb (in marketing parlance, to "verb up"). For example,

"I Facetimed my niece," or "I Fedexed the book." Popularizing a mark as a verb is antithetical to trademark law, which discourages using a mark as a verb. (When a mark functions so successfully as a trademark that the public eventually comes to believe that it is the name of the goods or service, not the trademark, the term may be classified as generic.)

In 2017, the Ninth Circuit refuted the conventional wisdom and greenlighted some brandverbing in a case where one party sought to prove that the Google mark had become generic for search engines. The Ninth Circuit held that the plaintiffs mistakenly assumed that verb use ("I Googled that") by a majority of the public, automatically converted the mark to generic. What matters, according to the Ninth Circuit, is whether the primary significance of the word "google" to the relevant public was as a mark identifying the Google search engine in particular. (*Elliott v. Google, Inc.*, 860 F.3d 1151 (9th Cir. 2017).)

cancellation of registration

See opposing and canceling a trademark registration.

certificate of registration

A certificate of registration is proof that a mark has been registered with the U.S. Patent and Trademark Office (USPTO) on the Principal Register. The certificate reproduces the mark and sets out the date of the mark's first use in commerce. In addition, the certificate lists:

- the type of product or service on which the mark is used
- the number and date of registration
- the term of registration
- the date on which the application for registration was received at the USPTO, and
- any conditions and limitations that the USPTO has imposed on the registration, such as restricting use to a certain marketing area to avoid conflict with another registered mark.

The certificate of registration substantially simplifies the task of obtaining relief from a court if it is necessary to file a trademark infringement lawsuit. Besides proving registration, the certificate will be accepted by a court as proof that the registration is valid and that the registrant owns the mark. The exclusive right to use the mark in commerce on the product or service is also specified in the certificate.

Trademark Law: Definitions

The Lanham Act: § 1057. (§ 7) Certificates of registration

(a) Issuance and form

Certificates of registration of marks registered upon the principal register shall be issued in the name of the United States of America, under the seal of the Patent and Trademark Office, and shall be signed by the Director or have his signature placed thereon, and a record thereof shall be kept in the Patent and Trademark Office. The registration shall reproduce the mark, and state that the mark is registered on the principal register under this chapter, the date of the first use of the mark, the date of the first use of the mark in commerce, the particular goods or services for which it is registered, the number and date of the registration, the term thereof, the date on which the application for registration was received in the Patent and Trademark Office, and any conditions and limitations that may be imposed in the registration.

Related terms: ownership of mark in the United States; presumption of ownership; protection of marks under state law and common law.

certification mark

A certification mark certifies regional or other origin, material, mode of manufacture, quality, accuracy, or other characteristics.

> EXAMPLE: The California Certified Organic Farmers have established a standard to certify that food is free of pesticides. Farmers who meet these standards may use the CCOF certification mark on their food.

Certification marks have been described as a "special creature" of trademark law because a certification mark is never used by its owner. For example, the CCOF mark is owned by a voluntary trade association based in Santa Cruz, California. The group never uses the CCOF mark on its own goods or services, because it doesn't sell products. Instead, California farmers who meet organic farming standards qualify to use the CCOF label in conjunction with their brand name. For example, if you purchased Molino brand tomatoes, you would see the CCOF certification mark as well as the Molino trademark on the tomatoes.

A certification mark might attest to different qualities. For example, the mark can certify:

- **Safety.** The certification mark UL indicates that electrical equipment meets safety standards of the Underwriters Laboratory.
- **Quality.** Grass seed that includes the Lawn Institute Seal of Approval is certified as being "capable of yielding a fine-textured lawn which is normally perennial in the climate where marketed."

- **Accuracy.** The certification mark SPER Certified guarantees the accuracy of weather-forecasting equipment.
- **Materials used.** Clothing with the certification mark Grown and Made in the USA guarantees the apparel was made in the United States with cotton grown in the United States.
- **Mode of manufacture.** The Log Splitter Manufacturer's Association certification mark indicates that a log-splitting device has been built according to the manufacturing standards established by the LSMA.
- **Regional origin.** The certification mark Roquefort authenticates that cheese was manufactured from sheep's milk in the caves of Roquefort, France, according to long-established methods.
- **Source of labor.** ILGWU—UNION MADE certifies that a garment was manufactured by the International Ladies Garment Workers Union.
- **Morality.** The Intelligent Sex Seal of Approval certifies that books and videotapes discuss or portray "sexual relations in a constructive and healthy manner as part of an intelligent nondegrading relationship between fully consenting adults."

Certification marks are registered under the Lanham Act. The certifier (that is, the organization granting the certification) is the only party permitted to file the certification mark application. The certifier must submit a copy of the certification standards (that is, what it takes to qualify to use the certification mark). However, the USPTO does not verify these standards. The owner of the certification mark is usually engaged solely in the certification process, but it is possible that the owner might also engage in sales or services. For example, the Rust-Oleum Company sells a rust preventive coating. The company also has a certification mark, Protected by Rust-Oleum, that certifies those who provide the rust preventive services.

Certification marks must be retained by the persons or groups originating them. Assigning or licensing a certification mark to others destroys any meaning the mark may have had and constitutes an abandonment of the mark. Certification marks might be registered in the United States under the Lanham Act in the same manner as other marks.

Related terms: geographic terms as marks; Lanham Act; trademark.

Trademark Law: Definitions

characters as trademarks

Fictional characters such as Mickey Mouse or Mr. Clean may serve as trademarks. All that is required is that the character, like any trademark, be sufficiently distinctive or have acquired secondary meaning. Trademarked characters can be graphic or "drawn" characters such as the Pillsbury Doughboy or characters portrayed by actors, such as "Mr. Whipple" (Charmin bathroom tissue).

classes of goods and services

See International Schedule of Classes of Goods and Services.

coined terms

See fanciful terms.

collective mark

A collective mark is a symbol, label, word, phrase, or other mark used by members of a group or organization to identify goods members produce or services they render. A common use of collective marks is to show membership in a union, association, or other organization. Collective marks are entitled to registration and the same federal protection as other types of marks.

A collective mark differs from a trademark or a service mark in that use of the collective mark is restricted to members of the group. The mark's primary function is to inform the public that specific goods or services come from members of a group, thus distinguishing them from products or services of nonmembers. However, the organization itself, as opposed to its members, cannot use the collective mark on any goods it produces. If the organization itself wants to identify its product, it must use its own trademark or service mark.

> EXAMPLE: The letters "ILGWU" on a shirt is a collective mark identifying the shirt as a product of members of the International Ladies Garment Workers Union and distinguishes it from shirts made by nonunion shops. If the ILGWU actually started marketing its own products, however, it could not use the ILGWU collective mark to identify them.

Related terms: Lanham Act.

color as an element of a mark

If registering a mark in which color is claimed as a component, the applicant must submit the image of the mark in color, not black and white, as well as a separate statement describing where the color(s) appear on the mark. The application must include: (a) a claim that the color is a feature of the mark (for example, "The color magenta is claimed as a feature of the mark,") and (b) a statement in the "Description of the Mark" field naming the color and describing where it appears on the mark (often referred to as a "color location" statement—for example, "The mark consists of the colors purple and red and literal or design elements on which the colors appear, that is a purple crown placed on a red velvet pillow"). When describing the color, the applicant can use the generic name and a reference to a commercial color identification system such as Pantone. The examining attorney has the discretion to require that the applicant indicate shades of a color, if necessary to accurately describe the mark. See the *Trademark Manual of Examination Procedures* Section 807.07 for further information.

Related terms: color used as mark.

color used as mark

In 1985, a federal appeals court ruled that a single color—pink—could function as a trademark for fiberglass products. (*In re Owens-Corning Fiberglass Corp.*, 774 F.2d 1116 (Fed. Cir. 1985).) This does not preclude every other business from using pink, only other makers of fiberglass and related products. In 1995, the U.S. Supreme Court ruled that a single color—green—could function as a trademark for ironing pads. (*Qualitex Company v. Jacobson Prods. Co.*, 514 U.S. 159 (1995).) The Supreme Court held that a single color is registrable if both are true:

- Over time, consumers have come to view the color as an identification or the source of the product (rather than the product itself).
- The color has no function.

EXAMPLE: In the *Qualitex* case (*Qualitex Company v. Jacobson Prods. Co.*, 514 U.S. 159 (1995)), the product in question was a green-gold pad designed for dry cleaning presses. The green-gold color was not associated with dry cleaning pads as such, had no functional purpose, and operated only to identify the pads as originating with Qualitex. Once these facts were established, the court saw no reason why the color couldn't qualify as a trademark as long as it could be shown that consumers relied on the color to identify the source of the pads.

The color green reappeared 25 years later in another trademark case.

EXAMPLE: The maker of light green (Pantone 2274C) medical gloves was denied registration on the Supplemental Register because the examining attorney determined there was a likelihood of confusion with the maker of dark green (Pantone 7488U) medical gloves. The TTAB reversed the decision noting the availability of numerous variations of green. ("If this appeal were a movie, it would be entitled 'Fifty Shades of Green.'") (*In re Medline Industries, Inc.*, 2020 USPQ2d 10237 (T.T.A.B. 2020).)

If, on the other hand, a color has a function—for instance, the color blue used to signify nitrogen content, or bright yellow used for tennis balls so they can be seen in limited lighting—it won't qualify as a trademark.

In 2012, the Second Circuit overturned a district court holding that a single color can never serve as a trademark within the fashion industry. The court indicated that a company could prevent others from marketing shoes bearing outsoles in a shade of red identical (or substantially similar) to plaintiff's red shoe sole trademark. (*Christian Louboutin S.A. v. Yves Saint Laurent Am. Holding, Inc.*, 696 F.3d 206 (2d Cir. 2012).)

In 2020, the Federal Circuit determined that a multicolor mark on product packaging did not have to meet the same standards as a single-color mark on product designs (the Qualitex standard). The Federal Circuit held that multicolor packaging marks could be inherently distinctive, and unlike the Qualitex standard, registrable without proof of secondary meaning. (*In re: Forney Industries, Inc.*, 955 F.3d 940 (2020).)

Related terms: color as an element of a mark; distinctive mark; trade dress; trademark.

commerce that Congress may regulate

To qualify for registration and/or protection of a trademark under the Lanham Act, a mark must have first been used "in commerce that Congress may regulate." The Lanham Act defines commerce as "all commerce which may lawfully be regulated by Congress." (15 U.S. Code § 1127.) Technically, this means that to qualify for protection under the Lanham Act, a business must do at least one of the following:

- ship a product across state lines, as do most manufacturers, wholesalers, e-commerce sellers, and mail order businesses

- ship a product between a state and a territory or a territory and another territory (for instance, between New York and Puerto Rico or between Puerto Rico and the Virgin Islands)
- ship a product between a state or territory and another country (for instance, between California and Hong Kong or between Puerto Rico and Cuba)
- conduct a service business across state lines, as do most trucking operations and 900 numbers
- conduct a service business in more than one state (such as Taco Bell, Chevron, and Hilton Hotels do) or across international or territorial borders, or
- operate a business that caters to domestic or international travelers, such as a hotel, restaurant, tour guide service, or ski resort.

Because the USPTO can register only marks that are "lawfully regulated by Congress," it cannot register marks that are used in *unlawful* commerce. Hence, in 2016, the Trademark Trial and Appeals Board (TTAB) affirmed the refusal to register POWERED BY JUJU and JUJU JOINTS for "smokeless cannabis vaporizing apparatus." Although the underlying technology was similar to e-cigarette technology, the TTAB refused to disregard Congress's intent to criminalize the marijuana industry. (*In re: JJ206, LLC, dba JuJu Joints*, Serial Nos. 86474701, 86236122 (T.T.A.B. Oct. 27, 2016).)

An applicant cannot attempt to circumvent the commerce requirement with a sweetheart sale—a transaction made solely to satisfy the interstate commerce requirement—for example, selling a carton of wine to a cousin in Alabama.

The reason for the "commerce" requirement is that Congress has power under the commerce clause of the Constitution to regulate U.S. businesses only to the extent they engage in interstate, interterritorial, or international activity. Thus, the Lanham Act (the statute governing trademark registration) can affect marks in commerce only as defined here. Because Congress has no power under the commerce clause to affect marks used in only one state, the regulation of such marks is up to the individual states.

As a general rule, the U.S. Patent and Trademark Office (USPTO) doesn't question a registration applicant's assertion that a mark is being used in "commerce," which means the issue of commerce will arise only if the validity of the registration is called into question in an opposition or cancellation proceeding or in an infringement lawsuit. Also, the prevalence of commerce on the Internet, which by definition crosses state, territorial, and international boundaries, has made the determination even less of an issue.

Related terms: Lanham Act; state trademark laws; use of mark.

commercial name

See trade name.

Commissioner for Trademarks

The Commissioner for Trademarks is the title of the person who manages the trademark division of the U.S. Patent and Trademark Office. The previous title for this position was the Assistant Commissioner for Trademarks.

Related terms: Director of the U.S. Patent and Trademark Office; U.S. Patent and Trademark Office (USPTO).

Community Trademark

In 1996, the European Union began accepting applications for a community trademark, a registration that is good in 28 EU countries. To qualify for registration, the proposed mark must be acceptable in all 28 countries. Applications are to be submitted to the Office for Harmonization of the Internal Market, in Alicante, Spain. For more information on the Community Trademark, visit the European Union Intellectual Property Office at https://euipo.europa.eu

competing and noncompeting products

When the sale of one product might preclude the sale of another, the products are said to be competing. For instance, if one company sells a car, it obviously competes with another company's ability to sell a similar car, but it might also compete with the sales of pickup trucks or motorcycles.

Products are noncompeting when consumers could reasonably purchase both items—that is, the purchase of one is not at the expense of the other. For example, perfume does not compete with long-haul trailer trucks.

If the marks used on two competing products or services are similar enough to potentially confuse consumers, the owner of the mark found to be infringed upon may sometimes be awarded money damages measured by the amount of profits the other mark's owner earned as a result of the infringement (called defendant's profits). The owner might also be entitled to prevent future infringing use of the mark by the infringing party.

When goods are found to be not competing but are related enough to warrant a finding of potential consumer confusion (for example, they are distributed in the same channels to the same consumer base), the mark's owner can collect any actual damages and also prevent the other party from using the mark in the future. However, the defendant's profits are ordinarily not awarded in this situation, because the infringer by definition did not earn its profits at the expense of the mark's owner.

Related terms: infringement (trademark); related products and services.

composite mark

Marks that consist of several words—for example, the slogan "Don't Leave Home Without It" owned by American Express—are sometimes referred to as composite or hybrid marks. The strength of a composite mark depends on the effect of the whole mark, not just its individual terms. That is, every term in the mark may be ordinary, and yet the whole may be a distinctive and therefore protectable mark.

When registering a composite mark with the U.S. Patent and Trademark Office, the applicant is usually required to disclaim ownership of the unregistrable parts in order to register the mark as a whole. This could mean that each individual term in the mark is disclaimed, even while ownership in the entire mark is asserted.

Related terms: disclaimer of unregistrable material.

concurrent registration

In some circumstances, two or more owners of identical or similar marks may be allowed to register their marks with the U.S. Patent and Trademark Office (USPTO). This can happen if both of the following are true:

- Both marks were in use in commerce before either owner applied for registration.
- The likelihood of consumer confusion is slight, either because the products or services to which the marks will be connected are not closely related or because they will be distributed in entirely different markets.

When allowing concurrent registrations, the USPTO may specify marketing and use limitations on each of the marks to preclude consumer confusion. For example, the USPTO may restrict the use of one mark to ten western states and allow the use of the other mark in the rest of the states. Or the use of the respective marks may be restricted to their original products or services.

Related terms: competing and noncompeting products; interference; related products and services.

confusion of consumers

See likelihood of confusion.

constructive notice of mark under Lanham Act

When a mark is placed on the federal Principal Register, the law assumes that all other mark users anywhere in the United States will know that someone else owns that registered mark. This means that even if a second user has no actual knowledge of the registered mark, such knowledge will be implied, because the Principal Register is a public record, available for inspection.

This constructive (assumed) notice precludes anyone else's legal use of the mark anywhere in the United States, unless such use began before the registration. Assuming the mark's owner affixed proper notice of registration to the mark (usually an "R" in a circle: ®), the constructive notice also means the trademark owner qualifies to recover large (treble) damages and perhaps attorneys' fees.

The courts commonly refuse to find infringement if the marks in question are used in geographically separate markets. However, this rule has less importance as Internet commerce increases, thus extending the geographic reach of most companies. If the owner of a registered mark later chooses to expand into a market in which the infringing mark is being used, the infringer will have to give up the mark, unless its use predated the registration. As a result, it is always wise to do a trademark search before selecting a new mark to make sure the mark is available in all regions and for all products anticipated.

Related terms: geographically separate market; infringement (trademark); Principal Register.

continuous use of mark

A mark that is continuously used for five years after placement on the federal Principal Register may qualify as "incontestable." That means that the mark may no longer be challenged by another user on the ground that it is too weak (ordinary) to warrant legal protection. Any showing of a substantial interruption in the use of the mark during the five-year period may, however, prevent the mark from becoming incontestable.

Related terms: duration of federal trademark registration; incontestability status.

contributory infringer

"Contributory infringement occurs when the defendant either intentionally induces a third party to infringe the plaintiff's mark or supplies a product to a third party with actual or constructive knowledge that the product is being used to infringe the service mark." (*Lockheed Martin Corp. v. Network Solutions, Inc.*, 194 F.3d 980, 983 (9th Cir. 1999).) Like a criminal accomplice, a contributory infringer is a party who furthers or encourages the illegal activity of another. For example, a store that sells records carrying an infringing mark is considered a contributory infringer, as is the wholesale distributor of the records and any other person or business whose actions contribute to the infringement.

Contributory infringers are not liable for damages or defendant's profits as long as they were innocent (they didn't know about the infringement), but they may be enjoined (barred) from any further contributory activity. Thus, the record store owner might have to stop selling the infringing records unless the offending mark was removed. A contributory infringer who knows of the infringement, however, can be held liable on the same basis and in the same amount as the principal infringer. For example, eBay was not found to be liable for sale of counterfeit Tiffany jewelry because eBay did not know or had no reason to know which sellers were infringing on Tiffany's marks. A district court determined that Tiffany—not eBay—had the burden of protecting its trademark at the auction site. (*Tiffany (NJ) Inc. v. eBay, Inc.*, 576 F. Supp.2d. 475 (S.D.N.Y. 2008).) The Second Circuit upheld the trademark ruling. (*Tiffany (NJ) Inc. v. eBay, Inc.*, 600 F.3d 93 (2d Cir. 2010).) In a different case, however, a district court held that an Internet Service Provider (ISP) that hosted several websites selling fake Louis Vuitton merchandise could be liable for contributory infringement. The district court likened the ISPs in this case to the proprietor of the flea market found liable for contributory infringement. (*Louis Vuitton Malletier v. Akanoc Solutions*, 591 F. Supp.2d 1098 (N.D. Cal. 2008).)

In 2019, Oakley, maker of Ray-Ban and Oakley sunglasses, sued a mall owner for contributory trademark infringement. The defendants owned and managed an indoor mall where counterfeit Oakley merchandise was sold. Despite three raids by law enforcement and numerous letters from Oakley, the mall owners refused to take any action, such as policing the mall lessees, and as a result, the Eleventh Circuit found the mall landlords liable as contributory infringers. (*Luxottica Group v. Airport Mini Mall, LLC.*, 932 F.3d 1303 (11th Cir. August 2019).)

Related terms: infringement (trademark); innocent infringer; publishers of advertising matter.

Trademark Law: Definitions

counterfeit

Counterfeiting is the act of making or selling lookalike goods or services bearing fake trademarks, for example, a business deliberately duplicating the Adidas trademark on shoes. Likelihood of confusion is self-evident in counterfeiting, because the counterfeiter's primary purpose is to confuse or dupe consumers. Even when a buyer knows that the product is a fake, the business is still liable for counterfeiting, because the product can still be used to deceive others. Counterfeiting is not limited to consumer products such as watches and handbags. A website that copied the Playboy Bunny logo for adult sex subscription services was assessed $10,000 for trademark counterfeiting. (*Playboy Enterprises Inc. v. Universal Tel-A-Talk Inc.*, 1999 U.S. Dist. LEXIS 6124 (E.D. Pa. 1999).)

Proving infringement is easier when dealing with counterfeits because there is usually no need to conduct a factor-by-factor analysis of likelihood of confusion. In a case involving two merchandising companies, the district court ruled that by their very nature, counterfeit goods cause confusion. (*Bravado International Group Merchandising Services v. Ninna, Inc.*, U.S. Dist. LEXIS 78040 (E.D.N.Y. October 6, 2008).)

The remedies for trademark counterfeiting under the Lanham Act are much harsher than for traditional trademark infringement and unless a court finds some mitigating circumstances, treble damages or profits and a reasonable attorney fee award will be awarded if the counterfeiter knew that the goods were counterfeit and intended to offer them for sale. In addition, the counterfeiter must have duplicated the trademark on the goods or services for which the trademark was federally registered. For example, it is not counterfeiting to put the Gucci mark on automobile seat covers, as these are not goods for which Gucci has a registered trademark.

An offer to sell counterfeit products can also trigger liability as a counterfeiter. For example, an individual offered to sell counterfeit jeans and provided a sample to an undercover police officer. Proof of actual production or sale of the jeans was not necessary to prove counterfeiting.

Similarly, an Internet Service Provider (ISP) that hosted several websites selling fake Louis Vuitton merchandise could be liable for contributory infringement. The district court likened the ISPs in this case to the proprietor of the flea market found liable for contributory infringement. (*Louis Vuitton Malletier v. Akanoc Solutions,* 591 F. Supp.2d 1098 (N.D. Cal. 2008).)

Related terms: likelihood of confusion; related products and services; same or similar mark.

Customs and Border Protection

Under the U.S. Customs Act, a trademark owner whose mark is on the Principal Register may record the mark with U.S. Customs and Border Protection (CBP). This authorizes customs inspectors to seize any products bearing infringing marks and to contact the mark's owner. If the infringing importer agrees to remove the offending mark, or the mark's owner waives the right to object, the goods will be released. Otherwise, they will be destroyed. As a practical matter, most customs enforcement occurs at the behest of trademark owners who conduct their own investigations and tip off the CBP to the arrival of infringing goods. Currently, the recording cannot be made electronically. However, CBP (www.cbp.gov) has prepared a Trademark Recordation Application Template that can be downloaded and mailed.

Related terms: Lanham Act; Principal Register.

cybergriping

See free speech and trademark law.

cybersquatting

Cybersquatting originated at a time when most businesses were not savvy about online commercial opportunities. Some entrepreneurial souls registered the names of well-known companies as domain names with the intent of selling the names back to the companies when the companies finally realized the Internet's economic potential. Panasonic, Fry's Electronics, Hertz, and Avon were among the early victims of cybersquatters. Opportunities for cybersquatters rapidly diminished once businesses learned the importance of registering domain names and once there were two legal mechanisms of wresting names from cybersquatters: the Anticybersquatting Consumer Protection Act, and domain name arbitration under the Internet Corporation for Assigned Names and Numbers (ICANN).

An apparent cybersquatter's failure to sell or offer the names is not the only evidence of bad faith. For example, in one case a company registered domain names that combined elements of Bank of America and Merrill Lynch—for example bofaml.com. The defendant argued that it didn't have a profit motive because it had never sold a domain name. The court rejected that argument, pointing out that the defendant had earned considerable sums by "parking" the domains—that is, by generating pay-per-click revenue. (*Webadvisor v. Bank of America Corp.*, S.D.N.Y. No. 09-cv-05769-DC, February 16, 2009).)

A common variation on cybersquatting is typosquatting, in which misspellings of a domain name are used to mistakenly attract or mislead consumers. Typosquatting can be lucrative when tied to the use of an Internet advertising scheme such as Google AdSense. For example, in a 2006 case a typosquatter purchased domain names such as lnadsend.com and landswnd.com, and then, after sending the customer to the legitimate Lands' End website, charged Lands' End, claiming that these were referrals under the Lands' End referral program (for which the typosquatter belonged under another, legitimate domain). Lands' End filed suit, and the defendant's attempts to dismiss the suit were rejected. (*Lands' End, Inc. v. Remy*, 447 F. Supp.2d 941 (W.D. Wis. September 1, 2006).)

Related terms: Anticybersquatting Consumer Protection Act; defendant's profits; dilution of mark; domain name; UDRP.

damages in trademark infringement cases

Upon finding that a mark was infringed, a court may award payments to the plaintiff (the trademark owner bringing the lawsuit) to compensate for the damage done. The Lanham Act permits awards of:

- actual damages—direct losses suffered by the plaintiff, for example, lost goodwill, or the cost of correcting the confusion
- defendant's profits—amounts the defendant earned from the infringing activity (though the court may not award defendant's profits and actual damages on the same lost sales, as illustrated in the example below.)
- attorneys' fees and costs—in exceptional cases, a court may award attorneys' fees and cost (see "attorneys' fees in trademark infringement actions"), and
- treble damages—in egregious cases of infringement, the court may award damages up to three times the actual money damages suffered due to the infringement (37 U.S. Code § 1117).

EXAMPLE: Barbara averages $5,000 a month in profit selling her trademarked Bar-Bar coffee beans at a farmers' market in Boston. Sales slow in July, and she only profits by $2,500. Then, she learns it's because Herbie, another vendor closer to the entrance, sells Ba-Ba coffee with a similar logo and font. Barbara sues for trademark infringement and wins. She learns that Herbie earned a total of $2,500 in July. She is entitled to claim her actual damages of $2,500 (that is, the profit she would have made if Herbie hadn't siphoned her customers). Alternately, she's entitled to Herbie's $2,500 in profits. But she isn't entitled to claim both her lost profits and Herbie's profits (a total of $5,000), because she suffered a loss of only $2,500, and that would amount to two payments for each lost sale of coffee beans.

The Lanham Act: § 1117. (§ 35) Recovery for violation of rights

This statute sets out the types of money damages that the owner of a registered or unregistered mark is entitled to recover in a trademark infringement lawsuit and provides for attorney fees to be awarded in exceptional cases.

(a) Profits; damages and costs; attorney fees

When a violation of any right of the registrant of a mark registered in the Patent and Trademark Office, a violation under section 1125 (a) or (d) of this title, or a willful violation under section 1125 (c) of this title, shall have been established in any civil action arising under this chapter, the plaintiff shall be entitled, subject to the provisions of sections 1111 and 1114 of this title, and subject to the principles of equity, to recover

(1) defendant's profits,

(2) any damages sustained by the plaintiff, and

(3) the costs of the action. The court shall assess such profits and damages or cause the same to be assessed under its direction. In assessing profits, the plaintiff shall be required to prove defendant's sales only; defendant must prove all elements of cost or deduction claimed. In assessing damages, the court may enter judgment, according to the circumstances of the case, for any sum above the amount found as actual damages, not exceeding three times such amount. If the court shall find that the amount of the recovery based on profits is either inadequate or excessive the court may in its discretion enter judgment for such sum as the court shall find to be just, according to the circumstances of the case. Such sum in either of the above circumstances shall constitute compensation and not a penalty. The court in exceptional cases may award reasonable attorney fees to the prevailing party.

Trademark Law: Definitions

(b) Treble damages for use of counterfeit mark

In assessing damages under subsection (a) of this section, the court shall, unless the court finds extenuating circumstances, enter judgment for three times such profits or damages, whichever is greater, together with a reasonable attorney's fee, in the case of any violation of section 1114 (1)(a) of this title or section 220506 of title 36 that consists of intentionally using a mark or designation, knowing such mark or designation is a counterfeit mark (as defined in section 1116 (d) of this title), in connection with the sale, offering for sale, or distribution of goods or services. In such cases, the court may in its discretion award prejudgment interest on such amount at an annual interest rate established under section 6621 (a)(2) of title 26, commencing on the date of the service of the claimant's pleadings setting forth the claim for such entry and ending on the date such entry is made, or for such shorter time as the court deems appropriate.

(c) Statutory damages for use of counterfeit marks

In a case involving the use of a counterfeit mark (as defined in section 1116 (d) of this title) in connection with the sale, offering for sale, or distribution of goods or services, the plaintiff may elect, at any time before final judgment is rendered by the trial court, to recover, instead of actual damages and profits under subsection (a) of this section, an award of statutory damages for any such use in connection with the sale, offering for sale, or distribution of goods or services in the amount of—

(1) not less than $500 or more than $100,000 per counterfeit mark per type of goods or services sold, offered for sale, or distributed, as the court considers just; or

(2) if the court finds that the use of the counterfeit mark was willful, not more than $1,000,000 per counterfeit mark per type of goods or services sold, offered for sale, or distributed, as the court considers just.

(d) Statutory damages for violation of section 1125 (d)(1)

In a case involving a violation of section 1125 (d)(1) of this title, the plaintiff may elect, at any time before final judgment is rendered by the trial court, to recover, instead of actual damages and profits, an award of statutory damages in the amount of not less than $1,000 and not more than $100,000 per domain name, as the court considers just.

defendant's profits

Profits earned by a defendant as a result of infringing a mark may be awarded to the owner of a mark federally registered under the Lanham Act.

Awarding defendant's profits to the injured party prevents an infringer from realizing any gain from infringement.

To recover defendant's profits, the owner needs to prove the amount the defendant earned from the sales of the goods or services. Then, the defendant is given the opportunity to establish his or her costs (for instance, cost of production, sales attributable to other factors, and so on) and deduct them from the gross sales amount to arrive at the amount of profits. The U.S. Supreme Court resolved a split in the circuits in 2020 when it ruled that willfulness is not required as a condition for obtaining an infringer's profits. In a case involving the accessory-maker Fossil, the jury did not find that Fossil acted willfully, and the district court refused to award Fossil's profits as damages. Reversing this decision, the Supreme Court stated, "Reading words into a statute should be avoided, especially when they are included elsewhere in the very same statute." (*Romag Fasteners, Inc. v. Fossil, Inc.,* 140 S. Ct. 1492 (2020).)

Related terms: competing and noncompeting products; damages in trademark infringement cases; related products and services.

deliberate infringer (or willful infringer)

As a general rule, an infringement will be deemed deliberate if it begins after the mark in question has been federally registered, because the infringer is deemed to have notice of the existing mark.

Related terms: constructive notice of mark under Lanham Act; contributory infringer; innocent infringer.

descriptive mark

Descriptive marks such as Healthy Favorites for dog food, or ChapStick for lip balm describe some quality, ingredient, or characteristic of the goods and services. Many businesses prefer to use weak trademarks because a descriptive mark provides information about the product to the consumer. However, descriptive marks are considered ordinary and therefore weak. Weak marks do not merit much judicial protection unless the owner can demonstrate sufficient sales and advertising. That's because a mark that describes the characteristics of a product or service does not effectively distinguish it from similar products or services offered by others. Protecting descriptive marks does not fulfill the primary purpose of the trademark laws, which is to protect marks that operate as indicators of origin. Also, the law doesn't want to grant a trademark owner the exclusive use of words and phrases that are in common use as descriptive adjectives, because that would limit others' legitimate need to use such a word in their advertising. A descriptive mark will be protected under trademark law only if it achieves secondary meaning—that is, it becomes distinctive because consumers associate the mark with specific goods or services.

Marks that are judged to be descriptive and do not have secondary meaning do not qualify for placement on the Principal Register under the Lanham Act. Instead, they are placed on a list called the Supplemental Register, which offers much less protection than the Principal Register. After a descriptive mark has been in continuous use for five years, however, it can be moved to the Principal Register under the theory that it has developed secondary meaning: It has become a well-known identifier of a product or service through public exposure. At that point, a descriptive mark does act to distinguish certain products or services from others.

If a descriptive mark is mistakenly placed on the Principal Register by the USPTO, another party may challenge the mark's validity up until the time it becomes incontestable (five years on the Principal Register). Once incontestability occurs, the mark is immune from a challenge on the ground that it is descriptive.

Related terms: incontestability status; secondary meaning; Supplemental Register.

dilution

Dilution occurs when someone uses a famous mark in a manner that blurs or tarnishes the mark. In other words, dilution diminishes the capacity of a famous mark to identify and distinguish goods or services, regardless of the presence or absence of:

- competition between the owner of the famous mark and other parties, or
- likelihood of confusion, mistake, or deception (15 U.S. Code § 1527).

Dilution is therefore different from trademark infringement, because trademark infringement always involves a probability of customer confusion, whereas dilution can occur even if customers wouldn't be misled. For example, if a person sells flannel sheets under the brand name "Micro-soft," consumers are not likely to confuse the sheet maker with the software company. But, because Microsoft has become such a strong and famous mark, the use of the word on sheets would dilute its strength by blurring its distinctiveness.

Until the Federal Trademark Dilution Act was enacted in 1996, (15 U.S. Code § 1125(c)), there was no federal law prohibiting trademark dilution and only about half the states provided some recourse—usually an injunction against further use of the mark. As with the state statutes, the federal law applies only to famous marks and provides primarily for injunctive relief (a court order requiring the infringing party to stop using the mark). However, if the famous mark's owner can prove the infringer "willfully intended to trade on the owner's reputation or to cause dilution of the famous mark," the court has discretion to award the owner attorneys' fees and defendant's profits as well as actual damages.

In 2003, in a case involving Victoria's Secret, the Supreme Court confirmed what many practitioners already knew: that the federal dilution law (unlike traditional trademark law) was not intended to protect consumers but rather to protect famous trademarks. The Supreme Court determined that in order to prevail on a federal dilution claim, the owner of a famous mark must demonstrate actual dilution has occurred, not the likelihood of dilution. In other words, dilution can be proven only by evidence of actual harm to the famous mark—for example, survey evidence or other direct proof that shows that consumers perceive the famous mark less favorably. (*Moseley v. V Secret Catalogue, Inc.,* 537 U.S. 418 (2003).)

Unfortunately, the Supreme Court did not provide much guidance on the type or amount of proof required to prove dilution. Since *Moseley* was decided, the owners of famous marks bringing dilution claims have had the best results when seeking to prevent dilution of an identical mark. In *Savin Corp. v. The Savin Group,* 391 F.3d 439 (2d Cir. 2004), the U.S. District Court of Appeals ruled that when the marks are identical, not merely similar, no further proof is required. Still, the issue of proof remained unresolved. In one case, for example, a district court rejected expert witness testimony based on assumptions and hypothetical consumers. (*Monster Cable Products, Inc. v. Discovery Communications Inc.,* 2004 WL 2445348 (N.D. Cal. 2004).)

The Trademark Dilution Revision Act. Much of this turmoil was resolved in 2006, when Congress enacted the Trademark Dilution Revision Act (TDRA). That revised the Lanham Act by eliminating the need to demonstrate actual or likely confusion, competition, or actual economic injury when the owner of a famous mark seeks an injunction to stop dilution by blurring or tarnishment. Still some confusion remains as to the standards required to prove blurring and tarnishment.

> EXAMPLE: In a 2010 case, the Second Circuit determined that the term "Charbucks" does not tarnish the reputation of the Starbucks mark merely based on the evidence of an association and a negative connotation. Charbucks could blur the Starbucks mark but the district court's requirement of substantial similarity was not appropriate—all that was required was a measurement of the degree of similarity. (*Starbucks Corp. v. Wolf's Borough Coffee, Inc.,* 588 F.3d 97 (2d. Cir. 2009).)

The revision defined a mark as being "famous" if it is widely recognized by the general consuming public as a designation of the source of the goods or services of the mark's owner, and it allows the court to consider all relevant factors when determining whether a mark is famous, including: (1) the duration, extent, and geographic reach of advertising and publicity of the mark; (2) the amount, volume, and geographic extent of sales of goods or services offered under the mark; (3) the extent of actual recognition of the mark; and (4) whether the mark was registered on the Principal Register.

The revision defined "dilution by blurring" as an association arising from the similarity between a famous mark and a similar mark or trade name that impairs the distinctiveness of the famous mark, and allows the court to consider all relevant factors when determining whether a mark or trade name is likely to cause dilution by blurring, including: (1) the degree of similarity; (2) the degree of inherent or acquired distinctiveness of the famous mark; (3) the extent to which the owner of the famous mark is engaging in substantially exclusive use of the mark; (4) the degree of recognition of the famous mark; (5) whether the user of the mark or trade name intended to create an association with the famous mark; and (6) any actual association between the mark or trade name and the famous mark. "Tarnishment" was defined as an association arising from the similarity between a mark or trade name and a famous mark that harms the reputation of the famous mark.

The TDRA also declared that certain acts are not actionable as dilution by blurring or tarnishment, including: (1) any fair use of a famous mark by another person other than as a designation of source for the person's own goods or services, including for advertising or promotion that permits consumers to compare goods or services, or identifying and parodying, criticizing, or commenting upon the famous mark owner or the owner's goods or services; (2) all forms of news reporting and news commentary; and (3) any noncommercial use of a mark.

And finally, the TDRA allows the owner of a famous mark to seek additional remedies in an action if the person against whom the injunction is sought:

- first used the mark or trade name in commerce after the date of enactment of this act
- willfully intended to trade on the recognition of the famous mark, or
- willfully intended to harm the reputation of the famous mark.

Ownership of a valid registration is a complete bar to an action under state common law or statute that seeks to prevent dilution by blurring or tarnishment, or that asserts any claim of actual or likely damage or harm to the distinctiveness or reputation of a mark, label, or form of advertisement.

In the first appellate case heard under the TDRA, the Fourth Circuit Court of Appeals held that the Louis Vuitton trademark was not diluted by the use of the term "Chewy Vuitton" for a pet chew toy that was "evocative" of a Louis Vuitton bag. The defendant produced a line of chew toys that parodied famous designers such as "Furcedes" (parodying Mercedes) and "Chewnel No. 5" (Chanel No. 5). The court determined that Chewy Vuitton was a parody and that a successful parody would not dilute the famous brand but in fact might make it even more famous. (*Louis Vuitton v. Haute Diggity Dog*, 507 F.3d 252 (4th Cir 2007).)

The TDRA preempts state claims of dilution against federally registered marks. In other words, you cannot sue the owner of a federally registered mark for dilution in state court. These claims must be brought in federal court under the TDRA.

The Lanham Act: § 1125. (§ 43c)

(c) Dilution by blurring; dilution by tarnishment

   (1) Injunctive relief

   Subject to the principles of equity, the owner of a famous mark that is distinctive, inherently or through acquired distinctiveness, shall be entitled to an injunction against another person who, at any time after the owner's mark has become famous, commences use of a mark or trade name in commerce that is likely to cause dilution by blurring or dilution by tarnishment of the famous mark, regardless of the presence or absence of actual or likely confusion, of competition, or of actual economic injury.

   (2) Definitions

   (A) For purposes of paragraph (1), a mark is famous if it is widely recognized by the general consuming public of the United States as a designation of source of the goods or services of the mark's owner. In determining whether a mark possesses the requisite degree of recognition, the court may consider all relevant factors, including the following:

   (i) The duration, extent, and geographic reach of advertising and publicity of the mark, whether advertised or publicized by the owner or third parties.

   (ii) The amount, volume, and geographic extent of sales of goods or services offered under the mark.

   (iii) The extent of actual recognition of the mark.

   (iv) Whether the mark was registered under the Act of March 3, 1881, or the Act of February 20, 1905, or on the principal register.

(B) For purposes of paragraph (1), "dilution by blurring" is association arising from the similarity between a mark or trade name and a famous mark that impairs the distinctiveness of the famous mark. In determining whether a mark or trade name is likely to cause dilution by blurring, the court may consider all relevant factors, including the following:

(i) The degree of similarity between the mark or trade name and the famous mark.

(ii) The degree of inherent or acquired distinctiveness of the famous mark.

(iii) The extent to which the owner of the famous mark is engaging in substantially exclusive use of the mark.

(iv) The degree of recognition of the famous mark.

(v) Whether the user of the mark or trade name intended to create an association with the famous mark.

(vi) Any actual association between the mark or trade name and the famous mark.

(C) For purposes of paragraph (1), "dilution by tarnishment" is association arising from the similarity between a mark or trade name and a famous mark that harms the reputation of the famous mark.

(3) Exclusions

The following shall not be actionable as dilution by blurring or dilution by tarnishment under this subsection:

(A) Any fair use, including a nominative or descriptive fair use, or facilitation of such fair use, of a famous mark by another person other than as a designation of source for the person's own goods or services, including use in connection with—

(i) advertising or promotion that permits consumers to compare goods or services; or

(ii) identifying and parodying, criticizing, or commenting upon the famous mark owner or the goods or services of the famous mark owner.

(B) All forms of news reporting and news commentary.

(C) Any noncommercial use of a mark.

The Lanham Act: § 1127. (§ 45) Construction and definitions; intent of chapter
The term "dilution" means the lessening of the capacity of a famous mark to identify and distinguish goods or services, regardless of the presence or absence of—

(1) competition between the owner of the famous mark and other parties, or

(2) likelihood of confusion, mistake, or deception.

Related terms: famous mark; Victoria's Secret case (*Moseley v. V Secret Catalogue, Inc.*).

Director of the U.S. Patent and Trademark Office

The Director is the top person at the USPTO. The official title is "Under Secretary of Commerce for Intellectual Property and Director of the USPTO."

Related terms: Commissioner for Trademarks; U.S. Patent and Trademark Office (USPTO).

disclaimer of trademark use

A disclaimer is a statement that disassociates any connection created by the use of another business's trademark. A disclaimer, by itself, cannot guarantee that a trademark use is permissible. However, courts have recognized prominently placed disclaimers as a factor in reducing consumer confusion. An effective disclaimer must be:

- **Prominently placed.** It must be reasonably close to the other business's trademark so that a consumer is likely to read the statement when viewing the trademark.
- **Permanently affixed.** Detachable tags and labels will not provide adequate notice.
- **Capable of being read and understood.** The disclaimer must provide a clear statement that the companies and their goods are not associated.
- **Have the effect of minimizing confusion.** Many courts seek proof that the disclaimer actually has the desired effect. For this reason, a company might want to test its disclaimer on consumers to be certain it will have the desired effect. Statements such as "unauthorized" might be too general to avoid consumer confusion.

EXAMPLE: A publisher advertised a Godzilla filmography book. The book's front cover included the statement, "Unauthorized." A brief disclaimer was included on the back cover. The owner of the Godzilla trademark sued for copyright and trademark infringement. The court ruled in favor of the trademark owner; the publisher's disclaimer was inadequate because the word "unauthorized" conveyed limited information. An appropriate disclaimer would have been: "The publication has not been prepared, approved, or licensed by any entity that created or produced the original Toho Godzilla films," and should have been printed on the front cover and spine of the book in a distinguishing color or typestyle. (*Toho Inc. v. William Morrow and Co.*, 33 F. Supp.2d 1206 (C.D. Cal. 1998).)

disclaimer of unregistrable material

Often a trademark will consist of a distinctive word (for instance, "Nolo") in combination with one or more unprotectable terms (such as "Press" as in Nolo Press, or ".com" as in Nolo.com). Or the entire mark may consist of unprotectable terms that taken together are distinctive because of how the terms are combined.

When owners of these types of marks seek to register them with the U.S. Patent and Trademark Office (USPTO), the USPTO examiner will normally require the applicants to "disclaim" (agree to give up any claim to) ownership of the unprotectable terms, even though the mark itself would be registered. Thus, the owner of "Snappy Salsa" would have to disclaim "Salsa." These disclaimers make it clear that other businesses are free to use the disclaimed terms, as long as they don't use them in a way that would conflict with the distinctive aspects of the registered mark.

Related terms: composite mark; geographic terms as marks; Lanham Act.

disparaging mark

See prohibited and reserved marks under Lanham Act.

distinctive mark

Only marks that are distinctive (or "strong")—that is, that distinguish products and services—can function as trademarks. Some marks are "born" distinctive (sometimes referred to as "inherently distinctive") because in the context of their use they are memorable—for example, the mark might consist of terms that are arbitrary (Target Stores), suggestive (Jaguar cars), or fanciful (Reebok shoes). In addition, mundane or common marks—typically people's names, geographic designators, and descriptive terms—can become distinctive if they become well known over time (such as Microsoft *Windows*).

Distinctive marks excel in distinguishing their products or services from competing ones, which qualifies them for maximum judicial protection under state and federal laws. Because of this protection, distinctive marks are considered to be legally stronger than are marks considered common or ordinary because they describe the product's qualities (descriptive marks), use the owner's name, or are in widespread use for the particular product or service (in common use).

For example, any mark using the term "Google" would be considered infringing, since "Google" is a very strong mark and has no meaning other than as a mark. (The Google trademark resulted from an unintentional misspelling of Googol, which means ten to the hundredth power.) On the other hand, a mark with a common term like "data" will probably not infringe on another use of "data," since that word is already in wide use among large numbers of high-tech businesses.

A mark must be distinctive in order to qualify for placement on the Principal Register under the Lanham Act. A descriptive mark will be protected under trademark law only if it achieves secondary meaning—that is, it becomes distinctive because consumers associate the mark with specific goods or services.

Related terms: arbitrary mark; descriptive mark; dilution; generic terms; Principal Register; secondary meaning; strong mark; suggestive mark.

domain names

Consider www.nolo.com. The letters www (that stand for "World Wide Web") are automatically a part of almost every domain name. The middle part—Nolo—is the unique name that was selected and registered for the business.

When it comes to what are referred to as the generic top level domains (TLD)—typically the last part of a domain name, for example, .com—there are many choices. Some of these include:

- .aero, for the air transport industry
- .asia, for people and entities in the Asia-Pacific region
- .biz, restricted to businesses
- .com, for commercial enterprises
- .coop, restricted to business cooperatives
- .edu, for educational institutions
- .gov, restricted to government agencies
- .info, for information providers
- .int, restricted to organizations endorsed by a treaty between two or more nations
- .jobs, for employment-related sites
- .mil, restricted to U.S. Military
- .mobi, for devices using mobile Internet
- .museum, restricted to museums and related persons
- .name, restricted to individuals
- .net, for network-related entities
- .org, for nonprofit organizations
- .post, restricted to Postal Administration
- .pro, restricted to licensed professionals
- .tel, for internet communication services
- .travel, for the travel industry, and
- .xxx for pornography.

The number of TLDs is constantly increasing. You can see a complete listing of existing and proposed TLDs at the ICANN website (www.icann.org).

Every country also has a country code that serves as a TLD. For example, the country code suffix for the United States is .us. For France it's .fr, and for Greece it's .gr. The rules for obtaining one of these vary from country to country. Your business might qualify for a country code suffix even if it's not physically present in that country.

Occasionally, a business will choose a country code because the letters have some supposed promotional value. For example, the country code for Tuvalu is .tv, making it possible to acquire www.comedy.tv as a domain name. Similarly, the country code for Moldova is .md, so a doctor can nail down www.johnsmith.md. The country code for Andorra is .ad, making it a popular choice for commercial advertising businesses.

For now, the use of country codes is considered a novelty, outside mainstream business practice. In addition, many nations place additional burdens on registrants—for example, to obtain an Andorran .ad, you must register the business name as a trademark in Andorra.

For up-to-date information about the status of TLDs, go to https://newgtlds.icann.org.

Keep in mind that the guidelines for many of these suffixes are not strictly enforced. For example, anyone can usually acquire a .com, .net, .org, .biz, or .info domain name regardless of the type of business they operate. But strictly enforced standards put the .edu and .gov suffixes in the hands of government and educational institutions, respectively. Similarly, the .name extension is for individuals, not businesses. The extensions .coop, .aero, .museum, and .pro are also restricted—for example, a .aero registration will be issued only to a business in the air transport industry.

Most U.S. companies have chosen a .com designation. In fact, registrations for .coms have outpaced any other by ten to one. A domain name can be acquired under several TLD suffixes—for example, nolo.com, nolo.net, and nolo.org.

Because each domain name must be unique—so that all the computers attached to the Internet can find it—it is impossible for two different businesses to have the same domain name. A simple way to check ownership of a domain is to use www.whois.net.

Beware that some registrants, especially those acting in bad faith, can supply false information about domain name ownership. In these cases, there's not much that can be done to track down the domain name holder. This lack of information should not stop those pursuing a cybersquatter—a speculator who is holding a domain name for ransom. There are ways to wrestle a domain name from a bad faith registrant even if the identity or location of the cybersquatter is unknown.

Keep in mind that even if a company owns a federally registered trademark, someone else might still have the right to own the domain name. For example, many different companies have federally registered the trademark Executive for different goods or services. All of these companies might want www.executive.com, but the first one to purchase it—in this case, Executive Software—is the one that acquired the domain name.

When registering a domain name, a company should be sure that nobody else is using it as a trademark for similar goods and services. If another business is selling similar goods or services with a similar name, the use of the domain name can be terminated under trademark law principles.

> EXAMPLE: Jim's catalog company, Ahab, has been selling ocean-themed artwork and merchandise since 1980. Jim has registered the Ahab trademark with the U.S. Patent and Trademark Office (USPTO). Bob registers the domain name ahab.com and uses it to sell artwork depicting whales. Jim can stop Bob's use of the domain name ahab.com. If Bob were using ahab.com to sell Ahab-brand educational software, Jim could not stop Bob's use of the domain name.

The purchase of a domain name can be accomplished at any of the approved domain name registrars. A complete list is provided at both InterNIC (www.internic.net) and ICANN (www.icann.org). An applicant completes the online domain name registration form indicating basic contact information (name, telephone number, and address). The fee is usually $5 to $35 per year, although some registrars offer lower rates. The whole procedure takes a matter of minutes and the domain name registrant is notified by email of the domain name ownership, which is effective immediately.

Payment of the annual fee for a domain name grants ownership of only an address on the Internet; it doesn't establish a website presence. In order to use it in conjunction with a website, a business must establish a Web hosting arrangement

Trademark Law: Definitions

with an ISP (Internet Service Provider), usually for a fee of approximately $5 to $20 per month. The business must also construct and upload a website and coordinate the reassignment of the domain name from the domain name registrar to the ISP. Usually an ISP will assist the company through the process. A domain name purchase grants exclusive title to the domain name owner, who can stop others from using it with the following exceptions:

- **Failure to pay annual domain name fees.** Domain name ownership, unlike trademark ownership, must be renewed either every year or every two years (depending on the initial arrangement with the registrar). Failure to pay fees will result in cancellation of the domain name ownership, which may eventually be sold to another buyer.
- **The domain name registrant is a cybersquatter.** If a domain name is registered in bad faith, for example, for the purpose of selling it back to a company with the same name, the domain name can be taken away under federal law or under international arbitration rules for domain name owners.
- **The domain name infringes a trademark.** If a domain name is likely to confuse consumers because it is similar to another trademark, the domain name use may be terminated. For example, if a company registered adoobie.com for the purposes of selling software, it's very likely that the Adobe company, makers of graphics software, would be able to stop the use.
- **The domain name dilutes a famous trademark.** If a domain name dilutes the power of a famous trademark, the owner of the famous mark can sue under federal laws to stop the continued use. Dilution refers to the fact that the domain name is being used for commercial purposes and blurs or tarnishes the reputation of a famous trademark. For example, if a company registered guccigoo.com for the purpose of selling baby diapers, the owners of the Gucci trademark could stop the use of the domain name under dilution principles.

Purchasing a domain name does not automatically create trademark rights. Domain name ownership, by itself, does not permit the owner to stop another business from using the name for its business or product. For example, if Sam acquires the domain name greatgrammar.com, that does not mean Sam can stop others from using Great Grammar for services or products online or off. It only means that Sam has the right to that Internet address.

A domain name will function as a trademark only if it is used in connection with the sale of goods or services and consumers associate the name with the Internet business. When that happens, the domain name owner can stop others from using a similar name.

Consider Amazon.com, a domain name that functions as a trademark because consumers associate the name with a certain company and its services. Amazon.com achieved trademark status because the company was the first to use this distinctive name for online retail sales, and the name has been promoted to consumers through advertising and sales. If another company sold books on the Internet or off under the name Amazon, the owners of Amazon.com could sue under trademark law to stop the use.

In short, to be protectable as a trademark, a domain name must be distinctive or must achieve distinction through consumer awareness, and the owner must be the first to use the name in connection with certain services or products.

A domain name owner can run into problems if the domain name legally conflicts with an existing trademark. For example, if a company launched a website with the domain name Xon.com to sell automobile accessories, that company could be stopped from using the name by the owners of the Exxon trademark. That's because Exxon has the right to stop lookalike and soundalike business names that are likely to confuse consumers of a wide range of auto products.

Whether a domain name would legally conflict with an existing trademark depends on which was first put into actual use and whether the existing mark is famous or use of the domain name would confuse customers regarding the existing mark. The legal standards used in these conflicts are no different from other trademark disputes.

Federal registration of a domain name. If a company has registered its trademark, for example "Starbucks," does it need to also register "starbucks.com"? For many businesses the answer is, no.

Unless a company is establishing some service unique to its Internet business—for example, downloadable audio services or assistance in filling out a mortgage application—there is usually little to be gained from registering the ".com" version of a federally registered trademark. The owner of a federally registered trademark can stop others from using the mark for similar goods or services whether they are sold online or off. In addition, the USPTO requires that applicants disclaim ".com" in order to prevent any person from claiming a proprietary right to this generic term. However, if the website provides services or products unique to the online experience—for example, if Starbucks.com offered a musical downloading service separate from its retail outlets—then the business might want to register the .com version of the name.

The USPTO previously had a *per se* rule against trademark registration for a generic term combined with ".com," on grounds that the combination was generic. Following this rule, a trademark examiner rejected registration for BOOKING. COM for a travel booking company. The Supreme Court struck down the rule that 'generic.com' terms are incapable of identifying a source. The Supreme Court concluded that, "Because 'Booking.com' is not a generic name to consumers, it is not generic." The takeaway: "Whether a compound term is generic turns on whether that term, taken as a whole, signifies to consumers a class of goods or services." (*USPTO v. Booking.com B.V.*, 140 S. Ct. 2298 (2020).)

Related terms: Anticybersquatting Consumer Protection Act; dilution; free speech and trademark law; initial interest confusion; keyword; likelihood of confusion; metatags; UDRP.

domain tasting

Domain tasting occurs when someone registers a number of domain names and then waits several days before paying for them. In the interim, the "buyer" checks website analytics to see which domain names attract the most visitors and then pays only for the popular ones. There are a few problems with domain tasting, most notably that it can be used as a springboard for typosquatting. In addition, during the period between registration and payment, the domain names are shown as being registered, which creates problems for legitimate businesses and trademark owners. Domain tasters commonly operate at high volume. For example, in one case, a domain taster registered, but did not pay for, 1,400 variations on "Verizon" misspellings. In that case, a court determined that the practice was a violation of the Anticybersquatting Consumer Protection Act. (*Verizon California, Inc. v. Navigation Catalyst Systems, Inc.*, 568 F. Supp.2d 1088 (C.D. Cal. 2008).)

duration of federal trademark registration

Once a trademark or service mark is placed on the Principal Register, the owner receives a certificate of registration. Although it's good for an initial term of ten years, the registration can lapse unless the registrant files a sworn statement within six years of the filing date (the "Sections 8 and 15 Affidavit") indicating that the mark is either still in use in commerce or not in use, but for legitimate reasons that do not constitute abandonment. (Note, if a mark's registration occurred before November 16, 1989, its initial term is 20 years, not ten.)

The original registration may be renewed indefinitely for additional ten-year periods if the owner timely files the required renewal applications (called Section 9 Affidavits) with the U.S. Patent and Trademark Office. Failure to renew does not void all rights to the mark; however, unless it is reregistered, the mark's owner will not have the benefits of federal registration, such as the presumed nationwide notice and the presumption of validity.

> **EXAMPLE:** Carolyn registers a service mark for her graphic design business on May 1, 2017. The registration is good for ten years, or until May 1, 2030. To keep the registration in force, Carolyn must file a Sections 8 and 15 Affidavit between May 1, 2022 (five years after her registration date), and May 1, 2023, and she must renew it between May 1, 2027, and April 30, 2028, and again between May 1, 2037, and April 30, 2038. By continuing to renew the mark in this manner, Carolyn can keep it on the Principal Register indefinitely.

The Lanham Act: § 1058. (§ 8) Duration of registration

(a) In general

Each registration shall remain in force for 10 years, except that the registration of any mark shall be canceled by the Director for failure to comply with the provisions of subsection (b) of this section, upon the expiration of the following time periods, as applicable:

   (1) For registrations issued pursuant to the provisions of this chapter, at the end of 6 years following the date of registration.

   (2) For registrations published under the provisions of section 1062 (c) of this title, at the end of 6 years following the date of publication under such section.

   (3) For all registrations, at the end of each successive 10-year period following the date of registration.

(b) Affidavit of continuing use

During the 1-year period immediately preceding the end of the applicable time period set forth in subsection (a) of this section, the owner of the registration shall pay the prescribed fee and file in the Patent and Trademark Office—

   (1) an affidavit setting forth those goods or services recited in the registration on or in connection with which the mark is in use in commerce and such number of specimens or facsimiles showing current use of the mark as may be required by the Director; or

   (2) an affidavit setting forth those goods or services recited in the registration on or in connection with which the mark is not in use in commerce and showing that any such nonuse is due to special circumstances which excuse such nonuse and is not due to any intention to abandon the mark.

(c) Grace period for submissions; deficiency

(1) The owner of the registration may make the submissions required under this section within a grace period of 6 months after the end of the applicable time period set forth in subsection (a) of this section. Such submission is required to be accompanied by a surcharge prescribed by the Director.

(2) If any submission filed under this section is deficient, the deficiency may be corrected after the statutory time period and within the time prescribed after notification of the deficiency. Such submission is required to be accompanied by a surcharge prescribed by the Director.

(d) Notice of affidavit requirement

Special notice of the requirement for affidavits under this section shall be attached to each certificate of registration and notice of publication under section 1062 (c) of this title.

(e) Notification of acceptance or refusal of affidavits

The Director shall notify any owner who files 1 of the affidavits required by this section of the Commissioner's acceptance or refusal thereof and, in the case of a refusal, the reasons therefor.

(f) Designation of resident for service of process and notices

If the registrant is not domiciled in the United States, the registrant may designate, by a document filed in the United States Patent and Trademark Office, the name and address of a person resident in the United States on whom may be served notices or process in proceedings affecting the mark. Such notices or process may be served upon the person so designated by leaving with that person or mailing to that person a copy thereof at the address specified in the last designation so filed. If the person so designated cannot be found at the address given in the last designation, or if the registrant does not designate by a document filed in the United States Patent and Trademark Office the name and address of a person resident in the United States on whom may be served notices or process in proceedings affecting the mark, such notices or process may be served on the Director.

The Lanham Act: § 1059. (§ 9) Renewal of registration

This statute sets out the procedure for renewing a trademark registration.

(a) Period of renewal; time for renewal

Subject to the provisions of section 1058 of this title, each registration may be renewed for periods of 10 years at the end of each successive 10-year period following the date of registration upon payment of the prescribed fee and the filing of a written application, in such form as may be prescribed by the Director. Such application may be made at any time within 1 year before the end of each successive 10-year period for which the registration was issued or renewed, or it may be made within a grace period of 6 months after the end of each successive 10-year period, upon payment of a fee and surcharge prescribed therefor. If any application filed under this section is deficient, the deficiency may be corrected within the time prescribed after notification of the deficiency, upon payment of a surcharge prescribed therefor.

(b) Notification of refusal of renewal

If the Director refuses to renew the registration, the Director shall notify the registrant of the Commissioner's refusal and the reasons therefor.

(c) Designation of resident for service of process and notices

If the registrant is not domiciled in the United States the registrant may designate, by a document filed in the United States Patent and Trademark Office, the name and address of a person resident in the United States on whom may be served notices or process in proceedings affecting the mark. Such notices or process may be served upon the person so designated by leaving with that person or mailing to that person a copy thereof at the address specified in the last designation so filed. If the person so designated cannot be found at the address given in the last designation, or if the registrant does not designate by a document filed in the United States Patent and Trademark Office the name and address of a person resident in the United States on whom may be served notices or process in proceedings affecting the mark, such notices or process may be served on the Director.

Related terms: incontestability status; Section 8 Declaration; Section 15 Declaration; Supplemental Register.

eTEAS

See TEAS.

exclusive right to use mark

See ownership of mark in the United States.

ex parte expungement

The Trademark Modernization Act (TMA) provides a process (Section 16A of the Lanham Act) for challenging a registered mark on grounds that it was never used in commerce as required. If successful, the mark will be expunged (removed from the trademark register). An ex parte expungement must include evidence of a reasonable investigation demonstrating non-use—that is, that the mark has never been used in connection with the goods and services. The petition can be filed after three years (but within ten years) of registration. A challenger can file an expungement petition for registrations older than ten years if the petition is filed within three years of the TMA's enactment.

Related terms: abandonment; opposing and canceling a trademark registration.

ex parte reexamination

Like the ex parte expungement procedure described above, Section 16B of the Lanham Act permits petitioning for reexamination of a registration on grounds that it was not used in commerce before the registration date. The petition can be filed within five years of registration and must provide evidence of a reasonable investigation demonstrating nonuse.

Related terms: abandonment, opposing and canceling a trademark registration.

expungement

See ex parte expungement.

fair use of trademarks

In trademark law, the fair use defense is classified in two ways: classic fair use and nominative fair use. Classic fair use occurs when the defendant asserts that the use is to describe the goods, not to trade off the trademark owner's goodwill. For example, the maker of an electric dishwasher may describe the "joy" of clean dishes without infringing the trademark Joy for dishwashing liquid. A company promoting toothpaste may state that it is the "choice of dentists" without infringing the trademark Dentist's Choice. And a fragrance company may include advertising copy using the term "love potion" even though that term is a registered trademark for fragrances. The classic fair use defense is set forth in the Lanham Act. (15 U.S. Code § 1115(b)(4).)

In 2005, the U.S. Supreme Court ruled that a defendant may assert the classic fair use defense even if the trademark owner has demonstrated likelihood of confusion. In other words, a court will permit some confusion if the use is considered a classic fair use. (How much is a matter to be decided by the courts.) (*K.P. Permanent Make-Up, Inc. v. Lasting Impression*, 543 U.S. 111 (2004).)

Other noncommercial uses of a trademark are lumped together as nominative fair uses. The following are examples of nominative fair use:

1. comparative advertising
2. journalistic accounts of the owner of the mark or the goods or services identified by the mark, and
3. parodies involving the mark.

For example, a California district court determined that an artist's project including nude Barbie dolls and imagery entitled "Malted Barbie" and "The Barbie Enchiladas" was a noncommercial fair use of the Mattel company's Barbie trademark. (*Mattel Inc. v. Walking Mountain Productions, Inc.*, 353 F.3d 792

(9th Cir. 2003).) In another case involving artwork, the Eleventh Circuit permitted the use of the University of Alabama trademarks in paintings depicting the football team. (*University of Alabama Board of Trustees v. New Life Art Inc.*, 683 F.3d 1266 (11th Cir. 2012).) In a 2016 case involving a certification mark, the Second Circuit held that nominative fair use should not be considered a defense, but instead should be incorporated within its eight-factor test for determining likelihood of confusion. This decision puts the Second Circuit at odds with the Ninth Circuit, which considers nominative fair use as a defense to infringement. (*International Information Systems Security Certification Consortium Inc. v. Security University LLC*, 823 F.3d 153 (2d Cir. 2016).)

The Ninth Circuit had more to say about fair use in 2017. The BIC company used the statement "The WRITE Pen Choice for 30 Years," and a company owned by BIC used "All-in-One." Marketquest, owner of ALL-IN-ONE and THE WRITE CHOICE trademarks sued for infringement. BIC claimed trademark fair use as a defense. The Ninth Circuit held that fair use is an affirmative defense that's considered only after likelihood of confusion has been determined. (*Marketquest Group v. BIC*, 862 F.3d 927 (9th Cir. July 7, 2017).)

In 2018, the Sixth Circuit weighed in with a trademark fair use ruling regarding whiskey. The defendant purchased the Old Taylor distillery and used it to manufacture whiskey under the mark, CASTLE & KEY. As a historic shout-out, the owners left the 400-foot sign "Old Taylor Distillery" on its barrel warehouse and referred to its location as the "Former Old Taylor Distillery." The property was also listed on the National Register of Historic Places. The court found that the owner of the OLD TAYLOR trademark had failed to overcome the defendant's trademark fair use argument. (*Sazerac Brands, LLC v. Peristyle, LLC*, 17-5997 (6th Cir. 2018).)

In 2019, SportFuel, a supplement company, sued Gatorade over its use of "GATORADE: THE SPORTS FUEL COMPANY." When Gatorade registered the mark, it disclaimed "Sports Fuel Company." The Seventh Circuit held that Gatorade's use of the "sports fuel" terminology was descriptive and trademark fair use. (*SportFuel, Inc. v. PepsiCo, Inc.*, No. 18-3010 (7th Cir. 2019).)

In 2020, the Second Circuit reversed a lower court summary judgment against Costco in favor of Tiffany's. (The district court awarded Tiffany's $21 million.) Costco had referred to a specific ring design as a Tiffany ring, and claimed trademark fair use as a defense. The Second Circuit reversed on the grounds that a determination of liability was inappropriate at the summary judgment stage. (*Tiffany & Co. v. Costco Wholesale Corp.*, No. 17-2798 (2nd Cir. 2020).)

Note, trademark fair use should not be confused with the fair use defense applied in copyright law.

Related terms: free speech and trademark law; parodies of trademarks.

false advertising

False advertising occurs when advertisers materially mislead and deceive consumers. A business that makes misleading advertising statements about its products or another company's products can be sued in federal court under Section 43(a) of the federal Lanham Act. (15 U.S. Code § 1125(a).) It is not necessary to have a federally registered trademark to make such a claim. All that is required is that a business has made false or misleading statements as to its own product or another's, that there is actual deception or at least a tendency to deceive a substantial portion of the intended audience, and that the advertised goods traveled in interstate commerce. The deception must be material, that is, likely to influence purchasing decisions, and there must be likelihood of injury to another company in terms of declining sales or loss of goodwill. In other words, if the false advertising has no impact on purchasers, goodwill, or sales, then the claim will be dismissed.

For purposes of Section 43(a), advertising is any commercial speech intended to influence consumers and disseminated to the relevant purchasing public. "Commercial speech" refers to statements generally made for the purposes of promoting a business or trade, not editorial or informational speech protected under free speech principles. For example, it is not commercial speech to make statements about a product in a newspaper article.

Deceptive advertising is generally categorized as either statements that are simply untrue (or "false on their face") or statements that are accurate but deceptive. An example of a statement that is false on its face would be inaccurately claiming that a motor oil additive will increase mileage. An example of a statement that is accurate but deceptive would be that a motor oil additive protects against engine corrosion, but failing to mention that the protection is for boat engines and not automobile engines. In cases of accurate but deceptive claims, a court must examine evidence, for example, to determine if a company's test results have been distorted or exaggerated.

In 2014, the Supreme Court provided guidance on two false advertising issues. First the Court held that a claim for false advertising under Section 43(a) could be brought even if the parties were not in direct competition. What was required was that the party bringing the claim could demonstrate: (1) a reasonable interest to be protected against the alleged false advertising and (2) a reasonable basis for believing that the interest is likely to be damaged by the alleged false advertising. (*Lexmark Int'l, Inc. v. Static Control Components, Inc.*, 572 U.S. 118 (2014).) Second, the Supreme Court held that it was not inconsistent for a company to comply with federal labeling laws and to still violate false advertising laws. In that case, Pom, maker of pomegranate juices, sued Coca-Cola, claiming that Coke's pomegranate-blueberry juice was falsely labeled. Coca-Cola claimed that it could not be sued for false advertising because it had complied with FDA labeling requirements. The Supreme Court disagreed with Coca-Cola and held that compliance with federal labeling regulations in the food and beverage industry did not preclude liability for false advertising under Section 43(a). (*POM Wonderful LLC v. Coca-Cola Co.*, 573 U.S. 102 (2014).)

At the same time, federal labeling requirements can help to avoid a false advertising claim. A California district court dismissed a false advertising complaint against a company that prominently featured pictures of pumpkin, quinoa, yogurt, and pomegranate on its packaging despite the fact that these were not the primary ingredients. The court held that the FDA-required ingredient list resolved any confusion about the product's content. (*Workman v. Plum Inc.*, No. 15-cv-2568 (WHA) (N.D. Cal. 2015).)

The Lanham Act: § 1125. (§ 43a) False designations of origin and false descriptions forbidden

(a) Civil action

    (1) Any person who, on or in connection with any goods or services, or any container for goods, uses in commerce any word, term, name, symbol, or device, or any combination thereof, or any false designation of origin, false or misleading description of fact, or false or misleading representation of fact, which—

        (A) is likely to cause confusion, or to cause mistake, or to deceive as to the affiliation, connection, or association of such person with another person, or as to the origin, sponsorship, or approval of his or her goods, services, or commercial activities by another person, or

        (B) in commercial advertising or promotion, misrepresents the nature, characteristics, qualities, or geographic origin of his or her or another person's goods, services, or commercial activities, shall be liable in a civil action by any person who believes that he or she is or is likely to be damaged by such act.

    (2) As used in this subsection, the term "any person" includes any State, instrumentality of a State or employee of a State or instrumentality of a State acting in his or her official capacity. Any State, and any such instrumentality, officer, or employee, shall be subject to the provisions of this chapter in the same manner and to the same extent as any nongovernmental entity.

(3) In a civil action for trade dress infringement under this chapter for trade dress not registered on the principal register, the person who asserts trade dress protection has the burden of proving that the matter sought to be protected is not functional.

Related terms: unfair competition; unregistered mark, protection of.

famous mark

Under federal law and most state laws, only owners of famous marks can file claims alleging dilution. Examples of famous marks include the NBA logo of a silhouetted basketball player, Saks Fifth Avenue for retail stores, Hyatt for hotel services, and Godzilla for entertainment services.

As a result of the Trademark Dilution Revision Act of 2006, a mark is "famous" if it is widely recognized by the general consuming public as a designation of the source of the goods or services of the mark's owner, and it allows the court to consider all relevant factors when determining whether a mark is famous, including: (1) the duration, extent, and geographic reach of advertising and publicity of the mark; (2) the amount, volume, and geographic extent of sales of goods or services offered under the mark; (3) the extent of actual recognition of the mark; and (4) whether the mark was registered on the Principal Register.

Related terms: dilution.

fanciful terms

Fanciful terms (sometimes referred to as "coined marks") are invented words or phrases with no other purpose than to act as a trademark. Coined terms generally are considered strong or distinctive marks and courts will tend to protect them against unauthorized use. The easiest way to assure protection for a mark is to make up, or "coin," a new word.

A coined term may consist of any combination of letters and/or numerals that are not already in use to identify or distinguish another product or service. Thus, "4711 water" is a coined phrase used as the trademark for a particular brand of cologne. Other examples of coined terms are Sybex (publisher of computer books), Kodak (cameras), Tylenol (analgesic), Maalox (antacid medicine), and Unix (computer operating system).

Related terms: strong mark.

Federal Trademark Dilution Act of 1995

See dilution.

federal trademark registration

Federal registration of a mark entails all of the following:

- The mark must be used in commerce (used across state, national, or territorial lines or used in a way that affects interstate, interterritorial, or international commerce).
- A registration application, a Statement of Use, or an Application Alleging Use (if an intent-to-use application was previously filed) must be filed with the USPTO.
- If the mark qualifies for the Principal Register, it will be published online in the *Official Gazette* by the USPTO.
- If another party claims ownership of the mark in a pending application, the USPTO may declare that an interference exists and schedule a hearing. Similarly, an interested party may file an opposition to the registration after publication in the *Official Gazette*, and the owner might have to refute or reply to the opposition.
- If there is no interference or opposition, the USPTO will issue a certificate of registration on either the Principal Register or the Supplemental Register.

Once a mark is registered, the trademark registration symbol "(®)" or "Reg. U.S. Pat. Off." should always appear next to the mark whenever it is used. Without this designation, it can be harder to collect damages if a federal court lawsuit is filed over an infringement of the mark.

Applications for federal trademark registration may be made electronically at the USPTO website (www.uspto.gov).

To qualify for federal registration, a mark:

- must not infringe another mark that is already registered, and
- cannot include certain types of pictures, words, and symbols—the U.S. flag; other federal and local governmental insignias; names of living persons without their consent; names or likenesses of dead U.S. presidents without their widows' consent; words or symbols that disparage living or dead persons, institutions, beliefs, or national symbols; deceptive geographical names; or marks that are judged immoral, deceptive, or scandalous. (However, although they're still part of the Lanham Act, the standards of disparagement and scandalousness have been declared unconstitutional by the U.S. Supreme Court.)

Trademark Law: Definitions

A trademark can be registered at the USPTO on one of two lists of registered trademarks and service marks:

- the Principal Register, or
- the Supplemental Register.

The Principal Register is reserved for distinctive marks and marks that have become distinctive through acquiring secondary meaning. There are many benefits to having a mark on the Principal Register rather than the Supplemental Register. Chief among these are:

- Potential competitors will be assumed to know that the marks are off limits.
- The mark can achieve incontestability status if it remains on the Principal Register for five years.

The Supplemental Register is for marks that are not yet distinctive and do not merit the same protection as Principal Register marks. However, registration on the Supplemental Register allows placement of the trademark registration symbol (®) on the mark, which is likely to scare away most potential copiers.

The Lanham Act: § 1051. (§ 1) Application for registration; verification

(a) Application for use of trademark

    (1) The owner of a trademark used in commerce may request registration of its trademark on the principal register hereby established by paying the prescribed fee and filing in the Patent and Trademark Office an application and a verified statement, in such form as may be prescribed by the Director, and such number of specimens or facsimiles of the mark as used as may be required by the Director.

    (2) The application shall include specification of the applicant's domicile and citizenship, the date of the applicant's first use of the mark, the date of the applicant's first use of the mark in commerce, the goods in connection with which the mark is used, and a drawing of the mark.

    (3) The statement shall be verified by the applicant and specify that—

        (A) the person making the verification believes that he or she, or the juristic person in whose behalf he or she makes the verification, to be the owner of the mark sought to be registered;

        (B) to the best of the verifier's knowledge and belief, the facts recited in the application are accurate;

        (C) the mark is in use in commerce; and

        (D) to the best of the verifier's knowledge and belief, no other person has the right to use such mark in commerce either in the identical form thereof or in such near resemblance thereto as to be likely, when used on or in connection with the goods of such other person, to cause confusion, or to cause mistake, or to deceive, except that, in the case of every application claiming concurrent use, the applicant shall—

  (i) state exceptions to the claim of exclusive use; and

  (ii) shall specify, to the extent of the verifier's knowledge—

     (I) any concurrent use by others;

     (II) the goods on or in connection with which and the areas in which each concurrent use exists;

     (III) the periods of each use; and

     (IV) the goods and area for which the applicant desires registration.

(4) The applicant shall comply with such rules or regulations as may be prescribed by the Director. The Director shall promulgate rules prescribing the requirements for the application and for obtaining a filing date herein.

The Lanham Act: § 1052. (§ 2) Trademarks registrable on principal register; concurrent registration

No trademark by which the goods of the applicant may be distinguished from the goods of others shall be refused registration on the principal register on account of its nature unless it—

(a) Consists of or comprises immoral, deceptive, or scandalous matter; or matter which may disparage or falsely suggest a connection with persons, living or dead, institutions, beliefs, or national symbols, or bring them into contempt, or disrepute; or a geographical indication which, when used on or in connection with wines or spirits, identifies a place other than the origin of the goods and is first used on or in connection with wines or spirits by the applicant on or after one year after the date on which the WTO Agreement (as defined in section 3501 (9) of title 19) enters into force with respect to the United States.

(b) Consists of or comprises the flag or coat of arms or other insignia of the United States, or of any State or municipality, or of any foreign nation, or any simulation thereof.

(c) Consists of or comprises a name, portrait, or signature identifying a particular living individual except by his written consent, or the name, signature, or portrait of a deceased President of the United States during the life of his widow, if any, except by the written consent of the widow.

(d) Consists of or comprises a mark which so resembles a mark registered in the Patent and Trademark Office, or a mark or trade name previously used in the United States by another and not abandoned, as to be likely, when used on or in connection with the goods of the applicant, to cause confusion, or to cause mistake, or to deceive: provided, that if the Director determines that confusion, mistake, or deception is not likely to result from the continued use by more than one person of the same or similar marks under conditions and limitations as to the mode or place of use of the marks or the goods on or in connection with which such marks are used, concurrent registrations may be issued to such persons when they have become entitled to use such marks as a result of their concurrent lawful use in commerce prior to

(1) the earliest of the filing dates of the applications pending or of any registration issued under this chapter;

(2) July 5, 1947, in the case of registrations previously issued under the Act of March 3, 1881, or February 20, 1905, and continuing in full force and effect on that date; or

(3) July 5, 1947, in the case of applications filed under the Act of February 20, 1905, and registered after July 5, 1947. Use prior to the filing date of any pending application or a registration shall not be required when the owner of such application or registration consents to the grant of a concurrent registration to the applicant. Concurrent registrations may also be issued by the Director when a court of competent jurisdiction has finally determined that more than one person is entitled to use the same or similar marks in commerce. In issuing concurrent registrations, the Director shall prescribe conditions and limitations as to the mode or place of use of the mark or the goods on or in connection with which such mark is registered to the respective persons.

(e) Consists of a mark which

(1) when used on or in connection with the goods of the applicant is merely descriptive or deceptively misdescriptive of them,

(2) when used on or in connection with the goods of the applicant is primarily geographically descriptive of them, except as indications of regional origin may be registrable under section 1054 of this title,

(3) when used on or in connection with the goods of the applicant is primarily geographically deceptively misdescriptive of them,

(4) is primarily merely a surname, or

(5) comprises any matter that, as a whole, is functional.

(f) Except as expressly excluded in subsections (a), (b), (c), (d), (e)(3), and (e)(5) of this section, nothing in this chapter shall prevent the registration of a mark used by the applicant which has become distinctive of the applicant's goods in commerce. The Director may accept as prima facie evidence that the mark has become distinctive, as used on or in connection with the applicant's goods in commerce, proof of substantially exclusive and continuous use thereof as a mark by the applicant in commerce for the five years before the date on which the claim of distinctiveness is made. Nothing in this section shall prevent the registration of a mark which, when used on or in connection with the goods of the applicant, is primarily geographically deceptively misdescriptive of them, and which became distinctive of the applicant's goods in commerce before December 8, 1993.

A mark which when used would cause dilution under section 1125 (c) of this title may be refused registration only pursuant to a proceeding brought under section 1063 of this title. A registration for a mark which when used would cause dilution under section 1125 (c) of this title may be canceled pursuant to a proceeding brought under either section 1064 of this title or section 1092 of this title.

The Lanham Act: § 1063. (§ 13) Opposition to registration

This statute sets out the procedure to be followed if a person or organization believes that a mark published for comment should not be registered.

(a) Any person who believes that he would be damaged by the registration of a mark upon the principal register, including as a result of dilution under section 1125 (c) of this title, may, upon payment of the prescribed fee, file an opposition in the Patent and Trademark Office, stating the grounds therefor, within thirty days after the publication under subsection (a) of section 1062 of this title of the mark sought to be registered. Upon written request prior to the expiration of the thirty-day period, the time for filing opposition shall be extended for an additional thirty days, and further extensions of time for filing opposition may be granted by the Director for good cause when requested prior to the expiration of an extension. The Director shall notify the applicant of each extension of the time for filing opposition. An opposition may be amended under such conditions as may be prescribed by the Director.

(b) Unless registration is successfully opposed—

(1) a mark entitled to registration on the principal register based on an application filed under section 1051 (a) of this title or pursuant to section 1126 of this title shall be registered in the Patent and Trademark Office, a certificate of registration shall be issued, and notice of the registration shall be published in the *Official Gazette* of the Patent and Trademark Office; or

(2) a notice of allowance shall be issued to the applicant if the applicant applied for registration under section 1051 (b) of this title.

Related terms: constructive notice of mark under Lanham Act; Lanham Act; Principal Register; Supplemental Register; trademark search.

filtering

Filtering is the process by which an individual can skip or mute over objectionable content in audio or video content of motion pictures. The technology was created to allow parents the ability to bypass content such as graphic violence, sex, nudity, and profanity during DVD playback. In September 2002, several Hollywood movie studios and directors sued the manufacturer of the process, claiming that the process violated trademark and copyright law. However, in 2005, the lawsuit was preempted when President Bush signed into effect the Family Entertainment and Copyright Act of 2005, which includes a provision, the Family Movie Act of 2005, creating an exemption from copyright or trademark infringement for anyone who uses this technology for home viewing.

See also Part 2 (Copyright): Family Entertainment and Copyright Act of 2005.

first-to-file countries

See prior registration countries.

first to register

See ownership of mark in the United States.

first to use mark in United States

See ownership of mark in the United States.

flags as marks

See prohibited and reserved marks under Lanham Act.

foreign language equivalent terms

See phonetic or foreign language equivalents for marks.

foreign nationals registering in United States

A citizen, permanent resident, or business of another country is entitled to federally register a mark in the United States if the other country affords reciprocal trademark rights to U.S. citizens and if the mark meets U.S. requirements for registration.

Registration of a mark by a foreign national in the United States may be accomplished if any of the following are true:

- The mark has been placed in use in interstate, interterritorial, or international commerce in the United States.
- The mark has been registered within the last six months in another country with which the United States has a reciprocal treaty.
- The mark has been the subject of an intent-to-use application filed in the United States.

If the basis for registration in the United States is a previous registration in another country, the date of filing in the other country establishes the filing date in the United States as well.

As of August 3, 2019, applicants, registrants, or parties to a trademark proceeding whose domicile is not located within the United States or its territories must be represented by a U.S. attorney. Foreign attorneys or agents can no longer seek reciprocal recognition to practice before the USPTO.

Related terms: Inter-American Convention for Trademark and Commercial Protection; international trademark rights; Paris Convention.

franchising, service marks

Over 750,000 businesses in the U.S. are franchises—privately owned businesses adhering to a corporate business model and built around principles of licensing and service marks. Examples of successful franchises are Subway, McDonald's, 7-Eleven, H&R Block, and Dunkin' Donuts. Among other fees, franchise owners (franchisees) pay a royalty for the use of the franchiser's marks. In return, the franchiser has an obligation to monitor the franchisee's use of the trademark (and its accompanying services) so that they adhere to standards of quality and consistency. For more on these standards, see the entry regarding "naked licenses."

fraud at the trademark office (fraud on the USPTO)

Statements made as part of a trademark application are made under oath, and fraudulent statements can result in the loss of trademark rights. For example, in one year, the USPTO canceled three trademark registrations after receiving evidence from a competitor that the trademark owner had made fraudulent statements regarding the dates of first use in commerce. (*Standard Knitting, Ltd. v. Toyota Jidosha Kabushiki Kaisha*, 77 U.S.P.Q.2d 1917 (T.T.A.B. 2006).) Note: not every false statement made on a trademark application amounts to fraud. For example, a misstatement regarding whether commerce was intrastate, or interstate did not amount to a fraudulent statement. (*Maids to Order of Ohio, Inc. v. Maid-to-Order, Inc.*, 78 U.S.P.Q.2d 1899 (T.T.A.B. 2006).)

The standard for judging fraud on a USPTO trademark filing was clarified in 2009 when the Court of Appeals for the Federal Circuit (CAFC) terminated its "should have known" standard for judging fraud—that is, the applicant should have known the statement was fraudulent. Henceforth, proving fraud on the USPTO required proving intent. (*In re Bose Corp.*, 580 F.3d 1240 (Fed. Cir. 2009).) Subsequent cases have followed this precedent—for example, when an applicant incorrectly listed "transmission of oil" as one of its services, the Trademark Trial and Appeal Board (TTAB) held that absent proof of "deceptive intent," there was no fraud. (*Enbridge, Inc. v. Excelerate Energy Limited Partnership*, 92 U.S.P.Q.2d 1537 (T.T.A.B. 2009).) And in *Asian and Western Classics B.V. v. Lynne Selkow*, 92 U.S.P.Q.2d 1478 (T.T.A.B. 2009), the TTAB stated that a pleading of fraud must include "an allegation of intent."

free speech and trademark law

Free speech laws permit the use of another company's trademark for purposes of commentary or criticism. For example, the owner of a newsletter can write an article critical of Microsoft and use the Microsoft logo. Two factors may convert such commentary and criticism into a lawsuit based on trademark infringement or dilution: The newsletter is offering goods and services as part of its criticism, or the newsletter is likely to confuse readers as to whether Microsoft is a sponsor of the newsletter. In addition, if the newsletter is making false statements regarding Microsoft, this might trigger additional claims including product disparagement, false advertising, and trade libel.

However, if it is clear that the use does not confuse consumers and is not being used deceptively, courts will permit use of trademarks for purposes of commentary.

> EXAMPLE: A disgruntled former customer of the Bally Health Club created a website featuring the company's logo over which appeared the word "sucks" and included a statement that the site was "Unauthorized." A court permitted this use because the site had distinguished itself from the legitimate Bally site by prominent use of disclaimers and the site was not offering competing goods or services. (*Bally Total Fitness Holding Corp. v. Faber*, 29 F. Supp.2d 1161 (C.D. Cal. 1998).)

The *Bally* case triggered widespread registration of "sucks" domain names (despite the fact that the defendant had not registered ballysucks.com) and opened up a world of "cybergriping" in which angry consumers maintained websites whose sole purpose is to complain about company practices or products. Disgruntled consumers of other companies registered domain names such as nikesucks.com, toysrussucks.com, walmartsucks.com, and cadillacsucks.com. In some cases, companies have successfully stopped the use of these "sucks" domain names either because they were determined to be in violation of the law or because the domain name owner refused to respond to the legal action. Keep in mind when using trademarks under free speech principles: Even though there is a right of free speech, this doesn't prevent a trademark owner from filing a lawsuit. The economics of litigation often silence company critics despite their free speech rights.

In 2003, free speech rights triumphed over trademark rights when the first cybergriping case reached a federal Court of Appeals. (*The Taubman Co. v. Webfeats*, 319 F.3d 770 (6th Cir. 2003).) In *Taubman*, a Web designer created a site in support of a nearby shopping center. The site also contained a link to the designer's girlfriend's T-shirt business. The owners of the shopping center complained of the site, even though it contained a conspicuous disclaimer indicating that the site was not affiliated with the center. Alas, the previously supportive designer became angry and registered several "sucks" domain names related to the shopping center, the company owning the center, and the lawyers for the center. The owners sued for trademark infringement. The designer discontinued the link to his girlfriend's business—thereby rendering his cybergriping sites as noncommercial—and prevailed in the subsequent litigation. The court in *Taubman* pointed out that the qualifying moniker "sucks" removes any confusion as to the source of the goods or services. Keep in mind that the rule enunciated in *Taubman* is unlikely to apply in cases in which the cybergriping site has a commercial purpose—that is, offers services or products for sale or provides advertising.

Free speech also triumphed in a 2012 case when the Eleventh Circuit permitted the use of the University of Alabama trademarks in paintings depicting the football team. (*University of Alabama Board of Trustees v. New Life Art Inc.*, 683 F.3d 1266 (11th Cir. 2012).)

In E.S.S. Entertainment 2000, Inc. v. Rock Star Videos, Inc., 547 F.3d 1095 (9th Cir. 2008), the Ninth Circuit permitted a parody under First Amendment principles noting that artistic use of a mark is permitted when (1) the use has artistic relevance to the work at issue (the video game), and (2) it doesn't explicitly mislead consumers as to the source of the mark or the work—a test adopted by the Ninth Circuit in *Mattel v. Walking Mountain*. In *E.S.S. Entertainment*, the video game "Grand Theft Auto: San Andreas" included a parody of the East Los Angeles strip club, "The Play Pen," (referred to as the "Pig Pen" in the game).

In addition to these rights, trademark law permits the use of trademarks for comparative advertising and for descriptive purposes.

The Supreme Court unanimously held that the "disparagement" provision of the Lanham Act violated the First Amendment's free speech clause. The USPTO had denied an Asian-American band's registration for SLANTS on the basis that the term was disparaging to persons of Asian descent. Acknowledging that speech that demeans on the basis of race is hateful, Justice Alito wrote that "the proudest boast of our free speech jurisprudence is that we protect the freedom to express 'the thought that we hate.'" (*Matal v. Tam*, 582 U.S. (2017).) Soon after striking down the Lanham Act restriction on registering "disparaging" marks, the Supreme Court—in a case involving "FUCT" for clothing—struck down as unconstitutional the prohibition against registering immoral and scandalous trademarks. (*Iancu v. Brunetti*, 139 S.Ct. 2294 (2019).)

Related terms: fair use of trademarks; parodies of trademarks.

generic terms

Words or symbols commonly used to describe an entire type of product or service rather than to distinguish one product or service from another are known as generic. Generic terms never receive protection because such terms cannot fulfill the function of a mark, which is to distinguish specific goods or services from competing ones. Therefore, they belong in the public domain rather than to an exclusive owner.

> EXAMPLE: "Raisin bran" is a generic phrase that describes a kind of cereal; it defines the product itself rather than its source. Several different cereal manufacturers produce raisin bran, each of which is identified by its own mark—for instance, Post Raisin Bran, Kellogg's Raisin Bran, Skinner's Raisin Bran. While each of these manufacturer's marks is entitled to protection, the words "raisin bran" are not.

Combining a generic term with other terms may sometimes result in a protectable composite mark. However, often, the generic term must be disclaimed before the USPTO will grant trademark registration for the composite mark. Combining a generic term with a top level domain such as ".com" can also result in a protectable composite mark. In 2020, the Supreme Court struck down the rule that 'generic.com' terms are incapable of identifying a source. The Supreme Court concluded in this case that, "Because 'Booking.com' is not a generic name to consumers, it is not generic." (*USPTO v. Booking.com B.V.*, 140 S. Ct. 2298 (2020).)

Some protectable marks may lose their protection by becoming generic. "Genericide" occurs when a mark is used widely and indiscriminately to refer to a type of product or service, rather than the service or product of one company. For example, "escalator" was originally a protected trademark used to designate the moving stairs manufactured by a specific company. Eventually, the word became synonymous with the very idea of moving stairs and thus lost its protection. Other examples of marks that have become generic are lite beer, soft soap, and cola.

Most companies don't have to worry about this issue, since few products or services are successful enough to produce a generic mark. The common strategy for companies facing a potential genericide is to make an effort advising the media and the public that the mark should not be used as a noun or a verb. That said, even if a majority of the public uses the trademark as a verb, that by itself does not trigger genericide, as Google demonstrated in a 2017 case. What matters, according to the Ninth Circuit, is whether the primary significance of the word "google" to the relevant public was as a mark identifying the Google search engine in particular. (*Elliott v. Google*, Inc., 860 F.3d 1151 (9th Cir. 2017).)

For ten years, Royal Crown had opposed Coca-Cola's ZERO trademark. The TTAB held that the ZERO mark was descriptive, not generic, but the Federal Circuit ruled that the TTAB failed to consider whether the term is generic when applied to a specific genus of "soft drinks, sports drinks, and energy drinks." If the term ZERO is understood "to refer to a key aspect of that genus" then it is generic. (*Royal Crown Dr. Pepper, and Seven Up v. Coca Cola*, 2016-2375 (Fed. Cir. 2018).)

Related terms: brandverbing; loss of mark; unfair competition.

geographic terms as marks

Geographic terms (sometimes referred to as geographic designations) are naturals for trademarks because they either identify regional origin (San Francisco Sourdough bread) or conjure up a quality (the image of Prudential's Rock of Gibraltar). Geographic terms can indicate a specific location such as a street (Park Avenue), river (Rio Grande), city (Hollywood), state (Wisconsin), or mountain (Everest), or even a nickname such as Quaker State for Pennsylvania. The manner in which a geographic term is used and the type of mark—for example, trademark, certification mark, and so on—affects protection. Geographic terms are generally categorized as follows:

Descriptive. A geographic term that describes the origin, location, or source of the product or service (for example, First National Bank of Omaha for a bank located in Omaha, Nebraska) is usually considered to be weak and is not protectable unless there is a demonstration of secondary meaning. The reason for this rule is that consumers cannot differentiate the Bank of Omaha from other banks in Omaha (or New York Life from other life insurance companies in New York) without some advertising or marketing effort.

Arbitrary or suggestive. A geographic term that is used arbitrarily (for example, Atlantic for a magazine) or suggestively to conjure up a regional feeling (for example, Arizona for an iced tea drink) is considered to be strong.

Misdescriptive. When a geographic term misleads consumers into believing that the product originates from a region when it does not, it is not protectable as a trademark—for example, Danish Maid Cultured Products is geographically misdescriptive because the cultured products were not from Denmark.

Many companies use "America" or "American" as a geographic term in their trademarks (for example, American Flyer for wagons and American Express for financial services). Most uses of "America" are weak (geographically descriptive), such as Bank of America or American Diabetes Association, because the terms primarily connote American origin. Some uses, however, are strong (arbitrary or suggestive), such as American Girl for shoes, because the use of America is not primarily to connote origin. In those cases, no proof of secondary meaning is required. Some uses are geographically misdescriptive and protection is denied (that is, "barred"). For example, American Beauty for a sewing machine was barred because the sewing machine was made in Japan.

In the mid-1990s, international makers of wines and spirits successfully lobbied the United States for a special amendment to the Lanham Act that prohibited registration of geographic marks that are inaccurate as to the source of the wine. Although the amendment reiterated the existing rules regarding geographically misdescriptive marks, above, it also reassured foreign winemakers that terms such as Champagne could refer only to a bubbly wine from the Champagne region of France.

Terms that are not primarily geographical in nature (do not refer to defined locations) may be used and protected as marks if they are distinctive in the context of their use or gain a secondary meaning through extended exposure in the marketplace—for example, Southern Comfort (whiskey), Metropolitan (life insurance), and Globe (realty).

Geographical terms are also acceptable in certification marks, and the owners of such marks are entitled to full protection under the Lanham Act.

Related terms: disclaimer of unregistrable material; prohibited and reserved marks under Lanham Act; secondary meaning.

geographically separate market

When goods or services coming from different sources are sold geographically far enough away from each other to preclude consumers from getting confused, they are said to be in geographically separate markets. In general, using the same or similar marks in geographically separate markets does not constitute infringement.

Related terms: constructive notice of mark under Lanham Act; infringement (trademark); ownership of mark in the United States.

goodwill

Goodwill refers to the tendency or likelihood of a consumer to repurchase goods or services based upon the name or source. In a sense, it is name recognition, or at least a recognition of buying habits—for example, consumers who are loyal to one brand of cola. A trademark is considered to be inseparable from its goodwill. When a trademark is infringed, the infringer gets a free unauthorized ride on another company's goodwill. Any assignment of trademark rights must include a transfer of the goodwill associated with the mark.

Related terms: assignment of mark.

gray market goods

U.S. trademark owners often authorize the manufacture and sale of their goods for non-U.S. markets. For example, a cigarette maker may authorize production and sale of its brand in Germany. Usually, the arrangement prohibits the export of those cigarettes to the United States (or other territories). When these goods are imported into the United States without the consent of the trademark owner, they are referred to as gray market goods (sometimes known as parallel imports). One problem for the trademark owner who files a trademark suit over gray market goods is that these goods are not counterfeit or infringing, since they were produced under the direction of the trademark owner. U.S. trademark owners have two major remedies to prevent the importation and sale of gray market goods: Section 42 of the Lanham Act (15 U.S. Code § 1124), blocking sale and import of gray market goods; and Section 526 of the Tariff Act (19 U.S. Code § 1526), prohibiting importation of gray market goods and permitting their seizure.

When ruling on issues about gray market importation, most courts follow the logic used by the First Circuit in *Societe des Produits Nestle v. Casa Helvetia*, 982 F.2d 633, 635 (1st Cir. 1992). The Court of Appeals deflected an analysis of likelihood of confusion, and instead supported a chocolate maker's ability to stop importation of gray market chocolate—nearly identical as a consumer product—based on a trademark owner's right to market "segmentation" and ability to "ensure territorial exclusivity."

hybrid mark

See composite mark.

ICANN

The Internet Corporation for Assigned Names and Numbers (ICANN) is the agency that oversees domain name registration and dispute resolution procedures (www.icann.org).

Related terms: cybersquatting; domain names; UDRP.

immoral marks

See prohibited and reserved marks under Lanham Act.

incontestability status

When a mark has been in continuous use for five years after being placed on the Principal Register, it may be classified as incontestable, or immune from legal challenge. (37 U.S. Code § 1065.) Because of the fact that incontestability can be challenged on several grounds, the term "incontestable" really means "somewhat difficult to contest" (as explained in more detail below).

A trademark owner seeking to make its mark incontestable must be able to demonstrate all of the following:

- No final legal decision has issued against the mark.
- No challenge to the mark is pending.
- A Sections 8 and 15 Declaration describing the mark's use was filed on a timely basis.
- The mark is not and has not become generic.

In essence, achieving "incontestability status" conclusively establishes ownership of the mark for the uses specified in the Sections 8 and 15 Declaration that is filed between the fifth and sixth year after the mark is placed on the Principal Register.

The issue of whether a mark is incontestable usually arises in a lawsuit for infringement where the party being sued attempts to defend by challenging the validity of the plaintiff's mark. If the plaintiff can establish that the mark is incontestable, the mark will be presumed valid unless the defendant can establish one or more of the following:

- The registration or the incontestable right to use the mark was obtained by fraud.
- The registrant has abandoned the mark.
- The mark is used to misrepresent the source of its goods or services (for instance, use of the mark involves palming off).
- The infringing mark is an individual's name used in his or her own business, or is otherwise prohibited or reserved under the Lanham Act.
- The infringing mark was used in commerce first—before the incontestable mark's registration.
- The infringing mark was registered first.
- The mark is being used to violate the antitrust laws of the United States.

Even though an incontestable mark can still be challenged on these grounds, it is safe from attack on the otherwise common ground that it lacks distinctiveness. Thus, when Park 'N Fly, Inc., sued Dollar Park and Fly, Inc., for trademark infringement, the U.S. Supreme Court ruled that because the Park 'N Fly mark had obtained incontestability status, Dollar Park and Fly, Inc., could not allege as a defense that its rival's mark is actually descriptive. (*Park 'N Fly v. Dollar Park and Fly*, 469 U.S. 189 (1985).)

The Lanham Act: § 1065. (§ 15) Incontestability of right to use mark under certain conditions

This statute defines the reasons that may be used to attack the validity of a mark that has been in continuous use for at least five years after its registration. Unless one of these reasons is present, the statute provides that the mark shall be considered incontestable.

Except on a ground for which application to cancel may be filed at any time under paragraphs (3) and (5) of section 1064 of this title, and except to the extent, if any, to which the use of a mark registered on the principal register infringes a valid right acquired under the law of any State or Territory by use of a mark or trade name continuing from a date prior to the date of registration under this chapter of such registered mark, the right of the registrant to use such registered mark in commerce for the goods or services on or in connection with which such registered mark has been in continuous use for five consecutive years subsequent to the date of such registration and is still in use in commerce, shall be incontestable: provided, that—

(1) there has been no final decision adverse to registrant's claim of ownership of such mark for such goods or services, or to registrant's right to register the same or to keep the same on the register; and

(2) there is no proceeding involving said rights pending in the Patent and Trademark Office or in a court and not finally disposed of; and

(3) an affidavit is filed with the Director within one year after the expiration of any such five-year period setting forth those goods or services stated in the registration on or in connection with which such mark has been in continuous use for such five consecutive years and is still in use in commerce, and other matters specified in paragraphs (1) and (2) of this section; and

(4) no incontestable right shall be acquired in a mark which is the generic name for the goods or services or a portion thereof, for which it is registered.

Subject to the conditions above specified in this section, the incontestable right with reference to a mark registered under this chapter shall apply to a mark registered under the Act of March 3, 1881, or the Act of February 20, 1905, upon the filing of the required affidavit with the Director within one year after the expiration of any period of five consecutive years after the date of publication of a mark under the provisions of subsection (c) of section 1062 of this title.

The Director shall notify any registrant who files the above-prescribed affidavit of the filing thereof.

Related terms: federal trademark registration; infringement (trademark); loss of mark.

infringement (trademark)

Trademark infringement is the unauthorized use of a trademark or service mark (or a substantially similar mark) on competing or related goods and services. The success of a lawsuit to stop the infringement turns on whether the defendant's use causes a likelihood of confusion in the average consumer.

When infringement occurs, a trademark owner (the plaintiff) may file a lawsuit against the infringing user of the same or similar mark (the defendant) to prevent further use of the mark and collect money damages for the wrongful use. An infringement action may be brought in state court or in federal court if the mark in question is protected under the Lanham Act, which applies to both registered and unregistered marks that are used in commerce that Congress may regulate.

The success of an infringement lawsuit normally turns on whether the defendant's use causes a likelihood of confusion and so weakens the value of the plaintiff's mark. A mark need not be identical to one already in use to infringe upon the owner's rights. If the proposed mark is similar enough to the earlier mark to risk confusing the average consumer, its use may constitute infringement if the services or goods on which the two marks are used are related to each other—that is, they share the same market. For more on the standards of confusion see the entry, likelihood of confusion.

The extent of damages awarded in an infringement action will usually depend on whether the infringement was willful and on the actual amount of harm that the plaintiff can prove.

Related terms: constructive notice of mark under Lanham Act; incontestability status; injunctions against infringement and unfair competition; laches (and trademark law); likelihood of confusion; opposing and canceling a trademark registration; trade dress; unfair competition.

ingredient, use of a trademarked product as an

Unless it's authorized, a company should not give undue prominence to an ingredient's trademark. For example, if a candy contains Grand Marnier liquor, advertisements should not lead a consumer to believe that the candy is a product of (or endorsed by) the Grand Marnier company. A prominently placed explanatory disclaimer can also help reduce consumer confusion.

Related terms: disclaimer of trademark use.

initial interest confusion

In a 1999 case, Internet surfers were temporarily misled by the use of metatags containing the term "movie buff." When they typed the term into a search engine, they received results that favored a rival video business rather than the trademark owner. Although consumers were not prevented from locating the desired search result, a judge ruled that this momentary search engine confusion—referred to as initial interest confusion—was enough to sustain a claim for trademark infringement. (*Brookfield Communications v. West Coast Entertainment*, 174 F.3d 1036 (9th Cir. 1999).) Many commentators have criticized the standard, claiming that Internet users are sophisticated enough to sort through these momentary search engine diversions. Those arguments, as well as the dwindling importance of metatags, and a 2011 Ninth Circuit ruling that seriously constrained the rule (*Network Automation, Inc. v. Advanced System Concepts, Inc.*, 2011 WL 815806 (9th Cir. March 8, 2011), were all believed to have signaled a death knell for the initial interest confusion principle. But then in 2015, to the amazement of trademark attorneys, the doctrine reappeared when the Ninth Circuit ruled against Amazon.com in *Multi Time Machine, Inc. v. Amazon*, No. 13-55575 (9th Cir. 2015). In that case, an Amazon consumer searching for watches by the trademark owner was also shown watches by competitors. Perhaps regretting its decision, in October 2015 the three-judge panel reversed its ruling without directly striking down the initial interest concept.

Related terms: free speech and trademark law; keyword; metatags.

initials as trademark

Initials can function as a trademark and can be registered on the Principal Register, provided they meet the traditional trademark standards—the initials serve as a distinguishable indicator for the goods or services. One issue that often arises is whether the initials are signifiers for a generic term. For example, it is unlikely that someone selling wire fabric can register the initials WWF because within the trade, these are the commonly used initials for welded wire fabric. However, WWF can function as a registered trademark for the World Wildlife Fund.

Some other issues to consider in regard to initials:

- **Initials of government agencies.** 15 U.S. Code Section 1052 (b) bars the registration on either the Principal Register or the Supplemental Register of marks that consist of insignia of the United States or any simulation of such symbols. However, TMEP Section 1204.02(d) states that initials, words, or letters that merely identify people and things associated with a particular agency or department of the U.S. government, instead of representing the authority of the government or the nation as a whole, are generally not considered to be "insignia of the United States" within the meaning of Section 1052(b). In other words, you can register FDA, FAA, or CIA unless specifically prohibited by a federal law. For example, 18 U.S. Code Section 709 prohibits the use of F.B.I. (or any colorable imitation). Technically the application is not refused because of these statutes. Instead, if someone not authorized on the statute uses the mark, the application will be refused on the basis that the mark is not in lawful use in commerce. (TMEP § 1205.01.)

- **Initials and surnames.** If initials are used with a surname, for example, P.J. Fitzpatrick, it is often easier to obtain a registration for the surname because the trademark conveys the impression of a personal name (a name associated with a specific person) versus merely being a surname (for example, "Fitzpatrick") which is considered a weak or descriptive mark. Curiously, a single initial, for example, I. Lewis Cigar Mfg., may be considered merely a surname. (TMEP § 1211.01(b)(iii).)

injunctions against infringement and unfair competition

The winner in an infringement lawsuit can obtain an injunction: a court order that prevents further infringing activity or unfair competition. The state and federal laws of trademarks, service marks, and unfair competition authorize courts to require or prohibit any action or inaction necessary to protect the owner of a mark from economic harm.

Because lawsuits often take years to resolve, the courts have the power to issue interim injunctions. Promptly upon filing the case, the plaintiff might be able to obtain a temporary restraining order if the judge is convinced that irreparable injury is occurring. A few weeks later, the court will hold a formal hearing and, if it appears that the plaintiff is likely to prevail when the case is finally decided and irreparable harm will result if the injunction is not issued, the court will issue a preliminary injunction that will last until the case is over.

In 2020, Congress made it easier for some parties to obtain an injunction (and resolved a split among the court circuits) when it enacted the Trademark Modernization Act. The Act provides for a presumption of irreparable harm when a party demonstrates likelihood of confusion.

If, after a trial, a court finds that infringement or unfair competition has occurred, it will issue a permanent injunction ordering the defendant to stop using the infringing mark. In addition, the defendant may be required to destroy items or labels carrying the offending mark if necessary to prevent its further use. In some cases, especially if the defendant was an innocent infringer, the court might allow some continued use of the mark in a particular locality, but bar it in other parts of the country.

Trademark Law: Definitions

The courts have broad powers ("equity" powers) to fashion their injunctions to obtain justice under varying circumstances. If necessary, an injunction that addresses the parties in a case may be enforced against other parties as well.

Related terms: infringement (trademark); preliminary injunction.

injury to business reputation

See dilution.

innocent infringer

An infringer who didn't know that he or she was infringing a mark is termed an innocent infringer. When an infringer is considered innocent, the owner of the infringed mark will usually be able to prevent future infringements but will not be able to collect money damages or defendant's profits. In some cases, the owner might not even be able to prevent the innocent infringer from continuing to use the mark, at least in a limited geographical area that doesn't create the risk of consumer confusion.

For example, a district court held that a manufacturer that printed unauthorized copies of trademarks on packaging could not claim "innocent infringer" status even if the printing was done at the customer's request. The court indicated that a manufacturer should conduct a reasonable investigation when reproducing the ® symbol on packaging. (*Timber Prods. Inspection, Inc. v. Coastal Container Corp.*, 2011 U.S. Dist. Lexis 123224 (W.D. Mich. Oct. 25, 2011).)

If a mark has been federally registered on the Principal Register before an infringement of the mark begins, the infringer cannot claim innocence. This is because the registration provides notice that the mark is already owned by someone else, and the infringer could have discovered this fact by doing a trademark search. However, if registration occurs after the infringing activity begins, the infringer might still be able to claim innocence until actually learning of the registration.

Related terms: contributory infringer; infringement (trademark); injunctions against infringement and unfair competition; unfair competition.

intent-to-use application

The Lanham Act permits the owner of a mark that hasn't been used in commerce to reserve that mark for later registration. This is accomplished by filing an intent-to-use (ITU) application (sometimes referred to as a "1b application") with the U.S. Patent and Trademark Office (USPTO). The initial reservation is for six months from the date the USPTO approved the mark (which could be six months to a year after you file your application) and can be extended for up to five additional six-month periods for good cause. The date of the original ITU application serves as the priority date in case of conflict, regardless of when the use actually begins, as long as the applicant completes the registration process.

Actual registration will occur once the owner begins to use the mark in commerce and files an Allegation of Use for Intent-to-Use Application informing the USPTO of that fact. Without the timely filing of one of these forms, or a purchase of an extension, the ITU application will lapse. Filing an intent-to-use application requires more than a desire to use the mark; it requires actual evidence of the intent—for example, business, advertising, or marketing plans. (*Intel Corp. v. Emeny*, T.T.A.B. Opposition No. 91123312 (May 15, 2007).) An applicant that was unable to provide any documents or other evidence of an actual intent to use a mark cannot claim rights as an "intent-to-use" applicant. (*L.C. Licensing, Inc. v. Berman*, 86 U.S.P.Q.2d 1883 (T.T.A.B. 2008).) A foreign registrant who "has not had activities in the U.S. and has not made or employed a business plan, strategy, arrangements or methods there," and "has not identified channels of trade that will be used in the United States," does not have a bona fide intent to use the mark. (*Honda Motor Co., Ltd. v. Friedrich Winkelmann*, 90 U.S.P.Q.2d 1660 (T.T.A.B. 2009).)

The initial intent-to-use application costs the same as an actual use application, plus an additional $125 for each additional six-month extension if filing electronically and $100 to file the Statement of Use—when you finally start using it in commerce.

The Lanham Act: § 1051. (§ 1(b)) Application for registration; verification

(b) Application for bona fide intention to use trademark

(1) A person who has a bona fide intention, under circumstances showing the good faith of such person, to use a trademark in commerce may request registration of its trademark on the principal register hereby established by paying the prescribed fee and filing in the Patent and Trademark Office an application and a verified statement, in such form as may be prescribed by the Director.

(2) The application shall include specification of the applicant's domicile and citizenship, the goods in connection with which the applicant has a bona fide intention to use the mark, and a drawing of the mark.

(3) The statement shall be verified by the applicant and specify—

(A) that the person making the verification believes that he or she, or the juristic person in whose behalf he or she makes the verification, to be entitled to use the mark in commerce;

(B) the applicant's bona fide intention to use the mark in commerce;

(C) that, to the best of the verifier's knowledge and belief, the facts recited in the application are accurate; and

(D) that, to the best of the verifier's knowledge and belief, no other person has the right to use such mark in commerce either in the identical form thereof or in such near resemblance thereto as to be likely, when used on or in connection with the goods of such other person, to cause confusion, or to cause mistake, or to deceive.

Except for applications filed pursuant to section 44 [15 U.S.C. § 1126], no mark shall be registered until the applicant has met the requirements of subsections (c) and (d) of this section.

(4) The applicant shall comply with such rules or regulations as may be prescribed by the Director. The Director shall promulgate rules prescribing the requirements for the application and for obtaining a filing date herein.

Related terms: Allegation of Use for Intent-to-Use Application, With Declaration; Principal Register.

Inter-American Convention for Trademark and Commercial Protection

This treaty provides reciprocal trademark rights between the United States and a number of Latin American nations that are not signatories to the Paris Convention. These countries are Brazil, Colombia, Cuba, the Dominican Republic, Guatemala, Haiti, Honduras, Nicaragua, Panama, Paraguay, and Peru.

Related terms: international trademark rights; Paris Convention.

inter partes proceeding

This type of an administrative hearing is conducted by the Trademark Trial and Appeal Board to resolve:

- conflicts between pending applications (called interferences)
- the merits of opposition and cancellation petitions, and
- disputes over decisions of the Commissioner of Patents and Trademarks about applications for registration under the Lanham Act.

Related terms: interference; opposing and canceling a trademark registration.

interference

When two or more marks awaiting registration in the U.S. Patent and Trademark Office (USPTO) appear to overlap or conflict with each other, an "interference" is said to exist, and the applicants are informed of this fact. Any applicant may then request that the USPTO set up an interference hearing to decide who should be the registered owner. Interference hearings tend to be expensive, lengthy, and rare. Most often, applicants facing an interference will simply withdraw their application and devise a new mark, which is then made the subject of a new application.

When an interference hearing is held, the USPTO uses a set of rules developed by the courts over the years to decide which applicant is entitled to the registration. The rules are based on such variables as:

- who was first to use the mark anywhere
- who was first to use the mark in commerce
- who was first to file the registration application, and
- if the first filer is not also the first user, whether the first filer knew or should have known of the previous use.

Related terms: *inter partes* proceeding; ownership of mark in the United States.

International Convention for the Protection of Industrial Property of 1883
See Paris Convention.

International Schedule of Classes of Goods and Services
All marks that are federally registered are classified by the U.S. Patent and Trademark Office according to a master list called the *International Schedule of Classes of Goods and Services* (used by virtually all countries). Classification allows marks to be efficiently stored and retrieved according to the class assigned to such product or service.

Because a mark's meaning is inseparable from the product or service to which it is attached, all registered marks must be classified by the category of goods or services they identify. Because many marks naturally fall into two or more categories, simultaneous registration in different classes is permitted, with an extra fee for each extra class.

If a mark has been registered for use on one type of product or service, and the mark's owner wants to use it on a type of product or service that falls in a different class, the mark must be registered anew.

> EXAMPLE: Sweets Inc., a candy manufacturer, attaches the trademark "TummyYummy Candies" to its line of chocolate candies. Later on, Sweets decides to enter the fresh fruit juice market. If it wants to use the trademark "TummyYummy Fruit Juice," it should obtain a new registration, since fruit juice and candy are in different classes.

International Schedule of Classes of Goods and Services

Goods

1. Chemicals

2. Paints

3. Cosmetics and cleaning preparations

4. Lubricants and fuels

5. Pharmaceuticals

6. Metal goods

7. Machinery

8. Hand tools

9. Electrical and scientific apparatus

10. Medical apparatus

11. Environmental control apparatus

12. Vehicles

13. Firearms

14. Jewelry

15. Musical instruments

16. Paper goods and printed matter

17. Rubber goods

18. Leather goods

19. Nonmetallic building materials

20. Furniture and articles not otherwise classified

21. Housewares and glass

22. Cordage and fibers

23. Yarns and threads

24. Fabrics

25. Clothing

26. Fancy goods

27. Floor coverings

28. Toys and sporting goods

29. Meats and processed foods

30. Staple foods

31. Natural agricultural products

32. Light beverages

33. Wines and spirits

34. Smokers' articles

Services

35. Advertising and business

36. Insurance and financial

37. Building construction and repair

38. Telecommunications

39. Transportation and storage

40. Treatment of materials

41. Education and entertainment

42. Computer, scientific, and legal

43. Hotels and restaurants

44. Medical, beauty, and agricultural

45. Personal and legal

See the accompanying list of "short titles" as a means to quickly identify the general content of numbered international classes. The titles are not designed to be used for classification but only as information to assist in the identification of numbered classes. To determine the classification of particular goods and services, refer to the *Alphabetical List of Goods and Services* at the USPTO website.

Related terms: federal trademark registration; Lanham Act; trademark.

international trademark

There is no such thing as an international trademark. It is possible to file one application for a group of countries using a procedure known as the Madrid Protocol. The Madrid Protocol includes 98 countries. In addition, you can file one application and obtain protection in 28 European countries (known as a Community Trademark). Otherwise, you must seek protection on a country-by-country basis.

Related terms: Community Trademark; Madrid Protocol.

international trademark rights

Trademark rights in each country depend solely on the trademark laws of that country; there is no set of international laws. Mark owners must start anew to establish rights to a mark in every new country they enter for commercial purposes, a concept known as "territoriality." In other words, previous use or registration in other countries is generally irrelevant.

In the United States, first use often decides who owns a mark. Most other countries, however, award ownership to whoever is the first to register a mark (although use on the same or related goods usually must follow within a reasonable time). As a result, if the seller of wood patio furniture under the mark "Sueno" wants to expand to a first-to-register country, it will have to pick a new mark if "Sueno" is already registered in that country. This is true even if the U.S. seller was first to use the mark and even if the company that registered that mark in the other country does not currently make related goods. This "registration" system often allows people to anticipate international marketing trends and to register the rights to valuable marks before another company thinks to do so.

In an attempt to correct some of these conflicts, in 2003 the Madrid Protocol, an international treaty, went into effect, allowing U.S. trademark owners to file for registration in member countries by filing a single standardized English-language application at the U.S. Patent and Trademark Office (USPTO). The

Madrid Protocol provides a truly international centralized trademark application system. Information regarding rules and membership can be found at the WIPO's website (www.wipo.int/madrid). The Madrid Arrangement on International Registration of Trademarks and the Madrid Protocol, use an international bureau, the World Intellectual Property Organization (WIPO), as a central registration office for trademarks in use in the member countries.

The territoriality rule (discussed above) has an important exception: Countries that have established treaty rights among themselves, like the United States and Syria, might permit nationals of other treaty countries to establish their right to a mark based on prior use or registration in their own country alone. In the United States, the Lanham Act allows nationals of the Paris Convention countries to register their marks in the United States based on registration in their native country without alleging use here first (if they allege a bona fide intention to use the mark in the United States within a reasonable time).

Related terms: foreign nationals, registering in United States; Inter-American Convention for Trademark and Commercial Protection; Madrid Protocol; Paris Convention; phonetic or foreign language equivalents for marks; prior registration countries.

Internet domain names

See domain names.

keyword

Keywords (or adwords or keying) are terms (words or phrases) sold by search engines to advertisers. When an Internet searcher types the keyword into a search engine, an advertisement related to the keyword appears. For example, typing the keyword "patent" might trigger specific ads by Nolo for its patent products. Trademark issues sometimes arise when keywords are trademarks—for example a competitor of Nolo buys "nolo" as a keyword.

The primary issue, as with most trademark disputes, is whether consumers are confused. When consumer confusion is not found to have occurred (as has been the common inclination of courts), the practice is permitted. (*Gov't Employees Ins. Co. v. Google*, 330 F. Supp.2d 700 (E.D. Va. 2004).) In a 2004 case, a district court held that consumers were not confused by Google's sale of the keyword "Geico." (*GEICO v. Google*, 330 F. Supp.2d 700 (2004).) In 2009, Google changed its adword/keyword policy to permit the limited use of trademarks in advertising text in four situations: (1) the sponsor is a reseller of a genuine trademarked product; (2) the sponsor makes or sells component parts for a trademarked product; (3) the sponsor offers compatible parts or goods for use with the trademarked product; or (4) the sponsor provides information about or reviews a trademarked product. Sellers of unauthorized versions of Rosetta Stone language-learning software took advantage of this rule and used "Rosetta Stone" as a keyword/adword and also used the trademark in its ads, even though they were not authorized resellers. The Fourth Circuit held that there was a triable issue of fact as to whether use of the Rosetta Stone trademark in competing ads was confusing. The court also struck down Google's defense that Google's use of competing trademarks in a search engine comprised a "functional" (and therefore, excusable) use of a company's trademark. (*Rosetta Stone Ltd. v. Google, Inc.,* 676 F.3d 144 (4th Cir. 2012).)

In 2011, the Ninth Circuit stated that it was time for a different standard to be used in keyword advertising cases (ruling in a case in which a company purchased a competitor's trademark—ActiveBatch). Holding that confusion was unlikely, the Ninth Circuit indicated that Internet users have become sophisticated enough to understand the difference between search results and listings found under headings such as "Sponsored Links." The Ninth Circuit also held that similarity of the marks, and marketing channels used, were not appropriate factors in keyword advertising cases. (*Network Automation, Inc. v. Advanced Systems Concepts, Inc.,* 638 F.3d 1137 (9th Cir. 2011).)

When a competitor's sponsored link is triggered by its trademark and also includes the trademark within the sponsored ad—for example, a competitor of Gucci buys the Gucci keyword and includes Gucci in its ad—a court is likely to halt the sale. (*Romeo & Juliette Laser Hair Removal, Inc. v. Assara I LLC,* WL 750195 (S.D.N.Y. March 20, 2009).) The issue becomes even more complex when companies do business outside the United States. A French court ruled against the sale of trademarks as keywords in 2005.

Related terms: initial interest confusion; metatags; pop-up advertising.

laches (in trademark law)

Laches is the "unreasonable, prejudicial delay" in commencing a lawsuit. The Lanham Act, the federal trademark law, contains no statute of limitations, and expressly provides for defensive use of "equitable principles, including laches." The test for laches is twofold: First, was the plaintiff's delay in bringing suit unreasonable? Second, was the defendant prejudiced by the delay?

The laches period. The laches period begins on the date when a plaintiff in a trademark infringement lawsuit knows or should have known about the likelihood of confusion of the trademarks. It ends when the plaintiff files suit. Reasonable justifications for a delay include exhausting remedies through administrative processes, evaluating and preparing complicated claims, and determining whether the scope of proposed infringement will justify the cost of litigation. Delay is impermissible, on the other hand, when its purpose or effect is to capitalize on the value of the alleged infringer's labor by determining whether the infringing conduct will be profitable.

Analogous state statutes. In false advertising and trademark infringement lawsuits, most federal courts apply the comparable state statute of limitations. If the claim is filed after the analogous limitations period has expired, the presumption is that laches bars the lawsuit. For example, the comparable state statute of limitations for Lanham Act trademark claims in California is the four-year statute of limitations for trademark infringement actions. For false advertising (§ 43(a)) claims, the similar California statute of limitations is three years.

> **EXAMPLE:** A cosmetic company used the trademark LUSH. Pinkette, a clothing company, registered the trademark LUSH for clothing in 2010, putting the cosmetic company on constructive notice. Four years and eleven months after Pinkette's registration issued, the cosmetic company filed an action at the USPTO, and Pinkette filed a declaratory lawsuit based on the trademark infringement claim. The Ninth Circuit applied the analogous California statute of limitations for trademark infringement (four years), and on that basis, said the cosmetic company was barred by laches. (*Pinkette Clothing, Inc. v. Cosmetic Warriors Ltd.*, 894 F.3d 1015 (9th Cir. 2018).)

> **EXAMPLE:** Fitbit launched in 2008. Fitbug believed Fitbit infringed on its marks and sent a demand letter in 2011. Fitbug finally filed suit against Fitbit in 2013. The court found that Fitbug knew or should have known of Fitbit after its launch in 2008. The period of Fitbug's delay was five years. The district court held that laches barred the claim based on the analogous state statute of limitations. (*Fitbug v. Fitbit*, 78 F. Supp. 3d 1180 (N.D. Cal. 2015).)

Constructive notice: the "should have known" standard. The laches clock begins ticking once the trademark owner knew or should have known about the infringement. The "knew or should have known" standard allows a laches defense to be based on either actual or constructive knowledge. Constructive knowledge is judged from an objectively reasonable person standard, meaning a trademark owner is chargeable with the information it might have received had due inquiry been made. In short, constructive knowledge is tied to an obligation to proactively police the trademark. For example, constructive knowledge might be attributed to the registration of a trademark at the USPTO, the release date of a movie, or sharing an industry channel or business contacts. Arguing that the delay was caused by gradual encroachment, that is, claiming a trademark owner should not have known about an infringer until the infringer was competing directly or within their home territory, will usually not succeed.

Prejudicial delay. If the defendant can prove that it has continued to build a valuable business around its trademark during the time that the trademark owner delayed, then the defendant has experienced a prejudicial delay.

Related terms: infringement (trademark).

Lanham Act

The Lanham Act is the main federal statute that governs trademarks, service marks, and unfair competition. It covers such matters as: (1) when owners of marks may be entitled to federal judicial protection against infringement of a mark by others; (2) the types of remedies for infringement that the federal courts are authorized to provide, such as injunctive relief, money damages, and defendant's profits; (3) procedures for registering marks with the U.S. Patent and Trademark Office (on the Principal Register or Supplemental Register); (4) guidelines for when trademarks become incontestable; and (5) remedies for activity that constitutes unfair competition.

The degree of protection offered to a mark under the Lanham Act (the federal statute that addresses trademark protection) depends on many variables, such as:

- whether the mark is listed on the Principal Register or the Supplemental Register
- the length of time the registration has been in effect
- whether the registrant is the senior user or the junior user, and
- whether the infringer had either actual knowledge or constructive know-ledge of the registrant's mark.

Protection under the Lanham Act varies in scope and effectiveness. The owner of a registered mark can prevent others from later using a similar mark if such use would likely confuse the average reasonably prudent consumer as to the source of the product or service.

In addition, owners of such marks can prevent persons in other countries from using the same or a similar mark on their goods or services anywhere in the United States where consumer confusion is likely to result. On the other hand, the owner of a registered mark might have to accept another's use of the same or a similar mark in a specific marketing area where the mark has already been in use by the other party.

Although state and federal statutes and court decisions offer unregistered marks some local protection against mark infringement, this protection is greatly expanded if the mark is federally registered under the Lanham Act. For example, by federally registering a mark that's in use in two or three states, its owner may reserve the rest of the country for the trademark, except in places where the same or similar mark is already in use.

Some provisions of the Lanham Act are available to unregistered trademarks. For example, Section 43(a) of the Lanham Act protects against unfair competition. It makes liable anyone who causes another business to suffer damages as a result of the use of a false designation of origin; a false description; or a misleading mark, word, symbol, or name on any goods or services in commerce, in a way that is likely to cause confusion. This is the section most often used when a plaintiff claims that its trade name, unregistered mark, or trade dress has been misappropriated.

Related terms: commerce that Congress may regulate; unfair competition; unregistered mark, protection of; use of mark.

licensing of marks

The owner of a mark (licensor) grants a "license" when the owner authorizes another party (licensee) (usually in writing) to use the mark for commercial purposes. Such licenses should be very carefully drafted to provide control over the use of the mark, because the unfettered use of a mark by another party can harm the mark's value as a reliable identifier of a particular product or service. In an extreme case, allowing someone to use a mark without adequate restriction and supervision could result in the mark being considered abandoned (a "naked" license).

What happens to a licensee in bankruptcy? Congress amended the bankruptcy laws so that a bankrupt licensee could continue to use licensed intellectual property. One problem with the revision was that the definition of intellectual property in the bankruptcy law did not include trademarks. The issue was resolved when, in an 8–1 decision, the U.S. Supreme Court held that a bankrupt company's decision to reject an existing license of its trademarks does not terminate a licensee's right to continue using the licensed trademarks. Although bankruptcy permits debtors to reject most contracts and to eliminate their obligations, revoking a trademark license triggers a case-by-case inquiry to determine whether the licensee's rights would survive a breach. (*Mission Products Holdings Inc. v. Tempnology LLC*, ___ U.S. ___ (2019).)

Related terms: abandonment of mark; assignment of mark; naked license; ownership of mark in the United States.

likelihood of confusion

In order to stop trademark infringement, the senior user—the first business to adopt and use a particular mark in connection with its goods or services—must prove likelihood of confusion. When determining likelihood of confusion, courts and the Trademark Trial and Appeal Board (TTAB) use several factors derived from a 1961 case. (*Polaroid Corp. v. Polarad Elecs. Corp.*, 287 F.2d 492 (2d Cir. 1961).) These factors, sometimes known as the "*Polaroid* factors," can vary slightly as federal courts apply them throughout the country. The factors are intended as a guide, and not all factors seem particularly helpful in any given case.

- Strength of the senior user's mark. The stronger or more distinctive the senior user's mark, the more likely the confusion.
- Similarity of the marks. The more similarity between the two marks, the more likely the confusion.
- Similarity of the products or services. The more that the senior and junior user's goods or services are related, the more likely the confusion.
- Likelihood that the senior user will bridge the gap. If it is probable that the senior user will expand into the junior user's product area, it's more likely there will be confusion.
- The junior user's intent in adopting the mark. If the junior user adopted the mark in bad faith, confusion is more likely.
- Evidence of actual confusion. Proof of consumer confusion is not required, but when the trademark owner can show that the average reasonably prudent consumer is confused, it is powerful evidence of infringement.
- Sophistication of the buyers. The less sophisticated the purchaser, the more likely the confusion.
- Quality of the junior user's products or services. In some cases, the lesser the quality of the junior user's goods, the more harm is likely from consumer confusion.

The "likelihood of confusion" standard is applied by both the TTAB (when determining whether a mark should be registered) and by the courts in an infringement case. In a dispute over two soundalike trademarks, Sealtight and Sealtite, the Supreme Court ruled that a finding of likelihood of confusion by the Trademark Trial and Appeal Board (TTAB) could preclude litigating the same issue in court. (*B&B Hardware, Inc. v. Hargis Indus., Inc.*, 575 U.S. ___ (2015).)

When a trademark examiner considers whether an applied-for mark is likely to be confused with a registered mark, the Trademark Examiner's guide (TMEP Section 1207.01) advises that the two key considerations are:

- the similarity or dissimilarity of the marks in their entireties as to appearance, sound, connotation, and commercial impression, and
- the relatedness of the products, that is, the goods or services as described in the application and registration(s).

The TMEP also indicates that the following factors may be relevant in a likelihood-of-confusion determination and must be considered if there is pertinent evidence in the record:

- The similarity or dissimilarity of established, likely-to-continue trade channels.
- The conditions under which, and the buyers to whom sales are made, that is, "impulse" rather than careful, sophisticated purchases (TMEP § 1207.01(d)(vii)).
- The number and nature of similar marks in use on similar goods (TMEP § 1207.01(d)(iii)).
- The existence of a valid consent agreement between the applicant and the owner of the previously registered mark (TMEP § 1207.01(d)(viii)).

EXAMPLE: A company was refused registration for the mark "Terrain" for towable recreational vehicles, because the mark was likely to be confused with the identical registered trademark "Terrain" for trucks. The TTAB reversed the decision, noting the differences in the goods (trucks and RVs) and their channels of trade and the high degree of purchaser care. Businesses in these two industries "believe that their respective goods are distinct enough that confusion between even identical marks is unlikely." (*In re Thor Tech, Inc.*, 113 USPQ 2d 1546 (T.T.A.B. 2015).)

Related terms: average reasonably prudent consumer; infringement (trademark); initial interest confusion.

loss of mark

Ownership of an otherwise valid trademark can be lost in several situations. This occurs when a mark is deliberately abandoned (nonuse), when it becomes the generic term for the goods (genericide), when it is used improperly (in violation of antitrust laws), or when an unfavorable decision is made in a cancellation or interference proceeding (which passes the mark's ownership to another party).

Related terms: abandonment of mark; generic terms; interference; opposing and canceling a trademark registration; Trademark Modernization Act of 2020.

Madrid Protocol

Prior to the U.S. becoming a party to the Madrid Protocol in 2003, a U.S. trademark owner (or applicant) had to apply for registration in each country, a process that required spending thousands of dollars for fees, agents, and translators. Under the Madrid Protocol, U.S. trademark owners can file for registration in various countries by filing a single standardized English-language application at the U.S. Patent and Trademark Office (USPTO).

Under the Madrid Protocol rules, any trademark owner with an application filed in or a registration issued by the USPTO (referred to as the "basic application" or "basic registration") and who is a national of, has a domicile in, or has a real and effective business establishment in the United States can submit an international application through the USPTO. The USPTO certifies that the same information is in the international application and the U.S. basic application and then forwards the international application to the International Bureau.

The applicant must pay the U.S. certification fees at the time of submission and identify at least one other nation (Contracting Party) in which a registration (referred to as "extension of protection") is sought. The certification fee is currently $100, per class, if the international application is based on a single U.S. application or registration.

The international registration isn't really a single registration; it triggers a process in which the application is individually examined in each country named in the registration. If a country has a basis for refusing the application, it must do so within 12 months. If an initial refusal isn't made within 12 months, the registration will automatically take effect in the designated country. If a country issues a refusal, the examination may be extended up to 18 additional months, and even more if an opposition is filed. International registrations have a duration of ten years and have one registration number. The result of all this is to speed up and simplify the international registration process.

This process doesn't preclude applicants from following the old path and filing a separate application in each country in which registration is sought. One big difference, however, is that if the owner of a U.S. mark uses the international registration, all resulting registrations around the world are dependent upon what happens in the United States for the first five years. In other words, international registrations end if the U.S. application is refused, canceled, or abandoned. All is not lost if a U.S. trademark is canceled, however. The owner can still file individual national applications within three months of the cancellation (and retain the benefit of the original filing date).

To file using the Madrid Protocol, start with the TEAS system at the USPTO website. If you later wish to add other nations to your application, you may do so by filing a "Subsequent Designation," also provided in TEAS format.

An international registration has a ten-year term, a single registration number, a single renewal date, and a single renewal fee. Likewise, any assignment or other such postregistration filing requires only one communication and one fee, payable in U.S. dollars.

Although the Madrid Protocol has primarily affected rules for international registration, it also affects U.S. trademark activity by:

- making the rules stricter for reviving abandoned applications and registrations
- providing for "partial abandonments" of trademark applications
- changing rules regarding the methods and time periods for opposing applications
- modifying rules regarding the submission of color trademarks, and
- establishing rules for the size of electronic images provided to the USPTO.

Related terms: abandonment of application.

mark

This book uses "mark" to refer broadly to:

- trademarks
- service marks
- certification marks
- collective marks, and
- trade dress (when used as a trademark or service mark).

The term "mark" ordinarily encompasses any means that a business uses to identify or distinguish its product or service from competitors in the marketplace. Features of the mark must be nonfunctional and may include symbols, shapes, designs, logos, phrases, colors, tunes, and smells.

Related terms: trademark.

mark dilution

See dilution.

metatags

A metatag is programming code used in the creation of a website. Metatags do not affect the appearance of a website and are not visible when you look at a webpage, but they provide information regarding the site's content, and they once had a direct effect on the frequency with which a search engine would find a website. This led many website owners to game the system by including rival sites' names and products in their metatags. One company went so far as to copy and use all of the metatags at a rival site. This kind of deceptive use of another company's trademark in a metatag is a form of trademark infringement when it confuses consumers. One judge described the practice as similar to a shop owner posting a sign with another company's trademark in front of its shop. (*Brookfield Communications v. West Coast Entertainment*, 174 F.3d 1036 (9th Cir. 1999).)

In some cases, using competing metatags was found permissible. Former Playmate Terri Welles created a website and used Playboy and Playmate in her site's metatags. This use of *Playboy*'s trademarks was permitted because Ms. Welles was using the terms to describe herself and to properly index the pages. In addition, the court was influenced by the fact that most of the free webpages at the site included a disclaimer at the bottom: "This site is neither endorsed, nor sponsored by, nor affiliated with Playboy Enterprises, Inc. Playboy, Playmate of the Year, and Playmate of the Month are registered trademarks of Playboy Enterprises, Inc." (*Playboy Enterprises, Inc. v. Welles*, 279 F.3d 796 (9th Cir. 2002).)

Within a decade of these decisions, most major search engines had eliminated or discounted metatags as a major factor in providing search results and legal issues regarding metatags have disappeared from the courts.

Related terms: fair use of trademarks; free speech and trademark law; keyword.

misuse of mark

See loss of mark.

money damages for mark infringement

See damages in trademark infringement cases.

naked license

A trademark owner who fails to supervise a licensee and maintain quality control over the licensed products or services has created a "naked license." A naked license can cause the owner to lose rights in the mark, a process known as "abandonment." This occurs when the mark is used on goods and services of varying quality so that it no longer identifies and distinguishes specific products and services from competing ones and does not indicate a particular level of quality attached to some product or service.

EXAMPLE: Barcamerica licensed its registered trademark, Leonardo DaVinci, to Renaissance Vineyards for the sale of wines. The licensing agreement did not contain a quality control requirement, and there was no evidence that Barcamerica controlled the quality of the licensed wine. When Barcamerica sued to stop another company, Tyfield, from using a similar mark, Tyfield argued that Barcamerica abandoned its rights as a result of its naked license. A federal court agreed and Barcamerica lost its rights to the Leonardo DaVinci mark and federal registration. (*Barcamerica International USA Trust v. Tyfield Importers, Inc.*, 289 F.3d 589 (9th Cir. 2002).)

EXAMPLE: A family owned the "Eva's Bridal" trademark. The family licensed the trademark to two people to open a Chicago store. After the license expired in 2002, the store owners continued to use the mark but stopped paying the trademark license fees. They claimed that they didn't need to pay; the mark had been abandoned because its owners had not maintained quality control (it was a naked license). The trademark owners claimed they didn't need to supervise or maintain quality control because the bridal gowns at the store were of the same high quality (and from the same suppliers) as the other Eva's Bridal shops. In other words, quality control wasn't necessary because the store's goods were of high quality. The court responded that it wasn't "high" quality that was demanded; it was consistent quality—for example, the kind of supervision that guaranteed the dressing rooms were clean and that the customer experience was consistent across the franchise. As the judge stated, "The trademark's function is to tell shoppers what to expect—and whom to blame if a given outlet falls short. The licensor's reputation is at stake in every outlet, so it invests to the extent required to keep the consumer satisfied by ensuring a repeatable experience." (*Eva Bridal Ltd. v. Halanick Enterprises Inc.*, 639 F.3d 788 (7th Cir. 2011).) A similar result was reached when an organization (The Freecycle Network) did not exercise contractual or actual control over a licensee. The arrangement was considered to be a "naked license," resulting in trademark abandonment and the loss of all trademark rights. (*FreecycleSunnyvale v. Freecycle Network*, 626 F.3d 509 (9th Cir. 2010).)

A trademark license agreement should contain language assuring quality control and permitting the trademark owner to inspect products and services—for example, many toy licensors require pre- and postproduction samples. In addition, the trademark owner of a franchise operation should perform personal inspections to guarantee consistency.

Related terms: abandonment of mark; licensing of marks.

names as marks

The use of surnames (family names) as trademarks is sometimes controversial, because some business owners believe they have an inalienable right to use their own name as a trademark. They are surprised when they cannot register their name or someone else has preempted the field. For example, anyone with the family name McDonald or Denny would be unable to obtain a trademark for restaurant services.

A mark that is primarily a surname does not qualify for placement on the Principal Register under the Lanham Act unless the name has become well known as a mark through advertising or long use—that is, until it acquires a secondary meaning. Until then, surname marks can be listed only on the Supplemental Register. To register a mark that consists primarily of a living person's surname (assuming the mark has acquired secondary meaning), the mark owner must have the namesake's written permission.

Surnames are treated this way because, theoretically, everyone should be able to use their own name to promote their own business or product. In practice, however, as soon as someone establishes secondary meaning for a surname, it becomes off-limits for all uses that might cause consumer confusion. Del Monte, Disney, Spiegel, and Johnson & Johnson are just a few of the hundreds of surnames that have become effective marks over time.

A trademark is "primarily a surname" if the public would initially recognize it as a surname. A trademark application for a surname will not automatically be denied simply because it is a surname, or similar in sound or appearance to other surnames. Examination of an application for a surname should focus on how many people have that same surname and thus would be affected by its registration. Extremely rare or obscure surnames—such as "Baik"—do not, however, necessarily require proof of secondary meaning. (*In re Joint-Stock Company "Baik,"* Serial No. 78341041 (T.T.A.B. 2006).) However, a mark that is part surname and part distinctive mark may be registrable if the mark as a whole is distinctive, or if the surname is disclaimed as unregistrable material.

For example, two names may be combined (Smith and Wesson), or a name used with a design might be registrable. The reason for this is that when a surname is used with other matter, the "other matter" can affect public perception, thus diminishing (or perhaps reinforcing) the impact of the surname. If a surname has a dictionary meaning (that is, it also functions as a word), it is treated like any other trademark. For example, King and Bird both have significance other than as family names.

Whether registered or not, if a name mark has become well known, even a person with the same name might not be able to use that name as a mark. Courts do, however, sometimes permit two conflicting uses of the same surname, with modifications to try to minimize consumer confusion. For instance, if McGuffy's Bar faces a crosstown competitor by the same name, the second McGuffy could be forced to use a modifier, such as McGuffy's Cross-Town Bar.

Someone who obviously tries to capitalize on a personal name to take advantage of an identical famous mark (for example, Fred Ford opens Ford's Muffler Service) can be forced to give up all use of that name.

Likewise, businesses that are based on the name of a founder can contractually give up rights to that name, preventing the founder from using it in connection with similar goods.

> **EXAMPLE:** Dress designer Hayley Paige Gutman transferred her trademark "Hayley Paige" to a couture company as part of an employment agreement. When the arrangement with the couture company went south in 2019, the designer resigned, locked the company out of her Haley Paige Instagram account, and used the account for promoting goods. After the couture company sued, a district court enjoined the designer from using the Hayley Paige "name, trademarks and any derivatives or anything confusingly similar in trade or commerce." (*JLM Couture, Inc. v. Hayley Paige Gutman*, 20-10575 (S.D.N.Y. 2021).)

Names that are primarily surnames are considered weak and cannot be listed on the Principal Register unless they acquire a secondary meaning (for example, Heinz, Macy's, Miller). First names and nicknames, unless very unusual or memorable as a mark (but not as a name), need to acquire secondary meaning by becoming very well-known over time before others can be stopped from using them.

EXAMPLE: "Henry's" is a mark used to advertise the Henry Weinhard's line of beers. Over time, "Henry's" has become associated in the public's mind with the underlying product and therefore has taken on a secondary meaning. If Henry Clark came along and used his first name to advertise his line of beers, the Henry Weinhard company could probably successfully claim infringement of its "Henry's" mark.

Related terms: prohibited and reserved marks under Lanham Act; secondary meaning.

noncompeting goods

See competing and noncompeting products.

nonprofit corporations and trademarks

A nonprofit corporation is entitled to the same protection as a for-profit entity for its trademarks and service marks.

Related terms: state trademark laws; trade name.

notice of trademark registration

To denote that a mark is registered with the U.S. Patent and Trademark Office (USPTO) under the Lanham Act, a symbol must be placed next to it. The most commonly used symbol in the United States is an "R" in a circle (®), but "Reg. U.S. Pat. Off." is equally valid. Both symbols indicate that the mark is registered with the USPTO on either the Principal Register or the Supplemental Register (a list of marks that didn't qualify for the Principal Register because they lacked distinctiveness).

If a mark owner systematically does not use one of these symbols to identify a registered mark when using it to promote a product or service, the owner cannot collect treble damages or defendant's profits for an infringement, unless he or she can show that the infringer actually knew the mark was registered.

Related terms: constructive notice of mark under Lanham Act; damages in trademark infringement cases.

Official Gazette

As part of the application process for placing a mark on the Principal Register, the U.S. Patent and Trademark Office (USPTO) publishes the mark in an online publication called the *Official Gazette* (OG), also available at the USPTO website (www.uspto.gov).

Trademark Law: Definitions

The OG contains lists of marks proposed for registration on the Principal Register, together with examples of their designs, to give other mark owners notice of the impending registrations. If any other mark owners believe the new mark would infringe on or dilute theirs, they can file an opposition to protest the registration.

If no one objects to the mark's registration within 30 days of the publication date, the USPTO will register the mark. If, however, any interested person files a timely opposition to the registration, the USPTO will schedule an administrative (*inter partes*) hearing to resolve the dispute.

Related terms: opposing and canceling a trademark registration; Principal Register; U.S. Patent and Trademark Office (USPTO).

opposing and canceling a trademark registration

Under the Lanham Act, any party who may be damaged by the actual or proposed registration of a mark is entitled to challenge the registration.

> EXAMPLE: A law professor filed an opposition for a trademark registration for RAPUNZEL for toys and dolls. The applicant sought to dismiss the opposition because the opposer was not a competitor. The TTAB disagreed and established that the professor, a consumer of dolls, had standing to oppose because as a consumer, "she has purchased and continues to purchase said goods and that registration of the applied-for mark by applicant would constrain the marketplace of such goods sold under the name 'Rapunzel,' raise prices of 'Rapunzel' dolls offered by other manufacturers." The TTAB held, "Consumers, like competitors, may have a real interest in keeping merely descriptive or generic words in the public domain." (*Rebecca Curtin v. United Trademark Holdings, Inc.*, Opposition No. 91241083 (December 28, 2018).)

The opposition must be in writing and be filed within 30 days of the proposed mark's publication in the *Official Gazette*. The U.S. Patent and Trademark Office (USPTO) may grant extensions of the 30-day period upon written request.

Under rules promulgated by the Madrid Protocol, if a party wants to oppose a trademark registration, the period for filing an opposition cannot be extended more than 180 days from the date the application was published. Those extensions must be requested in one of two ways after the first 30-day period, by either:

- requesting an extension of 30 days (granted upon request), followed by a second request for a further extension of 60 days (upon a showing of good cause), followed by a final further extension of 60 days (upon stipulation or written consent of the applicant), or

- requesting an extension of 90 days (upon a showing of good cause), followed by a final further extension of 60 days (upon stipulation or written consent of the applicant).

A party who intends to oppose a Section 1 or Section 44 trademark application can do so electronically or on paper. An opposition to a Section 66 application (an application under the Madrid Protocol) must be filed electronically.

If the mark has already been placed on the Principal Register, the party may petition the USPTO for cancellation of the registration. (15 U.S. Code § 1064.) A cancellation petition may be filed:

- within five years from the date the mark is published in the *Official Gazette*
- any time if the mark becomes generic or is abandoned or its use becomes fraudulent in some way, or
- anytime, if the mark is a certification mark and is being misused (for instance, the registrant no longer exercises control or the registrant begins to manufacture goods subject to the certification).

Marks proposed for placement on the Supplemental Register are not published for opposition. A party who believes that a mark's placement on the Supplemental Register might cause it harm can file an application with the USPTO to have the registration canceled. (15 U.S. Code § 1092.)

When a petition for opposition or cancellation is filed, or the USPTO declares an interference, an *inter partes* proceeding to resolve the dispute will be scheduled before the Trademark Trial and Appeal Board. (15 U.S. Code § 1067.) At the conclusion of this hearing, the Patent and Trademark Commissioner may:

- refuse to register the opposed mark (in an opposition case)
- cancel the registration of a mark or place restrictions on its use (in a cancellation case)
- refuse to register any mark, or some or all of several marks (in an interference case)
- register the opposed mark or marks of persons who are found to be entitled to ownership, or
- order concurrent registration of marks along with conditions or restrictions on their use designed to prevent consumer confusion in the marketplace.

The USPTO will cancel a mark on its own—without anyone asking for it—if the mark's owner fails to timely file a Section 8 Declaration showing that the mark is still in use. Because this form must be filed between the fifth and sixth year following the initial registration, and because the USPTO doesn't send a reminder, the registrations of many marks are canceled for this reason. And because the

USPTO also doesn't send notice of the cancellation, many trademark owners continue to use their marks in the belief that they are registered, when they're not.

The fact that a mark's registration is canceled in no way affects the right of the mark's owner to challenge its users on the basis of first use. But as long as the mark remains unregistered, the owner will not be entitled to the benefits of registration should a trademark infringement suit become necessary.

In order to deal with a wave of fraudulent trademark registrations, Congress enacted the Trademark Modernization Act of 2020 (TMA). The TMA created two new ex parte procedures that allow a third party (or the Director of the USPTO) to contest whether the registrant used the mark in commerce. If the USPTO determines that the registrant did not use it as claimed, and its decision is not overturned on review, the USPTO will cancel the registration.

The two new ex parte proceedings created by the TMA are for expungement and for reexamination. In an expungement proceeding, the USPTO determines whether the registered mark has never been used in commerce in connection with some or all of the goods or services listed in the registration. In a reexamination proceeding, the USPTO determines whether the the registered mark was in use in commerce in connection with some or all of the goods or services as of either the filing date of the application or amendment to allege use or before the deadline for filing a statement of use. The procedures for instituting the proceedings, the nature of the evidence required, and the process for evaluating evidence and corresponding with the registrant are expected to be essentially the same.

Related terms: ex parte expungement; ex parte reexamination; federal trademark registration; interference; ownership of mark in the United States; Trademark Modernization Act of 2020.

ownership, presumption of

See presumption of ownership.

ownership of mark, international

See international trademark rights.

ownership of mark in the United States

In the United States, ownership of a mark typically comes from first use. Use of a distinctive mark on goods or services in the marketplace is sufficient to establish ownership in that mark unless either of the following is true:

- Someone else is already using the same or similar mark on related goods or services.
- An intent-to-use (ITU) application has been filed for the mark.

If, however, a business that is first to use a mark does not federally register it, and a second business uses the mark in a geographically separate market (which means no consumer confusion is likely), it is possible for both businesses to concurrently own the mark.

As mentioned, ownership of a mark may arise from the filing of an ITU registration application, before a mark goes into use. The ownership vests (becomes effective) when the mark is put into use and the application process is complete, but ownership will begin on the date the ITU application was filed.

Whether derived from actual use or from the ITU application, ownership of a mark confers an exclusive right to use that mark in a certain way and in a certain place.

Ownership rights may last forever, unless the mark is abandoned or becomes generic. The fact that a mark is not registered or that a registration is canceled or not renewed does not affect the basic ownership of the mark, which is primarily based on use. However, additional remedies provided by federal registration will not be available to the owner of an unregistered mark if an infringement occurs.

Although the exclusive right to use the mark initially exists in the geographic area where the mark is being used, if someone uses the same or a similar mark in the United States, the scope of this right depends on the following factors:

- Which mark was first used anywhere in the United States?
- Which mark was first subject to a registration application under the Lanham Act on the basis of actual use or an intent to use the mark in the future?
- Was the first registrant under the Lanham Act the junior user or the senior user?
- If the first registrant under the Lanham Act was the junior user, did that party know of the mark's prior use by the senior user?
- Is there geographical proximity between areas in which two conflicting marks are used?
- Are the types of products or services to which the marks are attached related or unrelated?
- Is confusion of consumers likely to result from the use of the two marks?

EXAMPLE 1: Marcia markets her marshmallow cookies, "Marcia's Marvelous Mallows," in California only. Because there is no interstate use, Marcia is entitled to register her mark only under her state's trademark laws. Lou, who lives in Colorado, decides to market cookies exclusively in Colorado under the name of "Lou's Marvy Mallows." Although Lou's mark is confusingly similar to that used by Marcia, she probably would have no recourse as long as Lou's mark was confined to the Colorado market (there would be no likelihood of consumer confusion).

EXAMPLE 2: Suppose now that Marcia markets cookies only on the West Coast, while Lou markets his cookies only in the East. Even if Marcia federally registered her mark before Lou started using his mark, she will not be able to force Lou to stop using his mark unless she can show a likelihood of consumer confusion as a result of the two uses. But since Marcia is the national owner of the mark, if she later decides to start marketing her product in the East, Lou could be forced to stop using his mark.

EXAMPLE 3: Using the same facts, with a last wrinkle. If Lou federally registers before Marcia and Lou does not know of Marcia's prior use of the mark, Lou will become entitled to exclusive use on a national basis except where Marcia is already marketing. If Lou does know of Marcia's prior use or if she objects to the registration, however, his registration may be deemed fraudulent and set aside.

These priorities can be somewhat complicated and obviously depend greatly on the facts of each case. Trademark law as it exists today developed at a time when geography played an important role in resolving trademark conflicts. If the same trademark was used by different businesses in different parts of the country, there was no likelihood of customer confusion and therefore no need for intervention by a court unless and until one of the users expanded into the other user's territory. After the Internet developed, this concept of territory became less important because doing business on the Web automatically extended a business's marketing activity to all parts of the country and the world simultaneously.

Related terms: assignment of mark; infringement (trademark); Lanham Act; licensing of marks.

palming off

A person engages in palming off (also called "passing off") when he or she intentionally causes one product or service to be confused with another for commercial gain. Examples of palming off include:
- substituting one product for another—for instance, representing a computer as having one kind of microprocessor when it has another, or
- deliberately infringing a mark belonging to another—for instance, using "IBM" as a mark on a new computer line.

Although the phrase "palming off" is appropriate only in situations where there is an intent to confuse, it is sometimes used colloquially to designate any infringement where there is a likelihood of confusion, even where the infringer might not have intended it.

Related terms: infringement (trademark); innocent infringer; likelihood of confusion; reverse palming off.

Paris Convention

The primary treaty regulating trademark relations between the United States and other countries is called the Paris Convention. The Paris Convention provides that each signatory country will give members of other signatory countries the same protections regarding marks and unfair competition that it affords its own nationals.

Related terms: foreign nationals registering in United States; international trademark rights.

parodies of trademarks

A trademark parody occurs when someone imitates a trademark in a manner that pokes fun at the mark, for example, distributing a newspaper called *The San Francisco Comical* in order to poke fun at the *San Francisco Chronicle*. Below are some trademark parody court cases.

- A college student sold T-shirts at Myrtle Beach depicting a red, white, and blue beer can with the phrase, "This Beach Is for You." Anheuser-Busch, the owners of the Budweiser trademark, filed a lawsuit, seized all of the T-shirts, and raided the college student's home and his mother's business. A jury determined that the T-shirts were a parody, but the judge overturned the jury verdict and ruled for Anheuser-Busch. An appeals court ruled that the use was a parody. Seven years and several lawsuits later, the parties reached a settlement in which Anheuser-Busch granted a license for sales of the T-shirt. (*Anheuser-Busch, Inc. v. L & L Wings, Inc.*, 962 F.2d 316 (4th Cir. 1992), *cert. denied*, 113 S.Ct. 206 (1992).)
- During a half-time show, the "San Diego Chicken" mascot initiated a fistfight with Barney, the popular purple dinosaur. A court held the use of the Barney trademark a permissible parody because the aggressive manner in which Barney behaved was not likely to cause consumer confusion. (*Lyons Partnership L.P. v. Giannoulas*, 179 F.3d 384 (5th Cir. 1999).)
- A gaudy, '60s style nightclub in Houston used the trademark "The Velvet Elvis" and, after being sued by the owner of the Elvis trademark, claimed that the club's name was an Elvis parody. A court disagreed, pointing out that the intent of the club's name and decor was to parody the Las Vegas lounge scene and the velvet painting craze, not to parody Elvis. (*Elvis Presley Enterprises v. Capece*, 141 F.3d 188 (5th Cir. 1998).)

Trademark Law: Definitions

- In *E.S.S. Entertainment 2000, Inc. v. Rock Star Videos, Inc.*, 547 F.3d 1095 (9th Cir. 2008), the Ninth Circuit Court of Appeals permitted a parody under First Amendment principles noting that artistic use of a mark is permitted when: (1) the use has artistic relevance to the work at issue (the video game), and (2) it doesn't explicitly mislead consumers as to the source of the mark or the work—a test adopted in *Mattel v. Walking Mountain*, 353 F.3d 792 (9th Cir. 2003). In *E.S.S. Entertainment*, the video game "Grand Theft Auto: San Andreas" included a parody of the East Los Angeles strip club "The Play Pen" (referred to as the "Pig Pen" in the game).

- In the first appellate case heard under the Trademark Dilution Revision Act of 2006 (TDRA), the Fourth Circuit determined that Chewy Vuitton (for dog chews) was a parody, stating, "For trademark purposes, [a] parody is defined as a simple form of entertainment conveyed by juxtaposing the irreverent representation of the trademark with the idealized image created by the mark's owner." More importantly, the court held (1) that Chewy Vuitton was a parody that was not likely to confuse consumers as to its source, and (2) that a successful parody, such as Chewy Vuitton, would not dilute the Louis Vuitton brand but in fact might make it even more famous. The court stated, "[B]y making the famous mark an object of the parody, a successful parody might actually enhance the famous mark's distinctiveness by making it an icon. The brunt of the joke becomes yet more famous." (*Louis Vuitton Malletier S.A. v. Haute Diggity Dog, L.L.C.*, 507 F.3d 252 (4th Cir. 2007).)

- In a 2020 case, Jack Daniel's, sued the maker of "Bad Spaniels" dog toys (which resembled the trade dress and shape of a Jack Daniel's, whiskey bottle). The Ninth Circuit ruled against Jack Daniel's, citing the *Chewy Vuitton* case (above). (*VIP Products LLC v. Jack Daniel's Properties, Inc.*, 953 F.3d 1170 (9th Cir. 2020).)

- In yet another case in which Louis Vuitton failed to "get the joke" (as the district court put it), the defendant sold tote bags that read "My other bag is a Louis Vuitton" (as well as naming other high-end fashion designers). Louis Vuitton sued, claiming the tote bags diluted the Vuitton mark. The Second Circuit upheld the summary judgment against Louis Vuitton because the tote bags, though they mimicked LV, were clearly "a joke on LV's luxury image." (*Louis Vuitton Malletier, S.A v. My Other Bag, Inc.*, 674 Fed. App'x. 16 (2d Cir. 2016).)

Conflicting case law and the discretionary power of judges make it difficult to predict the outcome of a lawsuit based on trademark parody. It is also difficult to predict when a company will take action against a parodist. Some companies, like Anheuser-Busch, prefer to fight to the end, while others believe that chasing parodists generates negative publicity and prefer to let the parody run its course.

As a general rule, a trademark parody is less likely to run into problems if it:

- **Doesn't compete.** That is, the use of the parody product does not directly compete with the trademark product.
- **Doesn't confuse.** That is, the parody does not confuse consumers; they get the joke and do not believe the parody product comes from the same source as the trademarked goods.
- **Does parody.** Keep in mind that all humorous uses are not parodies. To avoid trouble, the use should specifically poke fun at the trademark.

Related terms: fair use of trademarks; free speech and trademark law; infringement (trademark).

partial abandonment

See abandonment of trademark application.

passing off

See palming off.

Patent and Trademark Depository Library

See trademark search.

phonetic or foreign language equivalents for marks

In trademark law, a word that sounds the same as another mark, or one that means the same in another language, will normally be treated similarly. If a word or phrase is descriptive or generic (ineligible for protection), simply misspelling or translating it will not make it distinctive (that is, eligible for protection).

EXAMPLE: If DateTime is too descriptive for a singles dating service, then Dayttyme won't work, either. Or, if GoodTimes is considered too descriptive for a party-catering service, then using the French equivalent BonTemps will not help.

Related terms: composite mark; generic terms; international trademark rights.

pictures and symbols used as marks

Pictures and symbols may be protectable as marks if they are distinctive rather than descriptive. For example, the Quaker man on Quaker Oats cereals is a strong, distinctive pictorial mark. Similarly, the apple shape on Apple computer products is very distinctive and nondescriptive. A generic illustration such as the no-smoking symbol—a diagonal bar through a burning cigarette within a circle—is not distinctive and would be barred from trademark use for an antismoking product or service.

Related terms: descriptive mark; secondary meaning; trademark.

pop-up advertising

Pop-up advertising occurs when a new window opens to display an advertisement while a viewer is visiting a website. In some cases, a pop-up can be generated by a competitor. In one case, a company selling contact lenses filed suit after visitors to the company's website saw pop-up ads appear for a direct competitor. In 2005, the Second Circuit Court of Appeals rejected this infringement claim, holding that the practice was not infringement because the use of the trademarked name—for the purpose of triggering a pop-up ad—did not amount to a "use" under the Lanham Act. (*1-800 Contacts, Inc. v. WhenU.com, Inc.,* 414 F.3d 400 (2d Cir. 2005).)

Related terms: keyword.

preliminary injunction

A preliminary injunction in a trademark case is a court order that requires one party to stop the use of an infringing or diluting mark, at least until the case has been resolved. Stopping an infringing use early provides a tactical advantage and usually encourages a speedy settlement. But to win a preliminary injunction, the party seeking it must demonstrate that it is likely to prevail when the case gets to trial and that it will suffer irreparable harm if the injunction is not granted. For example, in a 2011 case involving Apple and Amazon, Apple was unable to obtain a preliminary injunction stopping Amazon's use of the "App Store" because Apple failed to demonstrate that it would prevail at trial.

The requirement for proving irreparable harm exists even if the party establishes a likelihood of success on the merits. (*Herb Reed Enterprises LLC v. Florida Entertainment Management Inc.,* 736 F.3d 1239 (9th Cir. Dec. 2, 2013).)

In 2020, the Trademark Modernization Act (TMA) established the evidentiary burden for obtaining an injunction. The TMA resolved a circuit split by providing for a presumption of irreparable harm when a party demonstrates likelihood of confusion, making it easier for some parties to obtain an injunction.

Related terms: injunctions against infringement and unfair competition.

presidents' names and likenesses as marks

See reserved marks under Lanham Act.

presumption of ownership

If a trademark infringement suit is filed, a court will assume that the trademark owner who is listed on a certificate of registration on the Principal Register is the owner of the mark. This presumption means that the owner does not have to present further evidence to support the ownership claim unless the defendant offers evidence to the contrary. In that event, the certificate holder will need to introduce evidence to back up the ownership claim.

The presumption of ownership is not available for marks on the Supplemental Register (a list of marks that didn't qualify for the Principal Register because they lacked distinctiveness).

The Lanham Act: § 1057. (§ 7) Certificates of registration

(b) Certificate as prima facie evidence

A certificate of registration of a mark upon the principal register provided by this chapter shall be prima facie evidence of the validity of the registered mark and of the registration of the mark, of the registrant's ownership of the mark, and of the registrant's exclusive right to use the registered mark in commerce on or in connection with the goods or services specified in the certificate, subject to any conditions or limitations stated in the certificate.

Related terms: certificate of registration; infringement (trademark).

Principal Register

The Principal Register is the list on which distinctive trademarks and service marks approved for federal registration are placed. Benefits of placement on the Principal Register include all of the following:

- It provides official notice to all would-be copiers that the mark is in use on particular goods or services, and that someone claims ownership of the mark for that use.

- It gives the owner the right to file an infringement action in federal court.
- It creates a presumption, in the event of litigation, that the registrant owns the mark, requiring the other party to challenge the registrant's ownership. (Placing the burden of proof on the challenger can make the difference between winning and losing a lawsuit.)
- It gives the owner the right to seek an award of treble damages, defendant's profits, and attorneys' fees.
- It gives the owner the right to register in countries that afford reciprocal rights to the United States.
- It confers on the owner the right to exclusive use of the mark in all parts of the United States, except where a senior unregistered user may have already been using the mark at the time of registration.
- After the mark is on the Principal Register for five years, it gives the mark's owner the right to file for incontestability status. If granted, incontestability status prevents a challenger from challenging the registrant's ownership on the basis that the registered mark lacks sufficient distinctiveness to warrant protection.

Related terms: incontestability status; opposing and canceling a trademark registration; prohibited and reserved marks under Lanham Act; Supplemental Register.

prior registration countries

Most countries determine ownership of a mark by who registers first, instead of who uses it first. These are called prior registration countries (or first-to-file countries) to distinguish them from countries that base trademark rights on first use, such as the United States.

Related terms: international trademark rights.

profits

See defendant's profits.

prohibited and reserved marks under Lanham Act

As written, the Lanham Act (15 U.S. Code § 1052), prohibits the registration of various types of marks—for example, marks that are composed of "immoral, deceptive, or scandalous matter," or "matter which may disparage or falsely suggest a connection with persons, living or dead, institutions, beliefs, or national symbols, or bring them into contempt, or disrepute." For 70 years, the USPTO was the arbiter of morality and decency when it came to approving or rejecting such applications.

For example, when a company sought to register a bottle design "in the shape of a hand with the middle finger extended upward," the Trademark Trial and Appeal Board (TTAB) found the mark vulgar and obscene. (*In re Luxuria*, 100 U.S.P.Q.2d 1146 (T.T.A.B. 2011).) A similar result was reached when a company that sold lollipops sought to register a term commonly used to describe a sex act (the lollipops were sold in the shape of a rooster). The TTAB determined that the mark had "vulgar meaning that will be perceived by a substantial composite of the general public." (*In re Marsha Fox*, T.T.A.B. 12-1212 (T.T.A.B. 2012).) Ten years later, however, both of these marks would probably have been approved, as a result of Supreme Court decisions in 2017 and 2019.

Disparagement. In 2017, the Supreme Court held that the "disparagement" provision of the Lanham Act (15 U.S. Code § 1052(a)) violated the First Amendment's free speech clause. The USPTO had denied an Asian-American band's registration for SLANTS on the basis that the term was disparaging to persons of Asian descent. (*Matal v. Tam*, 582 U.S. ___ (2017).) The Supreme Court's decision applied to marks that disparage the members of a racial or ethnic group. Changing social norms, consumer pressure, and the legal climate caused the Washington Redskins football team to abandon the Redskins moniker after nearly 30 years of controversy.

Immoral, deceptive, and scandalous. In 2019, two years after striking down the Lanham Act restriction on registering "disparaging" marks, the Supreme Court. in a case involving "FUCT" for clothing, struck down as unconstitutional the prohibition against registering immoral and scandalous trademarks. (*Iancu v. Brunetti*, 139 S.Ct. 2294 (2019).)

Living persons and presidents. The Lanham Act bars registration of a mark having the name of an individual without written consent (§ 2(c)). The Trademark Trial and Appeal Board (TTAB) refused registrations for "Obama Bahama Pajamas," "Obama Pajama," and "Barack's Jocks Dress to the Left." The petitioner claimed that the marks had nothing to do with the President and were meant to conjure up the English translation of Barack ("blessed") and Obama ("to lean)." However, the TTAB disregarded this defense in light of the fame connected with the name, and the timing of the applications (filed weeks before the President's inauguration). The TTAB also indicated that the use of the entire name was not required as long it identified a particular living person. (*In re Hoefflin*, 19 U.S.P.Q.2d 1174 (T.T.A.B. 2010).)

Special situations. In addition to these prohibitions, certain organizations, such as the Boy Scouts and the U.S. Olympic Committee, have the exclusive right to use their marks and symbols mandated by statute. Similarly, the use of the character and name "Smokey the Bear" is reserved to the Department of the Interior.

Subject to the unenforceability and unconstitutionality of certain sections, the Lanham Act establishes that a mark may be refused federal registration if it:

- Consists of or comprises immoral, deceptive, or scandalous matter; or matter which may disparage or falsely suggest a connection with persons, living or dead, institutions, beliefs, or national symbols, or bring them into contempt, or disrepute; or a geographical indication which, when used on or in connection with wines or spirits, identifies a place other than the origin of the goods and is first used on or in connection with wines or spirits by the applicant on or after one year after the date on which the WTO Agreement (as defined in § 3501(9) of Title 19) enters into force with respect to the United States.

- Consists of or comprises the flag or coat of arms or other insignia of the United States, or of any State or municipality, or of any foreign nation, or any simulation thereof.

- Consists of or comprises a name, portrait, or signature identifying a particular living individual except by his written consent, or the name, signature, or portrait of a deceased President of the United States during the life of his widow, if any, except by the written consent of the widow.

- Consists of or comprises a mark which so resembles a mark registered in the Patent and Trademark Office, or a mark or trade name previously used in the United States by another and not abandoned, as to be likely, when used on or in connection with the goods of the applicant, to cause confusion, or to cause mistake, or to deceive ....

- Consists of a mark which (1) when used on or in connection with the goods of the applicant is merely descriptive or deceptively misdescriptive of them, (2) when used on or in connection with the goods of the applicant is primarily geographically descriptive of them, except as indications of regional origin may be registrable under Section 1054 of this title, (3) when used on or in connection with the goods of the applicant is primarily geographically deceptively misdescriptive of them, (4) is primarily merely a surname, or (5) comprises any matter that, as a whole, is functional.

Related terms: Principal Register; Supplemental Register.

protection of marks under state law and common law

See state trademark laws.

PTO

See U.S. Patent and Trademark Office (USPTO).

public domain

See generic terms.

public use doctrine

The Coca-Cola company did not coin the trademark, "Coke." The public popularized it as an abbreviation for the soft drink and the company eventually registered "Coke" as a trademark. This "crowdsourcing" of a trademark is referred to as "the public use doctrine," a principle that permits a trademark owner to claim rights in abbreviations or modifications of its trademark by the public. (*George & Co. LLC v. Imagination Entertainment Ltd.*, 575 F.3d 383 (4th Cir. 2009).) The doctrine has traditionally been applied to publicly adopted abbreviations or shorthand versions of trademarks (for example, "Bud" for "Budweiser" or "Amex" for American Express). In 2013, the USPTO broadened the doctrine when it permitted the New York Yankees to oppose registration of "Baseball's Evil Empire," a term which the public used to refer to the Yankees. The Yankees, however, had never adopted the mark and it was not a modification or abbreviation of an existing Yankees mark. The TTAB held, "a party need not have actually used a mark if the public nevertheless associates the mark with [its] goods or services." (*New York Yankees Partnership v. Evil Enterprises, Inc.*, Opposition No. 91192764 (T.T.A.B. 2013).)

publication of mark in *Official Gazette*

See Official Gazette.

publishers of advertising matter

If an infringement of a mark occurs in advertising copy carried in a magazine, newspaper, or other periodical, and the publisher has not been made aware of the infringement, the Lanham Act exempts the publisher from liability for money damages or profits. (15 U.S. Code § 1114.)

A court may bar (enjoin) the publication from any future advertising copy carrying the infringing mark unless the effect of the injunction would be to delay the normal publication, delivery, or distribution of a scheduled issue. Such a compromise is needed to prevent the injunction from harming the innocent publisher.

If a publisher engages in infringing activity after becoming aware of the infringement, it can be treated like any other deliberate infringer and money damages may be assessed.

Related terms: contributory infringer; false advertising.

puffery

When advertising claims are so broad that consumers do not take them seriously, they are referred to as "puffery," and they do not give rise to claims of false advertising. For example, grand and immeasurable statements such as "world's greatest detergent" or "the best hamburger in the world" are considered puffery. Consumers understand that these claims are generalities intended to "puff up" a product. However, if the statement is capable of being measured or the puffery is related to specific attributes, the statement may be subject to false advertising claims.

> EXAMPLE: Pennzoil advertised that its motor oil "outperforms any leading motor oil against viscosity breakdown" and provides "longer engine life and better engine protection." A court determined that these statements were measurable, went beyond puffery, and were "literally false." (*Castrol Inc. v. Pennzoil Co.*, 987 F.2d 939 (3d Cir. 1993).)

Related terms: false advertising.

punitive damages

In trademark infringement lawsuits, the Lanham Act bars a court from awarding punitive damages: in other words, civil damages that are intended to punish a wrongdoer and serve as an example to future potential wrongdoers. The Lanham Act does, however, authorize treble (triple) damages in instances of egregious and intentional infringement. Also, unfair competition and related laws of many states provide for either punitive or treble damages. Therefore, in an effort to qualify for more generous damages, it is common to charge an alleged infringer with violations of both the Lanham Act and any applicable state laws. The Ninth Circuit has held that a jury may award only punitive damages if there are also actual damages. (*Monster Energy Co. v. Integrated Supply Network, LLC*, No. 19-55760 (9th Cir. Jul. 22, 2020).)

Related terms: damages in trademark infringement cases; state trademark laws; unfair competition.

reasonably prudent consumer

See average reasonably prudent consumer.

reconditioned goods

A business selling reconditioned goods, for example, rebuilt Apple computers, must make obvious to consumers—unless authorized by the trademark owner—that the goods are reconditioned or contain generic, nontrademarked parts. The words "Repaired," "Used," or "Reconditioned" must be prominently displayed with an explanation on the cartons and all printed matter. A claim for false advertising, dilution, or infringement may result if consumers are misled to believe that the company is related to, or is an authorized representative of, the trademarked goods. If a reconstruction of goods is especially extensive, the trademark should be removed from the goods and all advertising.

> EXAMPLE: A company customized Rolex watches by replacing internal and external elements and adding diamonds to enhance the appearance. The company then advertised and sold these as Rolex watches. The owner of the Rolex trademark (Rolex Watch U.S.A.) sued the company, claiming that the addition of non-Rolex parts affected the quality of the watch and its waterproofing and the insertion of diamonds affected the functioning of the watch hands. A court prohibited the promotion and sale of the watches under the Rolex trademark, since the reconditioning was so extensive that it was a misnomer to call the resulting watch a Rolex. (*Rolex Watch U.S.A. Inc. v. Michel Co.*, 50 U.S.P.Q.2d 1939 (9th Cir. 1999).)

"Reg. U.S. Pat. Off." or "®"

See notice of trademark registration.

registered mark

Although the term typically refers to federally registered trademarks, technically, any trademark, service mark, certification mark, or collective mark that is placed on a state or federal list of protected marks is considered registered. Registered marks are usually entitled to a higher degree of protection than unregistered marks. However, under Section 43(a) of the Lanham Act, unregistered marks used in commerce receive protection comparable to that provided marks placed on the federal Principal Register. As noted, the phrase "registered mark" commonly is understood as applying only to federally registered marks, specifically marks placed on the Principal Register.

Trademark Law: Definitions

registrable matter

Under the Lanham Act, certain parts of a mark might meet the standards for registration while others do not. The parts that do are called registrable matter; those that don't are disclaimed as unregistrable.

Related terms: disclaimer of unregistrable material; Lanham Act; Principal Register.

registrant

A registrant is any person or business who registers a mark under the Lanham Act or under state registration laws. The registrant is also usually the owner at the time of registration.

Related terms: registered mark.

registration

See federal trademark registration; state trademark laws.

related products and services

Deciding whether goods or services are related is a key determination in trademark conflicts and in deciding whether a mark qualifies for federal registration. This is because the extent to which goods or services are related will determine whether marks used on them are likely to confuse consumers if the marks are the same or very similar to one another.

How closely related goods or services are considered to be depends on many factors, the most important of which are:

- The international product/service categories (international classes) to which the goods and services belong. If they are in the same class, they will be presumed to be related, and the U.S. Patent and Trademark Office will usually not register the second mark.
- Whether the goods and services pass through related marketing channels. For example, if goods are sold in similar outlets, marketed in similar media, placed near each other in stores, and generally considered similar by the consumer, they will be considered related.

The courts have developed a number of additional criteria to determine when one product or service is related to another, which are used in infringement cases. These are:

- the likelihood that the goods or services of one business will be mistaken for those of the other
- the likelihood that one business will expand its activities so that its goods or services will compete with those of another business

- the extent to which the goods or services of businesses have common purchasers or users
- the market relationship, if any, between the goods produced, or the services provided, by the two businesses
- the degree of distinctiveness of the mark in question when compared to a competing mark
- the degree of attention usually given to trademarks or service marks in the purchase of goods or services of the type provided by the two businesses
- the length of time during which the allegedly infringing business has used the designation, and
- the intent of the allegedly infringing business in adopting and using the mark in question.

When products or services are considered to be totally unrelated, the courts will normally find that use of the same or a similar mark does not constitute infringement. On the other hand, if the products or services are found to be related, infringement may be found to exist, assuming the other requirements for infringement are also present.

EXAMPLE: Ethereal Fragrance Company produces a line of very successful perfumes with the distinctive federally registered trademark "Ekbara Scents," which it markets nationally to boutiques. If Ruben Santiago opens a small printing company specializing in business cards and calls his product "Ekbara Cards," a court is unlikely to find the two products to be related. Purchasers of business cards will not likely think they come from a fragrance company. In addition, neither business is likely to begin competing with the other. Therefore, the uses are unrelated and there is no infringement. On the other hand, if Ruben had created a line of scented greeting cards and marketed them under the Ekbara mark to boutiques as well as card shops, he might have a more difficult time proving the two products are not related.

Although the use of the same or a similar mark might not result in a finding of infringement under the "related/unrelated" analysis, this does not mean that the alleged infringer may continue to use the mark. A court may rule that the use of the allegedly infringing mark constitutes dilution of the original mark and restrict its further use on that ground. However, the dilution rule applies only if the original mark is famous.

Related terms: competing and noncompeting products; dilution; ownership of mark in the United States.

Trademark Law: Definitions

renewal of registration

See duration of federal trademark registration.

reservation system for acquiring ownership of mark

See intent-to-use application; international trademark rights.

reverse confusion

In traditional trademark infringement cases, the second user of a trademark confuses consumers into believing that they are buying goods from the first user. However, it is possible that through massive advertising, a second user might create the impression that it is actually the first to use a trademark and that the real senior user is the infringer. This is known as reverse confusion.

> EXAMPLE: Big O Tires, a midsized regional tire distributor, began marketing a bias-belted tire under the unregistered mark BigFoot in early 1974. The tire giant Goodyear decided to market a radial tire under the BigFoot mark in late 1974. The larger company pumped millions of dollars into its advertising effort, which overlapped with Big O's advertising effort to some extent. As a result, the public began coming to Big O asking for Goodyear's tire. Angry and disappointed, consumers suspected Big O of stealing the idea from Goodyear. But, in fact, Goodyear had become aware of Big O's prior use of the same mark midway into its marketing plans and had unsuccessfully negotiated to buy the mark from them. Nevertheless, Goodyear continued to use the mark. Under a theory of reverse confusion, Big O was awarded a judgment of $4.7 million. (*Big O Tire Dealers, Inc. v. Goodyear Tire & Rubber Co.*, 408 F. Supp. 1219 (D. Col. 1976) *affirmed* 561 F.2d 1365 (10th Cir. 1977).)

The traditional likelihood of confusion factors are used in a reverse confusion dispute. The only difference is that the court focuses on the strength of the junior user's mark rather than the senior user's. That's because the essence of reverse confusion is that the senior user's mark might be less well known than that of the powerful junior user.

In a 2017 case, the BIC company used the statement "The WRITE Pen Choice for 30 Years" and a company owned by BIC used "All-in-One." Marketquest, owner of ALL-IN-ONE and THE WRITE CHOICE trademarks sued for infringement, but did not specifically plead reverse confusion. The Ninth Circuit held that alleging likelihood of confusion is sufficient for pleading reverse confusion. (*Marketquest Group v. BIC*, No. 15-55755 (9th Cir. July 7, 2017).) In 2021, the Ninth Circuit found reverse confusion over Dropbox's use of the "Smart Sync" trademark (registered to Ironhawk, a software company). (*Ironhawk Technologies, Inc. v. Dropbox, Inc.,* 2 F.4th 1150 (9th Cir. 2021).)

Related terms: likelihood of confusion; unfair competition.

reverse palming off

Palming off occurs when goods are marketed in a way that makes people think they are really manufactured by someone else; to do this, an infringer usually uses the true trademark on substitute goods—for example putting a Levi's label on non-Levi's jeans. Reverse palming off, on the other hand, occurs when a noninfringing label is placed on someone else's goods and the goods are then sold under the noninfringing name—for example, a designer takes the Levi's label off Levi's jeans and puts the designer's label on the Levi's.

Either way, the public is being deceived and the owner of the original goods or mark may file a lawsuit under Section 43(a) of the Lanham Act to prevent this type of activity and recover damages caused by it.

Related terms: palming off.

right of publicity

The right of publicity is the right to control the commercial exploitation of a person's name, image, or persona. This right is traditionally associated with celebrities, because the name or image of a famous person is used to sell products or services. For example, it is much easier to sell a T-shirt if there is a picture of Beyoncé or Adele on it. However, the unauthorized use of the image of Beyoncé or Adele for such purposes would infringe their right of publicity. This right extends only to commercial exploitation.

The use of the name, likeness, or persona for news, information, or public interest purposes is not a violation of the right of publicity. For this reason, Taylor Swift cannot prevent the use of a photo of her in the *National Enquirer*.

Although the right of publicity is commonly associated with celebrities, every person, regardless of how famous, has a right to prevent unauthorized use of his or her name or image to sell products. This right also prohibits any implication that a person endorses a product (without the person's permission).

The right of publicity extends to a performer's identifiable voice. For example, in two separate cases, advertisements that used vocal performances that sounded like singers Tom Waits and Bette Midler were found to violate the singers' rights of publicity. In both of these cases, the advertising agency had sought permission from the performer and, when it was not granted, hired someone to deliberately imitate the singer's voice.

Like other intellectual property rights, the owner of the right of publicity can exclude others from using the property.

However, unlike other forms of intellectual property, the right of publicity is not always "descendible" (that is, it does not always survive the death of the person who owns the right.) For example, a copyright lasts for the life of the author plus 70 years. Yet only about a dozen states recognize that the right of publicity survives death. Tennessee, the home of the late Elvis Presley, was one of the first states to recognize that the right of publicity could be passed to survivors. It is for this reason that the estate of Elvis Presley still controls the right to merchandise showing the name and image of the rock-and-roll star. Similarly, California recognizes the survivability of this right, and the estate of Marilyn Monroe acquired the right to exploit her name and likeness following her death.

The right of publicity is generally a matter of state law. Some states, such as California, Florida, Kentucky, Massachusetts, Nebraska, Nevada, New York, Oklahoma, Rhode Island, Tennessee, Texas, Utah, Virginia, and Wisconsin have passed statutes regulating these rights. Other states do not have "right of publicity" statutes, but have established common law rights under case law. Some states have neither a statute nor case law regarding the right of publicity.

Because the right of publicity can trigger a claim of false endorsement or false advertising, these claims are sometimes brought under unfair competition laws, such as Section 43(a) of the Lanham Act. (15 U.S. Code § 1125(a).)

Related terms: false advertising; infringement (trademark); unfair competition.

same or similar mark

Any mark that is enough like another mark in appearance or meaning to lead the average, reasonably prudent consumer to confuse the two under the circumstances is considered "the same or similar." Whether any mark is deemed the same as or similar to another mark is necessarily decided on a case-by-case basis.

Related terms: counterfeit; infringement (trademark); likelihood of confusion.

scandalous marks

See prohibited and reserved marks under Lanham Act.

secondary meaning

Marks that are not distinctive when they are first used can become so in the minds of the consuming public over time and through long, widespread use and/or intensive advertising. This distinctiveness arises from the fact that the mark has acquired a secondary meaning as a mark that transcends the literal meaning of its words.

> **EXAMPLE:** The mark "Dollar a Day" initially just described a service: car rentals for a dollar a day. However, over time, and with the help of an advertising campaign and virtually exclusive use of the phrase by the firm, the phrase lost its descriptive literal meaning and instead stood for a specific car rental service.

If the owner of a nondistinctive mark can show (usually through consumer polls) that the mark has acquired a secondary meaning, the mark will qualify for placement on the Principal Register. Even without such a showing, a mark that is kept in continuous and exclusive use by its owner for five years will be presumed to have acquired such secondary meaning and will qualify for registration on the Principal Register as a distinctive mark.

Related terms: descriptive mark; Principal Register; Supplemental Register.

secondary register

See Supplemental Register.

Section 8 Declaration

Sometime during the fifth year after federal registration, the trademark owner must file a Declaration of Use of a mark declaring the continued use of the mark (or an explanation as to the special circumstances for any period of nonuse). The declaration must also be filed at the time of trademark renewal. The requirements for the declaration are set forth in Section 8 of the Lanham Act. (15 U.S. Code § 1058.) The fee must be enclosed along with a specimen of the mark as it is currently used for each class of goods or services. In lieu of the specimen, the trademark owner may recite facts as to the sales or advertising that demonstrates that the mark is in use.

If the owner fails to timely file the Section 8 Declaration, federal trademark rights will be canceled. There are no extensions for filing the declaration. The only way to reclaim federal trademark rights is to file a new registration application. In

Trademark Law: Definitions

the event that the mark has been assigned to a new owner since registration, the Section 8 Declaration is filed by the current owner, and the change in ownership should be reflected by the current owner filing a copy of the assignment with the U.S. Patent and Trademark Office (USPTO). When the Section 8 Declaration is filed for the first time (between the fifth and sixth years of registration), it is usually combined with a Section 15 Declaration. The Section 8, Section 15, and combined Sections 8 and 15 Declarations can be completed and submitted online at the USPTO website (www.uspto.gov).

Related terms: Section 15 Declaration.

Section 9 Declaration

See duration of federal trademark registration.

Section 15 Declaration

After five years of consecutive use from the date of federal registration, a mark may be declared incontestable. An incontestable mark is immune from challenge except if it has become the generic term for the goods or abandoned for nonuse, or if the registration was acquired under fraudulent conditions. In order to achieve incontestability, a Declaration of Incontestability must be filed containing the requirements as provided in Section 15 of the Lanham Act. (15 U.S. Code § 1065.)

A Section 15 Declaration is not necessary for maintaining ownership or rights under trademark law, and the failure to file the declaration does not result in the loss of any rights. However, the filing of the Section 15 Declaration is recommended because it expands trademark rights by making it more difficult to challenge the mark. A Section 15 Declaration form can be completed and submitted online at the U.S. Patent and Trademark Office (USPTO) website (www.uspto.gov). The Section 8 Declaration and Section 15 Declaration can be combined into one declaration, and a copy of this combined declaration can be completed and submitted online at the USPTO website.

Related terms: Section 8 Declaration.

Section 43(a)

See false advertising; unfair competition; unregistered mark, protection of.

selling goods or services with infringing marks

See contributory infringer.

senior and junior users of marks

When a dispute exists over the ownership of a mark, the person (or entity) who first used the mark is called the senior user, and the second person or entity to use the mark is termed the junior user. Although the senior user will usually be found to be the owner of the disputed mark, this is not always so. For example, if the junior user did not know about the senior user and is first to register the mark under the Lanham Act or under state laws, the junior user might still be able to use the mark in areas other than where the senior user's mark is being used.

Related terms: infringement (trademark); ownership of mark in the United States.

service mark

A service mark distinguishes a service in the same way that a trademark distinguishes a product. Examples of services and their marks are Chipotle (food services), Blue Cross (health insurance services), Cirque de Soleil (entertainment services), and jetBlue (transportation services).

In the United States, the rules for determining when and how service marks qualify for protection are the same as those applicable to trademarks. This means that when you read this book or other sources of information on trademarks, every time you read "trademark" (or "mark") in relation to a product, you can substitute the words "service mark" and "service" instead. One exception to this rule is that some states will register trademarks but refuse to register service marks.

Note that a service mark is different from a trade name. A service mark is the name under which the service is promoted; a trade name is the name of the business that does the promoting. McDonald's Corp. (trade name) prepares and sells food under the service mark McDonald's and sells a specific product under the trademark Big Mac. Especially for small businesses, the service mark and trade name are often the same words, but used in different contexts. For instance, Universal Auto Repair is both the name of a business (it appears on the company checks, invoices, and stationery) and the name that appears on the sign designed to bring consumers into the shop (that is, a service mark).

Related terms: trade name; trademark.

similar marks, use of

See ownership of mark in the United States; same or similar mark.

slogans used as marks

Advertising slogans that function as marks may be protected as marks. To qualify as protectable marks, slogans must either:

- be inherently distinctive and creative, or
- have developed enough secondary meaning to immediately call a product or service to mind.

The more mundane the slogan, the more secondary meaning the owner will need to show in order to obtain protection from imitators. For example, the owners of Excedrin had to prove that "Extra Strength Pain Reliever" had developed a strong secondary meaning.

Related terms: composite mark; secondary meaning; strong mark.

sounds used as marks

Many companies have registered sounds (or "aural trademarks") including NBC (chimes), MGM (roaring lion), and 20th Century Fox (Alfred Newman's triumphant theme). Although there is no prohibition against claiming trademark rights in a sound, the applicant seeking registration faces hurdles. For example, the sound must create an exclusive association with the company, a hurdle that the Harley-Davidson motorcycle company found too difficult to overcome (the company pursued registration for the chugging sound of its well-known twin-engine sound for many years before throwing in the towel). In addition the sound must not be functional, a hurdle that an alarm clock company found equally difficult to overcome. (*In re Vertex Group LLC,* 89 U.S.P.Q.2d 1694 (T.T.A.B. 2009).) Finally, despite the fact that snippets of tones and music can be registered, musicians cannot register one of their signature songs as a trademark. When the Romantics, a pop group from the 1980s, attempted to claim trademark rights in one of its hit songs, a district court rejected the trademark argument as being unsupported by case law and an "unwarranted extension into an area already protected by copyright law." (*Romantics v. Activision Publishing Inc.,* 88 U.S.P.Q.2d 1243 (E.D. Mich. 2008).)

specimen

For purposes of filing a trademark application, the specimen is an actual example of the trademark being used on goods or in the offer of services. The specimen must be filed with the application, or, in the case of ITU applications, filed later, together with a document entitled "Amendment to Allege Use." An actual specimen, rather than a facsimile, is preferred. When filing electronically, the USPTO provides a means for attaching a digital image of the specimen. For products, a label, tag, or container for the goods is considered to be an acceptable specimen of use for a trademark. A letterhead or business card is unacceptable as a trademark specimen because it doesn't follow the goods through the stream of commerce. A webpage is an acceptable specimen for services or goods provided the specimen page submitted shows a way to order the goods or services.

> EXAMPLE: The USPTO rejected an applicant's specimen of a webpage that showed images of goods (and described applicant's services) because the page failed to provide a user with direct means to order the goods. In other words, there was no "Click to Buy" or "Click to Order" feature on the page. (*In re Quantum Foods Inc.,* 665 F. Supp.2d 727 (S.D. Tex. 2009).)

In July 2019, the U.S. Trademark Office released a new guide instructing its examining attorneys to carefully review specimens of use that appear to be digitally created/altered or mere mockups.

state trademark laws

In addition to the federal Lanham Act, all states have laws under which marks may be registered and receive judicial protection should infringement occur. State trademark protections are, like federal law, based on use. However, unlike federal law, no state offers registration on an intent-to-use basis; use of a mark must always precede its state registration. Registering with the state does not give a mark owner significantly greater rights, but it does offer notice to potential infringers who bother to search the registration list and, in a few states, might provide litigation benefits (for instance, attorneys' fees, presumptions of validity of the ownership claim, punitive damages).

Although the federal Lanham Act has pretty much replaced state law as the most important source of protection for marks on goods and services that move between states or across territorial or national borders, the state systems are still the only source of trademark or service mark protection for those businesses, nonprofit organizations, craftspersons, dance and artist groups, theater companies, and restaurants that operate on a solely local basis. Also, because the laws of many states provide for punitive damages in situations where the Lanham Act does not, it is common for an infringement action to claim violations of both federal and state trademark statutes. Finally, a number of states offer protection against dilution of a famous mark.

A listing of state trademark agencies can be found at www.uspto.gov/trademarks/basics/state-trademark-information-links.

Related terms: dilution; presumption of ownership; unfair competition.

Trademark Law: Definitions

Statement of Use

See Allegation of Use for Intent-to-Use Application, With Declaration.

statute of limitations

See laches.

strong mark

A mark that effectively identifies the origin of a product or service rather than its characteristics is a strong (good) mark, and a court can protect it from most or all uses by others. For example, the word "Cobalt" as a mark for a music recording label would be strong. Because it means a metal and a blue color, its use on music is original and in no way descriptive. Thus, it is distinctive and highly protectable. As a rule, strong marks are made up of terms that are:

- arbitrary (a term that is used for a purpose other than its plain meaning such as Owl Ice Co. or Diesel clothing)
- fanciful (a made-up term such as Rackafrax Wax), or
- suggestive (a term that suggests without describing the goods or services, such as 7-11 convenience stores or Coppertone sunscreen.

Only strong marks are entitled to be listed on the federal Principal Register; however, even unregistered strong marks are entitled to wide protections. Courts can enjoin (prevent) almost any infringing use of a strong mark. The test is whether the allegedly infringing use is likely to cause consumer confusion. The stronger the mark, the greater the likelihood that its use by another will confuse consumers. Because a strong mark stands out as the mark of a particular service or product, any imitation of it would be confusing.

Descriptive marks are weak, but can be made strong by use of advertising and the growth of consumer awareness (secondary meaning). The weaker the mark, the more reluctant a court will be to find it has been infringed, and the less protection it will receive.

Related terms: Principal Register; related products and services; secondary meaning; strong mark; weak mark.

"sucks" domain names

See free speech and trademark law.

suggestive mark

A suggestive mark is a lesser cousin of the family of distinctive marks, which also includes arbitrary and fanciful marks. Suggestive marks qualify for the federal Principal Register but are not as strong as their cousins. They escape being descriptive, however, because they suggest interesting qualities or concepts about a product or service rather than directly describing it. Examples of suggestive marks are "Roach Motel" insect traps and "Accuride" tires.

Whether a mark is descriptive or suggestive is a highly subjective determination, depending on how a consumer (or a judge) perceives the word in relation to the product or service. For example, the mark "Enduring" can be descriptive on lipstick, suggestive on a photographic service, and arbitrary on ice cream.

Courts use various tests to determine whether a mark is descriptive or suggestive. As a broad rule, the more brainpower it takes to see the descriptive qualities underlying a suggestive mark, the greater the protection it will receive.

> **EXAMPLE:** A company registered the mark, "Would You Rather ... ?" and sued a competitor over a similar mark. A district court determined that the mark was descriptive and lacked secondary meaning. The Ninth Circuit reversed. One acceptable test for distinguishing between descriptive and suggestive marks was the "imagination test," which asks whether a leap of imagination is required to understand the mark's relationship to the product. The Ninth Circuit held that the district misapplied this test and that the record lacked evidence in the form of consumer surveys. A second test was also considered—the "competitors' needs" test—that focuses on the need of competitors to use a similar mark. Another test was also examined—the "extent of use" test—that considers the extent to which other competitors have used the mark. Based on the application of these three tests, the Ninth Circuit determined that the mark was suggestive. (*Zobmomondo Entertainment, LLC v. Falls Media, LLC*, 602 F.3d 1108 (9th Cir. 2010).)

Related terms: descriptive mark; strong mark.

Supplemental Register

The federal Supplemental Register is a secondary list maintained by the U.S. Patent and Trademark Office for trademarks and service marks that do not qualify for the Principal Register. In a sense, the Supplemental Register is like a waiting room where owners of descriptive marks can bide their time until they qualify (after five years) for the Principal Register. Any name or symbol may be placed on the Supplemental Register as long as it is in actual use in commerce that Congress may regulate and can in some way distinguish the applicant's goods or services from others.

Descriptive, surname, and geographical term marks all qualify for the Supplemental Register. Generic terms do not qualify, since by definition a generic term calls to mind a type of product rather than a specific product. For instance, "Blue Jeans" means any pants made of blue denim, rather than a specific manufacturer's jeans. Marks that are barred from the Principal Register for reasons other than sheer descriptiveness are also barred from the Supplemental Register.

It is often difficult to prove infringement of a mark listed on the Supplemental Register, because such registration is an admission by the mark's owner that the mark is insufficiently distinctive to be placed on the Principal Register. Neither trademark nor unfair competition laws protect marks in any significant way unless consumer confusion is likely to result. Consumers are not likely to be confused by dual uses of any marks unless they are well known or memorable—in other words, distinctive. As a result, marks on the Supplemental Register do not receive all the protections given to those on the Principal Register. Specifically, placement on the Supplemental Register does not:

- provide constructive notice of ownership or a presumption of ownership in the event of infringement litigation
- support a later claim of incontestability status
- imply the right to exclusive use of the mark, or
- allow the mark's owner to request exclusion of imports by U.S. Customs officials.

On the other hand, supplemental registration does offer some benefits such as:

- the right to use the circled "®" or "Reg. U.S. Pat. Off." abbreviation to discourage would-be infringers
- the ability to register the mark in countries that offer reciprocal trademark rights, and
- the right to obtain injunctive relief, money damages, treble damages, and defendant's profits in the unlikely event that the mark owner wins an infringement action (assuming that the mark bore the proper notice of registration).

An applicant should always apply for the Principal Register first. If rejected, an applicant can then apply for the Supplemental Register.

The Lanham Act: § 1091. (§ 23) Supplemental register

This statute establishes a supplemental register for the purpose of registering marks that are insufficiently distinctive to warrant placement on the principal register. In addition, it sets out the procedures for applying to have a mark placed on the supplemental register.

(a) Marks registerable

In addition to the principal register, the Director shall keep a continuation of the register provided in paragraph (b) of section 1 of the Act of March 19, 1920, entitled "An Act to give effect to certain provisions of the convention for the protection of trademarks and commercial names, made and signed in the city of Buenos Aires, in the Argentine Republic, August 20, 1910, and for other purposes," to be called the supplemental register. All marks capable of distinguishing applicant's goods or services and not registrable on the principal register provided in this chapter, except those declared to be unregistrable under subsections (a), (b), (c), (d), and (e)(3) of section 1052 of this title, which are in lawful use in commerce by the owner thereof, on or in connection with any goods or services may be registered on the supplemental register upon the payment of the prescribed fee and compliance with the provisions of subsections (a) and (e) of section 1051 of this title so far as they are applicable. Nothing in this section shall prevent the registration on the supplemental register of a mark, capable of distinguishing the applicant's goods or services and not registrable on the principal register under this chapter, that is declared to be unregistrable under section 1052 (e)(3) of this title, if such mark has been in lawful use in commerce by the owner thereof, on or in connection with any goods or services, since before December 8, 1993.

(b) Application and proceedings for registration

Upon the filing of an application for registration on the supplemental register and payment of the prescribed fee the Director shall refer the application to the examiner in charge of the registration of marks, who shall cause an examination to be made and if on such examination it shall appear that the applicant is entitled to registration, the registration shall be granted. If the applicant is found not entitled to registration the provisions of subsection (b) of section 1062 of this title shall apply.

(c) Nature of mark

For the purposes of registration on the supplemental register, a mark may consist of any trademark, symbol, label, package, configuration of goods, name, word, slogan, phrase, surname, geographical name, numeral, device, any matter that as a whole is not functional, or any combination of any of the foregoing, but such mark must be capable of distinguishing the applicant's goods or services.

Related terms: commerce that Congress may regulate; prohibited and reserved marks under Lanham Act; unfair competition.

surnames as marks

See names as marks.

symbols and pictures as marks

See pictures and symbols used as marks; prohibited and reserved marks under Lanham Act.

tacking

Often a trademark owner wishes to vary a trademark in order to capitalize on marketing and cultural trends. However, an issue then arises as to whether this modification results in a new mark or whether it is a continuation of the first mark and can claim priority on that basis. If a trademark is properly "tacked," then the trademark owner claims the mark is a continuation of the earlier mark and is able to claim the date of first use of the earlier mark. Proper tacking requires that the two trademarks "create the same, continuing commercial impression, and the later mark should not materially differ from or alter the character of the mark attempted to be tacked." (*Van Dyne-Crotty, Inc. v. Wear-Guard Corp.*, 926 F.2d 1156, 1159 (Fed. Cir. 1991).) For example, attempting to tack by changing Ego to Alter Ego or changing Polo to Marco Polo were not found acceptable.

In 2015, the Supreme Court examined tacking in a case in which Hana Bank claimed that its use of Hana Overseas Korean Club could serve as its basis for priority for Hana Bank. The Supreme Court unanimously held that trademark tacking presents a question of fact appropriate for jury determination. (*Hana Financial v. Hana Bank*, 574 U.S. 418 (2015).)

TEAS

TEAS (Trademark Electronic Application System) is the system for electronic filing of trademark, collective mark, certification mark, Statement of Use/Amendment to Allege Use, or other application and post-registration forms. An electronic filing costs $250 to $350 per class depending on which filing option you choose. Your TEAS options are:

- **TEAS Plus:** This is the less expensive approach, with a filing fee of $250 per class of goods and/or services. The USPTO also considers this the "strictest" application and requires payment of the filing fee for all classes listed in the application and an identification of goods and/or services taken directly from the USPTO Trademark ID Manual. In addition, if applicable, the applicant must indicate if the application includes a (1) claim of prior registration(s); (2) translation; (3) transliteration; (4) consent of individual identified in mark; and (5) concurrent use claim. Failure to include this information will result in having to pay a $100 fee and the application being converted from TEAS Plus to TEAS standard.

- **TEAS Standard:** This option has a filing fee of $350 per class. The primary difference between TEAS Standard and TEAS Plus is that TEAS Standard applicants do not need to satisfy a few application requirements at the time of filing including selecting an identification of goods and/or services from the Trademark ID Manual. (This allows the applicant to customize goods and services.) Unlike the TEAS Plus applicant, the Standard applicant does not have to pay upfront the filing fee per class for all classes listed in the application.

Related terms: registration; TESS; TSDR.

TESS

TESS (Trademark Electronic Search System) is a database and search system enabling users to access federal trademark registrations and prior-filed applications.

Related terms: TEAS; TSDR.

TLD (top level domain)

See domain names.

TM

Although only marks that are federally registered can use the "®" symbol, any business that uses a mark can place the "TM" symbol after it to publicly claim ownership of the mark. The "TM" mark has no legal significance other than to notify the public that the mark owner views the words, design, and/or symbol as a protectable trademark. It also may serve as evidence against a claim of innocent infringement by a junior user, and thus enhance the possibility of collecting damages.

Related terms: damages in trademark infringement cases; infringement (trademark).

trade dress

Trade dress consists of all the various elements that are used to promote a product or service. For a product, trade dress may be the packaging, the attendant displays, and even the configuration of the product itself. For a service, it may be the decor or environment in which a service is provided—for example, the distinctive decor of the Hard Rock Cafe restaurant chain.

As with other types of trademarks, trade dress can be registered with the U.S. Patent and Trademark Office (USPTO) and receive protection from the federal courts.

To receive protection, both of the following must be true:

- The trade dress must be inherently distinctive, unless it has acquired secondary meaning.
- The junior use must cause a likelihood of consumer confusion.

For trade dress to be considered inherently distinctive, one court has required that it "be unusual and memorable, conceptually separable from the product, and likely to serve primarily as a designator of origin of the product." (*Duraco Products Inc. v. Joy Plastic Enterprises Ltd.*, 40 F.3d 1431 (3d Cir. 1994).)

The U.S. Supreme Court found that a Mexican restaurant chain's decor could be considered inherently distinctive because, in addition to murals and bright colored pottery, the chain also uses a specific indoor and outdoor decor based upon neon colored border stripes (primarily pink), distinctive outdoor umbrellas, and a novel buffet style of service. (*Two Pesos, Inc. v. Taco Cabana, Inc.*, 505 U.S. 763 (1992).) However, the Supreme Court ruled that product designs such as the appearance of a line of children's clothing are not inherently distinctive and can be protected only if they acquire distinctiveness through sales or advertising. (*Wal-Mart Stores, Inc. v. Samara Brothers, Inc.*, 529 U.S. 205 (2000).) Similarly, the "Cuffs & Collar" design mark used by Chippendale's exotic male dancers was found not to be inherently distinctive. (*In re Chippendales USA, Inc.*, 90 U.S.P.Q.2d 1535 (T.T.A.B. 2009), affirmed by the Federal Circuit in 2010.)

Functional aspects of trade dress cannot be protected under trademark law. For example, a company that claimed trade dress on a round beach towel lost its rights when the Seventh Circuit determined that the towel design was primarily functional (despite the fact that the trade dress had been registered and had achieved incontestable status). (*Jay Franco & Sons, Inc. v. Franek*, 615 F.3d 855 (7th Cir. 2010).) Only designs, shapes, or other aspects of the product that were created strictly to promote the product or service are protectable trade dress.

EXAMPLE: Many liqueur bottles have a unique shape designed for advertising rather than for any particular function. The tall, tapered shape of the bottle used for Galliano is not necessary to hold the product but helps to identify it and is therefore protectable as trade dress.

The trade dress aspect of packaging may be protected if a showing can be made that the average consumer would likely be confused as to product origin if another product is allowed to appear in similar dress. Legal protection is provided under the Lanham Act provisions relating to registered and unregistered marks.

For example, in a 2010 case, a bottled water company was able to stop a rival from using a similar packaging design by demonstrating its design was distinctive—a square shaped bottle, blue bottle cap, green tropical foliage, a rain drop, and a pink element (all of which were copied)—and because the goods and channels of distribution were identical and because consumers considered bottled water as an impulse purchase (thus exercising less discretion). (*Fiji Water Co. v. Fiji Mineral Water USA,* 741 F. Supp.2d 1165 (C.D. Cal. 2010).)

In 2016, the U.S. International Trade Commission ruled that not all of the trade dress associated with the iconic Chuck Taylor sneaker was protectable. Some parts of the sneaker's look—the rubber-toe band, toe cap, and stripes—were not proprietary to Converse, the owner of Chuck Taylor marks, because competitors had been using similar trade dress for decades. The ITC did agree to bar any sneakers that duplicated Converse's diamond-patterned outsole. (*In the Matter of: Certain Footwear Products,* ITC No. 337-TA-936 (2016).)

It's also possible to assert a claim of dilution based on unregistered trade dress. To do so under federal law the trade dress owner must prove: (1) the claimed trade dress, taken as a whole, is not functional and is famous; and (2) if the claimed trade dress includes any mark or marks registered on the Principal Register, the unregistered matter, taken as a whole, is famous separate and apart from any fame of such registered marks.

Related terms: Lanham Act; likelihood of confusion; trademark; unfair competition; *Wal-Mart Stores, Inc. v. Samara Brothers, Inc.*

trade name

Trade names are used to identify both nonprofit and for-profit business entities, whereas marks are used to identify products and services produced by such entities. Under the Lanham Act, a trade name is the name of any commercial firm, association, corporation, company, or other organization capable of suing and being sued in a court of law.

Trade names cannot be registered under the trademark and service mark provisions of the Lanham Act. However, they are entitled to protection under the unfair competition provision of the Lanham Act. (15 U.S. Code § 1125.) They are also protected under state unfair competition statutes and court decisions, if the public is likely to be confused by the use of the same or a similar name.

Companies frequently use their trade names as trademarks or service marks for their products and services—that is, as designators of origin in their advertising and on the products. For instance, Apple Computer Corporation uses the trade name "Apple" as a trademark, and the McDonald's fast food chain uses "McDonald's" as a service mark. In these situations, the trade name may be registered in its capacity as a mark and may receive additional protection under the Lanham Act's provisions applicable to infringement of marks.

Related terms: likelihood of confusion; service mark; trademark; unfair competition.

trademark

Manufacturers and merchants use trademarks to distinguish their products and services from those of others in the marketplace. A trademark usually consists of a word, phrase, logo, or other graphic symbol. Examples of trademarks are Honda (automobiles), Cap'n Crunch (cereals), Apple (computer equipment), and Tesla (automobiles). A trademark is not limited to a brand name or logo. It can also consist of a distinctive shape, letters, numbers, package design, sound, smell, color, or other aspects of a product that tend to promote it. Titles, character names, or other distinctive features of movies, television, video games, and radio programs can serve as trademarks when used to promote a product.

Many people use the term "trademark law" to refer broadly to all the laws that cover how businesses distinguish their products and services from those of others. This includes subjects like trade names, trade dress, commercial misappropriation, unfair competition, unfair business practices, and palming off. The above definition, however, focuses on the narrower meaning of "trademark" as a product identifier.

Related terms: federal trademark registration; *International Schedule of Classes of Goods and Services*; service mark; trade dress.

trademark dilution

See dilution.

Trademark Dilution Act of 2006

See dilution.

trademark infringement action

See infringement (trademark).

Trademark Modernization Act of 2020

The Trademark Modernization Act (TMA) provides several changes to trademark law:

- **It establishes the evidentiary burden for obtaining an injunction.** The TMA resolves a court circuit split by providing for a presumption of irreparable harm when a party demonstrates likelihood of confusion, making it easier for some parties to obtain an injunction.
- **It changes some procedures for trademark owners at the USPTO.** Third parties who object to an application can now submit evidence if it is connected to a ground for refusal. The TMA also provides Examining Attorneys with flexibility in setting response times, including deadlines shorter than six months.
- **It establishes procedures for canceling fraudulent and "deadwood" registrations.** To address a flood of fraudulent foreign trademark applications, Section 1 of the Lanham Act has been amended to include a process for submitting a letter of protest against registration of a mark. The TMA also establishes an "expungement" procedure that will allow third parties to seek cancellation of a registration on the grounds that the mark was never used with the claimed goods or services. At the same time, the TMA permits cancellation if the mark has never been used in commerce. Finally, the TMA creates a system for ex parte reexamination of a registration based on nonuse.

trademark owner

See ownership of mark in the United States.

trademark protection

See Lanham Act; state trademark laws.

trademark search

A trademark search is an investigation to discover any potential conflicts between a proposed mark and an existing one. Preferably done before a proposed new mark is used, a trademark search reduces the possibility of inadvertently infringing a mark belonging to someone else.

Trademark searches are extremely important. If a chosen mark is already owned and/or registered by someone else, the proposed mark might have to be replaced. Obviously, no one wants to discover that a new mark infringes another mark and must be changed, after having put time and expense into marketing, advertising, and implementing the mark's usage. In addition, if the earlier mark was registered under the Lanham Act prior to an infringing use, the infringing mark's owner might have to pay the mark's rightful owner any profits earned from the infringing use (defendant's profits).

Although the most thorough trademark searches are accomplished by professional search firms such as Thomson Compumark, it is also possible to conduct a preliminary online trademark search to determine whether a trademark is distinguishable from other federally registered trademarks. This can be accomplished using the U.S. Patent and Trademark Office's (USPTO's) free trademark database at www.uspto.gov, which provides free access to records of federally registered marks or marks that are pending (applications undergoing examination at the USPTO). Privately owned fee-based online trademark databases often provide more current USPTO trademark information.

It's also a good idea to check the Internet for a possible conflict with existing domain names as well as for names of firms already doing business there. The report issued by the searcher notes all uses of identical or similar marks and the products or services on which they are used.

If the search fails to disclose use of the same or similar mark by anyone in a related business, the mark owner can feel free to use it and register it federally (if used in commerce) or with the state (if used within only one state).

Related terms: damages in trademark infringement cases; domain names; federal trademark registration.

Trademark Trial and Appeal Board (TTAB)

An administrative arm of the U.S. Patent and Trademark Office, this body hears and decides disputes involving the registrability of, or conflicts between, marks. The Trademark Trial and Appeal Board consists of the trademark commissioner, the deputy commissioner, assistant commissioners, and members appointed by the trademark commissioner. In a case involving two soundalike trademarks, the Supreme Court ruled that a finding of likelihood of confusion by the Trademark Trial and Appeal Board (TTAB) could preclude litigating the same issue in court. (*B&B Hardware, Inc. v. Hargis Indus., Inc.*, 575 U.S. ___ (2015).) For a thorough reporting of decision making at the TTAB, see the TTABlog (www.ttablog.com).

Related terms: opposing and canceling a trademark registration; U.S. Patent and Trademark Office (USPTO).

TSDR

TSDR (Trademark Status and Document Retrieval System) is a database that combines the previous TARR and TDR systems to provide a database and search system enabling users to retrieve information about the status of an application or the status of registered marks and also offers the public an electronic portal to PDF viewing, downloading, and printing of an array of information and documents for more than 460,000 trademark applications totaling more than eight million document pages.

Related terms: TEAS; TESS.

typosquatting

See cybersquatting.

UDRP

The international agency that oversees domain names (ICANN) has established a dispute resolution procedure for trademark owners who believe that their domain name has been hijacked. The Uniform Dispute Resolution Procedure (UDRP) is a nonbinding arbitration procedure that is usually resolved within 60 days—much faster than any court decision would take. However, some commentators have argued that the UDRP procedure has become more cumbersome and expensive than originally intended, and occasionally unpredictable in its outcome. In addition, since the UDRP results are not binding, either party can take the case to a local court if unhappy with the result. Also, based upon past ICANN arbitrations, the odds seem to be stacked heavily in favor of the person who has or claims to have trademark rights. To review the ICANN dispute resolution rules, go to www.icann.org/udrp/udrp.htm.

unfair competition

Unfair competition is the legal umbrella that governs any commercial activity that tends to confuse, mislead, or deceive the public about the sale of products or services. Such diverse activities as trademark infringement, trade name infringement, simulation of trade dress and packaging, palming off, false advertising, false designation of origin, and theft of trade secrets all constitute unfair competition. Once a court defines any given activity as "unfair competition," it is ordinarily authorized to enjoin (judicially prevent) further activity from occurring and to award money damages.

Although most unfair competition law in the United States has been fashioned by legislatures and courts at the state level, Section 43(a) of the Lanham Act provides remedies for a broad range of activity generally described as unfair competition.

In 2016, the Fourth Circuit permitted the Swiss company, Bayer, to bring a Section 43(a) unfair competition claim to cancel registration and prevent use of the FLANAX mark. This was despite the fact that Bayer had never registered or used the FLANAX mark in the United States. Bayer had used FLANAX for its naproxen products in several countries including Mexico. Bayer claimed that the company registering the mark in the U.S. was doing so to confuse Mexican immigrants in America. The Fourth Circuit stated that there was no requirement that a party bringing a 43(a) claim have used or registered the mark. (*Belmora LLC v. Bayer Consumer Care AG*, 819 F.3d 697 (4th Cir. 2016).)

State unfair competition laws provide judicial relief in situations where a mark or trade name has been copied or simulated but where federal or state trademark infringement laws don't apply. Also, in most cases where trademark or service mark infringement is alleged, unfair competition claims are also raised as an alternative basis for judicial relief, in part because state law may offer the successful plaintiff the chance to get more money in the form of damages.

Related terms: false advertising; loss of mark; secondary meaning; unregistered mark, protection of.

unregistered mark, protection of

Unregistered distinctive marks are entitled under the Lanham Act to nearly as much protection from infringement as are registered ones. Federal registration does, however, make it easier to prove infringement and recover significant damages; thus strong marks should be registered.

The federal unfair competition statute, Section 43(a) of the Lanham Act (15 U.S. Code § 1125), is the main mechanism for protecting unregistered marks and trade names in interstate commerce. It prohibits two basic types of commercial activity (which are, in most cases, also treated as unfair competition under state laws):

- the use of a mark or label to designate falsely the origin of any product or service, and
- the description of a product or service in false terms (that is, false advertising).

If the products or services carrying the false designation or description were used in interstate commerce, anyone who engages in such activity may be sued in federal court by a person or business that can prove resulting economic injury.

This type of unfair competition suit for infringement of unregistered marks is not technically a trademark infringement action, due to the lack of registration. Such an action does, however, enable the owner of an unregistered mark to use the federal courts to stop the use of a similar mark that is likely to lead to consumer confusion. But the plaintiffs in such an action do not get some of the litigation benefits of federal registration, such as presumption of ownership, constructive notice, and incontestability. They are, however, entitled to recover triple damages and possibly attorneys' fees in case of a willful infringement.

Related terms: false advertising; Lanham Act; registered mark; unfair competition.

unregistrable material

See disclaimer of unregistrable material.

unrelated goods and services

See related products and services.

U.S. Patent and Trademark Office (USPTO)

The USPTO is the federal governmental wing of the U.S. Department of Commerce that governs trademark registration. As a practical matter, the USPTO determines the initial degree of protection that a mark is likely to receive in the courts. If registration of a mark is disputed, the Trademark Trial and Appeal Board, an arm of the USPTO, will hold hearings to resolve the dispute.

Related terms: federal trademark registration; *Official Gazette*.

use it or lose it

See abandonment of mark.

use of mark

The term "use" has a special meaning when it comes to protection and registration under the Lanham Act. As a broad rule, "use" means that the mark has been, is being, or will be actually utilized in the marketplace to identify goods and services. This doesn't mean that the product or service actually has to be sold, as long as it is offered to the public under the mark in question.

Trademark Law: Definitions

A mark is being used for a service if the service is being marketed under the mark and the service can be legitimately delivered upon request by a consumer.

A mark is used for goods if the mark is placed on the goods or on labels or tags attached to them and the goods are shipped to a store for resale. However, sales made only for the purpose of getting a mark into use don't count.

Related terms: commerce that Congress may regulate; service mark; trademark.

USPTO

See U.S. Patent and Trademark Office (USPTO).

Victoria's Secret case (*Moseley v. V Secret Catalogue, Inc.*)

Victor's Secret, a New Jersey store, sold adult videos, adult novelties, hosiery, temporary tattoos, and lingerie. Victoria's Secret—a lingerie and clothing company that distributes over 400 million catalogs annually—asked the New Jersey store to change its name. The store complied, altering its name to "Victor's Little Secret." When the store refused to modify the name further, Victoria's Secret sued for dilution, arguing that Victor's Little Secret tarnished and blurred their famous mark. The district court and court of appeals agreed with Victoria's Secret, but the Supreme Court reversed. The Supreme Court acknowledged that the Victoria's Secret trademark was a valuable and famous mark and that consumers made a mental association when seeing the two trademarks—Victoria's Secret and Victor's Little Secret. But the mental association, by itself, was not enough to prove dilution. In order to prove dilution, the Court ruled that the trademark owner must demonstrate more than the likelihood of harm; the owner must actually prove—through consumer surveys or other evidence—that the mark has been damaged. The case was remanded for a new trial. However, perhaps to head off any further litigation, the defendants changed the name of their shop to "Cathy's Little Secret." Many commentators believe that the ruling will make it harder for some famous marks to claim dilution, because the trademark owner will have to demonstrate that consumers actually believe that the mark is tarnished or blurred by the second use. (*Moseley v. V Secret Catalogue, Inc.*, 537 U.S. 418 (2003).)

Related terms: dilution; trade dress.

Wal-Mart Stores, Inc. v. Samara Brothers, Inc.

In *Wal-Mart Stores, Inc. v. Samara Brothers, Inc.*, 529 U.S. 205 (2000), the Supreme Court ruled that product designs, like colors, are not inherently distinctive. Samara created a line of children's clothing that featured one-piece seersucker outfits decorated with appliques of hearts, flowers, fruits, and the like. Wal-Mart authorized another clothing company to copy Samara's designs and then sold the knock-offs at a lower price than that offered by Samara. Samara sued Wal-Mart and a district court ordered Wal-Mart to pay Samara $1.6 million. The Supreme Court eventually overruled that decision, holding that the designs were not protected under trademark law because they were not distinctive. The result is that no matter how creative and clever a product design is made, it will be protected under trademark law only if the owner can demonstrate secondary meaning—that the public associates that product design with one source. (Note that Wal-Mart Stores, Inc. has since changed its name to Walmart Inc.)

weak mark

Trademark protection is based around a "strength" classification system. Strong trademarks are distinctive and are protectable. Weak trademarks are not distinctive. Weak marks cannot be registered or protected unless the trademark owner pumps up the mark with consumer awareness or "secondary meaning."

Broadly speaking, the more that the mark describes the goods or services (for example, Shake 'n Bake), the weaker or less distinguishable the mark. In some cases, if a mark is so descriptive that it is indistinguishable from the goods or service (for example, Light Beer for a beer low in calories), then it might be generic or too weak to ever obtain protection.

There are three common types of weak marks: descriptive marks that merely describe the nature, quality, characteristics, ingredients, or origin of a product or service; geographic marks that describe the origin or location of the goods or services; and family names (surnames) that are used as trademarks. All weak marks are capable of becoming strong if secondary meaning can be demonstrated.

Related terms: descriptive mark; generic terms; geographic terms as marks; surnames as marks.

willful infringer

See deliberate infringer (or willful infringer).

words in common use

See weak mark.

World Intellectual Property Organization (WIPO)

See international trademark rights.

zombie trademark

Abandoned trademarks that still have brand name recognition are referred to as zombie trademarks. Also known as "ghost brands," "orphan brands," and "graveyard brands," these revived marks pose a conundrum in trademark law. On the one hand, anyone is free to use an abandoned trademark; on the other, the new owner rarely replicates the quality formerly associated with the brand. Zombie marks are attractive to speculators who sometimes file intent-to-use applications to preclude others from using them. Some potential zombie marks include: Brim (coffee), Bonwit Teller (apparel), Coleco (toys and games), and Nuprin (analgesics). In 2020, AT&T salvaged the "Cingular" mark after another company attempted to register the term for wireless phone service. (*AT&T Mobility LLC v. Mark Thomann and Dormitus Brands LLC*, 2020 USPQ2d 43785 (T.T.A.B. 2020).)

Trademark Law: Forms

Preparing a Federal Trademark Application

In this section, we explain how to complete a federal trademark application and provide an example of a completed application. Applicants can also obtain help from the instructions provided at the U.S. Patent and Trademark Office (USPTO). The Trademark Electronic Application System (TEAS) offers two options:

- **TEAS Plus:** This is the less expensive approach, with a filing fee of $250 per class of goods and/or services. The USPTO also considers this the "strictest" application, and requires: (1) payment of the filing fee for all classes listed in the application; and (2) an identification of goods and/or services taken directly from the USPTO Trademark ID Manual. In addition, if applicable, the applicant must indicate if the application includes a (1) claim of prior registration(s); (2) translation; (3) transliteration; (4) consent of individual identified in mark; and (5) concurrent use claim. Failure to include this information will result in having to pay a $100 fee and the application being converted from TEAS Plus to TEAS standard.

- **TEAS Standard:** This option has a filing fee of $350 per class. The primary difference between it and TEAS Plus is that TEAS Standard applicants do not need to satisfy a few application requirements at the time of filing including selecting an identification of goods and/or services from the Trademark ID Manual. (This allows the applicant to customize goods and services.) Unlike the TEAS Plus applicant, the Standard applicant does not have to pay up front the filing fee per class for all classes listed in the application.

Before you begin your federal application, you'll need to figure out what theory it's based on. Most federal trademark applications are based on either "use in commerce" or an applicant's intention to use the trademark (referred to as an "intent-to-use" or ITU application). The process for both "in use" and "intent-to-use" application involves three steps:

- **Preparation and filing of application.** A trademark application consists of a completed application form, a drawing of the mark, the filing fee, and a specimen of the mark. You must file the application electronically and pay by credit card.

- **Examination by the USPTO.** Upon receipt, the trademark application is given a number and assigned to a USPTO examining attorney. If there is an error or inconsistency in the application, or if the examining attorney believes that registration is inappropriate, the attorney will contact the applicant to discuss the objection. The applicant can respond to the objections or can abandon the application. The examining attorney will either approve the mark for publication or reject it. If it is rejected, the applicant may challenge the rejection.

- **Publication in the *Official Gazette*.** Once the examining attorney approves the mark, it is published in the *Official Gazette*. The public is given 30 days to object to the registration. If no one objects, a trademark registration will be issued (or in the case of an ITU application, the mark is allowed pending use in commerce). If there is an objection from the public, the matter will be resolved through a proceeding at the USPTO.

The total time for an application to be processed can range from a year to several years, depending on the basis for filing and the legal issues that might arise in the course of examining the application. The registration expires ten years from the date of registration. You have certain obligations to maintain your trademark registration—for example, you must file a Section 8 Declaration of Continued Use between the fifth and sixth anniversary of the registration. Information about these maintenance requirements can be obtained at the USPTO website or by reviewing *Trademark: Legal Care for Your Business & Product Name,* by Stephen Fishman (Nolo).

The Trademark Application: the TEAS System

The online Trademark Electronic Application System (TEAS) located at the USPTO's website (www.uspto.gov/teas/index.html) is an interactive system in which the user is asked a series of questions. If a question is not answered or an essential element is not completed, the applicant is asked to correct the error. The system is easy to use and there's a low probability of error in preparing the form. The information provided below is intended for use on a standard TEAS application.

Basis for Application

On the trademark application, you will be asked the basis for your application. If you have already used the mark in connection with the sale of goods or services, then you would check "Yes" under "Use in Commerce." As for dates of use, you will need to provide the date (or your best guess as to the dates) you first sold goods or services using the trademark, anywhere. You will also need to provide the date when you first sold your work or services outside your state. If you have not yet used the mark but have a bona fide intention to use the mark, check, "Yes" under "Intent to Use."

Identification of the Class of Goods or Services

You will need to identify your class of goods. The USPTO uses the *International Schedule of Classes of Goods and Services* to group related goods. This helps it make appropriate comparisons of the mark. For example, glassware, porcelain, and earthenware are in Class 21. You can register your work in many classes, but each class registration costs between $225 and $400, depending on which TEAS form you use (check current fees at the USPTO website).

To identify the class for your goods, search the USPTO's goods and services manual online. Go the USPTO home page and click the Trademarks tab on the top of the page. On the drop-down menu, click "More tools & links," and then search for "Guides, Manuals and Resources." Then, select "Acceptable Identification of Goods and Services Manual (ID Manual) Next Generation," and type in the types of product or service that you sell. Two online sources for guidance in identifying goods are the *Trademark Examiners Manual of Procedure* (TMEP) and the U.S. Patent and Trademark Office *Acceptable Identification of Goods and Services Manual*.

Description of the Goods or Services

Along with the class for the goods, you will need to provide a description of the goods or services. This description is different from the listing of the International Class. For example, if you are selling key rings (International Class 6, "nonprecious metal goods"), the listing should state "key rings," not "nonprecious metal goods."

The description should be precise. If your description is too broad, the USPTO's trademark examining attorney will negotiate an appropriate description with you. (According to a USPTO survey, the applicant's identification of goods and services was questioned in more than 50% of trademark applications.)

Choosing the proper description is simplified because the TEAS system is electronically linked to the USPTO *Acceptable Identification of Goods and Services Manual*. An applicant can type in a word related to the goods and examine sample descriptions and lists of goods and services.

Identification of the Mark

If the mark is a word or group of words, identification of the mark is straightforward. For example, the mark could be identified simply as "Hooky Wooky Hats." (Note: For the broadest protection for a word mark, register it free of any lettering style. This will give you the ability to use the trademark in various fonts, rather than being restricted to your original presentation of the mark.)

If the mark is a stylized presentation of the word, a graphic symbol, a logo, a design, or any of the other devices permitted under trademark law, a statement must be provided that clearly identifies the mark. If you're using the TEAS system, type in the word "mark" or, in the case of a stylized mark, attach a JPG graphic file.

Information About the Applicant

The applicant—your business—can be an individual; a partnership; a corporation; an association such as a union, social club, or cooperative; or a joint ownership by some combination of any these forms. If you are acting on behalf of a partnership, include the names and citizenship of the general partners and the domicile of the partnership. If you are representing a corporation, include the name under which the business or group is incorporated and the state or foreign nation under which it is organized.

Your own citizenship is required, as well as a mailing address. If you are doing business under a fictitious name, that information should be provided, especially if it is included on any specimen furnished with the application. If the mark is owned jointly by two entities, that should be stated as well. Type the appropriate information into the online form. Drop-down menus and online help screens are available to guide you.

Declaration

You are required to provide a declaration, a sworn statement, or other verification that the facts in the trademark application are true. You, or an officer of your corporation or association, should sign the declaration. The TEAS application provides an all-purpose declaration that can be used for both ITU applications and for trademarks that are in use.

Disclaimers

Many trademarks include words or phrases that, by themselves, cannot be protected under trademark law. For example, no manufacturer of cars can claim an exclusive right to the word "car" or "automobile." To allow one person an exclusive right to use such terms would decimate the English language. Therefore, the trademark office usually requires a disclaimer as to certain portions of trademarks. For example, if an applicant selling baked goods wanted to register the mark Lucky Bakery, the applicant would be required to disclaim "bakery." This means that apart from the use as a part of the trademark, the applicant claims no exclusive right to use the word "bakery."

Specimen

If your application is based on actual use of your mark in commerce, you'll need to enclose a specimen—that is, an actual example of the trademark being used on your goods or in your offer of services. In the case of ITU applications, the specimen must be filed later, together with a document entitled "Amendment to Allege Use." An actual specimen, rather than a facsimile, is preferred. When filing electronically, you'll see that the USPTO provides a means for attaching a digital photograph of the specimen. For products, a label, tag, or container for the goods is considered to be an acceptable specimen of use for a trademark. Your JPG file size must be under two megabytes and it should be scanned at 300 DPI or higher. A letterhead or business card is unacceptable as a trademark specimen because it doesn't follow the goods through the stream of commerce.

Completing the Process

You will complete the process by paying the fees, authorizing your electronic signature, and validating the application. After you click "Pay/Submit" and your transaction is successful, you will receive a confirmation.

Later, you will receive email acknowledging the submission of your application. Hold on to that email, because it is the only proof you'll have that the USPTO has your application. It is also proof of your filing date and contains the serial number assigned to your application.

After Filing

The USPTO filing receipt explains that you should not expect to hear anything about your application for approximately three months. If you have not heard anything in three and a half months, it is wise to call and inquire as to the status of your application. There are three ways to do this:

- Check TSDR. The online Trademark Status and Document Retrieval system page (https://tsdr.uspto.gov) allows you to access information about pending trademarks obtained from the USPTO's internal database by entering a valid trademark serial number.
- If you want additional information or would prefer talking with a human, call the Trademark Assistance Center at 703-308-9400 and request a status check.

You will likely receive some communication from the USPTO within three to six months. If there is a problem with your application, you will receive what's called an "action letter." This is a letter from your examiner explaining what the problems are. Most problems can be resolved with a phone call to the examiner.

When the examiner approves your application for publication, you will receive a Notice of Publication in the mail. Your mark will then be published online in the *Official Gazette*. For 30 days following publication, anyone may oppose your registration. Only 3% of all published marks are opposed, so it is unlikely you will run into trouble.

Once your mark has made it through the 30-day publication period, and you are filing on an actual use basis, you will receive a Certificate of Registration. The USPTO sometimes has a difficult time moving applications through this long process. As a result, it can take a year or more to process your application.

If you filed on an intent-to-use basis, your mark will not be placed on the trademark register until you file an additional document with the USPTO when you put it into actual use. This form, available on the TEAS system, is called "Statement of Use/Amendment to Allege Use for Intent-to-Use Application." It tells the USPTO the date you started using the mark and completes the registration process. You must also provide a specimen at that time, showing how you are using the mark.

Communicating With the USPTO

The chances are good that you will be communicating with the USPTO after you have filed your application. Few applications sail through completely unscathed.

You are required to be diligent in pursuing your application. If you are expecting some action from the USPTO (the ball is in its court) and more than six months have elapsed without your hearing from it, immediately check the TSDR system or call the USPTO Status Line. If you discover a problem, bring it to the USPTO's attention. If you fail to respond in a timely manner to a request from a USPTO examining attorney, your application could be considered abandoned. If that happens, you may petition the Commissioner for Trademarks within 60 days to reactivate your application.

If the examiner wants you to change your application, such as claiming a different description of services or goods, there is usually some room for negotiation.

An examiner with a brief question might call you and then issue and mail you an examiner's amendment. This is a form on which the examiner records in handwriting a phone conversation or meeting with the applicant. Read the amendment carefully to make sure it matches your understanding of the conversation. If you disagree, or don't understand the amendment, first call the examiner, and then, if necessary, write the examiner a letter with your concerns, explaining your point of view on the communication.

Example of a TEAS Plus Application

The following data sheet reflects an application prepared using the new TEAS Plus system. The application is for the Nolo trademark as it is used in three classes: for books, software, and legal information services.

USPTO Generated Image

Trademark/Service Mark Application, Principal Register
TEAS Plus Application

NOTE: Data fields with the * are mandatory under TEAS Plus. The wording "(if applicable)" appears where the field is only mandatory under the facts of the particular application.

The table below presents the data as entered.

Input Field	Entered
TEAS Plus	YES
MARK INFORMATION	
*MARK	NOLO
*STANDARD CHARACTERS	YES
USPTO-GENERATED IMAGE	YES
LITERAL ELEMENT	NOLO
*MARK STATEMENT	The mark consists of standard characters, without claim to any particular font, style, size, or color.
APPLICANT INFORMATION	
*OWNER OF MARK	Nolo
*STREET	950 Parker Street
*CITY	Berkeley
*STATE (Required for U.S. applicants)	California
*COUNTRY	United States
*ZIP/POSTAL CODE (Required for U.S. applicants only)	94710
PHONE	510-704-2280
FAX	510-859-0027
EMAIL ADDRESS	rich@nolo.com
AUTHORIZED TO COMMUNICATE VIA EMAIL	Yes
LEGAL ENTITY INFORMATION	
*TYPE	CORPORATION
*STATE/COUNTRY OF INCORPORATION	California
GOODS AND/OR SERVICES AND BASIS INFORMATION	
*INTERNATIONAL CLASS	009
*DESCRIPTION	Computer software for the preparation of legal and business documents
*FILING BASIS	SECTION 1(a)
*FIRST USE ANYWHERE DATE	09/15/1987
*FIRST USE IN COMMERCE DATE	11/20/1987
*SPECIMEN FILE NAME	spec-6320712128-193107767 . Nolo_9.jpg
SPECIMEN DESCRIPTION	packaging for software product
GOODS AND/OR SERVICES AND BASIS INFORMATION	
*INTERNATIONAL CLASS	016
*DESCRIPTION	Books in the field of law and business topics
*FILING BASIS	SECTION 1(a)
*FIRST USE ANYWHERE DATE	06/01/1972
*FIRST USE IN COMMERCE DATE	06/01/1972
*SPECIMEN FILE NAME	spec-6320712128-193107767 . Nolo_16.jpg
SPECIMEN DESCRIPTION	cover of book

USPTO Specimens (Page 1)

PTO Form 1478 (Rev 7/2005)
OMB Control #0651-0009 (Exp. 09/30/2005)

Mark (USPTO-generated image for standard characters):

NOLO

Go Back

USPTO Specimens (Page 2)

PTO Form 1478 (Rev 7/2005)
OMB Control #0651-0009 (Exp. 09/30/2005)

Trademark/Service Mark Application, Principal Register

Serial Number: N/A

Class = 009

packaging for software product

Specimen:spec-6320712128-193107767_._Nolo_9.jpg

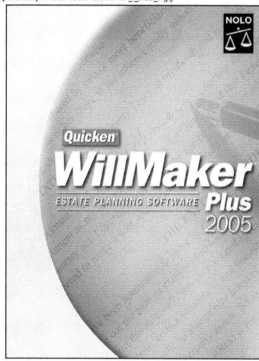

USPTO Specimens (Page 3)

Class # 016

cover of book

Specimen:spec-6320712128-193107767_._Nolo_16.jpg

NOLO

Law for All

4th edition

Marketing
Without
Advertising

**Inspire Customers to Rave About
Your Business & Create Lasting Success**

High-impact, low-cost marketing strategies

that will help you:

- attract new customers
- provide great service
- "spread the word"
- plan marketing events
- use the Web ethically & effectively

30 Years

*"Anyone who wants to make the most
effective use of customers for word-of-
mouth marketing needs to read what
Rasberry and Phillips have to say."*
—Tim O'Reilly
CEO of O'Reilly & Associates

by Michael Phillips & Salli Rasberry

USPTO Specimens (Page 4)

Class # 042

screen shot of Nolo web home page

Specimen:spec-6320712128-193107767_._Nolo_42.jpg

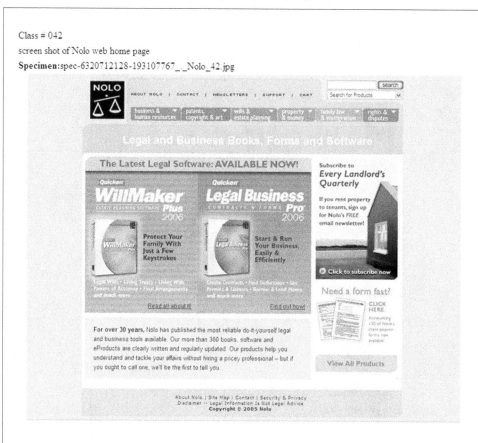

Back

Application Prepared for Review by Applicant

PTO Form 1478 (Rev 7/2005)
OMB Control #0651-0009 (Exp. 09/30/2005)

Trademark/Service Mark Application, Principal Register

TEAS Plus Application

To the Commissioner for Trademarks:

MARK: NOLO (Standard Characters, see mark)

The mark consists of standard characters, without claim to any particular font, style, size, or color.

The literal element of the mark consists of NOLO.

The applicant, Nolo, a corporation of California, residing at 950 Parker Street, Berkeley, California, United States, 94710, requests registration of the trademark/service mark identified above in the United States Patent and Trademark Office on the Principal Register established by the Act of July 5, 1946 (15 U.S.C. Section 1051 et seq.), as amended.

   International Class 009: Computer software for the preparation of legal and business documents

For specific filing basis information for each listed item, you must view the display within the Input Table. To access, click here.

   International Class 016: Books in the field of law and business topics

For specific filing basis information for each listed item, you must view the display within the Input Table. To access, click here.

   International Class 042: Providing information relating to legal affairs

For specific filing basis information for each listed item, you must view the display within the Input Table. To access, click here.

If the applicant is filing under Section 1(b), intent to use, the applicant declares that it has a bona fide intention to use or use through the applicant's related company or licensee the mark in commerce on or in connection with the identified goods and/or services. 15 U.S.C. Section 1051(b), as amended.

If the applicant is filing under Section 1(a), actual use in commerce, the applicant declares that it is using the mark in commerce, or the applicant's related company or licensee is using the mark in commerce, or the applicant's predecessor in interest used the mark in commerce, on or in connection with the identified goods and/or services, and lists below the dates of use. 15 U.S.C. Section 1051(a), as amended.

If the applicant is filing under Section 44(d), priority based on foreign application, the applicant declares that it has a bona fide intention to use the mark in commerce on or in connection with the identified goods and/or services, and asserts a claim of priority based on a specified foreign application(s). 15 U.S.C. Section 1126(d), as amended.

If the applicant is filing under Section 44(e), foreign registration, the applicant declares that it has a bona fide intention to use the mark in commerce on or in connection with the identified goods and/or services, and submits a copy of the supporting foreign registration(s), and translation thereof, if appropriate. 15 U.S.C. Section 1126(e), as amended.

The applicant hereby appoints Richard Stim, 950 Parker Street, Berkeley, California, United States, 94710 to submit this application on behalf of the applicant.

The USPTO is authorized to communicate with the applicant or its representative at the following email address: rich@nolo.com.

A fee payment in the amount of $825 will be submitted with the application, representing payment for 3 class(es).

Declaration

The undersigned, being hereby warned that willful false statements and the like so made are punishable by fine or imprisonment, or both, under 18 U.S.C. Section 1001, and that such willful false statements, and the like, may jeopardize the validity of the application or any resulting registration, declares that he/she is properly authorized to execute this application on behalf of the applicant; he/she believes the applicant to be the owner of the trademark/service mark sought to be registered, or, if the application is being filed under 15 U.S.C. Section 1051(b), he/she believes applicant to be entitled to use such mark in commerce; to the best of his/her knowledge and belief no other person, firm, corporation, or association has the right to use the mark in commerce, either in the identical form thereof or in such near resemblance thereto as to be likely, when used on or in connection with the goods/services of such other person, to cause confusion, or to cause mistake, or to deceive; and that all statements made of his/her own knowledge are true; and that all statements made on information and belief are believed to be true.

Signature: /rwstim/   Date: 08/19/2005
Signatory's Name: Richard Stim
Signatory's Position: Legal Counsel

 Back

Part 4: Trade Secret Law

Trade Secret Law: Overview..539

    What kind of information qualifies as a trade secret?...539

    How are trade secrets lost or stolen?...539

    Can you sell your trade secrets?...540

    How is trade secret protection enforced?...540

    What's new in trade secret law since the last edition?..541

    Trade secret resources..542

Trade Secret Law: Definitions...543

Trade Secret Law: Forms..599

  Preparing a Nondisclosure Agreement...599

    Explanation for Sample Nondisclosure Agreement...599

    Miscellaneous Provisions..608

Trade Secret Law: Overview

A trade secret is any information that has actual or potential commercial value, that has been maintained in confidence by a business, and that is not known by competitors. A business that owns trade secrets is entitled to court relief against those who have stolen the secrets or divulged them in violation of a legal duty—for example, after signing an agreement not to disclose (a nondisclosure agreement or NDA).

What kind of information qualifies as a trade secret?

Trade secrets can comprise all types of financial, business, scientific, technical, economic, or engineering information, including patterns, plans, compilations, program devices, formulas, designs, prototypes, methods, techniques, processes, procedures, programs, or codes. It doesn't matter whether they are tangible or intangible, or whether or how they are stored, compiled, or memorialized physically, electronically, graphically, photographically, or in writing.

Information is most likely to be considered a trade secret if it is:

- not known outside of the particular business entity
- known only by employees and others involved in the business
- subject to reasonable measures to guard the secrecy of the information
- valuable, and
- difficult for others to properly acquire or independently duplicate.

How are trade secrets lost or stolen?

Information that qualifies as a trade secret comes under legal protection (against theft and misappropriation) as a form of valuable property—but only if the owner has taken the necessary steps to preserve its secrecy. If the owner has not diligently tried to keep the information secret, courts will usually refuse to extend any help to the trade secret owner if others learn of the information.

Some activities that the courts will commonly treat as trade secret theft—which means the owner will be afforded some judicial relief, such as damages or an order preventing use of the stolen information—are:

- disclosures by key employees (current and former managers, scientists, and others occupying positions of trust) in violation of their duty of trust toward their employer
- disclosures by employees (current and former) in violation of a nondisclosure agreement entered into with their employer
- disclosures by suppliers, consultants, financial advisers, or others who signed nondisclosure agreements with the trade secret owner promising not to disclose the information
- industrial espionage, and
- disclosures by any person owing an implied duty to the employer not to make such disclosure, such as directors, corporate officers, and other high-level salaried employees.

When a disclosure is considered wrongful, the courts may also issue an order (injunction) preventing use of the information for a particular period of time.

Can you sell your trade secrets?

As with other types of property—such as goods, accounts receivable, patents, and trademarks—trade secrets may be sold by one business to another. Most trade secret sales occur as part of the sale of the business itself, but that is not mandatory.

How is trade secret protection enforced?

If the court finds that trade secret theft has occurred, it may issue an order (injunction) requiring all those wrongfully in possession of the information to refrain from using it or disclosing it to others. The court may also award the trade secret owner money damages to compensate for any monetary loss suffered as a result of the theft. In cases involving willful or deliberate theft, the court may also award punitive damages to punish the wrongdoer. A business can bring a trade secret lawsuit in state or federal court. All states except New York have adopted rules based on the Uniform Trade Secret Act (UTSA). New York bases its trade secret law on judge-made law (the common law). A business can also bring a lawsuit for misappropriation of trade secrets under the federal Defend Trade Secrets Act (DTSA). In some cases, the trade secret thief can be subjected to federal or state criminal prosecution.

What's new in trade secret law since the last edition?

Below are some important changes in trade secret law that have occurred since the last edition.

- **Supreme Court's "confidentiality" definition shields FOIA disclosures.**
  Despite the Freedom of Information Act (FOIA) mandate to disclose
  unreleased documents, an exemption prevents disclosure of "trade secrets
  and commercial or financial information obtained from a person and
  privileged or confidential." (5 U.S. Code § 552(b)(4).) A media company
  sued under the FOIA to obtain food stamp data from retail stores. The
  U.S. Department of Agriculture (USDA) refused to provide food stamp
  redemption data, citing the exemption. The Supreme Court agreed, and
  established two criteria for the exemption: (1) the information must be
  closely held by the person imparting it, and (2) the party receiving the
  information provides assurance that the information will remain secret.
  Because a store's redemption data is not customarily disclosed to the public
  and because the USDA promised the participating stores to keep their data
  private, the exemption prohibited disclosure. (*Food Marketing Institute v.
  Argus Leader Media*, 139 S.Ct. 2356 (2019).)
- **Bar is high for overturning permanent trade secret injunction.** The inventor
  of a shelf-life-extending formula for iceberg lettuce obtained a permanent
  injunction against a company founded by a former employee. The former
  employee's company sought to end the injunction after the ingredients
  for the formula were publicly disclosed. The appellate court refused to
  terminate the injunction, noting that knowledge of the ingredients didn't
  mean knowledge of the formula. (*The Global Protein Products, Inc. v. Le*,
  42 Cal.App.5th 352 (2019).)
- **DTSA statute of limitations begins once party is on notice of misappropriation.**
  A company, CMI, had noticed that its trade secrets were being used by a
  rival, but waited 14 years before bringing a lawsuit under the federal Defend
  Trade Secrets ACT (DTSA). The Eighth Circuit held that CMI knew or
  should have known that its trade secrets were being used and had a duty to
  investigate. The DTSA three-year statute of limitations began to run once
  CMI was on notice of misappropriation. (*CMI Roadbuilding, Inc. v. Iowa
  Parts, Inc.*, 920 F.3d 560 (8th Cir. 2019).)

- **"Head-start" damages upheld by Third Circuit.** A $1.1 million trade secret damages award by an arbitrator was based on the equitable "head-start" principle. Typically, the head-start remedy takes the form of an injunction prohibiting one company from using a trade secret for a period of time (usually the amount of time that it would take to develop the secret). In this case, the arbitrator awarded financial damages based upon the estimated head-start period. The defendant argued against this application of the head-start principle but the Third Circuit ruled that "head-start" damages were permissible and upheld the arbitrator's award. (*Sabre GLBL, Inc. v. Shan*, 779 Fed. App'x 843 (2019).)

- **Crime of "attempted" trade secret theft does not require actual trade secret.** An ex-employee of a cast-iron manufacturer was arrested leaving for China, where he planned to work for a rival cast-iron manufacturer. The ex-employee was carrying a hard drive on which he had downloaded 1,900 documents from his former employer. He was convicted of attempted theft of trade secrets under the Economic Espionage Act (EEA). The defendant claimed that the government never proved that the pilfered information constituted trade secrets. The court held that "an attempt charge allows the Government to charge not only individuals who are unsuccessful in stealing actual trade secrets, but also those who successfully steal information that they believe to contain trade secrets but in fact do not." (*United States v. O'Rourke*, No. 16-1594 (N.D. Ill., October 9, 2019).)

- **California business noncompetes treated differently than employee noncompetes.** Section 16600 of the California Business and Professions Code prohibits an employer from restraining an ex-employee from competing. In a case dealing with California noncompete law, the California Supreme Court was faced with the question: Does section 16600 void a contract by which a business (not an employee) is restrained from engaging in a lawful trade or business with another business? The court held that section 16600 applies to contractual restraints on businesses, but that restraints on businesses should be evaluated using the "rule of reason" standard (used for antitrust analyses). (*Ixchel Pharma v. Biogen*, 9 Cal.5th 1130 (2020).)

Trade secret resources

For more news and information on trade secret law and nondisclosure agreements, see Trade Secrets Watch (http://blogs.orrick.com/trade-secrets-watch).

Trade Secret Law: Definitions

B elow are concise definitions of the major concepts and terminology associated with explaining, protecting, and enforcing trade secrets.

accidental disclosure of trade secrets

If valuable business information is inadvertently disclosed to the public, courts commonly refuse to protect it as a trade secret. This means that accidentally disclosed information can be used by competitors without fear of a lawsuit by the information's original owner.

> EXAMPLE: Independent Robotics conducts a guided tour of its plant. One of the company's engineers accidentally leaves a top secret diagram of a new robot in full view, where it is seen by a competitor on the tour. This diagram (and the information contained in it) has lost its trade secret status due to the fact that it was discovered accidentally, without any intentional wrongdoing by the employee or the competitor.

Related terms: loss of trade secrets; reasonably precautionary measures to protect trade secrets.

advantage over competitors

See competitive advantage.

anticompetition agreements

See covenant not to compete by employee; covenant not to compete by owners of a sold business.

antitrust law and trade secrets

The primary purpose of antitrust law is to preserve a free, competitive marketplace by preventing companies from engaging in behavior that unduly dominates the marketplace or restricts free trade. Antitrust law:

- restricts businesses from engaging in practices with the intent to create a dominant or monopolistic market position, and

- prohibits businesses from making agreements with other businesses or individuals that impose significant restrictions or restraints on trade, such as price-fixing, territorial restriction agreements, bid-rigging, and tying arrangements.

In some circumstances, trade secret owners can violate the antitrust laws by using their trade secrets unfairly, to discriminate against other companies. For example, if a clothing manufacturing company that has discovered a new method for protecting cotton from shrinkage shares this secret with one competitor for the purpose of driving a third competitor out of business, the antitrust laws might have been violated (conspiracy in restraint of trade and monopolistic practices). In general, deciding whether a particular activity violates the antitrust laws involves such variables as the intent of the actors, the degree of harm done to other companies, and the level of commerce that is affected (local, state, national, or international).

In 2011, the Fourth Circuit ruled that a company that misappropriated trade secrets from DuPont regarding the production of Kevlar (and had subsequently been enjoined from marketing such products) was not prohibited from enforcing anticompetition laws against DuPont. (*E.I. DuPont de Nemours and Co. v. Kolon Industries Inc.*, 637 F3d 435 (4th Cir. 2011).)

Related terms: illegal restraint of trade; licensing of trade secrets.

attorneys' fees

Under the federal Defend Trade Secrets Act (DTSA) attorneys' fees can be recovered by the prevailing party if the claims are made in bad faith, a motion to terminate an injunction is made or opposed in bad faith, or the trade secret was willfully and maliciously misappropriated. The 49 states that have adopted the Uniform Trade Secrets Act (all but New York) typically provide for the recovery of attorneys' fees if a trade secret lawsuit is brought (or resisted) in bad faith. Attorneys' fees may also be recovered if a nondisclosure agreement provides for recovery of fees in the event of breach of the agreement.

Defend Trade Secrets Act, 18 USC § 1836(b)(3) (D). Remedies

In a civil action brought under this subsection with respect to the misappropriation of a trade secret, a court may, if a claim of the misappropriation is made in bad faith, which may be established by circumstantial evidence, or a motion to terminate an injunction is made or opposed in bad faith, or the trade secret was willfully and maliciously misappropriated, award reasonable attorney's fees to the prevailing party.

Uniform Trade Secrets Act: § 4. Attorney's Fees
If (i) a claim of misappropriation is made in bad faith, (ii) a motion to terminate an injunction is made or resisted in bad faith, or (iii) willful and malicious misappropriation exists, the court may award reasonable attorney's fees to the prevailing party.

beta testing and trade secrets

After new products and services are developed, they are often tested exhaustively under real-life conditions to make sure that they work properly before being released to the public. This reality check (known as beta testing) is especially important in the case of computer software, which is usually so complex that its performance in disparate real-life situations cannot accurately be predicted on the basis of the written code. To identify any potential problems and mistakes (bugs) in the software, the software developer will commonly allow a number of people to use the software in exchange for keeping track of any problems they encounter. To preserve the software as a trade secret during the beta test phase, the developer customarily requires beta testers to sign nondisclosure agreements containing a promise not to talk about the software with anyone unless authorized by the developer.

Related terms: nondisclosure agreement; software and trade secrets.

business information as trade secret

A business's internal information can qualify as a trade secret if its disclosure would negatively affect that business's competitiveness. For example, the following types of information commonly are considered to be trade secrets because they provide a business with a competitive edge:

- information concerning the characteristics of customers
- information relevant to the cost and pricing of goods
- sources of supply, especially if disclosure would divulge the nature of a secret ingredient
- books and records of the business
- mailing lists and other sales information
- customer lists
- information regarding new business opportunities (such as the price and physical characteristics of real estate)
- information regarding the effectiveness and performance of personnel, distributors, and suppliers, and
- methods of doing business.

On the other hand, business information is not protectable as a trade secret if it can be independently developed with little difficulty. Information that might not usually qualify as a trade secret includes general employee handbooks and personnel policies that discuss the rights and responsibilities of workers based on applicable federal and state law.

Related terms: competitive advantage; compilation of information as a trade secret; customer lists; databases as trade secrets; industrial secret; know-how.

clean room

In order to demonstrate that proprietary materials were developed independently, teams are isolated and monitored in "clean rooms." These facilities provide evidence that similarities to others' works or products are due to legitimate constraints and not copying.

commercial piracy

See piracy.

competition by former employees

See confidential employment relationship; covenant not to compete by employee.

competitive advantage

Trade secret information, by definition, provides a business with a competitive advantage. This means that the information can potentially be exploited to enhance the income or assets of a business. If the owner of information cannot derive economic benefit from the information, there is no trade secret. Conversely, if keeping the information secret will give its owner a competitive advantage, the item may qualify as a trade secret, assuming that secrecy is, in fact, maintained.

Related terms: trade secret, defined.

compilation of information as a trade secret

Trade secrets are often thought to involve a new approach, formula, device, or method for accomplishing a given end. However, a genuinely innovative structuring or reorganization of otherwise public information that creates a competitive advantage can also qualify as a trade secret if it is maintained as one.

Much existing information is now being reorganized so that it can be more easily stored in and retrieved from computer databases. Often referred to as "knowledge engineering," these new machine-searchable formats themselves might qualify as innovative compilations. They deserve treatment as trade secrets if maintained as such, because they enable a business to analyze old information in new ways that can lead to a competitive edge.

Related terms: business information as trade secret; customer lists; databases as trade secrets.

computer programs and trade secrets

See software and trade secrets.

confidential employment relationship

Much of trade secret law is concerned with how employees may act with respect to an employer's trade secrets during and after their period of employment, even if these matters are not set out in a written agreement.

Federal and state laws prohibit trade secret theft. Regardless of whether an employer uses a nondisclosure agreement, an employee can be legally prevented from making unauthorized disclosures. In some cases, an employer may obtain financial damages from the employee for such disclosures. Although it is always advisable to use a nondisclosure agreement, these state laws provide a second line of defense for when trade secrets are stolen.

In addition to federal and state laws prohibiting disclosure, certain management and high-level employees—for example, engineers, scientists, or corporate executives—who come into contact with trade secrets during the course of their work have a special obligation (referred to as a "fiduciary duty" or "duty of trust") to treat secrets as confidential. The higher the level of expertise or responsibility possessed by the employee, the more likely this special fiduciary relationship is to exist. This offers an employer another method of preserving trade secrecy.

Regardless of these laws and fiduciary duties, firms possessing trade secrets usually require all employees with access to trade secrets to sign nondisclosure agreements. Such agreements provide additional rights and obligations in the event of a trade secret theft.

Related terms: duty of trust; exit interview; nondisclosure agreement.

confidentiality agreements

See nondisclosure agreement.

Trade Secret Law: Definitions

copyright and trade secret law compatibility

A copyright consists of the exclusive right to reproduce, display, perform, distribute, and make alterations to an original work of expression. Simply put, copyright law protects the original expressions of ideas, but not the ideas themselves.

Copyright and trade secret laws sometimes protect the same kinds of information and sometimes are mutually exclusive of each other. Here are the salient points of how trade secret and copyright legal protections can work together under the Copyright Act of 1976:

- Trade secret and copyright protection are both available for unpublished works as long as the idea (or ideas) within the work is sufficiently innovative to qualify as a trade secret (is confidential information that provides a business with a competitive advantage) and the information is kept confidential.

- Trade secret and copyright protection may both be available for works that are distributed on a limited and restricted basis under a copyright licensing arrangement that requires the licensee (user) to recognize and maintain the trade secret aspects of the work. This dual protection is especially pertinent for the computer software business.

- Trade secret protection is normally not available for software if the source code is made available to the public on an unrestricted basis through such means as listing it in a computer magazine or on a medium of distribution.

- Works that are widely distributed without specific licensing agreements will ordinarily lose their trade secret status but might be entitled to copyright protection.

- The deposit of a physical copy of the work that is being registered with the U.S. Copyright Office operates to disclose any trade secrets in the work unless the deposit in some way masks the material that comprises the trade secret. For instance, it is possible to deposit samples of source code with major portions blacked out so that the parts of the code being maintained as a trade secret are not disclosed. There are several other methods for simultaneously registering a computer program and maintaining trade secrets. One common way is to withhold the source code altogether and deposit object code—which is impossible to understand when read in the U.S. Copyright Office.

- In some litigation involving trade secret and copyright claims, the trade secret claims may be preempted. ("Preemption" is the invalidation of a state claim because it conflicts with federal law.) This occurs if the basis for the trade secret claim falls within the subject matter of the Copyright Act and the rights asserted under state law are equivalent to those protected by the Copyright Act.

Related terms: ideas as trade secrets; reasonably precautionary measures to protect trade secrets; software and trade secrets.
See also Part 2 (Copyright Law): Copyright Act of 1976.

covenant not to compete by employee

Also referred to as a "noncompetition agreement" or "noncompete," this is legalese for a written promise by an employee not to compete with his or her employer, or to take employment with a competing business, for a specified length of time after the employer-employee relationship ends.

Noncompetition and nondisclosure agreements both have the same goal: to prevent a competitor from using valuable business information. The difference is that a nondisclosure prohibits revealing information to a competitor; a noncompete prohibits even working for a competitor or starting a competing business. In other words, the noncompete is broader and more heavy-handed in its approach. (So heavy-handed that some states restrict or prohibit them.)

In some cases, noncompetes and nondisclosure agreements complement each other. For example, an Internet business might use a noncompete agreement to prohibit employees from working for competitors for a period of six months. After that, the employees may work for a competitor but will still be prohibited, under the terms of a nondisclosure agreement, from disclosing trade secrets. The six-month noncompete period guarantees that short-term business strategies won't be compromised, while the nondisclosure agreement guarantees that fundamental long-term business information and methods won't be lost in subsequent years.

By delaying former employees from going to work for competitors or starting their own competing businesses, covenants not to compete minimize the risk that trade secrets will be disclosed or used to compete with the former employer.

Agreements restricting the right of employees to compete have often proved difficult to enforce in court, as courts tend to dislike contracts that restrict a worker's right to earn a living. Employees with high levels of responsibility are more likely to be held to their promise, while those with less important responsibilities might be able to escape from the restriction on the premise that they would not be in a position to harm the employer's interest, and it would more severely affect their ability to support themselves.

Covenants not to compete are banned in some countries and banned or greatly restricted in a few states, including California. However, if an employee enters into a legal noncompete in one state and then takes a job with a competitor in California, California courts will enforce the agreement.

> EXAMPLE: Medtronic, a manufacturer of implantable medical devices, hired Mark Stultz to work in its Minnesota branch office. Stultz signed a noncompete agreement—legal in Minnesota—and then, after a few years, resigned and went to work for Advanced Bionics, a California medical device manufacturer. Stultz and Advanced Bionics asked a California court to invalidate the Medtronic noncompete agreement, since California does not permit noncompetes. The California Supreme Court refused; Stultz was bound by the Minnesota agreement, even in California. (*Advanced Bionics Corp. v. Medtronic, Inc.*, 29 Cal.4th 697 (2002).)

Federal district courts in California have also held that forum selection clauses (provisions that determine where a contract will be litigated) can be enforced against California employees even if the end result is to enforce a noncompete. (*Hartstein v. Rembrandt IP Solutions*, 2012 WL 3075084 (N.D. Cal. July 30, 2012).)

Most state courts will, however, enforce covenants not to compete if they are seen as necessary to protect trade secrets and are drafted to minimize the restriction of the employee's right to work and/or engage in commerce.

A court is more likely to shorten the time periods for restrictive covenants when the employee works in an area of developing technology such as software or the Internet.

> EXAMPLE: An Internet employee's one-year restriction on working for a competitor was too long "given the dynamic nature of this [Internet] industry, its lack of geographical borders, and the employee's former cutting-edge position." (*EarthWeb, Inc. v. Schlack*, 71 F. Supp.2d 299, 313 (S.D.N.Y. 1999).) Another court limited an Internet employee's noncompete restriction to six months. (*DoubleClick, Inc. v. Henderson*, 1997 LEXIS 577 (Sup. Ct. N.Y. Co. 1997).)

Related terms: confidentiality agreements; reasonably precautionary measures to protect trade secrets.

covenant not to compete by owners of a sold business

As a condition of the sale of an existing business, its owners, officers, or directors are commonly required to promise in writing not to compete with the purchased business for a specific time period. These promises (or covenants) constitute recognition that part of the value of the purchased business consists of trade secrets. If former owners, officers, or directors were permitted to utilize this information in competing businesses, the purchasers of the existing business would not be getting their money's worth. For this reason, courts are usually willing to enforce these covenants. This is true even in California, which prohibits employee noncompetes.

criminal prosecution for trade secret theft

Several states and the federal government have passed laws that make the unauthorized disclosure, theft, or use of a trade secret a crime. Under these laws the government, not private businesses, arrests the perpetrators and brings criminal charges. The penalties—including imprisonment—can be much more severe than in a civil suit. For example, a person convicted of violating the federal Economic Espionage Act of 1996 (EEA) can be imprisoned up to ten years.

The filing of a criminal case does not prevent the trade secret owner from filing a civil lawsuit based on the same issues. For example, in a case involving the Avery-Dennison company, a Taiwanese competitor was ordered to pay $5 million in fines to the government as a result of criminal charges and $60 million to Avery-Dennison as a result of a civil lawsuit involving claims of trade secret misappropriation, RICO (Racketeer Influenced and Corrupt Organizations Act) violations, and conversion.

Criminal prosecutions of trade secret theft are rare because many businesses prefer not to bring law enforcement officials into the fray. Also, in some cases, law enforcement officials hesitate to prosecute because there might not be sufficient evidence to obtain a conviction. Keep in mind that the standards of proof for criminal cases are higher than for civil battles.

Two 2012 cases demonstrate the limits of bringing trade secrecy claims using federal criminal statues. The Ninth Circuit (in a split with other circuits) held that a former employee who downloaded trade secrets could not be convicted under the Computer Fraud and Abuse Act (CFAA) because the employee did not exceed his "authorized access." (*United States v. Nosal*, 676 F.3d 854 (9th Cir. 2012) (*en banc*).) And in another case, a man who uploaded high-speed securities trading software containing trade secrets to his new job was convicted under the National Stolen Property Act (which makes it a crime to transport or transmit goods, wares, merchandise, securities, or money). The Second Circuit Court of Appeals reversed the conviction, holding that the trade secrets were intangible and the statute sought to protect theft of tangible goods. (*United States v. Aleynikov*, 676 F.3d 71 (2d Cir. 2012).)

In 2019, a federal court held that the crime of "attempted" trade secret theft under the EEA does not require proof that the pilfered information was, in fact, a trade secret. The defendant claimed that the government never proved that the 1900 documents he secretly downloaded (before exiting to work for a Chinese competitor) constituted trade secrets. The court held that an attempt charge allows the government to charge individuals "who successfully steal information that they believe to contain trade secrets but in fact do not." (*United States v. O'Rourke*, No. 16-1594 (N.D. Ill., October 9, 2019).)

Although state criminal laws affecting trade secrets differ from state to state, the typical law applies to anybody who intentionally:

- physically takes records or articles reflecting the trade secret
- copies or photographs such records or articles
- assists in either of these acts, or
- discloses the trade secret to another after having received knowledge of the secret in the course of a confidential employment relationship.

Related terms: Economic Espionage Act of 1996; improper acquisition of trade secrets; improper disclosure of trade secrets.

customer lists

Companies are often eager to protect their customer lists with nondisclosure agreements, particularly when a former employee might use a customer list to contact clients. If a dispute over a customer list ends up in court, a judge usually considers the following elements to decide whether or not a customer list qualifies as a trade secret:

- Is the information in the list ascertainable by other means? A list that is readily ascertainable cannot be protected.
- Does the list include more than names and addresses? For example, a customer list that includes pricing and special needs is more likely to be protected because this information adds value.

- Did it take a lot of effort to assemble the list? A customer list that requires more effort is more likely to be protected under a nondisclosure agreement.
- Did the departing employee contribute to the list? If the departing employee helped create a relationship or had personal contact with the customers, it is less likely to be protected under a nondisclosure agreement.
- Is the customer list personal, long-standing, or exclusive? If a business can prove that a customer list is special to its business and has been used for a long time, the list is more likely to be protected.

EXAMPLE 1: A salesman worked for an insurance company selling credit life insurance to automobile dealers. When he switched jobs to work for a competing insurance company, he took his customer list and contacted the customers at his new job. A court ruled that the customer list was not a trade secret, because the names of the automobile dealers were easily ascertainable by other means and because the salesman had contributed to the creation of the list. (*Lincoln Towers Ins. Agency v. Farrell*, 99 Ill.App.3d 353, 425 N.E.2d 1034 (1981).)

EXAMPLE 2: Former employees took the client list of a temporary employee service. The former employees argued that the list could not be a trade secret since the information could be obtained through other means. A court disagreed and prevented the ex-employees from using the list, because it could not be shown, using public information, which companies were likely to use temporary employees, and because the list also included such information as the volume of the customer's business, specific customer requirements, key managerial customer contacts, and billing rates. (*Courtesy Temporary Serv., Inc. v. Camacho*, 222 Cal. App.3d 1278 (1990).)

Wholesalers' lists of retail concerns are often hard to protect as trade secrets. Retailers are usually easy to identify through trade directories and other sources, and a list of them ordinarily does not confer a competitive advantage. But there are exceptions—for instance, a list of bookstores that order certain types of technical books and pay their bills promptly might be highly valuable to a wholesale book distributor. But if the information is readily ascertainable through trade publications or other industry sources, it is not classified as a trade secret.

Trade Secret Law: Definitions

EXAMPLE: In a California case, a court determined that employees who left a business could use their former employer's mailing list to send out an announcement of their change of employment to former clients. The former employer's mailing list was not a trade secret because: (1) the clients became known to the ex-employees through personal contacts, and (2) the use of the customer list simply saved the ex-employees the minor inconvenience of looking up the client addresses and phone numbers. In other words, the information was easy to ascertain. (*Moss, Adams & Co. v. Shilling*, 179 Cal.App.3d 124 (1984).)

Related terms: business information as trade secret; databases as trade secrets.

damages in trade secret misappropriation actions

Under federal law (the Defend Trade Secrets Act), a trade secret owner who proves misappropriation can be awarded money (damages) for any actual losses (typically, lost profits) as well as any profits by the thief (to the extent they're not computed in the actual losses). Alternatively, a federal court may award a reasonable royalty to compensate for the disclosure. Special damages may be awarded if the theft was willful and malicious. These "exemplary" damages cannot be more than two times the damages actually suffered.

Under state laws, if a trade secret owner has suffered monetary loss as a result of a trade secret theft, the owner might be able to get a court to award either:

- money damages measured by the profits earned by the competitor as a result of the use of the trade secret, or
- money damages measured by the loss of profits by the trade secret owner due to the improper trade secret leak.

Further, if the theft was intentional, courts in many states may impose punitive damages (damages awarded to the plaintiff for the purpose of punishing the wrongdoer and providing an example to other would-be trade secret thieves). By contrast, in other states, treble damages (three times the amount of proven actual damages) is the most that can be awarded in a trade secret case. For example, in a state that allows punitive damages, a court might award the plaintiff $1,000,000, even if the trade secret owner only proves $10,000 worth of actual damages. But in states where punitive damages are defined as treble damages, the court could only award $30,000 in the same case.

Defend Trade Secrets Act, 18 USC § 1836(b)(3)(B)&(C). Remedies
In a civil action brought under this subsection with respect to the misappropriation of a trade secret, a court may: (B) award—(i)(I) damages for actual loss caused by the misappropriation of the trade secret; and (II) damages for any unjust enrichment caused by the misappropriation of the trade secret that is not addressed in computing damages for actual loss; or (ii) in lieu of damages measured by any other methods, the damages caused by the misappropriation measured by imposition of liability for a reasonable royalty for the misappropriator's unauthorized disclosure or use of the trade secret; (C) if the trade secret is willfully and maliciously misappropriated, award exemplary damages in an amount not more than 2 times the amount of the damages awarded under subparagraph (B);

Uniform Trade Secrets Act: § 3. Damages
(a) In addition to or in lieu of injunctive relief, a complainant may recover damages for the actual loss caused by misappropriation. A complainant also may recover for the unjust enrichment caused by misappropriation that is not taken into account in computing damages for actual loss.
(b) If willful and malicious misappropriation is shown, the court may award exemplary damages in an amount not exceeding twice any award made under subsection (a).

Related terms: injunction; trade secret misappropriation action.

databases as trade secrets

A database is information of any type organized in a manner to facilitate its retrieval. An encyclopedia, for example, is a database that is organized alphabetically and contains information that can be retrieved by subject.

The term "database" currently is understood as referring to computer databases. Computer databases usually consist of information linked in a way to allow its quick retrieval, either by specific item or in combination with other items.

Databases may be protected as trade secrets. For instance, a database that allows a book publisher to identify people who purchased certain categories of books in the previous year would qualify as a trade secret if it were kept confidential.

A database often contains component materials that are protected by copyright. Sometimes this copyrighted material is owned by someone other than the database owner, as in the case of a database of archived newspaper articles where the copyright in the articles is owned by their original authors or publishers. Even so, this type of database can still be a trade secret, because the way the materials are organized is at least as valuable as the materials themselves.

Related terms: competitive advantage; compilation of information as a trade secret; copyright and trade secret law compatibility; customer lists.

The Defend Trade Secrets Act

The Defend Trade Secrets Act (DTSA), signed into law in May 11, 2016, "federalizes" trade secret law by providing a procedure for trade secret owners to file civil lawsuits in federal court. Any company possessing a trade secret that is "related to a product or service used in, or intended for use in, interstate or foreign commerce" can take advantage of the provisions of the DTSA.

Prior to the DTSA, trade secret owners could bring civil lawsuits only in state courts, under state laws based on the Uniform Trade Secrets Act (UTSA). (Except for New York, every state has adopted some version of the UTSA.) In many important ways, the DTSA and state laws based on the UTSA are similar. For example, the definitions of trade secrets and misappropriation are the same, as are the statute of limitations (three years), and the remedies for theft (injunctive relief, compensatory damages).

But the DTSA can be more favorable to trade secret owners, because it creates access to federal courts and provides for seizing trade secrets without giving any notice to the defendant, a major change from the notice requirements of state laws based on the UTSA.

The DTSA will apply only if there is some violation occurring after the act's effective date. The DTSA also has some built-in protections for those accused of trade secret theft. These include:

Seizures. If a trade secret owner orders a trade secret seizure, there must be a hearing within seven days of the seizure order. At the hearing, the trade secret owner must prove the legal and factual basis for the order.

Employee injunctions. The DTSA sets limits on injunctions against former employees, particularly when an employer seeks to prevent an ex-employee from entering into another employment relationship. At least one court has held that the term "employment relationship" does not include independent contractors. (*Engility Corp. v. Daniels*, 2016 WL 7034976 (D. Colo. Dec. 2, 2016).)

Attorneys' fees for bad faith. A defendant accused of misappropriation can recover attorneys' fees from the trade secret owner if the claims were made in bad faith.

Finally, the DTSA includes a provision that can affect the disclosure of trade secrets during and after litigation, by preventing disclosures at trial and within court opinions unless the trade secret owner has first been briefed on the disclosure.

Nondisclosure agreements. Employers who want to take advantage of the Defend Trade Secrets Act's provision for obtaining punitive damages and attorneys' fees from an ex-employee or independent contractor must include a whistleblower provision in all nondisclosure agreements executed after the law's passage. The failure to include the provision does not prevent filing in federal court; it only prevents recovery of punitive damages and attorneys' fees. In other words, the provision is strongly recommended but not mandatory.

A sample provision would include this language:

> **Notice of Immunity From Liability.** An individual shall not be held criminally or civilly liable under any federal or state trade secret law for the disclosure of a trade secret that is made (i) in confidence to a federal, state, or local government official, either directly or indirectly, or to an attorney; and (ii) solely for the purpose of reporting or investigating a suspected violation of law; or is made in a complaint or other document filed in a lawsuit or other proceeding, if such filing is made under seal. An individual who files a lawsuit for retaliation by an employer for reporting a suspected violation of law may disclose the trade secret to the attorney of the individual and use the trade secret information in the court proceeding, if the individual (i) files any document containing the trade secret under seal; and (ii) does not disclose the trade secret, except pursuant to court order.

disclosure of confidential information during lawsuit

See litigation, disclosure of trade secrets during.

duty of trust

Over the years, the courts have recognized that certain business relationships require a higher-than-normal degree of trust between the parties. These are often referred to as "fiduciary relationships," and people or businesses in these relationships are said to owe a duty of trust to each other. They thus have an obligation to take the interests of another person or a business into account when engaging in commercial activity potentially affecting that person or business. For instance, an employer and a high-level employee or provider of a service (expert consultant, lawyer, accountant) have a duty of trust to deal fairly with each other under all circumstances.

If a person violates (breaches) a duty of trust, the courts are usually willing to grant whatever remedy is necessary to undo the resulting harm. For example, if a high-level executive breaches a duty owed to his or her employer by disclosing trade secrets to a competitor, the employer may go to court to prevent further breaches, to receive an award of damages from the employee, and to prevent the competitor from using the disclosed trade secrets.

Criminal prosecutions seldom are brought in breach of trust cases, which are almost always viewed as civil matters.

Related terms: confidential employment relationship; trade secret misappropriation action.

Economic Espionage Act of 1996

The Economic Espionage Act of 1996 makes the theft of trade secrets a federal crime. The Act prohibits theft of a trade secret by a person intending or knowing that the offense will injure a trade secret owner. The Act also makes it a federal crime to receive, buy, or possess trade secret information knowing it to have been stolen. The Act's definition of "trade secret" is similar to that of the Uniform Trade Secrets Act. The penalties for a violation of this statute include a potential prison term of 15 years and fines up to $5 million, depending on whether the defendant is an individual or a corporation.

A private party can still sue for trade secret theft even if the federal government files a criminal case under the Economic Espionage Act.

Since its adoption, the Economic Espionage Act has been enforced in several instances, including:

- an attempt to steal the process for culturing Taxol from plant cells (Taxol is used in the treatment of ovarian cancer)
- the theft of a new shaving system developed by the Gillette Company
- the sale of trade secrets about a Kodak-owned device (known as the 401 machine) that inexpensively produced the clear plastic base used in consumer film
- the theft of trade secrets by a Taiwanese company from the Avery-Dennison company
- the attempted theft of 1900 documents from a cast-iron manufacturer (for use by a Chinese rival)
- the theft of blueprints and bootlegged semiconductor parts from a Silicon Valley company, and

- the theft of trade secrets regarding the development of chloride-route titanium dioxide (TiO2) technology from E.I. DuPont and the sale of those secrets to the People's Republic of China (the first jury conviction under the EEA), resulting in a 15-year sentence.

Related terms: criminal prosecution for trade secret theft.

email and confidentiality

The transmission of email usually doesn't jeopardize confidentiality, because each email message is broken into packets of information and reassembled at the delivery point, making it difficult to intercept. Also, the nature of email requires that the address be typed exactly, and, if it is not, the email typically bounces back to the sender.

The danger from loss of confidentiality occurs when email is stored either on the sender's computer, a host computer (for example, an Internet Service Provider like Gmail), or the recipient's computer. These stored files can be acquired legally by employers, lawyers, or the police, or they can be acquired illegally by hackers. Email transmissions also pose a threat to confidentiality when the information is subsequently posted on a bulletin board or in a chat group. For this reason, businesses often institute trade secret procedures on company computers, including password protection and encryption of messages—a process that uses sophisticated software to garble the sender's words and then allows the recipient to unscramble and read them. In addition, companies prevent outsiders from penetrating the office network by the use of firewalls, protective computer hardware, or software systems.

Related terms: Internet and trade secrets.

employees, covenant not to compete

See covenant not to compete by employee.

employees, notice of trade secrets

See notice to employees of trade secrets.

employees' rights and duties toward trade secrets

See confidential employment relationship.

employment contracts and trade secrets

See covenant not to compete by employee; nondisclosure agreements.

Trade Secret Law: Definitions

evaluation agreement

This is a contract by which one party promises to submit an idea and the other party promises to evaluate the idea while maintaining its confidentiality. After the evaluation, the evaluator will either enter into an agreement to exploit the idea or promise not to use or disclose the idea.

Related terms: idea submission.

exit interview

An employer may conduct an interview with a departing employee in which the employee is reminded of the trade secrets he or she has knowledge of and warned that his or her unauthorized disclosure of these trade secrets may result in being held personally liable for damages.

Related terms: duty of trust; notice to employees of trade secrets.

federal trade secret statutes

See Defend Trade Secrets Act; Economic Espionage Act of 1996.

fiduciary duty and trade secrets

See duty of trust.

formulas as trade secrets

Product formulas that both are kept confidential and add to a business's competitive advantage may qualify as trade secrets. A formula can consist of any combination of ingredients that results in a particular product. Examples of the many formulas that have been granted trade secret status are those for soft drinks, butter flavoring, industrial solvents, floor wax, and rat poison.

Freedom of Information Act, exemption of trade secrets

In its regulatory capacity, the federal government often requires businesses to submit information that the businesses consider to be trade secrets, such as the precise formula used in a drug for which FDA approval is being sought. The Freedom of Information Act (FOIA), located in 5 U.S. Code Section 552, ordinarily provides the public with broad access to documents possessed by the executive branch of the federal government. However, to encourage businesses to file the appropriate records, trade secrets are exempt from the disclosure requirement otherwise imposed on the government by the FOIA. This means that businesses are able to comply with government regulations without necessarily giving up their secrets.

Although the government is not required to disclose trade secrets under the FOIA, it is often difficult, if not impossible, for an agency official to tell from the information itself whether or not it is considered a trade secret by the company that submitted it. So, to protect their trade secrets, companies submitting trade secret information should clearly label the material as such. If the agency receives a request for the information, the agency is then supposed to contact the company and give it a chance to argue why the information should not be disclosed. If, however, the agency chooses to release the information in question against the company's wishes, there is little that can be done about it. Courts have prohibited affected businesses from filing lawsuits against the agencies involved (called "reverse FOIA suits").

Despite the FOIA mandate to disclose unreleased documents, an exemption prevents disclosure of "trade secrets and commercial or financial information obtained from a person and privileged or confidential." (5 U.S. Code § 552(b)(4).)

> EXAMPLE: A media company sued under the FOIA to obtain food stamp data from retail stores. The U.S. Department of Agriculture (USDA) refused to provide food stamp redemption data, citing the exemption. The Supreme Court agreed, and established two criteria for the exemption: (1) the information must be closely held by the person imparting it, and (2) the party receiving the information must provide assurance that the information will remain secret. Because a store's redemption data is not customarily disclosed to the public and because the USDA promised the participating stores to keep their data private, the exemption prohibited disclosure. (*Food Marketing Institute v. Argus Leader Media*, 139 S.Ct. 2356 (2019).)

freedom of speech and trade secrets

The First Amendment to the U.S. Constitution prohibits the government from placing restrictions on a person's freedom of speech. One exception to this "prior restraint" rule is that a court may prohibit the publication of trade secrets that have been obtained in violation of an employment agreement. Courts weigh several factors when making a prior restraint determination, including the commercial interest in the trade secrets, the individual's right to speak freely, and the illegal behavior used to acquire the trade secrets.

EXAMPLE: A California man republished computer code from a Norwegian website. The code allowed users to bypass encryption and play DVDs on a computer—a method that was considered a trade secret by the DVD trade association. The California Supreme Court ruled that enjoining the republication of this trade secret did not violate the First Amendment. (*DVD Copy Control Association v. Bunner*, 2003 Cal. LEXIS 6295 (2003).)

Prohibiting publication is less likely if the trade secrets are obtained by legitimate means.

EXAMPLE: An attorney accidentally attaches trade secret information to a publicly filed court document. A reporter uncovers this inadvertent disclosure and arranges to publish the information in a newspaper. A court is unlikely to restrain this publication, since the information was obtained legally.

Keep in mind that some trade secret information, for example a business plan, may be protected under copyright law. In that case, the owner of the trade secret can sue, claiming copyright infringement as a result of the unauthorized publication, regardless of whether the information was obtained legally.

Journalists who republish trade secrets often seek to shield their sources under the First Amendment. In 2005, a California superior court ruled that bloggers who republished trade secrets owned by the Apple computer company could not claim this shield for their sources. The case—the first to assess the First Amendment rights of bloggers—indicates that writers for online publications might not be entitled to the same constitutional protections as traditional print and broadcast news journalists. (More information regarding free speech and trade secrets can be found at the Electronic Frontier Foundation website (www.eff.org).)

Related terms: copyright and trade secret law compatibility; injunction; protective order; temporary restraining order.

GATT (General Agreement on Tariffs and Trade)

The General Agreement on Tariffs and Trade (GATT) is a treaty among most of the world's industrialized nations addressing a number of factors affecting international trade, including how each signing country treats trade secrets belonging to businesses in the other signing countries. Under GATT, most industrial countries have pledged themselves to provide protection to trade secrets owned by residents of all signatory nations.

geographical licenses

See licensing of trade secrets.

head-start rule

A court will often order a business that improperly possesses trade secrets to stop using the trade secrets for a period of time. The time period might depend on the length of time it would have taken the offending business to independently develop the information that constitutes the secret. In other words, the rightful trade secret owner is provided with a commercial "head start" in the information's use. This head-start remedy recognizes that the essential value of a trade secret is the competitive advantage it affords its owner. In one instance, an arbitrator used the head-start period as a measurement for financial damages. A $1.1 million trade secret damages award by an arbitrator based on the equitable "head-start" principle was upheld by the Third Circuit. (*Sabre GLBL, Inc. v. Shan*, 779 Fed. App'x 843 (3rd Cir. 2019).)

Related terms: injunction; trade secret misappropriation action.

hiring employees from competitors to obtain trade secrets

See improper acquisition of trade secrets.

idea submission

People often come up with concepts that have not yet been exploited and might have economic value. For example, someone might conceive of an idea for a television show, but unless that person is in the business of producing television shows, the idea does not provide an advantage over competitors. In other words, it may not qualify as a trade secret. The key to protecting these idea submissions is to enter into an arrangement that respects the idea's potential value and justifies compensation.

Although the rules regarding protection of ideas vary from state to state, the best approach to protecting an idea submission is:

- maintain it with secrecy since, due to the vagaries of trade secret law, the idea may qualify as secret
- don't submit it to a company unless it has been solicited and it is clear that the arrangement is for compensation, and
- if possible, use an evaluation (or option) agreement to maintain secrecy and to demonstrate solicitation.

Trade Secret Law: Definitions

EXAMPLE: In 1983, two men submitted an idea to a movie studio: An African king comes to America, loses his memory, works in a restaurant, and marries an American woman and returns with her to his kingdom. The men entered into an agreement that if the studio ever produced a movie based on the idea, they would be compensated from the film's profits. The studio made *Coming to America*, a movie based on the idea, which grossed over $300 million. The studio claimed it had no obligation to pay the men because the movie was not based on their idea. The men sued and a court ruled in their favor because: (1) the movie studio had solicited the idea; (2) the parties had signed an agreement; and (3) $10,000 had been paid to the men when the idea was submitted. In the *Coming to America* case, no one factor was conclusive, but collectively these factors established that the idea submission was submitted in confidence and for economic benefit. (*Buchwald v. Paramount*, 13 U.S.P.Q.2d 1497 (1990).)

Although an evaluation or option agreement may create the presumption that an idea was solicited for compensation, a court will not always enforce it. If an idea is obvious within the industry, an agreement can be invalidated, because each party to a contract must contribute something of value. If the submitted idea has no novelty, it has no value, and therefore the contract is void. (*Nadel v. Play-by-Play Toys & Novelties, Inc.*, 208 F.3d 368 (S.D.N.Y. 1999).)

EXAMPLE: A company submitted a cross-marketing idea to the Mattel toy company and the National Basketball Association; the two entities would jointly market a Cabbage Patch Doll dressed in a basketball uniform. A court later determined that the company submitting the idea had no rights to compensation, because the idea was obvious to the NBA and Mattel. (*Khreativity Unlimited v. Mattel, Inc.*, 101 F. Supp.2d 177 (S.D.N.Y. 2000).)

Even if a company doesn't sign an evaluation or option agreement, it's still possible to get paid for the use of an idea. An agreement can be implied from the circumstances.

EXAMPLE: The Mattel toy company invited members of an animation company to submit ideas for licensed characters. The animation company presented several ideas, including its "Flutter Faeries" characters. Mattel asked to keep copies of the presentation and soon afterwards produced dolls with characteristics similar to Flutter Faeries. A court of appeals permitted the animation company to pursue Mattel over an implied agreement. (*Gunther-Wahl Productions, Inc. v. Mattel*, 104 Cal.App.4th 27 (2002).)

Under limited circumstances, the originator of an idea may stop someone to whom the idea is disclosed from misappropriating it if there is a "fiduciary relationship" between the parties and the idea was not generally known. In a fiduciary relationship, one person stands in a special relationship of trust, confidence, or responsibility. Fiduciary relationships are often defined by statute or case law. For example, the relationship of an attorney to a client is a fiduciary relationship, and stealing a client's idea would be a breach of that relationship.

Equally important is whether the parties are in a confidential relationship. If the parties have agreed not to disclose the secret without authorization, a presumption is usually created that the idea has economic value and deserves compensation.

ideas as trade secrets

Ideas alone can be protected as trade secrets only if they are generally unknown in the business community, offer a competitive advantage, and are treated confidentially. The real value of any idea will ultimately depend on its commercial success. An idea that offers the possibility of helping a business compete should be maintained as a trade secret until such time as it appears to lack feasibility or others independently think of it. Otherwise, a golden opportunity for obtaining an advantage over potential competitors might be lost.

Although the rules regarding protection of ideas vary from state to state, the maximum legal protection can be obtained by following these principles:

- Maintain an idea with secrecy and use a nondisclosure agreement.
- Don't submit it to a company unless it has been solicited and it is clear that the arrangement is for compensation.

Trade secret protection is also available for ideas that later become an invention, up to the time that a patent covering the invention issues. Once a patent issues, the underlying ideas become part of the patent. Patent information is available to the public and is no longer considered a trade secret. For example, in a case involving digital stamping technology, a California appellate court held that ideas are protectable under California trade secret laws, provided that information is sufficiently specific and secret. (*Altavion, Inc. v. Konica Minolta Sys. Laboratory, Inc.*, 226 Cal.App.4th 26 (2014).)

Trade secret protection for ideas should be contrasted with copyright protection, which protects only the actual expression of the idea and not the idea itself. Because of this difference, trade secret law can often best protect the conception and development stages of a work before it is finally fixed in a tangible medium and published, at which point copyright protection takes over.

Trade Secret Law: Definitions

Related terms: copyright and trade secret law compatibility; patent application, effect on trade secrets.

illegal restraint of trade

Commercial activity by one business showing a strong tendency to restrict or curtail the free flow of commerce is considered an illegal restraint of trade. Examples of illegal restraints are tying arrangements (requiring the purchase of one product as a prerequisite to buying another), price setting agreements (two or more businesses agreeing to set prices at a particular level), and territorial restriction agreements (private agreements to restrict the use of a trade secret to certain geographical areas).

Related terms: antitrust law and trade secrets; licensing of trade secrets.

implied duty not to disclose trade secrets

See duty of trust.

improper acquisition of trade secrets

This phrase describes the situation where a business obtained a trade secret through means that the law considers impermissible, such as:

- deliberate theft through misrepresentation, burglary, or industrial espionage, or
- knowingly obtaining or using trade secrets that have been obtained by theft or improperly disclosed by a person who breached a nondisclosure agreement, implied duty not to disclose trade secrets, or duty of trust.

Under these circumstances, an injured trade secret owner can file a trade secret lawsuit to stop the other company from using the information, and perhaps to recover money damages and punitive damages.

> EXAMPLE: The Bayside Graphics company develops and tries to keep secret a program that greatly improves the graphics capability of a popular business-forecasting package. A competitor discovers the information by illegally stealing Bayside's trash during a five-minute period when it is left unprotected. Improper acquisition has occurred and court relief can be obtained.

The U.S. government may also file criminal charges against the trade secret thief under the Economic Espionage Act.

The Uniform Trade Secrets Act (§ 1 Definitions) and the federal Defend Trade Secrets Act (18 U.S. Code § 1836(b)(6)(A)) both define "improper means" as including theft, bribery, misrepresentation, breach or inducement of a breach of a duty to maintain secrecy, or espionage through electronic or other means.

Related terms: damages in trade secret misappropriation actions; federal trade secret statute; industrial espionage; trade secret misappropriation action.

improper disclosure of trade secrets

When someone communicates trade secrets to others in violation of a nondisclosure agreement, duty of trust, or confidential employment relationship, it is known as an improper disclosure of trade secrets. Those who improperly disclose trade secrets may be held liable for all resulting harm to the trade secret owner's economic interests.

Related terms: damages in trade secret misappropriation actions; improper acquisition of trade secrets; nondisclosure agreement; trade secret misappropriation action.

independent conception, defense to trade secret claim

For a trade secret owner to obtain court-ordered relief against a competitor who is using the trade secret, there must be a showing that the competitor improperly acquired it. A trade secret is not improperly acquired if it is independently conceived of or is discovered by a competitor through parallel research. The Defend Trade Secrets Act specifically excludes "independent derivation" from its definition of "improper means."

To preserve their ability to raise independent conception as a defense to a trade secret infringement action, many large companies will not:

- sign a nondisclosure agreement tendered by an outsider who wants to sell something to the company, or
- examine any work developed by an outsider who hasn't signed a written statement giving up the right to treat the work as a trade secret.

Related terms: improper acquisition of trade secrets; parallel research; trade secret misappropriation action; unsolicited idea disclosure.

independently developed

See independent conception, defense to trade secret claim.

industrial espionage

In the trade secret context, industrial espionage consists of any activity directed toward discovering a company's trade secrets by such underhanded or illegal means as:

- electronic surveillance
- bribing employees to disclose confidential information
- planting a spy among the company's employees
- tapping of a company's phones, computers, or email, or
- theft of documents containing confidential information.

In the United States, an owner of trade secrets obtained by an outsider as a result of industrial espionage may recover large damages if the secrets are subsequently used by the guilty party. The thief is also subject to criminal prosecution under the federal trade secret statute. In some countries, however, trade secret theft through industrial espionage is tolerated as a normal part of doing business.

Related terms: Economic Espionage Act of 1996; improper acquisition of trade secrets.

industrial innovations as trade secrets

See competitive advantage; trade secret, defined.

industrial secret

Industrial secrets are trade secrets of a technical, technological, scientific, or mechanical nature. Secret processes, formulas, unregistered industrial designs, manufacturing techniques and methods, secret machinery, and devices are all examples.

The laws of some countries, such as Japan, distinguish between industrial secrets and commercial secrets. In the United States, however, courts tend to treat all trade secrets alike, regardless of their type. In other words, whether or not a trade secret is business information, industrial know-how, or an industrial secret is of no legal consequence in the United States.

Related terms: know-how; trade secret, defined.

inevitable disclosure rule (also known as the inevitability doctrine)

Even without a noncompete agreement, some businesses have been able to prevent ex-employees from working for a competitor under a legal concept appropriately titled the inevitable disclosure doctrine. This principle was popularized by a 1995 case in which Pepsico successfully argued that a former executive could not help but rely on company secrets at his new job with a rival. (*Pepsico, Inc. v. Redmond,* 54 F.3d 1262 (7th Cir. 1995).)

This principle, adopted in some form by the majority of states, allows a business to prevent an ex-employee from competing without the use of a noncompete agreement. From the employee's perspective, this rule is troubling because it allows a former employer to get a court order preventing employment without any proof of actual or even threatened theft or disclosure of trade secrets. In other words, the rule is used to prohibit employment, not disclosure. (*DoubleClick, Inc. v. Henderson,* 1997 N.Y. Misc. LEXIS 577 (N.Y. Sup. Ct. 1997).)

In many of the cases where it was applied, the courts have required more than an allegation of inevitability—for example, a showing of bad faith or underhanded dealing by the ex-employee.

Bringing a claim based solely on inevitable disclosure is likely to backfire:

EXAMPLE: An employer brought a trade secret claim against a former employee without any evidence and based solely on an argument that the employee would inevitably disclose the trade secret as part of his new employment. California does not permit inevitable disclosure claims and the employer was required to pay attorneys' fees and costs as a result of the bad faith claim. (*In Flir Systems, Inc. v. Parrish,* 95 Cal.Rptr.3d 307 (Cal.App.2d Dist. 2009).)

The Defend Trade Secrets Act (DTSA) states that a court may enjoin "any actual or threatened misappropriation … provided the order does not prevent a person from accepting an offer of employment under conditions that avoid actual or threatened misappropriation." (18 U.S. Code § 1836.) However, despite this language, several courts have issued injunctions based on inevitable disclosure. See, for example, *Mickey's Linen v. Fischer,* No. 17 C 2154 (N.D. Ill. Sep. 8, 2017), in which the court enjoined a former employee from working for a competitor because the ex-employee "would inevitably use or disclose" the ex-employer's trade secrets.

injunction

A court order directed at persons or businesses that have either improperly acquired trade secrets or who threaten to improperly disclose them is known as an injunction. Typically, an injunction is sought as part of a trade secret misappropriation action, to prohibit a defendant from using a trade secret belonging to the plaintiff (the party bringing the action) or from disclosing it to others. This type of judicial relief is common in trade secret litigation, since one of the trade secret owner's primary goals is to stop any further erosion of the competitive advantage gained by keeping the information secret.

Courts are authorized to issue emergency injunctions, called temporary restraining orders (TROs), when a trade secret owner shows that a trade secret is at risk of being lost as a result of the defendant's behavior. The court must then schedule a hearing at which all sides may be heard. If, after this hearing, the court still believes that a trade secret is at stake and that the trade secret owner will probably win at trial, it can issue a provisional or "preliminary" injunction. This order will continue to prevent the defendant from using or disclosing the trade secret pending a final decision in the case. As a practical matter, once a preliminary injunction is granted, the parties will often settle rather than fight through to trial and beyond. The Defend Trade Secrets Act (DTSA) uses a similar injunctive relief standard as the Uniform Trade Secrets Act, except that under the DTSA, an injunction cannot prevent an ex-employee from entering into another employment relationship.

Uniform Trade Secrets Act: § 2. Injunctive Relief

(a) Actual or threatened misappropriation may be enjoined. Upon application to the court, an injunction shall be terminated when the trade secret has ceased to exist, but the injunction may be continued for an additional reasonable period of time in order to eliminate commercial advantage that otherwise would be derived from the misappropriation.

(b) If the court determines that it would be unreasonable to prohibit future use, an injunction may condition future use upon payment of a reasonable royalty for no longer than the period of time the use could have been prohibited.

(c) In appropriate circumstances, affirmative acts to protect a trade secret may be compelled by court order.

Defend Trade Secrets Act 18 USC § 1836(b)(3)(A)—Remedies

In a civil action brought under this subsection with respect to the misappropriation of a trade secret, a court may (A) grant an injunction (i) to prevent any actual or threatened misappropriation described in paragraph (1) on such terms as the court deems reasonable, provided the order does not (I) prevent a person from entering into an employment relationship, and that conditions placed on such employment shall be based on evidence of threatened misappropriation and not merely on the information the person knows; or (II) otherwise conflict with an applicable State law prohibiting restraints on the practice of a lawful profession, trade, or business (ii) if determined appropriate by the court, requiring affirmative actions to be taken to protect the trade secret; and (iii) in exceptional circumstances that render an injunction inequitable, that conditions future use of the trade secret upon payment of a reasonable royalty for no longer than the period of time for which such use could have been prohibited.

Related terms: improper acquisition of trade secrets; improper disclosure of trade secrets; trade secret misappropriation action.

Internet posting of trade secrets

The online publication of confidential information will almost always cause the loss of trade secret rights regardless of whether it was done inadvertently or maliciously. The result of such a posting is that competitors who obtain the information legally, that is, those who did not violate trade secret laws to get the information, are entitled to use it.

There are many ways a trade secret is disclosed in cyberspace. Sometimes the disclosure is the result of revenge by an angry employee or contractor, sometimes it occurs because a hacker has uncovered information without permission of the website owner, and sometimes it is the result of carelessness—often by employees of the business who might discuss secrets in online chats.

There are exceptions to the "posting equals disclosure" rule. One court ruled that posting on the Web does not automatically cause the loss of trade secret status, because the posting might not result in the secret being "generally known." The court required a review of the circumstances surrounding the posting and consideration of the interests of the trade secret owner, the policies favoring competition, and the interests—including First Amendment rights—of innocent third parties who acquire information on the Internet. (*Religious Tech. Ctr. v. Netcom On-Line Comm. Servs. Inc.*, 923 F. Supp. 1231 (N.D. Cal. 1995).) In addition to violations of trade secret law, the improper online disclosure of trade secrets may lead to claims of copyright infringement.

In other cases, a defendant may argue that the posting of trade secret information is protected under free speech principles established in the First Amendment. However, this argument will not succeed if the court determines that protecting the commercial information outweighs disclosure. For example, the California

Supreme Court ruled that enjoining the republication of a software code that permitted unauthorized use of a DVD did not violate the First Amendment. (*DVD Copy Control Association v. Bunner,* 2003 Cal. LEXIS 6295 (2003).)

Related terms: copyright and trade secret law compatibility; email and confidentiality; freedom of speech and trade secrets; improper disclosure of trade secrets.

know-how

Know-how does not always refer to secret information. Sometimes it means a particular kind of technical knowledge that might not be confidential but that is needed to accomplish a task. For example, an employee's know-how could be necessary to train other employees in how to make or use an invention. Although know-how is a combination of secret and nonsecret information, businesses usually treat it as a protectable trade secret and require employees and contractors to whom it is disclosed to sign a nondisclosure agreement.

An organization called the International Chamber of Commerce defines "industrial know-how" to include applied technical knowledge, methods, and data that are necessary for realizing or carrying out techniques that serve industrial purposes. Industrial know-how differs from business know-how, which normally involves white-collar managerial and marketing techniques.

The kind of information encompassed by the term "industrial know-how" will qualify as a trade secret if it is specialized, is not generally known in the relevant business community, provides a company with a competitive advantage, and is maintained as a trade secret.

Related terms: industrial secret; methods and techniques as trade secrets.

licensing of trade secrets

A trade secret owner may license a trade secret by permitting others to use it in exchange for an agreement to treat it as confidential. Licenses commonly are limited to specific time periods, types or fields of commerce, and purposes. There are no government agencies that oversee trade secret licenses, but such licenses are subject to applicable antitrust prohibitions against monopolistic or restraint-of-trade activities.

Under a trade secret license, ownership of the trade secret remains with the original owner, while the licensee has the right to use the trade secret as long as it complies with the specific terms and time limits of the license. The license agreement should always include a clause stating that the trade secret in question is confidential information and must be maintained properly as a trade secret by the licensee.

One common type of license provides the owner with a royalty based on a percentage of the retail or wholesale price of each item sold that takes advantage of the trade secret. Many other compensation arrangements are possible. For example, the license could provide for a flat fee for each separate use of the secret, a monthly or annual fee, the reciprocal use of information belonging to the licensee, or some combination of all of these arrangements.

Related terms: antitrust law and trade secrets; trade secret owner.

litigation, disclosure of trade secrets during

State and federal laws establish rules regarding the use and disclosure of trade secrets during litigation. If one party requests trade secret information from another, a court will balance the interests of the litigants. If the failure to disclose would cause injustice or conceal a fraud, the owner of the trade secret will be required to disclose it. In order to preserve secrecy, the court will issue a protective order that requires all participants in the lawsuit—the litigants, attorneys, independent contractors—to maintain confidentiality. Protective orders can be made by order of the court, or the parties may agree to the protection of confidential information.

Related terms: injunction; protective order; temporary restraining order.

loss of trade secrets

Trade secrets, and the judicial protection their status confers, may be lost by any conduct that:

- releases the trade secret into the public domain, and
- does not constitute wrongful conduct such as theft, violation of a nondisclosure agreement, or breach of a duty of trust.

EXAMPLE: Sonoma Foods Inc. (SFI) conceives of a new way to lengthen the shelf life of jams and jellies. Initially, SFI takes careful steps to preserve its invention as a trade secret. However, over a few drinks at a trade show, SFI's chief executive officer tells an employee from another food company about the invention without first asking for a nondisclosure agreement. Such behavior might result in the loss of the idea as a trade secret, especially if the other company proceeds to implement the idea or tell others about it. Should SFI bring a misappropriation suit against the other company, the SFI officer's disclosure would likely constitute a successful defense.

Related terms: accidental disclosure of trade secrets; patent application, effect on trade secrets; public domain and trade secrets; public records and trade secrets; reasonably precautionary measures to protect trade secrets.

Trade Secret Law: Definitions

methods and techniques as trade secrets

Specialized business knowledge related to a specific process or method, commonly known as business know-how, can qualify as a trade secret in many countries if it is so treated. Examples of such know-how include specialized barbecue methods of cooking (including use of special cuts of meat and secret sauces) and methods and techniques for running group sessions of a how-to-quit-smoking organization.

On the other hand, general business knowledge or expertise not related to a specific process or method is usually not protectable as a trade secret. The courts rarely protect information that is widely known to, or available to, the business community and thus is not secret.

Related terms: know-how; processes as trade secrets; trade secret, defined.

misappropriation of trade secrets

Misappropriation of a trade secret occurs when secret information is acquired by improper means—for example, by theft, bribery, misrepresentation, or breach of a duty to maintain secrecy. Misappropriation can also occur if a trade secret is disclosed by someone who used improper means to acquire it. Misappropriation of trade secrets is sometimes mistakenly referred to as trade secret infringement. The Uniform Trade Secrets Act (§ 1 Definitions) and the federal Defend Trade Secrets Act (18 U.S. Code § 1836(b)(5)(A)) both define "misappropriation" as:

(i) acquisition of a trade secret of another by a person who knows or has reason to know that the trade secret was acquired by improper means; or

(ii) disclosure or use of a trade secret of another without express or implied consent by a person who

  (A) used improper means to acquire knowledge of the trade secret; or

  (B) at the time of disclosure or use, knew or had reason to know that his knowledge of the trade secret was

    (I) derived from or through a person who had utilized improper means to acquire it;

    (II) acquired under circumstances giving rise to a duty to maintain its secrecy or limit its use; or

    (III) derived from or through a person who owed a duty to the person seeking relief to maintain its secrecy or limit its use; or

  (C) before a material change of his position, knew or had reason to know that it was a trade secret and that knowledge of it had been acquired by accident or mistake.

money damages

See damages in trade secret misappropriation actions.

noncompetition clauses in employment contracts

See covenant not to compete by employee.

nondisclosure agreement

The term "nondisclosure agreement" is often used interchangeably with "confidentiality agreement" or "NDA." A nondisclosure agreement is a contract in which a person or business promises to treat specific information as a trade secret and not to disclose the information to others without proper authorization. If the trade secret is disclosed in violation of the nondisclosure agreement, the trade secret owner can file a trade secret lawsuit, obtain an injunction to stop further use of the trade secret, recover money damages, and possibly recover punitive or treble damages.

Nondisclosure agreements should be used whenever it is necessary to disclose a trade secret to another person or business for such purposes as development, marketing, evaluation, or fiscal backing. Through the conscientious use of nondisclosure agreements, trade secrets can be distributed to a relatively large number of people without destroying their protected status.

Nondisclosure agreements should also be used between employees and employers, in order to require that the employee treat as confidential all trade secrets learned about in the course of employment. If the employer later tries to prevent an employee from using information considered to be a trade secret, the nondisclosure agreement can establish that the employee recognized a duty to cooperate in this endeavor. Competitors who learn of trade secrets through an employee's violation of a nondisclosure agreement with a former employer may also be prevented from commercially using the information, even if they didn't know the employee had breached the agreement.

The drafters of the federal Defend Trade Secrets Act (DTSA) sought to protect whistleblower rights in the workplace. To encourage employers to notify employees of their whistleblower rights, the DTSA made employers ineligible for obtaining punitive damages and attorneys' fees from an ex-employee or independent contractor, unless a Notice of Immunity is included in nondisclosure agreements that are executed after passage of the law. The failure to include the provision does not prevent taking advantage of the DTSA's benefits, it only prevents recovery of punitive (exemplary) damages and attorneys' fees. In other words, the provision is not mandatory.

Trade Secret Law: Definitions

A nondisclosure agreement can also help establish that a business treated particular information as a trade secret—a necessary element to claiming legal protection.

Although nondisclosure agreements usually take the form of written contracts, they may also be implied if the context of a business relationship suggests that such agreement was intended by the parties. For instance, a business that conducts patent searches for inventors is expected to keep the information about the invention secret, even if no written nondisclosure agreement is signed, since the nature of the business is to deal in confidential information. A sample nondisclosure agreement is provided in the Forms section of this part.

Related terms: beta testing and trade secrets; trade secret misappropriation action.

Notice of Immunity (From Liability)

Employers who want to take advantage of the federal Defend Trade Secrets Act's provision for obtaining punitive damages and attorneys' fees from an ex-employee or independent contractor must include a whistleblower provision (known as a Notice of Immunity From Liability) in all nondisclosure agreements executed after the law's passage. Failure to include the provision does not prevent filing in federal court, it only prevents recovery of punitive damages and attorneys' fees. In other words, the provision is strongly recommended, but not mandatory.

A sample provision would include the following language:

> **Notice of Immunity From Liability.** An individual shall not be held criminally or civilly liable under any federal or state trade secret law for the disclosure of a trade secret that is made (i) in confidence to a federal, state, or local government official, either directly or indirectly, or to an attorney; and (ii) solely for the purpose of reporting or investigating a suspected violation of law; or is made in a complaint or other document filed in a lawsuit or other proceeding, if such filing is made under seal. An individual who files a lawsuit for retaliation by an employer for reporting a suspected violation of law may disclose the trade secret to the attorney of the individual and use the trade secret information in the court proceeding, if the individual (i) files any document containing the trade secret under seal; and (ii) does not disclose the trade secret, except pursuant to court order.

notice to employees of trade secrets

For information to qualify as a trade secret, employers must ensure that it is treated as confidential. All employees (and anyone else who might come in contact with the information) must know in no uncertain terms that the information is confidential and that they have an obligation not to disclose it.

The best way to give this notice is to require all employees coming in contact with the secret to sign nondisclosure agreements. However, an express written notice to employees regarding the status of the information and their obligation of confidentiality will also usually provide a basis for judicially protecting the information in the event of a later threatened or actual disclosure.

Companies often put employees on notice of trade secret status by using:

- signs in walk-in areas where trade secrets are being stored or used
- confidentiality labels on documents
- initial employment interviews in which the business's trade secrets are discussed and the need to keep them confidential is stressed, and
- exit interviews where departing employees are cautioned against disclosing the company's trade secrets in their new employment.

Related terms: confidential employment relationship; nondisclosure agreement; reasonably precautionary measures to protect trade secrets.

notice to former employee's new employer

When an employee with knowledge of his or her employer's trade secrets takes a new job with a competing company, the first employer will often send the new employer a letter. The first employer will emphasize that the former employee is legally bound not to disclose any trade secrets and that, if he or she does, any such disclosure may not be used by the new employer. If the new employer then makes use of the trade secrets, the first employer may obtain greater damages and other enhanced judicial relief.

Related terms: improper disclosure of trade secrets; trade secret misappropriation action.

novelty and trade secrets

For information to qualify as a trade secret, it must generally not be known or used in the relevant industry. Strictly speaking, information constituting a trade secret need not be novel in the sense of "new" or "innovative." It simply must provide its owner with a competitive advantage.

EXAMPLE: A marionette manufacturer rediscovers a principle of movement first pioneered by the 19th-century European moving doll industry. If this particular principle has been lost to the modern world, it can qualify as a trade secret, even though it is in no way novel. As long as the principle of movement provides its owner with a competitive advantage, it is legally identical to trade secrets that are independently conceived.

Trade Secret Law: Definitions

Related terms: competitive advantage; parallel research; trade secret, defined.

obligation of confidentiality

See duty of trust.

ownership of trade secret rights

See trade secret owner.

parallel research

Parallel research refers to situations where similar information or ideas are developed by two or more companies through their independent efforts. Especially where cutting-edge technologies are involved, many companies are likely to be engaged in similar research and development activity, which can be expected to produce trade secrets. This means that the same basic information may be properly viewed as a trade secret by many different companies.

> EXAMPLE: A new cola company inadvertently creates the exact cola formula used by an existing company. Both the new and old companies are entitled to protect their formulas as trade secrets, even though the second formula is not novel.

Related terms: head start rule; independent conception, defense to trade secret claim; unsolicited idea disclosure.

patent application, effect on trade secrets

To obtain a patent on an invention, the inventor must fully describe the invention in the patent application. The U.S. Patent and Trademark Office (USPTO) treats patent applications as confidential, making it possible to apply for a patent and still maintain the underlying information as a trade secret, at least for the first 18 months of the application period. Unless the applicant files a Nonpublication Request at the time of filing and doesn't file for a patent outside the United States, the USPTO will publish the application within 18 months of the filing date. Because a patent application is published by the USPTO, all of the secret information becomes public and the trade secret status of the application is lost.

However, if an applicant files a Nonpublication Request at the time of filing the application, the information in the patent application will become publicly available only if and when a patent is granted. If the applicant is not filing abroad and the patent is rejected, confidentiality is preserved, because the USPTO does not publish rejected applications. If the USPTO approves the patent application, it will be published in the *Official Gazette*. Inventors are willing to accept this trade-off—loss of trade secrecy for patent rights—because the patent can be used to prevent anyone else from exploiting the underlying information.

Publication after 18 months does provide one advantage for a patent applicant: If a patent later issues, the patent owner can later recover damages from infringers from the date of publication, provided that the infringer had notice of the publication.

In a dispute involving patented technology for an oil drill, a Louisiana district court permitted a trade secret claim to proceed to trial, despite the fact the USPTO had published the secrets 18 months after the patent was filed. The defendant argued that trade secret claims were moot because of the disclosure. The court disagreed, holding that the defendant could be liable for trade secret theft that occurred before the USPTO published the secrets. (*Cajun Servs. Unlimited, LLC v. Benton Energy Serv. Co.*, No. 17-0491 S (E.D. La. Apr. 3, 2019.)

In a case involving handguard attachments, the Court of Appeals for the Federal Circuit (CAFC) held that material disclosed in the written portion of an invalidated patent could still be a trade secret under Massachusetts state trademark law. (*Atlantic Research Marketing Systems, Inc. v. Troy*, 659 F.3d 1345 (2011).)

Related terms: loss of trade secrets; reverse engineering and trade secrets.

patterns and designs as trade secrets

Patterns and designs may qualify as trade secrets if they create a competitive advantage and are kept secret. Examples of patterns and designs that have been protected as trade secrets are advanced design plans for a new minicomputer, designs for electronic circuitry, and schematic plans for an innovative metal door frame.

Related terms: industrial secret; trade secret, defined.

physical devices, ability to maintain as trade secrets

Physical devices—for example, tools, products, and components—can qualify as trade secrets if they provide their owner with a competitive advantage and are kept secret. Such devices can easily be protected when they are used solely in the trade secret owner's manufacturing or production process. In addition, if distribution is limited and the devices are licensed rather than sold, the trade secret protection may be preserved if the license prohibits reverse engineering. However, the more the world shrinks and the faster information moves, the harder it will be to preserve trade secrecy by licensing restrictions.

Once products are widely distributed, trade secret status is usually impossible to maintain. Anyone could examine these products and figure out how they work—that is, reverse engineer them. When reverse engineering is accomplished, the trade secret enters the public domain.

EXAMPLE: Jason invents, manufactures, and distributes an artificial intelligence device that allows people to simulate performing surgical procedures. The device consists of a screen, handles, ports, and a central processing unit (CPU) and is marketed as "Cutaway." If Caryl were to open the CPU, examine the board, figure out how Cutaway works, and start manufacturing her own device, Jason would have no grounds for relief against Caryl under trade secret laws. Why not? Because Caryl lawfully obtained the necessary information through reverse engineering. If, however, Jason owns either a patent or copyright on some aspect of the Cutaway hardware or software that was copied by Caryl, Jason can obtain court relief on those grounds.

Related terms: licensing of trade secrets; reasonably precautionary measures to protect trade secrets; reverse engineering and trade secrets; trade secret, defined.

piracy

A colloquial term, "piracy" refers to any activity directed toward the improper acquisition of a trade secret or other forms of intellectual property that belong to another. The word has no legal significance.

Related terms: criminal prosecution for trade secret theft; improper acquisition of trade secrets; industrial espionage.

predetermination of rights in technical data

Before hiring a business or consulting firm for research and development projects likely to produce patentable inventions and trade secrets, the government routinely requires a contract that contains clauses predetermining who will own the rights to the patents and secrets in question. Predetermination of rights provisions are also typically found in agreements between universities and corporations and between corporations and independent contractors. (Also, note that under the Bayh-Dole Act, enacted in 1980, universities may claim patent rights in inventions created at the university with federal funding. The university may license these discoveries to private industry—a practice some critics have likened to corporate welfare.)

Although ownership of intellectual property rights can be a subject for negotiation, the government will typically demand ownership of all rights in the main product being developed but will allow the private party to own the rights to any "side-products," including information, that can qualify as trade secrets.

Related terms: trade secret owner.

preliminary injunctions in trade secret actions

See injunction.

premature disclosure

See loss of trade secrets.

price setting

See illegal restraint of trade.

processes as trade secrets

A "process" consists of a series of steps that lead to a particular result. Any process may qualify for trade secret status if it is generally not known in the industry, adds to a business's competitive advantage, and is maintained as a trade secret. Among the processes that have been afforded protection as a trade secret in the past are those involving photographic development, silk screening, centrifugal processing for blood plasma fractionation, and the manufacture of chocolate powder and tobacco flavoring. Processes can also be protected under patent law.

Related terms: know-how; methods and techniques as trade secrets; trade secret, defined.

professional client lists

See customer lists.

protecting a trade secret

See reasonably precautionary measures to protect trade secrets.

protective order

In the event a trade secret is disclosed as part of a lawsuit, the trade secrecy can be preserved by a protective order. This order prohibits the participants in the lawsuit from disclosing the secret, and it "seals" the court record pertaining to the trade secret, making it unavailable as a public document. Protective orders can be made by order of the court, or the parties can agree to (stipulate) the protection of confidential information. Protective orders are authorized under Section 5 of the Uniform Trade Secrets Act and under Federal Rule of Civil Procedure 26(c)(7).

The federal Defend Trade Secrets Act provides for protective orders in trade secret proceedings. It also prevents disclosures at trial and within court opinions unless the trade secret owner has first consented to the disclosure.

Defend Trade Secrets Act 18 USC § 1835—Orders to preserve confidentiality
(a) In General. In any prosecution or other proceeding under this chapter, the court shall enter such orders and take such other action as may be necessary and appropriate to preserve the confidentiality of trade secrets, consistent with the requirements of the Federal Rules of Criminal and Civil Procedure, the Federal Rules of Evidence, and all other applicable laws. An interlocutory appeal by the United States shall lie from a decision or order of a district court authorizing or directing the disclosure of any trade secret.
(b) Rights of Trade Secret Owners. The court may not authorize or direct the disclosure of any information the owner asserts to be a trade secret unless the court allows the owner the opportunity to file a submission under seal that describes the interest of the owner in keeping the information confidential. No submission under seal made under this subsection may be used in a prosecution under this chapter for any purpose other than those set forth in this section, or otherwise required by law. The provision of information relating to a trade secret to the United States or the court in connection with a prosecution under this chapter shall not constitute a waiver of trade secret protection, and the disclosure of information relating to a trade secret in connection with a prosecution under this chapter shall not constitute a waiver of trade secret protection unless the trade secret owner expressly consents to such waiver.

Uniform Trade Secrets Act: § 5. Preservation of Secrecy
In an action under this Act, a court shall preserve the secrecy of an alleged trade secret by reasonable means, which may include granting protective orders in connection with discovery proceedings, holding in camera hearings, sealing the records of the action, and ordering any person involved in the litigation not to disclose an alleged trade secret without prior court approval.

Related terms: injunction; litigation, disclosure of trade secrets during; temporary restraining order.

provisional relief in a trade secret action
See injunction.

public domain status of trade secrets

Trade secrets are considered to be in the public domain—where their owners have no legal recourse under trade secret law against disclosure and use by others—when the owner of the trade secret:

- is negligent or impermissibly sloppy in keeping it confidential
- fails to seek relief quickly in court if the trade secret becomes known to others through wrongful behavior (for instance, in violation of a nondisclosure agreement or through industrial espionage), or
- loses the rights to court protection of the trade secret by doing something forbidden under the law (for instance, using the trade secret in violation of the antitrust laws).

EXAMPLE: Microwave Systems wants to raise some capital to fund the promotion of its new mini satellite dish system, which it plans to sell to consumers for an affordable price. To accomplish this, it prepares a magazine article describing its revolutionary system, without intending to disclose its trade secrets. However, Manfred reads this article and learns enough details to start his own satellite dish business. Microwave would not be able to claim misappropriation of a trade secret, since its ideas became a matter of public knowledge through its own disclosure.

Even if the secret becomes public because of someone's improper actions, such as the breaking of a nondisclosure agreement or industrial espionage, it will still be in the public domain if the information becomes well known. In short, once a trade secret is disclosed, it is gone unless the owner can somehow manage to contain the disclosure. For example, if an ex-employee discloses the secret to a rival company, it might be possible to obtain a court order preventing the other company and the ex-employee from further disclosures, and thereby maintain the trade secret status. This would not be possible, however, if the ex-employee published the trade secret for the public to see, for example, on the Internet.

It is possible for information to be in the public domain for the purpose of trade secret law but still subject to restrictions under another set of laws. For instance, certain trade secrets in a computer program might pass into the public domain under trade secret law but still be entitled to a patent. If a patent is obtained, no one can use the invention comprising the former trade secret without the patent owner's permission. Similarly, an author may treat his or her novel as a trade secret while it is being written. Once the novel is published, the trade secret aspect of the novel falls into the public domain, but the novel itself will continue to be protected by copyright.

Related terms: loss of trade secrets; trade secret misappropriation action; trade secret owner.

public records and trade secrets

Any information contained in a public record (a document, tape, disk, or other medium that is open to inspection by the public) cannot qualify as a trade secret, since by definition it is not confidential. However, because companies are often required by state and federal governments to file documents that, of necessity, contain trade secrets, there are usually laws that allow the withholding of the precise data that make up the trade secrets, even if the rest of the document is released for inspection.

Related terms: Freedom of Information Act, exemption of trade secrets; litigation, disclosure of trade secrets during; protective order.

read-only memories (ROMs) and trade secrets

Internal operating instructions and other programs that are a physical part of the computing device (for instance, read-only memories or ROMs) do not usually qualify for protection as a trade secret once the device is marketed. This is because it is usually possible to figure out the design and logic of the ROM through reverse engineering, and any trade secrets that can become known in this manner are considered to be in the public domain.

Related terms: public domain and trade secrets; reverse engineering and trade secrets; software and trade secrets.

reasonably precautionary measures to protect trade secrets

Information will qualify as a trade secret only if its owner takes appropriate measures to keep it secret. What constitutes reasonably precautionary measures depends on the type of secret and the industry involved. This issue usually arises when a trade secret action is filed and the defendant claims that the information should not be considered as a trade secret because appropriate precautionary measures were not taken. If a court determines that the business claiming misappropriation has in fact taken appropriate measures to maintain the confidentiality of the information, it will be protected. If not, judicial relief will be denied and the information will no longer be considered a trade secret. Clearly, a certain amount of judicial discretion is involved in these decisions.

Measures typically considered to be reasonable precautions include:

- requiring employees to sign nondisclosure agreements
- requiring all outside persons with whom the information is shared to sign nondisclosure agreements
- restricting physical access to areas where trade secrets are located
- consistently enforcing specific rules formulated by the company regarding confidentiality of the information and physical access to it
- using encryption or other code-like devices to make sure that trade secret information cannot easily be understood, even if read by an unauthorized person
- giving notice to all persons coming in contact with the information that it is considered a trade secret
- posting warnings on the wall of areas where trade secrets are kept or used reminding employees about company rules regarding trade secrets
- conducting exit interviews with employees, specifically warning them against improper disclosure of trade secrets
- adequately protecting against unauthorized intrusion into computer databases that contain trade secrets
- shredding sensitive documents prior to disposing of them, and
- if the scope of the operation and the value of the secrets warrants it, taking such physical security measures as posting guards, maintaining tight control over keys (including keys to the photocopy machine), and requiring visitors to wear badges.

Not all of these measures are necessary in every context, although the more of them that are employed, the better position the company will be in to claim that it took reasonable precautionary measures to protect the trade secrets. Just what measures are considered to be reasonably precautionary in a given case will depend on the size of the company, the value of the trade secrets, and the nature of the technology involved.

Related terms: notice to employees of trade secrets; trade secret misappropriation action.

retail customer lists

See customer lists.

reverse engineering

The act of examining a product or device and figuring out the ideas and methods involved in its creation and structure is referred to as reverse engineering. Normally we think of engineering as the intellectual means by which something is built or an idea is transformed into practice. In this context, "reverse engineering" consists of taking apart and reducing a product or device into its constituent parts and concepts.

The idea of reverse engineering is of crucial importance to trade secret law. This is because of the rule that any information learned about an item through the process of legitimate reverse engineering is considered to be in the public domain for trade secret purposes and therefore no longer protectable as a trade secret. The federal Defend Trade Secrets Act specifically excludes "reverse engineering" from its definition of "improper means." However, the fact that a particular invention or technology can be figured out through reverse engineering has no effect on whether it is entitled to protection under the patent laws.

> EXAMPLE: Ivan creates a machine capable of producing holographic games (consisting of pictures projected onto three-dimensional space so that the images and characters appear realistic). Ivan treats the details of production as a trade secret. Once the machine is marketed, however, it will probably be possible to figure out through reverse engineering how it is constructed. The machine can then be freely manufactured and sold by the party doing the reverse engineering, without Ivan being entitled to any court relief on trade secret grounds. However, Ivan would be entitled to protection under the patent laws if he sought and obtained a patent on his invention.

There are two caveats with regard to performing reverse engineering:
- The reverse engineering should be performed only on an authorized copy of the work—for example, it is not permissible to reverse engineer illegally copied software code.
- Some companies prohibit reverse engineering through the use of end-user license agreements (also known as EULAs). EULAs are created when the customer either buys the product or first uses it. As a condition of use, the agreement may prohibit reverse engineering. A customer that violates this provision may be enjoined from further use and forced to pay damages. (*Bowers v. Baystate Technologies, Inc.,* 2003 U.S. App. LEXIS 1423 (Fed. Cir. 2003).)
  In 2012, a California district court held that breaching an end-user license agreement (EULA) by reverse engineering is not trade secret misappropriation.

A company breached its EULA by reverse engineering software. The court held that the action resulted in a breach of the agreement but did not result in trade secret misappropriation because reverse engineering was not an "improper means" of acquiring trade secrets under the Uniform Trade Secrets Act (UTSA). (*Aqua Connect Inc. v. Code Rebel LLC*, No. 11-5764 (C.D. Cal. 2012).)

Related terms: physical devices, ability to maintain as trade secrets; source code as trade secret.
See also Part 2 (Copyright Law): end-user license.

sale of business, covenant not to compete
See covenant not to compete by owners of a sold business.

screening incoming information for unsolicited disclosures
See unsolicited idea disclosure.

seizure of trade secret
The Defend Trade Secrets Act (DTSA) provides for the seizure of trade secrets without giving any notice to the defendant (*ex parte*). The purpose of such seizures is to prevent the dissemination of the secret or to prevent evidence from being destroyed. If a federal court orders a trade secret seizure, a hearing must be held within seven days of the seizure order. At the hearing, the trade secret owner must prove the legal and factual basis for the order.

Early cases under the DTSA indicate that courts are wary of issuing such seizures unless there are extraordinary circumstances. One such case was *Mission Capital Advisors LLC v. Romaka*, CV-05878-LLS (S.D.N.Y. July 29, 2016). In that case, the defendant evaded personal service five times and failed to appear for the preliminary injunction hearing. The court granted the plaintiff's *ex parte* seizure request based on the defendant's history of dubious behavior.

software as trade secrets
An innovative computer program will often qualify for trade secret status, at least during its development and testing stage. From a program's first conception, information and ideas about it often give an owner a competitive edge as long as they are kept secret. Once a program is fixed in a tangible medium of expression (that is, put down on tape, disk, or paper in tangible form), it might still remain a trade secret. In addition, its expression (not the ideas behind that expression) is protected under the copyright laws.

When a program is distributed, dual copyright and trade secret protections can continue if certain precautions are taken. For instance, if all "purchasers" of the program are required to sign a license forbidding disclosure of trade secrets, both trade secret and copyright protection could be available for distributed copies (the more limited the distribution is, the more likely the trade secret protection will exist). Or, if the owner of the program only distributes object code (usually the case except for programs written in BASIC) and keeps the source code locked in a secure place, it is similarly possible to maintain both trade secret and copyright protection for the program.

If the software owner registers the program with the U.S. Copyright Office, a printout of portions of the object code—or portions of the source code with critical parts blacked out—can be deposited as part of the registration. This will permit the trade secret to be maintained along with the registered copyright.

> EXAMPLE: Harry conceives of a utility that will analyze a computer user's daily usage and produce a report showing which programs were used and for how long, and the overall pattern of usage. Because such a utility would have commercial value, the basic ideas behind it will qualify as a trade secret as long as Harry treats them that way. Suppose that Harry decides to press ahead with his idea. All the information produced by the development process, including the first flowcharts, the written code (the source code), and the instructions to the computer produced by the compiler (the object code), separately and together, can properly qualify as trade secrets if they are treated as such.
>
> Once the program is up and running, Harry has others test it to see if it actually works and whether programming bugs need to be corrected. Because Harry still considers the program to be a trade secret, he has the testers sign nondisclosure agreements in which they agree to keep the program confidential and preserve its trade secret status. In addition, because the program is now fixed in tangible form, it is protected under copyright law without losing trade secret status. When Harry registers the program with the U.S. Copyright Office, he deposits the object code.

Whether using source code or object code, the applicant at the Copyright Office should declare its trade secrecy status concurrent with the filing. Later declarations might prove fruitless.

> EXAMPLE: A software developer registered software by submitting source code to the Copyright Office. Ten months later he submitted an email declaring that the material was a trade secret and he never checked for compliance with this request.

Because the submission was available to the public, trade secrecy was forfeited. (*Kema, Inc. v. Koperwhats,* 658 F. Supp.2d 1022 (N.D. Cal. 2009).)

Related terms: beta testing and trade secrets; copyright and trade secret law compatibility; reverse engineering and trade secrets; source code as trade secret.

source code as trade secret

The specific instructions written by a programmer to tell a computer what to do are referred to as the source code. The language used to write the source code cannot usually be read directly by the computer and must be translated by a compiler into language the computer can understand, which is called object code.

When software is sold to the public, it is in object code form—that is, it is already compiled. Because object code is mostly a series of ones and zeros, it cannot readily be figured out through reverse engineering (called "decompiling" in this instance). The source code, on the other hand, can be figured out, and any trade secrets that the software owner wishes to maintain in the code can be easily obtained. For that reason, source code is usually kept secret, locked in the owner's vault.

Related terms: reverse engineering and trade secrets.

specific performance of covenant not to compete

If a former employee or owner of a business threatens to violate a contract (covenant) not to compete with the business, a court may order the owner or employee to comply with the agreement. Whether a court will issue this type of order depends on a number of "fairness" or equity factors, such as:

- the length of time competition is prohibited
- in the case of employees, the effect of the agreement on the employee's ability to make a living, and
- whether the court concludes that the original covenant not to compete agreement was unnecessarily broad.

Noncompetition agreements that are limited in terms of time and scope have a better chance of being enforced than those that are open-ended. And a few states, including California, Colorado, Florida, and Oregon, severely restrict the ability of an employer to enforce a noncompetition agreement against a former employee.

Related terms: covenant not to compete by employee; covenant not to compete by owners of a sold business; injunction.

spoliation doctrine

Under this doctrine, a court can infer that theft of trade secrets has occurred when the defendant intentionally destroys trade secret evidence. The logic behind spoliation is that the defendant wouldn't have destroyed the information unless it indicated that trade secret theft had occurred. For example, in one case, a defendant destroyed all the files on his computer after being sued. Later, when a court-ordered image of the computer was required, the defendant deliberately left certain items out of the image, leading the judge to rule for the trade secret owner. (*Advantacare Health Partners, LP v. Access IV*, 005 U.S. Dist. LEXIS 12794 (N.D. Cal. June 14, 2005).)

statute of limitations

The federal Defend Trade Secrets Act requires that trade secret misappropriation cases be brought within three years of the discovery of the theft (or "by the exercise of reasonable diligence should have been discovered"). States that have adopted the Uniform Trade Secrets Act also typically provide that misappropriation actions be brought within three years after the theft is discovered (or should have been reasonably discovered).

> EXAMPLE: A company, CMI, had notice that its trade secrets were being used by a rival, but waited 14 years before bringing a lawsuit under the federal Defend Trade Secrets ACT (DTSA). The Eighth Circuit held that CMI knew or should have known that its trade secrets were being used, and had a duty to investigate. The DTSA three-year statute of limitations began to run once CMI was on notice of misappropriation. (*CMI Roadbuilding, Inc. v. Iowa Parts, Inc.*, 920 F.3d 560 (8th Cir. 2019).)

Defend Trade Secrets Act 18 USC § 1836(d)—Period of Limitations.

A civil action under subsection (b) may not be commenced later than three years after the date on which the misappropriation with respect to which the action would relate is discovered or by the exercise of reasonable diligence should have been discovered. For purposes of this subsection, a continuing misappropriation constitutes a single claim of misappropriation.

Uniform Trade Secrets Act: § 6. Statute of Limitations

An action for misappropriation must be brought within 3 years after the misappropriation is discovered or by the exercise of reasonable diligence should have been discovered. For the purposes of this section, a continuing misappropriation constitutes a single claim.

temporary restraining order

A court order that can be immediately obtained by a plaintiff in an intellectual property lawsuit with little or no advance notice to the defendant is a temporary restraining order (TRO). TROs place events in a holding pattern ("maintain the status quo") until the court can more fully determine what kind of protection is required, if any. Typically, TROs last for only a few days or, at most, two to three weeks. While the TRO is still in effect, a court will hear the argument of all sides to the dispute and more thoroughly consider the underlying issues.

Related terms: injunction; trade secret misappropriation action.

tools as trade secrets

See physical devices, ability to maintain as trade secrets.

trade secret, defined

In most states, a trade secret may consist of any formula, pattern, physical device, idea, process, compilation of information, or other information that both:
- provides a business with a potential or actual competitive advantage, and
- is treated in a way that can reasonably be expected to prevent the public or competitors from learning about it, absent improper acquisition or theft.

When deciding whether information qualifies as a trade secret under this definition, courts will typically consider the following factors:
- the extent to which the information is known outside of the particular business entity
- the extent to which the information is known by employees and others involved in the business
- the extent to which measures have been taken to guard the secrecy of the information
- the value of the information to the business, and
- the difficulty with which the information could be properly acquired or independently duplicated by others.

There is no crisp definition of what constitutes a trade secret. A trade secret is created and defined solely by reference to how certain information is handled, and to the value inherent in keeping it secret. Even if an item or piece of information otherwise qualifies as a trade secret, its moment-to-moment status will depend on how it is treated by its owners.

Uniform Trade Secrets Act: § 1. Definitions

(4) "Trade secret" means information, including a formula, pattern, compilation, program, device, method, technique, or process, that:

  (i) derives independent economic value, actual or potential, from not being generally known to, and not being readily ascertainable by proper means by, other persons who can obtain economic value from its disclosure or use, and

  (ii) is the subject of efforts that are reasonable under the circumstances to maintain its secrecy.

Related terms: ideas as trade secrets; reasonably precautionary measures to protect trade secrets; software and trade secrets; trade secret misappropriation action.

trade secret misappropriation action

The owner of a trade secret may bring a lawsuit, known as a trade secret misappropriation action, for the purpose of:

- preventing another person or business from using the trade secret without proper authorization, and
- collecting money damages for economic injury suffered as a result of the improper acquisition and use of the trade secret.

All persons and businesses responsible for the improper acquisition, and all those who have benefited from such acquisition, are typically named as defendants in misappropriation actions.

Among the most common situations that give rise to infringement actions are:

- Trade secrets are stolen through industrial espionage.
- An employee having knowledge of a trade secret changes jobs and discloses the secret to a new employer in violation of an express or implied nondisclosure agreement with the first employer.
- Trade secrets are improperly disclosed in violation of a nondisclosure agreement.

To prevail in a misappropriation suit, the plaintiff (person bringing the suit) must show that the information alleged to be a trade secret provides the plaintiff with a competitive advantage and has been continually treated by the plaintiff as a trade secret. In addition, the plaintiff must show that the defendant either improperly acquired the information (if accused of making commercial use of the secret) or improperly disclosed it (if accused of leaking the information).

The defendants in trade secret misappropriation cases commonly attempt to defend against the plaintiff's case by showing any of the following:

- The information claimed to be a trade secret was known throughout the particular industry, and thus was not a secret that should be subject to protection.
- The information was lawfully disclosed by a person having knowledge of it.
- The information was lawfully acquired through reverse engineering.
- The information was the result of an independent conception.
- The trade secret was being used by its owner in violation of the antitrust laws.

If the plaintiff can establish that a trade secret was, in fact, improperly used, disclosed, or acquired by a defendant, the court can enjoin (stop) its further commercial use. Sometimes such injunctions are permanent—that is, they are final court orders in the case. More commonly, courts will employ the head start rule. This operates to give the rightful owner of the trade secret a "head start" in commercially exploiting it, by prohibiting its use by the competitor for such period of time as the court decides it would have taken the competitor to independently develop the information.

Because lawsuits tend to drag on for years, courts are authorized to issue preliminary injunctions prohibiting the competitor from using the secret in question pending a final determination in the case. These preliminary orders are often viewed by the parties as harbingers of how the case will finally turn out and, accordingly, form the basis of a settlement (which precludes a full-scale trial).

In addition to injunctive relief (both provisional and final), a court may award damages suffered by the original trade secret owner. These can consist of lost profits resulting from sales by the trade secret thief, profits realized from the wrongfully acquired trade secret, and, occasionally, punitive or treble damages, depending on the state where the action is being tried.

Trade secret misappropriation cases can be brought under state or federal law. State law cases are brought under the Uniform Trade Secrets Act, as adopted by 49 states (all but New York). Federal cases are brought under the Defend Trade Secrets Act.

Related terms: damages in trade secret misappropriation actions; independent conception, defense to trade secret claim; injunction; litigation, disclosure of trade secrets during; reasonably precautionary measures to protect trade secrets; reverse engineering and trade secrets.

Trade Secret Law: Definitions

trade secret owner

The owner of a trade secret has a right to seek relief in court in the event someone else improperly acquires or improperly discloses the trade secret. The trade secret owner is also entitled to grant others a license to utilize the secret, or even to sell it outright.

Ownership of a trade secret is usually determined by the circumstances of its creation. In general, these ownership rules apply:

- Trade secrets that arise from research and development activities conducted by manufacturing concerns belong to the company sponsoring the research and development.
- Retail customer lists belong to the business or individual who compiled the list.
- Trade secrets developed by an employee in the course of employment belong to the employer.
- Trade secrets developed by an employee on his or her own time, and with personal equipment, usually belong to the employee.

EXAMPLE: A chef develops a special recipe and baking process for cheesecake during her off-work hours, and in her own kitchen. Even though she bakes the cheesecake for a restaurant, she would probably be entitled to preserve the recipe and process as her own trade secret. If, on the other hand, the recipe and process were developed at work using the restaurant facilities, the restaurant would own the trade secret.

Related terms: business information as trade secret; licensing of trade secrets.

trade secrets and antitrust laws

See antitrust law and trade secrets.

under seal

See protective order.

Uniform Trade Secrets Act (UTSA)

This model legislation was prepared for the ultimate purpose of creating similar trade secret laws in all states. At present, 49 states and the District of Columbia have adopted it. New York remains the only holdout (although there is still some debate as to whether North Carolina has adopted it). Overall, the provisions of the Uniform Trade Secrets Act are consistent with the principles of trade secret law adopted by the courts under the common law (law established by court case decisions). (Portions of the Uniform Trade Secrets Act are included in the relevant definitions in this section.)

unique ideas as trade secrets

See ideas as trade secrets.

unjust enrichment and trade secrets

Some courts deciding cases involving the improper acquisition of a trade secret have ordered the guilty party to pay the trade secret owner all profits earned from the trade secret in question. The legal theory underlying this type of relief is that the wrongful possessor has been unjustly enriched by profiting from these trade secrets.

The unjust enrichment approach has also been used as a theoretical basis for providing judicial protection to trade secrets. Courts have long been willing to entertain disputes where one party was being unjustly enriched at the expense of another, so the improper acquisition of a trade secret is by nature the type of unjust enrichment that deserves judicial relief.

Related terms: damages in trade secret misappropriation actions; trade secret misappropriation action.

unsolicited idea disclosure

Although many people have creative brainstorms, they usually must share their ideas with others to enlist their help in commercially developing or promoting the idea. This process frequently involves approaching a well-known company to see if it is interested in the unsolicited idea.

Although a company might benefit from ideas generated by outside parties, it often will decline to be informed about such ideas. This is because the company might already be working on a similar idea and want to avoid later accusations of ripping off the outside party.

Companies tend to be particularly reluctant to consider ideas presented by outsiders when asked to sign a nondisclosure agreement, which treats the idea as a trade secret belonging to the outsider. In that situation, if the company rejects the idea but later markets a product or service that appears to incorporate the idea, the company could be vulnerable to charges of trade secret theft and forced into an expensive lawsuit.

Trade Secret Law: Definitions

Probably the best way to get past a company's mechanisms for insulating itself from outside ideas is to trust the company. Very few companies are interested in ripping off creative people; most can be counted on to play straight. On the other hand, if trust does not seem an appropriate approach for one reason or another, companies are usually willing to examine an invention if either a regular patent application or a Provisional Patent Application has been filed on it (in either case, the invention is said to have "patent pending" status).

Related entries: evaluation agreement; ideas as trade secrets; idea submission; independent conception, defense to trade secret claim; trade secret misappropriation action; waiver agreement for unsolicited idea disclosure.
See also Part 1 (Patent Law): Provisional Patent Application (PPA).

waiver agreement for unsolicited idea disclosure

Companies routinely require anyone presenting an unsolicited idea to sign a waiver agreement giving up the right to sue for trade secret infringement. If the "idea person" does not want to sign the agreement, the company will not examine the secret. Many companies go to great lengths to make sure ideas don't get past the front door absent the signing of such a waiver.

Related terms: evaluation agreement; ideas as trade secrets; idea submission; unsolicited idea disclosure.

whistleblower

An ex-employee had retained trade secrets, as part of a legal claim against the former employer. The employer counterclaimed for trade secret misappropriation. A Pennsylvania court ruled that the ex-employee was immune from liability, becoming the first federal court to grant immunity to a whistleblower under the Defend Trade Secrets Act. (*Christian v. Lannett Co.*, No. 16-963 (E.D. Pa. Mar. 29, 2018).)

To encourage employers to notify employees of their whistleblower rights, the DTSA made employers ineligible for obtaining punitive damages and attorneys' fees from an ex-employee or independent contractor, unless a Notice of Immunity is included in nondisclosure agreements that are executed after May 11, 2016. Failure to include the provision does not prevent taking advantage of the DTSA's benefits; it prevents only the recovery of punitive (exemplary) damages and attorneys' fees. Under the DTSA, a whistleblower is someone who discloses trade secrets "solely for the purpose of reporting or investigating a suspected violation of law." (18 U.S. Code § 1833(b)(1).)

Related terms: Defend Trade Secrets Act (DTSA).

World Intellectual Property Organization (WIPO)

This organization was formed to facilitate international agreements regulating intellectual property. WIPO is a policy-making body only, with no delegated authority to make binding decisions or impose sanctions. WIPO's membership consists of representatives from countries, and groups of countries, including:

- most European countries
- countries that are members of the United Nations body UNESCO
- Japan, and
- the United States.

Related terms: GATT (General Agreement on Tariffs and Trade).

wrongfully disclosing trade secrets

See improper disclosure of trade secrets.

wrongfully obtaining trade secrets

See improper acquisition of trade secrets.

Trade Secret Law: Definitions

Trade Secret Law: Forms

Preparing a Nondisclosure Agreement

In this section we provide a sample nondisclosure agreement (NDA), followed by an explanation. A nondisclosure agreement will assure your right to sue someone who discloses secrets in violation of the agreement and demonstrates your diligence in protecting secrets. Keep in mind that you can never rely solely on a nondisclosure agreement as a basis for protecting confidential information. You must also be able to prove that you took reasonable steps to protect your secret and that the secret has not become known to the public. If you are given an NDA to sign, you can evaluate the agreement by comparing it to the model provisions.

Explanation for Sample Nondisclosure Agreement

Optional Provision for Employees and Independent Contractors

If you are drafting a nondisclosure agreement for an employee or independent contractor, you may wish to include an additional provision (shown below). This provision is not mandatory but if it is *not* included and a lawsuit is filed under the Defend Trade Secrets Act, you (as the trade secret owner) will not be permitted to seek punitive damages and attorneys' fees from an ex-employee or independent contractor.

A sample provision would include the following language:

Notice of Immunity From Liability. An individual shall not be held criminally or civilly liable under any federal or state trade secret law for the disclosure of a trade secret that is made (i) in confidence to a federal, state, or local government official, either directly or indirectly, or to an attorney; and (ii) solely for the purpose of reporting or investigating a suspected violation of law; or is made in a complaint or other document filed in a lawsuit or other proceeding, if such filing is made under seal. An individual who files a lawsuit for retaliation by an employer for reporting a suspected violation of law may disclose the trade secret to the attorney of the individual and use the trade secret information in the court proceeding, if the individual (i) files any document containing the trade secret under seal; and (ii) does not disclose the trade secret, except pursuant to court order.

Who Is Disclosing? Who Is Receiving?

In the sample agreement, the "Disclosing Party" is the person disclosing secrets, and "Receiving Party" is the person or company who receives the confidential information and is obligated to keep it secret. The terms are capitalized to indicate they are defined within the agreement. The sample agreement is a "one-way" (or in legalese, "unilateral") agreement—that is, only one party is disclosing secrets.

If both sides are disclosing secrets to each other, you should modify the agreement to make it a mutual (or "bilateral") nondisclosure agreement. To do that, substitute the following paragraph for the first paragraph in the agreement.

This Nondisclosure agreement (the "Agreement") is entered into by and between [*insert your name, business form, and address*] and [*insert name, business form, and address of other person or company with whom you are exchanging information*], collectively referred to as the "parties" for the purpose of preventing the unauthorized disclosure of Confidential Information as defined below. The parties agree to enter into a confidential relationship with respect to the disclosure by one or each (the "Disclosing Party") to the other (the "Receiving Party") of certain proprietary and confidential information (the "Confidential Information").

Sample Nondisclosure Agreement

Nondisclosure Agreement

This Nondisclosure Agreement (the "Agreement") is entered into by and between
_____ , with its principal offices at
_____ ("Disclosing Party"),
and _____ ,
located at _____ ("Receiving Party"),
for the purpose of preventing the unauthorized disclosure of Confidential Information as defined
below. The parties agree to enter into a confidential relationship with respect to the disclosure of
certain proprietary and confidential information ("Confidential Information").

1. **Definition of Confidential Information.** For purposes of this Agreement, "Confidential
   Information" shall include all information or material that has or could have commercial
   value or other utility in the business in which Disclosing Party is engaged. If Confidential
   Information is in written form, the Disclosing Party shall label or stamp the materials with the
   word "Confidential" or some similar warning. If Confidential Information is transmitted orally,
   the Disclosing Party shall promptly provide a writing indicating that such oral communication
   constituted Confidential Information.

2. **Exclusions From Confidential Information.** Receiving Party's obligations under this
   Agreement do not extend to information that is: (a) publicly known at the time of
   disclosure or subsequently becomes publicly known through no fault of the Receiving
   Party; (b) discovered or created by the Receiving Party before disclosure by Disclosing
   Party; (c) learned by the Receiving Party through legitimate means other than from the
   Disclosing Party or Disclosing Party's representatives; or (d) disclosed by Receiving Party
   with Disclosing Party's prior written approval.

3. **Obligations of Receiving Party.** Receiving Party shall hold and maintain the Confidential
   Information in strictest confidence for the sole and exclusive benefit of the Disclosing Party.
   Receiving Party shall carefully restrict access to Confidential Information to employees,
   contractors, and third parties as is reasonably required and shall require those persons to
   sign nondisclosure restrictions at least as protective as those in this Agreement. Receiving
   Party shall not, without prior written approval of Disclosing Party, use for Receiving Party's
   own benefit, publish, copy, or otherwise disclose to others, or permit the use by others for
   their benefit or to the detriment of Disclosing Party, any Confidential Information. Receiving
   Party shall return to Disclosing Party any and all records, notes, and other written, printed,
   or tangible materials in its possession pertaining to Confidential Information immediately if
   Disclosing Party requests it in writing.

Trade Secret Law: Forms

Sample Nondisclosure Agreement (continued)

4. **Time Periods.** The nondisclosure provisions of this Agreement shall survive the termination of this Agreement, and Receiving Party's duty to hold Confidential Information in confidence shall remain in effect until the Confidential Information no longer qualifies as a trade secret or until Disclosing Party sends Receiving Party written notice releasing Receiving Party from this Agreement, whichever occurs first.

5. **Relationships.** Nothing contained in this Agreement shall be deemed to constitute either party a partner, joint venturer, or employee of the other party for any purpose.

6. **Severability.** If a court finds any provision of this Agreement invalid or unenforceable, the remainder of this Agreement shall be interpreted so as best to effect the intent of the parties.

7. **Integration.** This Agreement expresses the complete understanding of the parties with respect to the subject matter and supersedes all prior proposals, agreements, representations, and understandings. This Agreement may not be amended except in a writing signed by both parties.

8. **Waiver.** The failure to exercise any right provided in this Agreement shall not be a waiver of prior or subsequent rights.

This Agreement and each party's obligations shall be binding on the representatives, assigns, and successors of such party. Each party has signed this Agreement through its authorized representative.

Signature: _____

Typed or printed name: _____

Date: _____

Signature: _____

Typed or printed name: _____

Date: _____

Defining the Trade Secrets

Every nondisclosure agreement defines its trade secrets, often referred to as "confidential information." This definition establishes the subject matter of the disclosure. There are three common approaches to defining confidential information: (1) using a system to mark all confidential information; (2) listing trade secret categories; or (3) specifically identifying the confidential information.

What's best? That depends on your secrets and how you disclose them. If your company is built around one or two secrets—for example, a famous recipe or formula—you can specifically identify the materials. You can also use that approach if you are disclosing one or two secrets to a contractor. If your company focuses on several categories of secret information, for example, computer code, sales information, and marketing plans, a list approach will work with employees and contractors. If your company has a wide variety of secrets and is constantly developing new ones, you should specifically identify secrets. Here's an example of the list approach.

Definition of Confidential Information Example

"Confidential Information" means information or material that is commercially valuable to the Disclosing Party and not generally known or readily ascertainable in the industry. This includes, but is not limited to:

(a) technical information concerning the Disclosing Party's products and services, including product know-how, formulae, designs, devices, diagrams, software code, test results, processes, inventions, research projects and product development, technical memoranda, and correspondence

(b) information concerning the Disclosing Party's business, including cost information, profits, sales information, accounting and unpublished financial information, business plans, markets and marketing methods, customer lists and customer information, purchasing techniques, supplier lists and supplier information, and advertising strategies

(c) information concerning the Disclosing Party's employees, including salaries, strengths, weaknesses, and skills

(d) information submitted by the Disclosing Party's customers, suppliers, employees, consultants, or coventure partners with the Disclosing Party for study, evaluation, or use, and

(e) any other information not generally known to the public that, if misused or disclosed, could reasonably be expected to adversely affect the Disclosing Party's business.

Trade Secret Law: Forms

Using a list approach is fine, provided that you can find something on the list that fits your disclosure. For example, if you are disclosing a confidential software program, your nondisclosure agreement should include a category such as "programming code" or "software code" that accurately reflects your secret material. Although the final paragraph in the example above includes "any other information," you will be better off not relying solely on this statement. Courts that interpret NDAs often prefer specificity.

If confidential information is fairly specific—for example, a unique method of preparing income tax statements—define it specifically.

Definition of Confidential Information Example

The following constitutes Confidential Information: _business method for preparing income tax statements and related algorithms and software code,_

Another approach to identifying trade secrets is to state that the disclosing party will certify what is and what is not confidential. For example, physical disclosures such as written materials or software will be clearly marked "Confidential." In the case of oral disclosures, the disclosing party provides written confirmation that a trade secret was disclosed. Here is an appropriate provision taken from the sample NDA in the previous section.

Definition of Confidential Information Example

(Written or Oral). For purposes of this Agreement, "Confidential Information" includes all information or material that has or could have commercial value or other utility in the business in which Disclosing Party is engaged. If Confidential Information is in written form, the Disclosing Party shall label or stamp the materials with the word "Confidential" or some similar warning. If Confidential Information is transmitted orally, the Disclosing Party shall promptly provide a writing indicating that such oral communication constituted Confidential Information.

When confirming an oral disclosure, avoid disclosing the content of the trade secret. An email or letter is acceptable, but the parties should keep copies of all such correspondence. A sample letter is shown below.

Letter Confirming Oral Disclosure

Date:

Dear Sam,

Today at lunch, I disclosed information to you about my kaleidoscopic projection system—specifically, the manner in which I have configured and wired the bulbs in the device. That information is confidential (as described in our nondisclosure agreement) and this letter is intended to confirm the disclosure.

William

Excluding Information That Is Not Confidential

You cannot prohibit the receiving party from disclosing information that is publicly known, legitimately acquired from another source, or developed by the receiving party before meeting you. Similarly, it is not unlawful if the receiving party discloses your secret with your permission. These legal exceptions exist with or without an agreement, but they are commonly included in a contract to make it clear to everyone that such information is not considered a trade secret.

Exclusions From Confidential Information Example

Receiving Party's obligations under this Agreement do not extend to information that is: (a) publicly known at the time of disclosure under this Agreement or subsequently becomes publicly known through no fault of the Receiving Party; (b) discovered or created by the Receiving Party prior to disclosure by Disclosing Party; (c) otherwise learned by the Receiving Party through legitimate means other than from the Disclosing Party or Disclosing Party's representatives; or (d) disclosed by Receiving Party with Disclosing Party's prior written approval.

In some cases, a business presented with your nondisclosure agreement might request the right to exclude information that is independently developed *after* the disclosure. In other words, the business might want to change subsection (b) to read, "(b) discovered or independently created by Receiving Party prior to *or after* disclosure by Disclosing Party."

Trade Secret Law: Forms

By making this change, the other company can create new products after exposure to your secret, provided that your secret is not used to develop them. You might wonder how it is possible for a company once exposed to your secret to develop a new product without using that trade secret. One possibility is that one division of a large company could invent something without any contact with the division that has been exposed to your secret. Some companies even establish clean room methods.

Although it is possible for a company to independently develop products or information without using your disclosed secret, we recommend avoiding this modification if possible.

Duty to Keep Information Secret

The heart of a nondisclosure agreement is a statement establishing a confidential relationship between the parties. The statement sets out the duty of the Receiving Party to maintain the information in confidence and to limit its use. Often, this duty is established by one sentence: "The Receiving Party shall hold and maintain the Confidential Information of the other party in strictest confidence for the sole and exclusive benefit of the Disclosing Party." In other cases, the provision might be more detailed and include obligations to return information. A detailed provision is provided below.

The simpler provision is usually suitable when entering into an NDA with an individual such as an independent contractor. Use the more detailed one if your secrets might be used by more than one individual within a business. The detailed provision provides that the receiving party has to restrict access to persons within the company who are also bound by this agreement.

Provision Establishing a Duty of Nondisclosure Example

Receiving Party shall hold and maintain the Confidential Information of the Disclosing Party in strictest confidence for the sole and exclusive benefit of the Disclosing Party. Receiving Party shall carefully restrict access to Confidential Information to employees, contractors, and third parties as is reasonably required and only disclose confidential information to persons subject to nondisclosure restrictions at least as protective as those set forth in this Agreement. Receiving Party shall not, without prior written approval of Disclosing Party, use for Receiving Party's own benefit, publish, copy, or otherwise disclose to others, or permit the use by others for their benefit or to the detriment of Disclosing Party, any Confidential Information.

In some cases, you might want to impose additional requirements. For example, a Prospective Software Licensee Nondisclosure Agreement might contain a prohibition against reverse engineering, decompiling, or disassembling the software. This prohibits the receiving party (the user of licensed software) from learning more about the trade secrets.

You can also insist on the return of all trade secret materials that you furnished under the agreement. In that case, add the following language to the receiving party's obligations.

Return of Materials Example

Receiving Party shall return to Disclosing Party any and all records, notes, and other written, printed, or tangible materials in its possession pertaining to Confidential Information immediately if Disclosing Party requests it in writing.

Duration of the Agreement

How long does the duty of confidentiality last? The sample agreement offers three alternative approaches: an indefinite period that terminates when the information is no longer a trade secret; a fixed period of time; or a combination of the two.

Unlimited Time Period Example

This Agreement and Receiving Party's duty to hold Disclosing Party's Confidential Information in confidence shall remain in effect until the Confidential Information no longer qualifies as a trade secret or until Disclosing Party sends Receiving Party written notice releasing Receiving Party from this Agreement, whichever occurs first.

Fixed Time Period Example

This Agreement and Receiving Party's duty to hold Disclosing Party's Confidential Information in confidence shall remain in effect until _____ .

Fixed Time Period With Exceptions Example

This Agreement and Receiving Party's duty to hold Disclosing Party's Confidential Information in confidence shall remain in effect until _____ or until one of the following occurs:

(a) the Disclosing Party sends the Receiving Party written notice releasing it from this Agreement, or

(b) the information disclosed under this Agreement ceases to be a trade secret.

The time period is often an issue of negotiation. You, as the disclosing party, will likely want an open period with no limits; receiving parties want a short period. For employee and contractor agreements, the term is often unlimited or ends only when the trade secret becomes public knowledge. Five years is a common length in nondisclosure agreements that involve business negotiations and product submissions, although many companies insist on two or three years.

We recommend that you seek as long a time as possible, preferably unlimited.

But realize that some businesses want a fixed period of time and some courts, when interpreting NDAs, require that the time period be reasonable. Determining "reasonableness" is subjective and depends on the confidential material and the nature of the industry. For example, some trade secrets within the software or Internet industries might be short-lived. Other trade secrets—for example, the Coca-Cola formula—have been preserved as a secret for over a century. If it is likely, for example, that others will stumble upon the same secret or innovation or that it will be reverse engineered within a few years, then you are unlikely to be damaged by a two- or three-year period. Keep in mind that once the time period is over, the disclosing party is free to reveal your secrets.

Miscellaneous Provisions

The sample NDA includes four miscellaneous provisions. These standard provisions (sometimes known as "boilerplate") are included at the end of most contracts. They actually have little in common with one another except for the fact that they don't fit anywhere else in the agreement. They're contract orphans. Still, these provisions are very important and can affect how disputes are resolved and how a court enforces the contract.

Trade Secret Law: Forms

Relationships. Your relationship with the receiving party is usually defined by the agreement that you are signing—for example an employment, licensing, or investment agreement. To an outsider, it might appear that you have a different relationship, such as a partnership or joint venture. It's possible that an unscrupulous business will try to capitalize on this appearance and make a third-party deal. That is, the receiving party could claim to be your partner to obtain a benefit from a distributor or sublicensee. To avoid liability for such a situation, most agreements include a provision like this one, disclaiming any relationship other than that defined in the agreement. We recommend that you include such a provision and take care to tailor it to the agreement. For example, if you are using it in an employment agreement, you would delete the reference to employees. If you are using it in a partnership agreement, take out the reference to partners, and so forth.

Relationships Example

Nothing contained in this Agreement shall be deemed to constitute either party a partner, joint venturer, or employee of the other party for any purpose.

Severability. The severability clause provides that if you wind up in a lawsuit over the agreement and a court rules that one part of the agreement is invalid, that part can be cut out and the rest of the agreement will remain valid. If you don't include a severability clause and some portion of your agreement is deemed invalid, then the whole agreement may be canceled.

Severability Example

If a court finds any provision of this Agreement invalid or unenforceable, the remainder of this Agreement shall be interpreted so as best to effect the intent of the parties.

Integration. In the process of negotiation and contract drafting, you and the other party might make many oral or written statements. Some of these statements make it into the final agreement. Others don't. The integration provision verifies that the version you are signing is the final version, and that neither of you can rely on statements made in the past. *This is it!* Without an integration provision, it's possible that either party could claim rights based upon promises made before the deal was signed.

Trade Secret Law: Forms

A second function of the integration provision is to establish that if any party makes promises after the agreement is signed, those promises will be binding only if they are made in a signed amendment (addendum) to the agreement.

Integration Example

This Agreement expresses the complete understanding of the parties with respect to the subject matter and supersedes all prior proposals, agreements, representations, and understandings. This Agreement may not be amended except in writing when signed by both parties.

Waiver. This provision states that even if you don't promptly complain about a violation of the NDA, you still have the right to complain about it later. Without this kind of clause, if you know the other party has breached the agreement but you let it pass, you give up (waive) your right to sue over it. For example, imagine that the receiving party is supposed to use the secret information in two products but not in a third. You're aware that the receiving party is violating the agreement, but you are willing to permit it because you are being paid more money and don't have a competing product. After several years, however, you no longer want to permit the use of the secret in the third product. A waiver provision makes it possible for you to sue. The receiving party cannot defend itself by claiming it relied on your past practice of accepting its breaches. Of course, the provision swings both ways. If you breach the agreement, you cannot rely on the other party's past acceptance of *your* behavior.

Waiver Example

The failure to exercise any right provided in this Agreement shall not be a waiver of prior or subsequent rights.

Signatures. The parties don't have to be in the same room when they sign the agreement. It's even fine if the dates are a few days apart. Each party should sign two copies and keep one. This way, both parties have an original signed agreement.

Index

A

Abandonment (full or partial) of trademark application, 396–397, 529

Abandonment of patent application
definition of, 21
notice (office action) of application rejection, 21
petition to USPTO to set aside, 21
Request for Continued Examination (RCE), 145
as statutory bar, 153
substitute application, 21, 155
time requirement to avoid, 21
utilize another form of IP protection, 21
will not serve as prior art reference after, 140
See also Patent application prosecution; Patent claims

Abandonment of trademark
overview, 385, 395–396, 405
ex parte expungement for never being used in commerce, 391, 396, 397, 435, 482, 515
ex parte reexamination for nonuse before registration, 396, 397, 436, 482, 515
failure of obligation to monitor use of mark ("naked" license) resulting in, 447, 470, 476–477
zombie trademarks, 522

Abridged works. *See* Derivative works

Abstract (patent application), 21, 162, 174

Abstract ideas not patentable
Alice/Mayo Test for, 15, 24, 94, 100
Section 101 ineligibility, 15, 18
software patents denied for, 18, 23, 35

Abstraction-Filtration-Comparison test for copyright infringement, 279, 334

Accelerated Examination Program (AEP), 22, 130

Acceptable Identification of Goods and Services Manual (USPTO), 397, 525, 526

Accused device, 21

ACPA (Anticybersquatting Consumer Protect Act), 398–399, 432

Actual reduction to practice. *See* Reduction to practice

Adaptations. *See* Derivative works

Administrative Patent Judges (APJs), 15

Advertising (trademarks)
awards and ratings, use of another company's mark to promote, 402
comparative, fair use and, 436, 449
definition of advertising, 438
as fair use, 436
false advertising, 438–440, 494, 495, 499–500, 518–519
keyword sales, 466–467
periodicals publishing infringing ads, 493–494
pop-up advertising, 488
puffery, 494
as trademark dilution exception, 422

Advertising injury, liability insurance, 199

AEP (Accelerated Examination Program), 22, 130

Aesthetic functionality, 398

Affirmative rights, 199

Aharonian, Gregory, 19

AHRA (Audio Home Recording Act), 204–205

AIA. *See* America Invents Act

AIPLA (American Intellectual Property Law Association), 22

Aircraft, temporary presence patent infringement exception, 155

AIR. *See* Automated Interview Request

Algorithms, not patentable, 23, 148

Alice Corp. v. CLS Bank International, 18, 23, 24, 37–38, 94, 148

Alice Test/Mayo Test, 15, 94, 100, 104

Allegation of Use for Intent-to-Use Application (trademark), 388, 396, 398, 441, 461, 529

Allowance. *See* Patent approval (allowance)

Altai test for copyright infringement, 279, 334

Amazon, 37, 93, 290, 311, 431, 458, 488

America Invents Act (AIA) assignees may apply for patent, 26, 31–32

"best mode" infringement defense eliminated, 26, 65

business-method patents, review of, 27

commercial use of less than one year as infringement defense, 26

covered business method patents (CBMs), 27, 38, 90

derivation hearing for fighting earlier effective patent filing, 27, 59–61

experimental use of an unpatented invention, 72–73

false marking, revision of, 26, 100

fees for non-electronic filers, 26

first-to-file replacing first-to-invent, 27

human organism may not be patented, 26, 80–81

inter partes review, 25, 26–27

inventor's oath, 26

joinder of unrelated accused infringers, 26

post-grant reviews, 26–27

PTAB changes, 27

supplemental exams, 27

tax strategy patents disallowed, 26

third-party submission of publications during prosecution of patent, 27

virtual website patent marks, 26, 100

American rule (attorneys' fees), 15, 32

Annotations and copyright as derivative works, 239

of state laws, not protected, 190, 286

Anonymous authors defined, 200

duration of copyright, 188, 200, 247–248

named by person with interest in the copyright, 248

name of author disclosed in records, 200, 248

Anthologies. *See* Collective works

Anticipated inventions (not patentable)

claims as fully met by (read on/recite), 28–29, 79

defined, 28

design patents and, 64

one-year limited grace period for inventor-led disclosures, 27, 28, 29, 110–111, 113, 134–135, 136

patent specification used to determine, 150

placing the invention on sale (offers of sale) as, 28, 135, 142

printed publication as, 28–29

public use or display of the invention as, 28, 135

Anticompetitive effects. *See* Competitive injury

Anticybersquatting
    Consumer Protect Act
    (ACPA), 398–399, 432
Antishelving clause
    (commercial use deadline),
    29
Antitrust law (federal) and
    patents
    overview, 29–30
    concerted refusal to deal,
        30, 46
    exclusive dealing
        agreements, 30
    patent pools and, 123
    patent thickets, 30, 126
    pay-for-delay (reverse
        payment), 30
    price-fixing, 30, 133
    requirements contracts, 30
    territorial restrictions, 30
    tying agreements, 30,
        55–56, 156–157
    See also Patent misuse
Antitrust law and trade
    secrets, 543–544, 566
    illegal restraint of trade, 566
    licensing and, 572
    violation of, and loss of
        trade secrets to public
        domain, 583
AOTW (Assignments on the
    Web), 400
APIs (application
    programming interface
    codes), 335, 349–350
APJs (Administrative Patent
    Judges), 15

Apple, 64, 243, 294, 311,
    488, 514, 562
Apple Computer, Inc. v.
    Franklin, 201, 282, 334
Apple Computer, Inc. v.
    Microsoft Corp., 201, 334
Apple iTunes, 294, 309, 311
Applicant Initiated
    Interview Request Form.
    See Automated Interview
    Request
Application programming
    interface codes (APIs), 335,
    349–350
Arbitrary marks, 384, 399,
    426, 452, 506
Arbitration
    anticybersquatting, 399,
        415, 517
    derivation hearing, 61
    domain names, 399, 415,
        517
Architectural works, 192,
    201–202
Article III standing, 16, 90,
    151
    See also Standing
Articles of manufacture. See
    Manufacturers
Artificial intelligence, cannot
    be the inventor, 16–17, 95
Artistic use of trademarks
    fair use, 436–437
    free speech, 449
Art Resource
    (clearinghouse), 213

Artworks. See Artistic use
    of trademarks; Pictorial,
    graphic, and sculptural
    works (copyright); Visual
    Artists Rights Act
ASCAP, 213, 311, 322
Asserted Truth Doctrine,
    254
Assignment. See Copyright
    assignment; Patent
    assignment; Trademark
    assignment
Assignor estoppel, 13, 32
Attorneys
    as fiduciary, 565
    foreign attorneys may
        not seek reciprocal
        recognition to practice
        before the USPTO, 447
    trademark registration
        by nonresident foreign
        national required to have,
        447
    See also Attorneys' fees;
        Patent attorneys
Attorneys and Agents
    Registered to Practice
    Before the U.S. Patent
    and Trademark Office
    (USPTO), 119
Attorneys' fees
    copyright cases and award
        of, 186, 203–204,
        209–210, 280–281
    litigation misconduct and
        award of, 32
    patent cases and award of,
        15, 32, 87, 128, 159

trademark cases and award of, 401–402, 416

trade secret cases and award of, 544–545, 556, 575, 596

USPTO may not recover, 15, 32

Attribution of authorship

artists' right of (VARA), 360, 363–364

copyright infringement and, 204, 231

Creative Commons "Founders' Copyright" and need for, 231

credit line, 231

public domain works not requiring, 204

Audio Home Recording Act (AHRA), 204–205

Audiovisual works and copyright

overview, 223

copyright management information and, 227

copyright registration, 268

defined, 205

registration form (Form PA), 229

Aural trademarks, 504

Automated Interview Request (AIR) Form, 33

Average reasonably prudent consumer test (trademarks), 402, 471

B

Bankruptcy

and trademark assignment, 399

and trademark licensing, 470–471

Bayh-Dole Act (1980), 33–34, 580

Berne Convention, 5, 190, 206, 271, 284, 293, 296

duration of, 190, 246

"Best mode" patent infringement defense (no longer available), 26, 65

Bilski v. Kappos, 35, 37, 93–94, 148

Biotechnology (genes and genetic engineering)

overview, 80–81

Accelerated Examination Program (AEP) and, 22, 130

Alice/Mayo Test for patents that include laws of nature, 15, 24, 94, 100

as compositions of matter, 45

the human organism and genes not patentable, 26, 80–81, 104

minor improvements considered too trivial/ obvious to be granted a patent, 82

researchers allowed to use others' patents without permission, 80

sequence listing attachment to patent application, 146

utility patents for plants, 131

BitTorrent, 207, 308, 309

Blank forms, not protected by copyright, 207–208, 319

Blocking patent, 35

Blogs, 192, 208, 348–349

group of entries, copyright registration, 268, 365

trade secret limitations on, 562

See also Websites

BMI, 213, 311

Board of Patent Appeals and Interferences (BPAI) (discontinued in 2012), 35

Books. *See* Literary works

Bootlegging, 208, 221, 271, 310

Brandverbing (trademark verbing), 402–403, 451

Breaches of trust (trade secrets), 558, 566–567, 573, 574

Breaking (or busting) a patent, 36

Broadcasting

copying programs with VCRs, 258

and copyright management information (CMI), 227

display right distinguished from, 310

ephemeral recording, 252

live transmissions, as fixed by recording of, 267

performance rights and, 309

See also Digital music providers; Performance rights and royalties

Broadest reasonable interpretation (BRI) of patent claims, 36, 41

Browserwrap agreements. *See* End-user license agreements

Buenos Aires Convention, 200, 208–209

Building and testing inventions. *See* Reduction to practice (building and testing inventions)

Business information as trade secret
overview, 545–546
business know-how (of processes), 574
compilations of information, 546–547
customer lists, 552–554, 594
independent development information not protectable, 546
know-how of administration not protectable, 572, 574
See also Trade secret(s)

Business know-how (of processes), 574

Business method patents
overview, 37–38, 93–94
Alice Corp. v. CLS and, 18, 23, 24, 37–38, 94, 148
Bilski v. Kappos and, 35, 37, 93–94, 148
covered business method (CBM) reviews, 27, 38, 90
defined, 37
expansion of applications, 37
State Street case and, 37, 93, 151–152
"useful, concrete, and tangible result" standard for, 93
See also Software patents

C

CAFC. *See* Court of Appeals for the Federal Circuit

California
business noncompete agreements, 542, 551
forum selection clauses, 550
ideas as trade secrets, 565
noncompete agreements severely restricted for employees, 542, 550, 589

California Resale Royalty Act (CRRA) (struck down), 265, 293, 362

Camcorders, 240

Cancer, Accelerated Examination Program, 22, 130

Cannabis industry, inability to get trademarks, 409

Cartoonbank (clearinghouse), 213

Cartoons, permissions clearinghouse for, 213

CASE Act (Copyright Alternative in Small-Claims Enforcement Act), 209–210

CBMs (covered business method patents), 27, 38, 90

CD copying, 205

CD-ROMs, 205, 297

Cease and desist letter (copyright disputes), 210

Celebrity photos
copyright violation, 242
derivative use of, 195, 314
fair use of, 193, 194, 250, 314
right of display violation, 249–250

Center for Global Innovation/Patent Metrics, 19

Certificate of correction, 39

Certification marks
overview, 404–405
cancellation petition filed for misuse of, 481
and fair use, 437
geographical terms in, 452
as mark, 474
trademark law applies to, 404, 405, 495
See also Trademark(s)

Chemical formulas, processes, and procedures, 44–45

Choreography, and copyright, 212–213

CIP. *See* Continuation-in-part application (CIP)

Class Definitions (patents), 42

Classification
goods and services, 525
patents, 42, 74
trademarks, 397, 463–465

Clean rooms, 546

Clickwrap agreements. *See* End-user license agreements

Clip art, 312

Coauthorship, and copyright
collaboration agreement for, 214
collective works, 214
defined, 213
derivative works, 214
duration of copyright for, 247
federal jurisdiction over, 191
joint works, 213, 247, 285

Coinventors, 42–44
micro entity status and, 102
need not have a complete conception of the invention, 43–44, 45
as patent applicants, 43, 164
See also Inventor

Collaboration agreement (coauthor agreement), 214

Collective marks, 406, 474, 495
See also Trademark(s)

Collective works
coauthorship and, 214
compilations distinguished from, 214
copyright registration, 269
creativity of organizing and selecting material, protection for, 214–215, 229
damages (statutory) for infringement of, 234
defined, 214, 215
derivative works distinguished from, 239
ownership of copyright is retained for underlying elements, 214, 229
permissions by copyright owners of constituent parts, 214
permissions of copyright owners for publishing in new media, 296–297
public domain materials in, 214
registration form (Form SE), 229
separate protection for underlying elements of, 214
See also Compilations

Color in trademarks
as an element of a mark, description of, 407

functional color, 398, 408
multicolor marks as inherently distinctive, 393, 408
used as a mark, 407–408

Combination patent (no longer in effect), 44

Combination patents (terminated), 44

Comedy, and fair use, 257

Commentary and criticism
as DMCA exception for override of copy-proof technologies, 244
fair use (copyright), 189, 255, 256, 257, 259, 260
fair use (trademark), 422

Commerce, first-to-use requirement (trademarks), 387, 408–409, 483–484
See also trademark cancellation

Commercial distribution, as condition of copyright preregistration, 319

Commercial speech, 438

Commercial success, as factor in nonobviousness, 106

Commercial use (patents)
antishelving clause (commercial use deadline), 29
defined, 56–57
lack of, and compulsory licensing (international), 159
pay-for-delay (reverse payment) to avoid, 30

prior use of more than one year, as infringement defense, 26, 38, 56–58
as working a patent, 159
See also Offer of sale; Patent licensing; Public use
Commissioned works under a work-made-for-hire agreement (copyright)
overview, 187, 356
categories of works that qualify for, 283, 357–359
duration of, 188, 223, 247–248, 358
ownership of copyright, 187, 205, 223, 356
written agreement for commission, 358
Commissioner for Patents, 44
Commissioner for Trademarks, 410
Common law
right of publicity, 500
state copyright (common law copyright), 215, 330
trademark law, 4, 384, 422
trade secret law, 4, 540, 594–595
Common law copyright, 215, 330
Communications Decency Act (CDA), 215–216
Competitive advantage, trade secrets defined by, 546, 591

Competitive injury
and damages for infringement, 50
false marking claims require proof of, 26, 100
patent misuse claims require, 56, 121
Competitor copying, and nonobviousness analysis, 17
Compilations
authors not named in registration may bring infringement actions, 191
collective works distinguished from, 214
on copyright registration application, 373
and creativity, insufficient, 263, 303
creativity of organizing and selecting materials, protection for, 216
defined, 216
derivative works distinguished from, 239
not protected by copyright, 303
preexisting materials as independent of copyright on, 216–217, 263
See also Collective works
Composite marks, 411, 426, 450
Composition of matter, 44–45, 67
Compulsory copyright licenses, 217–218, 291–292
clearinghouses for, 218
defined, 217

innocent copyright infringer granted, 218
musical arrangements and, 218
music licensing collective (MLC) to collect and distribute fees for, 218, 295, 355
performance rights not covered by, 218
permission not required for, 217
for physical copies and digital downloads, 218, 291–292
for recording music (mechanical license), 217–218
for reliance parties (who used foreign works in the public domain before restoral), 328
statutory fee for, 217
for translation of work by a government, 218
Compulsory licensing of a patent (international), 45, 159
Computer databases. *See* Databases
Computer Fraud and Abuse Act (CFAA), 551
Computer games
copyright and, 205, 319
trademarks in, 449, 486
Computer graphical user interfaces (GUIs), 201, 292, 334

Computer graphics, 276

Computer hardware, 13

Computer hardware and
peripherals
attempts to apply DMCA
anti-copying rules,
242–243
See also Software *entries*

Computer operating systems,
201

Computer semiconductor
chips, 292, 331–332, 334

Computer Software
Protection Act, 202–203

Conception of the invention
coinventors and, 43–44,
45
proof of, as date of
invention, 52

Concerted refusal to deal,
30, 46

Condensations. *See*
Derivative works

Confidentiality agreements.
See Nondisclosure
agreements

Confidentiality of patents
for first 18 months after
filing, 4, 46, 47, 108
Nonpublication Request
to preserve, 46–47, 108,
578
patent applications and
trade secrets, 4, 46, 108,
274–275, 578–579

Confidentiality of trade
secrets
during litigation, 556, 573,
581–582

email confidentiality, 559
establishing and
maintaining, 576–577,
582, 583, 584–585,
591–592, 599
licenses and, 572
NDAs as establishing
protection of, 576
patent applications and,
4, 46, 108, 274–275,
578–579
See also Employees, trade
secrets and confidential
employment relationship;
Nondisclosure
agreements; Trade secret
status; *specific types of
trade secrets*

Continuation application
(patents), 47, 68, 77, 139,
145

Continuation-in-part
application (CIP), 48, 104,
139

Contributory infringement
copyright, 220–221
patents, 48
trademarks, 392, 412–413,
414

Convention for the
Protection of Industrial
Property. *See* Paris
Convention

Cooperative Patent
Classification (CPC), 42

Copies and copying
archival copies, 202–203,
209, 242, 251, 297

bootlegging, 208, 221,
271, 310
cached copies, 209
of collected works onto
new media, 297
course packs, 259, 313–314
defined, 221
ephemeral recording, 252
and fair use, end-user
license agreement
waiving right to, 252
by libraries and archives,
during last 20 years of
copyright term, 261
linking and, 290
of music, from originals
only, 205
photocopies, 313–314
verbatim copying, 197
See also Digital rights
management (DRM);
Fair use; Reproduction
right (copyright)

Copyfraud, 222

Copyleft movement, 222

Copyright & Fair Use
website, 196

Copyright
overview, 222–224
author, defined, 205
as bundle of separate
exclusive rights, 187,
222–223, 252–253, 343
commercialization of. *See*
Copyright assignment;
Copyright licensing
common law copyright,
215, 330

creation of work, defined, 230

criteria required. *See* Creativity; Fixed in a tangible medium of expression; Original work of authorship

drafts of works are protected by, 230

dual trade secret/copyright status, concurrent declaration with copyright filing, 548, 587–589

expiration of. *See* Copyright duration

freedom of speech as limited by, 270–271

ideas or facts not protected, only the unique expression is protected, 185, 192, 201, 223, 273–274, 292

limited publication and, 289, 323

new versions of works receive copyright protection, 230

published work, defined, 323–324

registration not a requirement for, 186, 325

resources for, 196

simultaneous publication (obsolete), 332

small claims forum (Copyright Claims Board), 209–210

thin copyright, 342

types of works. *See* Audiovisual works; Coauthorship; Collective works; Compilations; Factual works; Literary works; Musical works; Parody and fair use (copyright); Periodicals; Pictorial, graphic, and sculptural works; Software and copyright; Unpublished works; Work made for hire

See also Coauthorship; Copyright assignment; Copyright duration; Copyright infringement; Copyright law; Copyright licensing; Copyright management information (CMI); Copyright notice; Copyright ownership; Copyright permissions; Copyright registration; Fair use; Fees (copyright registration); Internet (copyright); *specific types of works and mediums*

Copyright Act (1909), 224–225

Copyright Act (1976), 224, 225

Copyright Alternative in Small-Claims Enforcement Act (CASE Act), 209–210

Copyright and Fair Use (website), 260

Copyright application. *See* Copyright registration

Copyright assignment
advance assignment by software programmers, 223
defined as transfer of all or part copyright rights unconditionally, 187, 203
grant of rights, 272
recordation of transfers, 187, 304, 324, 344
termination rights of authors, 203, 341–342
transfer process, 343–345
See also Copyright licensing; Copyright ownership

Copyright Claims Board, 209–210

Copyright Clarification Act (1990), 337

Copyright Clearance Center, 213

Copyright clearinghouses, 213, 218

Copyright duration
overview, 246–248
anonymous authors, 188, 200, 247–248
author, individual, 188, 224, 246, 247
Berne Convention and, 190, 246
chart of, 247
death of author, presumption of, 248
death of author, reported, 248

Eldred v. Ashcroft challenge
to extensions of, 222, 249
extension for works
published after January 1,
1998, 335
GATT treaty and, 246
international copyright,
190, 246, 351
pseudonymous authors,
188, 200, 247–248
by publication date, 188,
247
semiconductor chips (by
statute), 331
text of law, 247–248
Universal Copyright
Convention and, 351
unpublished works, 352
works by employees
(employer owned), 188,
224, 247–248, 358
works commissioned with
work-made-for-hire
agreement, 188, 224,
247–248, 358
works created prior to
1978, 188, 246, 335
works owned by the
author's employer, 188,
224, 247–248
Copyright infringement
overview, 188–189,
276–279
access, proving, 197–198,
277
attribution of author and,
204, 231
contributary infringement,
220–221

defined, 276–277
factors determining, 277
filtering movies for
objectionable content as
exempted from, 261, 263,
445–446
Internet service providers
and "notice and
takedown" procedures,
209, 241–242
"inverse ratio" doctrine of
evidence (rejected), 191,
198, 285
liability insurance for, 199
plagiarism, 317
preregistration of works
historically subject to,
318–319
similarity standard. *See*
Substantial similarity
standard
small claims forum
(Copyright Claims
Board), 209–210
standing (to sue), 338
vicarious liability, 354
See also Copyright
infringement actions;
Criminal copyright
infringement
Copyright infringement
actions
overview, 188–189,
280–281
abstraction test, 317–318
affirmative claims against
copyright owners
who misrepresent
infringement, 241

cease and desist letter, 210
certificate of registration as
evidence in, 210
compilations authors not
named in registration
may bring, 191
registration of copyright
as legal presumption of
copyright validity, 186,
210, 325
registration of copyright as
mandatory prior to, 210,
253, 280, 319, 327–328
statute of limitations on,
192, 237, 338–339
See also Copyright
infringement action
defenses; Copyright
infringement remedies;
Damages for copyright
infringement
Copyright infringement
action defenses
overview, 189, 237–238
authorized use, 189, 206,
238
copyright estoppel,
253–254
de minimis (insubstantial)
copying, 236–237
independent creation of
allegedly infringing
work, 189, 237, 276
innocent infringement
(mitigation of damages),
189, 218, 234, 283, 301,
302
no substantial similarity,
194

plaintiff doesn't own the copyright, 238
public domain, 238
statute of limitations defense, 189, 237
See also Fair use
Copyright infringement remedies
compulsory license/royalty payments granted to innocent infringer, 218, 302, 332
impoundment and destruction of infringing material, 281, 320
injunctions (temporary, preliminary, permanent), 242, 271, 280, 281–283
See also Damages for copyright infringement
Copyright law
overview, 3, 185
basis of, 4, 190, 225
changes to law since last edition of this book, 190–196
overlap with patent, 5, 225–226
overlap with trademark, 4, 5
overlap with trade secrets, 275, 337, 548–549, 555, 565, 583–584, 587–589
See also GATT and copyright; International copyright protection; Visual Artists Rights Act
Copyright licensing
overview, 287–289

challenges to copyright by licensee, 101–102
conflicting/overlapping licenses, 304, 324, 344
defined as transfer of limited number of copyright rights, 187, 203
of derivative works, 239
divisibility of each right, 223
exclusive licenses, 187, 223, 288, 304, 341–342, 343–345
grant of rights, 272
implied, 192, 289
nonexclusive licenses, 187, 288–289, 304
open source licenses, 302–303
recordation of rights transfers in the U.S. Copyright Office, 187, 304, 324, 344
restriction of rights by agreement for, 251
revocation of, 329
separate sales of each right, 223
site licenses, 333
sublicenses, implied, 192, 289
sublicenses not granted by terms-of-use agreements, 193–194
termination of exclusive licenses (35–40 years later), 329, 341–342
trade secret overlap with, 548

transfer process for exclusive licenses, 343–345
See also Compulsory copyright licenses; Copyright assignment; Copyright ownership; End-user license agreements; Royalties (copyright)
Copyright management information (CMI), 227, 231
Copyright management systems, recording devices, 205
See also Digital rights management
Copyright notice
overview, 298–299, 301–302
"all rights reserved" (obsolete), 200, 209
Copyright Act (1909) and requirement of notice for protection, 224–225, 237
Copyright Act (1978) and curing of lack of notice, 224
copyright bug, 186, 237
correct form of, 237
defective notice, 237
foreign works lacking, restoral of copyright to, 225, 271, 272, 301, 322, 328
form of, 186, 298, 299
fraudulent use of, 222–223

innocent infringement as precluded by, 298, 299, 300, 301, 302, 324

no requirement for use of (March 1989), 224, 237, 284, 298

position of, 298, 299

registration not required for use of, 186

removal, 302

for sound recordings, 237, 299–300

text of law, 298–300

Universal Copyright Convention requirement for, 284, 351

usefulness of, 298, 301–302

See also Copyright management information (CMI)

Copyright ownership

overview, 186–187, 228–229

of all or part of the bundle of rights, 343–344

by assignee of copyright, 121, 164, 187, 226, 343–345

as author for copyright purposes, 205

by the author who created the work, 186, 205, 224, 228, 229, 343–344

as claimant of copyright, 226, 373

collective works, contributions to, 214, 229

by commissioning party of independent contractor with a written work-made-for-hire agreement, 187, 205, 223, 356

on copyright registration application, 372, 373

by employer (works made for hire), 187, 205, 223, 229, 356

as grant of rights, 223

involuntary transfers of, 344

by licensee of exclusive rights, 226, 228–229, 288, 343–345

limitations on scope of rights transferred, 343

orphan works (hard-to-find copyright owner), 304

text of law, 229

transfers of, 343–345

See also Copyright duration

Copyright permissions

overview, 311–312

clearinghouses for, 213, 218, 312

for derivative works, 238–239, 240

for freelancers' material published in new media, 296–297

from friends and family, 311–312

obtaining, as preferable to fair use, 189

oral consent, 312

recording artists seeking, instead of compulsory license, 217, 292

for sampling, 330

written consent preferred, 312

Copyright registration

overview, 186, 224, 325–328

certificate of registration, 210

claimant, 226, 373

Copyright Office guidance, 366

copyright protection exists without, 186, 325

cover letter, 337

damages for infringement easier to obtain with timely, 186, 224, 234, 280, 325, 342

de minimis changes too small to warrant a new registration, 236

electronic filing (eCO system), 229, 248, 332–333, 337

electronic filing, application instructions, 369–370

electronic filing, screenshots of, 367–368

error correction (supplemental registration), 267, 340

errors not invalidating copyright, 320

expedited registration (special handling), 253, 374

false representations in, 222, 233, 260, 270, 320, 374

filing group registrations, 268, 365

forms for, 229, 267–269, 326, 370

legal presumption that the copyright is valid created by, 186, 210, 325

as mandatory prior to suing for copyright infringement, 210, 234, 280, 326–328

not required to file suit for works of visual art (VARA), 327

not required to file suit in non-U.S. Berne Convention countries, 326–327

paper application instructions, 370–374

paper application sample forms, 375–380

paper filing, 229, 326, 365

preregistration of unpublished works, 261, 318–319

process of, 325–326

sample forms, 375–380

single application, 332–333, 369

single registration rule, and exceptions, 333

special relief (exemptions from formal requirements), 275, 337

standard application, 337, 369

supplemental registration, 333, 340

"the rule of doubt," 300, 329, 336

timely registration, benefits of, 186, 224, 234, 325

timely registration, defined, 342

See also Deposit of works with U.S. Copyright Office; Fees (copyright registration); Library of Congress, deposits to

Copyright Remedy Clarification Act (CRCA), 190

Copyright renewal, on works first published prior to January 1, 1978, 268

Copyright Royalty Board (CORB), 354, 355

Counterfeiting
overview, 414

contributory trademark infringement, 392, 412–413

damages for, 418

and likelihood of confusion (trademarks), 414

PRO-IP Act and, 320

Course packs, 259, 313–314

Court costs, copyright infringement and, 203, 280–281

Court of Appeals for the Federal Circuit (CAFC)
overview, 49

on dual terminology of claim limitations/ elements, 39

pronunciation of acronym, 49

standing required for (Article III), 16, 90, 151

Court of Customs and Patent Appeals (CCPA), 38

See also Court of Appeals for the Federal Circuit (CAFC)

Covenants not to compete. See Noncompetition agreements

Covered business method (CBM) patents, and review, 27, 38, 90

Creative Commons, 230–231

Creativity, as copyright criterion
collective works, 214–215, 229

compilations, 216, 263, 303

the Copyright Office as making decision about, 303

criterion of "original work of authorship" as referring to, 303

defined, 185

factual databases, 185, 219, 263, 335

fiction as more susceptible to infringement claims than factual works, 223

thin copyright, 342

Credit line, 231

Criminal copyright infringement

overview, 231–233

commercial gain, 231

counterfeiting, 320

false representation on copyright registration, 233

fines, imprisonment, forfeiture, 231, 232–233

fraudulent use of copyright notice, 232–233

innocent infringers not subject to, 232

knowingly placing protected works on a computer network for the purpose of public copying, 232, 261, 295, 308

people who aid violators, 232

prosecutions under DMCA, 242

streaming unauthorized material, 232, 339–340

ten or more copies of a certain retail value, 231

text of the law, 232–233

videotaping or transmitting signals from inside a movie theater, 232, 261

willful violators of the Digital Millennium Copyright Act, 232

Criminal prosecutions for theft of trade secrets, 542, 551–552, 558–559

Cross-licensing, 9, 49–50, 82

Customer lists (trade secrets), 552–554, 594

Cybergriping, 448–449

Cybersquatting, and protections from, 398–399, 415–416, 429, 432

D

Damages for copyright infringement

overview, 189, 280

actual damages, 233, 235, 242

attorneys' fees, 186, 203–204, 209–210, 280–281

collective works and, 234

Copyright Claims Board limits on, 209–210

court costs (full costs), 203, 280–281

enhanced damages, 236, 242, 320

for infringement misrepresentation, 241, 255

innocent infringement as mitigating factor in, 218, 234, 283, 301, 302

photographs and, 315

profits, 233–234, 235, 320–321

PRO-IP Act and strengthening of, 320

statutory damages, 234, 235, 280, 323, 325

timely registration and ability to obtain, 186, 224, 234, 280, 325, 342

violations of DMCA, 242

willful infringement, 234, 242

Damages for patent infringement

overview, 50–51

actual notice and, 87, 99

attorneys' fees, 32, 87, 128, 159

date of patent mark on invention and, 87, 99

design patents, 64

extra damages, 51, 87, 147

lack of product mark on invention and, 99

lost income/defendant's profits, 50–51, 87

royalties as, 50–51

time limit on obtaining, 56, 86, 152

and U.S. companies exporting infringed components for assembly, 51

willful infringement and enhanced damages, 51, 85, 87, 159

Damages for trademark infringement

overview, 416–418

actual damages, 392, 410–411, 416, 417

actual harm and, 457

attorneys' fees, 401–402, 416

defendant's profits, 390, 391, 410, 411, 414, 416, 417, 418–419

exceptional cases, 401

innocent infringement as mitigating factor in, 460

money damages, 388, 398

punitive damages (via state laws), 392, 414, 494, 505, 518

punitive damages prohibited in federal law, 494

statutory damages, 418

treble damages, 416, 418, 494

use of the registration mark affecting recovery of, 390, 479

willful infringement and, 388, 390, 413, 419, 457

willfullness not required for obtaining profits, 391, 419

See also Trademark infringement remedies

Damages for trade secrets. See Trade secret misappropriation remedies

Dance, choreography, 212–213

Databases

copyright protection for, 219–220

copyright registration of, 220

creativity requirement for copyright and, 185, 219, 263, 335

defined, 219

legal databases, 348

permission to publish existing freelance articles on, 296–297

public domain and copyright-protected material on, 219, 555

searchable, as transformative fair use, 256, 348, 349

as trade secret, 555

DAT players, 204–205

Dear Rich: Nolo's Patent, Copyright & Trademark Blog, 19, 196, 393

Declaratory judgments, patents, 19, 52

Deep links, 290

Defamation, 314

Defendant's profits

copyright infringement, 233–234, 235, 320–321

patent infringement, 50–51, 87

trademark infringement, 390, 391, 410, 411, 414, 416, 417, 418–419

trade secret misappropriation, 593

Defend Trade Secrets Act (DTSA)

overview, 540, 556–557

attorneys' fees awards, 544, 556, 575, 596

damages, 554, 555

employee injunctions, 556

improper means, defined, 567

and inevitability doctrine, 569

injunctive relief, 570–571

litigation and protection of trade secrets, 556, 582

misappropriation definition, 574

reverse engineering excluded from "improper means," 586

seizure orders and hearing, 556, 587

state law as basis of, 556

statute of limitations for misappropriation actions, 541, 590

whistleblower provisions, 557, 575, 576, 596

Defensive publication (patents), 59, 153

De minimis (insubstantial) copying as copyright infringement defense, 236–237

De minimis changes too small to warrant a new copyright registration, 236

Dependent claims, 40, 59, 150–151, 162

Deposit of works with U.S. Copyright Office

overview, 238

account for frequent registrations, 373

"best edition of a work" standard, 206–207, 238, 287

electronic filing and submission of, 238, 369, 370

failure to submit, fines for, 238

hand delivery of, 370

"identifying material" satisfying requirement of, 274

number of copies required, 238

obligation to deposit work with Library of Congress and, 287

resource for, 207

software and source- vs. object code, 274–275, 300–301, 336, 588

special relief (exemptions from formal requirements), 275, 337

special relief for individual deposits, 275

and trade secrets, protection of, 274–275, 337, 548

uploading, 369, 370

U.S. postal service delivery of, 369, 370

See also Copyright registration

Derivation hearing (patents), 27, 59–61

Derivative works

overview, 238–240

artworks as, 314, 350

in bundle of copyright rights, 239

celebrity photo, 195, 314

coauthorship of, 214

copyright protection for, 239

on copyright registration form, 373

defined, 238, 239

distinguishing independent creation from, 276

examples of types of, 239

fictional characters as, 210–211

fictionalizations as, 239

framing on websites as, 270

licensing of right to, 239

permission from copyright owner of preexisting work required, 238–239, 240

substantial similarity and, 279

termination of license for preexisting work does not affect, 342

text of law, 239–240

Derwent, 124

Descriptive trademarks

overview, 419–420

becoming distinctive over time (secondary meaning and qualification for Principal Register), 385, 386, 420, 426, 501

defined, 388

five-year period and presumption of secondary meaning, 389, 420, 501

geographic terms, 451, 452, 492, 508

mistakenly placed on the Principal Register, 420

phonetic or foreign language equivalents for, 487

rejection of, 386

suggestive marks, tests to distinguish from, 507

on Supplemental Register, 386, 389, 420, 508

trade dress, 512

as weak marks, 386, 419, 426, 506, 521

"Designing around" a patent, 61–62, 66, 99

Design patents, 62–64

anticipated by prior art, 64

application for, preparation of, 179–182

assignment of, 179–180

claims for, 16, 63

classification of, 42

copyright protection overlap with, 225

damages for infringement, 64

Declaration, 181

defined, 3, 10, 62

designer/inventor as applicant for, 179

drawings for, 63, 179, 180–181, 182

duration of, 12, 62, 179

Fee Application Transmittal Form, 181

infringement of, ordinary observer test for, 64–65, 86

international, 62

as limited by the claims language, 16

no maintenance fees for, 98

ornamental requirement, 63

patentability qualifications, 128

patent specification for, 180, 182

point of novelty test (terminated), 63–64

professional assistance with, 179

reproduction requirement, 62–63

resource for, 181

sample application, 182

Statement Regarding Federally Sponsored R&D, 180

timeline of application, 179

transmittal form, 181

utility patent also sought for same device, 63

visual sense requirement of, 62–63

Design. *See* Design patents; Pictorial, graphic, and sculptural works (copyright); Product design; Visual Artists Rights Act

Digital Millennium Copyright Act (DMCA)

overview, 240–243

affirmative claims against copyright owners who misrepresent infringement, 241

archival copies of computer programs, 242

attorneys' fees, award of, 204

civil remedies for violations of, 242

copyright management information (CMI), 227, 231

criminal prosecutions under, 242

and digital rights management, 240

Internet service providers, safe harbor rules for, 240–242, 285

novel attempts to apply, 242–243

prohibiting devices and services that circumvent copy-proof technology, 240, 243–245

Digital music providers

criminal penalties for unauthorized streaming, 232, 339–340

new licensing rules for, 218, 295, 354–355

new music licensing collective (MLC) for handling royalties from, 218, 295, 355

performance rights royalties paid by, 218, 310, 311, 354–355

small webcasters, 354–355

Digital rights management (DRM), 243–245

copy-proof technologies, DMCA rules prohibiting circumvention of, 240, 243–245

defined, 243

DMCA exceptions allowing for override, 244–245

Digital transmissions

bootlegging of live performances, 208, 221, 271, 310

criminal penalties for unauthorized use, 232, 261, 295, 308

ephemeral recording, 252

live transmissions as fixed, 596

podcasts, 192, 318

streaming, 232, 339, 339–340

See also Broadcasting; Digital music providers; File sharing; Music downloads; Website *entries*

Director of the U.S. Patent and Trademark Office, 64, 425

Disclaimer of trademark use, 425, 448, 449, 457, 475

Disclaimer of unregistrable material (trademarks), 411, 426, 450, 527

Disclosure Document Program (DDP) (eliminated), 65

Display right (copyright)
in bundle of copyright rights, 245
defined, 245
embedding as infringement of, 193, 249–250
performance right distinguished from, 310

Distinctive trademarks
overview, 426–427
descriptive marks that become distinctive over time, 385, 386, 420, 426, 501
geographic terms in, 452
incontestable marks not vulnerable to challenges as, 455
inherently distinctive marks, 384, 393, 426
multicolor trademarks as inherently distinctive, 393, 408
pictures and symbols as, 488
state laws, 426
as status required to be placed on the Principal Register, 427
as strong marks, 384–385, 426, 506
trade dress, 512
See also Principal Register

Divisional application (patents), 65–66, 67, 105, 115, 139

DMCA. *See* Digital Millennium Copyright Act

Doctrine of competitor standing, 16, 90

Doctrine of equivalents, 62, 66–67, 74, 86
converse of (negative doctrine of equivalents), 86, 104

DOCX file format, 70, 161

DOJ. *See* U.S. Department of Justice

Domain names
overview, 427–432
country codes, 428
cybersquatting and anticybersquatting action, 398–399, 415–416, 429, 430, 432
dilution of a trademark by, 430
dispute resolution with ICANN, 399, 415
domain tasting, 432
fees for, 429
fees for, failure to pay, 430
likelihood of confusion with a trademark, and termination of domain name, 429, 430, 431
purchase of, 429
"sucks" domain names, 448–449
top level domains (.com, etc.), 427–428

as trademark, 430–431
trademark registration of ".com" version, 431
trademark registration of generic terms with ".com," 431–432, 450
trademark rights not acquired with, 430
trademark search to rule out conflicts, 429, 516
typosquatting, 416, 432
as unique, 428
and Web hosting arrangements, 429–430
website construction and upload with, 430

Domain tasting, 432

Double patenting, 67, 105, 139

Drafts of works (copyright), 230

Dramatic works
copyright registration, 268
defined, 245

Dramatizations. *See* Derivative works

Drawings. *See* Pictorial, graphic, and sculptural works (copyright); Visual Artists Rights Act

DRM. *See* Digital rights management (DRM)

Droit moral. See Moral rights

DTSA. *See* Defend Trade Secrets Act

Duty of candor and good faith, 68–69

Duty of trust (trade secrets)
  overview, 547, 557–558
  breach of, as improper
    acquisition of trade
    secrets, 558, 566–567,
    573, 574
  clause of NDA, 606–608
  duration of, 607–608
  as fiduciary relationship, 557
  higher-level employees and,
    547, 557
  remedies for, 558, 575
DVD technology, 240, 243

E
eBay, 87, 127, 280, 282, 413
Economic Espionage Act
  (EEA), 542, 551, 558–559
Editorial revisions. *See*
  Derivative works
Education
  course packs, 259, 313–314
  fair use and, 189, 256, 257,
    259, 260
EFS-Web, Accelerated
  Examination Program
  using, 22
Eldred v. Ashcroft, 222, 249
Electronic circuits, 98
Electronic Filing System
  (EFS-Web), patents, 69–70,
  118
Electronic Frontier
  Foundation, 562
Electronic Signatures in
  Global and International
  Commerce Act (2000), 252
Email confidentiality, and
  trade secrets, 559

Embedding
  overview, 249–250
  celebrity photos, 193, 194
  defined, 249
  as display right
    infringement, 193,
    249–250
  as fair use, 194, 249, 250,
    259
  "server test" for, 249, 250,
    270
  sublicenses not granted by
    terms-of-use agreements,
    193–194
  thumbnail images on
    websites, 259
  See also Social media;
    Website *entries*
Employees, and copyright.
  See Employer-owned
  copyright (employee
  authored under work made
  for hire)
Employees, and patents
  assignments to employer
    (obligated), 31–32, 70,
    121
  "employed to invent"
    doctrine, 70
  outsider-inventors refused
    by employers, 109
  ownership of patent
    transferred with
    assignment, 121, 164
  shop rights of employer,
    122, 146
  state laws prohibiting
    mandatory assignment of
    independent inventions,
    121–122, 132–133

university patents made
    with federal funding and
    compensation to, 34
  written employment
    contract, 70, 132–133
Employees, trade secrets and
  confidential employment
  relationship
  overview, 540, 547
  email confidentiality, 559
  exit interviews, 560, 577,
    585
  improper disclosures by
    employees, 540, 547
  inevitable disclosure rule,
    569
  injunctions against former
    employees, 556, 569
  Internet chats, 571
  NDAs for current or
    former employees, 547,
    575, 585
  noncompetition
    agreements for
    employees, 549–550, 589
  notice of trade secret status
    to, 576–577, 585
  notice of trade secret status
    to new employers, 577
  ownership of employee-
    developed trade secrets,
    594
  whistleblower protections,
    557, 575, 576, 596
  See also Duty of trust;
    Nondisclosure
    agreements; Notice of
    Immunity From Liability

Employer-owned copyright
(employee authored under
work made for hire)
overview, 187, 356
duration of, 188, 224,
247–248, 358
employment relationship,
factors determining,
356–357
ownership of copyright,
187, 205, 223, 229, 356
work by employee authored
outside the scope of
employment, 356
Employers, notice to former
employee's new (trade
secrets), 577
Encyclopedias. *See* Collective
works
End-user license agreements
(EULAs)
overview, 250–252
assent as requirement of,
193, 251
for nonsoftware products,
252
notice as requirement of,
193, 251
for products marked
"copyright-free," 312
reverse engineering
prohibited by, 252, 586–
587, 607
and sale of individual
components of software
package, 252

site licenses, 333
sublicenses not granted by,
193–194
trade secrets, structure
of license to forbid
disclosure of, 548, 588
as valid contracts, 251, 252
waiver of Copyright Act
rights in, 251, 252
See also Software
Energy, Accelerated
Examination Program
(AEP) and, 22, 130
Environmental quality,
Accelerated Examination
Program (AEP) and, 22,
130
Estoppel
assignor, 13, 32
copyright, 253–254
file wrapper, 54–55, 75–76
EULAs. *See* End-user license
agreements
European Patent
Convention, 71
European Patent Office, 71,
93
European Union
community trademarks,
410, 465
Intellectual Property
Office, 410
patent law, 71
Exclusive dealing
agreements, 30
Exhaustion. *See* First-sale
exemption

Exit interviews, 560, 577,
585
Experimental use of an
unpatented invention,
72–73
Expert witnesses, and patent
litigation, 73, 106
Extrinsic-intrinsic test for
copyright infringement,
278

F

Factual works (copyright)
overview, 254–255
creativity of, 335
"fictionalized" facts in, not
protected by copyright,
191, 254
greater similarity required
for infringement, 278
merger doctrine, 292
narrower protection given
by copyright, 223,
254–255
Fair use (copyright)
overview, 189, 255–260
amount and substantiality
of portion used, as factor,
257–258, 346
analysis of, as required
prior to issuing a DMCA
notice, 241, 255
application programming
interface codes (APIs)
and, 335, 349–350

case-by-case basis,
determination of, 189,
255, 259
celebrity photos as, 193,
194, 250, 314
as defense to copyright
infringement, 189, 237,
255, 260
defined, 189
derivative uses not
protected by, 195
end-user license agreement
waiving the right to, 252
factors determining,
general discussion of,
255–260
failure to exploit a market
and, 259
fanfiction and, 261–262
file sharing as precluding
defense of, 260, 308–309
informational vs.
entertaining nature of
the copyrighted work, as
factor, 257
innocent infringement
distinguished from, 283
market or profitability
affected by, as factor, 195,
224, 258–259, 262
obtaining permission as
preferable to, 189
online resource for, 196
photograph cases, 193–194,
249–250, 258–259, 314,
347, 348–349, 350–351

as resolving conflict
between free speech and
copyright, 271
resources on, 260
sampling, 329–330, 345,
349, 350
screenshots as, 195, 258
shortest possible snippet
not necessary to, 195,
258
software and, 194, 257,
272, 335
text of law, 260
unpublished works and,
257, 260, 324, 352
See also Parody and fair
use; Transformative use
standard (copyright fair
use)
Fair use (trademarks)
overview, 436–438
classic fair use (descriptive
terminology), 392–393,
436, 437, 449
comparative advertising,
436, 449
journalistic accounts, 436
and likelihood of
confusion, 436, 437
nominative fair uses,
436–437
parodies, 436–437
as trademark dilution
exception, 422
False advertising, 438–440,
494, 495, 499–500,
518–519

False endorsement, 499, 500
Family Entertainment and
Copyright Act (2005),
criminal copyright
infringement, 232, 261,
263, 308, 446
Family Movie Act (2005),
263
Family of patents, fraud
or inequitable conduct
invalidating, 17, 78
Famous marks, 421–422,
440
See also Trademark dilution
Famous people, and right
of publicity, 314, 318,
499–500
See also Celebrity photos
Fanciful marks, 384, 426,
440, 506
Fanfiction, 261–262
Fashion industry, 408
Federal laws, as basis of IP
law, 4
Federal Trade Commission,
proceeding to bar the
importation of infringing
devices, 73
Fees (copyright registration)
electronic registration
(standard eCO
application), 186, 332, 365
electronic registration for
one work with one author
(single eCO application),
186, 332
expedited registration and
recording, 253

paper registration, 186, 365, 374

payment of, 369, 370, 374

updates for current, 366, 374

for using the Single application inappropriately, 369

Fees (patents)

overview, 163

continuation application, 47

Credit Card Transmittal Form, 163

Fast-Track Appeals Pilot Program, 18

Fee Transmittal Form, 163

online resource for, 31

patent fees, unpaid, 12, 84

patent fee total required to fully maintain, 12

patent filing fee, 118, 161

patent filing fee, non-electronic filings, 161

patent issue fee, 12, 95, 140

patent maintenance fees, 12, 98

patent pending status and, 141

Provisional Patent Application (PPA), 141

Request for Continued Examination, 145

substitute application, 21

Track One: Prioritized Examination, 156

Feist Publications Inc. v. Rural Telephone Service Co., 263, 335

Festo v. Shoketsu, 39, 66–67, 74

Fictional characters

derivative copyright for, 210–211

fanfiction and, 261–262

and parody as fair use, 211–212

as trademarks, 406

Fictionalizations, as derivative works, 239

Fictionalized facts, 191, 254

Fiction, as more susceptible to invention claims, 223

Fiduciary relationships, and trade secrets, 565

See also Duty of trust

File sharing (copyright)

BitTorrent as infringing, 309

contributory infringement and, 220–221

criminal penalties for, 295

fair use defense precluded in, 260, 308–309

MP3s, 294–295

owners of networks liable for infringement, 261, 294–295, 308, 309

peer-to-peer networks, 308–309

vicarious liability for, 354

See also Digital music providers; Music downloads

File wrapper, 74–75, 118

File wrapper continuing application. *See* Continuation application

File wrapper estoppel, 54–55, 75–76

Film. *See* Movies

Filtration test for copyright infringement, 279, 334

Financial service patents. *See* Business method patents

First Amendment. *See* Freedom of speech

First-sale exemption

overview, 263–266

as copyright infringement defense, 252

defined, 263–264

end-user license agreements prohibiting, 252

exceptions to, 265

imported goods and, 265

as patent infringement defense (exhaustion), 54, 72, 131

plant patents and, 72, 131

and resale of legally purchased copies, 252, 263–265

state laws giving artists the right to a commission on resale (struck down), 265, 293, 362

text of law, 266

Fixed in a tangible medium of expression

overview, 266–267

as copyright criterion, 185, 223

copyright protection arises the instant a work becomes fixed, 186, 224, 230, 267

defined, 267

live transmissions, 267

tattoos, 341

See also Copyright notice;
Copyright registration

Flags, prohibited from
trademarking, 441, 443, 492

Flow charts, 267

FOIA (Freedom of
Information Act), trade
secret protection, 541,
560–561

Food and beverages
formulas as trade secrets,
560, 573

labeling rules and false
advertising, 439

trademarked ingredients,
use of, 457

wine and spirit labels, and
geographic marks, 452

See also Products
(trademarks)

Form 1449, 84–85

Form CA (copyright
registration), 267

Form CO (discontinued
copyright registration), 268

Form GRAM (Group
Registration for Works
on an Album of Music)
(copyright registration),
268, 365

Form GRTX (Group
Registration of Short
Online Literary Works)
(copyright registration),
268, 365

Form GRUW (Group
Registration of
Unpublished Works)
(copyright registration),
268, 365

Form PA (copyright
registration), 268, 326,
375–376

Form RE (copyright
registration), 268

Form SB/01 (Declaration)
(patent application), 181

Form SB/17 (Fee
Transmittal) (patent
application), 181

Form SB0018 (Design Patent
Application Transmittal),
181

Form SB28 (patents), 22

Forms, blank, not protected
by copyright, 207–208, 319

Form SE (short, regular,
and group) (copyright
registration), 269, 326

Form SR (copyright
registration), 269, 326

Form TX (copyright
registration), 269, 326,
377–378

Formulas
chemicals, patents and,
44–45

mathematical, as not
patentable, 10, 23

as trade secrets, 560

Form VA (copyright
registration), 326, 379–380

Forum selection, 550
"shopping", elimination in
patent actions, 86, 128

Franchise businesses, 447,
476–477

FRANDS (Fair, Reasonable,
and Non-Discriminatory
terms), 77–78

Fraud (copyright)
copyright notice, 232–233

false representations on
registration application,
222, 233, 260, 270, 320,
374

invalidation of copyright
registration due to, 270

removal of copyright
notice, 233

See also Criminal copyright
infringement

Fraud (patent application)
failure to disclose
knowledge of prior art as,
13, 68–69, 78, 84–85

family of patents
tainted by "infectious
unenforceability," 17, 78

invalidation of patent due
to, 13, 17, 78, 85

See also Antitrust law
(federal) and patents

Fraud (trademarks), 391,
447–448, 482

Freedom of Information Act
(FOIA), and trade secret
protection, 541, 560–561

Freedom of speech
copyright as limiting,
270–271
parody and, 305
trade secret limitations on,
561–562, 571–572
See also Freedom of speech
(trademarks)
Freedom of speech
(trademarks)
artistic use of marks, 449
commentary or criticism
using another company's
trademark, 448–449
commercial speech
distinguished from, 438,
448
cybergriping ("sucks"
domain names), 448–449
disclaimer of trademark
use and, 448, 449
"disparagement"
prohibition of Lanham
Act found in violation of,
449–450
"immoral and scandalous"
trademark prohibition
found in violation of, 450
parody, 449
See also Fair use
(trademarks)
Freeware, 312
Functional vs. aesthetic,
division of intellectual
property rights into, 3
Functional features,
exclusion of
copyright. *See* Useful
articles

design patents, 10, 63, 128
trade dress, 387, 513–514
trademarks, 387, 398, 408,
504
Functional features required
for utility patents, 5, 10,
101, 128, 147

G

GATT (General Agreement
on Tariffs and Trade)
overview, 79, 271–272
patent provisions, 45, 79
trade secret provisions, 5,
562
and WTO, 160
See also GATT and
copyright
GATT and copyright
overview, 190
Berne Convention
mandated by, 206, 271,
284, 352
bootlegging protection, 271
computer programs as
literary works, 271, 284
copyright and import-
export of infringing
material, 272, 275
import-export of infringing
materials, 272, 275
infringement penalties and
damages, 272
restoral of copyright to
foreign works, 225, 271,
272, 301, 322, 328
software rentals, protection
from, 272

Trade Related Aspects of
Intellectual Property
Rights (TRIPS), 271
General public license (GPL
and LGPL), 302
Generic terms and symbols
(trademarks)
overview, 385–386,
450–451
combinations with .com
no longer generic, 392,
431–432, 450
composite marks
including, 450
key aspects of a genus as,
451
phonetic or foreign
language equivalents of,
487
pictures and symbols as
marks, 488
in the public domain, 450
trademark becoming
(genericide), 386,
402–403, 450–451
Genes and genetic
engineering. *See*
Biotechnology (genes and
genetic engineering)
Geneva Act (Hague
Agreement), 62
Geographically separate
markets (trademarks), 412,
453, 470, 483–484, 496
Geographic licenses
copyrights, 223, 287, 343
patents, 9, 30, 71, 81

Geographic limitations on trademark rights, 387, 403, 411, 483–484
  imposed as remedy, 390, 459
Geographic terms as trademarks, 451–452, 492, 508, 521
Getty copyright clearinghouse, 213
Good faith
  and fair use analysis prior to ISP takedown requests, 241
  patent applicants' duty of candor and, 68–69
Goodwill (trademarks), 395, 399, 453
Google
  copyright cases involving, 194, 209, 249, 257, 270, 272, 335, 349–350
  Google AdSense, 416
  Google Patent Search, 124, 125
  patent cases involving, 38
  and trademarks, 384, 385, 395, 403, 426, 451, 466–467
Google v. Oracle, 194, 257, 272, 335, 349–350
Government edicts doctrine, 190, 296
Government employees
  copyright infringement liability, 337
  patent infringement liability, 142

Government insignia, trademark exclusions on, 458–459
Governments. *See* Local governments; State governments; U.S. government
Graffiti art, 196, 361, 362
Graham v. John Deer, 81, 112
Graphical user interfaces (GUIs), 201, 292, 334
Graphic works. *See* Pictorial, graphic, and sculptural works (copyright)
Gray market goods, 453–454
Grokster (Metro-Goldwyn-Mayer, Inc. v. Grokster Ltd.), 294, 308, 309
GUIs (graphical user interfaces), 201, 292, 334

H

Hague Agreement (design patents), 62
Harry Fox Agency, 213, 218
HathiTrust, 256, 348
Head-start rule (trade secrets), 542, 563, 593
HIV/AIDS, Accelerated Examination Program, 22, 130
Holographs, 274
Hot news doctrine, 273
HTML (Hypertext Markup Language), 273, 355
Hulu, 339
Humans/the human organism no patents for, 26, 80–81, 104

as tangible medium of expression, for tattoo copyright, 341
Hybrid mark. *See* Composite mark

I

ICANN (Internet Corporation for Assigned Names and Numbers), 454
  dispute resolution procedures (UDRP), 399, 415, 517
  TLDs list, 428
  website, 428
Ideas (trade secrets)
  evaluation agreements, 560, 563, 564
  fiduciary relationships and, 565
  idea submissions, 560, 563–565
  as trade secrets, 274, 565
  unsolicited idea disclosures, 595–596
  waiver agreement for unsolicited idea disclosure, 596
Ideas and patents. *See* Abstract ideas not patentable
Ideas not copyright protectable, only the expression of those ideas, 185, 192, 201, 223, 273–274, 292
  abstraction test, 317–318
  merger doctrine and, 292
  See also Creativity, as copyright criterion

IDS (Information Disclosure Statement), 84–85, 137, 163

Illegal conduct. *See* Fraud (patent application)

Implied duty not to disclose trade secrets. *See* Duty of trust

Imported goods
first sale doctrine and, 265
gray market goods, 453–454
manufacturing clause (defunct), 291
patent infringement, 51, 55, 73, 79, 275
trademark infringement. *See* Counterfeiting
trademark owners' right to exclusion/seizure of, 556, 587

Improper acquisition of trade secrets
overview, 566–567
breach of duty of trust as, 558, 566–567, 573, 574
defined, 567
industrial espionage, 542, 551, 552, 568, 583, 592
"piracy" as term for, 580
and public domain status of trade secrets, 583
relief for misappropriation dependent on finding of, 567
reverse engineering exception, 586–587

unjust enrichment theory, 595
See also Trade secret disclosures

Improper disclosure of trade secrets, 540, 574, 583, 592
defined, 567
precautionary measures, 584–585
See also Trade secret disclosures

Improvement inventions, 10, 13, 82, 153

Incontestability status of trademarks, 412, 420, 442, 455–456, 490

Indecent or immoral works, not protected by copyright, 275

Independent conception (trade secrets), 567
as defense to misappropriation action, 567, 593
parallel research, 578

Independent contractors. *See* Commissioned works under a work-made-for-hire agreement (copyright)

Independent creation (copyright), 189, 237, 276

Independent inventions made by employee, 121–122, 132–133

Independent patent claims, 40, 83, 162

Index of U.S. Patent Classification, 42

Indian Civil Rights Act, 149

Inducing patent infringement, 83–84

Industrial espionage, 542, 551, 552, 568, 583, 592

Industrial know-how, 572

Industrial secrets, 568

Inequitable conduct. *See* Fraud (patent application)

Inevitable disclosure rule, 569

Infectious unenforceability (of patents), 17, 78

Information Disclosure Statement (IDS), 84–85, 137, 163

Initial interest confusion principle, 457–458

Initials as mark, 458–459

Injunctive relief
copyright infringements, 242, 271, 280, 281–283
patent infringements, 12, 87, 127
trademark dilution, 420, 421
trademark infringements, 391, 459–460, 488–489
trade secret misappropriation, 541, 542, 556, 569, 570–571, 593
unfair competition (trademarks), 459–460

Innocent infringement of copyright
overview, 283
copyright notice as precluding use as defense for infringement, 298, 299, 300, 301, 302, 324
criminal copyright prosecutions not made for, 232
as defense to copyright infringement (mitigation of damages), 189, 218, 234, 283, 301, 302
fair use distinguished from, 283
license/royalty payments granted as infringement remedy, 218, 302, 332
recordation of copyright transfers as constructive notice against, 324
of semiconductor chips, 332
Innocent infringement of trademark
overview, 460
allowed continued use of mark, with geographic limits, 459, 460
contributory infringement and, 413
damages as mitigated by, 460
placement on the Principal Register as constructive notice of mark, 460
Instagram, 193–194

Instructional texts, 283, 357–358
Integrity, artists right of (VARA), 360–361, 362, 363–364
Intellectual property (IP)
definition of, 1, 2
functional vs. aesthetic elements of the creation, 3
overlapping forms for same creation, 4–5
turning to another form if your first application doesn't succeed, 21
Intellectual property law
overview, 2–3
affirmative rights, 199
basis of, 4
determine what rights apply to your work, 2–5
international, basis of, 5
Intent-to-use (ITU)
trademark registration
overview, 460–462
electronic filing of, 524, 525–529
evidence of actual intent needed, 461
fees, 461
first use established by, 387, 483
process of, 524
specimen, 504–505
Statement of Use/ Amendment to Allege Use for Intent-to-Use Application, requirement to file, 388, 396, 398, 441, 461, 529

text of law, 461–462
time limits for, and extensions, 461
See also Trademark registration
Inter-American Convention for Trademark and Commercial Protection, 462
Interference proceedings for patents (discontinued in 2013), 92, 96
See also Derivation hearings
International Bureau of the World Intellectual Property Organization, 92, 93
International copyright protection
overview, 5, 190, 284
"all rights reserved" (obsolete), 200, 209
Berne Convention, 5, 190, 206, 246, 271, 284, 293, 296
deep linking of websites, 290
duration of, 190, 246, 352
first sale doctrine does not apply to goods made and first sold outside the U.S., 265
import-export of infringing material, 272, 275
reciprocal protections (national treatment), 284, 296, 351

restoral of copyright to
foreign works, 225, 271,
272, 301, 322, 328
simultaneous publication
(obsolete), 332
transfers of ownership, 345
Universal Copyright
Convention (U.C.C.),
218, 284, 351–352
See also GATT and
copyright; Moral rights
International Patent
Classification (IPC), 42
International patent
protection
overview, 13, 92–93
all patents are considered
prior art, 129
basis of laws for, 5, 13
classification of patent, 42
compulsory licensing, 45,
159
design patents, 62
disclosure of filing to
USPTO, 47
European Patent
Convention, 71
European Patent Office,
71, 93
filing date, 49, 76
foreign manufacture and
sale unless patented in
that country, 55
International Bureau of
the World Intellectual
Property Organization,
92, 93

Nonpublication Request to
preserve confidentiality
requires statement not to
file, 46, 47, 108
opposition proceeding, 114
Paris Convention, 5, 13,
49, 76, 93
Patent Cooperation Treaty,
5, 13, 49, 76, 92, 119–
120, 158
patent searches and, 119
separate filings in each
country, 93, 119
single filing with
International World
Intellectual Property
Organization, 93
U.S. company exporting
infringing parts for
assembly or importing
infringing devices, 51,
55, 73, 79
utility model, 158
International Registration
of Industrial Designs
(Geneva Act of the Hague
Agreement), 62
*International Schedule
of Classes of Goods and
Services,* 463–465, 525
International Trade
Commission, and
importation of infringing
works, 275
International Trademark
Association, 393

*Acceptable Identification
of Goods and Services
Manual* (USPTO), 397,
525, 526
International trademark
rights
overview, 465–466
assignment of trademark,
401
attorney required for
nonresident registrations
in the U.S., 447
classification of goods and
services, 496
classification of marks,
463–465
community trademark
(EU), 410, 465
each country has its own
rules (territoriality rule),
465, 466, 474
first-to-file (prior
registration) countries,
465, 490
foreign attorneys may
not seek reciprocal
recognition before the
USPTO, 447
inaccurate geographic
marks prohibited, 452
infringement in the U.S.
by foreign nationals, 470
intent-to-use foreign
applicants, 461
Inter-American Convention
for Trademark and
Commercial Protection,
462

keyword sales and
advertising, 466–467
Madrid Protocol, 5, 397,
465–466, 473–474, 480,
481
Paris Convention, 466, 485
Principal Register giving
reciprocal rights, 490
reciprocal trademark
rights, 446
registrations by foreign
nationals in the U.S.,
446–447
single application under the
Madrid Protocol, 473–474
treaty members permitting
foreign nationals to
establish trademarks
without alleging
commercial use first, 466
International trade secret
law, 5, 550, 568
Internet (copyright)
e-contracts, 251, 252
and expansion of business
method patents, 37
HTML (Hypertext
Markup Language), 273,
355
"published work"
requirement and, 323
radio station simulcasts
on, 354
See also Blogs; Digital
music providers; End-user
license agreements; File
sharing; Internet service
providers (ISPs); Music
downloads; Social media;
Websites (copyright)

Internet (trademarks)
commerce requirement
and, 409
geographic reach of
companies as expanded
through, 412, 484
Internet service
providers, contributory
infringement by, 413, 414
See also Domain names;
Search engines; Websites
(trademarks)
Internet (trade secrets)
email confidentiality, 559
free speech rights of
bloggers, 562
posting of trade secrets,
571–572
working in, and state
enforcement of employee
NDAs, 550
Internet patents, 37, 93–94
See also Business method
patents; Processes (or
methods), category of
patents; Software patents
Internet service providers
(ISPs)
overview, 285
affirmative claims against
misrepresentation
of infringement by
copyright owners, 241
agent to accept service of
legal papers, requirement
of, 241
awareness of infringement
does not trigger a duty to
police, 242

burden of proof and, 242
contributory infringement
by (trademarks), 413, 414
Digital Millennium
Copyright Act "safe
harbor" provisions for,
240–242, 285
email and trade secrets,
559
as escaping liability for
third-party content,
215–216, 285
fair use and, 241
"notice and takedown" rule
for copyright infringing
material, 209, 241–242
Inter partes proceedings
(trademarks), 462, 480,
481
Inter partes review (IPR)
(patents), 88–92
as administrative hearing,
88
all claims of petitioner to
be resolved in, 89
appeals to the CAFC, 16,
90
authorization rules, 25,
88, 92
constitutionality of, 89
defined, 88
federal government not
a "person" for purposes
of, 90
filing deadline, 26–27, 88,
90, 91
no appeal from denial of,
14, 88, 90

no federal court review of, 25

novelty and nonobviousness as sole issues for petitioners, 26–27, 90

for pre-AIA patents, 89

and printed publication as statutory bar, 26–27

prior art as basis of, 26–27, 88

prohibited if filing party has filed a civil action, 27

real-party-in-interest inquiry, 89

Section 101 patentability and, 16, 90

sovereign immunity not applicable to, 89, 149

text of law, 91–92

Invasion of privacy, 314

Invention(s)

date of, 52

defined, 94

field of, 74

improvement inventions, 10, 13, 82, 153

new-use inventions, 105, 108

"not invented here" syndrome, 109

"teach the invention," 155

as term, 10

as worked. *See* Public use

See also Patent(s); Reduction to practice (building and testing inventions); Statutory subject matter

Inventors

advisers not qualifying as, 43

as applicant for patent, 117, 164

builders not qualifying as, 43

conception of invention, 45, 52

defined, 95

natural person requirement, 16–17, 95

notebook of, 109

oath by (Patent Application Declaration), 31, 117, 118, 140, 163

as patent owner, 121–122

of university patents created with federal funding, 34

See also Coinventors; Reduction to practice (building and testing); Work made for hire

IP.com, 124

IPR. *See Inter partes* review

Irreparable harm

as burden of proof to get an injunction, 488–489

likelihood of confusion creating presumption of, 391, 459, 489

ISPs. *See* Internet service providers

J

Joint inventors. *See* Coinventors

Joint works, 213, 247, 285

See also Coauthorship, and copyright

Journalism

as copyright fair use, 257

as trademark fair use, 436

trade secret disclosures, 562

See also Blogs; News reporting

Judicial opinions as not protected by copyright, 286

K

Keyword sales and advertising, 466–467

Know-how, 572, 574

KSR v. Teleflex, 96, 107, 112

L

Laches (copyright), 339

Laches (trademarks), 467–469

Laches defense (terminated in patent law), 56

Landlords, contributory trademark infringement and, 392, 413

Lanham Act (trademarks), 384, 469–470

See also Trademark *entries; individual topics for specific provisions*

Large entities

defined, 96

as licensee for university patents created with federal funding, 34

patent filing fee, 12, 161

patent issue fees for, 95, 96

Provisional Patent
Application fee, 141

See also Employees, and
patents

Latin American nations, 462

Laws, judicial opinions,
and model codes as not
protected by copyright,
286

Laws of nature exception to
patents

overview, 10, 97

algorithms and, 23

Alice/Mayo Test to test for
patentability, 15, 24, 94,
100

See also Section 101
(natural law exception)

Lawyers. *See* Attorneys

Lay observer test for
copyright infringement,
278

Leahy-Smith America
Invents Act. *See* America
Invents Act

Led Zeppelin, "Stairway to
Heaven," 191, 198, 285

Legal databases using legal
briefs, 348

LexisNexis, 124, 296–297

Liability insurance,
advertising injury, 199

Libraries and archives,
copying works during the
last 20 years of copyright
term, 261

Library of Congress, deposits
to, 287

Likelihood of confusion
(trademarks)

overview, 386, 471–472

and anticybersquatting
action, 398

average reasonably prudent
consumer test, 402, 471

competing products and,
410

consumer polls and, 402

counterfeiting and, 414

disclaimer of trademark
use, 425, 448, 449, 457,
475

domain names and, 429,
430, 431

factors in determining, 471

and fair use, classic, 436

false advertising, 438–440,
494, 495, 499–500,
518–519

finding by Trademark Trial
and Appeal Board can
preclude litigating the
issue in court, 516

geographically separated
markets and, 412, 453,
470, 483–484, 496

infringement lawsuits
normally turn on, 457

irreparable harm,
presumption of, 391, 459,
489

noncompeting products
and, 410–411

palming off (passing off)
and intent to confuse,
484

reverse confusion, 498–499

same or similar marks, 457,
500

strong marks and, 506

trademark examiner's
considerations for, 472

Linking, 290

Literal similarities (copyright
infringement), 277–278

Literary works and copyright

overview, 223, 290–291

copies of (course packs),
259, 313–314

end-user license
agreements for, 252

flow charts as, 267

plots as copyright
protected, 317–318

preregistration of
unpublished, 319

registration form (Form
TX), 229, 269, 326

scanning/digitization
of books to create a
searchable database, as
fair use, 256, 348, 349

short online works, group
registration of, 268, 365

stock elements of works
(scènes à faire), not
protectable by copyright,
331

titles of works not
protected, 303

as trade secret until
completed, 583–584

See also Derivative works;
Fair use; Parody and fair
use; Unpublished works

Litigation misconduct, and award of attorneys' fees, 32

Living persons. *See* Names of persons in trademarks

Local governments
employees of, liable for copyright infringement, 337
employees of, liable for patent infringement, 149
no sovereign immunity for, 149, 337

M

Machines, 67, 97, 98, 153

Madrid Protocol, 5, 397, 465–466, 473–474, 480, 481

Magazines. *See* Collective works; Periodicals

Mall landlords, contributory trademark infringement and, 392, 413

Mandatory deposit of works. *See* Deposit of works with U.S. Copyright Office

Manual of Classification (patents), 42

Manual of Patent Examining Procedure (MPEP), 98

Manufactures, category of patents, 22, 64, 67, 98, 130

Manufacturing clause (defunct), 291

March-in rights, 98

Markman v. Westview Instruments, 86, 100

Mathematical formulas, as not patentable, 10, 23

Mayo v. Prometheus, 24, 80–81, 100

Means plus function clause, 101

Mechanical rights (reproduction), 217–218, 291–292

Medical accessories and devices, 75–76

MedImmune v. Genentech, 101–102

Merger doctrine, 292

Metatags, 457–458, 475

Methods. *See* Processes (or methods), category of patents; Processes and methods as trade secrets

Microcode, 292

Micro entities
defined, 102
fee reductions for, 31, 95, 102, 141
and multiple inventors, 102
patent filing fee, 161
See also Large entities; Small entities

Microfilm and microfiche, 297

Microsoft, 334

Minidisc players, 204–205

MMA. *See* Music Modernization Act

Model codes as not protected by copyright, 286

Moral rights
defined, 293
as exception to international adherence to the Berne Convention, 206, 271, 293

VARA providing visual artists with rights of attribution and integrity, 360, 363–364

More discerning observer test for copyright infringement, 278–279

Movies
actors' film reels, 195, 258
as audiovisual works, 205, 294
based on preexisting work. *See* Derivative works
copyright registration, 268, 294
fair use and, 257–258, 348
fanfiction, 261–262
filtering for objectionable content, as exempted from copyright and trademark claims, 261, 263, 445–446
preregistration of unpublished, 319
rentals of, 264
trade secrets and, 564
training films, 268
videotaping or transmitting video signals from inside a movie theater, 232, 261

MP3.com, 294

Multimedia products, copyright registration, 268

Musical arrangements and copyright, 218, 223, 239

Musical works
copyright clearinghouses, 213, 218

lyric origin is a question of fact, 191

preregistration of unpublished, 319

sampling, 276, 329–330, 345, 349, 350

sound recordings distinguished from, 296

See also Digital music providers; File sharing; Mechanical rights (reproduction); Music downloads; Music licensing; Performance rights and royalties; Photorecords; Songs; Sound recordings

Music clubs, performance royalties paid by, 310–311

Music downloads

compulsory licenses for, 218

legitimate sites, 294, 309

MP3s, 294–295, 311

permanent downloads, sale of, 311

unauthorized, 294–295

See also Digital music providers; File sharing

Music licensing collective (MLC), 218, 295, 355

Music Modernization Act (MMA)

music producers collect royalties directly, 295

new licensing rules for digital music providers, 218, 295, 355

pre-1972 recordings protection by copyright, 295

Music publishers, 295

N

NAFTA (North American Free Trade Association), date of invention and, 52

Names of persons in trademarks

composite marks formed with, 478

first names and nicknames, 478–479

initials as mark, 458–459

of living persons and presidents, as barred, 491, 492

loss of use of personal name in trademark conflict, 478

surname marks and secondary meaning, 477–478, 521

surname marks listed on the Supplemental Register, 477, 508

Napster.com, 294, 354

National Film Preservation Act, 261

National Stolen Property Act, 551–552

National treatment (international reciprocal copyright), 284, 296, 351

Native Americans, limited sovereignty and, 89, 149

Natural phenomena excluded from patentability

Alice Test for, 15, 24, 94, 100

See also Laws of nature exception to patents

Natural substances as nonpatentable

overview, 10, 80, 103–104

genetic engineering as exception to, 80, 103–104

human organism not patentable, 26, 80–81, 104

NDAs. *See* Nondisclosure agreements

Negative doctrine of equivalents, 86, 104

Netflix, 339, 383

New matter (patents)

amendments to application cannot contain, 112

continuation-in-part application (CIP) for, 48, 104, 139

Newspapers. *See* Collective works; News reporting; Periodicals

News reporting

as dilution of trademark exception, 422

fair use cases and, 255, 257–258, 260, 347, 350

hot news doctrine, 273

as right of publicity exception, 499

trade secrets and, 562

New-use inventions, 105, 108

New York Time v. Tasini, 296–297

Noncompetition agreements (covenants not to compete)
for businesses, 542, 551
for employees, 549–550, 589
international laws limiting, 550
prevention of employment without (inevitability doctrine), 569
state laws limiting, 542, 549, 589

Nondisclosure agreements (NDAs)
overview, 575–576
attorneys' fees for breaches of, 544
beta testers of software, 545
confidentiality established with, 576
for current or former employees, 547, 575, 585
customer lists, 552–554
for galleys of unpublished works, 352
idea evaluation agreements, 560, 563, 564
for idea submissions, 560, 563–565
implied agreements, 576
mutual NDA, 600
noncompetition agreements compared to, 549
Notice of Immunity From Liability, 575, 576, 596, 599

preparation of. *See* Nondisclosure agreements, preparation of
remedies for violation of, 575
unpublished works and, 352
and unsolicited idea disclosures, 595
violations of, 540, 575, 592
whistleblower provision in, 557, 575, 576, 596
See also Confidentiality; Employees, trade secrets and confidential employment relationship; Improper disclosure of trade secrets; Nondisclosure agreements, preparation of; Trade secret disclosures

Nondisclosure agreements, preparation of, 599–610
overview, 599
disclosing and receiving parties, 600
duration of the agreement, 607–608
duty to keep information secret, 606–607
excluding nonconfidential information (with modification you might be asked to make), 605–606
identifying confidential information, 603–605

integration, 609–610
miscellaneous provisions (boilerplate), 608–610
mutual NDA, 600
optional additional requirements (e.g. Software Licensee Nondisclosure Agreement), 607
optional provision for employees and independent contractors (Notice of Immunity From Liability), 599
optional provision to allow the disclosing party to certify what is and is not confidential, 604–605
oral disclosure confirmation, 604–605
relationships, 609
return of materials provision, 607
sample agreement, 601–602
severability, 609
signatures, 610
waiver, 610

Nonfiction. *See* Factual works

Non-literal similarities (copyright infringement), 277–278

Nonobviousness standard (patents)
overview, 10, 11, 105–107
AIA changes to, 27
analysis guidelines to determine, 81

and claims, narrow vs. broad scope of, 41

and claims, secondary factors must be related to, 15

common-sense determinations of, 107

competitor copying and, 17, 106

defined, 81, 105–106

filing date as point of determination for, 106

invalidation of patent for failure to show, 53

obviousness, defined, 111–112

"ordinary innovation" as obvious and not patentable, 96, 107

patent examiner analysis, 106, 138

patent infringement actions and, 106–107

a person with ordinary skill in the art as standard for, 106, 129

secondary factors to consider, 15, 81, 106

text of law, 107

in USPTO notice of rejection, 138

Nonprofit corporations, trademark protections for, 479

Nonprofit laboratory use (patents), 57

Nonpublication Request (NPR), 4, 46–47, 108, 578

Nonstatutory subject matter, 108–109

Nonuse of trademark. *See* Abandonment of trademark

Notice of Immunity From Liability, 575, 576, 596, 599

Notice to employees of trade secrets, 576–577, 585

Notice to former employee's new employer (trade secrets), 577

"Not invented here" syndrome, 109

Novelty requirement (trade secrets), 577

Novelty standard (patents)
overview, 110–111

AIA changes to, 27

and claims, narrow vs. broad scope of, 41

defined, 110

invalidation of patent for failure to show, 53

patent examiner analysis, 110, 138

plant patents and, 130–131

point of novelty test (terminated), 63–64

text of law, 110–111

in USPTO notice of rejection, 138

See also Anticipated inventions (not patentable); Prior art (previously existing inventions)

O

Object code (copyright and trade secrets), 201, 300–301, 329, 334, 336, 548

Objective/subjective test for copyright infringement, 278

Obviousness analysis. *See* Nonobviousness standard (patents)

Offer of sale
one-year rule (on-sale bar) (terminated), 27, 29, 113

as public use/prior art, 28, 135, 142, 153

Official Gazette (OG, USPTO), 112, 158

patents published in, 46, 112–113

trademarks published in, 388, 441, 479–480, 524, 528

One-year limited grace period for inventor-led disclosures, 27, 28, 29, 110–111, 113, 134–135, 136

One-year rule (on-sale bar) (terminated), 27, 29, 113

Online resources
Accelerated Examination Program, 22

Center for Global Innovation/Patent Metrics, 19

copyright, 196

copyright clearinghouses, 213

copyright forms, 370

copyright registration for websites, 356

Creative Commons, 231

Dear Rich: Nolo's Patent, Copyright & Trademark Blog, 19, 196, 393

deposits of works to Copyright Office, 370

domain name conflict arbitration, 399, 415, 517

Electronic Frontier Foundation, 562

fair use, 196, 260

ICANN.org, 454

Manual of Patent Examining Procedure (MPEP), 98

mechanical royalty rate, 292

Nolo.com, 196, 393

Official Gazette of USPTO, 112–113

patent attorneys, 22

patent classification, 42

Patent Cooperation Treaty, 120

patent fees, 31

patents, 19

patents, defensive disclosure programs, 59

patent searches, 124

Software Patent Institute, 59

Technical Disclosure Commons, 59

trademark application, monitoring progress of (TSDR system), 396–397, 517, 528

trademark classification, 397

trademark classification of goods and services, 525

trademark recordation with U.S. Customs and Border Protection, 415

trademark resources, 393

trademark searches, 389

Trade Secrets Watch (blog), 542

updates for this book, 5

U.S. Copyright Office, 196, 260, 353

USPTO website, 19

Online service providers. *See* Internet service providers

Online services

copyright infringing materials posted via, 216

as escaping liability for third-party content, 216

Online works, short works, group copyright registration of, 268, 365

Open Source Initiative (OSI), 302

Open source software, 302–303

Operability requirement for utility patents, 114

Oracle, 281, 335

Google v. Oracle, 194, 257, 272, 335, 349–350

"Ordinary innovation" as obvious and not patentable, 96, 107

Ordinary observer test for design patent infringement, 64–65, 86

ordinary observer test for substantial similarity (copyright), 278

Ordinary skill, person with. *See* Person with ordinary skill in the art (POSITA or PHOSITA)

Originality. *See* Creativity, as copyright criterion

Original work of authorship, as copyright criterion
overview, 185, 303
categories that do not qualify as, 303
independent creation as defense to infringement claim, 276
lyrics, as matter of fact, 191
See also Creativity, as copyright criterion

Orphan works, 304

P

PAC (Patent Assertion Company), 127–128

Paintings. *See* Pictorial, graphic, and sculptural works (copyright); Visual Artists Rights Act

Pandora, 218, 295, 311, 339, 355
See also Digital music providers

Pantomime, and copyright, 212–213
Parallel research (trade secrets), 578
Paris Convention (international)
 patent rights, 5, 13, 49, 76, 93
 trademark rights, 466, 485
Parodies of trademarks
 court cases, 436–437, 485–487
 defined, 486
 as fair use, 436–437
 as free speech, 449, 486
 general guidelines for, 487
 as trademark dilution exception, 422, 423, 486
Parody and fair use (copyright), 211–212, 256, 347
 elements of parody not found, 195, 306
 humor ruled to be unnecessary to, 307–308
 qualification for copyright, 308
 transformative quality as determining, 305–306
PatBase, 124
Patent(s)
 blocking, 35
 challenges to. *See* Patent reexaminations
 classification of, 42, 74
 commercialization of. *See* Patent assignment; Patent licensing
 defined, 9, 115–116

double patenting, 67, 105, 139
duration of, 12, 67–68, 79
duration of, USPTO delays and extension of, 68
enforcement of rights. *See* Patent infringement actions (lawsuits)
first-to-file replacing first-to-invent rules. *See* Patent filing date
in force, defined, 84
patentability qualifications, 128
patentable subject matter. *See* Statutory subject matter
patent pools, 123
patent thickets, 30, 126
public domain technology, patents based on improving, 13
reissue patent, 94, 140, 144
standard-essential patents (SEPs), 77–78
submarine patent, 154
types of. *See* Design patents; Plant patents; Utility patents
unenforceable. *See* Patent invalidation; Patent misuse
See also International patent protection; Invention(s); Patent application; Patent expiration; Patent infringement; Patent law; Patent markers; Patent searches; Public domain inventions

Patent agents, 116, 126, 179
Patent and Trademark Resources Centers (PTRCs), 116
Patent application(s)
 overview, 11–12, 117–118, 161–163
 abstract, 21, 162, 174
 accelerated processing. *See* AEP (Accelerated Examination Program); Petition to make special (PTMS); Track One: Prioritized Examination
 amending to use provisional application filing date, 141
 assignee as applicant, 26, 31–32, 95, 117, 164
 caution against admissions by inventor, 17, 22, 54–55, 75–76
 confidentiality of. *See* Confidentiality of patents
 duty of candor and good faith, 68–69
 filing by mail, 69, 118, 161, 162–163
 filing deadline, 11
 filing electronically, 69–70, 118, 161, 162
 Information Disclosure Statement, 163
 inventor(s) as applicant, 117, 164
 list of documents for, 117
 negative statements about invention, avoidance of, 75

new matter (information)
not included in,
continuation-in-part
application for, 48, 104,
139

Nonpublication Request
(NPR), 4, 46–47, 108,
578

as parent application,
114–115

Patent Application
Declaration (PAD), 31,
117, 118, 140, 163

preparation for design
patent, with sample,
179–182

preparation for utility
patent, with sample,
161–178

professional help with.
See Patent agents;
Patent attorneys; Patent
drawings; Patent searches

receipt postcard, 118

reduction to practice date
established by filing of,
47

resource for, 164

return receipt postcard,
118, 163

samples of, 165–178, 182

substitute application, 21,
155

Transmittal Form(s), 163

for university patents
created with federal
funding, 34

See also Fees (patents);
Patent application
prosecution; Patent
assignment; Patent
claims; Patent disclosures;
Patent drawings; Patent
filing date; Patent
pending period; Patent
specification; Provisional
Patent Application;
Publication of patent
application

Patent Application
Declaration (PAD), 31, 117,
118, 140, 163

Patent application
prosecution (process with
USPTO)
overview, 11–12, 138–140

appointment with
examiner, request for, 33

delays in, and extension of
the patent term, 68

new matter submission
during (continuation-
in-part application), 48,
104, 139

operability requirement,
114

patent examiner, 11, 33,
120

preissue submissions from
third parties, 27

Request for Continued
Examination and, 145

timeline for, 11, 68, 138,
139, 140

See also Abandonment
of patent application;
Anticipated inventions
(not patentable);
Nonobviousness
standard; Novelty
standard; Patent
application rejections;
Patent approval
(allowance); Patent
claims; Prior art
(previously existing
inventions); Statutory
subject matter

Patent application rejections
overview, 25, 138–140

admissions by inventor
and, 22

amendment of application
in response to, 25, 77,
103, 112, 139, 146

appealing to PTAB, 41,
77, 139

contesting via amendment,
25

continuation application
after, 47, 68, 77, 139, 145

divisional application after,
65–66, 67, 105, 115, 139

final office action and,
76–77, 139–140

final office action, time
limit (and extension) for
response to, 140, 145

first office action and, 77,
112, 138–139, 146

first office action, time limit (and extension) for response to, 139

prior art references provided by examiner, 25, 109, 137, 138

reconsideration request, 139, 143

Request for Continued Examination (RCE) following, 139, 145

scientific evidence lacking, 18, 154

shot gun rejection of claims, 147

supplemental examination, 27

See also Abandonment of patent application

Patent approval (allowance)
overview, 11–12, 25

amendment to broaden claims, reissue patent for, 140

grant (issuance) of patent, 81

issue fee, 12, 95, 140

minor corrections to application after (certificate of correction), 39, 140

Notice of Allowability, 25, 109, 140

patent deed issued by USPTO (letters patent), 115–116, 120, 140

patent number issued by USPTO, 121

Supplemental Declaration (of amendments to claims), 140

Patent assignment
overview, 9, 164

assignee as applicant for patent, 26, 31–32, 95, 117, 164

assignor estoppel, 13, 32

cover sheet for, 163

defined, 31

design patents, 179–180

filing after receiving serial number for the application, 164

filing deadline as prior to paying issue fee, 117

form for, 163

by independent inventor, 31, 121

ownership of patent and, 121, 164, 187, 226

in patent application, 163

for university patents created with federal funding, 34

See also Employees, and patents; Patent licensing

Patent attorneys
overview, 119

AIPLA (American Intellectual Property Law Association), 22

design patent assistance from, 179

finding, 119

patent searches by, 126

USPTO licensing of, 119

utility patent application assistance from, 164

Patent claims
overview, 39–41, 162

amending, 25

amending after final office action, 139

amending after RCE filing, 145

amending after reconsideration rejection, 614

amending, and use of doctrine of equivalents, 66–67, 74

amending during prosecution process, 25, 77, 103, 112, 139, 146

amending, Supplemental Declaration of, 140

amending to broaden a claim (reissue patent), 94, 140, 144

amending to narrow a claim, 103, 144

broadest reasonable interpretation (BRI) of, used by examiners, 36, 41

correction of significant errors, 144

dependent claims, 40, 59, 150–151, 162

design patents, 16, 63

incorrectly formulated, rejection for, 139

indefiniteness of, invalidation of patents for, 128, 157

independent claims, 40, 83, 162

limitations (elements) of, 39, 97

limitations (elements) of prior art as anticipated invention, 28–29, 79

means plus function clause, 101

multiple claims, 103

printed matter doctrine, 134

product-by-process claims, 138

read on, 142

recite, 143

reissue of patent due to changes in, 94, 140, 144

samples of, 172–175, 182

scope of (broad vs. narrow), 40–41, 75–76, 101

scope of, and "designing around" a patent, 61–62, 101

scope, rejection as too broad, 139

secondary factors must have a connection to, 15

standard for claims review by a court, 41

USPTO requirements for each, 40

Patent Cooperation Treaty, 5, 13, 49, 76, 92, 119–120, 158

Patent disclosures

"best mode" requirement for patent applications, 65, 68, 161

defensive, 59, 153

duty of candor and good faith for, 68–69

enabling a person with ordinary skill in the art to build it, 65, 71, 129, 150

Information Disclosure Statement (IDS), 84–85, 137, 163

of international filing, 47

invalidation of patent for inadequate, 68–69

prior to filing application, one-year limited grace period for inventor-led disclosures, 27, 28, 29, 110–111, 113, 134–135, 136

for university patents created with federal funding, 33

See also Patent specification; Prior art (previously existing inventions)

Patent drawings

overview, 67

design patents, 63, 179, 180–181, 182

prior art, distinguishing differences from, 67

professional help for, 162, 181

resource on, 162, 181

samples of, 175–178

Patent expiration

overview, 12–13, 84

expired markers on products, 26, 100

term expires, 12, 67–68

unpaid maintenance fees, 12, 84

See also Patent invalidation; Public domain inventions

Patent filing date

overview, 76

amending the application to use the earlier provisional date, 141

continuation application preserving original, 47, 139

derivation hearing fighting earlier effective filing date, 27, 59–61

early, Provisional Patent Application establishing, 11, 76, 118, 138, 140

in filing receipt from USPTO, 76

first-to-file replacing first-to-invent, 27, 36–37, 52

international, 49, 76

as nonobviousness reference point, 106

prior art established by early provisional date, 141

prior to March 2013, remaining importance of date of invention, 52

Patent infringement

overview, 85–86

Accelerated Examination Program (AEP) and, 22, 130

accused device, 21

claims read on (describe) all elements of the infringing device, 142

contributory infringement, 48

"designing around" a patent and, 61–62, 66, 99

design patents, 64

direct infringement, 83–84

doctrine of equivalents and, 62, 66–67, 74, 86

exportation of infringing parts by a U.S. company, 51, 55

importation of infringing material into the U.S., 55, 73, 79, 275

inducing infringement, 83–84

notice, actual, 99

notice, patent marks as, 99, 100

ordinary observer test for design patents, 64–65, 86

the patent pending period and, 99, 122

search to determine if proposed invention infringes (infringement search), 88, 124

temporary presence exception, 155

See also Patent infringement actions

Patent infringement actions overview, 12, 86–87

declaratory judgments, 19, 52

defendants, joinder of unrelated, 26

defined, 86

the doctrine of equivalents applied, 86

expert witnesses, 73, 106

"forum shopping", elimination of, 86, 128

injunctive relief, 12, 87, 127

judge as responsible for interpeting patent claims, 86, 100

judge trial, 86–87

jurisdiction for, 86, 128

jury trials, 86–87, 100

lay judge in, 97

licensing negotiations ongoing during, 19, 52

the negative doctrine of equivalents applied, 86

by "patent trolls," 127–128

plaintiff's claim examined on whether it fully describes the defendant's device or process, 86

presumption of validity in, 133

as risky for the patent owner, 87

time limitation on damages (effective statute of limitations), 56, 86, 152

See also Damages for patent infringement; Patent infringement action defenses

Patent infringement action defenses, 52–58, 87

"best mode" (terminated), 26, 65

breaking (or busting) a patent with, 36

commercial use more than one year prior to filing date (prior user defense), 26, 38, 56–58

dissimilarity of inventions, 53

exhaustion (first-sale exemption), 54, 72, 131

file wrapper (prosecution history) estoppel, 54–55, 75–76

foreign manufacture and sale, 55

inequitable conduct by patent owner, 54

intervening rights due to reissue of patent, 94

laches (terminated), 56

repair doctrine, 54, 144

See also Patent invalidation; Patent misuse

Patent invalidation overview, 157

assignor estoppel, 13, 32

declaratory judgment, 19, 52

inadequate disclosures, 68–69

indefiniteness, 128, 157

infectious unenforceability, 17, 78

insufficient patent application, 13

inventors inaccurately
identified, 43
by licensee of patent,
101–102
nonobviousness standard
not met, 53
novelty standard not met,
53
validity search by accused
infringer, 85, 88, 124, 159
See also Fraud (patent
application); Patent
infringement action
defenses; Patent misuse;
Patent reexaminations
Patent law
overview, 2–3
acronyms used in, 14
basis of, 4, 13
changes to law since last
edition of this book,
14–19
overlap with copyright, 5,
225–226
overlap with trademark, 5
overlap with trade secret
law, 4, 46, 108, 274–275,
565, 578–579, 583
resources for, 19
See also America Invents
Act (AIA); Antitrust law
(federal) and patents;
International patent
protection
Patent licensing
overview, 9, 97
antishelving clause
(commercial use
deadline), 29

compulsory licensing
(international only), 45,
159
cross-licensing, 9, 49–50, 82
defined, 9
exclusive, 9, 71, 81
geographic patent license,
9, 71, 81
illegal conduct and
invalidity of patent, 13
improvement inventions
and, 82
length of time of, 9
licensee, 9
negotiations ongoing
during infringement
action, 19, 52
nonexclusive, 9, 105
patent pools and, 123
patent trolls and, 127–128
sublicenses, 9
submarine patent, 154
for university patents
created with federal
funding, 33–34, 580
use limits, 9
See also Patent assignment;
Royalties (patents)
Patent litigation
admissions by inventor
used in, 17, 22, 54–55,
75–76
derivation hearings, 27,
59–61
expert witnesses, 73, 106
Federal Trade Commission
proceeding to bar
importation of infringing
devices, 73

patent trolls, 127–128
See also Patent
infringement *entries*
Patent markers
overview, 99–100
date of marking, and
damages collection, 99
expired patent numbers on
products, 26, 100
false markers, 26, 100, 157
as notice to infringers, 99,
100
number assigned by
USPTO, 121
"Patent Pending" or "Pat.
Pend.," 99, 122
unmarked inventions, 99
unnumbered marks, 99
virtual (website) marking,
26, 100
Patent misuse
overview, 55–56, 120–121,
157
breaking (or busting) a
patent due to, 36
competitive injury required
for claims of, 56, 121
curing (purging), 120–121
infringement actions
unavailable, 55
"rule of reason" standard
for, 56
"unenforceable patent"
declaration due to, 120,
157
See also Antitrust laws
(federal) and patents;
Patent invalidation

Patent Misuse Amendments (1988), 56
Patent pending period
  overview, 122
  as allowing inventors to avoid rip-offs when showing the invention to developers, 122
  filing application (regular or provisional) creates status of, 122, 141
  infringers cannot be stopped during, 99, 122
  marking with "Patent Pending" or "Pat. Pend.," 99, 122
  notice to infringer, 99, 122
  Provisional Patent Application and status of, 122
  publication of patent application by USPTO and, 99, 122
  royalties for infringing use during, 99, 122
Patent pools, 123
Patent reexaminations
  confidentiality of requester's identity, 143–144
  covered business method (CBM) reviews, 27, 38, 90
  ex parte reexamination, 143–144
  federal government not a "person" for purposes of, 90

as open to any person, 90
  sovereign immunity not applicable to, 89, 149
  vacated, previous prior art admissions as binding, 17, 55
  See also Inter partes review (IPR); Post-grant reviews (PGR)
Patent searchers, 125–126
Patent searches
  overview, 123–125
  classification of patents, 42
  infringement search, 88, 124
  international, 119
  keywords for, 125
  obtaining a copy of a patent following, 125
  online search engines, 124
  patentability search, 88, 124, 129
  at Patent and Trademark Resources Centers, 116
  pre-1972 searches, 124–125
  professional assistance with, 125–126
  by USPTO, 84–85
  validity search (by accused infringer), 85, 88, 124, 159
Patent specification
  contents of, 150, 161–162, 180
  samples of, 165–174, 182
  text of law, 150–151

See also Patent claims; Patent disclosures; Patent drawings
Patent thickets, 30, 126
Patent Trial and Appeal Board (PTAB)
  overview, 126–127
  AIA changes to, 27
  appeals division, 126
  appeals of decisions by. *See* Court of Appeals for the Federal Circuit
  Fast-Track Appeals Pilot Program, 18
  no appeal from denial of *inter partes* review, 14, 88, 90
  Section 101 authority of, 16
  trial division, 126
  See also Patent reexaminations
Patterns, as trade secrets, 579
Pay-for-delay (reverse payment), 30
PDF file format, 70
Peer-to-peer networks. *See* File sharing
Performance rights and royalties (copyright)
  overview, 309–310
  bootlegging protection, 208, 221, 271, 310
  collection and distribution of royalties, 310–311, 322
  compulsory licenses not available for, 218

and copyright management information, 227

definition of performance, 309

definition of public, 309, 322–323

digital music providers and, 218, 310, 311, 354–355

examples of public performance, 309

mechanical rights distinguished from, 291

music played at a business, 310

for pre-1972 sound recordings, 295

ringtones as exempt from, 322

vicarious liability and, 354

Performing arts, copyright registration of (Form PA), 268, 326

Performing rights societies, 310, 322

Periodicals

archiving, 297, 555

copyright form for, 269

deep linking, 290

fair use cases, 346–347, 350–351

as literary works, 291

permission needed to reproduce freelancers' work in new media, 296–297

as publishers of infringing marks in advertising, 493–494

See also Collective works; News reporting

Permanent downloads (DPDs), 311

Personal planners, 192, 208

Person with ordinary skill in the art (POSITA or PHOSITA) (patents)

overview, 129

anticipated inventions and, 29

disclosure on the application for building the invention by, 65, 71, 129, 150

and the nonobviousness standard, 106, 129

Petition to make special (PTMS), 22, 130, 163

superceded by AEP (Accelerated Examination Program), 22, 130

Pharmaceutical companies, 34, 89, 149

Phone directories, 185, 219, 263, 335

Phonorecords

all sound recordings labeled as, 324

compulsory license allowing, 218

copyright registration, 313

defined, 312–313

mechanical rights (reproduction), 217–218, 291–292

notice of copyright on, 299–300

photographs and artwork accompanying, 313

See also Musical works; Sound recordings

Photocopies, and copyright, 313–314

Photographs and photography

derivative use of, 195, 314

fair use, 193–194, 249–250, 258–259, 314, 347, 348–349, 350–351

group registration of, 315

marketing photographs, preregistration of, 319

permissions clearinghouse for, 213

protectable elements of, 314–315

of publicly visible architecture, 192, 201

as qualifying for VARA protection, 360

rendition and timing, 314–315

reproduction rights of, 314–315

as "slavish reproductions," 315

subject of photograph, as preventing reproduction, 314

thin copyright, 342

See also Celebrity photos; Pictorial, graphic, and sculptural works (copyright); Visual Artists Rights Act

Phrases as trademarks
  composite marks, 411, 426, 450
  disclaimers of unregistrable material, 411, 426, 450, 527
  titles, 383
Phrases, copyright not protecting, 303
Pictorial, graphic, and sculptural works (copyright)
  overview, 316
  copies or images sent with registration application, 374
  copyright notice on, 299
  as derivatives, 314, 350
  design patent overlap with copyright for, 225
  designs of useful articles, 353–354
  expressive vs. functional purposes of, 316, 353–354
  fair use and, 256, 258, 259, 314, 346, 350
  first sale doctrine and disallowance of state laws giving artists the right to a commission on resale, 265, 293, 362
  first sale doctrine and use of artworks in new artworks, 264
  permissions clearinghouse for, 213
  with phonorecords, 313

registration form (Form VA), 229, 269
substantial similarity standard of infringement, 279
thin copyright and, 342
See also Visual Artists Rights Act
Piracy, 316, 580
Plagiarism, 317
Plant patents
  overview, 130–131
  classification of, 42
  defined, 3, 10
  duration of, 12, 68
  duration of, extension, 126
  as exception to rule against patents the involve natural materials, 80
  exhaustion (first-sale doctrine) and, 72, 131
  no maintenance fees for, 98
  novelty standard and, 130–131
  patentability qualifications, 128
  public depositories for seeds or plant tissue, 131
  utility patents for plants, 131
Plant Variety Protection Act, 131
Plays, 211, 239, 255, 257, 303, 309, 317, 318, 349
Plots of fiction as copyright protected, 317–318

PME (Patent Monetization Entity), 127–128
Podcasts, 192, 318
Point of novelty test (terminated), 63–64
Post-grant reviews (PGR)
  for covered business method (CBM) patents, 27, 38, 90
  federal government not a "person" for purposes of, 90
  fees for, 132
  prohibited if filing party has filed a related civil action, 27
  PTAB as handling, 132
  requirements for, 26–27
Preinvention assignments. See Employees, and patents
Premarketing regulatory review (patents), 57
Presidents of the U.S., no trademarks of, 491, 492
Price-fixing, 30, 133
Principal Register (trademarks)
  overview, 388, 489–490
  acquired second meaning of descriptive marks and placement on, 385, 386, 420, 426, 501
  as constructive notice of mark, 412, 442, 460, 489
  descriptive mark mistakenly placed on, and challenges to, 420

incontestability status after
five-year period on, 412,
420, 442, 455–456, 490
presumption of ownership
for marks on, 489, 490
presumption of secondary
meaning and placement
on (five-year period), 389,
420
presumption of willful
infringement for marks
on, 388
See also Trademark
registration
Printed forms, not protected
by copyright, 207–208, 319
Printed matter doctrine
(patents), 134
Printed publication as
statutory bar (patents)
overview, 134–135
anticipation doctrine
triggered by, 28–29
definition of statutory bar,
152–153
inter partes hearings
(reexamination) based
on, 26–27
one-year limited grace
period for inventor-led
disclosures, 134–135
public accessibility rule,
134
user manuals, 18
Prints. *See* Pictorial, graphic,
and sculptural works
(copyright); Visual Artists
Rights Act

Prior art (previously existing
inventions)
abandoned applications do
not serve as, 140
admissions of, as binding,
17, 55
all patents are considered
prior art, 129
anticipation as, 28–29
date of assessment
determined by filing
date, 106, 138, 141
defensive publication as,
58–59, 153
defined, 135
drawings must distinguish
from, 67
failure to disclose
applicant's knowledge of,
as fraud, 13, 68–69, 78,
84–85
as fully meeting patent
claim, 79
inter partes review as based
on, 26–27, 88
one-year limited grace
period for pre-filing
inventor-led disclosures,
27, 28, 29, 110–111, 113,
134–135, 136
patented status not
required for, 28, 84,
124–125, 129
preliminary look at, 133
rejection due to, 25
as statutory bar, 152
text of law, 135–137
user manuals as, 18

See also Anticipated
inventions (not
patentable); Patent
searches; Printed
publication as statutory
bar; Prior art references;
Public use
Prior art references
as anticipated inventions,
28–29
with close date, and
reduction to practice
date, 79
defined, 136
as fully meeting patent
claim, 79
Information Disclosure
Statement (IDS) listing,
84–85, 137, 163
Notice of Prior Art
References, 109, 137, 138
provided by patent
examiner with rejection,
25, 109, 137, 138
Prioritizing Resources
and Organization for
Intellectual Property Act of
2008 (PRO-IP Act), 320
Processes (or methods),
category of patents, 10, 67,
79, 137
"useful, concrete, and
tangible result" standard
for, 137
See also Business method
patents
Processes and methods as
trade secrets, 574, 581

Product-by-process claim, 138

Product design
copyright protections for, 225, 353–354
as trade secret, 579
See also Design patents

Products (trademarks)
collective marks for, 406, 474
competing, 410
noncompeting, 410–411
related vs. unrelated, analysis of, 496–497
See also certification marks; Food and beverages; Trade dress

Prosecution history estoppel, 54–55, 75–76

Protecting Lawful Streaming Act (2020), 232

Provisional Patent Application (PPA)
overview, 11, 140–141
deadline for formal patent application following, 11, 79, 141
fee for, 141
filing date established early with, 11, 76, 118, 138, 140
filing date establishes prior art references, 141
filing date from, amendment of patent application to utilize, 141
patent pending status and, 122, 141

prosecution of patent process does not apply to, 138

reduction to practice date established by (constructive reduction), 47, 79, 143

resources for, 164

transmittal letter with filing date, for patent application, 117

Pseudonymous authors
overview, 321
duration of copyright, 188, 200, 247–248
named by person with interest in the copyright, 248
name of author disclosed in records, 200, 248

PTAB. *See* Patent Trial and Appeal Board

Publication of inventions. *See* Printed publication as statutory bar (patents)

Publication of patent application
confidentiality until time of (first 18 months after filing), 4, 46, 47, 108
information provided in, 112–113
international filings not allowed under Nonpublication Request, 46, 47, 108

Nonpublication Request (NPR) to preserve confidentiality, 46–47, 108, 578
in *Official Gazette,* 46, 112–113
and royalties obtained from infringers during patent pending period, 99, 122
trade secret confidentiality and, 4, 46, 108, 274–275, 565, 578–579
trade secrets disclosed via, 46
trade secret violations prior to, 46, 579

Publication of trademarks (*Official Gazette*), 388, 441, 479–480, 524, 528

Public domain
generic terms in trademarks and, 450
loss of trade secrets to, 573, 580, 583–584
See also Public domain inventions; Public domain works (copyright context)

Public domain inventions
overview, 142–143
defensive publication and, 59, 153
patents for improvements to, 13
patent termination and, 13

Public domain works
(copyright context)
overview, 321–322
attribution not required for
use of, 204
copyfraud and, 222
Creative Commons and
dedication of works to,
230–231
date of entry into, by
publication date, 188,
247
as defense to copyright
infringement, 238
defined, 141
as element of copyrighted
works, 214, 219, 303
facts considered to be in,
254–255, 263
government works, 359
laws of nature considered
to be in, 97
reliance parties (on public
domain of later-restored
foreign works), 328
restoral of copyright to
foreign works, 225, 271,
272, 301, 322, 328
unpublished works, 352
works consisting entirely of
information from, 303
Publicity, right of, 314, 318,
499
Public records, and
protection of trade secrets,
560, 584
See also Freedom of
Information Act

Public use
anticipated inventions and,
28, 142
defined, 142
experimental use
exception, 72–73, 142
foreign uses, 142
NDAs as exception to, 142
prior art and, 28, 135
sale or offer of sale as, 28,
135, 142, 153
as statutory bar, 153
See also Commercial use
Public use doctrine
(trademarks), 493
Puffery, 494

Q

Qualitex standard for
trademarks, 393, 407, 408

R

Radio
performance royalties paid
by, 310–311
played in a business, 310
podcasting, 227
simulcasts on the Internet,
354
Read on, 142
Read-only memories
(ROMs), 334, 584
Reasonably precautionary
measures to protect trade
secrets, 584–585
See also Trade secret status
Receipt postcard (patent),
118

Recite, 143
Recombinant DNA,
Accelerated Examination
Program (AEP) and, 22,
130
Reconditioned goods, sale
of, 495
Recordation
of copyright assignments
and licensing, 187, 304,
324, 344
of trademark assignment,
400
of trademark, with U.S.
Customs and Border
Protection, 415
Record companies, 296
Recording Institute of
America (RIAA), 294
Reduction to practice
(building and testing
inventions)
overview, 36–37, 143
date of, actual reduction to
practice, 47, 143
date of, as less important
due to first-to-file system,
36–37, 45, 143
date of, established by
filing patent application
or Provisional
Patent Application
(constructive), 47, 79, 143
inventor status and, 43
in NAFTA or WTO
countries, date of
invention and, 52
See also Patent(s)

Reissue patent, 94, 140, 144

Related vs. unrelated products and services (trademarks), 496–497

Repair doctrine (patent infringement defense), 54, 144

Reproduction, control by subject of photographs, 314

Reproduction right (copyright)
 assume that all art, music, and writings are protected, 312
 "copyright-free" materials and (e.g. clip art), 312
 each new media requires authorization, 312
 RSS feed does not imply, 192

Request for Continued Examination (RCE), 139, 145

Requirements contracts, 30

Research
 in biotechnology, as allowed to use others' patents without permission, 80
 fair use and, 189, 255, 256, 260
 scientific support, patents refused for lack of, 18, 154
 See also Universities

Res judicata, 392

Reverse confusion (trademarks), 498–499

Reverse engineering
 allowed under DMCA exceptions for override of copy-proof technology, 244
 copyright and, 580
 as defense to trade secret misappropriation action, 579–580, 584, 593
 defined, 586
 legitimate, and loss of trade secret status to the public domain, 579–580, 584, 586–587
 patents and, 145, 580, 586
 prohibited by end-user license agreement, 252, 586–587, 607
 prohibited by Prospective Software Licensee Nondisclosure Agreement, 607
 prohibited by trade secret license, 579
 and source code guarded as trade secret, 589

Reverse palming off (trademarks), 499

RICO (Racketeer Influenced and Corrupt Organizations Act), 551

Right of publicity, 314, 318, 499–500

Ringtones, 322

ROM chips, 334, 584

Royalties (copyright)
 innocent infringer ordered to pay, 218, 332
 mechanical royalty, 217, 291–292
 music producers given direct access to, 295
 music publishers and, 295
 for music streaming, 218, 295, 354–355
 for pre-1972 sound recordings, 295
 See also Performance rights and royalties (copyright)

Royalties (patents)
 attempt to pay artists a royalty on resale of their work, 265
 awarded as damages (full or apportioned), 12, 50–51
 FRANDS as contracts among industries regarding, 77–78
 for licensing agreements, 9
 patent pending period, infringers paying, 99, 122
 smallest-saleable patent practicing unit (SSPPU) theory, 78

Royalties (trademarks), franchise licensing and, 447

RSS feed, 192

S

Sampling (music), 276, 329–330, 345, 349, 350

Satire, 347, 348–349

Scènes à faire doctrine, 331

Scholarship
 fair use and, 189, 255, 256, 260
 See also Commentary and criticism; Education

Schwimmer, Martin, Trademark Blog, 393

Scientific support, patents refused for lack of, 18, 154

Screenshots, 195, 258

Sculptural works. *See* Pictorial, graphic, and sculptural works (copyright); Visual Artists Rights Act

Searchability, and transformative fair use standard, 256, 348, 349, 351

Search engines
 framing, 269–270
 Google trademark brandverbed for, 403, 451
 initial interest confusion principle, 457–458
 keyword sales and advertising, 466–467
 metatags and deceptive use of marks, 475
 thumbnail images as fair use, 259

Secondary infringement. *See* Contributory infringement; Vicarious liability

Secondary meaning rule (trademarks)
 overview, 501
 defined, 385
 descriptive marks becoming distinctive over time, 385, 386, 420, 426, 501
 geographic terms and, 452, 521
 presumption of, after five years on the Supplemental Register, 389, 420, 501
 surname marks and, 477–478, 521

Section 8 affidavit (Declaration of Use), 396, 481–482, 501–502, 524

Sections 8 and 15 affidavit combination, 432, 455, 502

Section 9 Affidavit, 43

Section 15 affidavit (Declaration of Incontestability), 501

Section 101 (natural law exception in patents), 15, 16, 18, 90

Semiconductor Chip Protection Act (1984), 331–332

Separability test for useful articles (copyright), 353

Serials. *See* Collective works

Service marks
 overview, 503
 defined, 383, 474
 duration and renewals of, 433
 franchise businesses, 447
 "SM", as optional, 89
 states that will not register, 503
 trademark law applies to, 383, 495, 503
 trade names distinguished from, 503
 See also Trademark(s)

SESAC, 311

Shareware, 312

Ships, temporary presence patent infringement exception, 155

Shop rights of employers, 122, 146

Shrinkwrap licenses. *See* End-user license agreements

Simultaneous publication (obsolete), 332

Site licenses, 333

Slogans
 not protected by copyright, 303
 as trademark, 504

Small entities
 Accelerated Examination Program (AEP) for biotechnology applications filed by, 22, 130

assigning patent to large entity, 95, 147

defined, 147

fee reductions for, 12, 31, 95, 141, 147

Fee Transmittal Form and, 163

as licensee for university patents created with federal funding, 34

patent filing fee, 161

See also Large entities; Micro entities

Smart money, 147

Smartphones, 64, 387

Social media

group of posts, copyright registration, 268, 365

See also Embedding

Software

open source, 302–303

rental of programs, prohibition of, 265, 272

See also Software and copyright; Software and trade secrets; Software patents

Software and copyright

overview, 333–335

Altai/filtration test for infringement, 279, 334

application programming interface codes (APIs), 335, 349–350

archival copies of, 202–203, 209, 242, 251

artificial intelligence, 16–17, 95

BitTorrent, 207

as category, 223

collective works copyright and, 215

deposit of works with U.S. Copyright Office, 274–275, 300–301, 336, 588

DMCA restrictions on circumventing copy-proof technology, 240

dual trade secret/copyright status, concurrent declaration with copyright filing, 548, 587–589

fair use, 194, 257, 272, 335

graphical user interfaces (GUIs), 201, 292, 334

merger doctrine and, 292

microcode, 292

object code, 201, 300–301, 329, 334, 336, 548

patents overlap with, 226

preregistration of unpublished, 319

programmers and assignment of ownership prior to completion, 223

registration form for (Form TX), 229, 269

resale of individual components from bundle of, 252, 264

rewriting into a different programming language, as derivative work, 239

ROMS, 344

and "rule of doubt" on registration, 300, 329, 336

semiconductor chips, 292, 331–332, 334

shareware and freeware, 312

site licenses, 333

source code, 300–301, 329, 336, 548

structure, sequence, and organization of, 334

trade secrets overlap with, 548–549

See also Digital rights management (DRM); End-user license agreements

Software and trade secrets, 587–589

overview, 587–589

beta testing and NDAs, 545

dual copyright/trade secret status, concurrent declaration with copyright filing, 548, 587–589

employees and noncompetition agreements, 550

freedom of speech limitations and, 571–572

knowledge engineering, 546–547

licensee protection of, and copyright, 548, 588

reverse engineering and, 586–587, 589, 607, 608

ROMs, 584

source code and, 275, 300–301, 336, 548

source code handled as trade secret, 588, 589

Software Patent Institute, 59

Software patents

overview, 93–94, 147–149

abstract ideas not patentable, 18, 23, 35, 37–38, 94, 148

algorithms not patentable, 23, 148

Alice Corp. v. CLS Bank International and, 18, 23, 24, 37–38, 94, 148

Bilski v. Kappos and, 35, 37, 93–94, 148

copyright overlap with, 226

defensive publication, 59

hardware-involved, 147–148

merging of existing ideas not patentable, 23

and nonobviousness standard, 149

requirements for patentability, 18, 23, 93–94

State Street case and, 37, 93, 151–152

"useful, concrete, and tangible result" standard for, 23, 93, 147, 151

See also Business method patents

SongFile (clearinghouse), 218

Songs

derivative works from, 238–239

music publishers and, 295

performance royalties and, 310–311

substantial similarity standard and, 277, 278

trademarks unavailable to, 504

See also Mechanical rights (reproduction); Musical works; Sound recording

Sonny Bono Copyright Term Extension Act, 335

SoundCloud, 218, 295, 355

SoundExchange, 295, 311, 355

See also Digital music providers

Sound recordings

artwork and notes packaged with, copyright registration, 313

audiobooks, 265

copies made from original, 205

copyright notice for, 237, 299–300

copyright ownership for, 296

copyright registration form (Form SR), 229, 269

ephemeral recordings, 252

group of works, copyright registration of, 268, 313

home recording devices, 204–205

Mechanical rights (reproduction), 217–218, 291–292

musical works distinguished from, 296

as "phonorecords," regardless of medium, 324

pre-1972 recordings, 242, 295

preregistration of unpublished, 319

producers given direct access to royalties for, 295

rental of, as prohibited, 265, 272

resource for, 313

sampling, 276, 329–330, 345, 349, 350

unpublished, 269

See also Musical works; Phonorecords; Songs

Sounds, as trademarks, 504

Source code (copyright and trade secrets), 275, 300–301, 329, 336, 548, 588, 589

Sovereign immunity
  Congress may not
    terminate, 190, 337
  states cannot be held
    liable for copyright
    infringement, 336
  USPTO administrative
    hearings not subject to,
    89, 149
Spoliation doctrine (trade
  secrets), 590
Sporting goods, 11
Spotify, 218, 295, 311, 339,
  355
  See also Digital music
    providers
Standard-essential patents
  (SEPs), 77–78
Standard-setting
  organizations, and patents,
  77–78
Standing
  for appeals to CAFC
    (patents), 16, 90, 151
  defined, 16
  doctrine of competitor
    standing, 16, 90
  to sue for copyright
    infringement, 338
State courts
  FRANDS enforced as
    contract claims, 78
  trademark infringement
    actions in, 457
State governments
  employees of, liable for
    copyright infringement,
    337

employees of, liable for
  patent infringement, 149
See also Sovereign
  immunity
State law
  annotations of, not
    protected by copyright,
    190, 286
  as basis of intellectual
    property law, 4
  Copyright Act of 1976 as
    preempting, 225
  copyright, artists' right to
    commission on resale of
    their work (struck down),
    265, 293, 362
  copyright of pre-1972
    sound recordings, 242
  patents, mandatory
    assignment prohibited for
    independent inventions
    by employees, 121–122,
    132–133
  preemption of, 225, 318,
    423, 549
  sovereign immunity, 149,
    337
  Uniform Computer
    Information Transaction
    Act (UCITA) (model
    code), 252, 351
  See also State law
    (trademarks); State law
    (trade secrets)
State law (trademarks)
  overview, 505
  dilution, 420, 422, 423,
    440, 505

  distinctive trademarks, 426
  false advertising, 468
  litigation benefits, 494,
    505
  for local entities with no
    interstate use, 483–484,
    505, 516
  as notice to infringers, 505
  online list of state agencies,
    505
  punitive infringement
    damages, and actions
    brought on both federal
    and state statutes, 494,
    505
  registers, 389, 495
  registration, 496, 503, 505
  right of publicity, 500
  service marks not
    recognized in some
    states, 503
  statute of limitations, 468
  trademarks, 388, 457, 470,
    483
  trade names, 514
  unfair competition. *See*
    Unfair competition laws
  unregistered marks, 470
State law (trade secrets)
  common law, 4, 540,
    594–595
  criminal laws, 552
  ideas as trade secrets, 565
  inevitability doctrine, 569
  injunctions, 459
  laches, 468
  litigation and trade secrets,
    573

misappropriation remedies, 554

noncompete agreements, 542, 549, 589

noncompete agreements for business, 542

trade secret disclosures, prohibition of, 547

uniform law. *See* Uniform Trade Secrets Act

Statement of Use/ Amendment to Allege Use for Intent-to-Use Application (trademark), 388, 396, 398, 441, 461, 529

State Street Bank and Trust v. Signature Financial Group, 37, 93, 151–152

Statutes of limitations copyright infringement, 192, 237, 338–339

as defense against copyright infringement action, 189, 237

false advertising, 468

patent infringement claims (effective), 56, 86, 152

trade secret misappropriation actions, 541, 590

Statutory bars to patentability, 152–153

See also Abandonment of patent application; Anticipated inventions; Prior art *entries*

Statutory Invention Registration (SIR) (terminated), 153

See also Defensive publication

Statutory subject matter (patents) overview of five categories of, 10, 153–154

composition of matter, 10, 44–45, 67, 153

improvements on existing ideas, 10, 13, 82, 153

machines, 67, 97, 98, 153

manufactures, 22, 64, 67, 98, 130

processes or methods, 10, 67, 79, 137

See also Nonobviousness standard; Novelty standard

Stock elements of works (scènes à faire), not protectable by copyright, 331

Streaming defined, 339

unauthorized, as criminal copyright infringement, 232, 339–340

See also Digital music providers

Submarine patent, 154

Substances. *See* Natural substances as nonpatentable

Substantial similarity standard (copyright) defined, 277

in different media, 279

and factual vs. fictional works, 278

filtration (Abstraction-Filtration-Comparison or *Altai* test), 279, 334

lay observer (ordinary observer test), 278

literal vs. non-literal similarities, 277–278

more discerning observer test, 278–279

objective/subjective (extrinsic-intrinsic test), 278

Substitute patent application, 21, 155

Suggestive marks, 384, 426, 452, 506–507

Superconductivity materials, Accelerated Examination Program (AEP) and, 22, 130

Supplemental copyright registration, 333, 340

Supplemental Declaration (patents), 140

Supplemental Register (trademark) overview, 507–509

cancellation petition for mark placed on, 481

descriptive marks placed on, 386, 389, 420, 508

limitations and benefits of placement on, 508

no presumption of ownership for marks on, 489

presumption of secondary meaning after five years on, 389, 420

surname marks listed on, 477

text of law, 509

trademark registration symbol may be used on trademarks in, 442, 508

See also Principal Register; Secondary meaning rule; Trademark registration

Surnames. *See* Names of persons in trademarks

Synergism (no longer in effect), 44

T

Tacking (variation on original trademark), 510

Tattoos, 341

Tax strategies, no patents for, 26

"Teach the invention," 155

TEAS and TEAS Plus electronic filing system (trademark registration) overview, 387, 510–511

fees, 523

preparing an application, 523–529

sample application, 529–535

USPTO examination process, 524, 526, 528–529

See also Trademark registration application

Technical Disclosure Commons, 59

Television

fair use cases of material from, 257, 258, 349

fair use of items in set designs, 259

home recordings of, 258

no longer covered by in-force patents, 13

performance royalties paid by, 310–311

played in a business, 310

substantial similarity standard of infringement, 277–278, 279

See also Performance rights and royalties

Territoriality rule (trademarks), 465, 466, 474

Territorial restrictions (patents), 30

See also Antitrust law

Terrorism, Accelerated Examination Program, 22, 130

TESS (Trademark Electronic Search System) database, 389, 511, 516

Thin copyright, 342

Thumbnail images, 259

Titles of creative works

no copyright, 303

as trademarks, 383

TM Act. *See* Trademark Modernization Act of 2020

Top level domains (TLDs), 427–428

Track One: Prioritized Examination, 156

Trade dress

overview, 383, 512–513

distinctive vs. descriptive, 512, 520–521

false advertising action and, 440

functional aspects not protected, 387, 513–514

likelihood of confusion and, 512, 513

as mark, 474

and trademark dilution, 513

trademark law applies to, 512

website design as, 356

See also Trademark(s)

Trademark(s)

overview, 514

abbreviations or modifications of, public use doctrine and, 493

arbitrary marks, 384, 399, 426, 452, 506

brandverbing (trademark verbing), 402–403, 451

composite marks, 411, 426, 450

defined, 383

domain names as, 430–431

famous marks, 421–422, 440

fanciful marks, 384, 426, 440, 506

goodwill and, 395, 399, 453

mark, defined, 474

permissions for use of, 312, 402

registered mark, defined, 495

resources for, 393

strong marks, 384–385, 426, 506

suggestive marks, 384, 426, 452, 506–507

tacking (variation on original trademark), 510

use of mark, defined, 519–520

weak marks, 386, 419, 426, 506, 521

See also Abandonment of trademark; Certification marks; Collective marks; Domain names; Service marks; Trade dress; Trademark law; Trademark ownership; Trademark registration; Unregistered marks, protection of

Trademark assignment

overview, 399–401

certification marks may not be assigned, 405

electronic recordation with ETA system, 400

goodwill and, 399, 453

searches for, 400

text of law, 400–401

written agreement required, 400

See also Trademark licensing

Trademark cancellation

abandoned marks, 481

any party who may be damaged may file, 480

certification marks being misused, 481

descriptive marks mistakenly placed on the Principal Register, 420

for dilution, 445

effects on use of trademark, 482, 483

ex parte expungement for never being used in commerce, 391, 396, 397, 435, 482, 515

ex parte reexamination for nonuse before registration, 396, 397, 436, 482, 515

fraudulent use of marks, 481

generic marks, 481

incontestability status and immunity from, 412, 420, 442, 455–456, 490

inter partes proceeding to resolve, 462, 481

interruption of continuous use of mark and, 412

marks placed on the Supplemental Register, 481

notice not sent about, 481–482

possible outcomes of, 481

times for filing, 481

used if the mark has already been placed on the Principal Register, 481

USPTO canceling for failure of owner to timely file the Section 8 Declaration, 481–482, 501–502

Trademark challenges. *See* Trademark cancellation; Trademark opposition

Trademark dilution

overview, 390, 420–424

cancellation proceeding, 445

damages for, 420

defined as blurring or tarnishing a famous mark, 420, 422, 520

domain names and, 430

exceptions to, 422–423, 486

famous mark, definition of, 421–422, 440

identical marks as proof of, 421

infringement distinguished
from, 420
injunctive relief for, 420,
421
proof requirements,
421–422
related/unrelated analysis
and, 497
sale of reconditioned goods
and, 495
state laws, 420, 422, 423,
440
text of law, 423–424
trade dress and, 513
Trademark Dilution Act
(1996), 420–421
Trademark Dilution
Revision Act of 2006
(TDRA), 421–423, 440
Trademark duration
agent designated for those
living abroad, 434, 435
initial 10-year term, 432
mandatory filing of Section
8 and 15 Declarations
(six year time limit), 432,
433–434, 481–482,
501–502
for registrations before
November 16, 1989, 432
renewals of (Section 9
Affidavit), 433, 434–435
*Trademark Examiners
Manual of Procedure*
(TMEP), 472, 525
Trademark exclusions and
prohibitions
overview, 441, 490–492

certain organizations given
exclusive right to their
marks and symbols, 492
confusingly similar
marks. *See* Likelihood of
confusion
disparaging marks (found
unconstitutional),
449–450, 491
functional features, 387,
398, 408, 504, 512
immoral and scandalous
marks (found
unconstitutional), 450,
491–492
living persons and
presidents, 491
misdescriptive geographic
marks, 452, 492
nonuse. *See* Abandonment
of trademark
songs, 504
text of Lanham Act,
443–445, 492
unlawful commerce, 409
U.S. government insignia
(initials, words, or
letters), 458–459
weak marks, 386
See also Descriptive
trademarks; Generic
terms and symbols;
Trademark dilution
Trademark infringement
overview, 456–457
authorship,
misrepresentation of, 293

certificate of registration
as proof of mark validity,
403
competing products, 410
contributory infringement,
392, 412–413, 414
dilution distinguished
from, 420
filtering movies for
objectionable content as
exempted from, 261, 263,
445–446
geographically separate
markets and, 412, 453
initial interest confusion
principle, 457–458
jurisdiction and, 457
liability insurance for, 199
noncompeting products,
410–411
palming off (passing off)
and intent to confuse,
484
related vs. unrelated
services analysis,
496–497
sale of recondition goods,
495
senior and junior users,
503
See also Advertising;
Artistic use of
trademarks; Fair use
(trademarks); Internet
(trademarks); Likelihood
of confusion; Parodies of
trademarks

Trademark infringement actions, 390, 457
  laches defense (plaintiff's delay), 467–469
Trademark infringement actions, defenses to
  for cybersquatting, 399
  fair use, 437
  invalidity of incontestable mark, 455
  laches (delay of lawsuit), 467–469
  res judicata does not bar a defense in a subsequent suit, 392
  See also Innocent infringement of trademark
Trademark infringement remedies
  competitor allowed to use the mark within geographical limits, 390, 459
  competitor barred from using the mark, 410, 411
  destruction of infringing material, 459
  injunctive relief, 391, 459–460, 488–489
  surname marks, modification to work in same market, 478
  See also Damages for trademark infringement

Trademark interferences, 441, 462–463
  hearings, 462–463
  inter partes proceeding to resolve, 462, 481
Trademark law
  overview, 3, 384, 514
  basis of, 4, 384
  changes to law since last edition of this book, 391–393
  goals of, 383
  overlap with copyright, 4
  overlap with patent and trademark, 5
  trademark litigation. *See* Trademark dilution; Trademark infringement; Unfair competition laws
  types of marks protected by, 474
  See also Fair use (trademarks); Freedom of speech (trademarks); International trademark rights; State law (trademarks)
Trademark licensing
  overview, 470–471
  bankruptcy and, 470–471
  certification marks may not be licensed, 405
  challenges to trademark by licensee, 101–102

  failure of obligation to monitor use of mark ("naked" license), and loss of trademark rights, 470, 476–477
  for franchises, and obligation of franchiser to monitor use of the mark, 447, 476–477
Trademark Modernization Act of 2020 (TM Act)
  overview, 391
  examiners given flexibility in response times, 391, 515
  ex parte expungement for never being used in commerce, 391, 396, 397, 435, 482, 515
  ex parte reexamination for nonuse before registration, 396, 397, 436, 482, 515
  letters of protest against registration of a mark, 391, 396, 515
  presumption of irreparable harm if likelihood of confusion is demonstrated, 391, 459, 489, 515
Trademark notice
  overview, 479
  lack of, as limiting availability of damages, 389–390, 441, 479

may not be used before registration, 389, 389–390

Principal Register placement as constructive notice, 412, 442, 460, 489

symbol and text used for, 441

"TM" and "SM" marks, as optional prior to registration, 389, 511

Trademark opposition
any party who may be damaged may file, 480
conflicting marks, 388
filing the petition, 480, 481
inter partes proceeding to resolve, 462, 480, 481
letters of protest from third parties, 391, 396
possible outcomes of, 481
text of law, 445
third parties submitting evidence, 391
time limits and extensions of, 480–481
for use prior to issuance of trademark, 441, 481, 524, 528
written petition required, 480
See also Trademark cancellation; Trademark interferences

Trademark ownership
overview, 482–483
certificate of registration and presumption of, 489
date of first use, 387, 403
first-to-use in commerce requirement, 387, 408–409, 483–484
geographic limitations on rights of, 387, 403, 411, 483–484
intent-to-use (ITU) registration establishing, 387, 483
joint ownership, 527
obligation to proactively police the trademark, 446–447, 469, 470
registrant, 496
use limitations on rights of, 411
See also Trademark assignment; Trademark duration; Trademark licensing

Trademark registration
overview, 387–389, 441–445
basic elegibility requirements, 388, 441
certificate of registration, 403–404, 441, 489, 528
of certification marks, 404–405
concurrent registration, 411, 481
as constructive notice, 412, 442, 460, 489

disclaimer of unregistrable material, 411, 426, 450, 527
examination process with USPTO, 524, 526, 528–529
first use, "in commerce that Congress may regulate," 388, 408–409
recordation with U.S. Customs and Border Protection, 415
registrable matter, 496
registrant, 496
related vs. unrelated products and services, analysis of, 496
of slogans, 504
of sounds, 504
state law, 389, 495, 496, 503, 505
text of law, 442–445
trade dress, 512
See also Color in trademarks; Descriptive trademarks; Distinctive trademarks; Generic terms and symbols; Likelihood of confusion; Names of persons in trademarks; Principal Register; Secondary meaning rule; Supplemental Register; Trademark duration; Trademark exclusions and prohibitions; Trademark notice; Trademark registration application; Trademark searches

Trademark registration
application
abandonment (full or
partial) of application,
396–397, 529
abandonment of, partial,
397
applicant information,
526–527
Application Alleging Use
(if intent-to-use was filed)
filing, 441
classification of goods or
services, 496, 525
classification of
trademarks, 397,
463–465
color as an element of a
mark, description of, 407
declaration verifying the
facts are true, 527
description of goods or
services, 526
disclaimer of unregistrable
material, 527
email receipt, importance
of, 528
examination process with
USPTO, 388, 524, 526,
528–529
examiner from USPTO,
391, 472, 505, 526
false statements in,
447–448
fee payment, 528
fees for, 387, 523, 525

filing electronically. *See*
TEAS (Trademark
Electronic Application
System)
fraudulent statements on,
447
identification of the mark,
526
monitoring of progress
by USPTO Status Line
(phone), 528, 529
monitoring of progress
online (TSDR system),
396–397, 517, 528
Notice of Publication, 528
publication in the *Official
Gazette,* 388, 441,
479–480, 524, 528
specimen, 504–505, 527
specimen samples,
531–534
Statement of Use filing,
441
timeline for processing,
524, 528, 529
See also Intent-to-use
(ITU) trademark
registration
Trademark searches
overview, 389, 515–516
assignments, 400
domain name search to
avoid conflicts, 429, 516
preliminary search, 389,
516
private fee-based databases,
389

professional searchers, 389,
516
TESS database of USPTO,
389, 511, 516
Trademark Trial and Appeal
Board (TTAB), 516
inter partes proceeding held
before, 462, 481
*Trademark Examiners
Manual of Procedure*
(TMEP), 472, 525
See also Trademark
cancellation; Trademark
opposition
Trade names
defined, 513
protected by unfair
competition laws, 514
service marks
distinguished from, 503
as trademark, 514
Trade Related Aspects of
Intellectual Property
Rights (TRIPS), 271
Trade secret(s)
competitive advantage as
defining, 546, 591
confidentiality as defining,
539, 591–592
databases as, 555
defined, 539, 591–592
dual copyright/trade
secret status, concurrent
declaration with
copyright filing, 548,
587–589
industrial know-how, 572

industrial secrets, 568

licensing, 572–573, 579, 594

novelty and, 577

patterns and designs as, 579

physical devices as, 579–580

processes and methods as, 574, 581

sale of, 540

See also Business information as trade secret; Confidentiality of trade secrets; Duty of trust; Employees, trade secrets and confidential employment relationship; Ideas (trade secrets); Internet (trade secrets); Software and trade secrets

Trade secret disclosures

accidental disclosures, 543

as breach of duty of trust, 558, 566–567, 573, 574

deposit of copy of work with U.S. Copyright Office and, 274–275, 337, 548

during litigation, 556, 573, 581–582

email, 559

exit interviews to caution employees about, 560, 577, 585

Freedom of Information Act requests, 541, 560–561

freedom of speech and, 561–562, 571–572

improper disclosures, defined, 567

on the Internet, 559, 571–572

protective orders, 573, 581–582, 583

publication, 548, 583

public domain status due to, 573, 579, 583–584

state and federal laws prohibiting, 547

by vendors or consultants who signed a nondisclosure, 540

in violation of an NDA, 540, 575, 592

whistleblowers situations and protections, 557, 575, 576, 596

See also Improper disclosure of trade secrets; Nondisclosure agreements; Trade secret misappropriation

Trade secret law

overview, 3, 539–540

basis of, 4

changes to law since the last edition of this book, 541–542

GATT protections, 5, 562

international, 5, 550, 568

loss of trade secrets to the public domain, 573, 579–580, 583–584, 586–587

misappropriation and enforcement basics, 539–540

overlap with copyright, 275, 337, 548–549, 555, 565, 583–584, 587–589

overlap with patent application, 4, 46, 108, 274–275, 565, 578–579, 583

resource for, 542

trade secret defined, 539, 591–592

See also Antitrust law and trade secrets; Defend Trade Secrets Act; Economic Espionage Act (EEA); State law (trade secrets); Uniform Trade Secrets Act

Trade secret litigation

protection of trade secrets during, 556, 573, 581–582

whistleblowers filing suit for retaliation by employer, and disclosure of trade secrets, 576

See also Trade secret misappropriation actions

Trade secret misappropriation

overview, 574

antitrust law and, 544

criminal prosecution and penalties, 542, 551–552, 558–559

customer list disputes, 552–553

defined, 574

failure to seek relief resulting in loss to public domain, 583

of idea submissions, 564

industrial espionage, 542, 551, 552, 568, 583, 592

spoliation doctrine, 590

See also Improper acquisition of trade secrets; Nondisclosure agreements; State laws (trade secrets); Trade secret disclosures; Trade secret misappropriation actions

Trade secret misappropriation actions

overview, 592–593

burden of proof for the plaintiff, 592

common situations giving rise to, 592

confidentiality of trade secrets during, 556, 573, 581–582

defendants, 592

federal or state law may be used, 540, 556, 593

patent publication does not affect, 46, 579

as preempted by copyright claims, 549

preliminary injunctions, 593

statute of limitations for, 541, 590

See also Trade secret misappropriation defenses; Trade secret misappropriation remedies

Trade secret misappropriation defenses

overview, 592–593

failure to take reasonably precautionary protection measures, 584–585

independent conception, 567, 593

lawful disclosure, 593

parallel research, 578

prior disclosure, 593

reverse engineering, 579–580, 584, 593

use by owner in violation of antitrust laws, 593

Trade secret misappropriation remedies

overview, 540

attorneys' fees, 544–545, 556, 575, 596

damages, 554–555, 557, 558, 575, 593

defendant's profits, 593, 595

head-start rule, 542, 563, 593

improper acquisition finding required, 567

industrial espionage, 551, 552, 568

injunctions, 541, 542, 570–571, 593

notice to former employee's new employer, as affecting damages, 577

royalties, 554

seizure orders, 556, 587

temporary restraining orders (TROs), 570, 591

unjust enrichment theory, 595

whistleblower provision rule affecting damages, 557, 575, 576, 596

willful theft and, 540

Trade secret ownership

overview, 594

as determined by the circumstance of its creation, 594

licensing trade secrets, 572–573, 579, 594

loss of rights, 573

predetermination of rights in technical data, 580–581

selling trade secrets, 540, 594

See also Trade secret misappropriation action

Trade secret status

after patent issuance, 565, 578–579

before patent issuance, 4, 46, 108, 274–275, 578–579

clean rooms as proof of, 546

duration of, 3

establishing and maintaining, 576–577, 582, 583, 584–585, 591–592, 599

industrial secrets, 568

for invalidated patents, 579

loss of, 573, 580, 583–584

notice to employees of trade secrets, 576–577, 585

notice to former employee's new employer, 577

reverse engineering and loss to the public domain, 579–580, 584, 586–587

Trade Secrets Watch (blog), 542

Trade secret theft. *See* Improper acquisition of trade secrets; Trade secret misappropriation

Transformative use standard (copyright fair use), 256–257, 345–351

  court decisions, 193, 194–195, 250, 256–257, 260, 272, 305–306, 309, 314, 330, 335, 345–351

  See also Fair use (copyright)

Translations of works

  compulsory license to governments for, 218

  permission required from owner of earlier work, 238

  See also Derivative works

Tribal sovereign immunity, 89, 149

TRIPS (Trade Related Aspects of Intellectual Property Rights), 271

TSDR (Trademark Status and Document Retrieval System), 393, 397, 517

TTABlog, 393

TTAB. *See* Trademark Trial and Appeal Board

2 Live Crew sampling case, 345

Tying agreements, 30, 55–56, 156–157

Typosquatting, 416, 432

U

UCITA (Uniform Computer Information Transaction Act) (model code), 252, 351

UDRP (Uniform Dispute Resolution Procedure), 399, 517

Unauthorized use of trademark, and disclaimer of trademark use, 425, 448, 449, 457, 475

Unfair competition laws (trademarks)

  overview, 470, 517–518

  false advertising, 438–440, 494, 495, 499–500, 518–519

  false endorsement, 499, 500

  federal law (Lanham Act Section 43a), 457, 470, 495, 518–519

  injunctions against, 459–460

  as providing relief where trademark infringement laws don't apply, 518

  reverse palming off, 499

  right of publicity claims brought under, 500

  state laws as basis of, 518

  trademark law as subset of, 384

  trade names, 514

  unregistered marks protected under, 470, 518–519

  See also Trademark infringement

Uniform Computer Information Transaction Act (UCITA) (model code), 252, 351

Uniform Dispute Resolution Procedure (UDRP), 399, 517

Uniform Trade Secrets Act (UTSA)

  overview, 540, 594–595

  attorney fees recovery, 544, 545

  DTSA compared to, 556

  improper means, defined, 567

  injunctive relief, 570

  litigation, protection of trade secrets during, 582

  misappropriation definition, 574

misappropriation remedies, 555

reverse engineering not "improper means," 587

statute of limitations of misappropriation actions, 590

trade secret, defined, 592

United States Code Title 35 (patents), 155

Universal Copyright Convention (U.C.C.), 218, 284, 351–352

Universities

permitted to license patents created with federal funding (Bayh-Dole Act), 33–34, 580

and prior commercial use as infringement defense, 57, 58

See also Employees, and patents

Unjust enrichment (trade secrets), 595

Unlawful commerce, excluded from trademarks, 409

Unpublished works

overview, 352

common law copyright, 215

copyright protection gained the instant it becomes fixed in a tangible form, 224

deposit of works with U.S. Copyright Office, 369

displaying a work is not publication, 352

fair use and, 257, 260, 324, 352

group copyright registration of, 268, 365

limited publication of a work, 289

new copyright registration when published, 333

preregistration of, 261, 318–319

public domain status and, 352

published work copyright compared to, 323–324

restricted distribution not publication, 352

sound recordings, 269

timely copyright registration of, 342, 352

trade secret protection for, 548

as works made for hire, 352

Unregistered marks, protection of

overview, 518–519

ability to stop the use of a similar mark, 470, 519

cancelled registered marks become, 482, 483

as comparable to marks on the Principal Register, 495, 506

dilution and, 513

Lanham Act as covering, 457, 470, 495

remedies for violation of, 417, 519

and reverse confusion, 498

as senior to a newer registered mark, 490

state law, 70

strong marks, 506

trade dress, 513

unfair competition laws, 470, 518–519

See also Trademark(s)

Unsolicited idea disclosures, 595–596

U.S. Constitution, 4, 190

U.S. Copyright Office

overview, 353

Copyright Claims Board, 209–210

extensive help available from, 366, 369

fair use database of cases, 260

form downloads, 370

mailing address, 353

recordation of transfers, 187, 304, 324, 344

Register of Copyrights, 325

website, 366

See also Fraud (copyright)

U.S. Copyright Office Circular 65, 220

U.S. Copyright Office Circular 66, 220, 356

U.S. Customs and Border Protection agency (CBP), preventing import of infringing material, 275, 415

U.S. Department of Justice (DOJ)
    criminal copyright infringement prosecutions, 231, 232
    patent pool approvals by, 123
Useful articles (copyright)
    design of, copyright protection for, 352–353
    not protected by copyright, 193, 316, 353–354
    separability test, 353
User manuals, 18
U.S. government
    employees of, patent infringement as individuals, 149
    initials and insignia of, prohibited as trademark, 458–459
    no sovereign immunity for, 149, 337
    not a person for purposes of *inter partes* reviews, 90
    public domain status of works prepared by officers or employees of, 359
    trade secret protection and FOIA requests, 541, 560–561
    See also Public records
U.S. government funding
    consulting firms hired by, and predetermination of rights in technical data, 580–581

march-in rights for unused patents, 98
universities permitted to license patents created with (Bayh-Dole Act), 33–34, 580
U.S. Patent Classification system (USPC), 42
USPTO (U.S. Patent and Trademark Office), and patents
    overview, 158
    Attorneys and Agents Registered to Practice Bedfore the U.S. patent and Trademark Office, 119
    classification of patents, 42
    Commissioner for Patents, 44
    confidentiality of patent applications, 4, 108, 578
    copies of patents, obtaining, 125
    Director of, 64
    DOCX file format used by, 161
    Electronic Filing System (EFS-Web), 69–70, 118
    Fast-Track Appeals Pilot Program, 18
    form downloads from, 181
    group art unit, 82
    Manual of Patent Examining Procedure (MPEP), 98
    patent agents licensed by, 116

Patent and Trademark Resources Centers (PTRCs), 116
patent attorneys licensed by, 119
Patent Cooperation Treaty applications, 158
patent examiners, 11, 33, 120
patent searches on website, 124
retaining copy of patent (patent copy or soft copy), 116
Track One: Prioritized Examination, 156
website of, 19
See also Patent application prosecution; Publication of patent application; USPTO notices, patents (office actions)
USPTO notices, patents (office actions)
    overview, 112
    final, 76–77, 112, 139–140
    first, 77, 112, 138–139, 146
    Notice of Allowability, 25, 109, 140
    Notice of Prior Art References, 109, 137
USPTO (U.S. Patent and Trademark Office), and trademarks, 519
    appeals of decisions, 386
    Commissioner for Trademarks, 410

Director of the USPTO, 425

examiners, 391, 472, 505

International Schedule of Classes of Goods and Services, 463–465, 525

international trademark applications (Madrid Protocol), 465–466

Patent and Trademark Resources Centers (PTRCs), 116

rejection of weak trademark, 386

TESS (Trademark Electronic Search System) database, 389, 511, 516

TSDR (Trademark Status and Document Retrieval System), 393, 397, 517

See also TEAS and TEAS Plus electronic filing system; Trademark interferences

Utility patents

defined, 2, 10, 158

design patent also sought for the same device, 63

duration of, 12, 67–68, 79

exceptions to patentable inventions, 10

operability requirement, 114

patentability qualifications, 128

for plants, 131

procedure for applying, 11

types of inventions qualifying for, 10–11

See also Nonobviousness standard; Novelty standard; Patent application(s); Provisional Patent Application; Statutory subject matter

V

VARA. *See* Visual Artists Rights Act

Vicarious liability (copyright infringement), 354

Victoria's Secret case (*Moseley v. V Secret Catalogue, Inc.*), 421, 520

Video cassette recorders, 240

Videodiscs, 205

Videos and videorecording, 235, 240, 261, 264, 267

Videotapes, 205

Virtual reality, 274

Visual Artists Rights Act (VARA)

attorneys' fees, award of, 204

attribution right, 360, 363–364

copyright registration not required to file infringement suit, 327

damages for violations of, 362

definition of "work of visual art," 359–360

excluded types of artworks, 362, 363

first sale doctrine as limited under, 265

and the moral rights of artists, 360–361

prevention of destruction of art of "recognized stature," 196

"recognized stature" requirement, 362

right of integrity (prevent mutilation or modification of work), 360–361, 362, 363–364

rights not transferable at death of the artist, 361

temporary works protected by, 196, 361

text of law, 363–364

unfinished artworks, 362

waiver of right of integrity, 361

and work made for hire, 361

W

Wal-Mart Stores, Inc. v. Samara Brothers, Inc., 520–521

Web browsers, HTML (Hypertext Markup Language), 273, 355

Webcaster Settlement Act (2008), 355

Webcaster Settlement Act (2009), 355

Webcasting, 354–355

See also Digital music providers

Websites (copyright)
cached copies, 209
copyright registration of, 356
deep links, 290
defined, 355
design of, protection as trade dress, 356
fair use and, 208, 347, 351
framing and, 269–270
"incorporation test," 270
linking, 290
patent marking (virtual marking), 26, 100
permissions required for reproduction of protected materials, 208, 355
as "published work," 323
renewal of registration, three-year requirement, 241
resource for, 356
"server test," 249, 250, 270
See also Embedding; Internet service providers (ISPs); Search engines
Websites (trademarks)
metatags, 457–458, 475
new construction with domain name purchased, 430
permissions required for, 312
pop-up advertising, 488
specimen page for trademark registration application, 505

trademarks with .com in name, 392
See also Domain names; Search engines
Whistleblower protections (trade secrets), 557, 575, 576, 596
Wiki. *See* Collective works
Willful blindness, 83
Willful infringement
of copyright, 234, 242
of patents, 51, 85, 87, 159
of trademarks, 388, 390, 413, 419, 457
Willful noncompliance with patent disclosures, 69
Willful trade secret misappropriation, 540
Wine and spirit labels, 452
WIPO. *See* World Intellectual Property Organization
Work made for hire
overview, 356–359
categories of works that qualify as commissioned works for hire, 283, 357–359
defined, 356
duration of copyright, 187, 188, 223, 247–248, 356
by employees within the scope of employment, 187, 356–357
employment relationship, factors determining, 356–357

by independent contractor commissioned under written contract, 187, 223, 356, 357–358
ownership of copyright, 187, 223, 229, 356
unpublished, and the public domain, 352
work by employee authored outside the scope of employment, 356
work of visual art as, 361
written agreement for commission, 358
Work-made-for-hire written agreements, 358
Works of visual art, defined, 359
See also Visual Artists Rights Act (VARA)
World Intellectual Property Organization (WIPO), 62, 597
International Bureau of, 92, 93
Patent Cooperation Treaty, 5, 13, 49, 76, 92, 119–120, 158
website, 120
World Trade Organization (WTO), 52, 160, 271

Z

Zombie trademarks, 522

On Nolo.com you'll also find:

Books & Software

Nolo publishes hundreds of great books and software programs for consumers and
business owners. Order a copy, or download an ebook version instantly, at Nolo.com.

Online Forms

You can quickly and easily make a will or living trust, form an LLC or corporation,
apply for a provisional patent, or make hundreds of other forms—online.

Free Legal Information

Thousands of articles answer common questions about everyday legal issues,
including wills, bankruptcy, small business formation, divorce, patents,
employment, and much more.

Plain-English Legal Dictionary

Stumped by jargon? Look it up in America's most up-to-date source for
definitions of legal terms, free at nolo.com.

Lawyer Directory

Nolo's consumer-friendly lawyer directory provides in-depth profiles of lawyers all
over America. You'll find information you need to choose the right lawyer.

PCTM17